Y0-ATI-806

REVOLUTIONS AND MILITARY RULE IN THE MIDDLE EAST: THE ARAB STATES

REVOLUTIONS AND MILITARY RULE IN THE MIDDLE EAST: THE ARAB STATES PT. I: IRAQ, SYRIA, LEBANON AND JORDAN

GEORGE M. HADDAD

University of California, Santa Barbara

Volume 2

ROBERT SPELLER & SONS, PUBLISHERS, INC.

10 EAST 23rd STREET

NEW YORK, N. Y. 10036

Library of Congress Catalog Card No. 65-20537

First Edition

SBN 0-8315-0060-3

Printed in the United States of America

DEDICATED TO
SHUKRI AND JOSEPH
My Elder Brothers

TABLE OF CONTENTS

LIST OF ILLUSTRATIONS

PREFACE

The first volume of this work on revolutions and military rule in the Middle East, published in 1965, dealt with the non-Arab countries of the northern tier – Turkey, Iran, Afghanistan and Pakistan – after a general background on the nineteenth century. The second and third volumes are devoted to the study of fifty-nine revolutions and coups d'etat in eight Arab countries of the Middle East – Iraq, Syria, Lebanon, Jordan, Egypt, the Sudan, Yemen and Libya – beginning with the first military coup of October 1936 in Iraq and ending with the fifty-ninth coup of September 1969 in Libya. The present volume contains a study of thirty-nine coups and revolutions in the Arab states of the Fertile Crescent: Iraq, Syria, Lebanon, and Jordan. The following volume – the third in the series – deals with twenty coups and revolutions in Egypt, the Sudan, Yemen and Libya. The study does not include the revolutions for national independence during the period of colonial rule. It deals with the military and popular movements that have forced, or attempted to force a change in government and institutions after the countries had become independent – with or without treaty – and it covers developments until the end of 1969.

The coups d'etat and revolutions of each country have been studied in separate chapters. Comparisons have been made between the coups of each country and also between those of the various countries in order to emphasize the similarities and contrasts in their motives, patterns and results. In the study of each individual coup the background and causes were analyzed, the role of the officers and their civilian partners in planning and carrying out the coup was outlined, the new institutions and changes that followed the coup were critically described, and the account was ended with an analysis of how and why the regime established by the coup was destroyed. In each case the personality and character of the leaders involved in the coup as well as their methods, achievements and failures have been assessed. Controversial problems related to certain coups have been treated, and the reactions and opinions of native and foreign observers and scholars have been recorded.

The first chapter of this second volume contains a general description of the tensions, ideologies and problems of the Arab Middle East after the first world war and outlines the position of the Arab radicals, civilians and military, who played a role in the various revolutionary movements. The other five chapters deal with the upheavals in the four Fertile Crescent countries, with two chapters on Syria. The conclusion at the end of the following third volume sums up the motives and patterns of the revolutions and coups d'etat as well as the characteristics and results of military rule in the Arab states. It ends with a critical comment on the record of the military rulers and their socialist revolution, and with a statement on the return of the officers to their barracks and the restoration of liberal democratic rule.

The author's purpose in writing this work was, first, to contribute to the understanding of the recent history of the Arab world and its present problems and turmoil by making a comprehensive study of its revolutionary movements and their background; second, to present an object lesson drawn from the record of events on the consequences of the intrusion of the military into radical politics and the results of the controversial innovations and policies they imposed at a critical period in the history of the Arab nation. The author had the unpleasant duty of presenting some blunt facts and comments on leaders and rulers among whom he counted several friends and acquaintances. He had no other choice, because the record had to be set straight in order that the lesson might be useful and the understanding of the present situation and of future developments might be clear.

The author is grateful to the authorities of the University of California and their General Research and Humanities Institute grants and to the Ford Foundation and its Non-Western Studies grants for their unfailing support of his research. He feels deeply indebted to the many scholars and writers whose researches and insights on the subject have been of invaluable help. Their names and publications are referred to in the notes. The author at one time lived through some of the events described in this book, and he later went back to the area for observation and study in 1966-67. He has appreciated the kindness of several persons who answered his questions on various developments in which they were personally involved or on which they were well informed. In the diligent and patient work of typing the manuscript I am pleased to thank Mrs. Melva McClatchey for her unfailing kindness and competence. For providing the needed publications and illustrations on the subject I am indebted to the kind cooperation of the acquisitions and inter-library loan departments of the university library at Santa Barbara and the university photographic service.

Except for certain familiar names for which the most commonly used and accepted spelling has been adopted, I have generally followed the standard system of transliteration of Arabic names and terms. For various reasons I have rarely used diacritical marks.

George M. Haddad

Santa Barbara, California
April 1970

CHAPTER I

General Background
Tensions, Ideologies and Army Officers

The revolutions and coups d'état which this volume attempts to study were the result of tensions, frustrations and weaknesses either inherited by the emerging Arab states, or engendered in the course of their independent existence.[1] The tensions had their source in the differences on foreign policy and the attainment of national aspirations, and also in the functioning of parliamentary rule and the problems of political and social reform. The issues of foreign policy and the external pressures that accompanied them ended by influencing the attitudes towards parliamentary government and rulers while new ideologies and ideological conflicts played their role in exacerbating the tensions. The military upheavals, however, were not all directed against the civilian rulers and their democratic or autocratic regimes. In the majority of cases the officers mounted their coups against the ruling military colleagues either to take their place or to restore civilian constitutional government.

I. The Peace Settlement and the Emerging States: Geopolitics, Power Politics and Arab Frustrations

When the First World War began the Arab countries of the Middle East were either a part of the Ottoman Empire, or under the protection or influence of Britain. Only Nejd in central Arabia was independent under the Saudi princes.

Yemen was an autonomous entity under its own dynasty of Imams, but it was officially an Ottoman province. Hejaz, under more direct Ottoman rule, was a province that the Sultan could not afford to lose on account of the religious importance of its holy cities, Mecca and Medina. The Sherif of Mecca, however, added to the prestige of being a descendant of the Prophet a certain measure of autonomy within the holy city, and in the Ottoman protocol he held the same rank as the Grand Vizier and the Khedive of Egypt. The sultanates and sheikhdoms of southern Arabia and the Persian Gulf were under British protection. Egypt was a separate entity and had its own dynasty, but it was occupied by Britain in 1882 and became officially a British protectorate in 1914. The Sudan had been under the direct and joint rule of Britain and Egypt since the Condominium agreement of 1899. In the Fertile Crescent neither geographic Syria nor Iraq existed as separate entities. Each of them included three provinces of the Ottoman Empire—Aleppo, Syria (Damascus) and Beirut in geographic Syria, and Mosul, Baghdad and Basra in Iraq. The sanjak (sub-province) of Mt. Lebanon inhabited by Druzes and Maronite Christians had been autonomous since 1861 under an Ottoman Christian district governor who was responsible directly to Constantinople.[2]

In the course of the war, Sherif Hussein of Mecca placed himself at the head of the Arab national movement when he declared a revolt against the Turks in June 1916 and accepted Britain's help after he had obtained a qualified British pledge to secure the independence of the Arab countries after their liberation from the Turks. The Sherif's sons commanded the Arab fighting units and were joined by Arab officers who had served in the Ottoman army, while the members of the secret Arab national organizations in Syria and Iraq gave their moral support and advice to the leadership of the revolt. Shortly after the British pledge had been given to Sherif Hussein, Britain made other pledges that were viewed by the Arabs as a betrayal of their national cause. In May 1916 Britain concluded the Sykes-Picot agreement with France for the partition of the Fertile Crescent into British and French zones of occupation and influence, and on November 2, 1917 Britain issued the Balfour Declaration promising its support for a national home for the Jews in Palestine.[3]

The peace settlement in the Fertile Crescent was essentially the work of Britain and France and was roughly an implementation of the secret Sykes-Picot agreement of 1916. It was disappointing to most of the Arabs and their national aspirations. In the conference of San Remo in April 1920 Britain and France agreed that the French would rule the central and northern regions of geographic Syria (present Syria and Lebanon) under a kind of trusteeship of the newly created League of Nations known as the mandate system. Britain obtained a mandate to rule Iraq and the southern regions of geographic Syria (Palestine and Transjordan), but the official confirmation of the mandate of both Britain and France to rule the territories that they had already awarded themselves was given by the League of Nations in 1922 with a provision to implement the Balfour Declaration in the mandate over Palestine. In the meantime the Syrian Congress had met in Damascus in June 1919 and decided, on the basis of the principle of self-determination advocated by President Wilson, upon the rejection of the Balfour Declaration, and the independence of geographic Syria with an economic union with Iraq. The same congress later proclaimed Prince Faisal, third son of Sherif Hussein, king of Syria on March 8, 1920 and thus created the first independent Arab kingdom after the war. Faisal's kingdom, however, was not destined to survive, particularly after Britain's agreement with the French at San Remo in April. It collapsed on July 25, 1920, less than five months after its establishment, when the French forces advanced from the coastal region and occupied Damascus and the rest of internal Syria.[4]

On September 1, 1920 the French announced the creation of Greater Lebanon as a separate state by adding to the sanjak of Mt. Lebanon the adjoining cities of the coast and the Beqa plain. Greater Lebanon became the first Arab republic in modern times when it was given a republican constitution in 1926. It remained under French mandate until its effective independence in 1943. The equal numeric strength of its Christian and Muslim population has generated in Lebanon various problems of confessional politics, national identity, and political orientation which have continued to produce tensions and crises after independence. Lebanon, moreover, is surrounded on the north and the east by the State of Syria and cannot communicate by land with the outside world except through Syrian territory on account of the closed border with Israel. Crises and tensions have consequently developed whenever Syria closed its borders with Lebanon as a result of differences in policy and orientation that strained the relations between the two countries.

In the rest of Syria under French mandate France created in September 1920 the states of Damascus, Aleppo and Latakia, and two years later the Jabal Druze was separated from the State of Damascus and became a separate entity. At the same time, in 1922, a Syrian federation of the states of Damascus, Aleppo, and Latakia (called the Alawi state) was formed. It was ended in 1924 when the states of Damascus and Aleppo were united to form the State of Syria that included the autonomous sanjak of Alexandretta in the north inhabited by a large Turkish minority.[5] While still a mandatory power over Syria, France surrendered this Syrian sanjak or sub-province to Turkey in 1939 and caused an influx of Arab and Armenian inhabitants of the sanjak to Syria and strained relations between Syria and Turkey. The State of Syria became a republic in 1930 and obtained effective independence in 1943. It was only then that the two states of the Alawis and the Druzes (Jabal Druze) were united with the Syrian republic.

Before and after its independence, the Syrian republic had to face constantly the problems arising from its important geographical position and the presence of the Christian, Druze, and Alawi minorities in a country of overwhelming Sunni Muslim population. The French had already exploited the religious differences for the fragmentation of Syria, and later, in the age of military coups, the Alawi officers from the rural regions used their military power to enforce measures that offended and weakened the urban Sunni Muslim majority. The problems of identity and alignment became particularly acute after independence, and tensions arose because of the pressures of the Arab neighbors in Jordan, Iraq, Egypt and Saudi Arabia and the various attitudes of Syrian leaders towards the Arab blocs and the implementation of Arab unity. Besides its role as a standard bearer of the Arab national movement and its ability to influence the balance of power between rival Arab states, Syria enjoys a strategic location that allows her to control the communications of its neighbors with the Mediterranean. Because of Arab hostilities with Israel, it is not conveniently possible for Jordan and Iraq to reach Lebanon and the Mediterranean by land and by air except through Syria. The pipelines that carry the oil of Iraq and Saudi Arabia to the terminals on the Mediterranean have to pass through Syrian territory. This has been an advantage which Syria has used against its Arab neighbors and against the foreign powers involved in the oil enterprise, but these same powers have also tried to influence Syrian policy and have caused tensions to rise as a result of their interventions and pressures.

Britain's policy in the eastern Arab world was dictated by the strategic importance of the region and the concern about the security of British communications with India, East Africa and the Far East through the Suez Canal and through the land and air routes between the Mediterranean and the Persian Gulf. Egypt and its Canal Zone, as well as Palestine, Iraq and a corridor joining the two were consequently kept under British control. Britain, however, was confronted in 1919 with a nationalist uprising in Egypt when it refused to abolish the protectorate and exiled the Egyptian leaders who asked for independence. Similarly a national revolution against British rule began in Iraq in May 1920. Britain, as a result, found it more convenient to relax its control over the strategic areas and at the same time safeguard its basic interests under an autonomous local rule. In the Cairo Conference in March 1921 British experts on the Middle East under the direction of Colonial Secretary Winston Churchill decided to establish national governments in Iraq and in a new entity called Transjordan that joined Iraq and the Persian Gulf to Palestine, the Mediterranean and the border of Egypt. Prince Faisal, who had lost his throne in Syria, became king of Iraq in August and his elder brother Abdallah became prince (Emir) of Transjordan in April, 1921. The new principality with about one-third of a million inhabitants had been a sub-province (sanjak) of the province of Syria (Damascus) in Ottoman times.[6] The decision of the conference to end the protectorate in Egypt was officially announced later in the Declaration of 28 February 1922 that gave Egypt a restricted independence under a constitutional monarchy. Unlike Syria and Lebanon and the other entities of the Fertile Crescent, Egypt had no problems of identity or unity. Its territory was well defined, it had been a modern nation state since the early nineteenth century, and its people were aware of their Egyptian identity. Its main problem was the removal of the restrictions on its independence, and its tensions were essentially a product of the disagreements between its nationalist party—the Egyption Wafd—the British, and the king of Egypt on the questions of Egyptian sovereignty and royal power.[7]

The British and the French thus succeeded in setting up governments in their own image in the territories under their control—constitutional monarchies in Egypt, Iraq and Transjordan and constitutional republics in Syria and Lebanon. Only Palestine was not given a national government and remained under direct British rule because the overwhelming majority of its population was Arab, and Britain was committed to build up the Jewish national home which the Arabs opposed. The problem of Palestine, that consisted of Arab opposition to large scale Jewish immigration and acquisition of land and the eventual establishment of a Jewish state produced tensions in Palestine itself and in the neighboring

Arab states. It had its influence on the Arab image of Britain, the United States and the West in general and on the emergence of radical ideologies and the search for new friends and allies who could lend their support to the Arabs. The standing and the authority of the native Arab rulers were eventually compromised and challenged by the critics among the new Arab generation, and the Palestine question became a convenient instrument in the hands of opportunists and demagogues for building up an artificial leadership and for hurling accusations against the men in power. The Palestine problem was partly responsible for producing the tensions and the conditions that enabled certain military officers to seize power and to retain it. It also became the excuse for far reaching changes in the political and social order in some Arab countries.

The two Hashemite rulers of Iraq and Transjordan and their descendants were destined to remain an object of suspicion and derision in radical Arab circles because of the circumstances of their appointment and the policy of friendly cooperation with Britain that was not without its advantages to them and to their countries. In assuming the role of king maker, the British government thought it was fulfilling part of its war time promises to Sherif Hussein and the Arabs and rewarding the Sherif's sons for their cooperation with the Allies. It expected the cooperation to continue and in this respect it was not disappointed. Tensions in Iraq and later in Transjordan had their source precisely in the disagreements on the nature and extent of that cooperation which the radical nationalists viewed as subservience and treason.[8] Another cause of tensions was the exploitation of the rich Iraqi deposits of oil by British-French-American interests represented by the Iraq Petroleum Company and the differences of opinion on questions of royalties, nationalization, utilization of oil revenues, and granting concessions to other companies. The common source of tensions in the entire Fertile Crescent and in the Arab Middle East in general was the hostility of Egypt, Saudi Arabia and Syrian radicals to the attempt of Emir (later King) Abdallah of Transjordan to rule geographic or Greater

Syria with autonomy for certain regions and to the desire of Iraq to achieve a Fertile Crescent federal union with Syria.[9] Although Arab nationalists, particularly in Syria-Palestine, never forgave Britain for the fragmentation of geographic Syria and the Fertile Crescent and for supporting the Jewish national home in Palestine, they opposed constantly the Great `r Syria and the Fertile Crescent projects that could have restored the unity and integrity of Syria and perhaps prevented the establishment of the Jewish state, and would have been a notable step towards a larger Arab federation. The projects had their partisans in the Syrian republic and throughout geographic Syria. Those who fought them did so supposedly out of concern for the republican form of government in Syria and because Iraq and Transjordan had treaties of alliance with Britain. They evidently did not foresee that the British alliance and the Hashemite rulers themselves could not remain forever and that in the meantime unity and strength could have been achieved.

Those who fought the Greater Syria and the Fertile Crescent projects and thus became responsible for the tensions in the Fertile Crescent countries included a group of politicians, administrators and officers who were moved by their vested interests within the solidifying frontiers of the newly created states because they were determined to keep their lucrative positions and independent local prestige. Many of them were also serving the interests of external forces in Egypt, Saudi Arabia and France that were opposed to that unity while Britain and the United States did not give it their support. France wanted Syria to remain divided and hoped to maintain at least some cultural and economic influence in the Syrian and Lebanese republics. Its policy coincided with that of the Christians of Lebanon who wanted their state to remain independent and sovereign. Egyptian aspirations for Arab leadership under the monarchy and later under the republic were best served by keeping Syria divided and by preventing a Syrian union, or even a close relationship, with Iraq. Saudi Arabia traditionally opposed the formation of a stronger and larger state ruled by the rival Hashemites in Iraq and Transjordan after it had occupied their ancestral Hashemite domain in Hejaz in 1925. The United States preferred to act in favor of her Saudi Arabian ally and probably feared the impact of a united Syrian state or of a Fertile Crescent federation on the projected Jewish state.

In the Arabian Peninsula, Yemen became automatically independent with the fall of the Ottoman Empire and kept its traditional theocratic institutions under the absolute rule of the Zaydi Imams. It remained distant and isolated, and its problems grew mainly out of the challenges of rivals to the rule of Imam Yahya and his descendants, and out of the formation of an enlightened opposition that wanted to modernize and develop Yemen and give it a constitutional form of government. The momentous development in the Peninsula was the emergence of Saudi Arabia as a large and rich kingdom, and the discovery of oil in its eastern regions and in other smaller entities along the Persian Gulf. The Wahabi emirate of Nejd under Abdul Aziz al-Saud became the Sultanate of Nejd in 1921 after the annexation of the northern areas. Following the conquest of Hejaz and the ousting of the Hashemites, the Sultan of Nejd and its dependencies became also the king of the Hejaz in 1926, and in September 1932 the entire area under his control was called Saudi Arabia. The new kingdom remained a traditional Muslim state with no constitution. The extraction of oil in the late 1930's and in particular after the Second World War by American corporations represented in the Arabian American Oil Company was one of the factors that brought the United States into Middle Eastern politics and into close friendship with Saudi Arabia. The expansion of American oil interests, the construction of the Daharan air base, the building and protection of the pipeline that carried the oil to the Mediterranean, and the security of transportation and communications along the sea and air routes of the Middle East had their impact on American policy in the area and were at the same time influenced by the tensions in the Arab states and by the

Arab pressures on Saudi Arabia. The United States had to maintain friendly relations with the Arabs while it supported Israel, and because of this support it was accused of various sinister actions and conspiracies against Arab governments. The Saudi occupation of Hejaz led the Saudis to remain until 1957 suspicious of the Hashemite states along their northern border and made them pour generously the gold of oil royalties into the pockets of Syrian and other Middle Eastern politicians and journalists to keep the Hashemites away from Syria and to preserve the status quo and the fragmentation established by the peace settlement. Saudi Arabia thus became one of the external forces that were responsible for instability and tensions in the Fertile Crescent. It became later the target of the attacks of the Egyptian and other revolutionary regimes after it had supported them against the Hashemites because they now aimed at operating a political and social change in Saudi Arabia and the entire Peninsula. Saudi Arabia as a result had to watch carefully the revolutionary developments along its borders, the southern border in particular after the revolution in Yemen in 1962. Its rule of Hejaz and its guardianship of the Holy Places in Mecca and Medina gave it prestige and power to speak on behalf of traditional Muslim values and made of her a major contender in the cold war between Arab revolutionaries and conservatives.[10]

II. National Independence and Parliamentary Regimes

The two outstanding aspects of Arab activity between the two wars were first, the struggle for national independence in the countries under foreign control in Egypt and the Fertile Crescent, and second, the modernization and development of the political, social, economic, and intellectual life in the same countries. The leaders of the national crusade against foreign rule were the pioneers of the pre-war period and the surviving members of the Arab clubs and secret societies that were active during the last years of the Ottoman regime. Some of them were former officers, others were civil servants, professionals and notables who lived on the income of their landed property. They were joined by other notables, officials, and religious leaders when the Ottoman empire collapsed. In addition to their maturity, courage and experience, these national leaders also possessed the means that allowed them to spend time and money to organize parties, inspire and incite the masses, and stand in the face of the foreign rulers with all the material and physical risks involved, but their incentive to oust the foreign overlord was by no means simply to run the country in their own interests.[11] In Egypt, most of the leaders were former government executives, lawyers, and landlords and some of them had been involved in Egyptian national affairs in the pre-war period. A new phase began during and after the peace settlement with the participation of the masses in the national struggle as illustrated by the Egyptian revolution in 1919, the Iraqi revolution in 1920 and the Syrian revolution in 1925, and with the role played by students and shopkeepers in the strikes and demonstrations that were the two effective instruments of pressure on the foreign ruler.

The Arab states and political entities that emerged after the peace settlement worked each for its own cause and by its own means against foreign rule but not without mutual moral support. The leading parties that were organized primarily to support the demand for independence were mass parties in which there was no formal system of membership. The two best known examples were the Wafd party founded in 1919 in Egypt under the leadership of Saad Zaghlul followed by Mustafa al-Nahas, and the National Bloc in Syria organized in late 1927 and led successively by Ibrahim Hanano, Hashem al-Atassi and Shukri al-Quwatli. The constitution of the National Bloc proclaimed that "the entire nation considers itself a part of the Bloc and dedicates all that it possesses for the national struggle." Allegiance in these parties was not merely to the person of the leaders but to a specific and simple nationalist ideology and program that consisted of liberation from foreign rule and the establishment of a free independent state. The disparate elements in the mass parties were united by the common struggle against colonialism for the achievement of political independence. It was only at a later stage and particularly after political independence had been won that various definitions and concepts of nationalism appeared under the influence of a younger Arab generation that had played no essential role in the national struggle, and under the impact of new radical ideologies and political developments. The clash between the varied definitions and interpretations of the nationalist ideologies resulted in tensions and difficulties that contributed to the intrusion of the military into politics.

The leaders of the mass parties who for twenty years organized the resistance against foreign domination recognized the value of negotiation and compromise and were by no means as negative as they have been portrayed. In Syria, the leaders of the Bloc tried to cooperate with the French on four occasions–in 1928, 1931, 1936 and 1943–and in one of them they signed the treaty of 1936 that the French parliament never ratified. The Bloc was able to obtain full independence for Syria without the provisions of a treaty in 1946. In Egypt the Wafd government conducted negotiations for a treaty with the British in 1930 as other governments had done earlier but with no success, and finally it signed the treaty of 1936 by which Egypt won full independence but granted Britain certain privileges. The rulers in Iraq and Jordan also compromised and signed treaties that gave them restricted independence but then maneuvered and watched for occasions to modify them and obtain better terms until they won complete independence in accordance with King Faisal's famous policy of "take and then ask for more." Iraq became independent when it signed its fourth treaty with Britain in 1930 and was admitted to the League of Nations in 1932 before any other Arab country. The treaty and the privileges accorded in it to Britain were abolished in 1955. Emir Abdallah of Transjordan similarly started with a treaty with Britain in 1928 and gained independence in the third treaty in 1948 which was ended in 1957 under his grandson King Hussein. In the meantime the Arab Legion that was organized, trained and financed by Britain became an important fighting force and in 1956 its British commander was replaced by a Jordanian. Differences of opinion between parties and factions on the wisdom of compromise and of signing treaties of alliance or other agreements with the former foreign ruler created bitter tensions and conflicts in the Arab countries and provided the Young Arabs with pretexts to attack the older leaders and accuse them of unpatriotic behavior and even of treason.

The nationalist leaders of the post-war period in the Fertile Crescent also thought of independence as a step towards Arab unity and the first movement in that direction was made by the Syrian Congress in 1919 when it set as its goal the unity of geographic Syria and economic union with Iraq. This same goal was revived in 1943 by Emir Abdallah of Transjordan and Nuri al-Said of Iraq in the form of a united Syria that would join Iraq in a federation or a league that would be open to other Arab states.[12] The plan, known as the Fertile Crescent project, was opposed and was never given a chance to be implemented. Two years later in March 1945 the League of Arab States was formed and under the influence of Egypt and certain other Arab countries, the unity projects were discarded. The Arab League consisting of seven charter members emphasized in its Article VIII the respect for the sovereignty of other member states, and in Article IX it allowed "closer cooperation and bonds" between member states that desire them in the future. Political unity was thus rejected in favor of regional organization and Arab solidarity, but Arab unity, nevertheless, remained, as it has been said, "the sacred cow of the League, it gave little nourishment but no one dared to kill it."[13] Projects for Arab unity by gradual steps were presented by Arab leaders from Syria and Iraq in the early 1950's but were shelved by the League. In 1950-51 the League members signed a collective security pact that instituted an Arab defense council, and since then several defense pacts between two or more League members have also been made. But the general result of the discussions about unity and of the defense pacts and other defense projects was to create at times more Arab disunity and more tensions between the states or between parties and factions within each state. Yet, it cannot be denied that the older Arab leaders in forming the League have provided the Arab world with an instrument for various aspects of cooperation and solidarity and for the settlement of disputes between Arab states. The younger Arab leaders found themselves obliged to maintain this instrument in spite of its shortcomings because of their inability to create anything more effective. At the same time they aggravated Arab tensions and disputes through their irresponsible handling of the question of Arab unity that became only a pretext to attack and discredit their rivals in the game of the struggle for power. They also found it convenient to accuse the colonial western powers of standing in the way of Arab unity even after foreign domination had ended and the affairs of the Arab states had been placed in Arab hands.

The older nationalists of the post-war period who struggled for, and achieved independence for their countries were liberal according to the Western tradition, and for them nationalism and independence were associated with freedom and the guarantee of civil liberties under a constitution. They believed the parliamentary system to be desirable and useful since it was the most effective means of national self expression and as such it would serve as an instrument for combating foreign domination. At the same time it was a sign of political maturity and of equality with the foreign ruler, and it therefore carried prestige with it in as much as it was a sign and proof of a modern independent state.[14] While they were still under foreign rule, the various Arab countries except Palestine pressed for and obtained constitutions, conducted elections for representative assemblies, and formed cabinets responsible to these assemblies. Sometimes the constitution was prepared by the colonial power and in other cases it was the work of local constituent assemblies. The foreign ruler directly or indirectly through his influence on the local authority often suspended the constitution and dissolved parliament in order to avoid criticism and to defeat the maneuvers of the nationalists. In Egypt a constitution was promulgated by royal decree in April 1923 following the recommendation of a constitutional committee. It was revoked by King Fuad in 1930 and a new constitution giving more power to the king was proclaimed but it was unpopular. The old constitution was restored in 1935 and remained in effect until the military abolished it in 1953. The powerful Wafd party that was active for over thirty years and won majorities in the elections was able to hold power only for eight years while anti-Wafd cabinets often ruled. The constitutions of Iraq and Syria were drafted by constituent assemblies in 1924 and 1928 respectively and that of Iraq was promulgated by King Faisal in March 1925 and was maintained until the military coup of 1958. The Syrian constitution of 115 articles provided for an independent republican regime in a united Syria and was consequently unacceptable to the French. It was drafted by the National Bloc that dominated the assembly and refused to omit the six articles to which the French objected. In 1930 the French high commissioner promulgated the constitution after adding Article 116 that made the six articles ineffective. It remained, with several interruptions under the French mandate, until 1950 but Article 116 was never recognized by the Syrians. The constitution of 1950, drafted four years after complete independence, was more elaborate in its bill of rights and more modern. It was abolished by the military and then was restored several times, but since 1963 it has not been functioning. Syria was effectively the first Arab country to have a constitution in the post-war period before French rule began. That was the constitution of 1920 drafted by the Syrian Congress for Faisal's monarchy and it provided for a modern democratic parliamentary government, but it ended with the end of Faisal's rule.[15]

Lebanon obtained its republican constitution in 1926. It was presented to the Lebanese representative council by the French high commissioner who promulgated it after the approval of the council. It was amended in 1927 and 1929, and in May 1932 it was suspended and replaced in 1934 by a new constitution promulgated by the French high commissioner. In 1937 the old constitution of 1926 was restored and has remained in effect since then with important amendments in 1943 when the country became independent, and in 1947. In the case of Transjordan, the first constitution or organic law of the Emirate was promulgated in 1928. It was replaced in 1946 by the constitution of the Hashemite kingdom of Jordan and in 1952, Jordan obtained another constitution. In the Arabian Peninsula, the two independent states, Yemen and Saudi Arabia, were monarchies with no constitution and representative institutions of the western type but they had consultative councils and religious laws. They were theocratic states with an old but constantly evolving administration especially in Saudi Arabia.

The major criticism directed against the system of parliamentary rule was that it was not a true democracy but rather an oligarchy where the landlords, tribal chiefs and wealthy bourgeois of the urban centers monopolized power. Parliaments therefore did not express the wishes of the nation and had to be subservient to the executive or else they could be dissolved. Cabinets rarely resigned as a result of a vote of confidence and parliaments in some of the countries rarely finished their term while the division and the balance of powers which is the basis of parliamentarism did not exist. Among the features of this democracy the following were noted: uncontested or managed elections accompanied by bribery and violence and amounting to what has been called "election without representation," absence of stable parties and of active and loyal opposition, subordination of public to private interests, scandals, corruption, patronage and the role played by confessional, regional, family and personal considerations.[16] Rulers and parties, moreover, in their jealousies and struggle for power, exploited the various issues of the time, external as well as internal–such as colonialism, Zionism, and Arab unity as well as confessional, tribal, labor and student problems–for their own benefit.

In analyzing these charges against parliamentary democracy, it is necessary to make a distinction between the functioning of constitutional government and the behavior of nationalist leaders before and after the winning of independence. While colonial rule still existed in one form or another, the colonial power and those of the local rulers who cooperated with it did their best to make the parliamentary regime serve as the instrument of their policy. The colonial rulers were thus the ones who fixed the elections, suspended parliaments or dissolved them or used force against them and even suspended the constitution itself. The nationalists at that time formed the opposition and acted on behalf of all classes. They wanted the elections to be honest because they were confident of public support. In the elections of December 20, 1931 to the Syrian chamber of deputies, for example, the French authorities tried to interfere in a number of cities and bloody clashes took place where some lost their lives. When a draft treaty of restricted independence was proposed to the elected Chamber on November 25, 1933, the mandatory power tried to intimidate the members and force their consent to the treaty by surrounding the Chamber with troops but the nationalists of the Bloc prevailed on the majority to refuse it. The Chamber was dissolved as a result and the constitution was suspended. In January, 1942, when Egypt was independent on the basis of treaty relations with Britain, the British Ambassador, Sir Miles Lampson (later Lord Killearn), urgently asked King Farouk to dismiss the Hussein Sirri Pasha cabinet and to call on Nahas Pasha, the king's personal enemy, to form a cabinet. King Farouk had to submit on February 4 because of a threat to depose him by force while his palace was surrounded by British armored units. These and other incidents of the same kind were bad precedents and not very edifying lessons in the exercise of constitutional government. The nationalist leaders became themselves the rulers of their respective countries after independence, but while their leadership was unquestioned by the various class interests during the period of national struggle, they now found themselves in the presence of an opposition asking for its share in the privileges and responsibilities of government and demanding due attention to its problems.

It should be recognized, moreover, that while the people of the Fertile Crescent countries and the Arabs in general shared certain moral and mental attitudes, they did not share the same socio-economic conditions and the same political experience. The percentage of literacy, the standard of living, the natural resources and other sources of wealth, the relative strength of religious, racial and tribal minorities, the size of the middle class, and the degree of civic responsibility differed in the various Arab countries and had their impact on the functioning of parliamentary democracy.

It can be noted, furthermore, that no democratic or other political regime has ever functioned to perfection. Some of the same criticisms already mentioned have been directed against much older and well established democracies. The differences sometimes seem to be ones of degree not of kind. When the military issued their verdict that democracy was a complete failure and seized power with the applause of flatterers and apologists, democratic parliamentary life was in most cases only a few years old and in a period of trial and error. The country was gaining experience, and progress was being achieved in various spheres of economic and social life. The Arab countries and the Middle East in general had been going through a period of transition from medievalism to the modern age, and the change which they have undergone has carried them in a few decades through the successive revolutions that took Europe several centuries to experience. The change, however, began and had gone a long way before the intervention of the military in politics.

It will become evident in this study of military as well as popular upheavals that they were not provoked so much by internal corruption and the malfunctioning of the democratic regime as by new political developments and external pressures and by new ideologies and attitudes bearing on the role of the state, the structure of the social order and the relations of the Arab states with each other and with foreign powers.

III. Doctrinal Movements and Parties

In the 1930's while the Arab countries were struggling for complete independence from Britain and France, certain movements and groups appeared in the Fertile Crescent and in Egypt that took on some of the trappings of European Fascism and showed attraction to the totalitarian regimes of Italy and Germany. The Syrian National Party of Antun Saadeh, the Young Egypt or Green Shirt movement of Ahmad Hussein, and the *Futuwa* or militaristic youth movement of Iraq with Sami Shawkat as chief advocate, were all militaristic and exalted power and discipline. They all spoke of the will of the people and of the need to remove class and religious barriers in order to achieve social unity and emphasized martyrdom for the country's cause. They all worked for some kind of unity but each in its own way: the Syrian National Party aimed at the unity of geographic Syria which was extended later to include Iraq and Cyprus; the Green Shirts expected Egypt to be the leader of a federal Arab union, and the *Futuwa* believed that a united Arab nation would ultimately emerge with Iraq as the leader.[17] The three groups showed their admiration for Germany and Italy as examples of efficiency and strength while the Axis propaganda undoubtedly played its role in stirring anti-British feeling. For a whole decade before the end of the Second World War, certain Arab nationalist circles based their hope of emancipation on the possible support of the Axis powers but these hopes were shattered by the victory of the Allies.[18]

One of the three movements with Fascist tendencies, the

Futuwa, had its impact on the fostering of the army as an object of popular devotion and on the spread of pan-Arab sentiments in it. The Young Egypt movement turned into a socialist group and had its influence on Egyptian officers. The Syrian National Party (later on the Syrian Social National Party or SSNP) was essentially opposed to Communism.[19] It became distinctly pro-Western in the post-war period and played a significant role in the armed forces in Syria, and to some extent Lebanon. The doctrine of the SSNP as formulated by its founder and leader, Antun Saadeh in 1932 in Beirut rests on the initial principle that "Syria belongs to the Syrians and the Syrians form a complete nation.[20] The unity of the Syrian nation is not based on a community of language or religion, but on sharing a common history and common interests and a well-defined homeland. In contrast with the Arab nationalists, who believed in the existence of one indivisible Arab nation that groups all the Arabic-speaking countries, the Syrian nationalists believed in the existence of a separate Syrian nation which is a part of the Arab world but has its own personality and characteristics. Although they held that Arab unity was impracticable, they accepted the formation of an Arab front based on the common interests of the nations of the Arab world. For reaching its goals, the party depended on its strong hierarchical organization under a powerful leader, its system of political education and propaganda and the support of a trained party militia. Its cohesiveness and secrecy allowed it to survive for about a quarter of a century and to play a minor role in Syrian and Lebanese politics. Its membership consisted mostly of Christians, Alawis and Druzes; few Sunni Muslims joined its ranks. Syrian unity could not be achieved under its direction because of its totalitarian aspect and its negative attitude towards Arab unity, both of which did not appeal to the majority of the Syrians. The party had to face the opposition and sometimes violent attacks of three major groups: the Lebanese ultra-nationalists represented by the Phalangist movement founded in 1937, the radical Arab nationalists represented by the Arab *Baath* (Renaissance)

Party, and the Communist Party. It came under violent Syrian attack in the mid-fifties when the radical Baath Party in active cooperation with the Communists and Nasserists led an active campaign against Fertile Crescent unity and against all pro-Iraqi and pro-Western policies and groups.[21]

Prominent among the doctrinal parties was the Communist Party that had one or more Marxist organizations in almost every Arab country. The Communists and their parties, however, were unable to play any important role while the Arabs were under foreign rule in the inter-war period. Their proclaimed goal was liberation from colonial rule and the establishment of a democratic regime that guarantees freedom to all, but they effectively followed and served faithfully the policies of the Soviet Union even when these policies disagreed with Arab national goals as in the partition of Palestine in 1947. The Communist parties took advantage of the wartime alliance of the Soviet Union and the West and of the resulting establishment of Soviet legations in Arab states to intensify their activities. Their position was strengthened by the prestige gained by the Soviets after their exploits in the war and their emergence as a world power. Communist policy in the Arab states as in other underdeveloped countries subject to Western influence was to adopt popular nationalist slogans and try to turn nationalist agitation into revolutionary channels. The problem of Palestine offered the Soviets great opportunities to oppose Western policy—after they had voted for partition and recognized Israel—and win Arab friendship, while the Arabs thought they found a successful and influential world power on whom they could depend. The Communists capitalized on the various expressions of Soviet-Arab amity particularly after the Egyptian arms deal in 1955. But even before the military usurpation of power, the Communists were able to cooperate with the left wing of the Wafd in Egypt and with the Baath and other radical parties in Syria and Iraq who sought to take advantage of the cold war and challenge Western influence. Certain Communist goals coincided with those of the radical nationalists and worked for the

Marxists' advantage. They included the undermining of the Western position in the Arab world and preventing the Arab states from joining the Western Bloc, the introduction of agrarian reform, and the weakening or destruction of the Arab ruling elite.

The radical nationalist parties, including the doctrinal ones, were soon able to adopt the Marxist kind of demagogy and made full use of Marxist slogans and of the superior technique of Communist agitation. The anti-government demonstrations of February 1946 in Egypt were mounted by the Communists of the Egyptian Movement for National Liberation (EMNL), and the increasing Communist influence was seen in the period that followed the repudiation of the treaty with Britain by the Wafd government, and in the riots of "Black Saturday" in Cairo on January 26, 1952. Two of the "free officers" and future members of the Revolutionary Command Council—Yusif Saddiq and Khalid Muhieddin—were members of the EMNL while Lt. Col. Gamal Abdel Nasser was mentioned as a sympathizer.[22] In Syria, Communist activities and cooperation with the radical Baath party were at their climax in the 1955-1958 period before the unity with Egypt. Syrian politicians who spoke out against the rising leftist pro-Soviet tide were arrested and tried and the officer, Col. Afif al-Bizri, who presided over the court-martial that tried them in 1957 was a Communist. Syria then became a refuge for the Communists who had to leave Iraq and other Arab countries.

Three other doctrinal parties or groups appeared in the inter-war period and during the Second World War, and they all advocated some radical change in the social order and provoked popular and military unrest. One of them, the *Ahali* (People) group appeared and remained within Iraq. The other two, the Muslim Brethren and the Arab Baath, were born in Egypt and Syria, respectively, but influenced other Arab countries. The *Ahali* group was organized in 1931 in Baghdad by a number of educated youngmen who worked for a brand of socialism under the name of populism and emphasized democracy and human rights. It cooperated with the military who mounted the first coup d'état in Iraq and in the modern Arab states in 1936, but it soon collapsed after the fall of the military regime that it had supported.[23] It was succeeded, however, during the post-war period of the early 1950's by the National Democratic Party led by Kamil Chaderchi. The new party advocated socialism and, along with the *Istiqlal* (Independence) Party, it insisted on neutralism and the abrogation of Iraq's treaty of 1930 with Britain.

The movement of the Muslim Brethren began in 1928 in Egypt under the leadership of Sheikh Hasan al-Banna, a devout Muslim teacher and dynamic orator and organizer. It spread into Syria and the other Fertile Crescent countries in the late 1930's.[24] In contrast with most other parties and movements, it did not patronize any military coup d'état and it gave no support to any military regime. It was critical of military government and opposed dictatorial rule. Its leader represented those Muslims who had no Western training and who resented westernization and the decline of Islamic values. He entered the political struggle in order to denounce corrupt government and build a just and prosperous Muslim society. The Muslim Brotherhood fought colonial rule and, like most doctrinal parties, called for social reform. But it was primarily an Islamic movement that conceived of a state ruled by the dictates of the Sacred Law and viewed Western democracy inferior to Islamic egalitarianism. The state was expected to exercise, among other things, control over education and morals and to provide for public welfare in accordance with Islamic law and tradition. The socialism that the advocates of this movement preached was an Islamic socialism based on the Koran. It emphasized social justice but did not call for the subversion of the social order.[25] The movement drew its membership mainly from the underprivileged and the religious intellectuals. In Egypt, it played a role in politics in the last years of the monarchy and it turned to terrorist activity. It was suppressed in 1954 by the Egyptian revolutionary regime. In Syria it fought the excesses and abuses of personal power and opposed radical socialism under the various military dictatorships.

Among the ideological parties that appeared in modern Syria, the Arab Baath (Renaissance) Party has attracted most attention, first, because of its comprehensive and revolutionary doctrine of Arab nationalism and its association of nationalism with socialism; second, for its influence on Arab youth, its connections with army officers particularly after its merger with the Arab Socialist Party of Akram Hourani, and its role in Syrian crises and military coups; third, for its role in the formation of the United Arab Republic in February 1958, and in the rule of Syria immediately before and after that unity; and fourth, because it was the only doctrinal party to reach power in Syria, and also in Iraq, in early 1963.[26] The party has also received attention for a different set of causes: first, its unscrupulous and conspiratorial methods for reaching power; second, the contradictions between its principles, as laid in its constitution, and its actual practice of power; third, the limited stature of its leaders and its inability to gain a mass following; and fourth, its open partisanship during its periods of rule, and its harsh methods of enforcing obedience to its policies.[27]

The two founders of the Arab Baath Party, Michel Aflaq and Salah al-Din Bitar, were both middle class Syrians from Damascus who had studied at the Sorbonne as bursary students in the early 1930's, and were later appointed teachers in Syrian government secondary schools under the French mandate. They both gave the impression of being frustrated and dissatisfied with their careers.[28] They belonged to that category of young intellectuals whose ambitions by far exceeded their achievement and their readiness for constructive work.

During his student years in France, Aflaq came under the influence of Marxism which was to have its permanent impact on him and on his party. He was associated with a group of Communist intellectuals and issued in collaboration with them a leftist literary magazine called *al-Taliah* (The Vanguard) in 1935. As long as the French mandate lasted, he never raised his voice against colonial rule which he and his party attacked so vehemently only after it had ended in Syria, or when it was in its last stages in other Arab countries. In the early 1940's, Aflaq began timidly to spread his ideas about Arab nationalism and rebirth among his students. Without abandoning his Marxist creed, except for that part of it which rejects nationalism, he had come by then under the influence of German idealistic nationalism and Hegelian totalitarianism and also under the spell of the rising Hitlerist star. The fall of the government of the French Popular Front followed by the collapse of France itself and the German initial successes against Russia must have had their impact on Aflaq's change of mind and heart and on his break with his Communist friends.

In 1942 Aflaq had to resign from the ministry of education because of his involvement in indoctrination at the expense of his teaching. His close friend and colleague, Bitar, resigned at the same time and suddenly, but tragically, the two isolated themselves completely from their former colleagues and acquaintances who came to refer to them derisively as the "prophet" and the "disciple". Aflaq was endowed with a good imaginative intellect, but he was eminently cynical, conceited, sarcastic and somewhat eccentric. In his hesitant and tiny person, he concealed a craving for fame and recognition which, under the circumstances, he could satisfy only by entering the open career of politics. Although his awkward personality and his Christian birth hardly fitted him for political leadership, he was able to maintain his position as the national secretary-general of the Baath Party and its recognized theorist.

The growth of Aflaq's party was slow, and until the mid-forties it was restricted to high school students and graduates. It was only in July 1946, a few months after the evacuation of foreign troops, that the party issued its newspaper, *al-Baath,* and rented a party headquarters. On April 7, 1947, the first party conference was held and its constitution was approved. This was the official date for the founding of the party. By the late 1940's many high school graduates who belonged to the Baath had become civil servants or had entered the university or the Military Academy. In the early 1950's the Baath could count among its members or sympathizers a few officers and a sizeable number of teachers and other civil servants. The party never succeeded, however, in having a mass following, and even at the height of its power in early 1964 its membership did not exceed 10,000 persons.[29] Outside Syria, its membership was largest in Iraq and Jordan where its ideology was disseminated by students who had studied at the Syrian university.

In 1949 the Baath Party received official recognition when Aflaq became member of a coalition cabinet that grouped representatives of almost all Syrian parties after the second coup d'état. Aflaq's tenure as minister of education—the first and last cabinet post he occupied—lasted less than three months and was marked by confusion and open favoritism for the party members. In the elections to the Constituent Assembly in that same year, Aflaq was unsuccessful. In 1954 the Arab Baath Party merged with the Arab Socialist Party which had been founded in 1950 by Akram Hourani, a young practical politician from Hama, who had encouraged and advised most of the leaders of military coups in the preceding four years and also had quarreled with them. Hourani's party stood for socialism and pan-Arab unity and had a popular following among the youth of his home town and in the rural areas where he advocated agrarian reform. The two parties were called after their merger the Arab Socialist Baath Party.

The doctrine of the Baath Party rests on the principles of the unity and freedom of the Arab nation, its capacity for self-renewal and its eternal mission, hence the Baathist slogan, "one single Arab nation with an eternal mission".[30] The Baath Party differed from the other Syrian parties that proclaimed Arab unity as their goal in that, first, it was a socialist party. Article 4 of its constitution declares that "socialism is a necessity that emanates from the depth of Arab nationalism itself," and it will help the Arab people realize their potentialities. Second, the Baath Party is a revolutionary party. Revolution in Baath doctrine is a means for realizing the renaissance of Arab nationalism and for the establishment of socialism. The party considers that Arab unity can be realized only by the Arab people, and revolution is the only way to insure reform and thus lead to the people's emancipation. Revolution and struggle, moreover, are necessary, according to Aflaq, not only to remove and change vitiated conditions but "so that the nation may recover its unity in this struggle also."[31] Third, the Baath Party is a universal Arab party. Although it started in Syria, it soon established branches in the Arab countries with regional committees in each country and an elected central or national committee for the whole Arab world. The party defines the "Arab" in Article 10 of its constitution as anyone whose language is Arabic, who has lived on Arab soil and who believes in his belonging to the Arab nation.

The Baath Party leadership has resorted to the classical methods of fault finding and rabble rousing in order to gain popularity and reach power. It concentrated on negative criticism and blackmail, and at the same time it made fine promises to the public and used attractive slogans. It took full advantage of the constitutional freedoms to make its attacks against the ruling regime, but whenever that regime was a military dictatorship it preferred not to raise its critical voice, and its leaders found safety in leaving the country. Four times at least Aflaq abandoned the struggle as well as the spiritual fulfillment that he could have derived from it, according to his revolutionary theory: the first time under Colonel Husni al-Zaim in 1949 when he wrote him a letter announcing his withdrawal from politics after having spent a few days in jail; the second time under Colonel Shishakli in 1952 when he left the country along with his colleagues; the third time under Abdel Nasser and the United Arab Republic in 1959-1961; and the fourth time under the post-Nasserist regime in 1962. The Baath Party succeeded in reaching power only by conspiracy and with the help of military coups, not by public consent.

Once in power, it followed a strict partisan policy in appointments and promotions and tried to win adherents by indoctrination and patronage. It worked for the party, as one of its former admirers said, more than for public interest. Many young men joined the Baath, as Professor Sati al-Husri found out, not by conviction but for profit.[32] The party organized its own militia under the name of the National Guard, and it even had its own commando units for repressive or terrorist action. It denied its opponents the constitutional freedoms which it enjoyed when it was in the opposition. In suspending the constitution and ruling by decree under martial law, it violated Article 14 of its constitution which defined its regime as one of constitutional parliamentary rule, and it thus established a virtual one-party dictatorship.

In its determination to reach power, the Baath Party has followed what seems to be an opportunistic course of action or, according to a more favorable view, it has operated a series of tactical changes in policy. In the course of the Second World War the party was pro-Fascist and it incurred the hostility of the former Communist friends of its founder. In the early and mid-fifties, it followed an inflexible anti-Western policy exceeding even that of the local Communists. The various issues such as the Baghdad Pact in 1955, the Suez crisis in 1956 and the inter-Arab problems and crises were exploited to redouble its attacks against imperialism and certain Arab rulers. The party was enabled through its alliance with the notorious Colonel Sarraj, Chief of Army Intelligence, to purge its opponents in a series of treason trials and to wield power. It capitalized largely on Abdel Nasser's popularity and became his ally. It also cooperated so closely with the Communists that many of its members came to be known as fellow travellers. The party leaders then became frightened by the growth of Communist activities and popularity, and with the help of the army officers they precipitated the merger of Syria and Egypt and the formation of the United Arab Republic in early 1958. When it became clear, after a short period of Baath partisan rule, that they could not dominate the Syrian

Region, they turned against Nasser and expressed their approval of the secession of Syria from the UAR in September 1961.

When constitutional rule was re-established after Syrian separation from the UAR, the Baath Party found itself discredited for its responsibility in the merger, and its leaders, except for the Akram Hourani group in Hama, were defeated in the elections of the Chamber of Deputies. The party then split in 1962 into its two original component parts: the Arab socialists of Hourani became determined anti-Nasserists and opposed any Arab unity under a dictatorial regime, while the Baath socialists of Aflaq and Bitar strove to reach power at any price and became again Nasser's allies and fifth-columnists in Syria. They fought separation and conspired against the Syrian constitutional government. When the Baathist-Nasserist clique in the army overthrew the remnants of the constitutional regime in March 1963, the Baath leaders of Syria along with those of Iraq immediately opened negotiations for union with Nasser, in order to guarantee his support and that of the local Nasserists in the two countries. But they soon quarreled with him and with his followers because of disagreement about the question of leadership in the union, and about the status of their party. In this quarrel they were supported by the majority of the Syrians who opposed Nasser's socialist and authoritarian regime and considered Baathist rule the lesser of two evils. But no sooner had the Baathists consolidated their power by purges in the army and violent suppression of opposition than they proceeded to establish their strict one-party dictatorship and their radical socialist system.

Among the flagrant contradictions in the Baathist ideology, and between Baathist theory and practice are first, the emphasis in the Baath constitution and slogans on freedom, constitutionalism and popular sovereignty on the one hand, and the subordination of freedom in all its manifestations to the all-powerful Baathist socialist state on the other. Second, the contradiction between Baath strict theory of the unity of the Arab nation and its emphasis upon the existence of regional differences and special regional conditions. This emphasis is really motivated by Baath opposition to any kind of unity that does not insure its own domination of Syria. The party thus ceased to be, as Professor Husri said, "a doctrinal party that holds to principles and spreads faith in the unity of the Arab nation, and has become an ordinary political party that strives to rule and sacrifices its principles for the sake of ruling."[33]

The Baath Party's position on secularism and Islam is opportunistic and confused. In its constitution there is no indication of its attitude towards religion and its place in the state: Its revolutionary socialistic program which calls for "the overthrow of the present faulty structure," differs from other reformist programs in that it does not advocate the separation of religion and the state. In spite of certain Platonic and flattering statements on Islam, the party seems to depart from the orthodox religious attitude that considers Islam a divine revelation, and speaks of it as an Arab movement that was created out of the heart of Arabism. Rather than view Arab expansion as the result of the spread of Islam, it emphasizes Islam's indebtedness to the Arabs for its rise and expansion. Because of its opposition to fundamentalist and traditionalist Islam, its general radicalism and its placing Arab nationalism above the Muslim religion, the Baath Party has never enjoyed popularity in orthodox Muslim circles and has been combatted by the Muslim Brethren.[34]

The greatest damage exercised by the Baath Party has been its subversion and indoctrination of army officers and students at all levels and the creation of division, hatred, intolerance and a spirit of conspiracy in their ranks. Under its influence, graduates of schools and universities relied more on partisanship and patronage to reach high public office than on personal efficiency and necessary qualifications. There is even evidence to prove that those who belonged to the party received, while they were still students, favorable treatment in examinations and in the award of state scholarships for admission to normal schools and study abroad. Another damaging influence of the party stems from the "chosen-party" complex of its members, the boastfulness of its leadership and their contempt for other Arab nationalist movements and their leaders. According to Aflaq, a new era of heroism began in the Arab renaissance when the Baath Party appeared, and the Baath movement thus became the destiny of the Arab nation in this age. Aflaq described his party members as the original bearers of the idea of nationalism and the ones who are more able than others to carry on the struggle for it.[35] The Baath Party thus gave itself a monopoly of both true nationalism and the ability to achieve progress. It did more than any other party or group to discredit the generations of nationalist leaders in the country and to distort the modern history of the Arab national movement.

It is significant that shortly after the Baath Party had come to power in 1963 differences appeared between its radicals of the younger generation, and its moderates and older members and founders who, like Bitar, were now considered conservatives and reactionaries of the old generation. The disputes between the party leaders, their struggle for power, their disagreements about government policy, and the series of purges and exclusions of members from party leadership followed by their reintegration in a series of tumultuous congresses have given a picture of the chaos and lack of maturity in the Baath Party and among its members. Because of its fanatic dogmatism and extremism, its reliance on intrigue, conspiracy and violence, the Baath Party has enjoyed neither the respect of the responsible elements of the population nor the support of the masses. It could not attract or develop leaders of any great caliber. Its exercise of authority has always remained tragically dependent on the fortunes of its military supporters.

In the late 1930's another doctrinal movement for Arab liberation and unity appeared in Beirut and later spread mainly through graduates of the American University into the various Arab countries. It was known as the Arab Nationalists'

Movement and was not organized into a formal party. It had neither formal membership nor recognized leadership, but at least one of its leaders, George Habash, a physician from Palestine, came to be known as it became more active following the Palestine war of 1948 and the disagreements and clashes with the government of Jordan. The movement began with a moderate nationalist group and its activity consisted mainly of meetings and talks in the various Arab cultural clubs in the Fertile Crescent countries, and in university student circles and camps of Palestinian refugees. It favored the union of Syria, Iraq and Jordan and postponed the discussion of socialism until after the realization of unity mainly because its members were disagreed about the social order to be established.[36] It turned left after the Baghdad pact in 1955 and the Nasserist offensive in the Arab world and became an advocate of neutralism and of Nasserist Arab policy. It supported the United Arab Republic and continued to subscribe to Arab unity under Nasser's leadership after the secession of Syria and to Nasser's socialism until the June war of 1967. Since then it has asserted its independence in organizing the guerilla group known as the Popular Front for the Liberation of Palestine.

The years that immediately followed World War II witnessed a singular mushrooming of parties with socialist epithets. In addition to Hourani's Arab Socialist party, there appeared in the Syrian Constituent Assembly of 1950, a group under the leadership of Sheikh Mustafa al-Sebai known as the Muslim Socialist Front. In Lebanon, Kemal Junblat, best described as a "feudal socialist" and a temporal head of the Druzes, organized the Progressive Socialist party in 1947. In Iraq, the Socialist *Umma* (Nation) party was founded by Saleh Jabr in 1951. Jordan witnessed the rise of the National Socialist party which held power in the eventful period that followed the Suez crisis. Most of these parties were not strictly socialist but could be termed progressive, for they tended to equate progress with socialism. The term socialist was in vogue and many politicians and parties used it demagogically to win the votes of the laboring classes. There was, however, a sincere desire for social and economic reform that could be seen not only in the programs of parties that called themselves socialist but also in others drawn from bourgeois circles like the People's party of Syria which was founded in 1947. The interest in socialism and the adoption of more or less radical socialist measures became a feature of almost all the military regimes after the mid-fifties.

IV. The Young Arab Radicals and the New Issues

The recently independent Arab states were faced after the Second World War with some important external as well as internal tension-raising issues. Some of them were related to Arab unity and Arab alignment in the cold war, others were concerned with reform, economic and social change, and the relevance of democratic parliamentary government. These issues were not entirely new but they became more lively and more crucial as a result of Arab defeat in the Palestine war in 1948. The concept of Arab nationalism itself was no longer the same, for it came to mean not only the achievement of political independence but also the quest for dignity and strength and complete emancipation from foreign influence. Such new expressions and slogans as social justice and progressism (*al-taqaddumiyah*) became objects of discussion. Disagreements soon arose on the nature and extent of the desired reform and change between those who wanted a revolution in the political and social order and were referred to as the "dynamic" or radical nationalists or the "new men," and those who favored moderate and gradual reform and were called by their opponents "static" or conservative nationalists or "elder politicians" but in reality continued to represent the liberal democratic Western tradition.[37] The great debate between the two sides involved such other issues as the power structure in the state, the nature of inter-Arab relations, and the question of Arab relations with the foreign powers. The radical "dynamic nationalists" believed that the old leadership consisting largely of socially prominent wealthy landlords and businessmen was inadequate for presiding over the destinies and directing the policies of the newly independent Arab states, as the Palestine fiasco proved. They wanted to transform society, raise the standard of living and mobilize the masses of peasants and laborers for participation in the national effort. Their nationalism included a socialist program that would distribute land among the peasants, nationalize industry, abolish capitalism and give the masses a better life. It involved also the formation of an Arab union in which the existing states would surrender their sovereign status. The new nationalism, likewise, aimed at a neutralism in foreign policy that would enable the Arab states to conduct their relations as they pleased and with whomever they pleased and avoid the problems of the cold war and the adhesion to pacts that would make of them satellites of the great powers.[38]

What the "dynamic nationalists" actually desired was a kind of modernity which, as Professor Shils has explained, means sovereignty, influence and a respected place on the world scene. It involves democracy and universal suffrage even though democracy is not representative but egalitarian and "the suffrage is exercised through the acclamation of a single-party ticket" while the ruler is answerable to a collective will instead of a legislature. Modernity also means republican instead of monarchic government, and it includes economic advance, scientific knowledge, industrialization and planning as well as the dethronement of those who enjoyed wealth or privilege.[39]

Most of the radical "dynamic nationalists" belonged to the younger generation that had grown up during and after the period of nationalist struggle for independence but did not take part in it. Some of them had participated as students in the street demonstrations against the foreign rulers and had gained a rebellious and rather negative spirit. They did not all belong to one party and they remained as divided as the elder politicians on questions of leadership and procedure. Some of the aims they advocated had been already envisaged by more moderate politicians under whom industrialization and labor legislation began, legal reform and expansion of education had taken place, and the Arab League was established. Already under British and French rule, but particularly after independence, the very low cost of higher education at home and the large number of scholarships given by the various Arab states for study abroad enabled thousands of youths from the humble social strata in the rural areas and urban centers to join the ranks of the intelligentsia and become a part of what has been called the "new salaried or would-be salaried middle class."[40] The state needed their services and appointed those of them who were qualified in various government positions. They benefited from the rise in personal income, and they progressed economically and socially even more than those men of wealth and family who stayed behind because Muslim society had no barriers between social classes and people moved freely forward as their financial, intellectual and public position improved. Some of the educated youngmen were attracted to public life and aspired to the kind of social prestige that was enjoyed by the holders of political power. They joined the existing parties and some of them became members of parliament and cabinet ministers. Others viewed with bitterness their former humble condition and were unwilling to cooperate with the older political leaders and the political and social order that they represented.[41] During their years of study abroad—during which sometimes very little studying was done—some of them came under the influence of various radical doctrines and became inclined to introduce them into their own country. They were, moreover, too ambitious and too impatient to accept anything less than those positions of leadership which their seniors reached only after spending the best years of their lives and, sometimes, the best part of their fortunes in the national struggle. Their ambitions were not always commensurate with their abilities, and they often chose the seemingly easy but prestigious career of politics out of unpreparedness to do anything else, or out of mediocrity in what they were trained to do as teachers, lawyers and physicians. Some of them became the founding members of doctrinal parties and others joined later, but the membership remained small and ineffective until it gained the support of a few army officers.

The doctrinal parties thus owed their emergence to the ambitions, frustrations, prejudices, jealousies and impatience of the educated and half educated young Arab nationalists and also to the influence of imported ideologies. They were aided by various political developments and crises such as those related to the Palestine problem and by the financial support of interested sources as well as by the existence of a relatively free press under the constitutional regimes which they attacked. The doctrinal parties eventually succeeded in molding a certain sector of the youth into instruments of political and sometimes violent action. They led a blunt attack against liberal traditions and democratic representative government and claimed that it symbolized a monopoly of power and the ascendancy of a corrupt ruling class although it was only later when the young radicals succeeded in seizing power that total authority was monopolized by them under a single party system.[42] Democracy to them was no longer to be defined in terms of individual freedom, and the multi-party system was condemned on the ground that it was divisive. Their radical nationalism gave them the liberty to pass judgment on all human activities and values including freedom and thus they and their nationalism ended by becoming tyrannical and totalitarian.[43]

The Arab radicals concentrated their efforts on seizing the reins of government at any price and without any scruples. Their technique for gaining popularity and speeding their assumption of power was to undermine and discredit the rulers by exploiting the continuously and sometimes artificially erupting problems and issues and to organize demonstrations and hold the rulers responsible for every setback or failure in the country's internal or external policy. At the same time their propaganda was intended to make the people doubt the patriotism and honesty of the older leaders, and it called on them to revolt and to overthrow the ruling regime. The incitements and agitation of the young radicals entailed no sacrifice or risk on their part because the older leaders under the liberal democratic regimes were generally tolerant, except when the state security was threatened, and refused to take the kind of harsh measures that were applied later by the radicals themselves when they became the rulers. The standards of heroism and leadership at this time degenerated to the level of being able to write a fiery article attacking the administration or making a harsh speech in a mass gathering denouncing the local ruler or some foreign power. The Western powers, imperialism, and the United States came often under attack in order to inflame the feelings of the masses by making them believe that the imperialists were constantly plotting against the Arab countries and that the so-called reactionary ruler was helping them restore or maintain their influence. The anti-imperialist tirades were useful in creating the tensions that were beneficial for the success of the young radicals' plans and they gave the radical leaders the moral satisfaction of being able to attack, defy and insult a great Western power especially when the denunciation gained the applause of the opponents and enemies of the West. The Western powers and the United States in particular were denounced also for their support of Israel and for the mere fact that they were capitalist and free democratic countries at a time when the young radicals were advocating a system diametrically opposed to capitalism and liberal democracy and drawing closer to the Soviet Union.

In their persistent effort to seize power, the radical Young Arabs made attractive promises to the people and represented themselves as the trustees who spoke in the people's name. They forgot, however, that the trustee is obligated to act in the interest of the minor or of the person for whom the trust was made and to respect the implications of the law. The radical leaders, one writer commented, "praised the people and flattered their virtues wholesale and then oppressed them and insulted them in retail.'"[44] The only laws that they respected were those that they themselves made on the basis of the principle that they cannot do wrong. The techniques used and the campaigns led by the Young Arab radical leaders against the older liberal rulers eventually did not succeed in giving them a large popular following and did not allow them to reach power by popular support. The only time they were able to rule was when they became the allies of a military usurper of power, and the only measure of rule they were able to obtain was what their military ally was willing to give them.

Among the sources of tensions in the Arab world, the issue of inter-Arab relations was one that the military and their radical allies often used as a pretext for intervention in politics. In the division of the Arab Middle East until 1957 into a Saudi-Egyptian camp and a Hashemite camp that included Iraq and Jordan, Saudi gold and Egyptian intrigue kept Syria on the Saudi-Egyptian side. Relations between the two camps and between them and such neutral states as Lebanon nevertheless remained polite and friendly until radical "dynamic nationalism" entered the scene. The era of friendliness, decency and outward cordiality ended when Iraq signed the Baghdad Pact with Turkey in February, 1955 and became associated with the Western-sponsored Middle East Treaty Organization. The military rulers in Egypt particularly took exception to Iraq's independent action, and in the Arab League meeting of January, 1955 they tried to have the Arab states condemn Iraq for her proposed alliance but they refused. Jordan complained against the corruptive and subversive use of Saudi payments to its leaders and press, while Iraq became the target of virulent Egyptian radio and press attacks. Saudi Arabia continued its subversion by gold against the Hashemites and the policies of Western pacts until it realized in early 1957 the seriousness of the Egyptian revolutionary threat to her own existence. Arab alignments then underwent a change and Egypt would have been isolated if it were not for the unity with Syria in February, 1958 which was preceded by close cooperation between the radical Baath party and the Syrian radical officers with Egypt.

The Soviet Union began its drive since 1954 to win over the Arab world to its side or at least to dissociate it from the West after it had failed to gain influence in Turkey and Iran in the post-war period. Under the pretext of supporting Arab nationalist aims, it became the ally of the Egyptian and Syrian ruling authorities particularly after the conclusion of the arms deals at the end of 1955. Communism consequently gained in strength and the Communists became the allies of the "dynamic nationalists," especially those of the Baath party. In establishing itself as the champion of the Arab people against colonialism, the Soviet Union profited from the fact that it was not established in the Middle East and the Arabs had not experienced its colonial rule. In the Bandung Conference in April, 1955, the split became clear between those Arab countries that remained pro-Western like Iraq and Lebanon, and those that were now pronouncedly neutralist like Egypt and Syria. The neutralist Arab states started an accelerated campaign of invective against the other governments or leaders who did not subscribe to their neutralist policy and to their socialist ideology. For the first time in modern Arab history, Arabs were openly accusing other Arabs of treason and inciting the people to revolt and even assassinate their leaders. Instead of becoming a period of great expectations for Arab unity, the era became one of great accusations and incitement. At this stage and particularly after the Suez crisis of November 1956, the United States feared the impact of Soviet penetration into the Arab world. In early 1957 it proclaimed what is known as the Eisenhower Doctrine which expressed American readiness to aid those countries that were the object of Communist agression or threat of agression.[45] The Eisenhower administration had supported Egypt in the Suez crisis but now it came to be accused of trying to fill the vacuum created by the withdrawal of Britain from the Arab area. The neutralist Arab states claimed that the vacuum could be filled by Arab forces and that the Soviet threat to the

Arab East did not exist. The ra 'ical young Arab nationalists particularly in Syria and Egypt now blamed all the ills of the Arab world on the West, and their campaigns against the "Western imperialists" became even more violent than when imperialism actually occupied the area. The attacks against and defiance of the West became a mark of genuine nationalism while those who withheld their tongue were considered traitors to the Arab cause. This attitude along with the campaigns of hatred, accusation and incitement inaugurated by the radicals in Egypt and Syria against those who did not follow their policy resulted in the weakening of authority in the countries that remained pro-Western and were largely responsible for the civilian and military upheavals of 1958. Differences in orientation or in opinion among Arab states or among individuals within these states were no longer tolerated. It became evident, as Francesco Gabrieli has remarked, that while in the Italian Risorgimento—and for that matter in the Arab countries also until the advent of the "dynamic nationalists" to power—civil liberties grew with the growth of the nation, in this Arab movement civil liberties diminished and totalitarianism increased.[46] It is ironic that while freedom was thus denied and sacrificed to nationalism, the radical nationalists continued to speak of freedom and to attack those regimes in the other Arab countries that had to restrict it for purposes of self-defense against subversion. It is no less ironic that the Young Arab radicals who assumed power proceeded to change the facts of contemporary history in order to make genuine nationalism begin with them. They eventually became more violent and ostentatious, more closely allied with foreign powers—those of the Communist bloc—and less respectful of human dignity and of the rule of law than the older nationalist rulers whom they had so harshly denounced.

V. The Army Officers and the Palestine Problem

The present national armies of the Arab Middle Eastern

states had their early beginnings under the rule of the European powers, Britain and France, who established military academies for graduating officers, and trained and controlled the local troops until the various states became independent. The Arab officers of these local foreign-dominated auxiliary units did not play any role in the winning of independence; they showed no active interest in politics, and organized no secret national or ideological parties or clubs as long as foreign domination lasted. In this respect they were different from the Arab officers of the Ottoman Empire who cooperated with the civilian national leaders in the drive for autonomy and independence after 1909. The Arab national struggle against British and French domination between the 1920's and the 1940's, moreover, was different from that of such countries as Algeria, Israel, and Cyprus where the national movement included an essential combating force or military wing that became the nucleus of the national army after independence.[47]

The Arab armies shared one common feature after independence. They all expanded their services, increased the number of their officers and men, and tried to modernize their equipment and training, particularly after the Palestine war of 1948. The degree of expansion, however, differed between Lebanon and the Sudan on the one hand and Egypt, Syria, Iraq and Jordan on the other. The Sudan kept a relatively small army which by 1965 numbered 18,000 soldiers after it had been 12,000 in 1958 and 5,000 in 1925. While its population was about half that of Egypt, its army in 1965 was one-tenth of the Egyptian army. The Syrian-Lebanese native troops, known as the *troupes spéciales* under the French mandate numbered 13,500 officers and men. But whereas the Lebanese army after independence increased from 4,000 in 1948 to 13,000 in 1965, that of Syria increased from 8,000 to 60,000 in the same period. Compared to Jordan, Lebanon was more populous but its army was one-fourth of the Jordanian army in number. The reason is that Lebanon has remained partly dependent on the international community for external defense, and the mission of its small army has been mainly a domestic one designed to police and mediate between the conflicting confessions and groups and insure internal security. The Arab Legion in Transjordan was organized in 1922 for police duty but it was later used in 1941 as a fighting force outside the country. From a small force of 1,350 it was increased to 8,000 in 1945, and after the Palestine war it almost tripled in number in 1959 to 23,000 and reached 45,000 in 1965.[48] It was the only armed force that remained under British command after the treaty that ended the British mandate–in 1946–and it continued to be subsidized by Britain until the end of the treaty in 1957. Its commander until 1956, General Glubb Pasha, and several other British officers served the Jordanian government under contract. The Arab Legion was regarded as the best fighting force in the Arab world.

With the exception of the Egyptian army, the army of Iraq was the oldest among the regular forces of the emerging Arab states after 1920. It was also the first army to play a role in politics and to mount the first coup d'état in 1936 partly because Iraq was the first Arab country to obtain independence by treaty in 1930 and to become a member of the League of Nations two years later. The Iraqi army was reorganized and purged of anti-British officers after the short military rebellion against the British ally in 1941. The army forces were expanded after the Palestine war and reached 40,000 in 1954, and by 1965 they numbered 80,000 officers and men. Like the other Arab states, such as Egypt and Jordan, that had treaties of preferential alliance with Britain, Iraq was dependent on Britain for its military equipment.

The situation in Yemen was different from that of the other Arab states in two ways: First, Yemen became a completely independent state after the end of the First World War and its armed forces were neither controlled nor trained by a foreign power; Second, Yemen had no regular army and its tribal levies furnished by the warlike Zaydi tribesmen of the internal highlands were nearly the exclusive source of military power at the Imam's disposal and their number fluctuated. Under Imam Yahya and later under his son, Imam Ahmad, a royal guard was formed and became the nucleus of a regular army that counted not more than 4,000 soldiers in the 1950's. Even after the coup of 1962, the republican army remained small and did not exceed 10,000 in 1967.

The composition and the role of the armies and their officers were not the same in the new independent Arab states. They differed in their recruitment, in the homogeneity of the society in which they were recruited, and in the officers' concept of their role and the extent to which they became politicized. In Jordan the officers were carefully chosen and watched during Abdallah's rule (1921-1951) as emir and as king. Political reliability was an important criterion for enlistment and promotion. The greatest majority of soldiers until 1945 were from the beduins of southern Transjordan. As the army expanded, officers and soldiers were taken from other areas including the annexed west bank (or the remaining Arab part of Palestine) but the elite units and commands remained largely tribal and were loyal to the ruling dynasty.[49] It was these tribal elements who overcame the attempts of various conspirators, civilian and military, against the regime. The Jordanian army thus continued to play a decisive role in the protection of the monarchy even after the death of King Abdallah in 1951 and the departure of the British in 1956. In Lebanon the army was essential for defending the Lebanese system of parliamentary democracy and free economy and for acting as mediator in the internal conflicts. The military service was not obligatory in Lebanon, but in the recruitment of career soldiers and in the preparation of officers, the sectarian balance had to be respected and a certain proportion between the various confessions had to be observed. The Lebanese officers, among whom Maronites have held the higher posts have refused to be involved in politics. They mostly belonged to the bourgeois class and have not been attracted by the radical ideologies.

The general tendency in the Arab states with expanding

armies and obligatory military service such as Egypt, Syria and Iraq was to make the military academy easily accessible to all classes exactly as in the case of the university and the civil service. The military career appealed particularly to the poorer classes who found in it security and prestige after a short period—two years in the military academy following high school—of free training. The officers as a result came to represent the underprivileged sector of society while the youngmen of the bourgeois class remained a minority because their parents preferred for them a professional or business career. The new officers generally belonged to the same class as that of the discontented civilians, and their commitment to the ruling regime was weaker than that of the senior officers. Some of them either because of frustration and youthful impatience and conceit, or because of dislike for a ruling elite to which they and their elders did not belong, were attracted to the radical parties that worked against the regime. Parliamentary government with its rivalries, controversies and crises sometimes discredited the political leaders and their rule, and the officers either independently or under the influence of the young radical nationalists or of foreign agents decided that a change was necessary. They eventually made their military coups and imposed their will on the civilian population by breaking the social and economic position of the ruling elite which had naively allowed the military to manage their own affairs and could not keep a watchful eye over the recruitment and promotion of the officers and over their loyalty and political reliability. Many officers remained or wished to remain neutral and were disinclined to engage in politics, but they had eventually to adhere to the ruling radical clique of officers or else be purged. Those who dissented sometimes indicated their disapproval by mounting a coup against their military colleagues.

In Egypt youngmen belonging to the lower middle class were admitted increasingly to the military academy after the independence treaty of 1936 with Britain. The members of the executive committee of "free officers" who later made the coup of 1952 were almost all graduated between 1938 and 1940 and they held the ranks of major or lieutenant-colonel at the time of the coup. The officers who became involved in politics and presided over the destinies of the revolution were all Egyptian Arabs of the Sunni Muslim faith and their homogeneity reflected that of the native Egyptian population where very few members of the Coptic Christian minority joined the officers' ranks. This was a potent factor in the peaceful teamwork of the ruling officers and in the absence of frequent serious quarrels among them. The situation was different in Syria and Iraq where disagreements and conflicts of loyalty were partly caused by religious and ethnic diversity. Under the French mandate, the "special troops" were recruited mainly from the Syrian ethnic minorities of Kurds, Circassians, and Armenians, and from the religious minorities of Christians and non-Sunni Muslims. Even after independence, the Sunni Muslim youngmen of the urban middle and upper-middle class showed little interest in a military career. The result was that while the Arab Sunni (Orthodox) Muslims formed the overwhelming majority of the Syrian population, most of the officers were Alawis (members of an extreme Shia sect) and Druzes (members of a post-Islamic indirect offshoot of the Shia sect) of the mountainous and rural areas, and Christians of the urban centers, in addition to the Sunni Kurds and Circassians and the Christian Armenians. This religious diversity and the large increase in the number of officers from under-developed rural areas eventually produced social differences and tensions within the army and made it easier for the radical ideological parties to infiltrate the officers' ranks. Factional and personal quarrels made the army look like "a divided but armed parliament" after the mid-fifties.[50] In Iraq the overwhelming Muslim majority was almost evenly divided between Shiis and Sunnis. The Kurds represented a large ethnic minority of about one-fifth of the population. The army officers were drawn from all three groups, Sunni Arabs, Shia Arabs, and Kurds but the Sunnis were dominant and their dominance was resented by the other groups.

The army officers became the guardians of national sovereignty after the independence of the various Arab states. Defeat in the Palestine war of 1948 did not impair their standing as the defenders of the Arab homeland against Israel. As they became increasingly conscious of their own importance they acquired more independence in the control of military affairs. While they refused to admit any responsibility for their defeat in the war, they accused the ruling civilian leaders of incompetence and corruption and joined the young radicals in their criticism of the existing regime. The first series of military coups that followed the Palestine war occurred in Syria in 1949, but it should be remembered that the army began meddling in politics in independent Iraq and staged its first coup in 1936, twelve years before the war in Palestine. The continued state of belligerency with Israel gave the officers the opportunity to continue their intervention in politics and allowed the young Arab radicals to press their appeal for revolution and change and to enlist the help of the young officers for overthrowing the "old regime" in the Arab countries. But it was only in the mid-fifties through the encouraging example of Egypt and in response to the call of the Egyptian revolutionaries that the other Arab officers and their civilian allies began their active intervention and their conspiracies to break the power of the old ruling elites. More military defeats in the wars with Israel in 1956 and 1967 did not diminish the control of the officers over internal affairs, and the defeats were followed by still more military coups that overthrew existing civilian regimes as in the Sudan and Libya in May and September 1969, or replaced one military–civilian radical group by another as in Iraq and South Yemen in July 1968 and June 1969, respectively.

The Palestine war of 1948 and the continued hostilities with Israel that led to other Arab disasters have had their impact on the staging of military coups and on the call for revolutionary reforms in several ways. First, they raised doubts in the people's minds about the competence and integrity of the civilian political leaders and about the effectiveness of the entire democratic parliamentary regimes in the Arab states. They consequently allowed the radical critics and their military allies not only to oust the political leadership but also to destroy the entire constitutional democratic structure in most of the Arab countries. Although the military disasters that came after the initial defeat of 1948 were the responsibility of the new military regimes, they did not lead to the overthrow of the military rulers but on the contrary they resulted in more radicalism and in the destruction of other remaining civilian democratic governments. Second, the Palestine war of 1948 and the subsequent developments of the Palestine problem created a hostile attitude towards the West that made all Arab governments and political leaders who had any friendly relations with the Western powers suspect and gave the Arab radicals a pretext to attack them and seek their displacement through military coups. The newly established regimes eventually sought and obtained support from powers opposed to the West, the Soviet Union in particular, and intensified their campaign against the Western presence in any part of the Arab world. Third, the Palestine war of 1948 and the feeling of frustration and weakness after the Arab defeat created in the officers a desire to reform and strengthen the military establishment and remove the old regimes that became the scapegoat for the military failure because they were considered responsible for the weakness of the army. The officers consequently bought arms from the Communist countries when they could not obtain them from the West, accepted Soviet technical aid and military advisers, and promoted friendly relations with the Soviet Union that resulted in more attacks against the West and its remaining Arab friends and in more encouragement for the Arab radicals to change the political and social order in the Arab states along totalitarian socialist patterns. The officers were no longer contented with their role as guardians of national sovereignty and defenders of the Arab homeland. They now claimed to be the people's trustees and the guardians and defenders of the people's interests. Their eventual quarrels among themselves on the ways and means of exercising that supposed trusteeship led to more military coups.

The result of the Palestine war of 1948, in the fourth place, produced a shock that moved certain sincere and thoughtful Arabs to propose a cure for the weaknesses of Arab society, while the Arabs in general looked for a leader who would defend Arab dignity and satisfy the Arab desire for power and outside admiration. The military strongmen who staged the coups against the old regimes at various times were expected to exercise that leadership and were given, in certain cases, ample time to prove themselves but they all failed. The atmosphere of crisis generated by the Arab-Israeli conflicts and tensions gave the Young Arab radicals—many of whom were mediocre, impatient and ambitious climbers—a splendid opportunity to subvert and destroy the liberal political and social institutions and values in the hope of presiding with military support over a better stronger, and more equitable order.

The Arab army officers did not constitute a separate caste or class, but they had certain interests which they intended to defend and a special position acquired by the circumstances of the war with Israel which they cleverly exploited. Otherwise, they shared the same interests and ambitions as those of the middle or lower-middle class from which they came. They also had the same attitudes and displayed the same weaknesses as those of the other Arabs. The army naturally stressed discipline, honesty, loyalty, decisiveness and competence because these are basic foundations of the soldier's profession, exactly as they are also important in the medical, legal, and educational professions. But this does not mean, as some have implied, that when the officer becomes a politician or a ruler he would necessarily display more discipline, honesty, competence and decisiveness than the civilian political leader. Nor can it be implied that the ruling officer is more interested in reform, or more modernistic and progressive than his civilian counterpart, although it is true that he disposes of the means of violence that can force the speedy implementation of reform. Moreover, the notion that the army has a sense of national mission that transcends parochial, regional or economic interests and kinship ties does not make the officer more qualified for holding political power. The fact is that Arab politicized officers have been influenced by regional and material interests and by religious and kinship ties to the same extent as their civilian counterparts.[51] The Arab officers have also used their power to lead a class struggle against their opponents of the old ruling elite under the pretext of reform and under the influence of imported ideologies. Furthermore, the general education of the Arab officers has generally been of a lower standard than that of the university graduates especially those who studied abroad. The result, contrary to what is generally believed, was that the officer had less knowledge, culture, experience and maturity than the average educated civilian. The young military officers lacked in particular the wisdom, the sound judgment and the respect for the rule of law that are needed for the exercise of power.

CHAPTER I

Notes

1. See discussion for the underdeveloped countries in general in Edward Shils "The Military in the Political Development of the New States" in *The Role of the Military in Underdeveloped Countries,* ed. John J. Johnson (Princeton: Princeton University Press, 1962), 8ff.
2. See Sati al-Husri, *al-Bilad al-Arabiyah wal Dawlah al-Uthmaniyah* (The Arab Countries and the Ottoman Empire), 2nd ed. (Beirut, 1960).
3. For details on the Hussein-McMahon correspondence, the Arab revolt, the pledges and counter-pledges and secret agreements, and the Balfour Declaration see George Antonius, *The Arab Awakening* (New York: G. P. Putnam's Sons, 1946), chs. 9-13; A. L. Tibawi, "Syria in War-Time Agreements and Disagreements," in *Middle East Forum* vol. 43 nos. 2-3 (Beirut, 1967), 77-109.
4. Antonius, ch. 14; Harry N. Howard, *The King-Crane Commission* (Beirut: Khayat's, 1961).
5. For these divisions, Albert H. Hourani, *Syria and Lebanon,* A Political Essay (London, 1946); J. Achkar, *Evolution Politique de la Syrie et du Liban, de la Palestine et de l'Iraq* (Paris, 1935).
6. Antonius, ch. 14 on the Cairo conference.
7. Royal Institute of International Affairs, ed., *Great Britain and Egypt* 1914-1936 (London, 1936).
8. These problems will be discussed in detail in Chapter 2 on Iraq and Chapter 6 on Jordan.
9. See Majid Khadduri, "The Scheme of Fertile Crescent Unity: A Study in Inter-Arab Relations," in *The Near East and the Great Powers,* ed. Richard N. Frye (Cambridge: Harvard University Press, 1951), 137-177. Other details will be given in Ch. 3 section 1 on Syria.
10. Details will be given on this Arab cold war in vol. 3 Chs. 2 and 4 on Egypt and Yemen respectively.
11. See the opinion on this "traditional bourgeoisie" in Manfred Halpern, *The Politics of Social Change in the Middle East and North Africa* (Princeton: Princeton University Press, 1963), 209.
12. See Nuri al-Said's blue book *Arab Independence and Unity* (Baghdad, 1943) and the plan supported by Emir Abdallah for a general Arab federation in Muhammad Khalil, *The Arab States and the Arab League: A Documentary Record* vol. II (Beirut: Khayat's, 1962), 14-15, 9-12.
13. See Robert W. Macdonald, *The League of Arab States* (Princeton, 1965), 41-44.
14. See a discussion on these points in Pierre Rondot, "Parliamentary Regimes in the Middle East," *Middle Eastern Affairs* (August-Sept., 1953), 257-265; William Thomson, "The Problems of Muslim Nation-

alism," in *Islam and the West,* ed. Richard N. Frye ('s-Gravanhage: Mouton & Co., 1951), 53.

15. For the Arab constitutions and their amendments see *Dasatir al-Bilad al Arabiyah* (Constitutions of the Arab Countries) (Cairo: Arab League Institute of Arab Studies, 1955).
16. See George Grassmuck, "The Electoral Process in Iraq 1952-1958," *The Middle East Journal* xiv, 4 (1960), 413; Caractacus (pseud.), *Revolution in Iraq* (London: Gollancz, 1959), 29ff; Arnold Hottinger, "Zuama and Parties in the Lebanese Crisis of 1958," *MEJ*. xv, 2 (1961), 127ff.
17. See Elsa Marston, "Fascist Tendencies in Pre-War Arab Politics," *Middle East Forum,* May, 1959; Speech of Sami Shawkat in 1933 on "The Art of Death" in Majid Khadduri, *Independent Iraq* (London: Oxford University Press, 1951), 166.
18. Details on contacts of Arab politicians with the Nazis in M. Khadduri, 164-235.
19. The name of the party was incorrectly translated into French as Parti Populaire Syrien or PPS and it is often mentioned under this name.
20. Among the publications of Saadeh: *Nushu' al Umam* (The Rise of Nations), (Damascus 1951), and *al-Muhadarat al-'Ashr* (The Ten Lectures), (Damascus, n.d.); for details on party see monograph of Labib Zuwiyya-Yamak, *The Syrian Social National Party* (Cambridge: Harvard University Press, 1966).
21. During this period, the theorist of Arab nationalism Sati al-Husri who was living in Cairo wrote his critique of Saadeh and his party in *al-Urubah Bayna Duatiha wa Muaridiha* (Arabism Between its Protagonists and its Opponents), (Beirut, 1957), 69-138, and in *Difa 'an al-Urubah* (Defense of Arabism), (Beirut, 1956), 15-63. More will be said on the fortunes of this party in Chs. 3 and 5 on Syria and Lebanon.
22. See for Egypt Jean and Simonne Lacouture, *Egypt in Transition* (New York: Criterion Books, 1958), 257-265; for Communism in general, Walter Z. Laqueur, *Communism and Nationalism in the Middle East* (London, 1951); Muhammad Harb Farzat, *Al-Hayat al-Hizbiyah fi Suriyah* (Political Parties in Syria), (Damascus, 1955), 194, 243.
23. See Majid Khadduri, "The coup d'etat of 1936: A Study in Iraqi Politics", *MEJ* II (July, 1948), 270-292.
24. In Syria it was first known under the name of *Shabab Muhammad* (Muhammad's Youth) and was later organized in 1944 under one central committee and one guide. See Farzat, 246 ff; for details on the Muslim Brotherhood in general see, Ishaq Musa al-Husaini: *The Moslem Brethren* (Beirut: Khayat's, 1956; Christine Phelps Harris, *Nationalism and Revolution in Egypt* (Stanford: Hoover Institution Publications, 1964).

25. See Mustafa al-Sebai, *Ishtirakiyat al-Islam* (Islamic Socialism) 2nd ed. (Damascus, 1960).
26. Among the studies on the party, Leonard Binder, "Radical Reform Nationalism in Syria and Egypt," *The Muslim World* IXL (April and July, 1959), 96-110, 213-231; Farzat, 232-241; Kemal S. Abu Jaber, *The Arab Baath Socialist Party* (Syracuse, 1966).
27. Among the critics of the party: Muhammad Hassanein Haikal, *Ma Lladhi Jara fi Suriyah* (What Happened in Syria), (Cairo, 1962), 40, and his numerous editorials in *al-Ahram* 1963-1966; Sati al-Husri, *al-Iqlimiyah: Judhuruha wa Budhuruha* (Regionalism: Its Roots and Its Seeds), (Beirut, 1963),
28. The author draws this information from his recollections on the two leaders as fellow students at the Sorbonne and colleagues in the Syrian public schools.
29. This estimate was given by Salah Bitar in Cairo and was quoted in *al-Hayat* (Beirut), January 25, 1964.
30 For the constitution, doctrines and declarations of the Baath Party see *Nidal al-Baath* (The Struggle of the Baath), vols. 1-5 (Beirut: Dar al-Taliah, 1963-65); Michel Aflaq, *Fi Sabil al-Baath* (For the Baath), 3rd ed. (Beirut, 1963); Sylvia G. Haim, *Anthology on Arab Nationalism* (Berkeley and Los Angeles: University of California Press, 1963), 62-70, 233-241.
31. See Michel Aflaq, *Maarakat al-Masir al-Wahed* (The Battle for a Common Destiney), (Beirut, 1958), 33 ff; Aflaq's "Aspects of Revolution," in Sylvia Haim, 245.
32. See Husri's critique of the Baath in his *al-Iqlimiyah,* 242-245.
33. *Ibid.,* 53.
34. See L. Binder, in *Muslim World,* (April, 1959), 107; S. Haim, 62 ff.
35. Husri, *al-Iqlimiyah,* 183 ff., 203 quoting from Aflaq's *Fi Sabil al-Baath.*
36. See Lucien George and Toufic Mokdessi, *Les Partis Libanais en 1959* (Beirut, 1959), 44-51, Arabic section, 56-66.
37. See for details: Fayez Sayegh, *Arab Unity: Hope and Fulfillment* (New York: Devin-Adair Co., 1958), Ch. 11 entitled "The Great Debate"; see also his "Arab Nationalism: The Last Phase," *Middle East Forum* (November, 1957), 7ff.; Hisham Sharabi, "The transformation of Ideology in the Arab World," *Middle East Journal,* XIX (Autumn, 1965), 471-486.
38. See on question of neutralism, Georgiana G. Stevens, "Arab Neutralism and Bandung," *MEJ.,* XI (Spring, 1957), 139-152; *The Dynamics of Neutralism in the Arab World,* ed. Fayez Sayegh, (San Francisco, 1964).
39. Edward Shils, *loc. cit.,* 9-11
40. M. Halpern, *Politics of Social Change, op. cit.,* 209; his "The

Character and Scope of the Social Revolution in the Middle East," in William R. Polk ed., *The Developmental Revolution* (Washington D.C.: The M.E. Institute, 1963), 14.

41. Some notions on the feelings of the returning educated youngmen in William Polk, *The United States and the Arab World* (Cambridge, Mass.: Harvard University Press, 1965), 225.
42. See for these claims and attacks, Sharabi, *loc. cit.* 486, 483.
43. For the notions and attitudes of these young angry nationalists and other radicals, see Malcolm Kerr, "Arab Radical Notions of Democracy," *St. Antony's Papers, Middle Eastern Affairs no. 3,* ed. Albert Hourani (Carbondale, Ill., 1963?), 9-40.
44. In the review of Adnan al-Atassi's book "Progressist Democracy and Revolutionary Socialism," by Zuhair al-Shulaq in *al-Hayat,* October 24, 1965.
45. See John C. Campbell, *Defense of the Middle East* (New York: F. A. Praeger, 1960), Ch. 9 entitled "From Doctrine Toward Policy."
46. Francesco Gabrieli, *The Arab Revival* (New York: Random House, 1961), 165 ff.
47. See Clovis Maksoud, "Democracy and Military Regimes," *Middle East Forum,* April 1960.
48. See for these figures on the Arab armies the statistical tables in J. C. Hurewitz, *Middle East Politics: The Military Dimension* (New York: F. A. Praeger, 1969).
49. *Ibid.*, 308-315.
50. Halpern, *Politics of Social Change,* 268
51. On these notions, see *Ibid.* 257 ff., 271; W. Polk, *The United States and the Arab World,* 222-227.

CHAPTER II

Coups d'Etat and Military Rule in Iraq

In 1932 Iraq was the first modern Arab state to become independent and its army officers were consequently the first among the Arab military to become actively involved in politics. They staged their first coup d'état in 1936 and ended the first series of interventions in 1941. A new era of military upheavals marked by external incitement and radical internal change opened with the revolution of July 14, 1958 and the fall of the monarchy. The Iraqi military, much like those of Syria, have been unable since then to disengage themselves from politics and to avoid the struggle for power that resulted in another series of coups and in more internal instability and economic weakness.

I. Government and Society Under the Hashemites

Iraq is the largest and richest of the Fertile Crescent states that were created by the postwar settlement. Its population is overwhelmingly Arabic speaking and Muslim, as in the other Arab countries, with a large number of smaller ethnic and religious minorities, but it presents certain special features that were to generate internal tensions and weaken national unity. The Muslims of Iraq, in the first place, are almost equally divided between Sunnis and Shiis and each of the two sects resents being dominated by the other. In the second place, Iraq contains a compact ethnic and linguistic minority of Kurds, estimated at about one-fifth of the population, who live in the northeastern regions of the country. They have raised the banner of rebellion on various occasions and expressed the desire for autonomy. The tribal segment of the population, in the third place, is numerous and powerful, and the rebellions of its turbulent leaders, the great landholding sheikhs, constituted a challenge to the central authority in the first decade of Iraq's independent existence. In the fourth place, Iraq's society, in contrast with that of Syria and Lebanon, had no significant urban middle class, and the gap was great between the restless poor urban masses and the peasantry on the one hand, and the relatively small wealthy groups, on the other.

In addition to the heterogeneity of the population and the features of the social structure as potential sources of tension, one can mention the functioning of the parliamentary regime in the new state, and the conflicting views of Iraqi leaders on the relationship with Britain. The tensions led to military intervention particularly when the officers were urged to act by internal and external political forces.

Iraq became a kingdom in 1921. It was in the conference of Cairo in March 1921, under the British Colonial Secretary Winston Churchill, that it was decided, in the wake of a violent Iraqi rebellion against the British mandate, to establish an autonomous constitutional monarchy in Iraq and offer the throne to King Faisal who had been ousted by the French from his short-lived kingdom of Syria in July 1920. Faisal was then thirty-eight years old and was recognized as an all-Arab leader. Britain desired to fulfill some of her pledges to Faisal's father, Sherif Hussein of Mecca, and to reward Faisal for his military action as commander of the Arab contingent that fought against the Turks in Hejaz and then in Syria. Britain also expected Faisal to be a friendly and cooperative ruler in a strategically important and oil rich country. Faisal enjoyed, in addition to the prestige of his national and military leadership, that of being a Hashemite Sherif or direct descendant of the Prophet. Observers also have praised Faisal's wisdom, patience, farsightedness and simple democratic manner.[1]

Faisal was officially proclaimed King of Iraq on August 23, 1921 after his nomination had been approved in July, in spite of some opposition, by the Council of State, and confirmed by a favorable national referendum. The monarchy was declared to be "constitutional, representative and democratic."[2] The constitution of Iraq was promulgated in March, 1925 and the first parliament, consisting of an elected Chamber of Deputies and an appointed Senate, met in July. According to the constitution, the king was given the right to adjourn and dissolve parliament and to select the prime minister, but until the amendment of 1943, he was not permitted to dismiss his cabinet.

It has been claimed that the monarchy was alien to the people of Iraq and that the Hashemites were not wanted. Before, and particularly after their fall in Iraq, the Hashemites were even called tools of the imperialists and servants of Britain.[3] King Faisal, himself, was described by one writer as incapable and without will.[4] One thing is obviously certain; Faisal gained the throne of Iraq with the help of the British, and certain elements of the population, particularly among the Shiis, did not show enthusiasm for a Sunni king who, moreover, had no previous ties with the country. At certain times, King Faisal was even denounced as a traitor by extreme nationalists because he negotiated and signed a series of treaties with Britain that gave Iraq less than complete independence although each of them surrendered more British privileges. The fourth treaty, implemented in 1932, gave Iraq independence and sovereignty and made her an ally of Britain. The Hashemite kings intended to be faithful to their alliance, but as a judicious British author remarked and thereby put his finger on the main source of their trouble, "they became ineradicably marked with the stigma of foreign domination."[5]

The rulers of Iraq, however, with Faisal I at their head were neither servants of imperialism nor traitors to the Arab cause. Responsible nationalists in Iraq and in the Arab world never doubted Faisal's sincerity, patriotism and wisdom. In Iraq Faisal was generally accepted and admired. When he died in 1933, he was mourned both in Iraq and in the other Arab countries and his prestige as founder of modern Iraq grew even more. The fourth treaty with Britain sponsored by his prime minister, Nuri al-Said, in making Iraq the first modern independent Arab state in the postwar period, became the ideal and the example for struggling Arab nationalists elsewhere. How many times in the 1930's, the nationalists of Syria under the French mandate, as this writer recalls, shouted in the face of the French authorities, "We want a treaty like that of Iraq!" This ideal, however, along with many others, was bound to change with the change in circumstances. Already before the Second World War but particularly in the years that followed it, international rivalries gave the rising nations new opportunities to demand and obtain complete independence. Alliance with a great power became a sign of servitude. The creation of national armies accompanied by a change in nationalist ideology and a pressing demand for reform gave certain politicians the occasion to draw the army into politics and help discredit the national leaders as well as the parliamentary regime and then establish a partnership with the military for the rule of the country.

In the parliamentary regime in Iraq under the monarchy, several features can be noted, and some of them were not too different from those of other Arab countries. The change of cabinets, in the first place, was rather frequent. Iraq had fifty-nine cabinets in thirty-seven years, fourteen before independence (1921-32) and forty-five after independence (1932-58).[6] The frequent change was partly due to army intervention. In the second place, the Iraqi constitution, in spite of the military coups, was never suspended and parliament met regularly from 1925 until the revolt of 1958. Parliaments, however, rarely finished their regular term, and out of the fifteen Chambers elected throughout the monarchical period, only two, those of 1939 and 1948, finished their four-year term.[7]

This leads to the third feature, namely, the control of the elections and of parliament by the cabinet which never resigned as a result of a vote of non-confidence but often dissolved the Chamber.

Many deputies in the fourth place were drawn from among the tribal leaders and wealthy landowners who were naturally against reform and supported authority only because it protected their interests. The liberals, including those who wanted to reach positions of power quickly and easily, in addition to some communists, appealed to the masses and exploited their condition as a pretext to provoke disorder and gain popularity. In 1931 a group of these liberals appeared under the name of the *Ahali* (People) with a democratic and socialistic program and were succeeded in the following decade by the National Democratic Party. The conservative elements and elder statesmen, some of whom had been military officers under the Turks and later on participated in the Arab revolt, were not inclined for some time to allow the younger generation to share authority, but at the same time they were divided among themselves. Some of them, like those who formed the *Ikha' al-Watani* (National Brotherhood) group in 1930, were against the treaty with Britain, while others were faithful to it.

Party life, in the fifth place, was not disciplined and persons changed parties according to their ambitions and their interest. For being refused a cabinet post or for being offered one, politicians changed party allegiance. Personal rivalries and the struggle for power were sometimes ruthless and employed damaging methods such as inciting revolts among the tribes in order to weaken the ruling party or group of parties. One of the features of the parliamentary regime was the dependence of the government on the army to silence its rivals in the opposition, and the attempt of the opposition to turn the loyalty of the army officers from the government and cause them to stage a rebellion and bring about its downfall. The pretexts ordinarily used in the appeal of the opposition to either the army or to the masses were the need for reform involving the sensitive issue of the people's welfare, and the urgent need to defend the country's independence and prestige against an alleged foreign threat. Both pretexts were sometimes used.

Although the social and economic conditions in Iraq were not much suited for democratic parliamentary government, local conditions were changing and progress was being achieved in adjusting to the new democracy. Under Faisal's leadership, efficiency and experience among civil servants were growing and public opinion was well guided.[8] After his premature death, considered by some writers as one of the worst disasters that had befallen Iraq, the process of adaptation and adjustment to the democratic form of government was interrupted by the growing personal differences among politicians, the poor leadership of Faisal's young son, King Ghazi (1933-39), and especially by the officers' desire to play their role in politics.

II. A Succession of Coups d'Etat 1936-41

Active army intervention in Iraqi government affairs began in 1936, four years after Iraq's independence and one year after the national conscription law had gone into effect. It brought seven cabinet changes in the period 1936-1941 in a succession of seven coups d'état. The seven military interventions, it must be noted, were not all accompanied by violence. Only in three of them, the first (October, 1936), the second (August, 1937) and the seventh (April, 1941), was violence used while threats and intimidation were sufficient in the other cases. In all of these episodes, there was no question of overthrowing the monarchy or changing the parliamentary system of government and establishing a military dictatorship.

The occasion for engaging in politics at the beginning was the question of reform. The example of two successful military rulers in neighboring Turkey and Iran was an encouraging factor. The officers of the first coup soon disappointed the liberals who had sought their help. Military intervention then became a struggle for power between factions in the army or between these and the political leaders. After the fourth coup, the occasions for military intervention were all related to Iraq's foreign policy, its attitude towards the British ally, the question of alignment with or against the West during the world struggle, and the impact of Iraqi and pan-Arab nationalism on these attitudes. The officers, as usual, had also their own private motives and personal ambitions. They were influenced, moreover, by foreign propaganda directed mainly by the Axis powers, but subversion never attained the proportions it was to attain after 1954 with the advent of Nasserism in Egypt or with the Soviet drive to gain influence in the Middle East.

The most significant of the seven initial coups in their motivation and their ultimate effects on Iraq's political life were the first and the seventh. The coup d'état of October 29, 1936, was the first military intervention in Iraq and in the rest of the emerging Arab states after the First World War. Its object was to remove the cabinet of Yasin al-Hashimi that had taken office in March, 1935, because its "sole object," as the military commander's proclamation to the people of Iraq said, "has been to promote its own personal interests without paying any attention to the welfare of the public," and to replace it by a cabinet "composed of sincere men under the leadership of Hikmat Sulaiman, who holds a high position in the eyes of the nation and is esteemed for his noble career."[9]

Hikmat Sulaiman was a rather opportunistic elder politician who had belonged to Hashimi's National Brotherhood party, but broke with it partly because he was refused the post of minister of the interior. He called himself a "reformist" and admired Kemal Ataturk. In late 1935 he joined the socialistically inclined *Ahali* group and led a campaign to unseat Yasin al-Hashimi's cabinet and presented petitions to King Ghazi urging him to dismiss it. Hashimi's cabinet silenced the opposition by its control of the press, arrested some communist members of the *Ahali* and stubbornly remained in office. Unable to overthrow the government by legal means, Hikmat sought and obtained the cooperation of General Bakr Sidqi, commander of the Second Army Division, and acted as the liaison between the *Ahali* group and the officers.

Bakr Sidqi had emerged as a glorious national hero after his unglorious massacre of the Assyrians in August, 1933. His harsh action against both the Assyrian rebels and the small Assyrian civilian minority was approved and even urged by Hikmat Sulaiman who was then minister of the interior in the *Ikha* or National Brotherhood cabinet. When in early 1935, the tribes of the Middle Euphrates revolted with the complicity of the *Ikha* party which was then in the opposition, the chief of General Staff, who was the brother of the opposition leader, Yasin al-Hashimi, refused to act against the rebels because their revolt was caused by party intrigues and should receive, as he said, a political solution. The same chief of General Staff, however, took a different stand when further tribal disturbances occurred after his brother had become prime minister in March, 1935. The resistance of the tribes was now ruthlessly crushed and General Sidqi again gained prestige for his leading role in ending the rebellions.

It now became evident to the army officers with Bakr Sidqi at their head that the government depended on the army to maintain its position and authority. While this gave them an idea of their own importance, they were not happy with the feeling of being used as instruments of repression against the cabinet's opponents and of having to fight rebellions inspired by the intrigues of politicians against each other. Another factor of a personal selfish character influenced the officers' decision. The officers around Bakr Sidqi thought he should become chief of staff as a result of his successes, and in this capacity he could benefit his friends. This was not feasible, however, as long as Yasin al-Hashimi was prime minister, for his own brother held the post.[10] The officers also thought that the appointment of Bakr Sidqi as Chief of Staff would help strengthen the army. This was particularly needed in view of the Pan-Arab nationalist sentiments in the army and the expectation that Iraq should become the nucleus of a unified Arab state.

Bakr Sidqi took advantage of his position as Acting Chief of Staff in the absence of the titular Chief, General Taha al-Hashimi, who was on leave in Turkey, to lead the rebellion. He told the commander of the First Army Division, General Abdul Latif Nuri, about his plan only one week before the coup. At the same time Hikmat Sulaiman talked to the *Ahali* group and dissipated their fears of a possible military dictatorship. The *Ahali* opposition then prepared the text of a letter to the king asking him to dismiss the cabinet and it was signed by the two generals. The opposition also prepared a proclamation to the "noble people of Iraq" signed by Bakr alone, who called himself the chief of the "National Reform Force." The proclamation assured the Iraqi citizens that the army had no other objective except the people's welfare and the strengthening of the country.

On the morning of October 29, 1936, as Bakr's forces moved towards Baghdad and the planes of the Iraqi Royal Air Force dropped the proclamations over the capital, Hikmat Sulaiman went to the Palace to deliver the letter to the king. The letter requested King Ghazi to save the country and appoint a cabinet under Hikmat Sulaiman and to reach a decision within three hours. When the three hours had passed and no decision had been reached, four bombs were dropped by the Air Force on various places in Baghdad and some civilians were killed and wounded. The king was then meeting with the cabinet and showed no inclination to resist army demands after the officers had given him assurances of loyalty to his throne. Yasin had therefore to resign in order to avoid civil war. His letter of resignation was courageous and critical of the army's action. No cabinet has been able since then and under such circumstances to accuse the officers and their allies of greed and lack of experience and to say that their action will lead to evil results, as Yasin's statement did.

One of the shocking incidents connected with the coup d'état of October 29, 1936 was the assassination of the minister of defense, Jaafar Pasha al-Askari. He was concerned about the discipline and reputation of the army which he helped create in the early twenties. He believed that the advance of the army to Baghdad was unnecessary and decided to have a personal talk with Bakr Sidqi after obtaining a letter from the king advising Bakr against any further movement.[11] Bakr, however, was determined to march to the capital in order to remove any danger against the coup and to satisfy his vanity by receiving the people's recognition as a national hero and saviour. He suspected Jaafar's motives and intentions for coming and decided to dispose of him. When he found no volunteers to murder him, he ordered four officers to carry out the mission. They intercepted his car on the road to the northeast of Baghdad, ordered him out of the car and shot him. The coup of 1936 thus began with a crime and Bakr gained enemies instead of winning friends. It so happened that the victim of the first criminal act committed by the military was the very person who, because of his work for the army, was called "the father of the Iraqi army." He was also the first minister of defense in Iraq.

The coup of October, 1936 did not achieve its goals of reform, freedom and stability, nor did it enhance the prestige of Iraq or the cause of Arab unity. In its apologetic statement of policy over the radio on November 5, the government of the coup explained why its members cooperated with the "gallant army officers" and at the same time made an extensive list of promises of reform. It promised to strengthen the army, improve education and economic conditions and provide work for the unemployed in addition to allowing trade unions to function. It promised also to distribute uncultivated government land, appoint more competent officials and establish rule on the basis of justice and equality. The promises were met with transports of joy among the people who usually react with optimism to a change in government. The newspapers were also eulogistic in their tone, but it should be admitted that as a classical feature of military rule, the favorable attitude of the press and much of the public jubilation were inspired and even organized by the new regime.

The cabinet of Hikmat Sulaiman dissolved parliament and held new elections on February 20, 1937. The supporters of the previous cabinet were excluded and two-thirds of the members were new. Thirty of them were Bakr's own nominees. Bakr himself had no official position in the cabinet but he became Chief of Staff. The new cabinet granted the press the freedom to criticize and was patient with the comments of the opposition newspapers for less than three weeks, and then proceeded to suspend their publication. Disagreement between Bakr, backed by the army, and his partners who wanted certain reforms of a socialistic nature, led ultimately to the resignation of more than half of the cabinet on June 19, 1937 because the goals of the coup were not achieved. Hikmat Sulaiman thus parted with his friends, the reformists, and became Bakr's puppet. As for Pan-Arabism, it was supported by some nationalist officers who were against Bakr's immediate group, but neither Hikmat who was pro-Turkish, nor Bakr who was a Kurd were interested in it.

As in almost every military coup, the leader of the rebellion—and Bakr was no exception—promises the withdrawal of the army from politics as soon as the new regime is secure. The inner circle around Bakr, however, was not in favor of such a move for they wanted to take over the government from the politicians and reformists and establish a dictatorship. The followers of Bakr were ambitious, arrogant and inexperienced and at the same time, they were anti-democratic and opposed to Pan-Arabism. Bakr's own behavior became the object of bitter criticism. A contemporary writer has spoken of him as "a kind of Kurdish Goering."[12] He married a Viennese dancing girl and was involved in several secret assassinations and other affairs motivated by revenge. The army officers around him overindulged in cabarets and were compared, because of their licentiousness and outrages in public places, to the old Janissaries of the Ottoman Empire.

Bakr must have heard about certain plans to dispose of him and consequently prepared lists of opponents to be eliminated. This is why his enemies decided to strike. A junta of seven officers prepared to kill him and took advantage of his plan to stop in Mosul on his way to Turkey where he was invited to attend the Turkish army maneuvers. They induced a soldier to assassinate him in the airfield of Mosul on August 11, 1937. The two shots fired by that soldier ended his life as well as that of his commander of the air force, Muhammad Ali Jawad.

The assassination of Bakr Sidqi was a part of the second coup or counter-coup, but it did not bring about the automatic resignation of Hikmat Sulaiman's cabinet. An army rebellion in Mosul to which other centers rallied, defied Hikmat and the central army command in Baghdad. King Ghazi avoided civil war by accepting the demands of the rebel army leaders and removed Bakr's followers from power. Hikmat's cabinet had no other alternative but to resign on August 17, six days after Bakr's assassination. A moderate politician, Jamil al-Madfa'i, formed a new cabinet under which new elections were conducted and the new parliament met on December 23, 1937. The body of Jaafar Pasha, victim of the first coup, was brought to Baghdad on October 4 from its temporary burial by the roadside at the place where he was killed, and buried in the royal mausoleum with military honors.

The Madfa'i cabinet, coming as it did as a result of a counter-coup, did not mean the end of military intervention. Madfa'i found it difficult to keep the balance between factions in the army although he tried hard. He punished neither the assassins of Bakr nor those of Jaafar Pasha. Nuri al-Said was then intriguing with a secret group of officers—all of whom later on became his opponents—in order to overthrow the Madfa'i cabinet that had dealt kindly with such of his adversaries as Hikmat Sulaiman. The plotting officers decided to strike when they knew about plans to retire them. Having finished their preparations at the Rashid camp on the outskirts of Baghdad, they sent one of their number to warn Madfa'i of the impending coup so that he might resign without the use of violence, while the chief of staff told the king that the army had no more confidence in Madfa'i. This unique way of making a coup worked and Madfa'i immediately resigned on December 25, 1938 without offering any resistance. He had maintained himself in power for over sixteen months. Nuri al-Said then formed the new cabinet and General Taha al-Hashimi, Nuri's liaison with the officers, became defense minister. This third coup was thus motivated by personal rivalries and was carried out by a mere military threat of using force.

Nuri thus came to power through army pressure against Madfa'i, but that same pressure was applied later against other prime ministers including Nuri himself. The new cabinet hastened to dissolve parliament and ordered new elections which were completed in June 1939. In the meantime King Ghazi had died of a car accident on April 4, 1939. Prince Abdul Ilah, Ghazi's cousin and brother of his wife, was appointed regent for the young four-year-old King Faisal II. King Ghazi was one of the rare Hashemites who defied British influence, and was rather outspoken in his ideas. He thereby won popularity as a national figure in spite of his irresponsibility and inexperience.[13] Prince Abdul Ilah, on the other hand, was more reserved and calculating and more distant, and he had a high idea of the dignity and duties of kingship. He was described as the archetype of the Anglo-Arab, and as more English than most of the English.[14] As time went on, his dependence on the British alliance, his parody of British royal life and his influence in isolating his nephew, the king, from the people along with his indifference to public welfare combined to make him not only unpopular and hated, but even despised by the population and particularly by the nationalists.[15]

Nuri formed another cabinet on April 6, 1939 after the king's death. It was during the tenure of this cabinet that the

Second World War began. The government of Iraq broke relations with Germany on September 5, 1939. Nuri would have liked to participate in the war against the Germans, but Axis propaganda was strong and some officers in Iraq were pro-German. Nuri resigned on February 18, 1940 hoping that a new cabinet formed by the influential leader, Rashid Ali al-Gailani, might be prevailed upon to follow a policy more favorable to the Allies. Nuri and Taha al-Hashimi also expected to be included as ministers of foreign affairs and of defense, respectively, in the new cabinet. Military intervention came three days after Nuri's resignation and was a result of disagreement among senior officers about Nuri's participation in the cabinet. In this fourth coup, three officers, including the chief of staff, alerted their forces at Washash camp when the regent refused their desire to prevent Nuri's participation, while other officers alerted their troops at Rashid camp. When Gailani declined to become prime minister, the regent asked Nuri to reform the cabinet on February 21, 1940 and the three opposing officers were retired. The four colonels who supported Nuri—they were later nicknamed "The Golden Square"—now became all powerful in the army.[16]

Nuri's cabinet again resigned on March 31, 1940 to make place for a cabinet under Gailani in which Nuri was given the portfolio of foreign affairs while Hashimi obtained that of defense. Conditions in Iraq and on the war fronts were now tempting the new premier and the influential army officers to move away from the alliance with Britain and thus reverse Nuri's policy. In the first place, the collapse of France in June 1940 and the German victories of the summer of the same year made certain Iraqi leaders feel that the alliance with Britain was becoming a liability instead of an advantage for Iraq. Gailani and the High Defense Council desired to pursue a policy of neutrality and refused then to break diplomatic relations with Italy after she had entered the war on June 10. In the second place, Arab aspirations in Syria and in Palestine were frustrated, and the Mufti of Jerusalem, Haj Amin al-Husseini, who had come to Baghdad on October 16, 1939 was now gaining influence over the four colonels and other officers and over pan-Arab nationalists who included a number of Syrian political refugees.[17]

Contacts were established between the Gailani cabinet and the Italian ambassador Luigi Gabrielli in Baghdad as well as with Von Papen, the German ambassador in Ankara. A letter was even sent by the Mufti to Hitler dated January 20, 1941 through the Mufti's secretary Uthman Kemal Haddad. Even Nuri al-Said himself, we are told, made some flirtations with the Axis powers after his disappointment with Britain's failure to promise a favorable settlement in Palestine.[18] But on the whole, Nuri's insight and patriotism caused him to realize that the Axis powers could not give Iraq more than Britain had given, and that Britain and the Allies would ultimately win the war. He proved to be more far-sighted indeed than the other Arab leaders, with the Mufti and Gailani at their head, for Germany and Italy were planning to build a Near Eastern empire and to divide the Arab countries into spheres of influence, and some of the Arab leaders knew it. Nuri, however, was unable to convince the four colonels who were determined to support Gailani and the Mufti, although they knew that the Iraqi army could not hold long in case of conflict with Britain.

In early December 1940, the British began to complain about Gailani's lack of cooperation and tried to make pressure by refusing to supply Iraq with arms. They expressed the desire to have Gailani removed. The regent had no power to dismiss the prime minister,[19] but Nuri and a few other ministers resigned from the cabinet on January 21, 1941, and Gailani had to defend himself by appealing to the colonels to intervene, although in principle he was against inciting army officers to interfere in politics. The colonels went to meet the regent and asked him to keep Gailani. When he refused, they threatened to alert the army, but the Senate president, Muhammad al-Sadr, interceded and Gailani was retained in the premiership. When the Chamber of Deputies showed hostility to Gailani and attacked him in its session of January 30, 1941 he decided to dissolve it, but this was made impossible due to the regent's departure from Baghdad. Gailani was finally prevailed upon to resign on January 31, 1941. The pressure made by the colonels in this fifth military intervention was thus of no avail. The four colonels now wanted to impose General Taha al-Hashimi as prime minister and sent al-Sadr to communicate their wishes to the regent who was still outside the capital at Diwaniyah. Obliged to choose between civil war and compliance, the regent accepted to appoint Hashimi premier on February 1, 1941. This was considered the sixth coup and it was carried out, like many others, by a mere threat of using force.

The Hashimi cabinet tried to improve relations with Britain and made a timid attempt to disperse the four colonels by transferring some of them out of Baghdad. But neither Salaheddin Sabbagh of the Third Division nor Kamil Shebib of the First Division accepted the transfer. The officers now could not be restrained and they evidently made Hashimi premier in order to use him as their instrument of rule. They also gave themselves the power of judging whether the policy pursued was acceptable to the nation or not. On this basis, they refused to break relations with Italy. When Colonel Shebib was transferred to Diwaniyah on March 26, 1941, he not only refused but it is said that he tore the order of transfer.[20] The colonels brought pressure on Hashimi to keep him and he was kept in Baghdad, but Hashimi obtained, as he thought, a promise from the colonels that they would not interfere in politics. This was probably just to save the premier's face for they were preparing for their most serious interference which produced the seventh coup. It was designed to return Gailani to the premiership, for under the new premier they expected to enjoy more prestige and also to achieve the aims of Arab nationalism.

In agreement with Gailani and the chief of staff, the colonels sent an ultimatum on April 1, 1941, one day after the end of the parliamentary session, to Hashimi asking him to resign. The two officers who carried the ultimatum made him sign, under threat, a letter of resignation and sent it to the regent. The plotters this time sent army units to surround the regent's palace while other units seized the radio station and the government and other key positions in Baghdad. It is said that the officers who entered the regent's palace were armed with a certificate of death by heart attack.[21] The leaders of the coup might have aimed at arresting the regent and perhaps disposing of him, but it is doubtful if they desired at this stage the destruction of the monarchy or the end of Hashemite rule. Little King Faisal had to leave Baghdad with his mother Queen Aliya, the regent's sister, and an English nursemaid to a palace in the northeastern mountains. He was simply watched but was not molested. The regent was able to escape in disguise and spent the night in his aunt's house. In the early morning he crossed the Tigris and went to the American Embassy where the ambassador was preparing to go to the air base at Habbaniya to meet the new British ambassador, Sir Kinahan Cornwallis. The American ambassador took the regent with him and hid him under the rug of the back seat. From Habbaniya, the regent was flown to Basra where he was forced to embark in a British warship, and later he was flown to Amman in Jordan where he was joined by Nuri al-Said.

The seventh coup placed the officers in complete control of Iraq, but they needed to give the new government an aspect of legality and avoid placing direct rule in their own hands. They, therefore, formed a government of National Defense and made Gailani its leader. Gailani then convoked parliament through a call by the second vice-president, and in its meeting of April 10 he suggested deposing Abdul Ilah and appointing a distant relative, Sharif Sharaf, as regent in his place. Under the pressure of military rule, the Iraqi parliament lost its freedom of action and accepted the suggestion although it was the same parliament that had previously directed attacks against Gailani. The new regent accepted Hashimi's resignation and appointed Gailani prime minister, and thus a legal basis was found and the government of National Defense was ended. Along with the creation of the fiction of legal government, the officers needed also to give a justification for their action. They broadcast on April 3 a statement that contained the necessary inventions and exaggerations about the regent, and accused him of trying to obtain the Iraqi throne for himself, creating dissension among all ranks of the nation, subverting the national army, and violating the provisions of the constitution. The officers' statement even pretended that Hashimi's resignation, which they had imposed, was due to his indignation against the regent, and to his refusal to share responsibility in his actions.[22]

Under the rule of the officers and Gailani, hostilities began with Britain on April 29, 1941. The British ambassador cleverly caused the Iraqis to act before the Germans could be in a position to come to their help. He forced the issue of troop landings at Basra, while the Germans were trying to take Crete, and it took them eighteen days instead of two.[23] Shortly after, Hitler decided to begin his campaign against Russia before attacking the Middle East. The Mufti's call for *jihad* against Britain on May 9 had no great effect. The four colonels, stubborn and ignorant of their own country's possibilities, prevented any compromise. They even threatened to shoot Gailani, because he wanted to reach an understanding with Britain. King Ibn Saud advised them to support Britain, and even Von Papen himself in Ankara told them that their action was premature.[24] The Iraqi army did not have sufficient planes and weapons. Its unit commanders were disunited and remained largely inactive, while the command was poor and it had neither coordinated movements nor proper intelligence services.

In spite of German help that was neither adequate nor well timed, the Iraqis lost, and on May 30, 1941, Gailani and his followers crossed the frontier to Persia while, on the other hand, the regent came back to Baghdad on June 1. The Mufti and Gailani ultimately went to Berlin where they competed for the leadership of the Arab cause. At the end of the war, Gailani escaped to Saudi Arabia, while the Mufti made his way to Egypt. The four colonels and Gailani received death penalties in absentia from a court martial in January, 1942. As the colonels were turned over to the Iraqi government from various countries, their death sentences were confirmed and all four of them were hanged between May, 1942 and October, 1945. The last to be tried and hanged near the gate of the defense ministry was Salaheddin Sabbagh, one of the most prominent members of the so-called "Golden Square." The regent's vengeance on the four colonels was not forgotten by the people of Baghdad, and the memory of these "martyrs of nationalism" sustained the hatred of a whole Arab generation against the regent.

The seventh coup thus brought Iraq into war through the rashness and vanity of the officers. It gave birth to a revengeful spirit against the regent which undoubtedly affected the Iraqi view of the royal family and of the monarchy. On the other hand, the failure of the coup and the "second British occupation" of Iraq eliminated a good number of politically-minded officers, and it also put an end to Axis intrigues.

The series of military interventions between 1936 and 1941 achieved nothing worthwhile in the area of reform and in the realization of national aspirations. The military coups generated each other in rapid succession without a valid goal based on a thoroughly studied program, and with no political organization to implement that program. The blunders of the military were as bad, if not worse, than those of the civilian leaders. They were certainly more harmful to Iraq.

III. Popular Uprisings and Nasserist Incitement

After the seventh military coup of April 1941 and for seventeen years until the bloody coup of July 1958, no military intervention in politics took place. The army was seemingly allied to the government and loyal to the throne. The rulers sometimes resorted to the dangerous procedure of relying on the army to enforce their authority against the opposition. Under the impact of internal and external influences, the army was again becoming involved in politics. In the meantime, cabinets were overthrown on two occasions by popular upheavals, in the first case because of the issue of the treaty with Britain, and in the second over the question of internal reform. The revision or abrogation of the treaty of 1930 with Britain was among the demands of Iraqi nationalists. Egypt demanded the same in 1947 and asked the Security Council to order the withdrawal of troops from the Canal Zone. But whereas in Egypt the king's relations with the British were less than cordial, in Iraq the regent and the ruling circles solved their problems with Britain in a friendly manner. Under the cabinet of Saleh Jabr (after March 29, 1947), negotiations were conducted in London and Baghdad and a revised treaty was signed by Saleh Jabr and Ernest Bevin at Portsmouth on January 15, 1948. The treaty constituted an improvement on that of 1930; it provided for the evacuation of air bases, but stipulated that British troops could return in case of war or imminence of war. The Anglo-Egyptian treaty of October 1954 under Nasser provided for the same with regard to the Canal. The signature of the treaty, however, came less than two months after the United Nations' decision on the partition of Palestine which led to continuous demonstrations. On the other hand, the opposition parties in general and the nationalists of the Istiqlal party in particular made common cause with the radical elements, including the communists, against the moderate nationalists, and the treaty was a welcome pretext for agitation. It was condemned as contrary to national interests. In the violent student demonstrations that took place, the demonstrators asked for the repudiation of the treaty and the resignation of the cabinet. After several days, the people joined in the demonstrations and many casualties happened when police and students fired at each other. The regent, alarmed by the proportions of the uprising, announced on January 21 that the treaty did not realize the country's aspirations. On January 27, Saleh Jabr, after trying in vain to explain and defend his treaty and after more clashes, was obliged to resign and the treaty was repudiated.

The early 1950's witnessed a succession of revolutionary movements in the Middle East. Some were the work of the military such as the coup of Shishakli in Syria in November 1951, and the Free Officers' coup of 23 July 1952 in Egypt, while others were due to civilian pressure as in the dispute on the nationalization of oil in Iran (March 1951), followed by the Mossadegh regime, and the peaceful revolution in Lebanon, September 1952. The repercussions produced by these movements were felt in Iraq.

Nine days after Iran's Majlis had nationalized the oil industry, some deputies in the Iraqi parliament proposed that the same course be followed in Iraq. Oil, however, was not nationalized, but the oil agreement was revised later on February 3, 1952 under Nuri al-Said's eleventh cabinet. The two revolutionary movements in Egypt and Lebanon in July and September respectively encouraged the opposition parties to present a petition on October 28, 1952 demanding the limitation of the royal prerogative, direct elections,[25] abrogation of the treaty with Britain, rejection of Western Middle East Defense plans, and the distribution of land. Although the Mustafa al-Umari cabinet accepted to modify the electoral law, student demonstrations began on November 22, 1952 under the influence of leftist elements. The demonstrators were joined by the opposition parties and by the Peace Partisans. They used pistols while the police were unarmed and many of them were wounded. The prime minister resigned on the first day, but the riots continued more violently on the second day when the United States Information Office was attacked, while acts of savagery were committed against policemen who were killed in a police station, mutilated and burned in the streets.[26] As no politician was ready to assume responsibility, the army was called to handle the situation and a cabinet was formed under the army chief of staff, General Nureddin Mahmud.

The military prime minister was not one of those ambitious superior officers who aspired to usurp power and to establish a military regime. He was called by the regent to maintain order, and this he did after proclaiming martial law, closing schools and arresting leaders of the opposition parties and the Partisans of Peace. He then announced that the cabinet would implement some reforms demanded by the public including direct elections, which were actually decided in the new electoral law of December 16, 1952. Elections were held on January 17, 1953 and a pro-government majority won but, at the same time, the opposition gained twenty-one out of the 135 seats. General Mahmud resigned five days later and was made senator. The two popular upheavals of January 1948 and November 1952 proved that popular pressure could be applied in Iraq against the government and could obtain concessions, and that the government of Iraq did not close its ears entirely to the people's demands. Government concessions, however, were not adequate, and the opposition was still dissatisfied and demanded more reforms.

When young Faisal II became of age and assumed his responsibilities as king of Iraq on May 2, 1953, the government of Iraq was already beginning to concentrate on economic and domestic development. It was expected that development would reach a level that would allow the material benefits to pass to various strata of society and thus reduce political and social tensions.[27] The unsolved problem of reform was a minor one compared to the tensions that developed during the last five years of the monarchy, and to the agitation that was provoked primarily by outside sources. The key to these tensions must be sought in the inter-Arab entanglements and in the policies and actions of Gamal Abdel Nasser of Egypt, summed up under the term "Nasserism."[28] Most of the early trends in Nasserist policy centering around neutralism, Arab unity, and social reform had already been discussed and inaugurated in the Arab world before Nasser, but Nasserism followed an activist radical policy in implementing them and added the hitherto unfamiliar element of violent interventionism. It sought to impose Nasserist policies and views on other Arab countries by exploiting internal differences and appealing to the people, the radical parties, and even the army to overthrow their government. Nasserism was able to act as it did because of the national and international prestige attained by Nasser through his defiance of certain great powers with the help of the Soviet Union in the Czech arms deal in September 1955, and in the Suez Crisis of November 1956. Nasser was before these moves the leader of a strictly Egyptian revolution and a newcomer in the field of Arab nationalist struggle, but he became overnight the "pioneer" and leader of Arab nationalism and believed he should exercise a kind of trusteeship over the Arab peoples and unify the foreign, military and social policy of the Arab states under his direction. The Arab states and their leaders were now expected to fall in line with him or else they would be branded as traitors, reactionaries and servants of imperialism.

Against the Hashemite rulers of Iraq and the Iraqi statesman, Nuri al-Said, and other leaders, Nasserism led a campaign of hatred, abuse and incitement that contributed to alienating the loyalty of the army and the people from them. Nazi experts who had served under Goebbels are said to have helped in this and other campaigns.[29] The Iraqis were urged to overthrow their rulers and assassinate them. Broadcasts in Kurdish were even made by the Cairo radio inciting the Kurds of Iraq to revolt.[30] Among the principal crimes of Iraq's rulers in the eyes of Nasserism was the signing of the Baghdad Pact on February 24, 1955, and Iraq's involvement with the West in the Middle East Defense Organization for the containment of Russia. Nasser himself, it must be remembered, had indirectly linked Egyptian security and defense to that of Turkey and the West when he accepted—in the agreement of October 19, 1954 with Britain—to allow British forces to return to the Suez Canal base in case of an attack by an outside power against Turkey. Nasser's violent campaign against the Baghdad Pact and his unsuccessful attempt to have the Arab League states condemn Iraq stemmed from his fear of being isolated if the other Arab states were to join the Pact, and from Egypt's rivalry with Iraq over influence in Syria and Nasser's personal dislike of Nuri al-Said.[31] As time passed and Nasser's position was consolidated after the Suez affair, the attacks of Nasserism against the Baghdad Pact and against the Eisenhower Doctrine in early 1957 were now aimed at the destruction of Western influence and the elimination of the allies or friends of the West in order to strengthen Egyptian influence in the whole area.

Although Nasserism pretended to follow a neutralist policy, it became virtually anti-Western and its objectives coincided with those of the Soviet Union. Nasser's Arab opponents thought that he was being used as an instrument for driving the West out of the Middle East and even for introducing Soviet influence and making of the Arab states communist satellites. Without intending to do so, Nasserist policy indeed came very near to fulfilling Soviet hopes and aspirations, and many of Nuri's warnings about the Soviet threat to the Arab world have since then been vindicated, particularly after the Iraqi revolution of July 14, 1958. Nasserism, moreover, sought and received the support of communists for the implementation of its plans outside Egypt. The communist party was given a carte blanche to expand its activity in the Fertile Crescent countries, and to cooperate with the extremist nationalist parties allied to Nasser. When some communists left Iraq as a result of the ordinance of September 1, 1954 against the communists and their sympathizers, they were received in Syria which, under the influence of the Baathist supporters of Nasser, was on its way to become a Nasserist satellite. Moscow was thus allowed to use Egypt against Iraq exactly as later on it was allowed to use Iraq against Egypt after the revolution of 1958.[32]

In the meantime, Nuri al-Said, against whom most of the invective of Cairo was directed, dominated Iraqi politics and had been prime minister of Iraq for the thirteenth time between August 1954 and June 1957. He came back on March

3, 1958 as the prime minister of the Arab Union that included Iraq and Jordan. Nuri al-Said was born in 1888 and was the only son of a minor government official. He received a Turkish military education at a primary school in Baghdad and from the age of fifteen at the military college in Istanbul. In 1910 he married the sister of Jaafar al-Askari who in turn married Nuri's sister. Back in Istanbul at the Turkish Staff College, he joined the Arab secret society, *al-Ahd*, and later engaged in anti-Turkish activity in Iraq. When Turkey entered the war he was taken from British occupied Basra as a Turkish prisoner to India to be cured of lung trouble. He remained under open arrest by the British Indian authorities after the end of his treatment, and in December 1915 he was in Cairo at the invitation of the Arab national leader, Aziz Ali al-Misri. When the Arab revolt began in June 1916 he went to join Sherif Hussein's forces in Arabia and later in 1917 became chief of staff of Prince Faisal's forces that were commanded by Jaafar al-Askari. When the war ended, Nuri became the commander of the garrison in Damascus after October 1918 and was promoted to the rank of general. He accompanied Faisal in his visits to Paris and London, and in July 1920 he left Syria with him after the French invasion of Faisal's Syrian kingdom. When Faisal became king of Iraq, Nuri was made chief of staff of the army and Jaafar was named minister of defense. Nuri was appointed minister of defense later in 1925 and helped modernize Iraq's armed forces. "The story of Iraq until 1933" it was said, "was that of the partnership and understanding between Faisal and Nuri."[33] The two men succeeded in building a modern state in Iraq between the two wars.

Nuri al-Said, commonly called also Nuri Pasha, loved order and discipline and was known to have a calculated approach to public issues. This was perhaps due to the influence of his service under the autocratic Ottoman Empire and also to his long association with the British. He was a man of action and acted quickly and firmly in discharging public duties.[34] Two important objectives of his policy were to see that Iraq was secure from outside aggression and internally stable. It is said that he saw the Russian danger to Iraq when the Shah of Iran came as a fugitive to Baghdad in August 1953.[35] His drive against communist activity especially after 1954 ended only with his death. The Baghdad Pact which made him a target of Arab and Nasserist attacks was intended mainly to obtain Western support for the security of Iraq. Nuri's main objective in his policy with Syria was to have a friendly government in Damascus. His advocacy of union with Syria was probably motivated mainly by his preoccupation for the security of Iraq.[36] When the Syrian regime under Baathist and Nasserist influence turned leftist after 1956, Nuri wanted to reverse the trend and encouraged a change in the Syrian government but it was too late. His quarrel with Nasser over influence in Syria ended in Nasser's favor, and the danger to the Iraqi monarchy and to Nuri himself reached its most critical stage when Syria was united with Egypt in February 1958. Less than six months later, the Iraqi monarchy and Nuri himself were swept away. Nuri and most Iraqi leaders resented Nasser's attempts to impose his views on Iraq. "The trouble with Nasser," he said, "is that he wants to shine as the leader of all the Arabs."[37]

Nuri's public policies depended on the support of the Palace, the army, the secret police and press control. Nuri was also shrewd in his maneuvers among political leaders and parties, but he was unable to satisfy those who embraced various radical ideologies and wanted either the end of the monarchy or the end of Iraq's cooperation and friendship with Britain and the West. Under Nuri's authoritarian rule, elections were managed and political freedom was suppressed. The opponents of the government, who included leaders of the Istiqlal, National Democratic and Communist parties, were watched, jailed and sometimes exiled. In the elections of September 12, 1954, most of the candidates were elected without opposition and only 25 seats out of 135 were contested. Parties were dissolved shortly after, and opposition newspapers were suspended.[38] Nuri justified these measures by the need to protect the monarchy and its policies against the interminable maneuvers of the communists and other politically-frustrated elements supported by Nasserism. Nuri's regime, in spite of this, could not be termed tyrannical and Iraq was not, as certain critics have termed it, a police state.[39] Members of dissolved parties and leaders of the Partisans of Peace were able to pursue their activities even while in jail. The various opposition groups organized themselves in a National Front under Kamil Chaderchi, and established contacts with the military. Agents of various Iraqi parties encouraged people throughout the country to boycott the Baghdad radio and listen to the Voice of the Arabs of Cairo. Associations of communist students and a federation of youth were active, and there was a "reasonably generous freedom of movement, speech and enterprise."[40] Sometimes Nuri was called a "genial dictator." His dictatorship was described as hesitant and negligent, while a foreign diplomat who knew him well said that Nuri never resorted to dictatorial measures.[41] In Egypt, on the other hand, repression was more severe, freedom of speech and party activity did not exist, and police rule was supported by an elaborate spying network, and yet it was Nuri's regime that was deemed odious while Nasser's regime was popular.

The explanation lies mainly with Nuri's and the Hashemites' fidelity to the British alliance and their close relations with Britain and the United States. They were no intransigent nationalists and did not quarrel with the West or defy the "imperialists." For them there was no more imperialism since they ended their treaty relation with Britain in 1955 after signing the Baghdad Pact or even before. They directed their attention to constructive work within Iraq. Nasser, on the other hand, did defy the West and attack its interests with the support of Russia and the circumstances of the cold war. With every gain over the West, as in the nationalization of the Suez Canal Company, he was applauded by the rest of the Arab world, while the rulers who were on good terms with the West or did not attack it were overshadowed. Nasser knew also how to lend support to the parties that were opposed to the established regime in Iraq, and how to win over the masses by identifying himself with them. Nuri did not give public opinion much importance and the public entered little into his calculations. He did not appreciate the importance of public relations, but he was not indifferent to reform. His successful efforts to raise the standard of living and make life richer for the masses by carrying out major economic development projects were not given credit, although the most striking economic growth in the Middle East next to Kuwait was registered by Iraq. The country doubled its net per capita income between 1951 and 1956 at an annual rate of 20 percent, while Egypt's growth was by far slower.[42] It is also hardly remembered that efforts were made by the government of Iraq since 1945 to distribute state land, and that by 1954-55 about one million acres had been distributed.[43] Nuri's shortcomings in this respect, according to most writers on the subject, were that his long term planning did not leave a place for projects with short term results and popular appeal, and he did not handle modern methods of publicity as Nasser did. Nuri al-Said, nevertheless, was not an old aristocratic reactionary or, as he has been described, "the conservative aristocrat by career and outlook . . . the Ottoman Victorian Metternich."[44] At least one judicious scholar has given him the credit of surrounding himself with "a rather impressive team of competent specialists and administrators in the prime of life."[45] Moreover, Nuri was neither a landlord nor the son of a landlord. His bitter critic, the anonymous Caractacus, agrees that he was not after wealth and was not rich, but adds, "he was corruptor not corrupted."[46] Nuri also had neither the arrogance nor the vanity of the military dictators of his time.

Nor was Nuri al-Said a traitor and a puppet, as Nasser's invective and other attacks by Arab radicals called him. A British writer even tells us that "some people thought the British themselves were his deluded puppets."[47] Nuri was an honest servant of a dynasty and of a country which he helped build up, and many Arabs of sound judgment believed that he was one of the very few able statemen in the Arab world. He realized already in the days of King Faisal I, that the more closely they cooperated with Britain the sooner Iraq would achieve independence. In the first and second world wars and in the cold war that followed, he was of the opinion that Iraq and the Arabs would gain more by being on Britain's side and in the Western camp. To the radical Arab nationalists this was heresy because Britain was the colonial power that betrayed the promises to the Arabs, issued the Balfour Declaration, and dominated vast areas of the Arabian Peninsula. To the Arab socialists and communists and to Nasser, this was intolerable since their primary object was the destruction of Western interests and any connection or obstacle that could prevent the expansion of Nasserist or leftist influence or domination in the Arab Near East.

Nuri's close association with the Hashemite throne brought him the hatred of those who despised Crown Prince Abdul Ilah and disliked the Hashemites in general. Iraqi critics noted among other things how their rulers imitated certain aspects of British royal life. They thought it was undignified and ludicrous for an Arab king and a crown prince to wear plumed cocked hats and ride to open Parliament in a landau that belonged to Queen Victoria, and was bought by them from Hooper's in London.[48] Arab nationalists thought that Nuri served foreign interests and that he tied his destiny and that of Iraq with that of Britain. The British, according to one writer, "created" Nuri, and they also "killed" Nuri.[49] His serious source of disappointment and trouble in the last years was the Baghdad Pact. In the opinion of a well known Iraqi author and politician, Iraq's membership in the Baghdad Pact, its isolation and its feeling of loss of dignity were among the main causes of the inevitable revolution of 1958.[50]

Nuri made Iraq join the Baghdad Pact because he believed that the Soviet Union was a threat to Iraq and to the Arab world. He also expected that the Pact would be a means to obtain the support of its Muslim non-Arab members against Israel,[51] while his critics thought that membership in the Pact meant the renunciation of Arab rights in Palestine because the Western members and sponsors of the Pact were friends of Israel and were interested only in fighting communism, which the Arab leaders claimed was not a threat to their countries. It is needless to say that keeping away from the Baghdad Pact did not advance the Arab cause in Palestine and those who spoke most loudly against the Pact because it would have restricted the Arab freedom of action, never felt free or prepared to begin a second round against Israel.

It has been said of Nuri that "he was the most imposing of living Arabs," that he was "a man of big vision and great assurance," and that even his unfortunate opponents had to admit that he did at least have character."[52] Nuri indeed did have character. He did not allow himself to be led by the masses or to bc dominated by the passions and the trends in vogue. In the issues of Iraq's relations with Germany in 1941 and with Russia in 1955, his strong convictions which proved justified were guided by his dedication to the interests of Iraq. Had he wanted to play the demagogue, as a discriminating writer said, and follow the intransigent nationalist and leftist trend, he would have ended as his contemporaries Shukri al-Quwatli of Syria and Mustafa al-Nahas of Egypt in dignified impotence instead of losing his life in the streets of Baghdad.[53]

Iraq's membership in the Baghdad Pact as an ally of Britain became a liability and a source of embarrassment when the British and the French attacked Egypt in cooperation with Israel at the end of October 1956. It has been disclosed that soon after the nationalization of the Suez Canal, Nuri and the leading Hashemites of Iraq, who were then in London, pressed for action against Egypt and warned that if Nasser did not fall within a short time subversive elements would be let loose and the Baghdad Pact would be dissolved. They advised Eden, however, not to get involved with France or with Israel in any counteraction.[54] Nuri's government made the necessary moves when the tripartite attack began, to show its solidarity with Egypt. Iraq's forces were mobilized and some of them were sent to Jordan as a protection against a sudden Israeli attack. Iraq boycotted the meetings of the Baghdad Pact when they were attended by Britain and broke relations with France, but not with Britain. Nuri was shocked by Israel's participation which he did not expect. The measures taken by Iraq to prove its cooperation with Egypt, however, did not impress anybody, and the Syrian and Egyptian propaganda attacks against Iraq's rulers reached their maximum of violence at this time. The Iraqi government was criticized because the songs broadcast during the hostilities showed a spirit of revenge and spite against Egypt, and the prejudiced anti-Egyptian way in broadcasting the news produced a hostile reaction within Iraq.[55] The Iraqi opposition parties and groups took advantage of the general feeling of sympathy with Egypt and indignation against imperialism to present certain demands to the government including Iraq's withdrawal from the Baghdad Pact and stopping the flow of Iraqi oil to Britain, but the principal leaders of this movement were arrested. At the same time a Syrian military report was published in Damascus about an Iraqi government plot to overthrow the leftist regime in Syria. The Iraqi people reacted violently against the attitude of their government and began rioting, but the cabinet had learned its lesson from the disturbances of 1948 and 1952 and it consequently took immediate measures against the various forms of protest. In the town of Najaf two persons were killed in the demonstrations of November 24. Martial law was declared on December 1, but demonstrations nevertheless took place in Mosul, and a violent revolt broke out in Kut al-Hayy, south of Baghdad on December 21. The government was not overwhelmed and the riots failed to overthrow it. It is generally believed that although Nuri weathered the storm that followed the Suez crisis, it came close to bringing about his fall. It is also believed that until Suez, Nuri's regime stood the chance of survival, but since then he was regarded as the ally of a power that fought on Israel's side, and the Iraqis could not tolerate it.

Another great Nasserist success in early 1958 again fired

the enthusiasm of Arab nationalists and gave hope to the Iraqi opposition. This was the proclamation of unity between Syria and Egypt and the formation of the United Arab Republic on February 1, 1958. Iraq's government did not recognize this new state, and responded by creating the Arab Union of Iraq and Jordan on February 14. Nasser continued to incite the Iraqis to subversive action in order to cut off the government from its people. Writers have maintained as a result that "If an Iraqi opinion hostile to the government, to the Hashemites, and to the West was formed and modelled in the years preceding the revolution, it was Nasser who did it."[56] His propaganda machine created the emotional and mental climate for the development of the Iraqi army conspiracy.[57] But while the Nasserist brain-washing campaign[58] succeeded in creating a public opinion favorable to the overthrow of the monarchy, it did not succeed in preparing the Iraqis to join the United Arab Republic under Nasser's leadership, as the events of 1958 and the following years were to prove.

IV. The Coup d'Etat of July 14, 1958

The Iraqi coup d'état of July 14, 1958, followed by the abortive coup of March, 1959 and the successful coups of February and November, 1963, can be considered the most violent and bloodiest among the military and popular upheavals that have been witnessed so far in the Middle East, if one excludes the civil wars of Lebanon in 1958 and Yemen since 1962.

In the course of the seventeen years that passed since the coup of April 1941, the Iraqi army had been called upon to back the government and help in suppressing the riots of 1948 and 1952. It had also participated in the Palestine war in 1948 and shared the bitterness and humiliation of Arab failures which the officers everywhere attributed to incapable or even treacherous Arab rulers and politicians. Shortly after the attack on Suez at the end of October 1956, an Iraqi brigade was sent to Jordon to reinforce its position against Israel. On King Hussein's request, another brigade was ordered to be rushed to Jordan before mid-July 1958—during the civil war in Lebanon—to protect it against possible Nasserist activities which were expected to extend, after Lebanon, to Jordan and Iraq.[59] This movement of troops gave the officers who were conspiring against the monarchy their opportunity to make their coup.

Within the Iraqi army itself, the years that followed the Second World War saw the emergence of a new generation of officers who had no particular feeling of loyalty to the Hashemite dynasty. They were mostly drawn from the lower middle class and many of them had fallen under the influence of the extremist brand of nationalism that imagined the presence of imperialism and tools of imperialism everywhere and advocated radical social and economic change. They were particularly influenced since the mid 1950's by Nasserist propaganda and attributed all the aspects of injustice and corruption to imperialism because their rulers were the friends of the imperialists. Their road to reform and to the elimination of "imperialism" was therefore to overthrow the monarchy. The officers also believed that in joining the Baghdad Pact, they were serving the military purposes of the West and they were being isolated from the sister Arab states. They viewed Nasserist intervention with favor and resented the idea of sending a brigade to Jordan to protect its king against Nasserist action. Those of them who came in contact with the Syrian officers gave them assurances that the Iraqi brigade which was to be sent to Jordan would never take up arms against them. The officers even falsely told their troops, in order to justify the coup against the monarchy, that they were being sent to Lebanon to take sides against the pro-Nasserist rebels.[60]

The army coup d'état on the morning of July 14, 1958 was motivated neither by an impending danger or national emergency, nor by an unusually oppressive or corrupt regime. It was made under the impact of external, rather than internal causes. The extreme nationalists, socialists and other leftists who provoked or led the coup wanted to seize power in order to change the western orientation of their government and destroy the regime that allegedly brought them humiliation by abandoning strict Arabism in favor of foreign friends. In order to assure the success of the coup, the military leaders mobilized all the enemies of the Hashemite regime, civilians and military, communists and Baath socialists alike, and used all the means, no matter how inhuman to eliminate the monarchy and even its innocent sovereign, King Faisal II. The disparate elements that agreed on the negative aspects of the undertaking later fell into fighting among themselves about the policies to follow and the persons to be entrusted with the implementation of these policies.

In the planning of the coup of July 14, it is interesting to note a number of features and debatable questions that are closely connected with it. In the first place, it is known that there existed more than one group of Iraqi "free officers" before the coup, but there is a difference of opinion, colored by the quarrels that erupted after the success of the coup, on the membership of the groups and the date at which they merged.[61] It is recognized, however, that the coup was prepared after the Suez affair in 1956 when the two principal groups merged in a "Central Committee of Free Officers," and chose Brigadier-General Abdul Karim Kassem as chief of the movement.[62] It is also believed that Colonel Abdul Salam Aref always supported Brigadier Kassem, his former instructor at the Military College, and that he was the one who invented later the slogan, "There is no Zaim [leader] except Karim."[63] Kassem was then forty-two years old and commanded the 19th Brigade that went to Jordan during the Suez crisis along with a regiment of the 20th Brigade commanded by Aref. Kassem belonged to a lower-middle class family and was described as calm, reflective, secretive and with a martyr complex.[64] He was close to Nuri al-Said who by way of endearment called him "Karrumi," and he also enjoyed the confidence of Prince Abdul Ilah. Aref, on the other hand, was about thirty-seven years old and was emotional and excitable, talkative and noisy, vain and unbalanced. Nasser of Egypt is said to have been shocked by his crudeness when he visited Damascus in July 1958.[65] Another personality that played a role in the revolution was Wasfi Taher who was Nuri's aide since 1954. He was brought up by the Askari family, related to Nuri, but eventually turned pro-Communist. His position allowed him to make sure that no news reached Nuri about the plans for the conspiracy or about Kassem's intentions.

The coup, in the second place, was planned by the military in cooperation with the civilian party leaders who had organized the National Front and had to assure popular participation in the coup. The leaders evidently did what was expected of them as proved by the spontaneous reaction to Aref's call to the people to join the revolution in the early morning of July 14. The communist prisoners at Baaquba near Baghdad were released on the night before the coup and group leaders who were appointed among them were given instructions with placards and flags to be used on the following morning in rousing and managing the mob.[66] The response of the mob could be perhaps credited more to them than to the political leaders. The first communiqué proclaiming the coup referred to "the support of the faithful sons of the people and the assistance of the national armed forces" in liberating "the beloved fatherland from the domination of the corrupt clique that was installed by imperialism." Kassem eventually disappointed the civilian leaders and failed to form the council of revolution which, it is said, was mentioned in the revolution charter. The politicians, perhaps did not even expect Kassem and the military to assume the rule of Iraq, and in their view he usurped power. This is why some of them declined cabinet posts under him.[67] It seems that Kassem and Aref were both unwilling to establish the council of the revolution which civilians and officers were asking for. Aref might have thought that he was more intelligent and popular than Kassem, and that he would be the real ruler with Kassem as a front man.

A third question relates to the degree of support given by Cairo or Damascus to the Iraqi free officers, and whether the Iraqi conspirators envisaged union or unity with the United Arab Republic. It is evident from the various narratives that contacts were established between Kassem and Aref on the one hand, and the Syrian officers such as Bizri, Sarraj and Nufuri on the other, while they were in northern Jordan at the end of 1956. It is said that Kassem explained to his Syrian colleagues the plan of the Iraqi free officers. Contacts continued later through Iraqi emissaries to Sarraj before and after the formation of the United Arab Republic, and it is possible that a promise of support was given in case the coup succeeded.[68] Cairo consequently knew about the planned coup, and gave the Iraqi plotters its approval and encouragement and perhaps provided expert advice and sent some of its radio speakers to help in the broadcasting of news and comments, as the Egyptian accent of the speakers has indicated. The Iraqi officers, however, made the preparations by themselves and executed the coup. It has been even said that Kassem chose the morning of July 14 to attack Baghdad not only because he could trap the Iraqi rulers—the king, Abdul Ilah, and Nuri—on the day of departure for the Baghdad Pact meeting at Istanbul, but also because Nasser was then visiting Tito in Yugoslavia, and Kassem could use his absence as a proof that he had no role in the coup. Kassem was thus anxious to give the coup an exclusive Iraqi character without denying the influence of the Egyptian revolution which seems to have inspired him.[69] Nasser himself pretended that he was on his way back to Egypt from Yugoslavia when he knew about the Iraqi coup, and he therefore went back to Yugoslavia and from there to Moscow to study the situation in the light of the new developments. The former commander of the First Army of the United Arab Republic, General Afif al-Bizri,[70] has disagreed with all this and claimed that Nasser knew the exact timing of the coup, and that he made his visit to Yugoslavia at the time the coup was to take place in order to be able to go from there to Moscow and obtain its consent to making Iraq a part of the United Arab Republic.[71]

As for the question of unity or union, it seems from the evidence given by witnesses in the People's Court during the trial of Aref that the supreme committee of free officers studied the question of union of Iraq with other Arab states and decided to prepare the ground for it, but that immediate union or unity with the United Arab Republic was not envisaged except for the purpose of insuring the defense of the revolution in case it was threatened by the "imperialists" or by the old regime. The idea was therefore to leave the question for the moment and wait for developments.[72]

It seems, in the fourth place, that the officers discussed the fate of King Faisal and the high-ranking personalities in the state before the coup. There was consensus among them that Abdul Ilah and Nuri should be killed. Some wanted to save King Faisal's life in the hope that stability would be insured under the monarchy, while others saw in him an obstacle to Arab unity or were afraid that he might ask for foreign support. At the time the coup was made, an agreement might have been reached to kill the king with the rest, but it was not made known because some officers might have withdrawn from the movement. After the fall of Aref in November 1958, some former members of the central committee of free officers and even Kassem himself began to declare that Aref was responsible for the massacre of the royal family. They claimed that no decision to kill the king had been taken before the coup. The present writer was told by a retired high ranking officer and cabinet minister under Kassem that in view of the free officers' disagreement before the coup about the fate of the young king, it was left to be decided by the circumstances. He added that Aref later sent orders to kill the king and the entire royal family shortly after the coup d'état began because the royal guards were offering resistance at the Rahab Palace while the king and his family were endangering the movement in coming out of the palace with the Koran in their hands and appealing to the soldiers. Another source has mentioned that Colonel Abdul Salam Aref remained exceedingly nervous at the broadcasting station early in the coup until Captain Abdul Sattar al-Sab' came and told him "We killed them all," and Aref then gave him a warm embrace.[73] The decision to kill the king, it would seem, was tacitly taken by a small circle of leading free officers and its execution was left to the discretion of Colonel Aref who entered Baghdad with the 20th brigade on the morning of July 14, 1958. Kassem must have felt the revulsion caused by the crime and found it practical to say that the massacre of the king and of the Hashemites was not intended, as he told King Hussein of Jordan in October 1960. It is significant, however, that during the years that followed the coup not one voice was raised among the Iraqi officers to express regret for the king's murder. The only declaration made was the announcement, a few days after the coup, that Faisal's remains were transferred from a secret place to the royal cemetery.[74]

King Faisal II, as his cousin King Hussein of Jordan has said, perhaps with some exaggeration, "never harmed anybody and never had enough control of events to make a single major political decision that could have angered anybody."[75] Faisal grew up as an orphan since the age of four, and his father, King Ghazi, was a popular nationalist. At the age of twenty-three, Faisal was personally charming, decent and unpretentious. He lived with his uncle and the other members of the royal family a moderate bourgeois life in a small palace.[76] He had nothing of the scandals, extravagance and vice of King Farouk of Egypt. His unpopular uncle, however, was too close to him and still clung to his power. The young king had to bear the results of the resentment against the elder politicians and his own uncle. Nobody disliked him, as it has been said, but few felt close to him.[77] It has been claimed that "had the young king been left alone to choose the prime ministers from the party or parties that could command some popular support, his throne might have been saved."[78] This might be partly true, but the question was really no more one of how to appoint a cabinet and whom to choose for it. The frantic and relentless incitements to violence from outside the country, and the no less frantic army officers and civilian associates who responded favorably to them were determined at this stage to sacrifice the monarchy which, to them, was a vestige and ally of imperialism and an obstacle to Arab unity.

The conspiracy prepared by the Iraqi officers was known in many quarters, and warnings were addressed to the government and to the royal family about the impending coup d'état but they were not heeded. It is claimed that already in the maneuvers at Habbaniya in December 1957, a bomb intended to kill Faisal and Abdul Illah landed at a few yards' distance from them. When an investigation was ordered, it happened that those who were asked to conduct it were "free officers" and they naturally concluded that the affair was an accident. Reports were sent to the prime minister by the security department, and they contained the names of suspects, who turned out to be ultimately the authors of the coup, but neither Nuri nor the chief of staff, Muhammad Rafiq Aref, gave them any importance.[79] Other reports are said to have been sent by Bahjat al-Atiyah, Director of Security, to the minister of the interior who sent them to the crown prince. In June 1958, the king, it is said, found a letter on his desk at the Palace with full details on the conspiracy and the names of the participants, but on reviewing these names, they were found to be close to the rulers. Kassem was the protégé of Nuri, Aref was under the wing of the chief of staff, and Naji Taleb, another conspirator, was close to the court. It is even said that Nuri called Kassem and asked him jokingly, "Is it true, Karrumi, that you are plotting against us?" Kassem naturally pretended ignorance and denied the charge. Nuri was so confident during that period of calm that preceded the storm that he set free those who had engaged in subversive activities, on condition that they renounce their communism and become loyal citizens.[80]

The most serious warnings came from King Hussein of Jordan as a result of his thwarting a coup which was to take place simultaneously in Jordan and in Iraq. It is said that the

United States Central Intelligence Agency that helped thwart the plot in Jordan had a fragmentary knowledge about the conspiracy in Iraq and warned that Kassem could not be trusted.[81] A few days before the coup, King Hussein warned his cousin of Iraq on the basis of a full confession made by a cadet of the Fourth Tank Regiment named Ahmad Yusif al-Hiari, who was in charge of a plot to kill Hussein and some prominent Jordanian officials. The cadet spoke of a coup planned in Iraq for mid-July. The Iraqi chief of staff had to go to Amman where he was given the details, but his reaction was offensive and cynical. He evidently hated to see anyone doubt his competence and his control over the army. He not only refused to believe what he heard, but according to King Hussein he boasted of the tradition of loyalty in the Iraqi army and told the Jordanian king, "I feel it is we who should be concerned about Jordan, your Majesty.[82] King Hussein insisted that he convey the full facts to Baghdad, which he promised, and on Friday July 11 he left Amman. On Monday morning July 14, the coup which Hussein warned against took place.

Nuri's confident attitude towards the Iraqi army and his ignorance of the trends of public opinion are best illustrated in the order given in early July 1958 to the 20th Brigade to prepare to leave for the Jordanian border. It was commonly known that in the Baghdad Pact meeting scheduled for July 14 in Istanbul, which was to be attended by the king and Nuri, the possibilities of intervention against the Nasserist-supported rebellion in Lebanon would be discussed. Iraqi pro-Nasserists of all categories resented the idea of Iraqi intervention, and it is strange, under these circumstances, that neither Nuri nor the king and his uncle saw any danger in the movement of troops or took into consideration the possible reaction of the army against the rumors of intervention in Lebanon.[83] They did not even take the regular security precautions against the danger of the troop movements close to the capital.

The free officers took full advantage of the movement of

troops and decided to strike while all three—the king, the crown prince and Nuri—could be trapped in Baghdad. They were determined not to see a repetition of the experience of April 1941 when Abdul Ilah, who was then regent, was able to leave the country and then come back with the help of British troops. On the night of 11-12 July Kassem and Aref laid down the plan for action. Aref was the commander of one of the three regiments of the 20th Brigade that was to leave for Jordan. It was agreed that he should divert his units from the route and occupy Baghdad in the early morning of July 14, just a few hours before the king's departure to the meeting in Istanbul, while Kassem was to stay with his 19th Brigade outside Baghdad and watch the developments.[84] The 20th Brigade that came from the northeast had to pass a bridge on the Tigris near Baghdad before taking the road to Jordan. The Rahab Palace where the king and his uncle lived was at a short distance from the bridge and from the Jordan road but no emergency measures were taken by the army and the police. On the night before the coup, Aref distributed to his regiment ammunition which he either had carefully put aside during previous army maneuvers and stored for this occasion, or which he took from the infantry training school and other centers against orders. Troops were not allowed to march through the capital with ammunition and it seems that, contrary to certain assertions and rumors, Nuri did not authorize a full issue of ammunition from the start, although he was pressed to do so on the pretext that the army would thereby save time.[85] Aref ordered the arrest of one of his colleagues, Col. Yasin Muhammad Rauf, commander of one of the battalions, because he was against the movement and particularly against killing the king. Aref then dispatched a battalion of his regiment to Nuri's house, another under Captain Abdul Jawad Hamid to occupy the royal (Rahab) palace, and he proceeded with a third battalion to occupy the broadcasting station. The battalions left their last halting place in direction of Baghdad at 4 A.M. and in thirty minutes they were in the capital. The three following hours witnessed the fall of the monarchy, the extermination of the royal family, and the proclamation of the republic. Nuri al-Said survived for another thirty-three hours.

The coup of July 14 succeeded at the first stroke and met with almost no resistance. The Iraqi rulers were taken by surprise in spite of the many warnings they had received, including the ones that were given to Nuri and to the king on the evening before the coup by the director of security and by other persons who reported something abnormal in the movement of troops. This coup, the eighth among the Iraqi military coups d'état, has been known since its very beginning as "the Revolution of 14 July." Unlike the other seven that preceded it, it was one of the most violent episodes in the history of Iraq. Two factors contributed to that violence: First, the elimination of the royal family and of Nuri was considered a prerequisite for the success of the coup; second, Colonel Aref's appeal on the radio to the mob to take part in the attack against the Rahab palace, and the activity of communists and other agitators opened the door to lawlessness and chaos, and marked the course of events with bloodshed and terror ever since. The royal family was massacred in cold blood, women and children included. Apologists have claimed that Prince Abdul Ilah provoked the soldiers by firing at them, and others have said that the royal family perished in the course of a skirmish between the royal guards and the troops.[86] Evidence proves, however, that Colonel Aref had no desire to save the king's life or even that of the women and children. He did not want to save anyone to whom the officers opposed to the coup could be loyal. In his broadcast from the Baghdad radio he told the people, before the royal family had been killed, that he had removed their despotic rulers, and he incited them to support the army "in its bullets, its tanks, and the wrath that is pouring on the Rahab palace."[87] He announced at the same time that "the national government will be henceforward known as the Iraqi Republic."

The troops that took position near the palace began firing intermittently with small arms after 6 a.m. and then they stopped. The palace was not completely surrounded and the king's chauffeur reportedly tried to pursuade him to break out at the side and leave by car for Diwaniyah, but the king refused.[88] The troops did not try to storm the palace either because they did not have sufficient ammunition or because they feared an unequal battle with the royal guard. After 6:40 a.m. more troops came and two officers from the neighboring Washash camp reportedly received orders from Aref to open the arms stores and to begin a new phase in firing at the palace in which an infantry anti-tank 106 mm gun was used. The palace was shelled and some of the ammunition in it was set off and a fire started.[89] The palace was now surrounded and it was too late to escape. It is not known exactly to what extent the royal guard attempted to defend the palace. It is maintained by some writers that the guards were numerous and steady and that their commander offered to use force against the insurgents while it was still possible, but the king and the crown prince repeatedly refused to fire on their own subjects.[90] It is possible that the royal group asked for safe conduct to leave the palace and the country. Between 7 and 8 a.m., Captain Abdul Sattar al-Sabe' of the Washash camp advanced with a sergeant inside the palace grounds, after having received secret orders from Colonel Aref, and announced that he would offer safe conduct to the royal family through the troops to the palace cars and out of the country. The king and the royal group were suspicious but agreed to the proposal after some hesitation. They left the palace with their servants behind the captain and the sergeant who had their submachine guns at the alert position.[91] When they were halfway across the court near the steps before the fountain, Captain Sabe' turned about and sprayed the party with machine gun fire from right to left and in reverse until they all fell. They were killed instantly except the king who died shortly after without regaining consciousness, and Princess Hiyam, the crown prince's wife, who was wounded and saved by a NC officer.[92]

The king and the women, the servants, and at least one

child were buried by the army, but Prince Abdul Ilah's body was delivered to the mob that gathered around the palace. It included the hard core thugs released from jail and other hoodlums who were brought to Baghdad from the suburbs by trucks to give the coup a semblance of popular backing. The prince's body was mutilated and dragged through the streets, and then was tied up naked at the gate of the defense ministry where the Golden Square officers were once hanged by the prince's order when he was a regent after the coup of 1941. It was then run over by cars until nothing but a piece of the backbone remained. Royal bones were reportedly sold in the bazaar to souvenir hunters.[93] The king's body was taken after a few days to be buried at the royal mausoleum.

The King's death was announced officially over the radio only on the third day after the coup. This delay was not only out of a feeling of shame or in order not to produce a hostile reaction among the population, but also in order to prevent King Hussein from assuming his position as head of the Arab Union at a time when some army units in Iraq had not rallied and when the international atmosphere was not clear. Nuri al-Said at the same time was still alive—he was killed only on the afternoon of the following day. He was recognized because the pajamas he wore since his flight from his house on the preceding day showed beneath the woman's cloak in which he was disguised. The revolutionaries were concerned about his disappearance and feared that he might rally support against the new regime. This is why they placed 10,000 dinars as a price for his head. Nuri might have taken the coup for a temporary upheaval but when he heard the radio mention the killings at the palace, he realized that it was entirely different. He was then reported to have exclaimed, "They [the Iraqis] brought them here to kill them as they once brought their ancestor Hussein [martyr of Kerbela] and killed him." When he knew later the names of leaders of the coup whom he thought were his trusted officers he again reportedly said, "Evidently we have brought up vipers and scorpions."[94] The person who fired the fatal shot at Nuri was not known, but before he fell he shot and killed some of those who assailed him.[95] His body was given a secret night burial, but when the Communists discovered the place, they dug up the body, mutilated it, and attached it to a vehicle and dragged it to the city. They then pulled the body to bits and burned what was left of it. After forty years of service, one of the architects of Arab independence and of modern Iraq was not given even a grave. It is believed that Nuri could have escaped to Persia but he wanted to stay to find his son and to be sure about King Faisal. Some of the generals and their troops were loyal to the monarchy and one of them, Umar Ali and his division, refused to rally to the revolution, and other units elsewhere did the same until they knew that there was no longer anyone to whom they could be loyal.

On July 18 King Hussein of Jordan took charge of the Arab Union, but the international situation had changed by then. The American marines and British troops had landed in Beirut and Amman, respectively, on July 15 and it was feared in Baghdad that they would intervene against the new regime. But Robert Murphy, President Eisenhower's special envoy to the Middle East, reassured Kassem, and the British ambassador also visited the Iraqi ruler. As the Anglo-Americans accepted the revolution, intervention was not possible any more and, as Hussein said, there was no one left to save in case of intervention. The King of Jordan believed that if anybody should be fought, it should be those outside Iraq who master-minded the plot and not their innocent dupes.[96]

It is worth noting that in the various revolutions and military coups that had taken place until then in the twentieth-century Middle East, kings, sultans, khedives and presidents of republics were usually allowed to leave their countries in peace or to be held in confinement within the country. In other cases such as that of Celal Bayar of Turkey, the chief of state was tried before a special tribunal. During the First World War, in the course of a struggle for life or death, the Ottoman Turks brought the Arab nationalist leaders for trial in a court martial before convicting them. Such was not the case with Faisal II, his uncle, and Nuri al-Said. Under the Abbasid Caliphate of Baghdad, certain caliphs were either ruthlessly killed or blinded by their army commanders, but teachers in Arab schools, including this writer, have repeatedly told their students that the murderers were Turkish officers not Arab commanders. In the Hashemite monarchy of Iraq in July 1958, it was at the hands of Arab officers and with the orders of Arab commanders that the royal massacre took place and the victims included women and children. No service was held in memory of the murdered king and of Nuri in any Arab country. In Iran, the Shah declared mourning for King Faisal on July 17. When a service was held in London on July 30, 1958 to honor the king and the other royal descendants of the Prophet of Islam, the mourners met in a Christian church and not in the mosque at Regent's Park. The eulogy of the murdered king was spoken, not by a Muslim Imam but by an old British friend of the founders of modern Iraq.[97]

Writers and observers have noticed a faithful imitation of communist methods in the Iraqi revolution especially in the total destruction of the royal family. The planned nature of the attack on the royal palace and of the sequence of events on the morning of July 14, in addition to the secrecy of the planned plot led some Iraqis, among others, to believe that the plan was not an Iraqi one and that the Russians and the Egyptians were among the planners.

In the chaos that accompanied the coup, many innocent persons were killed for no valid reason such as those residents of the Baghdad Hotel who were arrested and later on attacked and killed by the mob. They included two Jordanian ministers of the Arab Union and three Americans. For two days the mobs had a free hand in the streets of Baghdad, and they were soon brought under the direction of the rival communists and Baathists. The British Embassy was partly burned and looted and one of its officers was killed. An estimate of the number of victims on July 14 was given as 186 killed including seventeen at the royal palace. Those who were known to be loyal to the former regime or who prominently served under it were hunted down and arrested. All generals in the Iraqi army and several brigadiers and colonels were dismissed. Hundreds of government officials who could not be replaced, including nearly every director general in the civil service, were retired and this caused a deterioration of the administrative machine under General Kassem's rule.

V. Kassem's Military Regime

A. The Instruments of Power

After the fall of the monarchy, the four and a half years of military rule under General Kassem were marked by internal strife which sometimes drowned certain cities in blood baths, by external quarrels particularly with Egypt, and by the absence of constitutional democratic rule. In his speech of July 14, 1958, Kassem told the people of Iraq that "the army that stems from you and is for you has undertaken to sweep away the tyrants." Four and a half years later, those who overthrew him on February 8, 1963 called him, "the mad dictator, the deceitful criminal and the enemy of the people."[98]

Iraq was proclaimed a republic on the very first day of the coup d'état of July 14, 1958, but the recognized leader of the coup, Abdul Karim Kassem, was not proclaimed president of that republic nor was he promoted, as others have been in various Arab countries, to the rank of field marshal or even to lieutenant general. He kept his rank of brigadier-general (zaim) until January 1959 when he became major-general (liwa'), and one month before his fall he was made a lieutenant-general (fariq) on January 6, 1963. Kassem became the commander-in-chief of the armed forces, while Abdul Salam Aref, his partner in the coup, became deputy commander-in-chief and deputy prime minister. The ill assorted cabinet included mostly unexperienced representatives of various parties of the opposition under the monarchy, but six of them were to resign a little more than six months later in protest against Kassem's policy.[99] A council of sovereignty was formed to fill the role of the presidency of the republic and approve the laws passed by the cabinet in the absence of a parliament. The council represented the religious and ethnic groups in the country: of its three members, one was an Arab Sunnite, another was an Arab Shiite, and the third was a Sunnite Kurd.[100] In contrast to most contemporary military regimes, Kassem did not set up a "council of the revolution" and Aref agreed to this for personal motives. A provisional constitution of thirty articles was promulgated on July 26. It mentioned Islam as the religion of the state, proclaimed Iraq a part of the Arab nation and spoke of the association of Arabs and Kurds in a united Iraq. The constitution also guaranteed private ownership.[101] The cabinet was given legislative as well as executive powers.

During the period of transition which the new regime announced, Kassem did not allow political parties to function. This was disappointing for the politicians who were counting on the restoration of normal political constitutional life. In his first press conference on July 26, 1958 Kassem announced that there would be elections in the not too distant future, but no elections were ever held during his regime. On May 1, 1959 Kassem emphasized the idea often expressed by the military and their partners that the army and the people have merged in a single entity, and declared that his party was the whole people and that he belonged to the party of the people.[102] Like other military leaders, Kassem believed that Iraq was not yet mature for democratic life. It is noteworthy, however, that Kassem did not found any special movement in the nature of an ancillary civilian organization under his direction, or a single party such as the National Liberation movement or the National Union in Egypt and Syria. It has been explained that in Iraq where the revolution was made against Nuri's dictatorship and in favor of the opposition parties, no single-party regime could be possible, whereas the Egyptian revolution was made against the powerful parties and so it evolved towards a single party. Kassem also had no systematic ideology or a clear doctrine or program, and thus the military government was left in presence of conflicting ambitions and plans of Communists and Arab nationalists with no political direction or dominant movement or group and no guiding doctrine for its action.[103] Kassem's power rested virtually on the support of the army on which forty percent of the budget was spent. He counted on his ability to balance the various forces and remain above the factions instead of being involved in any of them, and eliminate those who were against his personal rule.[104]

In banning political parties, Kassem's government was not as categoric as other military regimes. Kassem liked to be conciliating and to compromise without surrendering any real power. On Army Day, January 6, 1960, parties were allowed to function in accordance with a law on the associations, but on a limited scale. The transitional period was then said to have ended and Kassem boasted that it was the shortest known, for it lasted eighteen months.[105] The Baath and other nationalist parties oriented towards Egypt were not tolerated, and similarly the main body of the Communist party under Abdul Qader Ismail, but a minority Communist party under Daoud Sayegh was allowed to register and so were the Kurdish Democratic and the National Democratic parties. The latter, however, split on the issue of cooperation with the regime, and the group of Muhammad Hadid formed the Democratic Progressive Party which was recognized on June 30, 1960. The end of the transitional period, however, did not leave much freedom of action to the parties and was meaningless in the absence of a constitution and a parliament. Kassem was generous in making promises on the restoration of constitutional life. On July 14, 1961 he said that the convocation of a parliament will not take long. Shortly after, on September 4, 1961, he told the editor of *al-Thawrah* newspaper that Iraq will soon have a freely elected parliament for the first time in its history. In the millenary festival of Baghdad, December 1962, the Syrian nationalist leader, Dr. Abdul Rahman Kayali, was told that Iraq will have its constitution in 1963. On the same occasion, Kassem told a Syrian press delegation that no minister or deputy of the old regime would be elected to the future parliament, and that Iraq would depend on the Ulama and legal specialists, cultured youth, laborers and peasants. He also said that he coveted no position of authority and domination. He was overthrown less than two months later and Iraq did not have its constitution.

In his attempt to consolidate his personal power and gain popularity, Kassem strove to give his regime a neutralist, nationalist and revolutionary character. This was noticeable first on the international level by recognizing Communist China and re-establishing diplomatic relations with the Soviet Union and accepting its economic and military aid. He also seized every possible occasion to attack the imperialists and declared that the new regime would be non-aligned. After a few months, on March 24, 1959, Iraq withdrew from the Baghdad Pact.

Internally, the government of Kassem organized a people's militia under the name of "popular resistance forces" to help defend the revolutionary regime. On September 30, 1958, the agrarian reform law was passed. It allowed landowners a maximum of 250 acres (1,000 donums) of irrigated, and 500 acres of non-irrigated land, and required the confiscation of land in excess of that size and its distribution among landless farmers. Kassem hoped that this measure would insure a higher standard of living for the poor. He also spoke of social reform projects of various kinds and of bringing civilization to every house and village. A few months later, his cousin Colonel Fadel al-Mahdawi, declared in the People's Court, June 25, 1959, in one of his frequent digressions, that the government of the revolution has taken upon itself to give all citizens palaces and cars.[106] But even before hearing this declaration, the poor people's reaction to the revolution and the founding of the republic was to move to vacant lots and settle in them. One man, it is said, was surprised to find out that he would still have to pay his debts under a republic.[107]

The revolutionary government welcomed back all the exiles, Communists and anti-Nuri nationalists who were living in neighboring countries. They included the nationalist leader, Rashid Ali al-Gailani, who had left Iraq in 1941, as well as the Communist leader, Kamil Kazanji, who was deprived of Iraqi citizenship in 1955 and was living in Turkey. The Kurdish leader, Mulla Mustafa al-Barzani, and several hundred members of his tribe returned from the Soviet Union. They had left Iraq in 1943 when their national revolt was crushed by the Iraqi government. The stage was set for the concentration of forces of both Arab nationalists and Communists, and for violent rivalries and quarrels between the two groups that were to last until Kassem's fall. Before the quarrels began, however, there was a short honeymoon in which both were rejoicing at the dismissal of thousands of civil servants of the old regime and enjoying the trial and humiliation of its leaders.

The establishment of the Special Military Court, renamed later the People's Court, to try some 106 officials and leaders of the old regime followed the pattern common to all the revolutionary regimes. The object of the trials was to discredit the old leaders and the regime they served, make propaganda for the existing revolutionary government, and frighten its enemies. The Iraqi trials of "the plotters against national security and the corruptors of rule," however, were most unusual in the attitude and role of the judges, in the freedom allowed to the audience, and in subordinating legal proceedings to political considerations. The court consisted of a president and four members, all military, and its sentences were final. On July 21, one week after the revolution, the court judges were appointed. The president of the court was Colonel Fadel Abbas al-Mahdawi, a cousin of Kassem, but far less reserved, more vociferous, sharp-tongued and cynical, and displaying a sense of humor mixed with sarcasm. He played the role of judge and prosecutor as well as advocate of the new regime. The defendants were ridiculed by both the court and the audience, and the latter interrupted the proceedings to demonstrate, recite poems or make speeches. In the trial of Said al-Qazzaz, former minister of the interior, forty-one poems were recited against him in Arabic and in Kurdish and people cheered in both languages and asked for the head of the accused. Mahdawi cynically asked Qazzaz to translate the poems in Kurdish into Arabic because he was of Kurdish origin.[108] The proceedings of the court were broadcast over the radio and television and were held at night to ensure a large audience. They were made entertaining by the jokes and sarcastic comments of Mahdawi who was spoken of as a buffoon, and "an obscene bully," while his court was compared to a circus.

The People's Court began its sessions on August 20, 1958. In the first phase of the trials, Kassem's relations with Nasser and the United Arab Republic were normal, and the judges spoke of "our leader Nasser" and "the blessed United Arab Republic" and "dear Egypt." Defendants like General Ghazi Daghestani, deputy chief of staff, and Muhsin Muhammad Ali, deputy director of guidance, had to answer charges of attempting to overthrow the pro-Egyptian regime in Syria before 1958, or of serving imperialism by attacking the U.A.R. and Nasser. In the trial of certain radio speakers, Madhdawi told the defendants on September 11, 1958, "How did you dare attack Egypt, our elder sister, and our leader Abdul Nasser?'"[109] When the trial of Fadel Jamali, former prime minister, began on September 20, the charges were not only those of plotting against the security of Iraq, corruption of rule and helping to fix elections, but also those of plotting against Syria, aiding in imperialist plans, attempting to unify Syria and Iraq, attacking Nasser in the last session of the Security Council and calumniating the U.A.R. for alleged intervention in Lebanon. The trend was to represent the old leaders as agents of imperialism, and to describe the attempt to unify Syria and Iraq or to attack Nasser and spread news on the danger of communism as anti-national acts inspired by imperialism.

When the friendly relations of Kassem's regime with Egypt and its president soon deteriorated at the end of 1958 and various plots were made against the leaders of Iraq, the second phase of the trials began and the same Mahdawi who had spoken of Nasser as "our leader" became the spokesman for answering Nasser's charges against Kassem. From his court, he addressed insults against Nasser and gave him such epithets as "the contemptible tyrant," and the "Pharaoh of Memphis." Mahdawi's mood, which in the first phase was sarcastic and rather entertaining, turned more violent in the second phase because the trials now involved internal as well as external attmpts to overthrow the Iraqi regime. Moreover, the condemnations to death against the leaders of the old regime were either commuted or carried out several months later, while the sentences against the pro-Nasser nationalists, were mostly executed immediately and produced a wave of hostility against the regime within and outside Iraq. The People's Court was suspended after 1960, but its trials have remained a notorious feature of Kassem's regime, and Mahdawi's sharp tongue was silenced only after it had brought discredit upon that regime.

B. The Struggle for Power: Aref Versus Kassem and the Role of Nasserists and Communists

The trials and sentences of the People's Court in its second phase reflect another outstanding feature of the revolutionary government under Kassem. It is the crisis or series of crises over the relations with the United Arab Republic, and the internal struggle for power between Kassem and Aref and also between Communists and Nasserist nationalists. Among the aspects of the crisis and the struggles that went with it were the abortive military coup of March 8, 1959, the communist reign of terror, the attempts against Kassem's life, and finally the successful coup d'état of February 8, 1963 that ended Kassem's rule.

It must be remembered in this connection that Nasserist policies and Iraqi attitudes towards Nasserism were a primary factor in Iraq's struggles and in Kassem's seemingly inconsistent behavior towards communists and nationalists. For, in spite of Nasser's denials of any desire to unite Iraq to the U.A.R.,[110] it is believed that he expected this unity and worked for it immediately after the coup of July 14, 1958. It has been even mentioned that his interest in Syria was motivated by his hope of reaching Iraq and Kuwait and their immense oil resources, just as his interest in Yemen later was deemed to be caused by his desire to reach the oil of Saudi Arabia.[111] In the first days after the Iraqi coup, we are told that Nasser's messenger, Michel Aflaq, leader of the Baath party arrived in Iraq and was heard in Baghdad Hotel saying that those who desired anything less than complete unity or were contented with a federal union were traitors to the Arab cause.[112] At the same time loads of Nasserist propaganda material and of Nasser's photographs were sent to Baghdad for distribution.[113] In the Iraqi cabinet, Abdul Salam Aref, deputy prime minister and Kassem's partner in the coup, was strongly inclined towards unity. His radicalism, imprudence and somewhat irresponsible behavior annoyed his military colleagues. He traveled through the country and engaged in rabble rousing with violent speeches and looked like Iraq's strong man, while Kassem was timidly sitting behind in Baghdad. After Aref's return from Damascus where he met Nasser and concluded with him a military, economic and cultural agreement on July 19, 1958, the U.A.R. began to differentiate between him and Kassem and to describe him as the hero who first announced the revolution.[114] Kassem evidently was not interested in any form of unity after the success of the coup, and the officers seemed to have made no pressure on him in that direction. On September 12, 1958, less than two months after the coup, Aref was deprived of his function as deputy commander-in-chief of the army. On September 30, he lost his other functions and was appointed ambassador to Bonn. He refused the appointment, and at a certain moment on October 11, 1958, while several officers were pursuading him to leave because the country was divided due to him, it is said that he attempted to fire at Kassem in the latter's room in the ministry of defense. It is also said that Kassem forgave him provided he would leave. Aref finally did leave on October 12 and Kassem even went to the airport to greet him. Aref spent one night at Bonn, made a tour of western and central Europe, and returned to Baghdad on November 4. The second day, after refusing to leave Iraq, he was arrested "for plotting against national safety ' On December 8, 1958 it was announced that a conspiracy to overthrow Kassem's regime was discovered and that "it was the work of some corrupt elements with the help of foreigners outside," referring to Aref's followers and to the U.A.R.

Aref's trial began on December 27, 1958. He was accused of favoring the Baath party, publishing his own photographs in the newspaper *al-Jumhuriyah* which he founded and gave to the Baath party, working for himself without mentioning Kassem and plotting with the Baathists to overthrow him. He was accused also of working for unity with the U.A.R. under Nasser's leadership and allowing himself to be exploited by the Baathists who plotted against the republic and protected themselves with Aref's authority. One of the main charges against Aref was his attempt against Kassem's life that endangered state security.[115] Aref was condemned to death but the sentence was commuted to life imprisonment. He virtually spent about three years in jail after which he was pardoned by Kassem and released in late November 1961, and his salaries and pension for all that period were paid to him.[116] Soon after his release, he resumed his intrigues and plotting against Kassem. The old leader Rashid Ali-al-Gailani was also implicated in a conspiracy inspired and directed by Cairo. He was similarly condemned to death but was pardoned and released on July 14, 1961, when Fadel Jamali and other leaders of the old regime were also allowed to leave prison.

Writers and scholars have wondered since the conclusion of these trials whether the disgrace of Aref was the result of a struggle for power or the outcome of a difference in the ideology of the revolution. In attempting to explain Kassem's action, one should consider that he was probably not anxious to surrender his leadership over Iraq to Nasser, or to Nasser's candidate, Abdul Salam Aref, and that the officers, warned by the example of their Syrian colleagues after unity with Egypt, were not inclined to be dominated by Egyptians in a larger state. The Kurds who were striving for autonomy, were not willing to be submerged in a greater Arab state, nor were the communists willing to lose their freedom of action and see their party banned like all other parties in the U.A.R. It must be admitted also that Aref's behavior and Baathist impatience in spreading Nasserist propaganda provoked not only Kassem's personal jealousy, but also that of many Iraqi circles who were reluctant to recognize Egypt's leadership and were concerned about their oil revenues under a larger state. The struggle between Kassem and the Nasserists thus became an aspect of the old struggle between Iraq and Egypt, and Kassem before long was seen reverting to Nuri al-Said's Fertile Crescent scheme, probably in order to cause trouble to Nasser in Syria at a time when difficulties had already started in the Syrian region.[117] In late 1958 and early 1959, in reaction against the attempts of union with the U.A.R., a popular slogan that was ritually chanted in the various demonstrations proclaimed that "there is no *zaim* [leader] except Karim, we are a republic and we will not be an *iqlim* [province]."

In his struggle against Aref and the Baath Party, and all those who favored unity with Egypt, Kassem found precious support in the Communists. He was blamed later for his reliance on the Communists who committed horrible excesses. One should bear in mind, however, first, that Baathist-Nasserist propaganda left him no choice as long as Nasserists and Communists were the only well organized groups capable of any mass action; and second, that it was Aref who gave Communism the chance to develop its force when he invited the masses to participate in his coup without evidently measuring the force of the Communists and their organizations.[118] Aref was also still in power when the law of August 1, 1958 allowed the formation of the Popular Resistance forces and the distribution of arms to them. These forces became soon an instrument in Communist hands, and in alliance with the Peace Partisans, they controlled public security, terrorized the inhabitants of the big cities by arresting, trying and executing those whom they considered suspects, and boasted of the *sahl* operations that consisted of dragging the victims in the streets after tying them to vehicles. A notorious example of communist demagogy and opportunism was the career of a certain Hasan al-Rakka' (the Cobbler) who became the secretary of peasants' societies and head of a proletarian court. He issued orders to officials and had his own bodyguard from among the popular resistance forces in the town of al-Musayyab on the Euphrates.[119]

Between September 1958 and the end of 1959, Communist activity and influence reached their climax. The Communists tried to maintain an atmosphere of revolution and intimidated the middle class government by mass demonstrations, slogans and violence in the name of safeguarding the revolution. Courses were opened to teach Leninism-Marxism, several organizations such as student federations and the trade unions and many institutions and government agencies including that of information and propaganda, came to be controlled by Communists. It was early in this period–on December 23, 1958–that Nasser launched his first attack on the Communists of Syria and Iraq who had been his allies a few months earlier during Nuri's rule. It was evident that the reason for his change of attitude was his frustration at seeing the Communists fill the vacuum in Iraq which he intended to fill. It has been claimed that the Communists were capable of seizing power in 1959 but the Soviet Union did not allow them for reasons of strategy in the Arab countries.[120] Resistance to Communist influence in Iraq expressed itself on February 7, 1959 in the resignation of six cabinet ministers and in the dissatisfaction of nationalist elements, not necessarily Nasserists, who wanted an independent Iraq dominated neither by Nasserism nor by Communism.

C. The Abortive Coup of March 1959 and the Communist Atrocities

Less than eight months after the army coup of July 14, 1958 another military coup–the ninth in independent Iraq since 1932–was attempted, but this time it was against Kassem. This was the unsuccessful Mosul revolt of March 8, 1959. It was caused by nationalist opposition to Kassem's policies and by the encouragement of the U.A.R. and its right-hand man in Syria, Colonel Sarraj, who was then minister of the interior in the Syrian region.[121] The spark that started the revolt was the aggressive and provocative behavior of Communists in the mass rally of the Peace Partisans in Mosul, who were transported there by special trains provided by Kassem's government. The leader of the revolt was Colonel Abdul Wahab Shawaf, commander of the garrison of Mosul. The communiqué announcing the revolt was broadcast from a radio transmitter that was supposedly furnished by the U.A.R. and was located anywhere between Mosul and Aleppo. The announcement declared that Kassem was a traitor and that he was mentally deranged. He was accused of tyranny, of persecuting the liberal free officers, deviating from the policy of Arab cooperation, betraying the principles of the revolution and handing the rule of Iraq to a group known to have a certain political ideology, i.e. the Communists. Shawaf's movement, as it seemed, was hastily and poorly planned. It had no air cover for its forces, and its following was not large. Kassem moved quickly and ruthlessly against the revolt. He declared Shawaf dismissed from the service on the same day, and announced a grant of 10,000 dinars to whoever seized him dead or alive. He sent his air force to bombard Shawaf's headquarters, while his troops surrounded Mosul. Shawaf was killed in action and his movement soon collapsed.

In the People's Court, the prosecutor, Majed Muhammad Amin, sarcastically offered his condolences to Nasser and to the Baath leaders, Akram Hourani and Michel Aflaq, in Syria for the failure of the revolt. In Mosul, the Communists and Peace Partisans moved to liquidate the bourgeois families and leading personalities and to plunder and destroy their homes. They improvised proletarian courts in public squares and condemned to death all those who were denounced as "enemies of the people."[122] Thousands were hanged or dragged in the streets or were shot in groups outside the city, while police and army units watched. The prosecutor in the People's Court in Baghdad boasted of how the masses went to the "nests of treason" and killed "the dregs of the old regime, the aghas and the feudal lords of the Jalili, Umari, Yawer, Ani, Mufti and Bash Alem families."[123] It was said that the Chinese Muslim Communist leader, Burhan Shahidi, who was sent by Peking in an effort to help the Communists seize power in Iraq, was partly involved in the Mosul massacres.[124]

The Mosul revolt was followed by a series of trials of anti-Kassem officers implicated in the attempt. The revolution was now devouring its own children. Many of those who were tried and executed had participated in the July 14 coup against the monarchy. On March 30, 1959, four officers who were sentenced to death by the People's Court were shot. They were the first death sentences that were executed since the coup of July 14, 1958, for the civilians of the old regime who were condemned to death were still in jail. On April 20, 1959 another group of sixteen officers and one civilian who had also participated in what Mahdawi called "the dirty Nasserist Fascist revolt," were tried and six of them were condemned to death.[125] A third group was tried in early May, but the most sensational trial was that of General Nazem Tabaqchali, commander of the second division at Mosul who did not participate effectively in the Mosul revolt but was preparing to join. He challenged Mahdawi in the court, as his colleague Rifaat al-Hajj Sirri did, and openly criticized Kassem's regime. On September 16, he and three others were sentenced to death. Four days later, they were executed with thirteen others, including four civilians of the old regime, such as Said Qazzaz, minister of the interior, and Bahjat al-Atiyah, director of police. The four civilians were the first persons of the old regime to be executed, and that was done at the insistence of the Communists. In the meantime, the Communists who claimed that they saved Kassem's government by their victory over Shawaf, wanted a share in the rule of Iraq and were given three posts in the cabinet on July 14, 1959. On that same date and for three days (14-17 July), Communist terror reached its climax in the Kirkuk massacres when hundreds of persons perished, while the wounded were thrown in pits and were buried alive. Babies, it is said, were thrown in wells, people were dragged from their homes to be tortured and killed, and Communist Kurdish soldiers participated in the attacks of the Kurds against the Turcoman elements in Kirkuk after disarming them, while army officers on the spot disobeyed orders for ending the disturbances until the government finally sent its troops and restored order.[126]

The violence of Kassem's regime against its opponents thus exceeded by far any degree of violence under Nuri al-Said and the monarchy. The anarchy and lawlessness under the military rule that followed the coup d'état of July 14 had no equal in Iraq's contemporary history. Nationalist and pro-Nasserist elements found a valid pretext to criticize and challenge the Communists who were discredited by their excesses. The Baath Party began to enjoy some favor among the people because of Communist atrocities, and almost every enemy of the Communists was called Baathist.[127] Kassem became a target for attack particularly after the September 20 executions of Tabaqchali and other superior officers. On October 7, 1959 an attempt was made on his life as he was riding his car in the streets of Baghdad. He received wounds in his shoulder from the many shots fired at him and had to stay six weeks in the hospital. On the very first day of the attempt, he appeared on the balcony of the hospital to denounce the traitors and to tell the people, "I have pledged before God to die for your sake." The martyr complex in him now became more pronounced, and one of the objects of his boasting was his shirt stained with blood which he kept on exhibit in the ministry of defense in a glass case. The attempt on his life was made by Baath nationalists, and the People's Court became again busy on December 26 to try 76 persons of whom 21 in absentia. The United Arab Republic was accused of participating in the conspiracy against Kassem, and Mahdawi's explosions against Nasser redoubled in violence. The trial ended in late February 1960 with 17 sentences to death, including 11 in absentia. Before giving the verdict, Mahdawi recited a poem "To Kassem the hero who will not die from the bullets of hirelings."[128] None of those sentenced to death were executed, and after a short period in prison they were all released.[129] Kassem had a disposition to forgive; he imagined that he could win over those whom he pardoned. In 1960-1961 most of the convicted and imprisoned political and military personalities of the old regime were set free.

In late 1959 and in 1960, Kassem, without attacking the Communists openly, began to accuse those whom he called the "anarchists" of committing the crimes in Mosul and Kirkuk. He took various measures to curb Communist influence. Several extreme Communists who had taken part in the massacres were tried and sentenced to death but were not executed. Restrictions were imposed on the popular resistance forces and the Peace Partisans, while Communist influence in the syndicates and associations was reduced and nationalists began to gain the upper hand. Communist or pro-Communist ministers lost their cabinet posts. The main Communist party under the name of "the People's Union" (*Ittihad al-Shaab*) was denied recognition when party activity was allowed in January 1960. Kassem, however, remained friendly to the Communists who were his main support among the civilians until the very end, in spite of their complaints and those of certain circles in the Soviet Union about his change of attitude.[130] Kassem's relations with the Soviet Union and its satellites remained cordial, and he continued to depend on its economic aid and its experts for his development projects until his downfall.

The trials of nationalists and pro-Nasserists such as Aref,

the Mosul officers, and the Baath conspirators in the People's Court, and the atrocities of Baghdad, Mosul and Kirkuk gave the Nasserist regime and its powerful press and radio the opportunity to attack Kassem, who retaliated mainly through Mahdawi and the People's Court. The old hostility of Nasser against Nuri was now directed against Kassem, and the old rivalry of Cairo and Baghdad was now revived more than ever. The cause of hostility and rivalry in both cases was the refusal of the rulers in Baghdad to accept Nasser's leadership. The same charges of treason to Arab nationalism and of serving Zionism, imperialism and Communism were exchanged between Egyptian and Iraqi leaders, and the same efforts were made for winning over Syrian public opinion. Kassem spoke of the sad fate of the unfortunate Syrian people under the U.A.R. and reminded Nasser of the unglorious role of Egypt in the war against Israel in 1948 and 1956 and taunted him of accepting the presence of UN troops on his border. Kassem, moreover, adopted Nasser's slogans and propaganda themes, and became a champion of Arab nationalism and freedom and a promoter of social reform. Both Nasser and Kassem allowed Moscow to use them, as it has been said, for as Moscow had used Egypt against Iraq and the Baghdad Pact, so now it was using Iraq against Egypt, and as Nasser had been supported by the Communists of Syria and Iraq in the 1955-1958 period against Nuri's Iraq, so Kassem was now being supported by the Communists of Iraq and less openly by those of Syria against Nasser's Egypt.

In order to discredit Kassem and condemn his regime, Nasser's government called for a meeting of the Political Committee of the Arab League to discuss the dangerous situation in Iraq. Arab League foreign ministers met in Beirut in early April 1959, but Iraq, Jordan, and Tunisia sent no delegates. Those who attended refused, after six days' discussions, to agree to any form of intervention or censure advocated by the U.A.R. against Iraq, and the conference ended in failure for Nasser. In the attacks and counter-attacks made by Cairo and Baghdad, each party tried, even more so than in the days of Nuri al-Said, to outdo the other and to invent incriminating items and insulting nicknames. Nasser was called at various times, the Protégé of American Imperialism, McNasser, the First Criminal, the Killer of the Arabs, the Pharaoh, and Hulagu.[131] In his speeches, Nasser began a personal offensive against Kassem in early March 1959 and used his name, which could mean "divider" to call him "the Kassem [divider] of Iraq." As Kassem's prestigious title in Iraq was "the Sole Leader," so Nasser now parodied it into "the Sole Divider of Iraq." Kassem was also viewed as the tool of the Soviet Union and of the Communists, but at times he was also believed to be sold out to "the imperialists," because he did not nationalize Iraq's oil, although strangely enough, it was Moscow, according to Egyptian reports, that sent instructions to the Iraqi communist party not to nationalize oil.[132]

D. Kassem's Achievements and Failures

As in most coups d'état in the Middle East, the military leaders of the Iraqi coup and their civilian partners have sought to gain popularity and legitimacy by promising revolutionary changes for the people's benefit They were kept busy, however, by internal struggles for power and when Kassem emerged as the stong man, he again spent most of his energy in fighting internal and external conspiracies. In an attempt to gain prestige, he sometimes created unnecessary troubles for himself. The promised reforms and changes as a result received little attention, and the proclaimed revolution did not effectively take place. In addition to his troubles with Aref and with Nasser and the pro-Nasserists and even with the Communists, Kassem unwisely added new ones by claiming oil-rich Kuwait as a part of Iraq immediately after Britain's proclamation of Kuwait's independence on June 19, 1961. Kassem thus became hostile to Britain, and alienated those Arab and foreign states who accepted the exchange of diplomatic relations with Kuwait by withdrawing his ambassadors from them and causing them to withdraw theirs from Baghdad.[133] He also boycotted the Arab League because Kuwait was admitted as a new member. In the summer of 1961, the Kurdish revolt began under the leadership of Mustafa al-Barzani whom Kassem had invited to return from Russia after the coup of July 14, 1958. Barzani wanted autonomy, which Kassem allegedly had promised, for the Kurdish regions of Iraq. The revolt was seemingly quashed in September, but in March 1962 it began on a larger scale. Kassem was not able to end it in spite of the extensive destruction in the Kurdish region by the attacks of his air force and the general amnesty that he promised the Kurds in December 1962 if they should stop fighting. The Kurdish revolt became the basic cause of Kassem's unpopularity in the army. On Kassem's downfall, Barzani was able to declare that his rebellion was the main factor in ending Kassem's regime.

A third dispute started in the fall of 1961 with the Iraq Petroleum Company when Kassem's government drastically restricted its concession-granted area and asked for an increase in royalties and the surrender of twenty per cent holdings in its ownership to the Iraqi government.[134] In the fall of 1962 Kassem took measures for establishing an Iraqi national oil company to operate in all the stages of the industry outside the areas specified for the IPC.

Kassem, moreover, in spite of his simple Spartan living, his self-abnegation, and his declarations about being a son of the people, must have become affected, as most military rulers have been, by the disease of megalomania, and he evidently encouraged a cult of his own person.[135] Along with his title "The Sole Leader," which became synonomous with his name, Kassem was called in the press and radio even before the end of 1958, "the beloved of the people," "the genius leader," "the immortal, the inspired, the faithful, the loyal, the saviour leader," and "the giant of the July 14 revolution."[136] The anniversary of his leaving the hospital on December 3, 1959 after the attempt on his life became a day of celebration entitled, "The Day of Safety and Rejoicing."[137] When two boats were added to the Iraqi commercial fleet in May 1962, one of them was called, "The July Fourteen" and the other "Abdul Karim Kassem." His portraits were found by the editor of *The New Statesman and Nation* to be even more ubiquitous than those of Nasser. In one small office, he counted four portraits, one statuette, and three framed texts taken from one of his speeches.[138]

Kassem's regime, as it has been observed, was not a heavy-handed dictatorship. It had none of that perfection of total power, achieved under Nasser, which ruthlessly silenced persons suspected of working against the regime and eliminated any chances of criticism. Kassem, however, never presented the constitution he had promised, and a police-state atmosphere prevailed with an espionage system, a controlled press, and frequent, but short, political arrests. The regime also resorted to the usual frequent retirement and dismissal of army officers. On the other hand, Kassem tried to retain the goodwill of his officers by good salaries, promotions, and comfortable low-rent villas. The loyalty of the army was believed to be the main reason for the survival of Kassem's regime for more than four years, yet that loyalty, as it has been explained, was more to military principles of discipline than to Kassem's own person.[139]

Kassem's military rule had on record a number of reforms and projects. Some of them were partly motivated or timed by expediency. The agrarian reform, for example, was proclaimed on September 30, 1958 when Aref was deprived of his various functions and sent as ambassador to Bonn. Aref's arrest on November 5, 1958 was softened, as it has been remarked, by a timely decree allotting free seed for farmers, raising the pay of the armed forces, and even promoting to the next class all students who failed the examinations of the preceding year.[140] The distribution of confiscated land among the peasants was slow and the net result of the reform was the reduction in farm production and income. In spite of some 280 million dollars of oil revenues, Iraq had a deficit in 1961 and the two years that preceded it. Only fifty per cent of the oil revenues were assigned to development projects instead of seventy per cent under the monarchy. The Baathist minister of development, Fuad Rikabi, began immediately after the coup to wreck the proud development program initiated under the monarchy. Projects were halted, Western advisers and technicians were dismissed, business contracted, prices rose and unemployment increased. Economic stagnation in 1962 seems to have resulted partly from uncertainty about the future, uncoordinated economic projects, and spending on unproductive schemes, and it was manifested again in a slow private business pace and in unemployment.[141] Several projects that were completed during this period, like the Derbend Khan Dam, had been already started under the monarchy. Public buildings, roads and monuments were built; good houses, mainly for officers, and dwellings for workers were erected. A luxurious group of buildings for a new university was also started. Improvements were noticed in elementary education and public health. The five-year industrial plan that began in 1961, received support from the Soviet Bloc, and complete Soviet factories were sent to Iraq, but problems of buildings, labor, and communications delayed their functioning.[142] An estimated $200 million in economic aid and $300 million in military aid were advanced by the Soviet Bloc after 1958 along with 500 Soviet military technicians and 800 others for economic projects. Some 3,000 Iraqis, moreover, were sent to the Soviet Bloc countries for academic, technical and military training.[143] Although at various times Communists were jailed, especially for the strikes they inspired, they again became more active in 1962 and, among all the parties, they were the most likely to support Kassem in his struggle against Nasser and his partisans.

By concentrating power in his hands, Kassem had to make most of the decisions and to carry the whole burden of responsibility, but he evidently lacked the necessary experience and ability in spite of the high opinion he had of himself. His policy of playing Communists against nationalists succeeded for a short time, but he ended by alienating most political groups. His eccentricity and that of his cousin, Mahdawi, also contributed to discrediting his regime. In a comment on Kassem's rule and on the monarchy that preceded it, a judicious historian of Iraq has declared that the regime which was abolished in 1958 "would undoubtedly have been able to carry out a plan of reform in a more liberal, tolerant and sympathetic spirit than that shown by the present government."[144]

In June 1962, the atmosphere in Baghdad was described as one of fear, frustration and gloom, and it was already believed that Kassem's regime could not go on much longer.[145] Kassem himself became more suspicious as he felt that various forces were cooperating to overthrow him. In four and a half years, it is estimated that 2,000 officers were retired along with hundreds, if not thousands, of civil servants including important and experienced officials. It is supposed that his failure to send enough troops to quell the Kurdish revolt was caused by his fear that these troops might revolt. In December 1962, Kassem told foreign correspondents that thirty eight attempts had been made against him or his regime. It is claimed that he lived in maniac fear of assassination. In the streets of Baghdad, he drove in a bulletproof car, and he slept in the defense ministry building on a simple cot. He had spy holes in his bedroom and his glass windows were bullet proof. He pretended, however, that it was not true that he slept in the ministry of defense by fear for his life.[146] His trusted aides through whom he governed, were the heads of military intelligence, military police, and internal security. While Kassem's authority was being challenged militarily by the Kurds, it was also challenged in the last months of his rule by students' strikes that the National Union of Iraqi Students called for on December 24, 1962. In Baghdad University and in the secondary schools, the students wanted free student elections and the release of those of them who were under arrest. Students' strikes were accompanied by violent clashes with other students and with the police. On January 10, 1963 Kassem spoke of students' disorders as anarchistic and he claimed that agents of imperialism were behind them. He mocked the clandestine broadcast, known under the name of "the Voice of the Arab Nation," that spread propaganda against his regime. Five days later he accused Egypt of plotting against Iraq since the Mosul revolt. He also claimed that the Egyptian embassy in Baghdad printed propaganda leaflets and distributed money to destroy his regime.[147] On January 27 it was reported that an Egyptian diplomat was arrested for distributing subversive leaflets and that he was expelled from Iraq. A week later, the minister of culture and national guidance in Egypt issued a statement that U.A.R. diplomats in Baghdad were assaulted and kidnapped. He added that "the real significance of these barbaric acts indicate that the Iraqi government is no longer respecting itself and is no longer worthy of respect."[148]

VI. The Fall of Kassem and the Baath Interlude

A. The Coup d'Etat of February 8, 1963

Kassem's rule of republican Iraq lasted four years, six months and twenty-five days. By the end of this period Iraq was more disunited, economically stagnant, isolated, and less democratic, prosperous and secure than under the monarchy. On February 8, 1963, a military coup d'état—the tenth in thirty years of Iraqi independence—ended Kassem's regime and drowned the country again in a blood bath. The coup took place on a Friday, the Muslim weekly holiday, and on the fourteenth day of Ramadan, the Muslim holy month of fasting.[149] This timing evidently helped in the coup because many officers and soldiers were away from their regular duties. It was one of the very few military coups that were staged in broad daylight, starting in the morning and continuing into the night. The coup was a result of close cooperation between the civilian members of the Baath party and Baathist army officers. Several political parties and blocs, it was said at the time, had been waiting for an occasion to revolt, but the

Baath party struck first.[150] Certain retired officers were prominent in the conspiracy that planned the coup and they included Colonel Abdul Salam Aref who was now forty-two years old, and a thirty-five year old colonel in the paratrooper regiment called Abdul Karim Mustafa whom Kassem had dismissed three years before. In his press conference on February 14, Aref declared that he began preparing for the revolt with his colleagues since he left prison in late 1961, but the decision to strike was made on Monday, four days before the action began. The probable explanation is that the plotters, who included many officers in the active service, felt that they were compelled to act while they could before Kassem retires or transfers them or sends them to jail. He had already issued several retirement lists affecting some 120 officers in the preceding weeks and had arrested many Baath leaders.[151]

Several significant features can be mentioned about the new coup and its subsequent developments. First, there was an impression that it was conducted by junior officers, and this is why Cairo spoke of it as "the revolution of the lieutenants." The three air force officers who flew from the Habbaniya camp to attack the ministry of defense included two lieutenants and one captain. The other officers who led the movement or took active part in it, however, were colonels like Ahmad Hasan al-Bakr who became prime minister, and Taher Yahya who became chief of staff. Second, the coup was accompanied by considerable violence and bloodshed, and this was partly due to the resistance it encountered and to the spirit of revenge and retaliation against all those who were responsible for the assassinations and executions under Kassem's rule, particularly the Communists. Kassem was not expected to surrender, as the royal family had done on July 14, 1958, at the approach of the attacking forces, and the coup therefore was not declared successful in the first few hours after it had started. Airplanes from Kirkuk and Habbaniya attacked the defense ministry, where Kassem lived, from 9:30 A.M. till 5:30 P.M. by canon and rockets while anti-aircraft batteries on the roof of the ministry fired back and at one point shot down one of the attacking Hawker-Hunters. The rebels, it was said, burned nine planes on the ground because their pilots were pro-Kassem and could have used them against the revolt.[152] Tanks and troops converged on the defense ministry from Abu-Gharib and the Rashid military camp, near Baghdad, and from Habbaniya, thirty-five miles to the west. At 5:30 P.M., a tank attack forced the surrender of 600 men who were defending the ministry, but Kassem and some of his supporters continued the resistance inside.

During the night and on the following morning, Kassem is said to have telephoned to Aref and pleaded for mercy. He offered to surrender if he could be guaranteed a safe conduct to the Turkish frontier. Aref was not moved and is reported to have answered, "Did King Faisal obtain such guarantees?"[153] The only safe conduct that Aref offered him was to the radio station where a "council of the revolution" was meeting, and he accepted. Kassem was taken there in company with his cousin, the notorious Mahdawi, and two hated Communist aides who were in charge of military intelligence and police. A brief informal trial followed during which, it is said, Aref wanted Kassem to admit that he betrayed the revolution and to explain why he killed the persons listed on a sheet of paper that Aref held. The four were condemned to death and were shot at 1:30 P.M., on Saturday February 9, 1963. Their bodies were displayed on television, a "refinement" which was perhaps intended to remove any doubt about Kassem's death and avoid the kind of discussions that followed the Yemen coup of September 1962 on the fate of Imam al-Badr.[154]

The number of victims by the third day of the revolt was estimated at between 1,000 and 5,000 persons.[155] Included in these figures were those who fell in the actual fighting, as well as the Communists and officers against whom reprisals were taken. Among the latter, for example, were four high ranking officers who were executed on February 11 because "they violated the rights of the people." Some of them were Peace Partisans and had participated in the atrocities at Mosul. The sporadic fighting with the Communists continued for several days in the three main cities of Iraq. Bloody clashes occurred in Basra where an estimated 400 were killed and as late as February 14 fighting was going on in Baghdad. The members of the national guard that was formed by the new Baath regime after the coup and consisted mainly of armed students went around searching the homes for Communist foes and arrested about 4,000 of them. Kassem had on his side the Communists and the poorer elements of the population who considered him their champion. In the first hours of the revolt, the rebels appealed by radio for support against the resistance that they were encountering. They called on the people "to come to the streets to see that the criminal deception has been killed along with his tyrannical supporters." But in the early afternoon this order was reversed and a curfew was imposed because the street mobs cheered Kassem and it was feared that the Communists might take advantage and move against the rebellion.[156] After the success of the coup, those of the soldiers and officers who were known to have offered resistance were executed. The Baathists, it was believed, acted like bandits in pursuing their personal enemies, killing without trial and taking vengeance against Communists and other rivals. One month after the coup, the Baathists were as hated as the Communists had been under Kassem. Aref and the Baath coup did not enjoy the same unanimity of popular support which the revolt of July 14 enjoyed at the beginning. The people of Baghdad were largely indifferent to the change of regime, and the pictures of the new leaders that were distributed were not generally put up.

The clear anti-Communist drive of this revolt constituted its third distinct feature. Between the Baath and the Communists, the difference was not so much in the aspects of economic policy and methods of rule as in the question of national destiny and political ambition. The Communists after the coup of July 14, 1958 had stood in the way of Aref and the Baath and prevented them from reaping the fruits of the revolt, for the Baath, like the Communists, aspired to total power and would not have tolerated the preeminence or even the participation of another strong group in the rule of the country. The Communists were the only strongly organized party in Iraq who could challenge the Baath. Their elimination was therefore a first class necessity for the consolidation of Baathist rule and for the project of Arab unity and cooperation with Nasser from whom the Baathists drew moral support. The anti-Communist drive of the new regime reassured the Western powers, but it naturally endangered Iraq's relations with the Soviet Union on whom Kassem had leaned heavily. Executions and arrests of Communists stirred anti-Iraqi demonstrations in Moscow and provoked fighting even among the 1335 Iraqi students in Russia. The elimination of Communists nevertheless continued and as late as June 23, 1963, twenty-eight of them were executed by the firing squad for having participated in the bloodbath in Kirkuk in 1959.

Another feature of the revolt appears in the violent language used against Kassem in the first communiqué that contained the causes and goals of the new military intervention, and in the contradictions between the ideals and the actions of the new regime. Kassem was called "the enemy of God, the deceitful, the mad tyrant, and the enemy of the people." His supporters were spoken of as the "hirelings, the deviationists, the traitors, the executioners." Kassem and his "notorious band" were said to have exploited the resources of the country to satisfy their own desires and interests. They were accused of "stifling freedoms, trampling on human dignity, betraying the trust of the glorious July revolution, suspending the laws, and persecuting the citizens." Kassem was also accused of having "divided the country, murdered citizens, weakened the army and executed scores of officers." The revolutionary communiqué proclaimed that the new movement was a continuation of that of July 14 that was betrayed by Kassem whose "black rule led to the weakening of national unity and the isolation of Iraq from the sphere of liberal Arabism, and hurt the national aims." The declaration mentioned that in order to continue the march of the July revolution, the present revolt had to achieve two goals: first, national unity, and second, the participation of the people in directing the rule and the administration of the country. This, it was said, could be done only by restoring public liberties and guaranteeing the supremacy of the law. The declaration also called on the citizens to be above the hatreds and inherited animosities, and it repeated the Baathist slogan of "one Arab nation with an eternal message."[157] While it proclaimed these beautiful basic principles, the government of the new regime urged the people to take their revenge and it rejoiced at the acts of vengeance: "Today is the day of vengeance, so avenge, O people, your sons . . . Today the souls of the martyrs of your army flutter in the sky of Baghdad rejoicing at the vengeance which their brethren have taken."[158] When the cabinet was appointed, it seemed to be on a Baathist partisan basis. It was headed by a Baathist officer and its main support was military. While the new regime spoke of the rule of law, it prepared to confiscate the property and assets of about eighty prominent figures under Kassem's rule, and executions continued with or without trial. It must be also said that while stories were being circulated about Kassem's megalomania and self interest, the officers in control of the new regime were being promoted to the rank of general, and Colonel Aref himself was given on February 15 the rank of Field Marshal. While the new government spoke of restoring freedoms, it allowed its Baathist national guardsmen to invade people's homes and take the law into their own hands. It also began preparing for union with the authoritarian Nasserist regime in Egypt. The Syrian anti-Nasserist circles were quick to draw a comparison between the abuses of authority under both Kassem and Nasser and to emphasize the futility of dictatorial rule.[159]

A fifth significant feature of the revolt and of the revolutionary regime that followed it was the establishment of a "national council of the revolution" under the leadership of the Baath Socialist Party. It is significant that for the first time in its history, the Baath Party succeeded in gaining complete control of the government, and this was done only by conspiracy and with the help of a military revolt. The national council of the revolution was organized in order to avoid the concentration of power in the hands of one person and to avoid the mistake made after July 14, 1958. The organization and the membership of the council remained secret. It was this council that appointed Aref president of the Iraqi Republic. It should be remembered that Kassem never assumed the title of president but remained prime minister. The national council also appointed a cabinet of twenty-one members with a military prime minister, Ahmad Hasan al-Bakr, who was now promoted to the rank of Major-General. The cabinet included five other officers whose new ranks ranged from Brigadier-General to Major-General. About ten of the cabinet ministers were Baath party members, three were sympathizers and the rest were Arab nationalists more or less inclined to Nasser.[160] In his press conference of February 14, Aref declared that he and his colleagues were all working for unity, freedom and socialism. These three words became the slogan of the new regime and they were also the slogan of the Baath Party. Aref spoke of the national council as the legislative branch, while the cabinet was the executive branch of the government. He said that the revolt was against the cult of personality and self-glorification and that it had no one strongman.

The Baath leadership of the revolt evidently moved against Kassem after it had guaranteed the neutrality of the Kurds who had been fighting against Kassem for over a year. According to Mulla Mustafa al-Barzani who led the Kurdish rebellion, they sent an emissary to ask him if he would support the revolt and he agreed if the "rights" of the Kurds were recognized.[161] The Baath probably made some promises because their immediate interests centered on the success of their coup and the consolidation of their position in Baghdad and other cities, not on fighting the Kurds. Barzani declared later that the new regime withdrew the troops from Kurdish territory not to please the Kurds but to bolster their own position in Baghdad. After the revolt, a truce was announced, and a Kurdish delegation came to Baghdad for negotiations. Mulla Mustafa spoke of autonomy and he even threatened to declare independence and fight for it if the new Iraqi government did not grant Kurdish autonomy. He claimed that it was the Kurdish rebellion that inflicted a mortal wound on Kassem and all that was needed was to give his regime the *coup de grace.* In the declaration of March 1, 1963 the new government guaranteed the rights of the Kurds without mentioning autonomy which it might have promised. Granting autonomy to the Kurds would have been a grave compromise with a radical minority which no government in Iraq or in the other Arab countries had so far dared to make.

The last significant characteristic of the revolt relates to its repercussions in the Arab world and the position it took towards Nasser and Arab unity. Whether Nasser had a direct hand in the Iraqi coup or not, it was undoubtedly an impressive triumph for him, first, because of the tense relations between him and Kassem whom he attempted to overthrow, and second, because of the reactions it was expected to create in the other Arab countries such as Saudi Arabia, Jordan, and particularly Syria whose regime was hostile to him. The revolt was hailed in Cairo as "the dawn of a bright future for the Iraqi people and army," and as "the beginning of the revolution throughout the Arab world."[162] Egypt was the first country to recognize the new Iraqi regime, and Nasser's congratulations were telegraphed to Aref on the very first day of the revolt. The Baghdad radio played songs extolling Arab unity and included in its martial music such songs as "*Allahu Akbar*" which became an Egyptian favorite during the Suez crisis. It was easily noted, however, that the Iraqi leaders of the Baath, and President Aref himself, who was now more mature and was also responsible to a national revolutionary council, did not show the same spontaneous desire to unite with Nasser's Egypt as in the first days that followed the revolt of July 14, 1958 when the United Arab Republic of Egypt and Syria existed.

The Aflaq wing of the Baath-to which the Iraqi Baath

belonged—had maintained close relations with the Nasserist regime since the secession of Syria in September 1961, but at the same time it had learned from the Syrian experience that it had to exercise caution in any new unity venture with Egypt. The Iraqi Baath was not anxious to lose its position as a ruling party and fall under the domination of Cairo, but at the same time it needed some kind of unity in order to consolidate its power and retain the support of the pro-Nasserist elements who might otherwise attempt to overthrow it. Nasser evidently was the one who started the dialogue on unity. A few days after the revolt, he was reported to have sent a letter to Aref expressing the readiness of Egypt to establish close relations with Iraq in any form the Iraqi leaders wished. Aref was said to have replied that his country's relations with other states must be considered "in the light of Iraq's internal conditions." Nasser, it was said, sent a second letter carried by Michel Aflaq in which he expressed interest in a union that resulted from "a profound study of conditions in both countries."[163] Iraq subsequently sent a delegation to Egypt on the occasion of the fifth anniversary of the United Arab Republic that Egypt continued to celebrate on February 22 even after Syria had withdrawn from the U.A.R. In his speech on this occasion, the Iraqi deputy prime minister, Ali Saleh Saadi, spoke of the U.A.R. as the "mother republic." The negotiations for an Arab federation (of which more would be said in the following chapter) were conducted actively in Cairo after the change of regime in Syria following the Syrian coup of March 8, 1963. On April 17 a charter was signed in Cairo by the delegations from Egypt, Syria and Iraq to join in a new United Arab republic, and the Iraqi revolutionary regime approved the charter on April 22. The document, however, remained a dead letter, and the federation was never formed because of the continued suspicions and distrust between the Baathists and the Nasserist regime.

B. The Troubled Period of Baath Rule February–November 1963

The Baath party in Iraq was the first ideological party to dominate the government and monopolize power in any Arab country. Its domination, however, was entirely dependent on the power of the military, and it ended when the military withdrew their support. The Baath government in Iraq was, like that of Kassem, a military dictatorship. In Iraq, as well as in Syria, the Baath rulers were never able to restore representative democratic government and could never face the electorate in any kind of parliamentary elections. Their regime was troubled by pro-Nasserist and Communist attempts to overthrow the Baathists, and by disputes and disagreements between the Baath rulers themselves which, in addition to their serious blunders, led after nine months to the end of their rule.

In their drive for the exclusive exercise of power in Iraq, the Baath rulers were challenged by the Nasserists and other Arab nationalists who pressed for union with Egypt. The government campaign against the Communists consequently slackened a few months after the fall of Kassem, while the campaign against the Nasserists became more active in spite of the federation charter that was signed by Iraq, Syria and Egypt on April 17, 1963. Several Nasserist officers were dismissed in early May and others were transferred. The government arrested scores of Nasserists in Mosul and Baghdad. The Baath regime in Syria was having the same difficulties with the Nasserists. On May 11 Prime Minister Ahmad Hasan Bakr resigned after the withdrawal of five non-Baath ministers from his cabinet and three higher officers from the national council of the revolution. A few hours earlier the Baathist prime minister in Syria, Salaheddin Bitar, had resigned for the same reasons and under the same conditions. In Iraq one of the cabinet ministers who belonged to the pro-Nasserist Istiqlal party mentioned in his letter of resignation that the Baath violated the agreement that was reached between the various nationalist groups prior to Kassem's fall. It provided for the collective leadership of all the nationalist parties in the future government of Iraq.

On May 13, 1963 General Ahmad Hasan Bakr formed a new cabinet in which the Nasserists were completely left out. On the same day, Bitar in Syria formed a cabinet along the same lines. The Baathists were now in complete control of the government in both countries. President Aref who was himself suspect to the Baath party remained a figurehead until the end of the Baath regime. The other nationalist elements opposed to the Baath naturally resorted to intrigue and conspiracy. On May 25, the national council of the revolution announced that it thwarted a plot by officers and nationalist groups supporting Nasser, and that eighteen officers and eight civilians were arrested. A Reuter dispatch mentioned that eleven officers were executed by the firing squad.[164] The arrested officers of various ranks belonged to the 25th Armored Corps near Baghdad. Among those arrested on suspicion of supporting the plot was Colonel Aref Abdul Razzaq who was later to make more attempts in favor of Nasserism and against the ruling regime in Iraq. The arrested civilians whose property was confiscated, included representatives of the various pro-Nasser nationalist parties: The Istiqlal, the Arab Nationalist Movement, the Nationalist League, and the Socialist party. This last party was founded towards mid-April by Abdul Razzaq Shebib, president of the Iraqi Bar Association, and it nominated Nasser as its president for life. The conspiracy evidently was not in an advanced stage and the plotters were caught, as it was reported, while they were in the process of planning the overthrow of the Baath regime. Three days earlier on May 22, the Baath government in Syria claimed that it discovered a pro-Nasserist plot to overthrow the Syrian regime.

The Iraqi Communists attempted to seize power on July 3, 1963, in a badly prepared venture to take over the Rashid camp near Baghdad and they failed. The Iraqi national council of the revolution gave a description of the attempt and its failure. It said that the government had discovered a Communist cell and had learned from the confessions of its members that the Communists were ready to start a suicidal movement at the Rashid camp on July 5 for releasing some arrested Communist officers and allowing them to return to their units for further action. The date of the movement was consequently advanced to July 3 after the confessions had been made. On the morning of July 3 at dawn, a number of Communists dressed in false military uniforms with false ranks ranging from lieutenant to colonel were seen near the military jail. They broke into the training center and the guard center in the Rashid camp and helped themselves to the weapons. They arrested the minister of interior who reached the camp, as well as the minister for presidential affairs. The chief of staff, Taher Yahya, soon arrived with armored cars and attacked those who surrounded the military jail. An infantry unit arrested most of the rebels and released the two ministers. The Iraqi government communiqué said that the Communist attempt was ended after a half hour skirmish. It also claimed that the rebels had prepared eight proclamations addressed to the people of Iraq and signed by "the revolutionary command of the popular front." One of the proclamations would have restored the popular resistance forces and dissolved the Baathist national guard. Others would have announced the arrest of various personalities, reappointed most of the officers who had been dismissed after Kassem's fall, and established a Communist regime in Iraq.[165]

By the end of July 1963, a first group of twenty-one Communists were condemned to death as a result of the Rashid camp attempt, and the prosecutor asked the death penalty for a second group of fourteen. The director of security in Baghdad declared that the first secretary of the Bulgarian embassy, Constantine Nikoloff, supervised the plot that aimed at taking over the Rashid camp. The secretary and four officials of the embassy had to leave Iraq.[166] A Bulgarian company was at this time building the international airport in Baghdad.

A third attempt against the Baath regime was mentioned by the military governor of Baghdad on October 17, 1963. He reported the arrest of several retired superior officers who plotted with politicians of the old regime to overthrow the Baath government. The attempt was not as serious as the other two and the sentences were mild perhaps because they were given after the end of Baath rule. In early January 1964, the alleged plotters who included Brig. Gen. Rashid Jannabi, and General Saleh Mahdi al-Samarra'i received sentences of one to three years in jail. They were pardoned one month later.[167]

The truce between the Baath government and the Kurds lasted until June 10, 1963. The Kurds were not granted autonomy and the fighting consequently was resumed. It continued until the fall of the Baathists. In the course of the war it was reported that some Iraqi units commanded by anti-Baath officers defected to the Kurdish side.[168] The Nasserist regime later claimed that the Baath government kept the Baathist officers in Baghdad and sent the non-Baathists to fight against the Kurds. The Kurdish war helped make the Baath rulers more unpopular especially among the military because they realized that the promises of a quick victory made by the Baathist minister of defense, Saleh Mahdi 'Ammash, did not materialize and the Kurds took the initiative with the approach of winter. Several moderate army officers and some cabinet ministers were opposed to the costly campaign, while the deputy prime minister, Ali Saleh Saadi, of the Baath extremist left wing, was willing to shed blood for suppressing the Kurdish autonomy movement and for enforcing his policies in general.

The army became particularly disenchanted with the Baath government because it introduced partisanship on a large scale in the army, appointed Baathist officers in the best posts, and allowed the national guard to usurp certain rights and privileges that belonged to the army. Even the Baath officers became impatient with the lawlessness of the national guardsmen who freely arrested people and committed acts of torture and murder, and were sometimes referred to as the *Bashi Buzuks* (ruthless irregular troops under the Ottoman Empire) of modern Iraq. The national guard was regarded as the special army of the Baath and Deputy Premier al-Saadi gave it his full protection and often acted above the head of the government and the army.[169] By the end of the summer of 1963 the split was almost complete in the cabinet between the moderate premier, al-Bakr, and his radical and irrational deputy, al-Saadi and their respective supporters.

The Baath regime in the meantime ended its dispute with Kuwait and recognized its independence and full sovereignty on October 5, 1963. It received from Kuwait a loan of thirty million dinars without interest. Baathist Iraq began serious talks with Baathist Syria for establishing a union of the two countries after Nasser's speech of July 22, 1963 in which he officially announced Egypt's withdrawal from the proposed Arab federation. The plan for the Syrian-Iraqi union was announced on September 28 and it was expected to be achieved gradually. The first step was the agreement about a pact of military union between the two countries on October 8. A supreme defense council was created and the minister of defense of Iraq, Saleh Mahdi Ammash, became supreme commander of the two armies. Damascus was made the center of the supreme command. On the same day, as a symbol of the implementation of the military union, a Syrian force entered Iraq to help in the war against the Kurds. President Nasser had until then concentrated his oral and press attacks against the Syrian Baath regime, and hoped to win over the Iraqi regime. He gave up that hope after the Syrian-Iraq pact of military union had been signed and directed his efforts to overthrow the Iraqi Baath government. It was the division and disputes among the Iraqi Baathists, however, that brought the end of their rule.

As a result of the sixth national conference of the Baath party in Damascus on October 5-22, 1963 it was decided to begin the implementation of socialism in Syria and Iraq in accordance with the provisions of the Baath constitution. Differences developed between the Iraqi leaders on the application of socialist measures and the attitude towards capitalism and the West. When al-Saadi returned to Baghdad, he made declarations on the need for nationalizing companies and establishing a Marxian socialist system, but the prime minister gave reassurances to businessmen about their property. While al-Saadi sought to destroy the bourgeois class and win over the masses through socialism, the moderate leaders tried to avoid offending the wealthy middle class and the religious scholars. The opponents of al-Saadi, who included Prime Minister al-Bakr, the minister of the interior, Hazem Jawad, and the foreign minister Taleb Hussein Shebib, decided to act against their colleague. On Monday November 11, 1963 they called for an extraordinary party meeting in which the regional (Iraqi) command of the Baath party that included al-Saadi was removed, and a new command excluding al-Saadi and consisting of nine members—five military and four civilians—was elected. On the following day al-Saadi and four of his supporters were deported aboard an Iraqi military plane that took them to Spain.

On November 13, the partisans of al-Saadi attempted to overthrow the government, but their coup failed. The commander of the national guard, Mundher al-Wandawi, led the air attack against the ministry of defense and the presidential palace, while disturbances occurred at the Rashid camp. The government ordered its troops and armored units against the national guardsmen and the other rebels and in two hours—between 11 a.m. and 1 p.m.—the rebellion was crushed. This coup, or counter coup as it is sometimes called—on the basis that the deportation of al-Saadi following the elections of November 11 was the coup—was the first instance of fighting among Baath party rulers in which Baathists killed Baathists.[170] Premier al-Bakr called for an emergency national meeting of Arab Baath leaders in Baghdad to settle the crisis. In the evening of November 13, Michel Aflaq, national secretary-general of the Baath party, and such other members of the national command as Amin Hafez and Salah Jedid of Syria, arrived in Baghdad while other representatives came from Lebanon and Jordan. As a result of the deliberations it was decided that the elections of the regional command on November 11 were illegal and that both the old and the new regional (Iraqi) committees should be dissolved. Taleb Hussein Shebib and three other members of his moderate anti-Saadi faction accepted to leave Baghdad for Beirut on November 14 in accordance with the wishes of the national committee which declared itself alone authorized to punish "the party comrades" and became the de facto ruler of Iraq.

Writers at the time found it remarkable that the Baath party national committee consisting of Iraqis and non-Iraqis and presided by a Syrian could become the highest authority in Iraq with power to judge, deport and summon back members of the government. In Beirut, *al Nahar* expressed the surprise of many Arabs when its headlines mentioned, "Aflaq rules Iraq directly and dismisses both disputing factions." Others concluded that the Baath party had more substance than any political party had ever shown before in the Arab world and that political party unity in Syria and Iraq was very much a reality.[17] The truth, however, is that the power behind the resolutions of the national party committee was that of the generals, and in spite of their presence, the committee was not able to end the crisis. Its exercise of authority lasted only three days (14-17 November). The crisis in fact set the stage for the coup of November 18 and the fall of the Baath regime. The proof that the Baath party had basically no more substance than other political parties was that some of its leading military members turned against it and cooperated with President Aref to end its rule. The coup that followed was largely a reaction of the Iraqi army against the Baathists who came from Syria to dictate their decision. Another proof was that when the coup occurred, the Syrian Baath regime did not raise a finger to defend the Iraqi Baath or to help it regain power.

VII. Military Rule Under the Aref Brothers 1963-1968

A. The Anti-Baath Coup of November 18, 1963

The Baath party ruled Iraq for nine months and ten days. Its loss of power can be explained, first, by its unpopularity and general Iraqi hostility caused by its dictatorial rule, the crimes of its national guard and the violence of al-Saadi and his partisans; second, the impatience of President Aref with the Baath regime because he felt he was a powerless figurehead and he disapproved the policies and behavior of the Baathists; third, the officers' discontent because of the lack of respect accorded to their authority and their institution; fourth, the rivalries among the Baath factions and the crisis of November 11-17 that allowed the enemies of the Baath to unite; fifth, the cooperation of moderate Baath generals with President Aref in making the coup because they placed their allegiance to the army above their allegiance to the party.

In its final stage, the conflict that brought about the coup of November 18, 1963 was between the Iraqi regular army and the military arm of the Baath party or the Baath *Bashi Buzuks*. The national Baath party committee was attempting to solve the crisis between the factions (November 14-17) when it received an ultimatum from the army commanders, supported by President Aref, to disband the national guard, but the committee refused and the commanders as a result brought their troops to Baghdad and seized control. [172] They were concerned about the possibility of Saadi's return and the reinforcement of the national guard. In preparation for the coup, President Aref obtained the cooperation of the moderate Baath military leaders who felt that the 50,000-man Baathist national guard had to be dissolved because it had got out of control. The Baathist commander of the air force, Hardan al-Takriti, was particularly affronted by the behavior of the national guardsmen. His two colleagues, the Baathist chief of staff, Taher Yahya, and the military governor, Rashid Muslih, were also among the leaders of the military coup, but they were careful to mention that the movement was aimed against the national guard and "not against any faction or party."

The military coup of November 18, 1963 began before dawn when several infantry battalions supported by tanks, artillery and aircraft marched to Baghdad. President Aref's brother, Colonel Abdul Rahman Aref of the Fifth Division, led his troops from Baaquba into the capital and was joined by troops from the Rashid camp outside Baghdad. The national guard barracks, headquarters and outposts were attacked by aircraft, tanks and heavy artillery. The guardsmen had no heavy weapons, but they fought desperately and lost hundreds of men. An absolute curfew was ordered in Baghdad and truckloads of soldiers swept through the streets with automatic weapons directed toward upper windows on the alert for national guard holdouts. At the end of the day the national guard no longer existed. Its forces were subdued, disarmed, and disbanded. In his broadcast statement on the same day, President Aref denounced the national guardsmen as "the reckless butchers of the non-national guard whose offenses against the people's freedoms, disobedience of the laws, and damaging action against the state have become unbearable." On another occasion, President Aref attacked the Baath regime and its national guardsmen when he said, "They had taken the course of chaos and crime, inflicting heavy losses on Iraq, terrorizing the people, creating blood baths . . . We therefore had to wage the battle to get rid of them once for all."[173]

President Aref, as a result of the coup of November 18 and of the support given him by the army, emerged as Iraq's strongman after he had been a figurehead. The communiqué that announced the coup said that the national council of the revolution, "in response to the people's appeal and to the demands of the army" elected Aref president of that council, appointed him commander in chief of the armed forces, and gave him full powers for a year that could be extended automatically.

The members of the national committee of the Baath,

including Aflaq, Hafez and Jedid, were still in Baghdad when the coup occurred. They were flown back to Damascus on the following day. The first reaction of the Syrian Baath regime was to denounce the military coup in Baghdad as "suspicious," and to charge that it was backed by "oil monopolies, reaction, deviationists and imperialism." Although the Syrian council of the revolution placed "the Syrians' potentials" at the disposal of the national Baath committee, it took no action against the military movement that overthrew the Baath regime in Baghdad. The Baath party solidarity between Syria and Iraq proved to be a fiasco, and on the second day of the coup the Syrian Baath had to tone down its campaign against the new Iraqi regime. The Iraqi coup was at the same time a victory for President Nasser of Egypt although it was not intended to be a pro-Nasser coup. It ended the Syrian-Iraqi Baath cooperation and isolated the Syrian Baath regime. The Egyptian government broadcast a statement as soon as the coup occurred warning against any outside interference in Iraqi affairs, and the warning was aimed at the Syrian Baath regime.

In the history of the Baath party, the coup of November 18, 1963 which ended Baath rule in Iraq was a serious setback, exactly as the anti-Kassem coup of February 8 was the party's great victory.[174] Yet, because of the presence of many moderate Baathists in the cabinet that followed the coup, the anti-Baath blow was somewhat mitigated. The 21-man cabinet appointed on November 20 was a coalition cabinet of pro-Nasser Arab nationalists and moderate Baathists. The three Baath military leaders who helped crush the national guard were given leading cabinet posts: Taher Yahya became prime minister, Hardan Takriti defense minister, and Rashid Muslih interior minister. The former Baathist prime minister al-Bakr became vice-President of the republic. The two prominent Nasserists in the cabinet were Abdul Karim Farhan, the guidance minister, and Subhi Abdul Hamid, the foreign affairs minister. Eight members of the new cabinet were army officers.

B. Fluctuating Policies and Abortive Coups Under the Two Arefs November 1963-July 1968

The coup of November 18, 1963 against the discredited Baath rule created a relaxed atmosphere in Iraq and the people expected the restoration of authentic democratic government. Until then, the regimes that succeeded the revolution of July 14, 1958 were less democratic than the government of Nuri al-Said under the old regime. President Aref promised at least a return to the rule of law after the coup of November 18. His new government ordered an investigation of Baath crimes and called on the families of missing persons and the relatives of those who were murdered or tortured by the Baathist national guard to inform the proper investigation bureau.[175] Under the new regime, however, arbitrary arrests continued and the military tribunal remained the instrument of political purges. Freedom of expression was not tolerated and no legislative organ was created. Aref was no more inclined than Kassem or the Baathists to restore democratic representative government. He was unable to curb the power of the military who at various times attempted to put an end to his rule.

Aref had to follow the trend of announcing new provisional constitutions that seemed to be in vogue in the spring of 1964 under the revolutionary military regimes. Egypt announced a provisional constitution in March and was followed by Syria and Iraq. On May 3, 1964 the Iraqi premier, General Taher Yahya, read over the radio the 105 articles of the new constitution that canceled the provisional constitution of July 27, 1958. It declared that the Iraqi republic was a socialist and democratic state "deriving its democracy and socialism from Islam." The constitution did not allow any organization to form military or para-military groups, and forbade the military personnel from engaging in politics. It gave the Iraqi president the power to appoint and dismiss the prime minister and ministers, and allowed the "present president" to continue until a new president is elected under a permanent constitution after a transitional period of three years. The aim of the Iraqi people, declared the constitution, was complete Arab unity beginning with Egypt.[176] The provisional constitution thus tried to win for Aref the needed backing of Nasserist Egypt and to maintain Aref in the presidency as long as possible.

On various occasions, the new regime promised elections and the restoration of constitutional life exactly as Kassem had done, but the promises were never fulfilled. The reshuffled Taher Yahya cabinet of November 14, 1964 said that the change would take place in one year. Under the first Bazzaz cabinet in November 1965, the election of a chamber of deputies was promised for the end of 1966. After Aref's death in April 1966 and under the presidency of his brother Abdul Rahman, the new Bazzaz cabinet again spoke of plans for parliamentary elections. On January 28, 1967 under the Naji Taleb cabinet a draft law for the election of a parliament was issued. It allowed women to vote, and required the candidates for election to be literate and to "believe in the July revolution and its aims and principles." This electoral law, however, was not followed by elections.[177] A new phase began after the Six Day War of June 1967 when the educated elite were no longer satisfied with government promises and began to press for the restoration of parliamentary democracy. On January 12, 1968 the students at Baghdad University went on strike for lack of freedom and failure to establish a democratic representative regime. In May 1968 twenty-five civilian and military leaders, including former Premier Bazzaz, sent a note to the government demanding a constitution and free elections. Until the end of the Aref regime and the coup of July 17, 1968, the establishment of a constitutional democratic regime remained one of the main issues in Iraq's public life.

The two Arefs, like most military rulers, devised various means to reenforce their power and extend their period of rule. On September 5, 1965 the national council of the revolution was dissolved. It had included the commanders of military divisions along with the president and the cabinet, and its dissolution was thought to be an attempt to keep the army away from politics. When the term of President Abdul Rahman Aref expired in April 1967 after he had been elected for one year following his brother's death, the same body that elected him—the cabinet and the higher defense council—extended his term of office indefinitely. On May 3, 1967 the transitional period of three years that had been decided in May 1964 was extended to a fourth year. A week later, President Aref became his own prime minister in replacement of Premier Naji Taleb, and the constitution was easily modified to allow this action. The transitional period was further extended on May 10, 1968 for two years until 1970.

The Baathist leaders remained suspect to President Abdul Salam Aref even though some of them supported him in the coup of November 18, 1963. He consequently attempted to weaken their influence in three ways: first, by transferring them from ministerial and military posts to ones of less importance or to the diplomatic service where they would be presumably harmless; second, by retiring them from government service; third by arresting them when they later tried to plot against him.[178] On March 2, 1964 Hardan Takriti was relieved of his two posts of defense minister and deputy commander in chief of the armed forces and was appointed ambassador to Sweden. In a meeting held later in Vienna by the Baathist exiles in Europe under Takriti's leadership, the former defense minister reportedly vowed, "By the beard of the Prophet, I swear I will overthrow the traitor Aref."[179]

The Baathists indeed organized a plot to put an end to Aref and his regime by an aerial assault on Baghdad airport in the afternoon of September 4, 1964 when he was scheduled to depart for the second Arab summit conference in Alexandria. The aerial attack, it was said, was to be made by a squadron of six MIG fighters of the Iraqi air force that were to escort Aref's plane and whose six pilots were members of a Baathist cell. They had agreed to blast the presidential Viscount as it took off. At the same time, an armored brigade commanded by a covert Baathist was to storm into the city from the Rashid camp and occupy the radio station and government buildings with the support of former members of the national guard. The planned coup was evidently betrayed by one of the six pilots who was working for Aref but had passed himself off as a secret Baathist. On the eve of the planned coup, loyal army units and police made a surprise attack on the Rashid camp and arrested the conspirators. Ten air force officers including the five pilots were executed. Hundreds of Baathists were sent to jail, including former Premier Ahmad Hasan Bakr who took full responsibility for the plot.[180] On September 21, Takriti was retired from his post of ambassador to Sweden. Aref's brother, Abdul Rahman, was made deputy chief of staff.

In order to offset the pressures of the Baathists whom he forced out of power, and of thc Communists who had been suppressed by the Baathists, President Aref needed the backing of the local Nasserists and of Nasser himself. Similarly Nasser was prepared to support the Aref regime against any possible return of the Baath because he hated to see the return of close cooperation between the Baath regimes of Iraq and Syria. On May 26, 1964 the two presidents, Nasser and Aref, signed an agreement in Cairo that was said to be "the first step toward full Arab unity." It called for a joint Egyptian-Iraqi military command in time of war and the immediate establishment of a joint presidential council that was to hold quarterly meetings to coordinate the policies of the two countries. The talks that led to the agreement began during Aref's visit to Egypt to attend the ceremonies marking the completion of the first stage of the Aswan High Dam in which Premier Khruschev was the guest of honor. President Aref thus repeated the tactics of the Baath and precipitated Iraq into an association with Egypt without consulting the people. He evidently did not learn from the lesson of the Baathists who discovered that Nasser accepted unity only when he was assured of the possession of full power. Aref and the Iraqi nationalist leaders paid lip service to Arab unity but they certainly did not want their own power to be eliminated or their role to be reduced within their own country.[181] For the moment, however, they were preoccupied by the single thought of gaining strength with Nasser's help because of their precarious position in Iraq. On October 16, 1964 the creation of a "unified political command" was announced by Egypt and Iraq, but it was not until May 19, 1965 that the command first met in Cairo. It comprised the presidents of the two countries and six members from each country and was expected to take practical measures to achieve the constitutional unity of Iraq and Egypt.

President Aref had to pay the price of his dependence on Nasser. He tried to pattern Iraq's political and economic system on that of Egypt. Already in the constitution of May 3, 1964 Iraq was declared a socialist and democratic state. After the agreement of May 26, Aref sought to win the good graces of Nasser by putting his country on the socialist road although he had been opposed to socialism during the period of Baath rule. On July 14, 1964, the sixth anniversary of the 1958 revolution, Premier Taher Yahya surprised the Iraqi people when he announced the socialist measures that nationalized all private and foreign banks, insurance companies, and thirty industrial and commercial concerns. An Arab socialist union, similar to that of Egypt, was to be the sole political organization. The nationalized companies were to be operated by a state-owned organization. The new measures provided, as in Egypt, that staff employees and workers should receive 25 per cent of the profits of companies and should be represented on their boards of directors. The foreign oil companies in Iraq were not affected by the nationalization decree.

Nasserists and Communists welcomed the new socialist measures. The attitude of the Baathists was equivocal because of the hostility between the Baath regime in Syria and Aref's Iraq. Iraqi business circles, however, viewed the announcement of the new measures as cynical duplicity because two weeks earlier, on June 30, President Aref spoke of the rumors about nationalization as "tendencious maneuvers and calumnies," and said that they were circulated by "the enemies of the people, the imperialists and the enemies of Arabism." On July 8 the rumors were again denied by the information minister and on July 13, they were also denied by the prime minister. Responsible Iraqis knew very well that their government was unprepared to direct industry and that the nationalizations would hurt the Iraqi economy. It has been suggested that the socialist measures were partly the result of the deliberate non-cooperation of the Shia businessmen with Aref and of their hostility to Aref's dependence on Egypt.[182] The measures were therefore partly intended to punish the enemies of the regime and, as in other Arab socialist countries, they were employed as a political instrument in the hands of the military rulers. The hostility of the Shia increased after the socialist decree, and the Ulama of the Shia stronghold at Najaf sent a delegation to President Aref to complain about the new slide towards radicalism and socialism. The small merchants in general were hurt by the government monopoly of the importation of tea and sugar. Six months after the new measures had gone into effect, Iraqi merchants contended that sales fell by 60 per cent, while executives grumbled over government interference and inefficiency, and even workers in nationalized factories charged that their earnings were cut in spite of the profit sharing plan.[183] Future private enterprise was discouraged because businessmen remained suspicious of government assertions that there would be no more nationalizations beyond those announced on July 14, 1964.

The Nasserist regime responded to the Iraqi socialist measures of July 14 by giving President Aref more backing. An estimated one thousand Egyptian technical experts and teachers were sent to Iraq and on September 9, 1964 an armored unit arrived from Egypt to the Taji camp near Baghdad. The fact that the military force was sent a few days after the discovery of the Baathist plot of September 4 probably meant that the Egyptian troops came on Aref's demand in order to discourage any attempts against his regime by the forces in the camps around Baghdad. The

Egyptian military force and the entire Iraqi-Egyptian agreement of May 26, 1964 were viewed also as part of a pincer movement from Iraq and South Arabia towards the Persian Gulf, and as an instrument of pressure to obtain loans from Kuwait. The Egyptian troops were also a guarantee that Egypt would keep Iraq as a satellite in regional Arab politics. The ousting of General Rashid Musleh as interior minister and military governor when Premier Yahya reshuffled his cabinet on November 14, 1964 was viewed as a gain for the Nasserists because Musleh was not in favor of union with Egypt and did not want Iraq's resources to be dominated by Nasser.[184]

The projected union between Egypt and Iraq never went beyond the formation of the unified political command. Although the only alternative for President Aref was to maintain friendly relations with Nasser, in view of their common hostility to the Baathists in Syria, the Aref regime was evidently unable to adapt the Egyptian political and economic system to Iraq. Aref, moreover, disliked the increasing attempts of the Nasserists to curb his power. On November 3, 1965, he admittted that "the road to Arab unity is not easy," and that "the beginning of the road for Iraq is to strengthen its national unity."[185] In Iraqi ruling circles, unity was not achieved even after the expulsion of the Baathists from the government. The Nasserists soon became a source of dissension and intrigue. They wanted the full application of Arab socialism and further steps for unity with Egypt. On July 3, 1965 six Nasserist ministers resigned and the Taher Yahya cabinet was reshuffled for the second time. The resigning ministers claimed that Aref had slowed down steps for unity and that he was not genuinely socialist. The resignations were interpreted as a failure for Nasser. They occurred while Nasser was still preoccupied with the overthrow of Ben Bella in Algeria which took place two weeks earlier. On August 21, Aref denied that the steps for union between Egypt and Iraq were faltering. "These were the rumors of imperialist forces and their lackeys and world Zionism," he said.

The Aref brothers were never able to take a clear and

determined attitude towards union with Egypt and the establishment of the socialist system. In their fluctuating policy, they were undoubtedly influenced by the opposition of the majority of Iraqis to both socialism and unity. The two presidents and their cabinets regularly declared their policy of adherence to the agreement with Egypt, and they were evidently satisfied with the moral support that it gave them. Their cabinets defined their socialism as "prudent" or "fair" socialism, and attempted to halt the trend towards nationalization and to encourage free enterprise and the investment of private capital.[186] The socialist union that was announced on July 14, 1964 was never effectively organized as a one party organization and as the organ of a socialist system. As late as March 1967 preparations were being made for electing the general secretariat of the socialist union, and in February 1968 it was reported that the government was not having success in persuading all shades of parties to join the organization.

Nasser at the same time seems to have been contented with the limited aspects of unity as long as Iraq was on his side in regional Arab politics. He was perhaps less enthusiastic about complete unity than many Iraqi Nasserists, and when these attempted in more than one abortive coup to overthrow the Iraqi regime in order to declare union with Egypt, he usually succeeded in avoiding a crisis in the relations with the Iraqi government.

On September 6, 1965 President Aref accepted the resignation of Taher Yahya's cabinet and appointed the commander of the air force, Aref Abdul Razzaq, as prime minister. It was said that the president wanted to satisfy the Nasserists and he believed that Abdul Razzaq, who was known as a Nasserist plotter, would be less dangerous as prime minister than as commander of the air force. The ousted prime minister, Taher Yahya, was the last Baathist to survive the changes of cabinets. He was flexible and moderate, but it is possible that he had become suspect to President Aref. The new cabinet included as deputy prime minister

Abdul Rahman Bazzaz, a civilian who had been ambassador to London and at one time dean of the law school in Baghdad. One week after the formation of the cabinet, President Aref left for the third Arab summit conference at Casablanca. As a precaution against a possible coup, he formed a sort of defense committee consisting of his brother, who was then deputy chief of staff, the interior minister, and the prime minister to act for him during his absence. He was also assured of the loyalty of the director of police and of the commanders of the Baghdad garrison and the presidential guard. Premier Abdul Razzaq, on the other hand, was acting defense minister and had on his side the directors of security, of military intelligence and of the military college in Baghdad who were all Nasserists.

Brigadier Abdul Razzaq had been prime minister ten days when he decided to overthrow his own cabinet and the entire Aref regime in a military coup, and announce complete unity with Egypt. On Thursday September 16, 1965 at 10 a.m. a tank column left the Abu-Gharib camp near Baghdad under the command of the premier's supporters to occupy the Baghdad radio station. Premier Abdul Razzaq himself and his security and military intelligence officers waited in their offices for the broadcasting of the communiqué no. 1 about the coup in order to arrest the president's supporters and inaugurate their new regime. President Aref's brother and his group evidently were aware of what was happening because Abdul Razzaq's contacts with army commanders were no longer a secret and the entire preparations for the coup were described as awkward. As soon as the tanks left Abu Gharib, General Aref and other loyalist officers immediately ordered their forces to move against the rebels. The tanks coming from Abu Gharib were encircled by a superior force of loyalist tanks and surrendered after a short exchange of fire. At 11 a.m., after one hour of action, the coup ended in failure largely because of lack of determination and preparation.[187] The coup has been described as a comic opera coup and some have called it a "coup by phone" because it was said that Premier Abdul

Razzaq telephoned in gentlemanly manner to the higher officials to hand over the installations to the rebels, but the officials did not comply. It was disclosed a week later that sixteen military men and twenty civilians were arrested in connection with the coup and that twenty-nine left the country. Premier Abdul Razzaq was able to leave Baghdad with several high ranking officers. They arrived unexpectedly in Cairo in the evening after their coup had failed.

The Egyptians were embarrassed by the attempted coup and assured President Aref that they had no connection whatsoever with the rebels. Nasser's unofficial spokesman, Haikal, in *al-Ahram* called it the greatest surprise of the Casablanca conference. President Aref left the conference on September 18 and stopped in Cairo where he changed planes because he was warned that his plane might be shot down by some Iraqi air force supporter of Abdul Razzaq. He was flown on a special Egyptian plane from a military airport and his pilot was Nasser's brother, Lt. Hussein Abdul Nasser. When Aref arrived in Baghdad, he paid a tribute of praise to the Iraqi armed forces "which are frustrating the propagators of evil who work for division," and implored Allah to protect the nation against disunity and evildoers.

The abortive coup was followed by the formation of a new cabinet under Abdul Rahman Bazzaz, a moderate independent radical who became the first civilian prime minister in Iraq since the 1958 revolution. He spoke of cooperating with Egypt "while taking into consideration our own circumstances," and proposed to work for a federal union. He looked forward to a flourishing Iraq where there would be "no need for courts martial, coups d'état, and tanks in the streets." He attacked Marxism and advocated a prudent or well guided unimported socialism that would encourage private enterprise. His important achievement was his plan to solve the Kurdish problem and restore peace with the Kurds.

President Aref had reached an agreement with the Kurdish leader, Mustafa al-Barzani, about a ceasefire in February 1964 after the fall of the Baath regime. Aref evidently had made oral promises involving a measure of Kurdish local autonomy, but when the Iraqi government presented its terms for the settlement of the problem in June they were rejected by Barzani because they did not include autonomy. Barzani consequently formed a de facto autonomous government in the Kurdish region and when he later in March 1965 communicated his demands to Baghdad, the prime minister, Taher Yahya, reacted angrily by declaring that the demands were "a dangerous call for secession from a madman who lost his senses."[188] By the end of March 1965, Iraq had concentrated some 50,000 troops to attack the Kurds and the war was resumed. It continued until after Aref's death.

President Aref died on April 13, 1966 when his helicopter crashed and burned in a sandstorm on its way from Qurna to Basra in southern Iraq. To those who suspected that the Kurds might have caused the crash, Mustafa Barzani forwarded a denial of the charge from his Voice of Kurdistan radio. There were still some writers who held that Aref's death was engineered by his political opponents. A few hours after the funeral on April 16, Aref's brother, Abdul Rahman, was elected president by the cabinet and the national defense council. It is said that General Aref was inclined to refuse the succession to his brother, but Marshal Abdul Hakim Amer of Egypt who attended the funeral persuaded him to accept the nomination in order to insure the continuity of government policy. Premier Bazzaz, who was considered by certain Iraqi circles for the presidency, now formed a new cabinet on April 18 that included only two new ministers in replacement of the two who died in the crash with Aref.

In his attempt to solve the Kurdish problem, Premier Bazzaz declared in May 1966 that his government was ready to consider anything that would not mean the creation of a separate entity in the Kurdish region. On June 29, 1966 he announced over the radio a plan to end the war, and Barzani signified his approval. The plan proposed to give the Kurds local self government on the basis of a decentralization law that was being drafted. The Kurds were guaranteed the right of holding public positions in the military and civil services and representation in a future national assembly in proportion to their number. Their national and cultural identity was recognized in such aspects as the official use of their language, the publication of Kurdish newspapers and the existence of the Kurdish Democratic party. The plan promised the rehabilitation and economic development of the Kurdish areas. The Iraqi soldiers and officers who had deserted to the Kurdish forces were promised pardon if they reported to their former units within two months.[189] The cabinet of Bazzaz resigned in August 1966, but the twelve points of his program to which his successor Naji Taleb adhered were not implemented even after President Aref's meeting with Barzani in early November during his visit to the northern regions. Barzani indicated his dissatisfaction by sending strong protests against the failure of the Iraqi government to keep her promises, but the hostilities were not resumed and the truce was maintained until after Aref's fall in July 1968.

The conspiracies of Nasserists and Baathists against the regime of the two Arefs were continuous even after the failure of their former attempts in September 1964 and 1965. On October 29, 1965 it was reported that President Abdul Salam Aref foiled an attempted coup and arrested thirty officers who were trying to occupy important posts in the capital but were discovered on time and surrendered without serious combat. The officers were in favor of unity with Egypt.[190] Two weeks later, on November 14, the State Security Court charged 268 persons, military and civilian, with "forming a secret organization with the aim of planning a coup against the regime." The organization had been discovered in the preceding year and included the communist leader and former army officer, Lt. Col. Selim al-Fakhry who had been director of radio and television in 1959. Its members, except for 51 persons who were tried in absentia, were arrested before they could carry out their plot. In mid-December 1965 another trial involved 81 persons–11 in absentia–who had conspired against the regime with the help of the Communist party. Their aim was to place authority in the hands of Kassemites, National

Democratic party members, such as Kamil Chaderchi, and Communists. Security forces noticed at the same time a resurgence of Communist activity in the Middle Euphrates region and by December 8, about fifty prominent Communists had been arrested.[192] This series of plots by Nasserists and Communists was followed in March 1966 by a renewed Baathist attempt to overthrow President Aref. The Baath supporters were encouraged by the radical Baath coup in Syria in February and were aided by anti-Nasser elements as well as by partisans of former Premier Taher Yahya. In mid-March 1966 the government of President Aref consequently deported or retired twelve superior pro-Baath officers for plotting against the regime. They included Said Saleeby, commander of the Baghdad garrison who had foiled the pro-Nasserist attempt of Abdul Razzaq in September 1965, and a former security chief who had been an aide of Taher Yahya.[193]

Under President Abdul Rahman Aref only one serious coup was attempted before the one that brought his downfall. It was the abortive coup of Thursday June 30, 1966 that was staged by the same Aref Abdul Razzaq who nine months earlier had led the coup against the first Aref. He had returned to Iraq under an amnesty granted after the election of the new president in April. The attempt came at a time when a new period of stability was expected following the announcement of the plan for ending the five-year-old war with the Kurds on the night before the coup. Brigadier Abdul Razzaq and his Nasserist supporters apparently wanted to force a strictly socialist system on Iraq and proclaim its unity with Egypt. The people were relieved when the coup failed. The rebels first seized the airport of Mosul and sent military aircraft to attack the presidential palace in Baghdad. Seven air force planes raided the palace at half hour intervals for more than four hours. The rebels also briefly occupied the Baghdad radio station and in the name of a "revolutionary council," they appealed to President Aref to surrender quietly to avoid bloodshed. They accused his government of taking Iraq back to the days of the old regime before the revolution. The government regained control of the radio station after a few hours and its loyalist forces were able to overpower the dissidents and make them "scurry like rats," as President Aref said on the following day.[194]

The coup failed because of the loyalty of the garrison in Mosul and of the army units and the presidential guard in Baghdad. President Aref mentioned that eight officers and soldiers were killed and fourteen others were wounded in the attempt. He also said that this time there would be no pardon for the plotters and they would be tried in accordance with the law. The leader, Brigadier Abdul Razzaq, was described as a "traitor" and "coward." He was arrested with seventeen others including the former Nasserist minister Subhi Abdul Hamid and some members of the pro-Nasserist "Arab Nationalist Movement." The arrests, however, were not followed by a trial because of a decree issued on March 9, 1967 by Premier Naji Taleb. Abdul Razzaq's two attempts to overthrow the Aref regime thus went unpunished probably because of Egyptian intervention.

On August 6, 1966 the Abdul Rahman Bazzaz cabinet resigned and was replaced by a cabinet under General Naji Taleb. The retired army officers who were behind the new cabinet apparently forced the resignation of the civilian prime minister. They distrusted Bazzaz and accused him of violating the principles of the revolution of 1958 of which they considered themselves the custodians. They also disliked his popularity and independence. Naji Taleb was succeeded by President Aref who became his own prime minister on May 10, 1967. Two months later Aref asked General Taher Yahya, who had been his deputy prime minister, to form a new cabinet. With the exception of the short Bazzaz period of ten months, the Iraqi republic has been ruled by military prime ministers since the revolution.

Relations of Iraq with Egypt continued to be friendly under the younger Aref in accordance with the unified political command agreement. Iraq, however, continued to relax the trend toward nationalization and did not imitate Egypt or

Syria in imposing a strict socialist regime. It only withdrew the licenses of all sixteen privately owned newspapers on December 3, 1967 and replaced them by five nationalized dailies edited by state officials. Iraq under the younger Aref also felt free to establish friendly relations with Iran, Turkey and Pakistan, and was the only revolutionary Arab country to maintain such relations. When President Aref visited Iran on March 14-19, 1967, the Egyptian press ignored the visit, while the independent press in Lebanon described it in broad headlines.

Iraqi relations with Syria remained tense and the radical Baath Syrian regime spared no occasion to criticize or embarrass Iraq. When the abortive coup of June 30, 1966 took place in Baghdad, the semi-official Damascus daily *al-Thawrah* described the Iraqi regime as "provisional and unfit to survive." The program to settle the Kurdish problem was described as "a serious agreement with the secessionists," and the forthcoming visit of Dr. Bazzaz to Turkey in early July 1966 was called "a suspicious trip." In the Syrian dispute with the Iraq Petroleum Company between December 1966 and early March 1967, the IPC assets in Syria were seized and the flow of Iraqi oil through the pipelines in Syrian territory as well as the shipping of oil from the Syrian terminal at Baniyas were stopped, to the great discomfort of Iraq whose royalties from oil were estimated at eighty per cent of its national income. The purpose of the radical Baathist regime in Syria was not simply to increase the royalties paid by the IPC for the transit of oil, but also to make pressure on Iraq to allow Baath political activity and appoint Baath ministers in the cabinet, create economic trouble in Iraq and force the country to align itself completely with the revolutionary Arab states, and cause Iraq to take a violent attitude towards the IPC that could result in nationalizing the oil industry. During the crisis the Syrian Baath foreign minister, Ibrahim Makhous, irresponsibly discussed the question of finding markets for Iraqi oil as though it was about to be nationalized. In the free press in

Lebanon, it was said that Syria was ready to fight an imaginary battle against the IPC to the last penny in the Iraqi treasury.[195] Iraq resented the action of the Syrian Baath and succeeded in taking a reserved attitude in the dispute, and so did the Western powers who control the IPC.

The year that followed the Six Day War of early June 1967 was one of unrest and discontent in Iraq. There were criticisms of Iraqi handling of the forces that were sent to fight against Israel, and protests and demonstrations against Iraqi inaction in the Arab national efforts. Influential military and civilian leaders as well as trade union workers and students pressed for parliamentary elections under a constitutional democratic regime. Economic development in potentially rich Iraq was slow and the country suffered from decreased productivity and economic decline as a result of land reform and government regulations. The leftist parties claimed that the Aref regime was socially and economically conservative. Iraq concluded several agreements with France for the purchase of arms and for oil concessions between November 1967 and April 1968, but charges of corruption and bribery among higher officials followed these agreements. The Soviet leaders sought to strengthen their relations with Iraq and on May 11, 1968 a Soviet cruiser and other ships arrived in Basra for an eight day visit. In the face of Iraq's internal dissensions, its national, constitutional and economic problems and its complex foreign relationships, President Abdul Rahman Aref remained weak and indecisive. He was known as an honest man, but also as a waverer and ineffective leader. Among his critics was the former Baathist prime minister, Ahmad Hasan Bakr, who charged his regime with corruption and accused him of seeking to avoid change in order to retain power, and finally succeeded in overthrowing him in a military coup.

VIII. The coups d'Etat of July 1968 and the New Baath Regime

The coup of July 17, 1968 was the eighth among the attempted military coups—successful and abortive—after the revolution of July 14, 1958 and the sixteenth since Iraq became independent in 1932. It was carried out by the cooperation of the retired Baathist officer-politician, Ahmad Hasan Bakr, with two younger independent officers in the active service, Lt. Cols. Ibrahim Daoud, commander of the presidential guard, and Abdul Razzaq Nayef, deputy chief of military intelligence and liaison man between President Aref and the army. Two weeks later, on July 30, it was followed by another coup in which the Baathists ousted the two young officers who brought them to power.

The Baathist leader Bakr had cooperated with thirteen influential retired officers who had sent a note to the president on April 6, 1968 asking for the formation of a coalition cabinet and the establishment of a 30-man legislature until the election of an assembly in two years. The president did not answer the demands and determined to retain his prime minister Taher Yahya under whose rule, it was said, the country suffered from so much corruption that he came to be known as "the Thief of Baghdad."[196]

The coup was carefully planned by the two younger officers Nayef and Daoud and was executed by a mere threat of using force followed by the firing of two or more mortar shells over the presidential palace after which the president capitulated. In Baghdad, the coup, according to one report, had been expected for a week and the rulers were unable to head it off. The organizers of the coup had assured themselves of the control of the key army units and were aided by the general apathy among the military for defending the Aref regime. The president was reportedly awakened at 3 a.m. by a telephone call from Abdul Razzaq Nayef and Ahmad Hasan Bakr warning him that tanks were proceeding to the palace and asking him to resign. The shots that were fired were a confirmation of the threat. President Aref did not try to resist. He was placed aboard a special Iraqi plane that took him to London. The prime minister, Taher Yahya, also received a warning by telephone; it told him not to resist those who were coming to arrest him and he did not.[197] Among those who were arrested with him, in addition to the cabinet members, were twenty-six officials whose property was seized because they were said to have accepted bribes and commissions when a French state-owned oil company obtained concessions in November 1967 and February 1968 for the exploration and exploitation of oil in 10,800 square kilometers that were a part of the acreage expropriated from the Iraq Petroleum Company. The officials included Adib al-Jader, head of the board of directors of the Iraq National Oil Company that concluded the agreements, and six important Nasserists.

The new revolutionary command council that took over the government of Iraq proclaimed fifty-six-year-old Ahmad Hasan Bakr president of the republic. In its communiqué on the coup, it described the former rulers—Aref and his supporters—as "opportunists, thieves, ignorant, illiterate Zionist spies." Four days later, President Bakr told the troops that had participated in the coup that "bribery and corruption were rampant in Iraq," and that the country was plagued by "spreading chaos, espionage networks, economic deterioration and exorbitant prices." "Iraqi soldiers," he said, "were sent to war [against Israel in June 1967] without ammunition or even supplies." He added that the country's wealth was stolen and delivered into foreign hands for commissions, and the state treasury was depleted by widespread corruption and looting. The communiqué made no reference to Egypt, but it called for a definition of who was responsible for Arab defeat. The commander of the Iraqi contingent in Jordan was dismissed, but the Iraqi forces were to "remain posted on the fire line."

The cabinet of twenty-six ministers that was formed on July 18 and sworn in before President Bakr two days later consisted of Baathist leaders who belonged to a less extremist wing of the Baath than that which ruled in Syria, and of many non-Baathists of rightist inclination. The two young officers who masterminded the coup and emerged as the new strongmen were given important posts. Lt. Col. Abdul Razzaq

Nayef, thirty-four years old, thus became prime minister, and Ibrahim Daoud, thirty-nine years old, was given the defense portfolio and became lieutenant general and deputy commander of the armed forces. Among the Baath military leaders who had been retired under the preceding regime, Lieut. Gen. Hardan Takriti became army chief of staff, and Maj. Gen. Saleh Mahdi Ammash minister of the interior. The cabinet included four Kurdish ministers, two of whom were regarded as adherents of the Kurdish leader Mustafa al-Barzani. Several technicians who were in the ousted cabinet were appointed in the new one and thus moved from the prison to which they were sent directly after the coup to their new cabinet posts.

Seven military leaders who occupied supreme executive positions under the new regime were also the members of its revolution command council. Their names were disclosed on July 23. Three of them were Baathists: President Bakr, and Generals Takriti and Ammash. The four others were non-Baathists: Lt. Col. Nayef, Gen. Daoud, Brig. Saadun Ghaydan, commander of the presidential guard, and Lt. Col. Hammad Shehab, commander of the Baghdad zone. They were younger and had less political experience than their Baathist colleagues. Already in the first week that followed the coup, clear signs of disagreement were reported, and a split was rumored between President Bakr and the two military strongmen on the basis of their statements. While President Bakr declared that Iraq was following an Arab nationalist and socialist policy, the new prime minister, Lt. Col. Nayef, supported by General Daoud, the defense minister, questioned the future of socialism and the Arab socialist union that the Aref regime had tried to organize. He said that his government "would not adopt any policy which has proved to be a failure," which meant socialism, and he declared that "it was impossible to fix our position about the future of the socialist union before we establish our attitude toward socialism itself."[198] Premier Nayef also ordered the arrest of several Nasserists and other leftists including the former radical leader Ali Saleh Saadi. He indicated that the agreement with the French oil company would not be abrogated. Parties and parliamentary democracy were not to be restored, but a national council that would be chosen without regard to parties was announced.

The Baath leaders were not happy with the attitudes and policies of the young officers who brought them back to power. They now used the same unscrupulous maneuvers that the Baathists had employed elsewhere in order to oust Nayef and Daoud because they stood in the way of complete Baath control in Iraq. In Syria, the Baathists had succeeded in July 1963 in ousting General Ziad Hariri who executed the coup of March 8, 1963 that brought them to power, and in purging out the non-Baathist elements that took part in the coup. The Iraqi Baathists did not wait four months or even four weeks to remove those who made the coup against Aref. On July 30, 1968, two weeks after the coup, Col. Nayef and Gen. Daoud were dismissed from their posts and sent to exile by their Baathist partners. They were also retired from the armed forces. The twelve-day-old cabinet was dismissed. Colonel Nayef was arrested at noon in his residence in Baghdad and was later sent to Morocco, while the minister of defense, General Daoud, was treacherously purged out while he was performing a duty of his office outside the country. He was inspecting the 12000 Iraqi troops posted in Jordan. He returned to Baghdad on July 31 and had to fly back to Rome on the same day.

President Bakr accused his deposed prime minister and minister of defense of being reactionary and of "attempting to exclude progressive elements and replacing them by reactionary elements" in the government. He claimed that it was Daoud who imposed Nayef as prime minister and the revolutionary command council had to give in to avoid a massacre, and that the two wanted to make the cabinet a substitute for the revolutionary council. The two ousted strongmen were also said to have been in touch with counter-revolutionary elements and to have arrested people who should not have been arrested. The situation according to President Bakr reached an unbearable degree at the meeting of July 28 when oil policy was discussed. In his statement, Bakr pledged to follow a revolutionary unionist line insuring fundamental reforms, to exploit oil directly, settle the Kurdish problem peacefully, and pursue Arab unity. On July 31 the Baathists organized a demonstration of peasants, workers and intellectuals in support of their coup while the state-owned newspaper *al-Jumhuriyah* wrote an editorial against Nayef and Daoud and spoke of "the mercenaries who got on top and harbored spies and conspired to take the revolution of July 17 out of its way."[199]

President Bakr and the Baathists saw clearly that they could not possibly appoint their own men in key positions and pursue their Baath party policies in the presence of the two independent strongmen. Nayef and Daoud, on the other hand, were apparently not familiar with Baathist ruthless tactics and perhaps did not expect their partners to act so quickly against them. President Bakr, it was said, was able to execute his coup of July 30 because he began immediately after the coup of July 17 to strengthen his following in the army. He released the Baathists who had been in jail and brought back some 700 retired Baathist officers to the army and thereby turned the balance of power in favor of his party.[200]

The revolution command council appointed a new 26 man cabinet on July 31, 1968 with President Bakr as his own prime minister. The cabinet was of leftist outlook and included twelve persons who became ministers for the first time, while eleven members of the Nayef cabinet were retained. The minister of foreign affairs, Nasir al-Hani, described as a Nayef man, was not reappointed. He was assassinated on November 11, 1968. The new cabinet consisted mostly of moderate Baathists, and its two deputy premiers were the military Baath leaders, Gen. Hardan Takriti who became also minister of defense, and Gen. Saleh Ammash who retained his post of interior minister. The new cabinet released the

Nasserists and other leftists who were jailed by Nayef and later appointed the radical Baathist Ali Saleh Saadi on the five-member Arab relations bureau which was one of five advisory bureaus intended to help the revolution command council to run state affairs. The cabinet issued an amnesty for all persons involved in the Kurdish rebellion between 1961 and 1966 and announced its decision to establish a Kurdish university in the north even though the Kurdish region had not been pacified. The Baathist cabinet naturally abolished by decree the holiday of November 18 that celebrated the fall of the Baath under the Aref regime. The press was now free to speak of November 18, 1963 as the "November setback" and of the coup of July 17, 1968 as "the revolution of 17 July that came to rectify the black setback."[201]

On September 22, 1968 the revolution command council published a new provisional constitution of 95 articles that replaced that of 1964 issued under the first Aref. In its preamble it mentioned that it would remain in force until a permanent constitution is promulgated. The transitional period that had been extended twice since the publication of the constitution of 1964 was now extended indefintely. The first article declared Iraq a people's democracy whose ideals were based on Arab culture and the Islamic spirit, and the second article said that Islam was the state religion. The constitution also declared that the economic system aimed at achieving socialism "through implementing social justice in cooperation between the private and public sectors." It banned feudalism and prohibited non-Iraqis from owning agricultural land. The rights of the Kurds were recognized "within the unity of Iraq." The revolution command council of six members was recognized as the highest state authority and all its members became vice-presidents of the republic. It was given the power of choosing the president of the republic, appointing the prime minister and his deputies and the ministers, and endorsing the laws. It was also given authority over the armed forces and the right to supervise state affairs. The revolutionary council could dismiss any of its members by a two-thirds majority. The constitution required the members of the cabinet to be born of Iraqi parents coming from a family that had lived in Iraq since 1900.[202]

Shortly after the coup of July 30, 1968 the Baathists in power began to arrest their potential antagonists and resorted to their old ruthless tactics in order to stifle opposition by creating a climate of fear. Houses were ransacked before dawn and men disappeared, and those arrested were questioned under torture. Sometimes the prisoners died in jail as in the reported case of a local manager of the Coca Cola bottling concern whose body was returned to his family with such signs of torture as the hands without finger nails.[203] On September 27 the numerous arrests included eighty army officers. The purges and arrests caused the exodus of educated Iraqis and threw the upper levels of the civil service into chaos. The new Baathist regime imposed penalties on Iraqis who married foreigners. It took over the control of al-Hikmah University which the Jesuits had been running for thirty years, and purged out thirty-two American and German lecturers, most of whom were priests, on November 26, 1968. The justification given by the Baathist rulers for these and other purges and measures was to "uproot foreign influence, and liquidate the pockets of counter-revolution."

In January 1969 a large group of eighty-nine persons was brought to trial for espionage and for plotting to overthrow the Baath regime. It was the first major trial after the period of Kassem's rule. Fourteen of those who were accused of spying for Israel were convicted and publicly hanged on January 27 in Baghdad and Basra. They included nine Iraqi Jews. The public display of the executions was criticized by *al-Ahram* in Cairo in early February as harmful and inappropriate. The display only gave Israel a "great propaganda edge," as the former Iraqi representative at The United Nations said. Among those who faced trial were the former prime minister, Abdul Rahman Bazzaz, and the former defense minister, General Abdul Aziz al-Uqaili, who had been arrested in December 1968 when two Iraqis testified in court that they cooperated in a plot to overthrow the Baath regime in preparation for a peace pact with Israel. Bazzaz was said to have been supported in the plot by the American government and by the Central Treaty Organization (Cento).

The Baath regime has remained unstable, unpopular, and constantly fearful of a coup. In the power structure that emerged after July 30, 1968, certain dangerous rivalries that could lead to change were noticed. The two Baath military leaders, Hardan Takriti, the defense minister, and Saleh Ammash, the interior minister, were both deputy prime ministers, but it was Takriti who presided over cabinet meetings in President Bakr's absence. Moreover, Takriti was an old friend of Bakr and both were natives of Takrit, north of Baghdad, from which several officers came. Following the disagreement of Iraqi leaders about trying more spies after the executions of January 27, 1969, the Syrian press reported in early February that Takriti was arrested and stripped of his powers, but the Iraqi radio denied the report. The power struggle within the Iraqi leadership appeared in the continuous purging of superior officers. In late December 1968, the chief of staff, General Ibrahim Faisal al-Ansari, and four other senior officers were retired. On July 8, 1969 the Iraqi press mentioned that Ansari would be tried along with Bazzaz and eighteen others by a "revolutionary court" on charges of "conspiracy against the state." Rumors of arrests in Baghdad for an attempt to overthrow the Baath government of President Bakr were heard in mid-May 1969. On May 29, 1969 *al-Anwar* in Beirut reported that the Iraqi authorities sequestrated the property of forty-six persons and that in the preceding week twenty-five persons, including former ministers, officers, journalists, and businessmen, had received the same treatment.

The Iraqi Baath regime cooperated militarily with the Syrian Baath in the eastern command after March 1969 but the two wings of the party were not reconciled or united. The Baghdad Baathists who, in contrast to those ruling in Damascus, were known to be moderate, gradually began to take the lead in radicalism over the Syrian Baathists. In May, 1969 the

Iraqi revolution command council issued a decree halting compensation for expropriated land under the agrarian reform law. The RCC also prepared arbitrary laws that reached every aspect of the people's lives and allowed the state to direct anyone to any job in the national interest.[204] On May 1, 1969 the Baghdad radio announced that Iraq became the first non-communist state to extend diplomatic recognition to East Germany. Other Arab socialist regimes followed the step taken by Iraq. Syria was the third Arab state to extend that recognition. In early July 1969, Iraq was accorded a loan of eighty million dollars by East Germany for implementing major industrial projects.

The Iraqi Baath, in its search for exclusive power and in the presence of formidable opposition, has been particularly active in purging its enemies. The classical practice for discrediting the opponents was to accuse them of spying for Israel or for the American Central Intelligence Agency. The United States was made responsible for Iraq's troubles, and its sinister instrument, the CIA, was accused of fomenting unrest among the Kurds, recruiting spies, intriguing against Iraq and collaborating with the Iraqi treacherous elements. Iraqi propaganda has attempted to generate loyalty to the ruling Baath regime by creating an artificial atmosphere of fear, and appealing to the people to be vigilant against CIA conspiracy. Thirty-six persons were executed for espionage between January and May 1969. In early June, a former mayor of Baghdad, Brig. Gen. Midhat Hajj Sirri, confessed on television his collaboration for nine years with the CIA. Among the eighty Iraqis arrested in May on charges of spying for the CIA and plotting a coup backed by it was a former interior minister, Rashid Muslih, who confessed in a recorded broadcast that he had been a CIA agent since 1964 with several others.[205] Most of those implicated in the spying or the conspiracy had been military and civilian supporters of the Iraqi revolution against the monarchy and later served with the Aref brothers under whom the Baath party was discredited and banned.

The extensive purges and attempts to arrest Iraqi personalities on charges of spying led to what was described as the worst crisis between the Shia sect and the Iraqi government. In late June 1969 demonstrations took place in the Shia holy cities of Najaf and Karbala and an explosion damaged the railroad Baghdad-Diwaniyah. Among the causes of the crisis was the attempt to arrest al-Mahdi al-Hakim, son of the Mujtahid of Najaf, on charges of espionage for CIA, and the violation of the sanctity of the father's residence in searching for the fugitive son. A Shiite religious college was also closed in Najaf because of the arrest of a religious leader accused of being a CIA agent.[206]

The Kurdish problem was not settled by the new Baathist rulers and in mid-August 1968, Kurdish sources reported that relations between the government of President Bakr and the Kurdish nationalists had worsened. On November 19, 1968, a representative of the Kurdish leader Barzani asked Secretary-General U Thant of the UN to name a mediator so that the dispute between the Kurdish people and the Iraqi government could be settled in "a just and peaceful manner." Reports at the same time indicated that there was renewed conflict between the Kurds and the Iraqi troops.[207] At the end of 1968, the program that had been announced by Bazzaz on June 29, 1965 had not been implemented.

Republican Iraq has thus continued to be in turmoil and has witnessed nine coups d'état in the course of the ten years that followed the revolution of July 14, 1958. Each of the successive leaders has accused his predecessor of tyranny, but none of these "sons of the people" has dared establish a democratic representative rule where the voice of the people could be heard. The so-called tyrannical rule of Nuri al-Said under the monarchy was by far more democratic and humane than the rule of the military dictators under the republic, and the excesses of the Communists and Baathists who supported them had no equal since the darkest years of Ottoman and Mongol rule. Instability and unrest in addition to socialist measures and the fear of more socialism has ruined the economy of an otherwise rich country and certainly did not benefit the Iraqi masses. The Arab nationalists in Iraq, the Baathists in particular, who once accused the old regime of indifference to the interests and ideals of Arab nationalism, have made no contributions to those interests. They failed to achieve Arab unity even with those Arab states which called themselves socialist and revolutionary. Even when Iraq and Syria were ruled by the same party, the two countries made only a timid step towards unity. In the military effort of helping the Arabs against Israel, the Iraqi military regime under Aref and again under Baath rule have demonstrated their ineffectiveness and incompetence. Under the military dictatorships the reputation of the Arabs and that of Iraq have suffered to a large degree because of the massacres, the confusion, and the lawlessness that they witnessed. Arbitrary rule, discontent, and the danger of more coups d'état and more unrest still exist under the present Baath regime.

CHAPTER II
Notes

1. The author remembers the enthusiastic admiration that surrounded Faisal's visit to the city of Homs in Syria at the end of the war and the comments of those who, on seeing him, exclaimed "He has the dignity and charm of the Prophet!" See also Amin al-Rihani, *Faisal al-Awal* (Beirut, 1934), 199 ff, 126 ff. for Faisal's life and character.
2. This had been decided by the provisional government (the Council of State) in July, 1921 when the monarchical system was instituted. The provisional government itself was established by the British in October, 1920.
3. Hostile broadcasts and press articles especially in Syria and Egypt after 1955; see also Caractacus (Pseudonym),*Revolution in Iraq* (London: Gollancz, 1959), pp. 20, 68.
4. Elie Kedourie, "Reflexions sur l'histoire du royaume d'Irak 1921-58," *Orient*, No. 11 (1959, 3), 55-77.
5. James Morris, *The Hashemite Kings*, (London: Faber & Faber, 1959), 98.
6. Majid Khadduri, *Independent Iraq: A Study in Iraqi Politics 1932-1958*: 2nd ed. (London: Oxford University Press, 1960), 27.
7. *Ibid.*, 28; Stephen Hemsley Longrigg, *Iraq, 1900-1950* (London: Oxford University Press, 1953), 277.
8. Khadduri, 30; for an evaluation of Faisal's administration, qualities and democratic regime, see Longrigg, 162 ff., 200 ff., 223-225; 237.
9. For the text of the Commander's proclamation, see Khadduri, 84; Muhammad Khalil, *The Arab States and the Arab League*, I, (Beirut: Khayat, 1962), 3 followed by statements of Hikmat Sulaiman and his government. For the coup of 1936, Khadduri's article "The coup d'état of 1936," *The Middle East Journal*, II (July 1948), 270-292; Longrigg, 249; Yunis Bahri, *al-Iraq al-Yawm* (Beirut, 1938).
10. For these motives, Khadduri, "The coup d'état of 1936," 270 ff.; Longrigg, 249.
11. Longrigg, 250; for the text of the letter, Khadduri, *Independent Iraq*, 89.
12. James Morris, 154.
13. For an estimate of King Ghazi, see *Ibid.*, 145, 150.
14. *Ibid.*, p. 158
15. Caractacus, 20 ff.
16. The four colonels were Salaheddin Sabbagh, Fahmi Said, Mahmud Sulaiman, and Kamil Shebib. Those who were retired were Hussein Fawzi, General A. Umari, and Colonel Yamilqi. See for these developments Longrigg, 281; Khadduri, 153 ff.

17. The Arabs lost hope of obtaining a favorable solution of the Palestine problem after the failure of the semi-official Newcombe mission to Baghdad in July 1940. The Mufti had fled from Jerusalem during the Arab revolt in Palestine in October 1937 to Lebanon, and then left for Baghdad where Nuri's cabinet gave him 18,000 pounds sterling for expenses. See Khadduri, 162 ff.
18. See Khadduri, "General Nuri's Flirtations with the Axis Powers," *The Middle East Journal*, XVI, 3 (Summer, 1962), 328-336.
19. This right was given to the king of Iraq by the amendment of 1943.
20. Khadduri, 209; Longrigg, 287, says that the order was ignored.
21. Morris, 163.
22. For the text of this statement and that of Gailani on the same day, see *Tarikh al-Wazarat al Iraqiyah*, vol. V (Sidon, 1953), 184-186; English text in M. Khalil, I, 7-9.
23. Rashid Ali, under army pressure, prescribed conditions for the movement of British troops and refused the landing of more troops on April 29 before the departure of those who had landed on April 17.
24. Morris, 166; on the lamentable condition of the army, its disunity and lack of coordination, see Longrigg, 293; see also Uthman Kemal Haddad, *Harakat Rashid Ali al-Gailani* (Sidon, n.d.), 112-126, for the cowardice and arrogance of the colonels, the nervous breakdown of Sabbagh, the weakness of the army, and the disagreement between Sabbagh and Gailani.
25. Direct or one-stage voting allows the voters to elect the deputies directly instead of electing only the secondary voters or electoral college that elects the deputies.
26. George Lenczowski, *The Middle East in World Affairs* 3rd ed. (Ithaca: Cornell U. Press, 1962), 285; Khadduri, 283.
27. Lenczowski, 295.
28. For the definition of Nasserism and its characteristics, see Fayez Sayegh, "Nasser and Arab Nationalism," *Middle East Forum*, April 1959, pp. 15 ff.; the entire issue contains articles on the subject of Nasserism.
29. George Kirk, *Contemporary Arab Politics* (New York: Praeger, 1961), 143; Keith Wheelock, *Nasser's New Egypt* (New York: Praeger, 1960), 51.
30. Pierre Rondot, *The Changing Patterns of the Middle East*, (New York: F. A. Praeger, 1961), 188.
31. See Walid Khalidi, "Nasser and the Arab World," *Middle East Forum*, April 1959, pp. 30 ff.; it is even held that Nasser would have joined in a defense agreement with the west if Nuri al-Said had not become its spokesman and agreed to it before he did, as a former pro-Nasserist Syrian officer and cabinet minister under the United Arab Republic declared. See *al-Nasr*, January 10, 1963, for the

declaration of Amin Nufuri.

32. Marcel Colombe, "Panorama du trimestre," *Orient*, No. 12, (1959, 4), 7-12.
33. Anthony Nutting, *The Arabs* (New York: Clarkson N. Potter, 1964), 343; for an account of Nuri, read *Ibid.* ch. 28 "The Era of Nuri as-Said"; favorable biography by Lord Birdwood, *Nuri As-Said, A Study in Arab Leadership* (London: Cassell, 1959).
34. Estimate of Nuri al-Said by the former American ambassador in Iraq, Waldemar J. Gallman, *Iraq under General Nuri* (Baltimore: Johns Hopkins Press, 1964), 88-92, 219 ff.
35. Lord Birdwood, 239.
36. According to Khalil Kennah, former cabinet minister in Iraq, Nuri was not too enthusiastic about the union with Syria, while Prince Abdul Ilah was. See his *al-Iraq, Amsuhu wa Ghaduhu* (Iraq, Its Past and Future), (Beirut, 1966), 230. See also Khaldun S. al-Husry on Fadel Jamali's complaint that Nuri refused him one-quarter of a million dinars to bring about unity with Syria, in "The Iraqi Revolution of July 14, 1958," Part II, *Middle East Forum*, Winter, 1965, p. 27.
37. Lord Birdwood, 238.
38. George Grassmuck, "The Electoral Process in Iraq 1952-58," *MEJ*, XIV, 4 (1960), 410 ff.
39. Caractacus, 29; Benjamin Shwadran, *The Power Struggle in Iraq*, (New York: Council for Middle Eastern Affairs Press, 1960), 12; Freda Utley, *Will the Middle East Go West?* (Chicago: Henry Regnery Co., 1957), 42.
40. Brigadier Stephen H. Longrigg, "Iraq Under Kassim," *Current History* (April, 1962), 214; J. Heyworth-Dunne, "Partis politiques et gouvernement dans l'Irak d'aujourdhui," *Orient*, No. 15, 1960, 3), 71.
41. See Anthony Nutting, 340; Bernard Vernier, *L'Irak d'Aujourdhui* (Paris: Armand Colin, 1963), 59; Ambassador Gallman, 93.
42. A. J. Meyer, *Middle Eastern Capitalism*, (Cambridge: Harvard University Press, 1959), 3-4.
43. Pierre Rossi, "L'Irak devant la réforme agraire," *Orient*, No. 7 (1958,3), 85 ff; Lord Birdwood, 277 speaks of two and a half million acres distributed.
44. Khalidi, "Nasser and the Arab World, "*loc. cit.*, 30.
45. Lenczowski, 283.
46. Caractacus, 42; see also Lord Birdwood quoted in Kirk, 213 n. 15.
47. Morris, 182.
48. See al-Husry, *loc. cit.*, 29.
49. See Nasir al-Nashashibi, *Madha Jara fil Sharq al-Awsat* (What Happened in the Middle East), (Beirut, 1961), 23 ff.
50. Abdul Rahman al-Bazzaz, *Safahat Min al-Ams al-Qarib* (Beirut, 1960), 20 ff., 170 ff.

51. Khalidi, *loc. cit.*, pp. 30 ff.
52. Morris, 182-183.
53. Kirk, 143.
54. Nutting, 351; Gerald De Gaury, *Three Kings in Baghdad* (London, Hutchinson, 1961), 177.
55. During the trial of the officials of the old regime in August, 1958, the director of broadcasting was asked about these songs. See also Bazzaz, 20; Muhammad Mahdi Kubbah, *Mudhakkirati fi Samim al-Ahdath* 1918-1958 (Beirut, 1965), 368.
56. Heyworth-Dunne, *loc. cit.*, p. 74.
57. Lenczowski, 300.
58. Brainwashing has been defined by David Lawrence in his column of January 2, 1963, as "a form of persuasion by persistence. The theory is that if you say something again and again, it will make a lasting impression."
59. Lord Birdwood 264; De Gaury, 187.
60. Simon Jargy, "Une page d'histoire de la revolution Irakienne: le proces Abd al Salam Aref," *Orient*, No. 12 (1959, 4), pp. 85 ff.; Lord Birdwood, 266.
61. One version mentioned in the People's Court said that the movement began before 1956 but Aref joined on the recommendation of Kassem only in early 1957, and that Wasfi Taher, Nuri's aide, was in one group headed by General Muhieddin Abdul Hamid, while Kassem headed another group. See Jargy, "Une page d'histoire . . .," *loc. cit.*, pp. 85 ff. Another version contained in *Majzarat Qasr al-Rahab,* (The Massacre of al-Rahab Palace), (Beirut: Dar al-Hayat, 1960), pp. 40 ff., spoke of a cell formed by Colonel Rifat al-Hajj Sirri and of another cell formed by Kassem in which Aref was a member, and that both merged at the end of 1954. Still another version related that Kassem and Aref were in two different groups and that Wasfi Taher brought them together. See Heyworth-Dunne, *loc. cit.* p. 76. A fourth version was related by Fayek Samarrai and published in the Syrian press in late March 1959, after his quarrel with Kassem, to the effect that Kassem belonged to a smaller group infiltrated by Communists, while a larger group existed, but its members were discovered and transferred by Nuri, who knew about it, probably through a betrayal by the smaller group.
62. The names of the twelve members of the Central Committee are: Brig. Generals Abdul Karim Kassem, Naji Taleb, Abdul Wahab al-Amin, Muhieddin Abdul Hamid, Colonels Abdul Salam Aref, Abdul Wahab Shawaf, Abdul Karim Farhan, Rajab Abdul Majid, Rifat al-Hajj Sirri (retired), Taher Yahya (retired), Wasfi Taher, and Captain Muhammad Sabe'. See *Majzarat Qasr al-Rahab,* 42.
63. Jargy, 85 ff.

64. Shwadran, 14 ff.; Caractacus, 119.
65. Caractacus, 119; Jargy, 87 says that as a result of the meeting with Nasser in Damascus, July, 1958, Nasser spoke of him as "the baby" *(al-tifl)* and was shocked by his crudeness.
66. De Gaury, 190.
67. Heyworth-Dunne, 78. Hussein Jamil, for example, refused a cabinet post, and Kamel Chaderchi, leader of the National Democratic party, refused to enter the political arena, while Shanshal, after a short period as Minister of Information and Guidance, resigned.
68. See Muhammad Hassanein Haikal's article in *al-Ahram,* January 27, 1959, addressed to Kassem under the title "To the Sole Leader," where it is said that Nasser declared, when his support was asked, that the movement must be planned and executed by the Iraqi officers and then Cairo will provide support. In the People's Court, Aref was asked about his relations, and those of Kassem, with Nasser. He replied that they had meetings with the First Army command to establish a basis of cooperation. See Jargy, 90 ff. Gen. Afif al-Bizri, in *al-Nasr,* July 1, 1962, has admitted contacts with Kassem and Aref in the tent near the Mafraq airport in Jordan, but then he said that Sarraj carried on the negotiations behind the back of the Syrian command and reported to Nasser for whom he was working, so that Syria would not know the real situation in Iraq and would always be in a precarious position and therefore would ask for unity with Egypt—as it did.
69. Heyworth-Dunne, 80, quoting a pamphlet entitled "14 Tammuz," (July), says that Kassem, in a press conference ten days after the coup, thanked the UAR for being the first to recognize the Iraqi Republic and then went on to say, "My brother Gamal was absent and the world was amazed by this surprise operation executed at night and so well organized in details that nobody knew about it, not even our friends."
70. Gen. Bizri was Commander of the First Army in the Northern Region (Syria) after unity for a short time and then was placed in forced residence in Cairo where he was made a member of the Higher Planning Council, which he said was "an imaginary non-existing council." He became violently hostile to Nasser.
71. Bizri in *al-Nasr*, July 1, 1962, said that Nasser told Khrushchev that Iraqi revolutionaries were among his men and that he started that revolt against imperialism.
72. Jargy, 92; see also, Shwadran, 23, n. 9 for another version reported by the Egyptian *Akhbar al-Yawm* that said that it was decided to achieve unity with the UAR in November, 1958.
73. My interview with retired Maj. Gen. Ismail Aref in Beirut, March

1967; the other source is Yunis Bahri, *Sab'at Ashhur fi Sujun Baghdad* (Beirut, 1960), 103 ff.

74. *Majzarah* . . ., 48-50.
75. King Hussein I, *Uneasy Lies the Head,* (New York: Bernard Geis Associates, 1962), 198.
76. The palace housed the king, his uncle Abdul Ilah and his family, the king's aunt Abdiya, and the king's grandmother Queen Nafisa. A new and much larger palace for King Faisal was begun in 1955 and was to be finished in 1958. Faisal was to marry a Turkish princess named Fadila in late 1958.
77. Morris, 190.
78. Khadduri, 286.
79. *Majzarah* . . ., 26 says that Nuri did not want to disturb the Palace with these reports, and so the security department had to send them later directly to the Palace; see also De Gaury, 186, 190 ff. for attempted plots and warnings about the impending coup.
80. Kahdduri, 363.
81. Andrew Tully, *CIA: The Inside Story,* (New York: William Morrow & Co., 1962), 76, 82.
82. King Hussein I, 194 ff. It is also reported that Muhammad Rafiq Aref told King Hussein, "Do you want us to arrest 1,000 officers? All these things are lies!" See *Majzarah* . . ., 36.
83. Caractacus, 118 says that Nuri spoke openly of intervention in Lebanon, "against the universal sentiment of Arab society." The same author considers that the danger of being sent to fight against the UAR would have forced the soldiers to a moment of decision; see Gallman p. 165 for Nuri's interest in U.S. intervention in Lebanon.
84. When the relations between Nasser and Kassem deteriorated a few months later, Nasser charged, in a speech of March 15, 1959, in Damascus, that Kassem was prepared to enter Baghdad as a leader if Aref succeeded, but if he had failed, Kassem would have entered to declare his loyalty to the king. See Shwadran, 53. On the other hand, it was reported that Kassem allegedly told Aref to shoot him if the coup failed and to pretend that he did so by loyalty to the regime, and then wait for another opportunity. Caractacus, 120.
85. See Tully's assertion, p. 76, and de Gaury's denial of Nuri's permission, p. 190.
86. Caractacus, 127 ff., who writes favorably of the revolutionaries, says that the King began descending the outside stairs from the second floor and was ready to surrender, but Abdul Ilah fired at the soldiers and they returned the fire and killed the entire family. Another version says that Abdul Ilah fired at his nephew, the king, when he wanted to yield. Still another version relates that Faisal was wounded and taken to a hospital where he died, but before dying, he begged

the officers not to give his body to the angry mob. The officers were touched and wept and promised. Morris, 199, mentions other rumors. One of them says that Abdul Ilah shot Faisal, and had himself shot by a bodyguard of the King. Another rumor states that as a result of the battle between the rebels and the royal guards, Faisal and his uncle were accidentally killed. Morris also reports an alleged safe conduct that was given to the royal group, which was followed by the fusillade against the same group by machine gun fire. See also Tully, 77; Vernier, 57; Birdwood, 266.

87. The text of Aref's broadcast in *al-Hayat,* July 15, 1958 and in Khalil, I, 27. This quoted part of Aref's statement was later omitted from the official publication of the text.
88. De Gaury, 194.
89. *Ibid*; *Majzarat Qasr al-Rahab,* 82 ff.
90. De Gaury, 194; *Majzarah,* 64 ff.
91. The royal party included King Faisal, Prince Abdul Ilah, Queen Nafisa, Abdul Ilah's mother, Princess Abdiya, Princess Hiyam, Abdul Ilah's wife, a six-year old child named Ghaziya who was being raised by Abdiya, Lt. Thabit, an aide de camp, a black servant named Shaker, and a maid named Razqiya.
92. See for details De Gaury, 194-195; *Majzarah,* 96.
93. Robert Murphy, *Diplomat Among Warriors* (Garden City, N.Y.: Doubleday, 1964), 412; De Gaury, 195.
94. *Majzarah,* 120-122.
95. It was reported that Colonel Wasfi Taher came with the battalion entrusted with the storming of Nuri's house. He entered first and told a baking woman to warn Nuri against the danger. Nuri slipped out of the house in his pajamas. Taher's action was a precaution which would have saved his position if the revolt had failed. When Nuri fell on the following day, Taher came and shot him to insure his silence. See *Majzarah,* 122.
96. King Hussein, 199; see also Murphy, 412; De Gaury, 200.
97. On the service at the Chapel Royal Savoy in London, see De Gaury, 203 ff.
98. Communiques in *al-Nasr,* February 10, 1963.
99. Among these ministers were Saddiq Shanshal of the Istiqlal Party, Jaber al-Umar, and Fuad Rikabi of the Baath Socialist Party, and Muhammad Hadid of the National Democratic Party.
100. Gen. Najib al-Rubay'i, chairman of the Council, was a Sunnite Arab, Muhammad Mahdi Kubbah was a Shiite Arab, and Khaled Naqshbandi was a Kurd.
101. The first instance of a sovereign Arab country declaring itself part of

the Arab nation, occurred in the Syrian Constitution of 1950, Article 1, Section 3. See text of provisional Iraqi constitution in Khalil, I, 30 ff.

102. *The Iraq Times,* May 6, 1959.
103. H. B. Sharabi, *Governments and Politics in the Middle East in the 20th Century,* (Princeton: Van-Nostrand, 1962), p. 161; Marcel Colombe, "Panorama du trimestre," *Orient* (1958, 3), 7-15.
104. Shwadran, 17.
105. *al-Hayat,* September 5, 1961.
106. Shwadran, 79, n. 34.
107. Caractacus, 132.
108. *al-Nasr,* January 26, 1959. For a description of the trials, see Shwadran, 60 ff; for a full account of the proceedings of the court see *Muhakamat al-Mahkamah al-Askariyah al-Khassah* (Trials of the Special Military Court), 23 volumes (Baghdad: Ministry of Defense, 1959-1960).
109. Heard by the author in Damascus from Radio Baghdad on September 11, 1958.
110. Nasser's speech in Damascus on March 22, 1959; Muhammad Hassanein Haikal's articles in *al-Ahram,* April 2 and 4, 1959.
111. *al-Nasr,* Editorial of November 5, 1962; on August 22, 1959, Mahdawi, in his usual sarcastic manner, declared that Nasser has "a trunk-like nose with which he will continue to sniff at our oil until he dies." Shwadran, 68.
112. Declaration by Amin Nufuri, former Syrian minister in the UAR cabinet, to the Arab East News Agency, quoted in *al-Nasr,* August 30, 1962.
113. Gen. Bizri spoke of two planeloads, *al-Nasr,* July 1, 1962, while Nufuri mentioned two carloads, *al-Nasr,* August 30, 1962. Lord Birdwood, 272 says that after July 14, 1958 and in a few hours the photos of Nasser were selling at twice the price of those of Kassem.
114. Shwadran, 32.
115. Jargy, 85 ff. on the trial of Aref.
116. Radio Baghdad announced on November 25, 1961, that Kassem revoked Aref's death sentence and decreed his expulsion from the army. In so doing, Kassem was said to have acted according to the principle of returning kindness for injury. Kassem also ordered the payment of the rent of Aref's house during the three years when he was in jail. *al-Nasr,* December 14, 1961.
117. When Kassem insinuated, in October 1959, that the Fertile Crescent scheme was a part of Iraq's policy, Amer of Egypt warned that if anyone dares to put his foot in Syria, it will be cut off. Shwadran, 49-50.
118. Heyworth-Dunne, 80 ff.

119. See the book in Arabic by Shaker Mustafa Selim, *The Court of Hasan al-Rakka' and Other Events from the Record of Communism and Opportunism in Iraq* (Beirut: Dar al-Tali'ah, n.d.). See also Khaldun al-Husry,*The July 14 Revolution and the Truth About the Communists in Iraq* (Arabic), (Beirut, 1963).
120. On Nasser's hopes of replacing Britain and the United States, supplying manpower, technical assistance, schools and development projects for Iraq, see Frederick Harbison, "Two Centers of Arab Power," *Foreign Affairs,* vol. 37 (July 1959), 680; for the claim on Communist readiness to seize power, al-Husry, *Ibid.*
121. Article by "Muttali" (Pseud.) in *al-Nasr,* July 5, 1962, mentions that the revolt was prepared and directed by Nasser and the intelligence service of Sarraj; Amin Nufuri's declaration in *al-Nasr,* August 30, 1962, on the carloads of arms and bombs sent from Jazirah in Syria, and on the broadcasting station provided by Sarraj.
122. One of these courts was formed by a butcher named Abdul Rahman Sultan, who was tried by a military court a year later in Baghdad. See *al-Hayat,* April 8, 1960; see Khalil Kennah 342 on the ungratefulness of this Abdul Rahman who was once protected by the Sanjari family but later ordered killing eight of its members.
123. Broadcast from the Baghdad radio heard by the author on March 24, 1959. An Iraqi refugee who spoke from the Damascus radio on April 9, 1959, estimated the number of houses that were destroyed to be 150 to 200, and the number of those who were killed between six thousand and seven thousand; *al-Ahram*, September 25, 1959 estimated the number of victims in Mosul to be 3,600. A former Iraqi diplomat told me that a bride of the Umari family was dragged and hanged naked on a lamp post and when an Aneze Bedouin came to cover her with his cloak, he was shot.
124. Report from Baghdad by Selim Nassar in *al-Safa*, (Beirut) February 12, 1963.
125. One of the defendants was the imam of a little town called Aqra, who had spoken against the danger of the spread of Communism in Iraq. During the trial, Mahdawi asked him, "Do you know what Communism is? Did not Islam encourage kindness to the poor?" Heard by the author on April 20, 1959.
126. See *al-Ahram,* August 27, 1959, for Tabaqchali's testimony on the Kirkuk massacre; *al-Ahram,* September 25, 1959, for the number of victims and those who were obliged to dig their own graves; *,al-Hayat,* March 3, 1963 on the number of victims in Mosul and Kirkuk, estimated to be ten thousand.
127. See Muhammad Baqer Shirri, *Iraq in Revolution* (Arabic), (Beirut, 1963), 38.
128. Shwadran, 72.

129. *al-Hayat,* January 11, 1962 related that in December, 1961, Kassem declared a general amnesty and invited political refugees outside Iraq to come back.
130. In early 1961, four associations in the Soviet Union sent letters of protest to Kassem against what they called victimizing pro-communistic elements in Iraq. Some of these elements were dismissed from their jobs because they took part in the Kirkuk massacre. *The New York Times,* February 19, 1961.
131. Shwadran, 54 ff.
132. *Ibid.*; see also "La controverse Egypto–Irakienne," *Orient* No. 9 (1959, 1), 109-119 on the accusations of Ihsan Abdel Quddus, and the counter accusations of Dhul Nun Ayyub.
133. On December 27, 1961, the foreign minister of Iraq served notice that any state that established diplomatic relations with Kuwait would commit an unfriendly act towards Iraq.
134. Longrigg, "Iraq Under Kassim, *loc. cit.*, 219; *The Wall Street Journal,* January 5, 1962.
135. In mid-July, 1962, Kassem told the correspondent of *al-Hayat* that he had nothing but the shirt of his uniform. "Put your hand on this shirt," he said, "I have entered the army with it and led the revolution, and it will always be the object of my pride. I thank God that I have nothing but it." *al-Hayat* July 18, 1962.
136. Shwadran, 33, n. 14; *al-Safa,* February 20, 1963.
137. *Yawm al-salamah wal ibtihaj.*
138. Kingsly Martin, "Arab Socialism," *Middle East Forum,* (May, 1962), 37; see also Shirri, 70.
139. See D. A. Schmidt, *The New·York Times,* June 17, 1962; Shirri, 44.
140. *Time,* November 17, 1958.
141. *The New York Times,* January 9, June 17, 1962; Kingsly Martin, 37; Ambassador Gallman, 214-215.
142. *The New York Times,* June 17, 1962.
143. Hedrick Smith, *The New York Times,* April 11, 1963.
144. Khadduri, 32-33.
145. *The New York Times,* June 17, 1962.
146. Kassem's declaration in *al-Hayat,* July 18, 1962; see also Clare Hollingsworth, "The Baathist Revolution in Iraq," *The World Today,* XIX, 5 (May, 1963), 225-230.
147. Kassem's speeches in *al-Nasr,* January 11, 16, 1963.
148. *Mideast Mirror,* February 9, 1963.
149. On the coup of February 8, 1963 see Shirri, *al-Iraq al-Tha'er* (Iraq in Revolution); Yunis Bahri, *Thawrat 14 Ramadan al-Mubarak* (Revolution of 14 Ramadan the Blessed), (Beirut, 1963?); Ahmad Fawzi, *Thawrat 14 Ramadan* (Cairo, 1963); Clare Hollingsworth, "The Baathist Revolution in Iraq," *loc. cit.*, 225 ff.

150. *al-Hayat,* February 17, 1963. When the foreign minister in the new cabinet was asked about the role of the Baath in the revolt, he diplomatically answered that all the sectors of the population took part in it. See *al-Nasr,* February 14, 1963.
151. A list of officers about to be arrested was allegedly found after the coup on the director of Kassem's intelligence. See *al-Hayat,* February 17, 1963. It is also claimed that the younger officers of the air force at Habbaniya, who were in the plot, had refused an order of transfer, and that Brig. Gen. Jalal al-Awqati, commander of the air force and a pro-communist, was about to retire them and so they decided to act. *al-Safa,* February 12, 1963.
152. *al-Safa,* February 12, 1963.
153. *al-Nasr,* February 14, 1963; In his press conference on February 14, Aref mentioned that he urged Kassem to surrender and not to be another Tshombe (referring to how Tshombe caused division in the Congo); he also claimed that Kassem was ready to kiss more than his hands while pleading for mercy; see Shirri, 15 ff.; *Mideast Mirror,* February 16, 1963.
154. During the proceedings, Mahdawi was believed to have been slugged. Both he and Kassem were seated on a couch when they were shot. It is said that Kassem refused to have his eyes bound when he was shot and declared that he was the beloved hero of the Iraqi people. *al-Nasr,* February 14, 1963.
155. *The New York Times,* February 11, 1963; *al-Safa,* February 12, 1963 quoting Teheran reports.
156. *The New York Times,* February 9, 1963.
157. *al-Nasr,* February 10, 1963; *al-Safa,* February 12, 1963; text of communiqué also in *Middle Eastern Affairs* (March, 1963), 78.
158. *al-Nasr,* February 10, 1963; Khalil Kennah, 383 on appeal over the radio by the Baath regime for killing Communists.
159. See the editorial in *al-Nasr,* February 10, 1963, entitled "Logic Cannot Accept the Rule of Dictatorships in the Twentieth Century," and the column on February 11, 1963, under the title "The Revolt of Iraq is a Lesson for all Dictators."
160. *al-Safa,* February 9, 1963 mentioned seven Baathist members in the cabinet; see also *al-Hayat,* February 17, 1963.
161. Quoted by D. A. Schmidt in *The New York Times,* March 2, 1963.
162. *The New York Times,* February 11, 1963. Ten days after Iraq's revolt, a senior western diplomat was quoted saying that Syria would be caught by revolution in the next two weeks—and his prediction proved to be true.
163. D. A. Schmidt, in *The New York Times,* February 20, 1963.
164. Reported in *The New York Times,* May 27; *al-Hayat,* May 26, 1963. In Cairo the Middle East News Agency said that 60 officers and 120

civilians were arrested, and that ten retired officers and two civilians were executed in Baghdad.

165. Description of the attempt according to the Iraqi communiqué, in *al-Hayat,* July 4, 1963.
166. *al-Hayat,* July 28, 1963.
167. *al-Hayat,* October 25, 1963, January 12, February 13, 1964.
168. *The New York Times,* August 2, 1963.
169. See article in *al-Hayat,* November 17, 1963 on "al-Baath between extremism and moderation" (in Arabic); see also *al-Bayan* (New York) November 19, 1963; Khalil Kennah, 385 described al-Saadi as bloodthirsty and totally unrestrained.
170. For these developments see *al-Hayat* November 14, 1963; *The New York Times,* November 11-15, 1963.
171. See comments by Dana Adams Schmidt in *The New York Times,* November 16, 18, 1963.
172. *al-Bayan* (New York), November 19, 1963; *The New York Times,* November 20 and 21, 1963; *Time* November 29, 1963 for a description of the coup. See also Kennah, 391 for the statement issued on the day of the coup.
173. *Mideast Mirror,* August 21, 1965.
174. See an analysis of the causes of the setback in Iraq by the Baathist leader Munif al-Razzaz, in his *al-Tajribah al-Murrah* (The Bitter Experience), (Beirut, 1967), 76-83.
175. *Mideast Mirror,* April 4, 1964.
176. On the provisional constitution see *Ibid.*, May 9, 1964; *The New York Times,* May 4, 1964.
177. On this electoral law, see *The Middle East Journal,* XXI, 2 (Spring, 1967), 239.
178. See Ernest Francis Penrose, "Essai sur L'Irak," *Orient* no. 35 (1965, 3), 39.
179. *Time,* October 2, 1964.
180. See account of the plot in *al-Hayat,* September 8 and 10, 1964; D. A. Schmidt account in *The New York Times* September 23, 1964; *Time,* October 2, 1964.
181. On the agreement of May 26, 1964 see Penrose, 52 ff.; Marcel Colombe, "Vers une union Egypto-Irakienne," *Orient,* no. 31 (1964, 3), 75-82; *Arab News and Views* November 1, 1964; *The New York Times,* May 27, 1964.
182. See Penrose, 48-50 on this explanation and other comments on nationalization.
183. Reported by *The New York Times,* January 3, 1965; *al-Hayat* September 20, 1964.
184. See Penrose, 53, 57-58; D. A. Schmidt in *The New York Times,* November 22, 1964, January 15, 1965.

185. *Mideast Mirror,* November 6, 1965.
186. See the slogan *al-Ishtirakiyah al-Rashidah* under the Bazzaz cabinet after September 21, 1965 and the "fair socialism" of the Naji Taleb cabinet in August 1966.
187. Accounts of the coup in *al-Hayat,* September 18, 1965; *Mideast Mirror,* September 18 and 25, 1965; Penrose, 60-61.
188. *Mideast Mirror,* April 3, 1965; see D. A. Schmidt in the *N.Y. Times* November 12, 1964 for the autonomous Kurdish government.
189. Details on this plan in *Mideast Mirror,* July 2, 1966; see also the views of Bazzaz on the Kurdish problem in *al-Nahar* (Beirut) May 13, 1966 as told to its correspondent in Baghdad.
190. Reported in *al-Hayat,* November 2, 1965 according to an Iraqi source in Cairo.
191. *Mideast Mirror,* November 20, 1965.
192. *Ibid.,* December 18, 1965; *al-Hayat* December 9, 1965.
193. *The N.Y. Times,* March 30, 1966.
194. Account of this abortive coup in *Mideast Mirror* July 2, 1966; *L.A. Times, N.Y. Times,* July 1, 1967.
195. Jubran Shamiyeh in *al-Hayat,* January 7, 1967; see also *Ibid.,* December 17, 1966, January 14, 1967.
196. See for description of the coup, *Time* July 26, 1968; *The N.Y. Times* July 18, 21, 22 and *The Los Angeles Times* July 17, 20, 1968.
197. Report by Thomas F. Brady in *The N.Y. Times,* July 21, 22, 1968.
198. *Ibid.* July 26, 1968.
199. *Mideast Mirror,* August 3, 1968.
200. Joe Alex Morris Jr. in *The Los Angeles Times,* July 31, 1968.
201. *Mideast Mirror,* November 23, 1968.
202. For the new constitution see *Mideast Mirror,* September 28, 1968
203. *The N.Y. Times,* October 27, November 29, 1968.
204. D. A. Schmidt in *N.Y. Times,* May 24, 1969.
205. *N.Y. Times,* June 10; *Los Angeles Times,* June 18, 1969.
206. *L.A. Times,* June 30, 1969.
207. *Mideast Mirror,* November 23, 1968.

CHAPTER III

Coups d'Etat and Military Rule in Syria

The Syrian republic became completely independent in 1946. The officers of its young army staged their first coup d'état in March 1949 and have not been able since then to disengage themselves from politics. Their successive interventions were encouraged by local political parties and by external political forces. The military often ruled indirectly through a facade of constitutional civilian government with parties and parliaments. In the mid 1950's, radical elements in the army in alliance with radical ideological groups began to assert their influence. In 1963 the destruction of the parliamentary regime became complete at the hands of the radical Baath socialist party which has been ruling since then under the influence of its military members and without the help of any kind of freely elected representative institutions.

The record number of military coups in Syria—two of which have been called revolutions—and the triumph of leftist extremism in local and foreign policy might be understood after a brief study of the external and internal sources of tension in the country, the historical and psychological factors that have influenced its people, and the character of the military leaders who imposed policies and trends that do not represent the people's wishes.

I. General Background: Problems and Tensions

A. Tensions of External Origin: The Problem of Syrian Alignment

The present Syrian republic occupies only about one-half of natural or geographic Syria which also includes the state of

Lebanon, created as a separate entity in 1920, the state of Jordan, originally Transjordan at the time of its birth in 1921 before it acquired the left bank of the Jordan, and the state of Israel which emerged after the partition of Palestine in November 1947. The borders of the Syrian state were arbitrarily fixed by the two mandatory powers, Britain and France. In 1939 Turkey was allowed to annex the Syrian Sanjak of Alexandretta with the consent of the French mandatory power. Syrian hopes for the formation of a united Syrian state, with a measure of autonomy for certain regions, were thus frustrated, for in spite of the political division of geographic Syria and its domination by foreign powers in various periods of its long history, its inhabitants had preserved an awareness of its geographical and historical identity – under its name "Syria" or "al-Sham" – and of its particular needs and economic interests.

In addition to their consciousness of their Syrian identity, the Syrians were also conscious of their Arab-Islamic heritage and of belonging to an Arab nation. In fact it was under the banner of Arab nationalism that they struggled for independence against the Ottoman empire until 1918 and later against the French mandate until 1946. Syrian Arabism continued to draw strength for some time from the memories of the shortlived Arab kingdom of Faisal in Syria, as it has always drawn strength from the memories of the glorious Umayyad caliphate in Damascus. Under the French mandate and since independence, the present Syrian republic has remained the standard bearer of Arab nationalism and Arab liberation and unity. The trouble with the Syrians, once said Dr. Nazem al-Qudsi, the last constitutional president of Syria, is that "we are never concerned with just our own problems but with issues affecting all the Arabs. [1]It has been suggested that because of the division of Syria into several states, national feeling was turned outwards as it had no existing state to focus upon, and Syrian nationalism as a result became weaker after 1918. According to the same opinion, if Syria had remained undivided there would have been a balance between Arab and Syrian feeling as in Egypt and Iraq.[2]

When the Syrian republic became independent, its rulers who belonged to the National Bloc, and its people in general were reconciled to the present divisions of geographic Syria, but they accepted neither the loss of the Sanjak of Alexandretta nor the idea of the Jewish state which they regarded as an alien state created by imperialism. When the Arab League was formed in March 1945, Syria as well as Lebanon and Jordan became charter members, and the League Charter recognized the separate existence and sovereignty of each member state and forbade the intervention of one state in the affairs of another. Ideological and other political parties continued, however, to hold separate views on the future of the existing Syrian republic. The Syrian Social National Party worked for the formation of a Greater Syria that would include not only geographic Syria but also Iraq. The People's Party, centered mainly in Aleppo and Homs, was in favor of a union between the present Syrian republic and Iraq, while the Baath Socialist Party advocated pan-Arab unity and opposed any regional grouping with Iraq or Jordan because it could threaten the republican regime and extend British influence to Syria. The Syrians remained generally committed to the idea of Arab unity and responded with emotion to the appeal for its achievement and to the leader who would promise to achieve it. Yet, it must be said that the sentiment of Arab nationalism in Syria and even the dogmatism of the Baath party about Arab unity never were able to eradicate the feeling of Syrian patriotism and the consciousness of the Syrian identity.

Tensions developed in Syria before and after 1949 on account of the conflicting views on the future of the country. The army officers including both those who belonged to ideological parties and those who were neutral became interested in the arguments and activities of the various political groups. Some stood with the SSNP for a Greater Syria, others stood with the Baath against the SSNP goals and against the Fertile Crescent union of Syria and Iraq advocated hesitatingly by the Populists, while others, belonging to no party, preferred to preserve the status quo because they hated to be subordinated to a larger army in which they might lose their prestige and independence. The differences of opinion, and the tensions among officers and civilian groups led eventually to the staging of military coups.

Syrian tensions were aggravated by the rival ambitions of the Arab neighbors, Egypt, Iraq, Jordan, and Saudi Arabia, and by the conflicting policies of the great powers. Because of its strategic position, its role as the heart of the Arab national movement, and its ability to swing the balance of power between the rival Arab states, Syria was subjected to pressures from all sides, and cash payments were used to influence the decisions of its politicians and officers and to orient the propaganda in its press. But while Saudi pressure was directed to prevent the union of Syria and Iraq or the formation of a greater Syrian state and to maintain the status quo, Egypt, particularly after 1954 under Nasser, viewed Syria as the key in its struggle for Arab leadership and therefore tried to control Syrian foreign policy in order to be in a better position to put pressure on the other Arab states of Western Asia as far as the Persian Gulf. The Egyptian offensive in Syria between 1954 and 1958 aimed at preventing it from joining the Baghdad Pact and at aligning Syrian policy with that of Egypt. Egyptian success resulted in effectively freezing the Baghdad Pact and bringing Syria within the Egyptian sphere of influence.[3] Another result was that Britain became involved in the Iraqi attempts to change the regime in Syria in order to stop Nasser and assure the formation of a government that would be friendly to Iraq and the West. The United States also became involved when the Soviet Union joined Egypt in its Syrian offensive and when the inter-Arab rivalries revived Russian interest in the entire area and became a part of the cold war. Russia and Egypt, supported by Syrian members of the Baath and the Communist parties, inflamed Syrian hostility to the West when the Western powers and Iraq attempted to change the orientation of Syrian policy. Western and Iraqi action was interpreted as an effort to revive colonial rule and influence. Israel similarly reacted to the Egyptian offensive and answered every Egyptian success by an attack on either Egypt or Syria. In mid-December 1955, the heavy Israeli attack against Syrian positions east of Lake Tiberias was an answer to the military pact of October 20 between Egypt and Syria.

While the Saudis ended their pressure on Syria in 1957 and tended to cooperate with the Hashemites because they felt the danger of Egyptian revolutionary activity, the Egyptians under Nasser maintained their primacy in Syria and prevented her from following an independent policy. They created an atmosphere of crisis every time their ascendancy was threatened and whenever stability under a constitutional regime was about to be assured. Nasserist intervention in Syria, perhaps more than any other factor, contributed to the tensions, divisions, and hatreds that produced the coups d'état after the breakup of unity in 1961.

B. Internal Tensions: The Parliamentary System and the Problem of National Unity

The long series of Syrian coups d'état was thus, to a large extent, a product of tensions of external origin related to the problem of Syrian alignment that influenced the wave of radical Arab nationalism and raised artificially the spectre of an imperialist threat after imperialism had come to an end in Syria. The Egyptian revolution, as well as the Soviet Union and the leftist parties in Syria added another dimension to the tensions when they portrayed imperialism as a supporter of the so-called reactionary rulers and as an enemy of reform, and represented the national ruling elite as servants of imperialism. The Syrian officers and their radical civilian allies tried later to justify their coups d'état and the socialist policies and other innovations that they introduced by violently criticizing the ineptitude, corruption, and conservatism of the old rulers and by even accusing them of cooperation with the imperialists against the best interests of the country. Undue importance was thus given to the internal political and social sources of tensions. Foreign and local writers repeated the arguments of those who made the coups and directed their criticism against the old ruling elite and against the system of parliamentary democracy and concluded, as the authors of the coups did, that the system was a failure.[4]

The egotism, ineptitude and negativeness of what has been termed the "elder politicians" and "old oligarchs" have been unduly exaggerated. These terms and titles themselves, moreover, are misleading since most of those to whom they were applied were middle-aged men of liberal outlook, but they did not subscribe to the radical socialism nor to the revolutionary methods of certain doctrinal parties that were founded before and after independence. According to their record, the leaders of the National Bloc, who dominated Syrian politics before and shortly after independence, have demonstrated their capacity for positive action on more than one occasion and under unusually difficult circumstances. They often tried to cooperate with the French and conducted with them delicate negotiations. During the Second World War and after, they maneuvered skillfully at home and abroad and obtained for Syria complete sovereignty. It is to their credit that they turned to constructive work in the economic and social fields whenever their political activity was restricted under the French mandate. With the help of an active nationalist business group they organized, for example, the famous Fijeh Project for bringing drinking water to the City of Damascus, and completed it between 1924 and 1932 in spite of French obstruction. They also established spinning and weaving factories, and canning and cement industries. The outcome of the war in Palestine that came two years after independence has probably been viewed as the main proof for the alleged ineptitude of these politicians. They have certainly lacked foresight, initiative and determination in dealing with the problem, but it should be recognized that the Palestine problem was so complex and the causes of Arab defeat were so many-sided that it would be unfair to hold any one group of persons responsible for the disastrous results. In retrospect, after the Six Day War of June 1967, it can be clearly seen that in spite of their small forces and modest equipment, the old rulers fought honorably, and in contrast to the military rulers of the Baath regime who disposed of by far more time, fighting forces, equipment and funds, the "elder politicians" offered a stronger challenge to Israel in 1948, and their small army did not allow the invasion and occupation of Syrian territory.

In the course of the six years that followed their success in the elections of 1943, the leaders of the National Bloc showed respect for constitutional government and obeyed its rules. Prime ministers often resigned, as Saadallah al-Jabiri did in 1944, when they felt there was strong criticism of their tenure. The chambers of deputies normally finished their term and the president of the republic never exercised his prerogative in dissolving them. Syria placed no limitations on candidacy for the elections, and the opposition was given full freedom to voice its criticism. Some of the old leaders, it is true, were repeatedly appointed to cabinet posts because for many years they had led the national struggle, and under the circumstances of the first years of independence they were the men expected to fill the higher posts. They were, moreover, honest and experienced men. The ministers were generally well educated and only a small minority of them, estimated at eleven per cent, were from the rural landlord class. In the chamber of deputies there was, as it has been said, "continuous infusion of new and young blood" with a constantly rising proportion of deputies who had a university education.[5] It is unfortunate that some of the latter were the ones who showed least respect for constitutional government and proved to be the most factious and negativist among the members.

The Syrian parliamentary system, like that of other Arab

countries, suffered from certain drawbacks. One of them was the instability and fluidity of parties and the consequent frequent change of cabinets. Yet it can be noted that when Syria emerged as an independent country between 1943 and 1946, there was only one organization, the National Bloc, that survived after having witnessed after its foundation in 1927 the rise and fall of more than a dozen parties. It was natural that the National Bloc should disintegrate after independence, because its role in the national struggle was over. In the short period that followed and until the first coup of 1949, there were virtually two main parties, the National Party that ruled and the People's Party that formed the opposition. The doctrinal parties such as the Baath were then without large following and lacked influence. The party system was then somewhat new, and the parties needed time to stabilize themselves while their members could acquire experience and work out their programs. But military intervention, and foreign as well as inter-Arab intrigues with their divisive effects gave the parties no such time. They weakened party discipline and led to the emergence of new parties and factions. Another disturbing factor in the parliamentary system was the continuous increase in the number of independents, mostly in the following period of military intervention, who grouped and regrouped themselves in blocs with other parties according to the issues and interests and pressures of the moment. In all this, it is good to remember that parliamentary life under the independent regime was only a few years old, and experience was being gained. It was, therefore, too premature to issue a verdict declaring that democracy had failed.

The parliamentary system in Syria was also free from certain aspects of authoritarianism and corruption that were known in some neighboring countries. The Syrian constitution, for example, did not allow the President to dismiss the cabinet as in Lebanon and in Iraq. It denied him and the cabinet the right to dissolve the Chamber within a period of less than eighteen months after its election. The Chamber, moreover, was free from such confessional politics as existed, and still exist, in Lebanon, and from the large influence of feudalism or tribalism, or the pressures and interventions of a royal court as in Iraq and Egypt. The Syrian Chamber was the first to adopt the system of direct, instead of indirect or two-stage, elections in April 1947. The electoral campaigns and the elections themselves were not accompanied by violence and bloody clashes between rival clans, and by scandalous buying of votes, nor did they witness the uncontested success of entire lists of candidates in certain districts. Although about half of the deputies at this time were rural landlords or tribal notables, they had no great share or influence in the government. Their number, moreover, tended to decrease in the Chamber.

In addition to all this, Syria was, in contrast with the countries like Iraq and Egypt, a socially balanced country with a large and influential middle class, and with no revolting inequalities in wealth, position and opportunity between its social groups. Its lower classes were not as abjectly poor as in some other countries, and those of its peasants who owned no land, were not as inhumanly exploited.[6] For a whole decade after 1947, Syria was prosperous and its economic growth was among the most striking in the Middle East. Its national income grew at the rate of six per cent annually, and the rate of its investment, almost all in private local capital except for banks, as well as its per capita income were among the highest in the area in spite of the absence of oil revenues. Agricultural and industrial production and building activity expanded by private initiative, and the government helped with public works and with appropriate economic regulations. Syria was the first country in the Middle East to adopt successfully the modern techniques of mechanized farming particularly in the vast plains of Aleppo and Jazirah.[7] The Syrian laborer was faced with no grave problems of unemployment, and he was protected by a modern labor code that was adopted in 1947.

One of the common misconceptions about Syria is that it is a mosaic of races and religions and therefore has no national unity. It is true that throughout history, religions and religious heresies and schisms have appeared or were introduced into Syria, and waves of emigrants and conquerors have settled in the area or occupied it for some time. But the population of the present Syrian republic has been overwhelmingly Arabic-speaking and Muslim for many centuries. Ethnic minorities—Kurds, Circassians, and Armenians—do exist, and similarly various religious minorities, Muslim as well as Christian with their subdivisions into sects, still prosper. Their presence, however, did not create the type of ethnic and confessional problems experienced by its neighbors, Iraq and Lebanon. The reason is that the ethnic minorities are too small and dispersed in comparison to the overwhelming and compact Syrian Arab majority; they are moreover, fairly well integrated. The religious sects are similarly of very unequal numeric strength. The Christians constitute only 14 per cent of the population. The Sunni Muslims are by far the overwhelming majority among the Muslims and among the inhabitants as a whole. The Druzes form a compact minority of some three per cent, and the Alawis form another compact minority of some nine per cent. The presence of all these minorities was not without its problems and the French took advantage of the situation to divide Syria into separate little states along religious sectarian lines. Independent Syria preserved the system of proportionate confessional representation in parliament and handled with particular care the Druze region and its leaders. It was only under the military regimes that rebellions broke out in that region. Parties and political groups in Syria were not organized along ethnic or religious lines but along national lines, and the members of the minorities belonged to the various national and ideological parties. It was only during the period of military Baath rule after 1963 that sectarianism appeared in the struggle for power among the Baathist leaders themselves. Sectarianism also assumed a regional as well as an ideological aspect. Socialism imposed by the Baath party on Syria after 1963 was applied in a radical manner with the support of the Alawi officers in particular. Socialism was the revenge of the Alawi and Druze rural minorities on the Sunnite city dwellers. It was intended to impoverish the Sunnite majority in the cities and reduce them to the level of the village.[8]

C. Syrian Attitudes and Character

Under the influence of Syria's strategic geographical position and its long and varied historical experience, the Syrians have developed certain characteristic traits and mental attitudes that distinguish them from other Arabs. They have acquired, for example, a remarkable ability in trade and business enterprise with an adventurous love of travel and a resourceful spirit of private initiative. The socialist system that the Baath party imposed by force after 1963 would have never been accepted by a freely elected legislature or by the people's free choice. It would be probably rejected as soon as the military force that imposed it is removed. The rival Arab neighbors have exploited the Syrian's love for gain and money making in order to win friends and frustrate the designs of their enemies, with all the sad negative effects on Syrian unity and policy making. Another effect was the creation of a group of parasitic leaders who became accustomed to seeking wealth and influence through intrigue, subversion and rabble rousing for the account of foreign countries.

Unlike the Egyptian, the Syrian did not have to submit throughout his history to a strong central authority and to unrelieved absolutism, for Syria was seldom ruled by a unified and centralized administration, and even under foreign rule, its princes and governors exercised a large measure of freedom and autonomy. The Syrian was particularly individualistic and less dependent on his government for carrying out various economic and social projects. Resignation, apathy and docility are not as pronounced in his character as ambition, indiscipline and emotional enthusiasm. His experience with his rulers caused him to be astute, adaptable, suspicious and inclined to shifting loyalties. His strong individualism and ambition, especially when it was not sustained by effort and talent, provoked in him a spirit of jealousy and conceit, weakened his cooperation, and tended to make him impatient and fault finding. This is why certain writers have described the Syrians as "almost ungovernable" and impossible to please. Jealousies and resentments were aggravated when the wave of economic prosperity in the 1940's and early 1950's and political success gave certain people wealth and power while certain others were relatively less successful and were left behind. The Syrians have been known, moreover, for their addiction and passion for politics and have certainly missed the excitement of political action when they were brought under the rule of the military dictatorial regimes. Party life and free expression, as one writer put it, are "the breath of life for them."

Because of a certain subtleness and sophistication in their character and the need for stability in a society oriented towards gainful business activity, the Syrians have been known for their moderation and aversion to violence. It was only under the influence of the ideological parties–the socialist Baathists, the Syrian social nationalists, and the Communists–that the educated and semi-educated youth was molded after the Second World War into rival instruments of political action with imported ideologies and methods of violent opposition and revolt. The parties exploited the jealousies, hatreds, frustrations and all the other negative traits and attitudes of the youth and harnessed them for political ends. Violence erupted when the officers became members of the ideological parties or acted in their name to overthrow the political and social order. Military intervention, however, was almost bloodless until the Baath party came to power in 1963. The Baathists then disregarded all the positive traits and values of the Syrian and Arab past, all the subtleness, courtesies, moderation, respect and respectability.

It must be said that many of the negative traits that have influenced the Syrians' public attitudes and actions are not immutable since they are the product of specific variable conditions of rule. Under a different and better tradition of government and with superior and non partisan methods of education, they can be changed in view of the remarkable adaptability of the Syrian. Under the shadow of other governments and in a different milieu, the Syrian immigrant has actually modified, if not abandoned, his old attitudes and traits and adopted new ones. It is necessary therefore to emphasize that the transformation of the Syrian public attitudes and the shedding of the old negative traits for the purpose of insuring a more stable and competent rule can hardly be accomplished in the troubled atmosphere of repeated coups d'état and military rule or under the indoctrination and compulsion of a one-party dictatorial regime.

D. The Syrian Army Officers

The army officers in Syria, much like those of the other Arab states, did not participate in the struggle for independence in the interwar period, nor did they show an interest in politics as long as the French mandate lasted. This was in sharp contrast with the Syrian and Iraqi Arab officers in the Ottoman Empire who cooperated with the civilian leaders in the Arab national movement before the First World War. The Syrian officers also, it must be emphasized, had the same weaknesses, negative traits and attitudes as the rest of the Syrians. Contrary to what certain writers have claimed about Arab officers in general, they were neither the sole force for reform, nor the guardians of national virtue.[10] They had neither more knowledge and competence nor were they more progressive or even more disciplined than the Syrian civilians. They were generally less cultured than the average educated civilians, less mature, and less experienced. They were deplorably unprepared for the task of ruling.

The Syrian cadets who received their training at the Military Academy of Homs, as well as those who were sent to France for further training, were drawn either from the religious and ethnic minorities or from families of the Muslim majority who were not active in politics. Most of the Muslim Sunni and Christian cadets belonged to the urban middle class and very few came from the well-to-do landowning class, while Alawis and Druzes, as well as Kurds and Circassians came from the rural areas. The qualifications for admission to the Academy were particularly simple and, at one time in the 1920's, an elementary school certificate and a knowledge of French were the only requirements. Most of those who sought admission were attracted by the advantages and benefits of the military career that began with a free education and promised a secure future. The Syrian officers were restricted to the junior ranks, and the higher command of the locally-recruited *troupes spéciales* was in the hands of French officers.

The *troupes spéciales* became the nucleus of the national army after the withdrawal of the French forces in 1946, and their Syrian officers received immediate promotion but none of them, until 1949, was above the rank of *zaim* or colonel. The system of universal conscription was adopted after the Palestine war of 1948 and a larger number of cadets were admitted to the Military Academy as well as to the other specialized schools. An increasing number of these cadets, and consequently of the officers, came from the rural areas and from the lower and poorer urban middle class. Many of them were patronized by the radical leader in Hama, Akram Hourani, who began since this time to create a circle of supporters among the officers, while doctrinal parties, like the Baath, strove to admit their partisans or convert the cadets. The Syrian rulers were singularly unaware of the social, religious and doctrinal imbalance among the future officers. There is no evidence to show that ambitious men in Syria turned to the army, as they are said to have done in Iraq where teachers and lawyers left their professions, "believing that their ambitions can better be attained in the army," and entered military schools.[11] The military career, on the contrary, was chosen now as under the French, because it was easily accessible to those who either on account of their financial condition or their academic ineptitude were unprepared to attempt anything else.

The war in Palestine brought the army and its officers to the foreground as the defenders of the homeland against Israel. In the years that followed, the military budget was largely increased, and the army was given a modern organization and equipment. The officers' self-interest and independence in the direction of military affairs increased with the increasing feeling of their own importance. The assumption that they decided to seize power after the Palestine war because "they discovered that their rulers had failed them,"[12] or because of the rulers' incompetence and corruption, does not seem to be entirely true. The real relation between the Palestine war and the first chain of Syrian army coups in March 1949 seems to have been, first, that the Palestine war, as every unsuccessful war, resulted in profound popular discontent that led to rioting. The civilian authorities had to rely on armed forces to suppress the riots, and thus the army leaders, having succeeded in maintaining order and dominating the situation, came to entertain ideas of usurping rule. Second, the Syrian officers, like other officers under similar circumstances, were sensitive to the criticism of their conduct of the war, and it was their pride, frustration and attempt to find a scapegoat for their faults that led to the take-over.[13] The Palestine problem and the Israeli danger were also exploited by ambitious officers or military rulers in their attempt to seize or to maintain power. They raised the spectre of an Israeli attack, as the Baath military did in early May 1967, in order to put an end to internal rioting and opposition and, as Hamad Ubaid, the future Baath defense minister, said in 1962, "Everytime a military dictator wanted to impose his demands on the politicians, he pretended there was Israeli mobilization.[14]

The army leaders who tried to impose their rule in the first five years after the Palestine war belonged to no party and were moderate reformers. They were overthrown by their own colleagues and by the resistance of the civilian party leaders. After 1955, radical officers in alliance with civilian radicals, encouraged by the example of Egypt, decided to break the power of the traditional elite by subverting the social and economic order.

It is important to note that the army in Syria did not form a caste by itself, and the struggle, therefore, was not between military and civilians. The officers reflected the factionalism and divisions among the civilian leaders but they naturally had, at various occasions, to defend their own interests. Politicians and parties competed to win their support but, because of their underprivileged social and economic background, they were won over by radical, revolutionary ideologies, and thus the struggle they waged against their opponents assumed the character of a class struggle. In many cases the officers' coups were not attempted for questions of conviction or principle, but were the result of a struggle for power between contending military factions supported or prodded by rival civilian personalities and parties or by external forces.

II. The First Three Coups d'Etat: March-December 1949

A. The First Coup and the Dictatorship of Husni al-Zaim

Syria experienced the first direct intervention of her army officers in politics on March 30, 1949, three years after the winning of complete independence. President Shukri Quwatli was then in his second term of office. Formal fighting in Palestine between the Arab states and Israel had ended, but Syria had not as yet signed an armistice. The Arab failure in the battle for Palestine was perhaps most bitterly felt in Syria where frustration and unrest created a situation that was favorable for a seizure of power by the army. The first Syrian coup d'état thus illustrates the fairly well established truth that armies commonly seize power on the domestic scene after defeat on the battlefield, not after victory.[15] The other two coups of the same year were provoked by more varied causes and were staged by military leaders against one another with the cooperation of political factions.

The leader of the first coup, fifty-five year old Colonel Husni al-Zaim, was at the time chief of staff of the army. He was a native Damascene and his mother was an Arabized Kurd. According to a pattern that became almost classical, the coup was carried out before dawn when detachments of armored cars and infantry under Major Adib Shishakli and other officers marched on Damascus to surround the presidential palace, the home of the prime minister, the radio station and other important government installations. President Quwatli, Premier Khalid al-Azem and other key members in the government were arrested and taken to the military hospital in the Damascene suburb of Mazze. A proclamation over the radio and in the press contained the communiqué no. 1 that announced the causes of the *inqilab* or "upturn" of the regime. They were said to be the corruption of the leaders and their violation of the constitution at the expense of the people's interests.[16]

It is generally believed that the bloodless coup led by Zaim was the first in a series of military upheavals that occurred in the Arab countries as a reaction against government corruption and incompetence that led to Arab defeat and humiliation in Palestine. It is not certain, however, that Colonel Zaim and the officers who made the coup acted out of patriotic concern about the aspects of weakness displayed by the Quwatli regime in Syria. The authors of the coup, as it seems, were rather motivated by self-interest and they exploited the unrest that followed the disastrous war to their own advantage.

In December 1948, popular discontent was fanned by leftist parties over the outcome of the Palestine war and also over the negotiations between the government and American oil concerns for building a trans-Arabian pipeline (known as the Tapline) across Syria to the Mediterranean. This led to demonstrations and riots. Prime Minister Jamil Mardam Bey and his cabinet were forced to resign, and after a ministerial crisis that lasted two weeks, a cabinet was formed by Khalid al-Azem who asked the chief of staff, Colonel Zaim, to restore order. Zaim succeeded in restoring normal conditions by imposing martial law, issuing quieting proclamations, and holding talks in various cities. This success, in addition to the authority that martial law gave him, might have suggested to an impulsive and ambitious officer and adventurer of his kind the idea of displacing the government that sought his help.[17]

The coup d'état led by Colonel Zaim was basically the outcome of the resentment and indignation felt among the officers because certain members of Parliament criticized the armed forces and blamed them for the defeat in Palestine. The officers were also indignant because the cabinet proposed to cut army expenditures, demobilize a part of the armed forces and reduce the officers' allowances. They claimed that corrupt politicians were meddling in military affairs, especially when certain officers were arrested for corruption. The immediate cause of the coup could very well have been the concern of Colonel Zaim over the arrest of his personal friend, Colonel Antoine Bustani who, as a chief supply officer, was accused of closing his eyes on the inferior quality of cooking fat *(samneh)* furnished by contractors to the army. Zaim decided to carry out the coup not only because he could have been implicated in the cooking fat scandal, but also because his *amour propre* was offended by the aristocratic prime minister, Khalid al-Azem, who contemptuously refused Zaim's intercession for his friend Bustani and even at one time, declined to see him.

In their decision to stage a coup against the government, the military received encouragement from certain political groups. In early 1949, some younger political leaders who were opposed to Quwatli and his group of "elder politicians," opened negotiations with Zaim and he accepted to cooperate with them. Prominent among the civilian conspirators was Akram al-Hourani, a deputy from Hama, who became the grey eminence with various military rulers from Husni al-Zaim to Gamal Abdel Nasser. He supported them all and ended by quarrelling with them all. As a radical nationalist and anti-feudalist, he gained a small following in his home town and in some villages of northern Syria, and among the youth. His ambition and unscrupulous drive to gain power led him to seek the support of the army.

It is difficult to determine exactly the nature and extent of external encouragement or support of the Zaim coup. The Hashemites of Jordan and Iraq were probably happy to see the end of Quwatli's rule, because he opposed the Greater Syria scheme of King Abdallah and the Fertile Crescent union of Nuri al-Said. Zaim's first flirtations with Iraq, however, proved to be of very short duration, and his relations with Jordan became tense before the end of April. On the other hand, they became most cordial with Egypt and Saudi Arabia, as well as with France who was traditionally opposed to the Hashemite schemes and probably encouraged the coup. The United States was interested in the ratification of the Tapline agreement that was signed in February 1949 by the Azem cabinet but which the Syrian Chamber of Deputies was not able to ratify partly as a reprisal against American policy in Palestine, and partly due to the pressure of student demonstrations manipulated by radical elements mainly in the Communist and Baath parties. The agreement was signed later by Zaim on May 16, 1949 and American policy was sympathetic to the new ruler and might have had a hand in his coup.[18]

Zaim's military regime was one of direct personal rule through a supreme military council. His first concern after the coup was to gain recognition and legitimacy. For this he consulted with Faris al-Khouri, the Speaker of the Chamber of Deputies, and with some other deputies and expressed the desire to form a cabinet under a political leader. Faris told him that the coup was an anti-constitutional act and that he would not accept a post under his regime, but would help obtain legitimacy for it in the country's interest.[19] On April 1, the Chamber was convoked to a special session, but a little more than half of the members attended the meeting. Although the deputies present voiced their support for Zaim they refused to participate in a coalition cabinet. The Chamber was consequently dissolved, and Zaim announced the appointment of a commission to draft a new constitution after having suspended the constitution of 1930.

One week after the coup, the resignation of President Quwatli and his prime minister was announced, and on April 16, Colonel Zaim himself formed a cabinet in which he kept for himself the portfolios of defense and interior. He appointed the well-known nationalist leader, Emir Adel Arslan, deputy prime minister and minister of foreign affairs. The change of government was thus effected easily and without bloodshed. It was favorably received by the people and by the younger generation of nationalists who saw the need for reform. The mistakes of the former rulers under these conditions were unduly magnified, and the ability of the new leader to satisfy the high expectations of the people was also unduly exaggerated. Zaim had an attractive personality. His exuberant nature and fine promises in addition to his show of power perhaps led the people to see in him a new Kemal Ataturk. The ease with which Zaim's coup was effected and the favorable reaction to it at the beginning have led commentators at the time to draw conclusions about the shallow roots of Syrian political institutions and parties and about the people's joy for the removal of the "pseudo-democratic" regime.[20] Experience has shown, however, that the very people who usually express joy and hope at the overthrow of a government very soon turn against the new government when their high expectations are not realized. It should be noted, furthermore, that the successive changes of regimes in Syria were not a product of the people's resentment and revolt. While the military engineered their coups, the people often watched quietly and sometimes indifferently. Those who applauded were often hired in order to applaud. Even among the officers who made the change, it was not unusual to find some who were paid for their role in the upheaval, or who were promised promotions and high posts, and their support of the new regime often lasted as long as they continued to enjoy the profits and prestige of their new position. The people in general were neither over-enthusiastic over the rise of the new ruler, nor unduly sad at his downfall. It is to the credit of the deputies of the Chamber that they refused cooperation with a regime that they considered unconstitutional. To speak of "pseudo-democracy" and shallow roots of institutions and parties in a country that had been standing on its feet for a few years and that was faced in the first three years of its independence with a foreign war was premature.

Zaim and his cabinet began active work on various projects, some of which had been envisaged by the former rulers but had not received serious study. Under the dictatorial power of the new leader, many of them were approved. Among the most important were the financial and economic settlement with France (April 20), the abolition of private family *waqfs* (endowments) on May 16, the new Civil Code (May 18), which was perhaps the most permanent work of the regime and led to the weakening of the hold of Muslim law and religious judges.[21] Other contributions of Zaim's regime were the Euphrates Project for supplying Aleppo with drinking water (May 21) and the Latakia Harbor Project (August 10). Zaim also planned, in his draft constitution, to give women equal electoral rights with men and to separate the church from the state.[22]

The readiness of a military dictator to make changes and reforms is not in itself sufficient to consecrate his leadership or to legitimize his usurped rule or insure for him continuous general approval. Colonel Zaim forfeited the favorable reaction to his reforms when he made the same mistakes which all inexperienced and ambitious military leaders make sooner or later. His particular trouble was that he committed them too soon and simultaneously, and he thus revealed himself to the public within only a few weeks after his coup. In the first place, he adopted the normal arbitrary tactics of authoritarian rule. He suppressed opposition and criticism, persecuted the press, abolished all political parties, established a spying system and spied on his own cabinet ministers, and he sent hundreds of persons to jail.[23] On June 4, his government decreed that a referendum would be made for electing a president of the republic. Fifteen days later, he presented his candidacy for the presidency and was the only candidate. On June 25, less than three months after his coup, he was elected president as a result of the referendum. He had previously awarded himself the rank of field-marshal, a title which at that time looked ridiculous and caused widespread criticism, but which since then has become an inevitable title for the leaders of certain military revolts. Zaim did not forget to order in France a field-marshal's "baton," which after his tragic end has found its way to the Military Museum in Damascus. The new rank and title augmented his megalomania and his love of pomp, luxury and ceremony. His adviser was his prime minister, Muhsin al-Barazi, who has been aptly described as his "evil genius."[24]

Zaim, in the second place, offended his own military associates as well as various social groups by his arrogant, vain and unwise conduct. His colleagues in the army had not wanted a military dictatorship to be established and were now beginning to fear and distrust him. He lost the support of Akram Hourani because he became the ally of the Barazis of Hama, Hourani's opponents. Zaim also distrusted his former supporter in the coup, Colonel Shishakli, and dismissed him in early August 1949. In the cabinet he refused to listen to his ministers' opinions and comments. At the beginning of his rule, he was in constant disagreement with his minister of foreign affairs, Emir Adel Arslan, a proud Druze Arab nationalist. Zaim, moreover, lost the allegiance of the Druzes because of his anti-Hashemite policy and sent forces to Jabal Druze to intimidate them. He dealt roughly with the religious leaders who disliked some of his reforms and denied him their support. He leaned on minority groups in the army such as the Kurds and the Circassians and used some of them as spies. He employed them in the cities while the Arab troops were kept on the Israeli front.[25] His prime minister, Barazi, was of Kurdish origin and was interested in the Kurdish national movement. Zaim also violated Arab tradition and offended the Syrian Social National Party by betraying Antun Saadeh, its leader, who had been offered asylum in Syria after stirring a rebellion in Lebanon. Saadeh was invited to a dinner with the Syrian prime minister on July 6 and was later on arrested and turned over to Lebanon where a drumhead court martial tried him and condemned him to death. He was executed on July 8, 1949.

In the third place, Zaim followed a capricious and undiplomatic course in his foreign relations. After he had given the Hashemites hopes of cordial relations in the first three weeks of his rule and had been recognized by Iraq on April 17, he went suddenly to vist King Farouk in Egypt on April 21, and he returned completely changed. He began a propaganda campaign against King Abdallah of Jordan and against Iraq without consulting his foreign minister. He accused both, without good reason, of massing troops on the Syrian border. His external contacts were conducted above the head of the ministry of foreign affairs.[26]

Husni al-Zaim, like most military leaders in the Arab world, came to power with no background of a national reputation and with no plan for establishing a system of rule. It is said that when the coup succeeded and one of his aides told him, "Sir, all Syria is now in your hands," he exclaimed, "Woe to you! what shall I do with it!"[27] Zaim was accepted by the people on the basis of providing them with a more efficient and honest administration. They generally approved the few changes he introduced, but they could not forgive him for his arbitrary manner, his selfish conceit and vanity, his reckless and offensive relations with the Arab neighbors,[28] and his questionable contacts with France shortly after the end of the French mandate. As for his military colleagues, they realized that the man they placed at the head of their movement deviated from the original aims and was now following the same course of turning power to his personal ends as the one against which they revolted. Under the leadership of fifty-one year old Brigadier Sami al-Hinnawi who commanded the first brigade in southern Syria, they decided to eliminate him.

B. The Hinnawi Interlude: The Second Coup

The leading conspirators against Husni al-Zaim were probably encouraged by the Iraqi government who wanted a more friendly regime in Syria. The People's party centered in Aleppo and Homs could have influenced Hinnawi's decision to overthrow Zaim. Both Hinnawi and his brother-in-law, Asaad Talas, were natives of Aleppo and it is possible that Talas acted as a liaison between Iraq, the People's party, and Hinnawi. Among those who cooperated with Hinnawi were some Druze officers who were also members of the Syrian social national party and therefore hated Zaim. One of them, Lt. Fadlallah Abu-Mansur, who left us an account of the conspiracy and the coup, mentioned that he and his superior, Lt. Col. Amin Abu-Assaf, refused Zaim's order to move their armored battalion from Quneitra to Jabal Druze, and ended by moving it to Qatana at twenty miles southwest of Damascus after the coup had been decided in a meeting in early August between them and their commanding officer, Brigadier Hinnawi.[29]

In the early hours of Sunday August 14, 1949, before 3 a.m., several detachments of armored cars entered Damascus to occupy the military and police headquarters and the radio station, and to arrest Zaim, his prime minister, and his chief of military police, Ibrahim al-Husseini. Lt. Abu-Mansur occupied the presidential residence, arrested Zaim, slapped him on the face and taunted him for his betrayal of Antun Saadeh. He then carried him in an armored car to the suburb of Mazze where he was joined by other conspirators who had arrested

Premier Barazi. One of Barazi's captors, Captain Issam Mraiwed, told Abu-Mansur that the Army Command had sentenced Zaim and Barazi to death and that he should carry out the sentence immediately, whereupon the two were shot by the firing squad. Barazi's appeal for mercy was of no avail. One report claims that he died of heart attack before he was shot.[30] Egypt observed mourning for three days for Zaim's death.

The leaders of the second coup attacked, in their communiqués, Zaim's conceit and despotism, his wickedness and misdeeds, his offensive foreign policy and his plunder of the treasury. They declared that he betrayed the previous coup and therefore it had to be returned to its true aims. The communiqué no. 1 mentioned that the army saved the nation from the tyrant, and it ended with the classical statement that "the army will retire to its baracks."[31] Military authority after the second coup was invested in a supreme military council of eleven members under Hinnawi's direction. Hinnawi had no political ambition to rule and called on the political leaders to appoint a caretaker government in order to conduct elections for a constituent assembly that would draft a new constitution. The seventy-six year old former president of the republic, Hashem al-Atassi, was asked to preside over a cabinet that contained representatives of all the parties and trends with the exception of the National Party which stood for the restoration of the old Chamber dissolved by Zaim. Particularly prominent in the cabinet and in the new regime that followed the second coup was the People's Party that had the support of the new prime minister and former president, Hashem al-Atassi, who had been formerly a leader of the National Bloc. Akram Hourani was given the relatively unimportant ministry of agriculture, and for the first time the Baath Party was given recognition by entrusting its leader, Michel Aflaq, with the ministry of education.

Elections for the constituent assembly were preceded by an electoral law that gave the right of vote to educated women for the first time in any Arab country, and reduced the age requirement of the voter from twenty-one to eighteen. The National Party under Sabri al-Assali and Abdul Rahman Kayali proclaimed that it would boycott the elections on the basis that the Chamber elected in 1947 under Quwatli was still lawful and that the cabinet which was to direct the elections was a partisan cabinet. The elections took place on 15-16 November 1949 and gave the People's Party a plurality of about 49 out of 114 seats. Shortly after the elections, Aflaq resigned from his cabinet post and withdrew his party from the government coalition. He was the only minister in the caretaker cabinet who did not succeed in the elections and he blamed foreign conspiracies for his and his party's failure. The group led by Akram Hourani was not very successful but Hourani himself was elected with the help of his military friends. He later organized his group into the Arab Socialist Party. The new Assembly met on December 12 and elected the Populist leader, Rushdi al-Kekhia, speaker. Two days later Hashem al-Atassi was elected by 89 votes of the Assembly as provisional head of state until the promulgation of a new constitution.

Under the Hinnawi-Atassi regime, negotiations opened with Iraq for establishing closer relations between the two countries. In early October, Regent Abdul Ilah of Iraq had stopped in Damascus for talks on future relations with the new Syrian regime. A reversal of Zaim's policy had begun to take place and many political groups including the National Party came out in favor of union with Iraq. In the first meetings of the new Assembly, around mid-December, opposition to the project of union was voiced by Akram Hourani who was the spokesman of some strong groups in the army. Hourani objected to the text of the oath to be taken by the head of state and the deputies because it did not mention the republican regime. The majority, however, approved the text on December 17. It is doubtful if the union could have materialized easily in view of the People's Party's vacillation, the lack of genuine encouragement at this stage by Britain, the abundant flow of Saudi money to bribe the leaders against the union, and the lack of interest of Nuri al-Said. But further negotiations were expected to be held with the Iraqi leaders, and the Constituent Assembly prepared itself for an active discussion of the question.

C. The Shishakli Coup of December 1949

The issue between unionists and anti-unionists was not allowed to be settled in the assembly and in a constitutional manner. It was settled by the arrest and dismissal of Hinnawi in a military coup, the third in the year, on 19 December 1949, because he supported the pro-Iraqi policy of the People's Party. Before his fall, Hinnawi, we are told, sent his men to seek the officers' support for the Syro-Iraqi union, but some of the leading officers were determined to oppose the project. They included forty-year-old Colonel Adib Shishakli, who had been reappointed to the command of the first brigade after the Hinnawi coup, and was now cooperating with his boyhood friend from Hama, Akram Hourani. According to the account of Fadlallah Abu Mansur, who seems to have had a grudge against Hinnawi for not obtaining the rank and position he expected, Hinnawi watched his opponents and at one time thought of having them arrested.[32] Akram Hourani and his anti-Iraqi supporters consequently decided that the Hinnawi regime should end. Shishakli who was to be the leader of the coup then met with Abu Mansur at Qabun near Damascus to plan the military action, but the coup was carried out only after Hinnawi had appointed a new commander for the armored battalion at Qabun. The commander was arrested as he arrived to take his new post, and at 5:30 a.m. on December 19, 1949 the armored cars began rolling towards Damascus. The conspirators, including Abu-Mansur, arrested Hinnawi, his chief of military police, his military intelligence chief, and other supporters. The skirmish at the headquarters of the military police left three victims.

The civilian government under Atassi and the Constituent

Assembly were allowed to continue but Colonel Shishakli, with the modest title of deputy chief of staff, kept a watchful eye over the government. A new supreme military council was formed and Hinnawi was dismissed from his posts of chief of staff and commander in chief. Brigadier Anwar Bannud commander of the Aleppo garrison who rallied to the Shishakli coup became chief of staff. Hinnawr was rèleased in September 1950 and went to live in Beirut where he was assassinated on October 31, 1950 in the street by a relative of Zaim's prime minister, Muhsin Barazi, who was the victim of Hinnawi's coup.

In reviewing the three first military interventions that took place in Syria in the space of nine months, it becomes evident, in the first place, that they were to a large extent motivated by the self-interest of the military and their concern about their reputation, their independence and prestige, and their finances. Another dominant motive was the disagreement among military groups and political leaders on the nature of relations with the Arab neighbors, as well as the rival ambitions of the neighbors themselves. The trend to prevent a Syrian union with Iraq was in itself an aspect of military self-interest for the army officers resented subordination to a higher command in a larger and stronger military establishment under a larger state or federation. It can thus be said that while such older Syrian political leaders as Quwatli were accused of becoming jealous particularists after independence,[33] the army can be equally accused of that same particularism in spite of its enthusiasm for Arab unity.

It can be noted, in the second place, that in the regime of rule after the coups, one can differentiate between the direct military dictatorial rule of Zaim after the first coup, and the indirect rule after the second and the third coups under Hinnawi and the first part of Shishakli's regimes. In the third place, one can notice in the second and third coups, the recurrence of the theme of "deviation from the original aims of the coup" as a factor that justified military action. This theme of deviation from the original goals was fequently used later, particularly in the struggle for power among military factions.

III. The Shishakli Regime 1949-1954: The Fourth and Fifth Coups d'Etat

A. Indirect Military Rule and the Fourth Coup

The Syrian political scene was dominated by Colonel Adib Shishakli for over four years (December 1949-February 25, 1954) after the coup d'état of December 19, 1949. During the first two years military rule was of the indirect type through a parliamentary facade and with the complete organs of a civilian constitutional government. This first phase ended in the fourth coup on November 29, 1951 when Shishakli's personal military rule began.

The Constituent Assembly that was elected shortly before the third coup of December 1949 ended its work with the adoption of a new constitution on September 5, 1950. It then transformed itself into a Chamber of Deputies, and elected Hashem al-Atassi president of the republic. Parties and factions continued to function under Shishakli's indirect military rule, and debates in the Chamber were relatively free. The new constitution contained a detailed bill of rights and for the first time in any Arab constitution, it included clauses on social reform, social justice and the role of the state in achieving them.

Shishakli must have profited from the lesson of Zaim and did not advance himself immediately to a higher rank and position. It was only in April 1950 that he became brigadier general (Zaim) and chief of staff.[34] He did not even award himself the portfolio of defense, and it was long after the fourth coup that he became deputy prime minister in August 1952. Shishakli, however, did exercise power through his interventions in the formation of cabinets and in the conduct of foreign relations. On December 24, 1949 he vetoed the first cabinet formed by the Populist leader, Nazem al-Qudsi, after the meeting of the Constituent Assembly, because it did not give the portfolio of defense to Akram Hourani. President Atassi presented his resignation on December 27 as a result of this intervention, but it was not accepted. A coalition cabinet was formed two days later by the independent leader, Khalid al-Azem, and Hourani became minister of defense. He exploited his cabinet post to gain a larger following among the officers and to spread his socialist ideas and anti-western slogans in the army.

In the Chamber of Deputies, the People's Party had the greatest number of deputies, but it had no majority. The two cabinets formed by Qudsi in June and September 1950 had therefore to be coalition cabinets. Populists were strong only in Aleppo and Homs, and did not command popular support especially in Damascus. They were united neither on internal reform nor on foreign policy. In spite of this, the People's Party struggled timidly to curb military influence and to play the parliamentary game, but the Arab socialists of Hourani and the numerous independents who were allied to the military, as well as the hostile Baath and National parties helped Shishakli win the battle. Protests against army interference were voiced in the Chamber particularly by the Populist leader Rushdi al-Kekhia, by Husni al-Barazi, a tough political leader from Hama who happened to be Shishakli's cousin, and by the independent and learned law professor, Munir Ajlani. On one occasion, (August 8, 1951), Barazi scolded the deputies for their weakness and pointed to the exclusion of many politicians from the recently formed cabinet by his "cousin's red pencil."[35]

Under the indirect rule of Shishakli, government authority was weakened, civilian rule was discredited, and the parliamentary regime was corrupted. The army definitely became and remained an instrument of political action. The radical parties such as the Baath profited from the weakening of the traditional parties and their clash with the army. At the end of July 1951, government officials went on strike for a whole week and the second cabinet of Azem resigned. An independent and brave elder statesman, Hasan al-Hakim, became prime minister in early August. Two months later, a dispute erupted within the cabinet over the question of a Middle East Defense Organization proposed by the western powers. On November 7, 1951, the Hakim cabinet resigned and a ministerial crisis followed and lasted three weeks. The people then speculated, as this author recalls, on when a "communiqué no. 1" announcing a military coup would be issued. A courageous Populist from Aleppo, Maaruf al-Dawalibi, who was at one time a turbaned sheikh and was now a law professor at the Syrian University, accepted the president's offer to form a cabinet, and chose for himself the ministry of defense. This was a challenge to the army, especially when it became known that Dawalibi might transfer Shishakli or retire him from the army and place the gendarmerie under the ministry of interior instead of that of defense.

The Dawalibi cabinet that was formed on November 28, 1951 lasted some twelve hours. In the early morning of November 29, Shishakli executed the fourth coup in Syria, and his own second coup. Dawalibi and most of the members of his cabinet along with other political leaders were arrested, and Shishakli issued a series of communiqués, military orders, and decrees to justify his action and create the new organs of government, in the name of the Supreme Military Council over which he presided. Dawalibi was obliged to resign on December 1, 1951. President Atassi refused to dissolve the Chamber of Deputies and resigned on the following day. The Chamber was dissolved by Shishakli on December 2 for its "inability to assume the responsibilities of directing the government of the state." The People's Party was attacked for its alleged obstruction, destructive action, and attempt to weaken the army and destroy Syrian independence by trying to form a federation that would restore the monarchy.

B. The Personal Rule of Shishakli

With the fourth coup, Shishakli's personal rule began. It

was the second military dictatorship in Syria's recent history. Party rivalries and the short-sightedness and quarrels of politicians along with the accusations and attacks of Shishakli against the People's Party have been mentioned to explain the fourth coup.[36] This was only partly true, for the increasing rivalries of parties and the weaknesses of civilian rule that have been suggested as the causes of military coups were really the result of constant army interference in political affairs, often encouraged by petty politicians who found no other way to assume power and eliminate their rivals except through cooperation with, and dependence on the military. The dictatorship of Shishakli and the fourth coup that brought it had no valid reason. They were the outcome of the desire of an army strongman and his ambitious political allies to seize power.

Shishakli did not assume directly the titles of high office, but waited nineteen months before he became president of the republic under a new constitution. In the meantime, he retained his position of chief of staff and head of the supreme military council, while his colleague, Fauzi Selo, an Arab Kurd from Damascus, was made head of state by military order no. 1 on December 3, 1951. General Selo was also appointed head of the government whose departments were directed, in the absence of a cabinet, by under-secretaries. It was only in June 1952 that a cabinet was formed with Selo as prime minister and minister of defense.

Typical dictatorial measures were taken by Shishakli to consolidate his rule. One of them required all civil servants to promise under oath before a judge that they would not participate in political activities.[37] Students were prevented by decree from making demonstrations and going on strike. The number of newspapers was reduced and censorship of the press was reinforced. Political parties were dissolved on April 6, 1952 and their dissolution marked the end of Shishakli's cooperation with Hourani and his Arab socialists, and with the Baath Party. In December 1952 a plot was discovered in which some senior officers and radical politicians including the eternal plotter, Akram Hourani, were involved. Forty officers were either arrested or dismissed, as a result. They included the outspoken Baathist, Colonel Adnan Malki, and the pro-Iraqi Colonel Muhammad Safa who later went to live in Baghdad and established a free Syrian government in exile. In January 1953, Hourani and the two leaders of the Baath Party, Bitar and Aflaq, escaped to Lebanon and from there left for Rome.

On August 25, 1952, The Arab Liberation Movement was launched. It was intended to be the sole political organization in Syria, and to regroup, as Shishakli said, the good elements from all parties and all classes. It made generous use of the slogans of Pan-Arab nationalism and set for itself a wide program of economic and social reform. It was joined particularly by certain civil servants who sought to improve their standing, but it had no popular prestige and the higher officals who had to join it seemed to be reluctant or ashamed to admit openly their membership in it.

In late January 1953, Shishakli spoke of the army as an instrument of social democracy, as in Turkey under Ataturk, and promised the restoration of constitutional rule. Six months later, on June 21, 1953 the draft of a new constitution of the presidential type, prepared by a committee of junior civil servants, was published.[38] On July 10 it was accepted in a referendum in which Shishakli, who was the only candidate for the presidency of the Syrian republic, was also elected president. The voters represented only one-third of the entire electoral body. In appointing his cabinet, Shishakli indicated his concern for making his regime acceptable to the country's traditional leadership. General Selo was retired, and Brigadier Shawkat Shuqair, a Druze of Lebanese origin, became chief of staff. Political prisoners were released as a sign of goodwill on the part of the new regime.

Shishakli's conciliatory measures, however, were of no avail. Already before his election to the presidency, a joint statement by the leaders and members of political parties and independent personalities was addressed to him on June 20, 1953 denouncing his arbitrary rule and the draft constitution. Shishakli nevertheless continued his offers of cooperation and allowed political parties to function, subject to certain conditions. When the elections to the Chamber of Deputies took place on October 9 in accordance with the new constitution, only the Liberation Movement and the Syrian Social National Party, of which he was an old sympathizer, participated. Sixty seats out of eighty-two were won by Shishakli's Liberation Movement, one by the SSNP and the rest by independents. The Chamber elected a brilliant lawyer and member of a well-known Damascene family, Mamun Kuzbari, Speaker on October 20, 1953.

Shishakli succeeded in giving Syria a stable and forward-looking government. Reform measures and projects of great significance were initiated or completed during his period of rule. His decrees of October 1952 and January 1953 provided for the distribution of state domain lands. Serious efforts were made by the Directorate of Tribal Affairs to settle the nomadic tribes and improve their sanitary and educational conditions. In December 1952, the well-known German economist, Dr. Schacht, visited Syria by official invitation and recommended several economic and financial measures that included the establishment of a central bank. The fourth anniversary of the first coup, on March 30, 1953, was celebrated by the establishment of the Monetary and Credit Council, and the Syrian Central Bank. The banking system was reorganized and became completely independent from French financial control. The thirty-inch pipeline of the Iraq Petroleum Company to the port of Baniyas was inaugurated, and work on the Latakia harbor was carried on. The great agricultural boom that began in 1943 reached its climax during his regime. Mechanized agriculture expanded the production of cereals and cotton in Jazirah, the cotton bureau was established in 1952, and private industrial enterprise was encouraged.

The former political parties, both radical and moderate,

remained indifferent to Shishakli's progressive measures and conciliatory mood and moved to put an end to his rule. He did not attempt to destroy them by destroying the economic and social foundations of their power as the revolutionary socialists did later. His collaborators were mostly office seekers and nationally unknown personalities, and they did not add credit to his regime. Shishakli himself was absorbed by his presidential duties and lost some contact with the army officers, while the Army Intelligence services became less efficient. In mid-October 1953, the Arab Socialist and Baath leaders, Hourani, Aflaq, and Bitar returned from Italy, and in November a general meeting of all opposition parties was held in Homs. The opposition incited students and distributed pamphlets against the regime. A wave of students' strikes and demonstrations spread after December 10, 1953. Bomb explosions, intended to disturb the authorities, were heard almost nightly during this period. On January 27 a state of emergency was proclaimed, and the Syrian university was closed. Troops supported by tanks and airplanes had been sent to Jabal Druze to maintain order, and a ruthless three-day campaign (27-30 January 1954) during which the town of Swaida was bombarded, left more than one hundred dead and caused the resentment of Druze officers in the army. The Druze leader, Sultan Pasha al-Atrash, had to seek refuge in Jordan. At the same time, the prominent leaders of the National and People's parties and of the Baath and Arab socialist parties were arrested and the octogenarian ex-president Atassi was placed under house arrest in Homs. Iraq exploited the Syrian disorders and supplied certain opposition leaders with regular payments—as the trials of the Mahdawi court in 1958 in Baghdad showed—in its drive against Shishakli. It is even believed that the Iraqi government knew the timing of the coup that ended his rule.

C. The Fall of Shishakli: The Fifth Coup

By the end of January 1954, the political opposition was

curbed and the Jabal Druze was pacified, but the situation remained tense. The *Times* in London thought that the ease with which the disturbances were suppressed was a proof that the Liberation Movement was in control.[39] The army, however, decided otherwise and by its intervention sealed Shishakli's fate. The military coup of Thursday, February 25, 1954 began in Aleppo when Lt. Col. Faisal Atassi arrested his commanding officer, Col. Umar Khan Tamr, and other official personalities and sent his troops to occupy the radio station and other government buildings. Two hours later, at 6:30 a.m. Captain Mustafa Hamdun, a friend and disciple of Akram Hourani, broadcast a long statement announcing the coup and calling on "the criminal oppressor" to relinquish power and leave the country. He referred to the meeting of the party leaders who organized themselves in a "national front" in Homs in July 1953 and rejected Shishakli's "sinister rule," told the people to set up their own republican popular regime and to "help the army return to its ideal duty of protecting the fatherland."[40] At 8:30 a.m. Colonel Amin Abu Assaf in Deir ez-Zor rallied and thus in the first few hours three officers reflecting the opposition of three anti-Shishakli civilian groups cooperated against the common enemy: Lt. Col. Atassi representing the Atassis of Homs and the People's Party, Captain Hamdun representing Hourani and the Arab socialists, and Col. Abu-Assaf representing the Druzes.[41]

In the afternoon of February 25, 1954 all the other commanders in the provinces rallied to the movement. Shishakli had at his disposal the armored forces near Damascus and the heavy artillery in addition to ten thousand troops who were maintaining order in Jabal Druze. Many pilots from the Damascus area defected to the north under the pretext of combatting the rebellion. Under these conditions and in response to the advice of his cabinet and to the threats of the rebellious officers, Shishakli decided to resign in order to avoid civil war. He left Damascus at 10 p.m. for Beirut where he stayed at the Saudi embassy. The resignation of Shishakli did not bring his regime immediately to an end. On the morning of February 26 in the meeting of the Chamber of Deputies, the Speaker, Mamun Kuzbari, was preparing to resign and publish the letter of resignation which Shishakli had addressed to him when Captain Abdul Haq Shehadi, chief of the military police, and Hussein Hidde, who was in command of the armored brigade at Qabun near Damascus, erupted into the Chamber and convinced Kuzbari to withhold his resignation. Joined by several deputies, Shehadi insisted that the regime should be maintained and that Kuzbari should take over as acting president of the republic according to the constitution. The Chamber then, instead of dissolving itself, consented to Kuzbari's new title. The issue was finally decided by an order accompanied by a threat from the insurgent commanders that Kuzbari and the Chamber should resign or else the insurgents would march on the capital. At the same time a mass demonstration on the morning of February 27 against the Shishakli regime forced the hand of the deputies. The demonstrators forced their way into the Chamber, and insulted and beat some deputies, while the Speaker announced his resignation and that of the members of the Chamber. Brigadier Shuqair was then released and on the following day, after negotiations with the insurgent commanders at Homs, Kuzbari presented his resignation to Shuqair. The two captains surrendered and were sent that same night to London and Paris as military attachés.

Shishakli did not leave for Saudi Arabia on February 26. He received a message from his supporters in Damascus urging him to return. The Druzes in Beirut prepared to take action against Shishakli, with the encouragement of the Iraqi embassy, as a former Iraqi consular official in Beirut told this writer. President Chamoun was thus forced to press for Shishakli's departure. On February 27 he left on a Saudi royal airplane to Saudi Arabia. More than ten years after his fall, a Druze shot him dead in Ceres in Brazil on September 27, 1964, to avenge those of his relatives who died in Shishakli's campaign against Jabal Druze.

Shishakli's indirect and direct rule lasted four years and two months. So far this has been the longest period of continuous military rule in Syria under the same man. After Shishakli's fall, his constitution of 1953 was abolished, and the Chamber that he had disbanded in December 1951 was reinstated. Thirteen of its members who had accepted to be elected deputies in the Shishakli Chamber were excluded. The reinstated Chamber restored the constitution of 1950 with the approval of the National Party which had formerly refused to recognize it. President Atassi, who had resigned in early December 1951, resumed office because his resignation had not been presented to the Chamber and accepted. The Dawalibi Cabinet which was forced to resign was also considered still in office, and President Atassi now issued a decree accepting its resignation. In this way Syria was brought back to the institutions and conditions of 1951 with the full observance of constitutional forms and as if the Shishakli period had not existed. Many dismissed officers were called back to the service. It is believed that the committee appointed to discuss the dismissals made under Shishakli was dominated by the Baathist officer Adnan Malki and by Brigadier Shuqair. The officers who were reinstated, consequently, were from among the Baathists and socialists and their friends.[42] A new cabinet was formed by Sabri al-Asali, leader of the National Party, but it was dominated by the Populists who held the portfolios of interior, foreign affairs, and defense. The Arab Renaissance Socialist Party (Baath), which had recently come into being by the merging of the Arab Socialists of Hourani and the Arab Renaissance (Baath) of Aflaq, did not accept to participate in the cabinet and resumed the negative obstructive policy that had been hitherto followed by its two component parts.

In Syria as well as in Lebanon, certain political analysts predicted that Shishakli's fall would mark the end of military rule in Syria because the lessons of the past five years should have been sufficient for the Syrians. The military evidently thought otherwise. They believed it was their duty to watch the civilian government they helped to bring back and they always found civilian dependents who were willing to enlist their support and pay the inevitable price.

IV. The Hourani-Sarraj Diumvirate and the Unity with Egypt: The Sixth Coup d'Etat Q A. Military-Baathist Influence and Nasserist Impact

During the four years that followed the fall of Shishakli, Syria was officially under a constitutional parliamentary regime. Constitutional government, however, was weakened and then destroyed by the continued intervention of the army and its chief of military intelligence, Lt. Colonel Abdul Hamid Sarraj, whose alliance with the Baath leader, Akram Hourani, constituted what has been aptly called the Hourani-Sarraj diumvirate.[43] Military intervention culminated in the officers' peaceful coup d'état of January 14, 1958 that imposed the unity of Syria with Egypt.

After 1954, army officers were able to make their influence felt in the country, in spite of the general disillusionment with military rule in the 1949-1954 period, under the impact of certain internal and external conditions. Political life exhibited an absence of party discipline, division marked by opportunism in the ranks of the politicians, and readiness of certain parties to appeal to influential officers to support them against their rivals. The two moderate parties that were sometimes described as conservative, the People's Party and the National Party, won twenty-eight and twelve seats respectively out of a total of 142 seats in the elections of September 1954. Personal rivalries divided their leaders although their common interests and goals should have compelled them to cooperate. The leftist Arab Renaissance Socialist Party (Baath) succeeded in winning sixteen seats, not without the help of Baath elements in the army. Through its oportunistic alliance with certain military leaders and with the Communists, and its exploitation of Nasser's prestige, it came to exercise after 1955 a preponderant influence in Syrian politics. The Communists gained one seat, and their leader, Khalid Bakdash, the first Communist elected to an Arab parliament, gained influence with the increase of Soviet support of Syria and the Arabs. The Syrian Social National Party gained only one seat but could claim several officers in the army. More than half of the members of the Chamber conveniently called themselves Independents. They grouped themselves, however, in various blocs and participated in cabinets under various coalitions. One of these blocs was called the Democratic Bloc and consisted mostly of deputies from little towns. They were grouped around Khalid al-Azem, the wealthy aristocrat with no nationalist past, whose alliance with the radical pro-Sovietic elements was his only alternative to reach power. The new Chamber elected as speaker the Populist leader, Nazem al-Qudsi. He continued to be re-elected to this post until October 14, 1957, when the Baath leader, Akram Hourani, won the speakership by 63 to 57 votes and thereby consecrated the triumph of radicalism and of army influence.

Already before the election of a new chamber of deputies in September 1954, the army had expressed its impatience with Maaruf Dawalibi, the Populist defense minister in the Asali cabinet, and put pressure to force the resignation of the cabinet in June 1954. The People's Party threatened to boycott the elections because of the expected interference of Baathist officers, and the chief of staff had to issue public statements to reassure the rivals of the Baath that the military will not interfere. The important issue in the elections was neutralism which meant non-participation in the Western defense pacts against Communism and the Soviet Union. Egypt under Nasser was advocating neutralism mainly to maintain its primacy and remove the Western presence in the Arab states, while Iraq was preparing to join the Western system of defense pacts because it could not depend on the Arab collective security pact of 1950 for its own defense. The neutralist trend triumphed in the elections and the gains of the

People's Party that was friendly to Iraq were by far less than in 1949.

When the elections ended on October 5, 1954, the various factions could not agree on the formation of a cabinet and the distribution of cabinet posts. To end the deadlock, President Atassi asked the eighty-one-year-old nationalist leader Faris al-Khouri, who was not a member of the Chamber, to form a cabinet. It was formed on October 29 without the participation of the Baath party and the Azem group. The Baath immediately brought its student supporters to demonstrate in the streets surrounding the Chamber while Faris read his ministerial statement. Although he pledged not to join any foreign alliances, the demonstrators shouted offensive slogans against him and even denounced the venerable veteran nationalist as a traitor while their leaders within the Chamber led a turbulent discussion of the cabinet statement from 4 p.m. until about midnight. Khouri's cabinet was granted confidence by a large majority, but the Baath minority showed since that day its determination to discredit by violent action and unwarranted accusations any leader who would be likely to disagree with its radical views. In January 1955, Faris attended the Arab prime ministers' conference in Cairo to discuss Iraq's decision to join what became the Baghdad Pact. He was denounced by the Egyptian press and by the Baath because he refused to condemn Iraq, and had to resign on February 7, shortly after the conference ended. It was said that the Baathist influential officer, Col. Adnan Malki, was ready to make a coup against Faris if he had not given way.[44] Under the new Asali Cabinet, formed on February 13, with Khalid al-Azem as foreign minister, Syria became an active opponent of the Baghdad Pact and a subservient ally of Egypt. The first half of 1955 was thus decisive in shaping Syrian alignments and the military played their role in policy making. The result was that the Baghdad Pact was "frozen" as Syria entered the Egyptian sphere of influence and became involved in the cold war, while Soviet hopes and Western fears were raised.[45]

Although their position was weakened by the Baghdad Pact of February 25, 1955, the Populists obtained four seats in the Said Ghazzi cabinet (September 1955-June 1956) but they had to subscribe to a policy of neutrality in the struggle between the Egyptian-Saudi Arabian Axis and the Hashemites, and to sign the defense pact with Egypt (October 20, 1955) in which they really did not believe. In June 1956 two Baath ministers officially joined the third Asali cabinet and were given the two important portfolios of foreign affairs and national economy. With the reshuffling of the cabinet at the end of 1956, the elimination of the moderate Populists became complete and the Baath dominated the government and the Chamber through intimidation and blackmail and with the help of the army and the subservient national parliamentary coalition which the Populists refused to join. The National Party, after having cooperated with the Populists in electing Quwatli president in August 1955, and defeated Azem who was supported by the Baath, became itself the ally of the Baath. Its leader, Sabri al-Asali, remained prime minister in the crucial nineteen months that witnessed the apogée of Baath power and army influence before unity with Egypt. Asali was then only a front man for the Baath and the military. President Quwatli ended by letting down the Populists who had made him president and became the puppet of both the influential officers and the Baath and a helpless adherent of Nasser's policies.

The various issues of Syrian foreign policy including the problems of inter-Arab relations and the cold war helped more than anything else to strengthen the hold of the officers on Syrian political life and gave them the opportunity to intervene. Local parties and foreign states needed allies among the Syrian military, and secret subsidies as a result were paid to them by Arab governments and by the great powers. There was no dominant military figure to preserve army unity and to restrain the officers who indulged in political intrigue and grouped and regrouped themselves in factions and shifting alliances although the most influential among them were influenced by the Nasserist-Baathist currents of Arab unity, neutralism, opposition to Iraq and the West, and adherence to pro-Egyptian and pro-Soviet policies. The Egyptian ambassador, former Brigadier Mahmud Riad, who arrived in Damascus in January 1955 was on close friendly terms with military and Baathist leaders and obtained their cooperation against the Baghdad Pact and for the mutual defense pact signed with Egypt on October 20, 1955. The Egyptian arms deal with the Czechs in September 1955, followed by the Syrian arms agreement with the Soviets in early 1956, enhanced the position of the Syrian military leaders and their civilian allies, and at the same time increased pro-Soviet feeling and strengthened the prestige of the local Communists. The nationalization of the Suez Canal Company in July 1956, and the outcome of the British-French-Israeli attack on Egypt in late October strengthened pro-Nasserist sentiment in Syria and gave the military leaders more power under the martial law administration.

Among the leftist officers who dominated the civilian political scene some, like Mustafa Hamdun, were affiliated with Hourani and the Baath while others, like Amin Nufuri, had no party connections and called themselves independents, and at one time they were allied to Khalid al-Azem. Another faction including Ahmad Hunaidi vacillated between the Baath and the independents and like the others demanded a share in power, while the Damascus group under Akram al-Dairi had a simple regional basis. One prominent officer at least, Colonel Afif al-Bizri, was a reputed Communist but he spoke in terms of Arab nationalism and liberation. The best known among the officers and one of the youngest and shrewdest was thirty-year-old Abdul Hamid al-Sarraj who became chief of the second bureau (military intelligence) in March 1955. His title to fame was the role he played in discovering the conspiracies against the leftist Syrian regime and in handling the investigations. He did not identify himself with any Syrian faction but was a faithful servant of Nasser.[46] Without moving overtly to seize power through a military coup, Sarraj was thus the real power behind the scenes after 1956, and Syria under him was spoken of as a "concealed military dictatorship."[47]

B. Treason Trials and Political Purges

The opposition groups in the Chamber were strong enough to challenge the policies of the Baath and indicate their disapproval of army intervention. Conservative and moderate elements outside the Chamber also expressed their concern in the press about the leftist political trend and the growth of Communism. In the army itself there was a number of anti-Communist, anti-Nasserist, and neutral officers. Sarraj destroyed all these elements of the opposition, civilian as well as military, and terrorized the enemies of the Baath by a series of three trials that subordinated law and justice to his political ambitions and those of his allies.

The first of the three principal trials or political purges succeeded in liquidating the Syrian Social National Party that was basically anti-Communist and dedicated to the idea of Fertile Crescent unity. The pretext for its liquidation was the assassination of Colonel Adnan Malki, chief of the Army Third Bureau, on April 22, 1955 by an Alawi military police sergeant who belonged to the Syrian Social National Party. Colonel Malki was a Baath socialist and as such was responsible for the transfer and dismissal of several SSNP officers including the Alawi Lt. Col. Ghassan Jedid. After his death, Malki became overnight a martyr and a national hero. It was assumed that on account of his opposition to Syrian membership in the Baghdad Pact he was the victim of a Western plot that was planned by the SSNP with American backing. Although the assassination could have been provoked by personal motives, and in spite of the absence of conclusive proofs of party conspiracy, the SSNP as a whole was made responsible for the crime.[48] The party quarters were searched, its leaders were arrested and brought to trial for treason, while other members were dismissed from the army or from the civil service.

The trial of the Syrian Social National Party involved more than thirty-five of its prominent members, some of whom lived in Beirut or even in the United States. It began on October 25, 1955 after a long investigation during which the arrested members claimed they were tortured. In the long speech made by the prosecutor, and also in the highly charged statements of the lawyers who defended the government position, it was evident that those who were being tried were not only the accused members of the SSNP. The Syrian court was trying, at the same time, Nuri al-Said and the Baghdad Pact along with the Hashemite rulers of Iraq and Jordan and the Western "imperialists." The prosecutor requested a death sentence for thirty-one members. The attorneys for the defense, however, told the court without ambiguity that the trial was no more than the vengeance of a party against another rival party. On December 13, 1955, the court gave eight death sentences, five of which were in absentia. Three SSNP members were sentenced to twenty years in prison, and they included the widow of the founder of the party. Of the three who were under arrest and condemned to death, two were executed, but only after nine months had passed (September 3, 1956) and as a result of the pressure of the two Baathist ministers, Salah Bitar and Khalil Kallas in the Asali cabinet, on President Quwatli, who was known for his aversion to bloodshed. The Baath, with the approval of the army, and the opportunistic support of the Communists, proceeded to create a legend around the person of the assassinated Colonel Malki, who died, as it was then said, to save Arab nationalism from the danger of Western pacts. A mausoleum was erected for him in the capital and on the anniversary of his assassination impressive celebrations were organized by the government every year where speakers and poets competed in praising the victim, flattering the new Arab leaders, and pouring contempt on the West and the pro-Western Arab rulers.

The second treason trial, aimed at destroying the rightist

opposition in the Chamber and insulting its members, was the most sensational owing to the caliber of the persons who were tried, the ruthlessness of the methods employed in the investigation and during the trial, and the harshness of the sentences. In November 1956, Colonel Sarraj accused forty-seven politicians of conspiring to overthrow the government with the aid of the Iraqi authorities. The trials before a court martial began on December 22, and the sentences were given on February 26, 1957. The Asali cabinet had been in office since June 1956 and it included two Baathist members. The day the trial began, the cabinet resigned and was reformed under Asali, but it included no Populists or Liberal Constitutionalists. Its members were expected to be indifferent to the fate of those implicated in the "Iraqi plot." As it was said in Damascus at the time, the cabinet had to include ministers who would not object to seeing certain heads roll. Included in the cabinet was the "red aristocrat," Khalid al-Azem, as minister of state and acting defense minister.

The accusations and arrests involved such former cabinet ministers as Adnan Atassi of the People's Party and son of the former president of the republic, Mikhail Elian of the right wing of the National Party who left the country at the suggestion of his former close friend, Premier Asali, because he knew about Elian's impending arrest, and Munir Ajlani of the Liberal Constitutional Bloc and professor at the Syrian university law school. Some of the defendants were tried in absentia, and one of them, Sheikh Hayel Srur, tribal member of parliament, was later kidnapped from Beirut and placed under arrest, while another, Col. Ghassan Jedid, was hunted down and killed in Beirut on February 19, 1957 by the agents of Sarraj.

It must be said that in the course of the year and a half that elapsed between Malki's assassination and the second trial, Communist progress was unchecked and Soviet and Egyptian influence were steadily increasing. The Egyptian ambassador, Mahmud Riad, was already being referred to in Damascus, as the "High Commisioner." Damascus became at this time, and remained until after the unity with Egypt, the principal center of Soviet action against the West. The Baath party at the same time stepped up the activities of its student followers and continued its policy of "fighting to the last student."[49] The Asali cabinet recognized Communist China on July 1, 1956. On August 20, a cultural agreement was signed with Russia and was followed by an exchange of cultural delegations and the sending of hundreds of students to study in Russia and her satellite countries. Between September 4 and 15, a Soviet parliamentary delegation visited Damascus, and at the end of October, President Quwatli left on a state visit to Moscow and became the first Arab head of state to visit the Soviet Union. In the Chamber, the Communist deputy Bakdash engaged in verbal battles with members of the opposition who did not hesitate to call him "Soviet agent." Russian films began to appear in the theatres, and Egyptian newsreels, with their propaganda for the Egyptian regime, entirely replaced European reels of international events. The story of the oil refinery of Homs and the pressures applied by the army, the Baath Party and Nasser's Egypt from January 1956 to March 1957 to accept the Czech bid to build it over the more favorable bids of Western companies, was an example of the regime's hostility to the West.[50] In the ministry of foreign affairs. the officials spoke humorously of the meetings of their minister, Salah Bitar, with his under-secretary, Salah Tarazi, and the ousted foreign minister of Jordan, Abdallah Rimawi, who became a permanent fixture in Bitar's office, as the gatherings of the "Supreme Soviet Council."

It was under these circumstances that patriotic members of the Chamber of Deputies began to discuss among themselves and with other Arabs in Beirut the possibility of finding a way to stop the drift towards the left and to limit Egyptian and Sovietic influence and also to preserve civil liberties and democratic institutions. The Iraqi government, at the same time, resented Syrian hostility and Syria's involvement with the Communist world and was anxious to see the end of the Sarraj-Hourani diumvirate and its subservience to Nasserist policy. The Iraqi authorities consequently established contacts with Syrian politicians, exiled officers, SSNP leaders, and former President Shishakli to overthrow the dominant ruling clique in Syria, but the mismanaged conspiracy never materialized and was betrayed after long discussions that extended from March to November 1956. The hundreds of rifles that were smuggled from Iraq and discovered by the Syrian government would not certainly have helped produce a revolt.[51]

The trial of the forty-seven Syrian politicians and officers implicated in the Iraqi plot began on December 22, 1956 and was given the greatest possible publicity. It was held in the auditorium of the Syrian University where this writer held his lectures immediately after the end of the court martial sessions presided by his former student, Colonel Afif Bizri, and could see the smuggled rifles that were brought to the auditorium as evidence of the conspiracy. Invitations were issued to the public for the hearings. The president of the court martial took full advantage of his position to shame and revile the defendants and to reserve his sharpest sarcasm and insults for the highest-ranking among them. The twelve death sentences that were handed down on February 26, 1957, and the many long-term prison sentences were met with consternation by Syrian political circles, and were accompanied by President Quwatli's departure to Egypt in order to avoid meeting the delegations that came to the presidential palace to beg for clemency. In early March the death sentences of those who were in custody were commuted to life imprisonment. The failure of the conspiracy resulted in strengthening the radicals and the influence of their foreign allies, and in giving more power, but not more prestige, to Sarraj who purged some of the most honest critics of his regime and portrayed them as traitors.

The height of Baath cooperation with the Communists was reached in the by-elections of May 4, 1957 to fill the seats of those who were sentenced in the Iraqi plot. In Damascus, a young Baathist lawyer named Riad Malki, brother of the assassinated Adnan Malki, was the candidate against Sheikh Mustafa Sebai of the Muslim Brethren. The platforms of the two candidates were the same except that Sheikh Sebai opposed imperialism in all its forms—which meant Soviet as well as Western imperialism. The contest between Sebai and Malki was spoken of as "a contest between Muhammad and Stalin."[52] Riad Malki won the elections by about 20,000 against 18,000 votes. Sebai might have won if a rival Kurdish sheikh by the name of Ahmad Kaftaro had not swayed some 2,000 voters in his congregation because of an old grudge which he held against Sebai or for more material reasons. The Baathists made use of Nasser's photographs and prestige in their campaign. In one of the main women's precincts, the wife of the well-known nationalist leader, Faris al-Khouri, was insulted and falsely accused of distributing "dollars and pounds sterling" to buy votes for Sebai.[53] The Soviet Embassy in Damascus opened its doors to receive congratulations for the leftist victory.

Populist opposition did not disarm, in spite of the trials of the Iraqi plot. In the press, a few courageous editors published their criticisms of the authoritarian regime. Syrian economic circles, represented by the chambers of commerce, industry, and agriculture, voiced their protest against Baathist policy that placed the economy at the mercy of politics and party interests and thus led to the loss of Syrian markets in neighboring countries They asked to separate economy from politics.

In the army ranks, division and confusion were reflected in the various factions and cliques and the changing alignments of officers in the last two years of the diumvirate. In July, 1956, the Chief of Staff, Shawkat Shuqair, was removed and retired through the cooperation of the Baath Party with certain factions in the army. He was replaced by Brigadier-General Tewfik Nizameddin, a moderate who was agreable to most army goups. Between March and May, 1957, attempts were made by President Quwatli to transfer Sarraj to Cairo as military attaché, but they all failed owing to the opposition of Hourani and Azem and some military cliques.

On August 12, 1957 the Damascus Radio announced the discovery of an "American plot" to overthrow the Syrian government. This was the third plot under the diumvirate and it led to another purge that particularly touched the Syrian officers. Three officials of the American Embassy were ordered to leave the country. The American government retaliated by declaring the Syrian ambassador in Washington persona non grata, and similarly one member of his staff. The American ambassador, James Moose, who was then in Washington, was retained for consultations. Evidence was presented in the proceedings of the military court that tried the ten Syrian defendants between December 11, 1957 and February 16, 1958 that contacts were made with several Syrian officers and that former President Shishakli and the Syrian military attaché in Rome, Colonel Ibrahim Husseini, were involved in the attempt which never went beyond the recruiting stage.[54] The plot served as a pretext for the dismissal of several rightist officers and the retirement of the Chief of Staff, Brigadier-General Nizameddin, because he refused to sign the decrees of dismissal. He was replaced on August 16 by Colonel Bizri, who became Brigadier-General, with the support of the Baath Party and Sarraj, while Colonel Nufuri became his deputy.

One week before the American plot, Radio Damascus had announced the conclusion of an economic agreement—arranged by Deputy Premier Khalid al-Azem—with the Soviet Union for a loan of $200 million for Syrian development projects. In Washington as well as in Ankara, and even in Damascus it was feared that with a Communist chief of staff and tighter economic relations with the Communist Bloc, Syria was becoming a satellite of Russia. President Quwatli indicated his concern by going to Egypt to meet Nasser after having failed to keep the balance between the leftists and their opponents. There were even rumors that he resigned. An international crisis followed and the American government sent Deputy Under-Secretary of State, Loy Henderson, to the Middle East on August 24. He met with various leaders in Ankara and expressed alarm at the growing Soviet influence in Syria. Turkey felt threatened by the danger of being outflanked by the possible establishment of a Communist regime in Syria. Turkish troops were concentrated near the Syrian border and Turkish maneuvers were held in mid-September. In the General Assembly of the United Nations, the foreign minister of Syria presented a complaint against American and Turkish pressure.

C. The Military Coup of January 1958 and Unity With Egypt

Cooperation between the Baath Party and the Communists was close and their policies were almost similar during the three-year period that ended in October, 1957. The Baath Party and the Communists succeeded in destroying their mutual opponents while the Soviet Union was given the occasion to support Syria against the Turkish threat and saw with satisfaction the elimination of the friends of Iraq and the West from political life. The Baath leaders finally became aware of the extent of Communist gains in Syria and of Communist attempts to acquire more political advantage. The Baathists were alarmed by the prospect of municipal elections which were to take place in November, and of parliamentary elections in the summer of 1958. They had no more friends to seek their support in a showdown with the Communists. Under these circumstances, they postponed the municipal elections and decided that the union with Egypt was their only way for gaining victory over their rivals and averting the external dangers.

In the fall of 1957, Syria was virtually isolated from her neighbors as a result of Baathist policy encouraged by Nasser and the Communists. Four pro-Western states surrounded her: Iraq, Jordan, Lebanon and Turkey, in addition to Israel. An

Iraqi intervention or a military coup backed by Iraq could be expected as the revelations of the People's Court in Baghdad later indicated. Egypt also had no allies except Syria. At the end of 1957, its relations were strained with almost every Arab country as a result of its interventions in the Arab states. A Syrian change in policy or orientation as a result of internal or external pressure would have left Egypt with no Arab friend or ally whatsoever and would have destroyed all Nasser's dreams and plans in the Arab region. It is therefore inexact, in spite of the uncertainties of the Syrian situation at the end of 1957, to claim that Nasser's decision to unite with Syria was an act of sacrifice intended primarily to save Syria from the pressure of the Baghdad Pact.[55] It is also not quite exact to say, as Nasser and other highly placed Egyptians have claimed, that the union was forced on Egypt and that Egypt was avoiding it. Since the end of 1954, Nasser and his government did everything they could to align Syrian foreign policy with their own and to win over the Syrian army and the Syrian masses. Moreover, as early as March 1955, Salah Salem spoke in Damascus about the need to form a federal union without Iraq, and Nasser himself welcomed union with Syria in his speech of July 22, 1957.

Nasser's decision to unite with Syria was not only to save Egypt from the danger of complete isolation, but also to make up for his failure in achieving the unity of the Nile Valley, and to offset certain new successes of his opponents like the successful counter-revolution of King Hussein of Jordan in April 1957, and Chamoun's successful elections in June 1957.[56] He also expected to begin that *drang nach Osten* that would bring him the oil-rich countries of Iraq and the Persian Gulf and allow Egypt to play a leading role in the Arab world, and later on in the Muslim world and in Africa according to his theory of the three circles.[57] Nasser, however, was not interested in a federal union with Syria because a dictatorship could not very well federate with a parliamentary regime, and a federation would not have given him the absolute power to dissolve parties and put an end to factionalism in the Syrian army.

In Syria, the Baath party alone was actively planning for union. Already on June 5, 1956, three weeks after the two Baath ministers entered the Asali cabinet, the Syrian Chamber approved the nomination of a committee under the foreign minister, Salah Bitar, to negotiate a federal union with Egypt. On September 3, 1957, an economic agreement was signed to lay plans for a future economic unity. Egypt made a demonstration of its solidarity with Syria in October 1957 at the time of the Syrian-Turkish crisis by sending a token force of some 1500 soldiers to Latakia. Renewed manifestations of the desire to unite occurred when an Egyptian parliamentary delegation visited Damascus and attended the meeting of the Syrian Chamber of Deputies on November 18, 1957. A joint resolution was then voted urging the governments of the two countries to begin negotiations for a federal union.[58]

Until the end of December 1957 and early January 1958, the politicians and the press in Syria continued to concentrate their attention on the coming parliamentary elections. Syrian political circles, including the Baath, did not expect the formation of a unitary state of Syria and Egypt but thought in terms of a federal union. The Baathist leader Aflaq himself has admitted that what the Baath wanted was a strong federal state with effective local parliaments and governments, but events moved too fast, he said, for the consideration of their project.[59] The formation of the unitary state—the United Arab Republic—was the direct result of a coup d'état made by a group of Syrian officers and imposed on the cabinet and the Chamber. The coup was supported and probably masterminded by Colonel Sarraj in full understanding with the rulers in Cairo. The coup began in mid-January at a time when Syria seemed to be in a dangerous stalemate with its army split into rival factions, and the influence of Communists and fellow travelers increasing. It can be argued that the stalemate was the direct result of Cairo's policy of subversion supported by Sarraj and the unsuspecting Baath. Yet, even these dangers along with the disagreements among officers and the pan-Arab feeling of the Syrians cannot explain the unconditional surrender to Nasser. It can only be explained by the high-handed military action prepared by Sarraj and his clique of officers with the approval of the Baath leaders in the last stages.

The role of the Syrian army officers in the coup that produced unity was described by highly placed Egyptian and Syrian authorities. In the pro-Nasserite apologetic book, *What Happened in Syria,* written by Muhammad Hassanein Haikal after the break of unity in late 1961, the author related the story of the genesis of the United Arab Republic.[60] He mentioned clearly that the Syrian army took the initiative in the formation of Syro-Egyptian unity because it allegedly decided that there was no hope for a solution of the problem of Syria except through unity with Egypt. He described with evident exaggeration, how twenty-two officers "representing twenty-two blocs in the Syrian army" took the plane on January 14, 1958 to Cairo. On the evening of January 15 they met Nasser in his residence and explained to him why unity should be achieved. Nasser is said to have told the officers that he could not discuss these topics except with a responsible government. When he asked them if President Quwatli knew what they were doing in Cairo, they reportedly said that "he cannot object to anything we ask, for we will send him General Amin Nufuri to present the army's wishes and he cannot but accept." Nasser is said to have expressed his regrets and added that he could not agree under such conditions. The officers, consequently, decided to send a delegate to Damascus to find out the government's reaction. On the morning of January 16, a plane left for Damascus and returned in the afternoon with Salah Bitar, minister of foreign affairs, on it. He came to Cairo as a representative of the cabinet, and in the meeting that took place in the night of 16-17 January, Bitar informed Nasser that the Syrian government agreed to the establishment of unity, and the officers also approved. At this point, Nasser presented his three conditions for unity: a national referendum on the formation of a united Syro-Egyptian state, the end of party activity and the dissolution of parties in Syria, and the end of army intervention in politics. The officers readily accepted the first condition, but they had their reservations on the other two.

In his three conditions, Nasser implied that the unity he wanted should take the form of a unitary state, not that of a federal union. His talk about the difficulties that stood in the way of unity, and his alleged refusal at the beginning were a prelude to the presentation of his three conditions and a part of the process of hard bargaining. On January 18, 1958, the officers and Bitar left Cairo for Damascus. Thirteen days later a Syrian government delegation headed by President Quwatli went to Cairo to sign the formal announcement of the merger of the two countries. On February 1, 1958, it was signed by the two presidents, Nasser and Quwatli, and the United Arab Republic was born.

In a slightly different version of the military coup that produced unity, we are told that the delegation consisted of fourteen officers who left Damascus on January 12 with Bitar's encouragement because many politicians opposed the union. Sarraj, according to this version, delivered a note that resembled an ultimatum to the government explaining the officers' departure to Cairo as an attempt to seek a remedy for the hopeless situation in Syria. The cabinet was alarmed and sent Foreign Minister Bitar to see how far the officers went, but when he asked for instructions, President Quwatli and Deputy-Premier Azem refused to commit themselves, and it was evident that there was no concerted policy on the union. When Bitar arrived in Cairo on January 16 and met Nasser with the officers, he advanced no conditions after Nasser had mentioned his three conditions for unity. After Bitar's return to Damascus, the cabinet drafted a federal project and asked him on January 25, 1958 to present it to Nasser; but the Egyptian president rejected the project. In a decisive meeting of Mahmud Riad, the Egyptian ambassador in Damascus, with the Syrian officers at the end of January, they approved the merger of Syria and Egypt and the cabinet had to give its consent as a result. The final act that confirmed the military aspect of the coup was that General Bizri ordered a plane on February 1 and assembled the cabinet on it and left for Egypt. The rumor was that he gave the cabinet members two alternatives: to go to Cairo or to the Mazze prison near Damascus.[61]

After the proclamation of unity on February 1, the two presidents made a statement, in seventeen points, on the basic principles of the new state: it was to be a unitary state with a presidential democratic form of government, an executive council for each of the two regions, the northern (Syria), and the southern (Egypt), a national assembly half of whose members would be taken from the two dissolved national assemblies of the two regions, and a constitution which was expected to be drafted later. On the basis of these principles, the Syrian Chamber and the Egyptian National Assembly ratified the formation of the UAR on February 5. A referendum was held on February 21 in both Syria and Egypt on the principles of unity and the nomination of Nasser as president of the new state, and the result was almost unanimous approval by 99.99% of the voters in Egypt, and 99.98% in Syria.

The decisive role of the army in imposing unity is attested by a statement made by General Abdul Karim Zahreddin, commander in chief of the Syrian army, on October 2, 1961, after the break of unity, when he said that the unification was the work of the army and that army representatives wrote the very words of the proclamation of unity. Another authoritative statement on the role of the army was made by Nasser during the talks of March 1963 with some Baathist and other leaders when he said, "But unity, who made it? It was the officers who made it. They came before the cabinet knew." Bitar and Aflaq answered him at the time that they—the Baath leaders—were the ones who suggested to the officers to go to Cairo.[62] Egyptian and Syrian personalities admitted later—although they remained silent at the time—that the unity was premature. The Syrian veteran nationalist Faris al-Khouri said, "It was done in a minute, in a foolish minute."[63] The columnist of *al-Nasr* in Damascus put it more bluntly: "Unity was speedily concocted as if it were the marriage of a rich man to a maid or to a harlot for the purpose of saving her reputation."[64]

V. The Fall of the United Arab Republic: The Seventh Coup d'Etat, September 1961

A. Weaknesses and Handicaps of the New Unitarian State

The coup d'état of September 28, 1961 that ended the unity of Syria and Egypt was the first among the Syrian coups to be called a revolution. It opened a period of internal disagreements and struggles, and led to a series of military interventions.

The United Arab Republic that was proclaimed on February 1, 1958 contained at the very moment of its birth the elements of its own destruction. In the first place, it was created under the pressure of an irresponsible military group and the influence of the Baath Party that represented about ten per cent of the Syrian electorate. It was established in an atmosphere of fear and treason trials that could not possibly permit a free discussion of the conditions of its formation. In the army as well as in the party ranks and even in the delegation that attended the formal ceremony of its proclamation in Cairo, there was no unanimity about its creation, and yet dissident voices could not be heard. The chief of staff, Afif Bizri himself acted by opportunism although he was basically opposed to Nasser's conditions.[65] He was promoted to Lieut. General and made commander of the First Army (in the Syrian Province) but he was not destined to stay long in that position.

In the second place, the motives and goals of the leaders

and groups who accepted unity were negative, sometimes selfish, contradictory and based on false assumptions. They hoped, however, each in his own way, to accommodate themselves to the new conditions and to turn them to their own advantage. President Quwatli found in unity a relief from the headaches of army intervention in politics, and from Baathist and Communist excesses and gave himself the title of "first Arab citizen."[66] Unity, for the rulers of Egypt as well as for the Baathist leaders and their military allies, was a successful maneuver in the cold war against Nuri al-Said and the Hashemite monarchs, and a safeguard against the pressures of the Baghdad Pact. The Baath Party itself considered unity a triumph over its internal rivals and hoped to enjoy a privileged position in the new state and to be the virtual ruler of Syria. Its leaders believed that the dissolution of parties would apply only to the moderate conservatives and the Communists. Its theoritician, Michel Aflaq, was of the opinion that the new political organization, the National Union, that was created by the rulers in Cairo, would be animated by no other principles than those of the Baath. He also thought that the "Baath came to give Nasser a philosophy and an ideology."[67] Nasser was not prepared to share power with the Baathists and ended by dissociating himself from them when he realized their unpopularity. The association of the Baath and Nasser, as it has been said, was produced by common interests as to immediate goals, but the interests for long-term goals were divergent.[68]

Nasser was mainly interested in unity as an instrument of propaganda for the consolidation of his regime at home, and for weakening and embarassing his Arab rivals. The goal was hegemony in the Arab world, and Syria was to be, on account of its central strategic position, the stepping stone as well as the center for subversion and intrigue. The events that followed in the summer of 1958 have confirmed this view.

In the third place, unity brought together two countries that had no common frontier and that were different in their political and economic systems, in their standard of living, and in the character of their people. Syria, at this time, was under parliamentary rule and its economy was free and based on private enterprise. Its people were known for their individualism, impatience with despotism, and enthusiasm for the Arab national cause. The Syrian middle class was large and prosperous, and the general standard of living in the whole country was among the highest in the Middle East. The Syrian masses were carried away by the merger of the two countries owing to the usual Syrian attachment to the ideal of Arab unity, and to the intensive propaganda campaign that portrayed Nasser as the saviour of the Arab world. The Syrians also thought that unity would respect personal freedom, and would be based on the equality and brotherhood of the two united peoples. Even the Syrian businessmen, who were ultimately to suffer most from unity, first welcomed it not only as Arab patriots, but also in the hope that active economic relations between the two countries would be profitable to both sides.

The United Arab Republic was thus handicapped from the very beginning by the circumstances of its formation, the conflicting aims and assumptions of its founders, and the basic differences between the two countries and their people. Certain observers hastily predicted, one year after unity, that "the United Arab Republic has come to stay" because no organized group, civilian or military, was left to end it, but the prediction proved ultimately to be unwarranted, for it both underestimated the ability of the Syrians to organize the revolt against an unfavorable situation, and over-estimated the dominant role and power of the Egyptian leadership in Syria.[69]

B. Causes of Syrian Discontent

The military coup d'état of September 28, 1961 that broke up the United Arab Republic after it had lasted three years and eight months, was provoked by the awkward policies and excesses of the Egyptian partners who notoriously ignored the basic interests of the Syrians and insulted their dignity and their local national pride. The Syrians, in the first place, resented the military dictatorship that brought with it police rule and the loss of political freedom. The first disappointment came with the provisional constitution of March 5, 1958 that was issued by President Nasser after the referendum. It proclaimed in its Article I that the UAR was a democratic republic. In this "democratic republic," however, political parties were dissolved on March 12 and the country was ruled by a constitution that remained provisional until the break of unity, and without a parliament until an appointed national assembly was created on July 19, 1960. The only political organization allowed was a sort of a single party organization that had already been created in Egypt by the rulers and was known as the National Union. The new National Assembly as well as the general congress of the National Union exercised no real powers of legislation or criticism.

One of the most revolting aspects of the unitary regime was the network of spying systems and secret police that watched and denounced private persons, government officials and army officers, and even cabinet ministers. More than one government authority had power to throw persons in jail where they could be tortured or kept for months or years without trial. The Syrians resented the arbitrary rule of Lt. Colonel Sarraj who became minister of interior in the Syrian executive council, and later on became its president. After the secession of Syria in 1961 the new minister of interior, Adnan Quwatli, declared that 6500 secret agents and spies were employed under the UAR regime.[70]

The Syrians, in the second place, resented the aspects of Egyptian domination which were referred to as Egyptianization, pharaonization, or simply Egyptian colonialism. A facade of Syrian autonomy was maintained in the form of an executive council, or cabinet, for the Syrian region. The ministers in this council and their president, however, were appointed by President Nasser and were responsible to him.

In the central government, two of the four vice-presidents of the republic were Syrians, Sabri al-Asali and Akram Hourani. They were allowed to remain in Syria, but they had no real power. The central cabinet for the entire UAR in Cairo had only three Syrian ministers out of fourteen. The three included the two Syrian vice-presidents, and Bitar as minister of state. Shortly after unity, the Baath leaders met Nasser and complained that they did not feel they were participating in government at its highest level. Bitar is reported to have suggested to Nasser that, "Three of us [Hourani, Aflaq, Bitar] and three of you should form a higher council of state," but Nasser refused the suggestion.[71]

A government reorganization in Syria took place in the wake of the Iraqi revolution of July 14, 1958 in order to keep the Baath leaders away from Syria and from direct contact with the Iraqi leaders. In October 1958, Hourani was kicked upwards and transferred to Cairo after a struggle for power between him and Sarraj, his former partner in the diumvirate, in which he was the loser. Asali had already resigned as vice-president and retired from politics. The end of Baath influence in Syria was marked also by the appointment in late October 1959 of Field Marshal Abdul Hakim Amer, one of the two Egyptian vice-presidents and the minister of war, as Nasser's personal representative in Syria in view of Syrian complaints against Baathist administration. The Baath leaders, feeling that they were being watched and deprived of power, resigned from their ministerial posts in Cairo and in Damascus on December 23, 1959. Rivalry then developed between Sarraj and Amer, but Sarraj still enjoyed Nasser's confidence and on September 21, 1960 became the president of the executive council in the Syrian region. Further reorganization in the government of the UAR ultimately brought the transfer of Sarraj to Cairo as vice-president.

In Cairo the Syrian central ministers felt their insignificance, for they had no authority in their own departments. One of them, Dr. Bashir Azmeh, central minister of hygiene, declared that he and his colleagues were like actors on a stage, or like protocol officers or receptionists. On August 18, 1960, he resigned, and after the break of unity he said that declarations were sometimes made in his name without knowing anything about them until he read them in the newspapers.[72] The regime of executive councils for the two regions was abolished in August 1961, one month before the break of unity, and only the central cabinet remained. The aspect of autonomy which was more apparent than real thus disappeared.

In the ministry of education the Egyptians imposed changes in the programs of history teaching that emphasized the importance of the Egyptian revolution and its heroes at the expense of the outstanding figures of Arab history in general. The Syrians resented, among other things, the idolization of Nasser and his colleagues in the school books on every occasion and the disregard of Syrian national heroes. The number of Egyptian teachers artificially increased without real need for them, for as it was explained later, the Egyptian authorities augmented the weekly class periods in schools from twenty-eight to thirty-six, so that Syrian schools suddenly needed 25 per cent more teachers than they had been employing.[73]

The third and one of the most potent causes of Syrian discontent was the economic and financial policy imposed by the rulers in Cairo. The principles underlying the Egyptian economic policy in Syria were the subordination of the Syrian to the Egyptian economy, the lowering of the standard of living in Syria in order to reach that of Egypt, and the establishment of what was called the democratic, socialist, cooperative society whose basic goals were the destruction of capitalism and the emergence of a classless society. Restrictions on trade took the aspect of Egyptian economic imperialism, for they were designed either to force the importation of Egyptian products, or the importation of foreign products through Egyptian companies. Pressure was made to unify the two currencies, and this led to the resignation of the governor of the Central Bank of Syria.[74]

During the three winters of the period of unity, Syria had no rainfall, and crop failures caused great damage to the economy. To the opponents of unity, as well as to all those who were hurt by the economic measures of Nasser, the lack of rainfall was considered to be a heavenly sign and a divine punishment for Nasser's pride and conceit.[75] The first important socio-economic measure introduced in Syria after unity was the law of agrarian reform of September 27, 1958 that expropriated the lands of those who owned more than 200 acres. The Baathists who ruled during the first year and a half of the UAR utilized the agrarian reform, and especially the expropriation of landed estates, as an instrument of revenge against their political and personal opponents.[76] The distribution of expropriated land to landless peasant farmers was slow, but whenever it occurred it was exploited to portray Nasser as the saviour of the Syrian fellah from tyranny in a country where the landlord was fairly benevolent and democratic in his relationship with the peasant farmer.

The rulers encouraged class warfare and stirred hatred between the peasant and the landlord, the laborer and the employer, the merchant and the consumer and even between the civilian and the military.[77] The exaggerated picture of social differences was used as a means for gaining popularity and playing on the people's emotions. Industrialists and businessmen were described as exploiters, while in reality they had been pioneers and had opened large vistas of gainful work for thousands of laborers and employees. Syria had also to pay the price of Nasser's quarrels with the Arab neighbors. It lost its markets in those countries and became isolated economically.

Syrian impatience with the unitary regime reached its climax when Nasser issued his socialist decrees and made them applicable to both Egypt and Syria. The decrees of July 1961 fully nationalized a number of industrial and commercial companies, including all insurance companies and banks, and imposed state partnership in many others.[78] Syrian businessmen thus lost their independence and initiative, as well as the product of long years of thrift and hard work. The Syrian economy was disrupted and became stagnant. The laborer, at the same time, lost his extra hours of work and his freedom and became the servant of the new bureaucracy. The labor unions had already lost the right to strike and were watched by the secret police.

The fourth cause of discontent in Syria was perhaps the most potent on account of its direct relationship with the coup. It was the feeling of frustration and humiliation among the Syrian officers and their concern about the Egyptian designs with regard to the Syrian armed forces. The Syrian officers, who had been accustomed to impose their will on Syrian cabinets—partly through Egyptian encouragement before unity—now felt bitterly the loss of their power and resented the wholesale transfers to Egypt and to the Gaza Strip where they were isolated and had neither influence nor prestige, while the Egyptian officers who were transferred to Syria occupied sensitive posts in the First Army and its command. Some of them engaged in intelligence work that involved even their Syrian colleagues and communicated above the heads of their Syrian superiors with the high command in Egypt or with other Egyptian officers in Syria, in total disregard of the proper hierachical channels.[79] The first clash between General Bizri, Commander of the First Army, and Marshal Amer, the minister of defense, was caused by their disagreement on the transfers and dismissals of Syrian officers. It ended in Bizri's resignation on March 23, 1958.

Several Syrian personalities warned Nasser and his responsible representatives against the evil effects of the policy that was followed in Syria and towards the Arab states in general, but Nasser was not inclined to listen. Former President Quwatli said in this connection that "Nasser had a thousand eyes but could not see with one eye that while he needed the friendship of the people he was acting as the executioner of the people."[80] The vocal Baath party that usually showed its strength under the mild rule of democratic regimes by inciting its students to demonstrate, now completely lost its voice, while one of its leaders, Michel Aflaq, went to live in Beirut and remained there until unity ended.

Nasser must have certainly felt the Syrian disenchantment with unity, but he ignored it and tried to tighten the control over the country's administration and economy. Nasser's only support left was Sarraj and his secret police network, and those individuals who acquired undreamed-of positions under the unitarian regime. With the reorganization and centralization of the UAR government in mid-August, 1961, Sarraj was transferred to Cairo as one of the seven new vice-presidents of the republic, and placed in charge of internal affairs. He revolted against this "promotion" especially when he felt that he was ignored in Cairo and not allowed to fulfill his duty. His ambition was to rule Syria and wrest its control from his rival, Marshal Amer. On September 15 he returned to Syria and tried through his secret agents and some trade union members, and through National Union representatives to stir trouble and influence Cairo's decision.[81] It is even alleged that he tried to make a coup against Egyptian rule, but the army did not trust him and refused to cooperate. On September 26, 1961 he resigned after several fruitless meetings with President Nasser and returned to Damascus.

C. The Coup d'Etat of September 28, 1961 and the Restoration of Constitutional Rule

The disorganization of Sarraj's secret police network during his quarrel with Amer and his transfer to Cairo gave the Syrian officers their opportunity to revolt against the existing regime and thereby stage the seventh Syrian coup. They were generally agreed about the need for military intervention and were ready to support any garrison that would give the signal. In Damascus, the assistant director of officers' affairs of the First Army, Lt. Colonel Abdul Karim Nahlawi, helped prepare for the coup by transferring to the fighting units those officers who were in favor of military action. He had the support of his brother-in-law (his sister's husband), Muhib al-Hindi, staff officer of the brigade at Qatana, and of other officers of the Damascus region.

On Thursday September 28, 1961 at various intervals after 2 a.m. the mechanized desert forces centered near Dmeir, northeast of Damascus, under Lt. Col. Haidar Kuzbari, and the armored units from the camp of Qatana to the southwest of Damascus under Lt. Colonel Muhib al-Hindi began their march to Damascus. They entered the capital at 4 a.m. and were joined by the Damascus garrison according to a previous agreement. They took their positions in the city and occupied, among other important establishments, the broadcasting station. A small force that went to Marshal Amer's residence in the Abu-Rummane quarter clashed with the guards who eventually surrendered. The Army command at the General Headquarters where Amer stayed that night was surrounded. The leaders of the revolt then engaged in negotiations with Amer and presented some demands that would remove the causes of tension and discontent, and would preserve unity. Amer agreed to their demands and promised to issue a statement about the agreement after communicating with Cairo, on condition that the officers proclaim the end of the revolt. The leaders as a result broadcast their ninth communiqué that seemed to end the movement, but after a few hours they realized that Amer was only trying to gain time while Nasser prepared his forces to strike against the revolt. When Amer was pressed to issue the promised statement, he declared that Nasser refused any bargaining under pressure and thus the revolt continued.[82]

The first communiqué that announced the coup was broadcast from the Damascus radio at 7:15 a.m. in the name of the Supreme Arab Revolutionary Command of the Armed Forces. It announced that the army's movement was intended to "remove corruption and tyranny and return to the people their legal rights." The second communiqué spoke of the people of Syria and Egypt who, supported by the army, have undertaken to destroy deviation and deviationists. It denounced the domineering clique and its so-called revolutionary decrees, and it proclaimed the Arab people's determination to support Arab unity on a basis of equality, fraternity, and freedom. When the ninth communiqué, about 1:35 p.m., announced that the officers reached an understanding with Amer, it was thought that a setback or a countercoup took place. The tenth communiqué at 5 p.m. announced the failure of the negotiations and Amer had to leave for Cairo in the early evening. Most of the garrisons had already rallied to the revolt. In the evening, Aleppo rallied, and late at night the coastal region around Latakia joined the other garrisons. The number of victims on both sides was two guards at Amer's residence, and about thirty in clashes in Aleppo between the opponents and supporters of the coup.[83]

Several characteristics can be noted in the attitudes and actions of the leaders of what came to be called the revolution of September 28, 1961. The officers did not reveal their identity and issued communiqués in the name of a supreme Arab revolutionary command without even mentioning the name of Syria. This anonymity became a practice in subsequent revolts and was intended to avoid jealousies among the officers and to prevent anyone of them from assuming the title of leader of the revolt. It was also meant to be a protective measure for the leaders and their revolt. The names of those involved in the coup were, however, revealed when Nasser announced the dismissal of five leading officers in his speech from Cairo at the end of the first day at 7 p.m.[84] The officers were young and most of them were in their thirties or early forties.

The officers declared from the beginning, contrary to what the rulers in Egypt claimed later, that there were no civilian politicians or foreign states behind their movement, and that they were expressing the wishes of the people when they decided to interfere by force because the danger threatened not only the army, but also the entire people, for it was exposed to impoverishment, humiliation, loss of freedom and dignity, while its economy was being ruined.[85] The military therefore wanted to make it clear that theirs was not just the rebellion of a group of officers, as Nasser proclaimed in his two speeches on the first day, but that it was a revolution of the whole army and of the whole people. In order to dispel any misconceptions on the role of Sarraj the army spokesman said that Sarraj did not represent the interests or wishes of anybody, and his conflict with Amer was for personal reasons. Sarraj was actually arrested on the fourth day after the coup, because he changed residence and tried with his aides to exploit the revolt for personal ends.

Another feature of the officers' attitudes and actions was revealed in the restrained language of the first communiqués where Nasser was not even mentioned by name. There seemed to be since the very beginning disagreement among the leaders of the coup. It is probable that the moderate elements, who can be considered responsible for the ninth communiqué, changed their position at the end of the first day when Nasser announced the dismissal of the leading officers and declared his intention to crush the revolt by sending forces to Syria. With that, the restrained language of the communiqués ended. After the communiqué no. 13, Nasser was described as a tyrant and was accused of borrowing his socialism wholesale "from a country [Yugoslavia] whose president [Tito] was allowed to become the trustee of Nasser and of the people of Egypt and Syria." The people of Syria were told that "the era of tyranny is gone forever, for the army has broken the idol who betrayed you and made you submit to a destructive clique."[86]

A classical feature of all military coups—and the coup of September 28 was no exception—was the promise made by the officers to surrender power to the people. The Revolutionary Command declared since the first day that it did not intend to assume the responsibility of ruling the country. It was true to its promise, but only for a relatively short period. Early on the second day of the revolt, the communiqués17-19 entrusted Dr. Maamun Kuzbari with the formation of a cabinet that would rule the country and prepare the return to constitutional government. On the day of his nomination, he issued decree no. 1 appointing the eleven members of his all-civilian cabinet.[87] General Abdul Karim Zahreddin was appointed Commander in Chief of the Armed Forces of the Republic two days after the formation of the cabinet. The communiqué no. 25, on October 4, 1961, ended the series of communiqués issued by the Revolutionary Command. It proclaimed the return of the army to its barracks.

The cabinet took immediate steps to re-establish the constitutional regime. It also ordered the raising of the Syrian flag and the return to the Syrian national anthem and emblem. In its ministerial statement, it expressed the hope to give the country a stable, constitutional government within a maximum of four months.[88] On November 12, 1961, a provisional constitution of eight articles was drafted. It proclaimed the independence and sovereignty of Syria. On the following day the government announced that elections for a constituent-legislative assembly would take place on December 1, 1961, two months earlier than was planned.

Elections took place on the prescribed day. The 172 elected deputies were expected to draft a constitution for the third Syrian republic.[89] On December 12, the new assembly met and elected Dr. Maamun Kuzbari speaker. Two days later it elected Nazem Qudsi president of the republic by 153 out of 172 votes. A cabinet was formed on December 22 under the premiership of Dr. Maaruf Dawalibi, a courageous fighter for constitutional government, and a left-wing member of the People's Party. The transitional regime thus ended in a record short period of a little more than two months.

It is significant that the elections were the freest in the annals of Syrian electoral history, and that the army did not impose its will on the voters. The people elected an overwhelming majority of moderate right-wingers to the assembly. Although all party activity was banned, most of the deputies belonged to the parties that had hitherto ruled Syria. As the

Orient of Beirut declared, Syria did not change fundamentally, "she is today the same as she was twelve years ago."[90]

The moderate conservative deputies who dominated the new assembly were by no means reactionaries, nor were they opposed to Arab unity. They constantly assured the masses—as the transitional government did before them—of their belief in what they called "constructive" socialism, and "sound" Arab unity. The transitional government also reassured the laborers in the first days of the revolution that the rights given to them by the socialist laws of July 1961 would be respected. On October 16, the revolutionary command in cooperation with the cabinet issued a manifesto that explained the basis of the government's economic policy. The manifesto defined the respective roles of the individual and of the state in the national economy and announced the determination to maintain agrarian reform.[91]

The Syrian people in general reacted with enthusiasm to the revolution and showed their gratefulness to the army in demonstrations, poems and speeches. Following the coup, there was an outburst of declarations by various writers and leaders on the essential human need for freedom. This was accompanied by a vivacious expression of Syrian national pride and satisfaction at the failure of the Egyptian attempt to obliterate the Syrian identity. Political and intellectual leaders were all of the opinion that there could be no Arab unity without freedom, democracy and dignity. To those who wept about unity, a young nationalist lawyer said, "We were about to lose something more important than unity. We were about to lose freedom."[92] The Grand Mufti of Syria gave the revolution his blessing and that of the Ulama and religious men and absolved the people from allegiance to Nasser. A large group of nationalist leaders, including those who had signed the declaration of unity in February 1958, issued a statement that approved and supported the armed forces in their "blessed" revolution.[93]

A characteristic aspect of the revolution, and at the same time a proof of the moderation of both the transitional government and the revolutionary command, is the fact that no reprisals were made against the leaders of the unitarian regime. The country's leaders who suffered total eclipse under unity did not take revenge against their opponents, and avoided those long trials that had been the fashion under the Hourani-Sarraj diumvirate. Sarraj was neither prosecuted nor tried, and he finally escaped from jail on May 6, 1962, probably with the connivance of the army and the government under a different regime.

The Syrian revolution was a great shock to Nasser from which he never recovered. It was a serious blow to his leadership both inside, but especially outside Egypt. It was for his enemies in the Arab world and beyond an occasion for jubilation. For several years to come Nasser stubbornly refused to take the separation of Syria for what it really was.

In his attempt to suppress the Syrian revolution, Nasser used all the weapons at his disposal. He tried to send troops from Egypt, but had to order them back. He also tried, by an attempted diplomatic blockade, to prevent the various countries from recognizing the new regime by breaking relations with those who did. This is how he broke with Jordan and Turkey on the first day of the revolution.[94] He soon discovered the futility of this method because the great and the small powers gave their recognition. The United States recognized the new Syrian regime only on October 10 after consultations with Nasser. The attitude of the Lebanese government was pitiful but not surprising, for the prime minister was Saeb Salam, who had led the rebellion in 1958 with Nasser's men and funds and the Lebanese Muslims were Pro-Nasserists. It was only when Lebanon's stand became an object of ridicule in all but the Nasserist press and in the Lebanese Chamber of Deputies that the regime was recognized on October 13. Salam's cabinet was forced to resign on October 24, 1961.[95]

Having failed to bring Syria back to the United Arab Republic, Nasser announced the secession officially in a speech on October 5, 1961, the seventh day after the revolution. He continued, however, to call Egypt alone the United Arab

Republic. He refused to recognize any government in Syria if it did not represent, as he said, the will of the people.[96] Nasser refused to be convinced except of one thing, that the Syrians should turn against their government. On the eve of the elections, he urged the people of Syria to stay away from the polls. When the results of the elections and the referendum became known, he refused to recognize them and continued his boycott of Syria.

The one weapon that remained in Nasser's hands—and one in which his regime particularly excelled—was subversion. He employed his press and radio, and his generously paid agents to keep Syria weak and divided. His revengeful behavior was dictated by his desire to save his face and restore his influence, for Syria had become, as a writer put it, "Nasser's tendon of Achilles."[97]

In his speeches, especially that of October 5, Nasser tried desperately to justify his policy and rule in Syria by enumerating what he did during the three and a half years of unity. He also mobilized his writers to harp on the same theme of Syrian indebtedness to Egypt. The great literary figure, Taha Hussein, became a participant in the duel of words between Nasser and the Syrians. The "dean of Arabic letters" mentioned the works established by Egyptians and which "the Syrians could never have dreamed of."[98] The Syrian authorities answered these claims with facts and figures. They explained that the Egyptian officials and officers in Syria were paid from the Syrian budget and that they were mostly not needed. They said that the projects of which Nasser boasted had really started before unity, and that Egyptian agents, by their reckless spending, ruined the Syrian finances. They also claimed that all the standards in Syria, including those of education and morals, were weakened as a result of unity.[99]

VI. The Independent Constitutional Regime and the Coups of March-April 1962

A. Constitutional Rule and the Coup of March 28, 1962

In its twenty-fifth and last communiqué of October 4,

1961, the Supreme Arab Revolutionary Command in Syria announced that "all the officers of the revolutionary movement hereby take God and the people as witnesses that they are returning to their military duties." Those who read this communiqué on the sixth day after the revolution were optimistic and hopeful that the army would consider its mission ended after the elections and the restoration of constitutional rule. But the army never considered its mission ended, and through a combination of military factionalism and pressure aggravated by popular disagreements on the policy of the constitutional government and by Nasserist intrigue it finally destroyed the constitutional regime.

While the army claimed that it had no desire to be dragged again into politics, it wanted to make sure that the civilian leaders agreed on a basic internal and external policy. On November 9, 1961, the Revolutionary Command and the cabinet persuaded the leading politicians to meet and draw up a national pact relative to such basic questions as Arab unity, socialism, and democratic rule. The pact was made three weeks before the elections, and was signed by seventy political leaders at the officers' club in Damascus where the meeting took place.

The Revolutionary Command and in particular the officers who led the revolution, with Colonel Nahlawi at their head, believed that their role in that revolution entitled them to watch the civilian government and to present their views on the various issues in order to achieve the initial goals of their movement.[100] The cabinet ministers and the deputies tried to cooperate with the officers but they also believed that the elections gave them legal power to legislate and rule, and that military interference and imposition should not be tolerated. When Maamun Kuzbari was elected speaker of the Chamber, and Dawalibi became premier, the Army Command felt, as General Zahreddin put it, that "it was stabbed in the back," because it expected to be consulted and would have liked more desirable persons for these two key positions.[101]

The coup d'état of March 28, 1962 that ended the shortlived constitutional regime, and the several other coups that followed in rapid succession, were thus caused by the reluctance of the officers to allow the legitimate authorities to rule, and by the continued divisions among the officers that reflected disagreements among the civilians. The most aggravating factor, however, was Nasserist subversion and incitement to overthrow the new regime and prove, for obvious motives, that Syria was incapable of insuring stability without unity under Nasser's leadership. The Syrian government was unable to persuade Nasser to stop the destructive propaganda which he thought strengthened his position in Egypt, while its fabrications against Syrian dignitaries helped create trouble for the government in Syria because the people, including the officers, believed them.[102]

The Syrian cabinet that was formed by Dr. Dawalibi on December 22, 1961 did not include any Baath socialists. It gave the important portfolios to members of the People's Party and the right-wing of the National Party. In its ministerial statement of January 8, 1962, the cabinet made it clear, while explaining its economic policy, that the rights of the peasants and workers would be respected. It also intimated that the agrarian law would be modified to remove certain injustices, and that certain corporations would be denationalized. The cabinet won the confidence of the Chamber by 133 votes against 30, with 3 abstentions. On January 13-14 some students and laborers demonstrated in Damascus and Aleppo against the cabinet's statement relative to nationalization, and clashed with the police. The demonstrations were partly provoked by the Baath socialists whose leader, Akram Hourani, advocated in the Chamber the maintenance of nationalization and the removal of emergency laws. The Cairo radio and press took advantage of the troubles and spoke in exaggerated terms of the martyrs of the Damascus and Aleppo demonstrations.

In spite of the disorganized condition of the Syrian economy as a result of the socialist laws of July 1961, the transitional government that followed the revolution of September 28 did not move quickly to abolish or modify those laws. After the elections, the Dawalibi cabinet introduced in the Chamber at the end of January three draft laws relative to industrial establishments, agrarian reform, and banks. The law on the industrial establishments abrogated nationalization under certain reservations and conditions, and was accepted on February 14, 1962 by a large majority. The Baath socialists and the Nasserists voted against it. The new law on agrarian reform, that replaced the law of September 1958, was also passed. It removed certain injustices in the previous law and provided for better terms of repayment for the expropriated land and more allowances to the landlords. At the same time, it exempted the peasant beneficiary from paying his installments, and thus gave him the land free.[103] The army command was dissatisfied because the project it presented to the government was not strictly adopted, and it contained a larger measure of socialism. Since then, Zahreddin said, confidence was lost between the command and the cabinet.[104]

In its external relations, the new cabinet continued the policy of the transitional regime that ended Syrian isolation and established friendly relations with Iraq, Jordan, and Saudi Arabia. It moved cautiously in order not to antagonize Nasser and to avoid offending certain Syrian officers who disliked the establishment of close ties with Iraq without Egypt. On February 28 an Iraqi military delegation came to Damascus and two weeks later, President Qudsi and General Abdul Karim Kassem met at Rutbah (14-15 March, 1962) near the Iraqi-Syrian border, but no details were given on the results of the meeting which General Zahreddin evidently opposed and did not attend.[105]

On March 16, a violent Israeli attack was directed against the Syrian positions east of Lake Tiberias. There were rumors at the time that Iraqi troops were ready to come to help Syria against the Israelis. Premier Dawalibi explained later that Syria had warned the Arab League against the suspicious movements of Israel since the end of 1961, but "one Arab voice", he said, "made fun of us, and refused to give us back our planes, our arms, and our naval units, so we addressed ourselves to Iraq."[106]

The Nasserist regime in Egypt seized every opportunity to discredit and weaken the Syrian government. The tempo of Nasser's campaign against Syria rose when his socialist laws were revoked or modified by the Syrian Chamber. As the anniversary of the formal establishment of the United Arab Republic on February 22 approached, more Nasserist agents converged on Lebanon, which ironically became under President Shehab the center of subversion against Syria, after Syria had been three years before the great source of subversion against the Lebanon of President Chamoun. The sector of the Lebanese press that was generously subsidized by Egypt, joined the Egyptian press in denouncing the Syrian regime and in provoking disorder in Syria.[107]

Nasser's speech of February 22, 1962 against the Syrian leaders followed the classical pattern of calling those whom he wanted to destroy agents of imperialism and accusing them of receiving funds from foreign sources. The attacks against Speaker Maamun Kuzbari were so violent that the spokesman of the Syrian Nasserists in the Chamber, Rateb Hussami, challenged the Syrian leaders to answer Nasser's charges. His challenge led to a brawl in the Chamber in which he was wounded. This Nasserist campaign came at a time when Syria was raising the question of the Israeli diversion of the Jordan waters. Premier Dawalibi and many other Syrians consequently concluded that Nasser was no less dangerous to Syria than imperialism and Zionism.

Tension between the military Command and the moderately conservative cabinet and Chamber was growing in the meantime. The Command had been since December 1961 in the hands of a leftist bloc led by Colonel Nahlawi after the arbitrary arrest of Colonel Kuzbari, leader of the rightist bloc, on charges of receiving funds from Jordan for staging the coup of September 28 and of interference in the elections. Although the investigation proved his innocence, he was kept in jail by order of his colleague Nahlawi and was dismissed from the army.[108]

The leftist command disapproved of the economic laws passed by the Chamber. It was also against the conclusion of any special ties with Iraq, and was in favor of Nasserism without Nasser in order to take power from the civilians without giving it to Nasser. In January 1962, it opened talks with Cairo, and its delegates discussed with Nasser the conclusion of a military agreement and a political alliance, but Nasser refused even the resumption of diplomatic relations before the removal of the entire regime in power in Syria.[109]

The master-mind in the coup d'état of March 28, 1962 was Colonel Nahlawi, who had reportedly made the communiqué no. 9 in the September coup. With remarkable opportunism, he exploited Nasser's accusations against the civilian leaders in order to destroy them. He and his circle of Damascene officers were moved by a mixture of concern about the socialist laws and especially by a selfish desire to rule the country and dismiss the legitimate rulers.

On March 24, 1962 a majority of 132 deputies presented a petition to the Chamber for the retrial of the political leaders who had been convicted in 1957 by a court martial presided over by Colonel Bizri.[110] The officers objected to the demand. On the same day, Premier Dawalibi made a speech in the Chamber and openly accused the army of interference in government affairs. The army command then presented to President Qudsi several demands that included the dismissal of the Dawalibi cabinet and the dissolution of the Chamber but he rejected them. General Zahreddin was, by his own admission, against staging a coup and preferred negotiation and pressure on Qudsi, but when Nahlawi came to tell him that the coup was being carried out, Zahreddin made no objection although he knew that most of the officers in the command were opposed to the coup.

In the early hours of Wednesday, March 28, 1962, the planned coup, the eighth since 1949, was carried out without any bloodshed. The army units moved from their barracks after midnight to occupy the strategic points in Damascus, and to arrest about one hundred politicians and businessmen. The arrests continued until the late morning and included President Qudsi, former prime ministers Azem and Kekhia, Premier Dawalibi and the members of his cabinet, Speaker Kuzbari and many deputies, and some leading industrialists. The first communiqué of this coup was given the number 26 to indicate that the movement was only a continuation of the revolution of September 28. The communique mentioned that "The General Command of the Armed Forces, in order to realize the wishes of the people and preserve the gains, freedoms, security, and stability that the army had achieved in the revolution of September 28, 1961, declares that the army has taken the reins of government into its own hands since this morning in continuation of the September 28 revolution." The communiques 28 and 29 announced the dissolution of the Chamber and the resignation of the President of the Republic. The cabinet was dismissed by the military authors of the coup, but communiqué no. 30 announced that the premier and his cabinet presented their resignation and it was accepted.

The General Command, as usual, did not reveal the names of its members, but they were soon known in the course of events in the following days. They were, with the exception of Colonel Haidar Kuzbari, almost the same as those who made the coup of September 28. The ring-leader was the notorious thirty-five-year-old Colonel Abdul Karim Nahlawi, head of the First Bureau (Personnel) in the army. The General Command published a proclamation along with the communiques to explain and justify its action.[111] The proclamation contained accusations, misrepresentations of facts, and exaggerations that reflected the frivolity and irresponsibility of the officers and their determination to smear the constitutional regime and its personalities. Some of the exaggerations and slogans used were copied from the Nasserist propaganda and were intended to win over Egypt as well as the Syrian laborers and peasants. The proclamation ended with a description of the goals of the revolution which included the establishment of a just and constructive Arab socialist system that would also encourage private enterprise, and the preparation for Arab unity on a sound and clear basis with the "liberated" Arab countries, and particularly "beloved Egypt and sister Iraq."

The coup of March 28 was a bitter disappointment for those who had predicted that the Syrian army would stay out of politics after the elections of December 1961, and would allow the country to enjoy a period of stability and order. At the time when the new coup took place the Syrian economy and finances were beginning to recover from the effects of the policies that were followed under the unity regime. The government was proceeding in an orderly constitutional way and with the help of some dedicated and competent leaders to solve the country's various problems but it did not have the nerve to deal effectively with Nasserist subversion. It was handicapped by the intrigues and suspicions of the military and by the group of Baath socialists under Hourani who resumed their negative and obstructionist policy and helped in provoking opposition to the government decrees among the masses.

The coup of March 28, 1962 failed to win popular support. The politicians refused to cooperate with the authors of the coup, and for over two weeks no cabinet could be formed. Many civilians were shocked by the false charges against the responsible authorities and by the sudden end of the parliamentary regime accompanied by the sweeping arrests of its leaders. In the army, the coup of March 28 was condemned by the regional commands outside Damascus and by many military factions that reflected the divisions in civilian circles. For three days (28-30 March) those who made the coup did not know what to do with the power they had seized. The army rightists or legalists who believed in constitutional government combined with non-partisan officers and with Nasserists to overthrow Nahlawi and his clique. The regional commanders were partly moved by personal jealousies to oppose the leadership of what they called the opportunistic group of Damascene officers. For the Nasserists the coup of March 28 was only a preparatory step for staging their own coup that was to take place in the first days of April. Nasser is said to have encouraged Nahlawi to overthrow the constitutional regime and promised him help and cooperation, but he prepared at the same time to stab him in the back through another coup that would restore Egyptian rule in Syria and oust Nahlawi.[112]

B. The Abortive Nasserist Coup of April 1, 1962

The Nasserists in the army had long been preparing for a coup, and it was said that they were organized in secret cells in Aleppo.[113] Most of them were dismissed officers who formed the core of what was called the "free officers."[114] Their leader was former Colonel Jassem Alwan who organized most of the Nasserist conspiracies against the Syrian government. He operated on Lebanese as well as on Syrian territory. A few other officers in the active service were dissatisfied with their posts and rank such as Captain Hamad Ubaid who headed a movement for the dismissal of the Damascus command, the return of dismissed officers, and unity with Egypt.

Opposition to the Nahlawi coup of March 28 began on Friday night, March 30 and continued to Saturday March 31 in Homs under the leadership of Brigadier General Badr al-A'sar, commander of the Homs region in central Syria. By Saturday evening the other regional commands had rallied to oppose the domination of Nahlawi's group in Damascus. Jassem Alwan, though still a dismissed officer, took advantage of the situation and tried to dominate the opposition by distributing active commands among his fellow dismissed officers who flocked to Homs. In the Homs riots that followed, Nasserists and anti-Nasserists clashed and an estimated forty victims fell. Brigadier A'sar then ordered the dismissed officers to leave Homs and refused to allow his disagreement with Damascus to be exploited by the Nasserists. Consultations between the superior officers in various parts of Syria were then conducted in order to prevent further deterioration of the situation. The officers decided, with the consent of the Damascus command which was now in trouble, to hold a general military congress in Homs on April 1, 1962 to study the demands and problems of the military factions. The Nasserists evidently foresaw that the congress of Homs would not decide for immediate unity with Egypt, and therefore decided to act promptly and take over the city of Aleppo. This is where the dismissed officers had moved after their failure in Homs. They expected to be aided by the officers of the paratroop and commando regiments that had been ordered, on March 27, to move from their barracks outside Aleppo to the Army Headquarters in the city in preparation for the coup of March 28.

The Aleppo coup d'état—the ninth since 1949—was made by some fifteen officers, many of whom had been dismissed, and were living in Lebanon. The commander of the Aleppo region, Brig. Gen. Hisham Midani, had a vague foreknowledge of the planned coup. He ordered the paratroopers to return to their barracks at Rasm al-Abbud, east of Aleppo, but they refused. At the zero hour which was set for April 1 at 2 a.m. by Jassem Alwan, two Nasserist lieutenants of the paratroopers, accompanied by some aides, forced their way into the Command Headquarters and arrested Brigadier Midani. Although they met no resistance, they cruelly shot and killed four officers, including the commando captain, and one soldier in cold blood. Jassem Alwan arrived in Aleppo after this initial "success" and assumed unofficially the title of commander in Aleppo. He was joined later in the day by the commander of the eastern region, Colonel Louay Atassi, who brought with him a number of armored cars.

The authors of the Aleppo coup occupied the broadcasting station and prepared the atmosphere for the unity with Egypt while they waited for the outcome of the meeting at Homs. One of the rebel officers raised the flag of the United

Arab Republic over the Command Headquarters. Demonstrations were immediately organized with the help of soldiers in trucks while flags of the UAR and pictures of Nasser that had been smuggled in previous months were distributed among the demonstrators.[115] The army command in Damascus attempted to prevent demonstrations in Homs and Aleppo by diverting attention to the Israeli border and the danger of an Israeli attack. Volunteers were even invited to register but the officers and demonstrators were indifferent and the maneuver remained fruitless. The Congress of Homs met on Sunday, April 1 at 4 p.m., and continued until after 1 a.m. of the following day. It was attended by some one-hundred officers who represented all the military regions and the various arms and fighting units. Its minutes and its decisions were not officially published, hence the various accounts about its resolutions. One resolution is certain, and that was to exile the seven officers who led the coup of March 28 and to form a new army command. The Nasserists and the neutrals forced the passage of this resolution but for various motives. The Nasserists had a grudge against the seven officers because they were the authors of the coup of September 28, 1961 that ended unity, while the neutrals and the legalists wanted to punish them for having overthrown the legal constitutional government. The resolution on unity provided for either conditional unity with Egypt subject to a referendum, or a referendum on the form of unity with the "liberated" Arab states, Egypt and Iraq. It was also decided to form a transitional government and to study the cases of officers who were retired after September 28, 1961. The Congress probably discussed the question of recalling the arrested President Qudsi to the presidency.[116]

The resolution concerning the banishment of the seven officers was immediately implemented because of the pressure of neutral and Nasserist officers and of public opinion. The officers were placed on a plane on Monday afternoon, April 2, and left for Switzerland.[117] In Damascus, non-partisan officers who were acceptable to the regional commands, took over. In

Aleppo alone, the rebellion continued, partly because the Congress of Homs did not reinstate the dismissed officers and also because the extreme Nasserist wing in Aleppo was dissatisfied with the Homs resolution relative to unity. The Nasserists miscalculated in thinking that the departure of the seven officers of the Damascus command had improved their chances of success. When they proclaimed the re-establishment of the United Arab Republic on Monday-April 2, at 7 p.m., the protests of their colleagues and of the other commands condemning their action were so strong that they had to make another broadcast in the name of the Syrian Arab Republic. On Tuesday morning, at 7 a.m., the over-excited Nasserists seemed to have gained the upper hand and resumed their broadcasts in the name of the Syrian Region of the UAR, and the communiqués were now officially signed by Jassem Alwan, as spokesman of the First Army. Alwan's communiqué accused the Damascus command of not complying with the Homs resolutions. At 9 a.m., he addressed the Egyptian ambassador in Beirut, Abdul Hamid Ghaleb, by wireless, asking him to contact Cairo in order to send reinforcements. Ten minutes later, a broadcast addressed by "the free officers' command in Aleppo" to the general command of the army and armed forces in the Southern Region (Egypt) said "the planes of the separatists are attempting to bombard the radio transmission station at Saraqeb (near Aleppo), we have no planes for defense, help us."[118]

The Egyptian command did not send any help because the rebels had no following, even in northern Syria. Yet, Alwan thought that he could defend Aleppo against the impending action of the Syrian command. The command in Damascus finally issued its ultimatum at 10:25 a.m. on April 3 to the rebels asking them to surrender by noon, and dispatched the fifth armored brigade from Homs to Aleppo. Shortly before the ultimatum had been issued, Louay Atassi assumed the command of northern Syria and tried to mediate between the rebels and the Syrian command because he felt the rebellion was collapsing. When the armored brigade reached Aleppo, the dismissed officers, including Alwan, saw the futility of their resistance and left the city. They took refuge in Lebanon while the rebel forces withdrew to the barracks. At 6 p.m., Damascus announced the collapse of Nasserist rebellion in Aleppo. Those who were responsible for the Aleppo abortive coup and for murdering the other four officers, were subsequently arrested and tried in a Special Higher Security Court. They were charged with murder, treason, armed rebellion and attempt to detach a part of Syria. The sentences were pronounced on January 17, 1963 and included three condemnations to death, one of which was commuted to life imprisonment. Jassem Alwan was condemned in absentia to hard labor for life.[119]

The military coup of March 28, 1962, and the abortive attempt of April 1, which came as a coup within the coup, thus ended with the exile or arrest of their respective leaders only a few days after they had taken place. In both cases, the rebel officers were moved to action largely by personal interests and jealousies, but they were also influenced in varying degrees by the issues of socialism, social reform and unity with Egypt. At no time in the history of independent Syria, were military coups attended by as much division and deterioration of discipline and authority as in these two instances. At no time until then, was the country as humiliated and its reputation as damaged as in that week of March 28 to April 3, 1962. In Syria itself, the military came to be compared to the unruly and selfish Janissaries in the age of decadence of the Ottoman Empire. In Aleppo, for example, when the four officers were shot in cold blood at Army Headquarters, the paratroopers fell on their dead bodies like vultures to take their watches, wallets and fountain pens. The Syrian flag was pulled down by some soldiers who, under the eye of their officers, used it to wipe their shoes.[120]

The excesses of the Aleppo rebellion, and more specifically the insult to the country's flag and the proclamation of the UAR, helped restore the cooperation between the regional commands and Damascus. The radio in the capital again spoke on behalf of the garrisons and of all Syria when, on April 3, it described the "free officers" in Aleppo as "traitors serving their masters in Cairo."[121] For Nasser and for Egyptian official circles, the turn of events in Syria was particularly disappointing. When on April 5, the funerals of the four slain officers took place, the Damascus radio declared that "nothing but the sight of spilled blood can satisfy Nasser." On the following day, Friday, an impressive procession in Damascus denounced Nasser as "The enemy of God."[122]

VII. The Semi-Constitutional Regime Under Pressure April 1962 - March 1963

A. The Nasserist Challenge and the Failure of Appeasement

After the departure of the seven officers to Europe and the failure of the Nasserist coup in Aleppo, the Syrian army command was reorganized and Abdul Karim Zahreddin was again appointed chief of staff and commander in chief of the armed forces. The new command tried to, but could not, establish a transitional government of technicians and specialists because the civilians refused to cooperate with the military or work under their dominance. The officers, at the same time, were reluctant to assume power and General Zahreddin himself pledged, on April 7, that the army would not participate in the new cabinet. While the country was being administered by the under-secretaries in the various departments, the self-discipline of the Syrians prevented the spread of anarchy during the uncertainties of the period and gave another illustration of the people's ability to keep their balance when their rulers had lost theirs. The Syrians proved, as it was said, that they "have a knack for adjusting themselves to bewildering changes."[123]

General Zahreddin sought and obtained the advice of political leaders on the appointment of a new government. He was told that the first step was to recall President Qudsi, but as the arrested president insisted that the Constituent-Legislative Chamber that elected him be restored and refused to dissolve it, a face-saving solution was found. It was agreed that the Chamber would be recalled and that Qudsi would guarantee the resignation of its members. On April 13, President Qudsi consequently moved from the prison hospital to the Presidential Palace, and the press was told that the Army and the people refused his resignation. General Zahreddin expressed on this occasion the concern of the military for the achievement of a sound unity with the "liberated" Arab countries and particularly with Egypt and the establishment of social justice and "fair" socialism. He claimed that he made President Qudsi sign a statement in which he agreed to these goals.[124]

Constitutional government, however, was not really reestablished with Qudsi's return to the presidency, and the crude falsehood of the reinstatement and resignation of the Chamber did not restore to the government its legality and strength. President Qudsi's declaration that most of the members of the Chamber had presented their resignation was not true. The petition of resignation circulated by the Army command and by Rashad Barmada, minister of defense, among the deputies had obtained only seventy signatures by April 12.[125] On April 16 Qudsi signed a decree accepting the resignation of the Dawalibi cabinet and gave it the date of March 27, the day that preceded the coup. At the same time he signed another decree nominating a new cabinet of fourteen members under the premiership of Bashir Azmeh, a professor of chest diseases at the Syrian University Medical School and a former central minister of health during the first period of unity with Egypt.

The new cabinet that emerged after two weeks of military bewilderment was a leftist cabinet and except for its vice-premier, Rashad Barmada, no members of the traditional political elite that had formed the majority in the Chamber were included. The cabinet members were either Baath socialists, or independents and technicians. The Baath Socialist

Party that had at least three representatives in the cabinet, in addition to Premier Azmeh himself who was known as a strong Baath sympathizer, was no longer the same old united party. Shortly after the revolution of September 28, 1961 the party split into its two original component parts. As a result of the elections of December 1961 in which Bitar was defeated, and under the pressure of events and the feeling of isolation and loss of prestige, the bitter Aflaq-Bitar faction drifted away from the Hourani faction and issued a statement in May 1962 calling for the restoration of union with Egypt, while Hourani launched his attacks and accusations against Nasser. In the Azmeh cabinet, both factions were represented and the premier himself inclined more towards the Aflaq-Bitar group.

The Azmeh cabinet lasted about two months, and was followed by another reshuffled Azmeh cabinet on June 22 which was able to rule for about three months (until September 17, 1962). The two Azmeh cabinets maintained themselves mainly by the support of the military. They were supported also by a small minority that believed in a conditional unity with Egypt and particularly by those who wanted the implementation of the socialist laws of July 1961. The first Azmeh cabinet proceeded, with the encouragement of the army command, to implement its socialist program. On April 30, 1962 it abolished the decree no. 3 of February 20, 1962 passed under the Dawalibi cabinet that modified the first agrarian reform law passed under unity. In its new version, however, the new decree retained certain modifications made under the Dawalibi cabinet that were advantageous to both landlord and peasant.[126] No re-nationalization of industrial corporations was decreed, except for the United Industrial and Commercial Corporation (known as the Khumassiyé or Big Five Company) after long hesitation. The decision was taken on May 21.[127] Three days later a decree on banking appeared. It nationalized foreign banks, provided for state ownership of 25 per cent of the stock of other banks, and limited the value of stock owned by any shareholder to 175,000 Syrian pounds (about $50,000). The cabinet also issued a decree on May 19 regulating the distribution of 25 per cent of the profits of corporations among workers and employees.[128] In pressing his socialist program, Premier Azmeh aimed at wooing Nasser especially since he proclaimed his National Charter of Arab socialism on May 21, 1962.

The partial restoration of the Nasserist socialist laws was the only achievement of the Azmeh regime. The other two articles of the Azmeh program–conditional unity with Egypt and restoration of constitutional government–were not implemented. Nasserist officers tried to put pressure on the government to restore unity, and a quasi-rebellion of the officers of the 70th Brigade at Deraa took place in April. They asked the cabinet to implement the decisions of the Congress of Homs. President Qudsi and the command told them to be patient until after the Adha Feast (Feast of sacrifice), and when the feast had passed, the officers were sent to Mazze prison. Other officers at Homs refused to take jobs outside the country and they were also sent to jail. The official communiqué on April 24 mentioned nineteen imprisoned officers instead of the sixty-three which rumors had cited.[129]

Although the Azmeh regime with the support of the army command fought the extreme Nasserists who wanted immediate unity with Egypt, it tried in all sincerity to be friendly to Egypt and Nasser and demonstrated its readiness to discuss the conditions of a federal union. On May 19, a committee that represented various parties and views was appointed by decree to study the question of unity, but most of its members declined the appointment and the committee never met.[130] Azmeh then acted on his own, and in a nation-wide broadcast on June 6, 1962 he called for a federal union with Egypt at a time when Nasser's campaign of propaganda against Syria continued to rage.

Nasser did not respond to Azmeh's call, and he contemptuously neglected to make an official comment on it. His spokesman, Muhammad Hassanein Haikal, however, wrote an article in *al-Ahram* five days later entitled "The answer of Cairo to all those who call for unity in Damascus" in which he made it clear that Syria, and any other country that desired unity with Egypt, would have to follow her program of Arab socialism. The majority of Syrian political leaders expressed their disapproval of Azmeh's appeal to Cairo even before the unfavorable response came. On June 8, politicians met in the house of Khalid al-Azem and then went to protest to President Qudsi against Azmeh's proposal and his general policy.

While the Azmeh regime called for a federation with Egypt, it ironically had at the same time to defend itself against the inroads of the very country with whom it was seeking to federate. Measures indeed had to be taken to prevent the infiltration of Nasser's agents from neighboring Lebanon. The agents who consisted of certain dismissed Syrian officers, such as ex-Colonel Jassem Alwan, and Lebanese sympathizers and mercenaries, were then recruiting saboteurs and sending them to Syria. Nasser's alleged aim was to paralyze production in Syria by subverting labor, and to create disorder and civil strife as he did in Lebanon in the summer of 1958.

The activities of Nasserist agents in Lebanon and Syria were considerably stepped up later in July, and it was believed that Nasser was preparing for some sensational act in Syria in order to celebrate the tenth anniversary of the Egyptian revolution of July 23. On July 21, 1962, the Syrian security forces discovered the plan of a coup to overthrow the government and arrested most of the conspirators who had been in touch with the Egyptian Embassy in Beirut and included prominent civilian and military Baathists and Nasserists. Another plan for murder and destruction was to take place on July 28-29, but it was discovered and its leader, Yusif Muzahem, was arrested and disclosed its details.[131] On September 8 a bomb exploded in a coffee house in the city of Hama on Friday evening and twenty-five persons were injured.

Syrian anti-Nasserists of various parties and trends reacted against Nasserist propaganda and sabotage, and their opposition to any kind of union under Nasser's domination became more vocal. It was particularly the leaders of the Hourani wing of the Baath who led the counter-offensive against Nasser. Private citizens during this same period addressed open letters to the American ambassador in Damascus expressing their surprise at the contradiction between the American nation's love for freedom and the American support of the "little Pharoah who stifles freedom, usurps private property, and threatens the freedom and security of other countries."[132]

Hostility against the subversive activities of the pro-Nasserists in Syria was reflected by increased attacks on Nasser himself and his regime of rule. Nasser was compared to the false prophet Musailama the Liar of early Islamic history, and to Kafur, the Ethiopian eunuch who ruled Egypt in the tenth century. His caricatures in the form of a Don Quixote attacking a windmill, or in the form of a little boy sitting on the lap of Uncle Sam, appeared often in the press. Nicknames and titles given to Nasser by the hostile press included: "the sucker of blood," "the big drum," "the destroyer of Arab nationalism," and "the great deception." He was accused of applying in Syria the policy of "scorched earth" that the French applied in Algeria. A large group of men of letters and arts published an appeal to the people to make no truce with dictatorship that enslaves and exploits human endeavor.[133]

The nerveless regime of Dr. Azmeh helplessly watched the duel between pro- and anti-Nasserists in Syria. The army command significantly did not interfere in this contest. Nasser moved audaciously from subversion and plotting to open attack and intervention in his speeches of July 26 and 27 in Cairo and Alexandria. He attacked the Syrian government as reactionary and opportunistic, and spoke of Syria as the northern province of the United Arab Republic. The Azmeh regime had thus to move, not without some pressure, from an initial attitude of friendliness to that of hostility. The first Azmeh cabinet, it must be remembered, had represented at the time a reaction against excessive criticism of Nasser.

Azmeh was severely criticized when he gave a permit to his friend, Salah Bitar, to issue a newspaper that ultimately became an organ of opposition to the Azmeh regime itself and an instrument of propaganda for Nasser. During the whole Azmeh regime, the trial of the pro-Nasserist officers who were accused of murder, treason, and armed rebellion in the abortive coup of April 1, 1962, never went beyond issuing a decree of accusation on July 23. In spite of all this, neither Azmeh nor the army command were ready to submit to Nasser's domination or to accept his socialist system.[134] When Nasser ignored the independent existence and sovereignty of Syria in his July speeches, Azmeh's policy of compromise had to end. On July 29, 1962 the Azmeh cabinet called for a meeting of the Arab League Council to "consider the situation resulting from words and acts–made and provoked by the rulers in Cairo against the Syrian Arab Republic–that constitute a clear aggression against the sovereingty of Syria and the dignity of its people." The Council met on August 22 at Shtura, Lebanon, and the Syrian delegation presented seven documents that contained proofs of Egyptian appeals for disorder and revolt, of spending funds on sabotage and terrorism, and of plotting against the existence of Syria. The meetings were marked by the overwhelming attacks of the Syrian delegates against Nasser's rule in both Syria and Egypt, and by the sympathetic attitudes of the majority of Arab delegations towards Syria's complaints. The delegations, however, did not vote on Syria's draft resolution to condemn Egypt. The Egyptian delegation itself was strongly shaken by the Syrian charges and their incriminating evidence, and by the strong attacks of the Syrian delegates and therefore decided to withdraw from the meetings. The Council did not have sufficient courage to deal with the documented accusations against Nasser. It decided simply to expunge the offensive terms that were used during the debate from the minutes, and then preferred to dissolve itself leaving the question open without taking any resolution.[135]

B. The "Legal Coup" of September 13, 1962 and the Azem Regime

The Azmeh cabinet continued in office for two weeks after the end of the Shtura Conference. Its end was brought by what was considered a "quiet, legal coup" engineered by President Qudsi and the dissolved chamber of deputies with the reluctant consent of the army. It can be recalled that the Chamber that was dissolved by the military in the coup of March 28, 1962 never considered itself legally dissolved, nor did it believe in the fiction of its resignation at the time of Qudsi's return to the presidency on April 13. The weak and ambivalent policy of the two Azmeh cabinets gave the members of the Chamber reason to ask for the return of constitutional life and to protest against Premier Azmeh's call for a federation with Egypt on June 6, as well as his plans for preparing a constitution and making a draft electoral law. Opposition to the Azmeh cabinet became more stiff after Nasser's speeches in July. On August 14, the supreme guide of the Muslim Brethren, Issam Attar, denounced the cabinet because it stubbornly persisted to rule without representing the people, and he called on it to resign.[136]

In early September, President Qudsi evidently became convinced of the need for a cabinet change, but he wanted the appointment of a new cabinet to conform to constitutional parliamentary rules by submitting the choice to a vote of confidence of the Chamber. In his talks with the army command, he was told that the officers were opposed to the restoration of the Chamber and to its meeting in the parliament building but they would agree to a face saving device by which the Chamber would meet once and then dissolve itself.[137]

On September 11, 1962, the members of the dissolved Chamber were invited to meet in the mansion of Khalid al-Azem. They met for one hour and appointed a committee to study and report on certain needed amendments to the constitution of 1950 which they decided to revive. The committee drafted ten articles that contained the necessary amendments. They allowed the executive power to issue legislative decrees for a certain period. They also gave the President and his cabinet the right to dissolve the Chamber within a year after its election, and permitted the Chamber to grant confidence to the prime minister alone without waiting for the formation of the entire cabinet. These two last amendments were to be considered provisional measures. On September 12 a second meeting was held in which it became known that Khalid al-Azem had been asked orally by the President to form a cabinet. The third and last meeting which was attended by Hourani's socialists, took place on September 13. The Chamber–acting as a constituent assembly–approved the proposed amendments to the constitution. The deputy speaker, Rafiq Bashour, then declared the role of the Chamber as a constituent assembly ended, and announced its transformation into a legislative body or chamber of deputies. In the meantime, Azem had received a formal letter from President Qudsi appointing him prime minister. He therefore read his ministerial statement to the members and asked for their confidence which was granted before the formation of his cabinet by 156 votes against one single vote.[138] Four days later, the Azem cabinet was formed, and on September 20 it ordered, according to a previously made agreement, the dissolution of the chamber of deputies which had given it confidence one week before.

The Chamber was evidently under great pressure to finish its work with that singular speed. Its three meetings came to a climax on the third day with the so-called "quiet, legal coup d'état" of September 13, 1962 which was believed to have restored constitutional rule. In Beirut, *L'Orient* believed that "the Syrians have re-discovered the institutions best suited to their country: a liberal, representative, parliamentary regime.[139] The coup, which was in reality a constitutional face-saving device, was unusual in many respects. It was made by a Chamber that the army had dissolved more than five months before, and whose resignation was announced by the President of the Republic shortly after. It courageously brought to the premiership a man who was jailed by the army in the coup of March 28, and who had openly declared himself opposed to Nasser's socialist laws and to unity with an Egypt dominated by Nasser's regime. The coup of September 13, however, looked strange and illogical because the Chamber that made it after a long and silent preparation in order to restore constitutional rule, ended by accepting to be dissolved and by even providing the necessary amendments that enabled the executive to dissolve it. The coup, therefore, was made in order to provide for a constitutional dissolution of the Chamber and to allow the formation of a constitutional cabinet, but not to restore constitutional rule. One of its aims was also to reaffirm the validity of the secession that occurred on September 28, 1961 and which some thought was invalidated by the coup of March 28, 1962.

In allowing the coup to take place through a compromise with the politicians, the army command was assured that the Chamber would be dissolved, and that, as under the previous Azmeh cabinet, General Zahreddin would assume "the power and prerogatives of defense minister." It also secured the nomination of the leftist ex-premier, Dr. Azmeh, as deputy prime minister. The Command, moreover, gave the new premier a list of persons from which he could choose his cabinet ministers, and although he chose some ministers from outside the list, he had to observe the veto of the military on certain political leaders.[140]

The cabinet formed by Khalid al-Azem on September 17, 1962, was one of national union. Most of the known parties were represented, but the nominee of the Aflaq Baathists never took office and resigned. In his ministerial statement before the Chamber, Premier Azem declared that his cabinet would work for Arab unity, and that it would maintain the existing legislation—as amended by the previous cabinet—on agrarian reform, labor benefits and other economic matters.

The statement, however, stressed the encouragement of private initiative, the belief in democracy and in the preservation and defense of the country's beliefs and values.[141]

The new cabinet directed much of its attention to economic development. It succeeded in implementing some of the projects that had been planned before and during the period of unity and obtained in mid-January, 1963 a loan of $87 million (350 million marks) from West Germany to help in the construction of a great dam on the Euphrates. One week after his appointment as prime minister, Azem assured the business leaders that there would be no more nationalization of local industries. The new cabinet included a number of socialist ministers and demonstrated its interest in the welfare of the peasant and the laborer by a number of measures. In the first week of its tenure, it issued a decree exempting the beneficiaries of land distribution from half the price of their land, which meant that they obtained their holdings free since the preceding Azmeh cabinet had exempted them from the first half. At the same time, the distribution of expropriated land was accelerated by the socialist agrarian reform minister, ex-Colonel Nufuri. The government also honored its pledges to the workers by granting them, on February 18, 1963, an extra month's salary as an advance payment on the profits made by their factories.

The Azem cabinet was planning to restore political activity and parliamentary rule in March, 1963. On November 21, 1962, it was decided that the emergency law that had been applied since the days of unity would be abolished on the first of January, 1963. Premier Azem then announced on December 21, 1962, that there was no democracy without parties. He expressed the view that public opinion in Syria did not follow any one particular political group, whatever its force might be, and therefore the idea of one ruling party would not succeed. He was obviously referring to the attempts of the military regimes—and that of Nasser in particular—to establish one-party rule. His cabinet was thwarted in its attempt to restore political party activity and to continue its work of economic and social development by civilian disorders and military dissension provoked primarily by a relentless campaign of subversion from Cairo. Many of those who supported this campaign were retired Syrian officers and civil servants, and partisans of the Aflaq–Bitar wing of the Baath Party who adopted the slogan, "the mistakes made under unity do not justify the destruction of unity." They worked with Nasser to undermine the Azem cabinet and Syrian sovereignty, but they had no clear idea how unity should be restored.

Between October 1962 and February 1963, incidents against the Azem government increased in intensity, and Nasserist propaganda became more provocative. Early in October, the Cairo radio urged the students in Syria to demonstrate, strike, and riot. The same radio circulated rumors about dismissals of laborers from their factories and urged workmen to strike. About the same time, the scandal of school textbooks exploded. It was found out that certain textbooks, which were usually published and sold to students by the ministry of education, still contained extracts of Nasser's and other Egyptian leaders' speeches as well as statements favorable to personal dictatorial rule. They carried the seal of the "Service of Textbooks" and the name of the Northern Region of the United Arab Republic. They were dated 1962, one year after the end of unity. This meant that certain responsible elements in the ministry of education had been working for Nasser. After a short investigation, it was decided to suppress the objectionable pages in the school books. On January 12 and 13, 1963, secondary school students rioted in the little town of Deraa, seventy miles to the south of Damascus, and in the smaller town of Sanamein at thirty-five miles to the south of the Syrian capital. The students used pistols, for the first time, in these unusually violent riots that ended with the death of one student and with thirteen wounded. On Saturday and Sunday, January 26-27 rioting erupted at the Syrian University, and was instigated and led mainly by Jordanian and Palestininian students. The Nasserists attacked their neutral or anti-Nasserist colleagues in the Students' Union with stones, sticks, and iron chains. The riots ended with forty-three wounded and one killed.

The government was on the defensive in dealing with pro-Nasserist subversion. It suppressed Nasserist activities only when they threatened public order, and it issued defensive declarations over the radio only to answer Nasser's Voice of the Arabs and other broadcasts and their accusations and fabrications. The press, basically anti-Nasserist, supported the government, and certain authors even counter-attacked and wrote books exposing Nasser's damaging un-Arab activities. One of them was entitled "The Black Book" and sold an unusual 25,000 copies in two editions, and the other bore the title of, "Abdul Nasser Began in Damascus and Ended at Shtura." Political leaders spoke of Nasser as "the new imperialism in the service of the old imperialism," and accused him of helping Israel expand in Africa by allowing Israeli navigation through the Gulf of Aqaba.[143]

C. The Attempted Coup of January 13, 1963

The Azem government was supported in its suppression of pro-Nasserist riots by the army high command that seemed to be in firm control of the armed forces. Events later showed that the authority of the Command was more apparent than real, and Commander in Chief Zahreddin himself revealed that his director of military intelligence deceived him and plotted against the regime, and that there was no cooperation between the heads of internal security and military intelligence.[144] The attempt to disturb the relative peace that had reigned among the military since Azem took over power in September 1962 did not originate, however, with the Syrian officers at home. The leaders of the abortive coup of January 13, 1963—the tenth since the first coup of 1949—were the exiled officers who had been sent abroad as military attachés on April 2, 1962 as a result of the military congress of Homs. Their ring leader was that notorious Abdul Karim Nahlawi who had organized the two previous coups of September 28, 1961 and March 28, 1962. It was disclosed later that while these officers were in their diplomatic posts, they were approached by Nasserist agents and at times they forwarded demands of military and political nature to the government. In May 1962, the Azmeh cabinet had decided to retire them from the army and transfer them to the ministry of foreign affairs, but their supporters in the active service then protested and the decision was postponed. It was carried out, however, in early January 1963 in view of their continued political interventions. Nahlawi and his colleagues reacted immediately against the government decision. After arranging a rendezvous in Turkey, they crossed the border into Syria on Wednesday, January 9 and tried to enlist the support of their former units.

The returning officers had been assured of the cooperation of some junior officers of their group in the army units near Damascus. It is also claimed that other military factions such as that of Colonel Ziad Hariri, who was preparing to lead a coup d'état against the ruling regime, encouraged the Nahlawi group in order to involve them and then have them removed from the service after abandoning them to their fate. Similarly, the rightist group of officers that supported the government and included Colonel Muti' al-Samman, the director of security, is said to have encouraged the Nahlawi attempt in order to remove General Zahreddin from the Command and then turn against Nahlawi's young supporters. This is why Nahlawi and his friends were able to enter Syria through a police post near the Turkish border and to stay in Damascus undisturbed for six days.[145]

Before Nahlawi's return, General Zahreddin had warned the commanders of the units at Qatana, Qabun and Kisweh about the activity of the pro-Nahlawi junior officers in their camps. It is possible that the student riots at Deraa and Sanamein on January 12 and 13 were instigated by these officers after the return of Nahlawi and his colleagues in order to put pressure on the government and abolish the decree of their transfer to the foreign service.

In the afternoon of January 13, 1963 the pro-Nahlawi junior officers were able to surround their camps with tanks after the end of office hours, profiting from the absence of other officers. They then demanded from the government the reinstatement of Nahlawi and his friends in the army, the implementation of the Homs resolutions that included a referendum on the union with Egypt, and the reshuffling of the high command. The officers must have known that Nasser's condition for union was the acceptance of his socialist system and the completion of the political and social revolution in the country that sought union.[146] This meant a complete ban on political parties and amounted to the acceptance of Nasser's system of rule and domination. Neither the military leaders, nor the politicians were sure if they would accept these conditions. But, for Nahlawi and his colleagues, as well as for many others as events have amply proved, the demand for a union with Egypt had become an instrument of opposition to the existing government and a pretext for forcing a change in the military command, and in brief, a step forward on the road to the conquest of power.

Nahlawi and his colleagues had forwarded their demands to the government soon after their return. President Qudsi and the cabinet promised to give them due consideration in order to gain time. A committee of officers was sent by the Command, at Qudsi's suggestion, to advise the insurgent officers to end their rebellion, but when it was reported that some of their tanks had moved from the camps of Qatana and Kisweh towards Damascus, General Zahreddin ordered the commander of an armored battalion to defend the Army Headquarters and break the assault of the rebels. Zahreddin has related that he had been to the presidential palace in the late afternoon of January 13 to meet President Qudsi and protest against the indifference of the internal security administration and its failure to arrest Nahlawi, but he could hardly believe his eyes when he saw Nahlawi and his colleagues at the Palace. President Qudsi evidently received the returning officers in order to lecture them on the wrongfulness of taking the law into their hands. General Zahreddin in his turn warned Nahlawi that the forces on the southern front as well as those at Homs, Latakia and Jabal Druze were ready to support the Command. Zahreddin also reached the insurgent officers south of Damascus by phone and told them that they should surrender before dawn. Their number did not exceed thirty. They finally realized that the Command was ready to use its superior forces against them and that those who promised them support, like Colonel Hariri, abandoned them and even threatened to march to Damascus to oppose them. They consequently surrendered at about 3 a.m., twelve hours after their rebellion began. The armored battalion deployed by the Command was withdrawn from the army headquarters in the morning, and for some time, the press correspondents, and even the heads of some civilian departments believed that it belonged to the rebellious officers.[147]

The Nahlawi attempt to dictate government policy or even o overthrow the cabinet by the threat of force thus ended in failure. The adventurous officers who had arrived in Damascus on January 9 and plunged the country into a crisis, were not even jailed or tried. They were sent back on January 14 as counselors of embassy in various European capitals. The success of the civilian government in overruling the Nahlawi clique must be attributed to the cooperation of the army command, and to the opposition of the majority of officers to Nahlawi an his group of Damascene officers. At the end of the crisis, a conference of officers decided by a majority vote that those officers who participated in the abortive attempt on Nahlawi's side should be tried after they had been arrested, but due to the clemency of President Qudsi, they were kept in jail for only forty-five days. The conference also believed that the sentences passed on January 17 against the participants in the Aleppo coup of April 1, 1962 should be executed. President Qudsi, known for his cool temper and opposition to drastic measures, refused, and so did General Zahreddin. The sentences were still lying in Qudsi's drawer when his rule ended in the coup of March 8, 1963.

CHAPTER III

Notes

1. Reported in *Time,* March 15, 1963
2. See Albert Hourani,*Arabic Thought in the Liberal Age* (London: Oxford University Press, 1962), 317.
3. On the clash of rival powers in Syria, the Egyptian offensive and its results see Patrick Seale, *The Struggle for Syria* (London: Oxford University Press, 1965), 194, 213, 229, 249 ff.
4. See among others, Walid Khalidi, "Political Trends in the Fertile Crescent," in *The Middle East in Transition,* ed. W. Z. Laqueur (New York: Praeger, 1958); George Kirk, *Contemporary Arab Politics* (New York: Praeger, 1961), 24-26; H. B. Sharabi, *Governments and Politics in The Middle East in the 20th Century* (Princeton: Van Nostrand, 1962), 123.
5. See R. Bayly Winder, "Syrian Deputies and Cabinet Ministers 1919-1959" *Middle East Journal,* XVI (1962), 419 and XVII (1963), 41-42.
6. For details and comparisons especially with Egypt, see article by Awad Barakat, former Syrian minister of economy, in *al-Nasr* (Damascus), January 30, 1962.
7. For details on this economic growth see A. J. Meyer, *Middle Eastern Capitalism* (Cambridge: Harvard University Press, 1959), 3 ff.; R. S. Porter, "The Growth of the Syrian Economy," *Middle East Forum* (November, 1963), 17-22; Awad Barakat, *loc. cit.*
8. On sectarianism, the Baath and socialism see the book of the former Baath party secretary-general, Munif al-Razzaz, *al-Tajribah al-Murrah* (The Bitter Experiment), (Beirut, 1967), 158.
9. See Georgiana Stevens, *Egypt Yesterday and Today* (New York: Holt, Rinehart Winston, 1963), .128; Charles D. Cremeans, *The Arabs and the World* (New York: Praeger, 1963) 197; see also Muhammad Hassanein Haikal, *Ma Lladhi Jara fi Suriyah* (What Happened in Syria), (Cairo, 1962), 40 for the alleged warning that President Quwatli of Syria gave to Nasser on the difficulty of dealing with the Syrians at the time of unity in 1958.
10. See William R. Polk, *The United States and the Arab World* (Cambridge: Harvard University Press, 1965), 136, 222.
11. This was related by Majid Khadduri in "The Army Officer: His Role in Middle Eastern Politics," in *Social Forces in the Middle East,* ed. Sydney N. Fisher (Ithaca: Cornell University Press, 1955), 162 ff.
12. Among other writers on this assumption, Manfred Halpern, *The Politics of Social Change in the Middle East and North Africa* (Princeton: Princeton Univ. Press, 1963), 257.
13. For a general analysis of army attitudes, see Dankwart A. Rustow, "The Military in Middle Eastern Society and Politics," in *The Military in the Middle East,* ed. Sydney N. Fisher (Columbus: Ohio State University Press, 1961), 11-12.

14. See the report on the trial of Major Hamad Ubaid for his role in the pro-Nasserist coup of April 1, 1962 in Aleppo, in *al-Nasr* (Damascus), October 2, 1962.
15. See Dankwart A. Rustow, "The Military in Middle Eastern Society and Politics," *loc. cit.*, 10-11.
16. See The Middle East Journal, III (July 1949), 316-17; 327-28; Alford Carleton, "The Syrian Coups d'Etat of 1949," *MEJ* IV (January, 1950), 4; see the text of the communiqué in Muhammad Khalil, I, 521 ff.
17. See Nasser Nashashibi, *Madha Jara Fil Sharq al-Awsat,* (What Happened in the Middle East?), (Beirut, 1961), 55; see also *Memoirs of Muhammad Mahdi Kubbah* (in Arabic), (Beirut, 1965), 298; See P. Seale, 41 for the Bustani affair and the cooking fat scandal.
18. The present writer, however, heard from a highly placed person who worked for the U.S. Information Service in Lebanon at the time that the coup was encouraged by the French. The same person related that he went to Damascus to warn Quwatli, but the latter, in his confident mood, refused to believe and told him that Husni al-Zaim was like his own child, and that he was brought up under his protection.
19. Told by Faris to the author; see Hanna Khabbaz and George Haddad, *Faris al-Khouri, Hayatuhu wa Asruhu,* (Faris al-Khouri, His life and Times), (Beirut, 1952), 250.
20. Developments of the Quarter, in *The Middle East Journal,* III (July 1949), 316-27.
21. The code was adapted from the Egyptian civil code, which had been recently drawn from European models. For details on the reforms and activities of Zaim, see Fathallah Saqqal, *Min Dhikrayat al-Zaim Husni al-Zaim* (Memoirs on Colonel Husni al-Zaim), (Cairo, 1951).
22. *The Middle East Journal,* III (October 1949), 442.
23. Emir Adel Arslan, *Dhikrayat al-Emir Adel Arslan 'an Husni al-Zaim* (Memoirs of Emir Adel Arslan on Husni al-Zaim), (Beirut, 1962), pp. 43-46. On p. 60, Emir Adel refers to the absurd reports of spies which Zaim showed him. He also mentions that the number of spies was 1,500 of whom 200 were in Lebanon. Zaim seems to have thought that the coup against his regime could originate in Lebanon. Emir Adel also mentioned the close supervision imposed on Qudsi and Kekhia, the arrest of Ajlani and Aflaq, and forcing the latter to renounce his Baath principles.
24. Carleton,*loc. cit.*, 10.
25. *Ibid.*, 7.
26. Arslan, 30.
27. The colloquial expression which he was reported to have used was, "Yikhrib Baitak!" (May God ruin your house!) See Nashashibi, 59.

28. Among the expressions of his childish and reckless behavior, and his loose tongue, were his threats to hang King Abdallah of Jordan in the Marje Square in Damascus, and his calling the British Ambassador to tell him on one occasion, "We are declaring war on Britain." The Jordan radio retaliated by calling Zaim "bandit, sot, and tyrant."
29. See Fadlallah Abu-Mansur, *A'asir* (Storms), (n.p. Beirut?, n.d. 1959?), 56 ff; for his description of the coup and his role in it, 63 ff.; for his discovery that the conspirators acted with Iraq's inspiration, 80; see also Patrick Seale's description of the coup, 73-76.
30. See account of Nashashibi, 61-62 who gives a slightly different version on the arrest and execution of Zaim and Barazi.
31. See text of Communiqué no. 1 and 5 in Muh. Khalil, I, 528-531.
32, For details on the Shishakli coup vs. Hinnawi, see Abu-Mansur, 84-104.
33. Walid Khalidi, "Political Trends in the Fertile Crescent," in *The Middle East in Transition,* ed. Walter Z. Laqueur, (New York: F. A. Praeger, 1958), 122.
34. In 1949, when Husni al-Zaim made his coup, the rank of *zaim* that he had was equivalent to that of colonel. Shortly after, a redefinition of ranks took place and the rank of *zaim* became the equivalent of brigadier general, while *aqid* became the equivalent of colonel.
35. These and other details in this chapter were taken from the author's diaries. See also Nicola A. Ziadeh, *Syria and Lebanon,* (London: Ernest Benn, 1957), pp. 112 ff.; Gordon H. Torrey, *Syrian Politics and the Military 1945-1958* (Columbus: Ohio State University Press, 1964); Patrick Seale, 92 ff.
36. Sharabi, 128-129.
37. The present writer remembers the humiliating and comical experience that he and his colleagues of the Syrian University went through at the Department of Justice. Only three professors of the law school who were deputies in the dissolved Chamber did not comply and they were dismissed from their positions.
38. The presidential constitution of July 1953 and Shishakli's statement on the draft constitution can be seen in Muhammad Khalil, I, 560 ff.
39. *The Times,* February 4, 1954.
40. See the statement of Captain Mustafa Hamdun in M. Khalil I, 592.
41. See Patrick Seale, 141.
42. See Abu-Mansur, 127. Abu-Mansur himself was not reinstated; he had been dismissed by Shishakli in December 1952.
43. Simon Jargy, "Le declin d'un parti," *Orient,* No. 11 (1959, 3), 21-38; Lenczowski, *The Middle East in World Affairs,* 367, speaks of a triumvirate of Hourani, Azem and Sarraj; the BBC on November 25, 1956, spoke of Syria as being ruled in Soviet style by the trio, Bakdash, Sarraj and Bitar.

44. Reported by Patrick Seale, 239.
45. *Ibid.*, 223; Nashashibi, 369.
46. *The New York Times,* September 29, 1961 quoted a highly placed Egyptian official who spoke of Sarraj as "Nasser's faithful dog"; Haikal, 23, 103 says that Sarraj "could hear the ant if it crawled in Syria."
47. *The Times,* November 28, 1956.
48. According to a rumor, Malki had intimate relations with the assassin's sister and refused to marry her. It was said also that the SSNP secretary George Abdul Massih who lived in Damascus made the decision to eliminate Malki without consulting the party.
49. On August 31, 1956, Jalal al-Sayyid, a former Baath leader who became disenchanted with Baath politics, spoke in the Chamber of those politicians who hide behind the students and say "we shall fight to the last student."
50. The revelations by Nizar Raslan, agent of Procon Company that made the favorable bid, had to be presented in the press in the form of a paid advertisement on April 24, 1957.
51. Some details on the Iraqi conspiracy were revealed by the trial of officers of the old regime in Iraq: see *Proceedings of the People's Court* (in Arabic), I (Baghdad, 1958), 271; see also Patrick Seale, 263-280.
52. Reported by the leftist weekly, *al-Sarkha,* April 17, 1957.
53. Mrs. Faris al-Khouri told the author that at a certain moment in the course of the voting, which seems to have been fixed beforehand by the Baathist and Communist women, a group of girls who were campaigning for Malki, surrounded her, snatched her purse and began to shout, "Isterlini wa dolarat" (pounds sterling and dollars) in order to intimidate those who were voting for Sebai. The shouting of the slogan lasted more than one hour until the police came and escorted her to her home.
54. See Patrick Seale on the entire crisis in August, 291 ff.
55. See for this claim, Haikal, 16, 22.
56. On the need of "some new injection of prestige" felt by the Egyptian Junta, see Kirk, *Contemporary Arab Politics,* 101.
57. See Charles Issawi, "The United Arab Republic," *Current History* (February, 1959), 66; on the hopes of Nasser, see also Simon Jargy, "La Syrie province de la republique arabe unie," *Orient,* No. 8 (1958, 4), 24; see also Nasser's *Egypt's Liberation: the Philosophy of the Revolution,* (Washington D.C.: Public Affairs Press, 1956), 88 ff., 109 ff.
58. F. Sayegh, "Arab Unity," (New York: Arab Information Center, 1958), 7-15.
59. See Patrick Seale, 318.

60. Haikal, *op. cit.*, 29-41.
61. See this version in P. Seale, 314-326; see also Abdul Karim Zahreddin, *Mudhakkirati 'an Fitrat al-Infisal* (My Memoirs on the Period of Separation), (Beirut, 1968), 17-18.
62. Text of Zahreddin's declaration in *Haqiqat al-Thawrah wa Ahdafuha* (The Truth on the Revolution and Its Aims), (Damascus: Publications of the Directorate of General Affairs and Moral Guidance of the Arab Syrian Army, 1961), 62; Nasser's statement and Bitar's explanation in *Proceedings of the Sessions on Unity Discussions* (Cairo, 1963), 99-100.
63. Quoted by P. Seale, 326.
64. *al-Nasr,* August 24, 1962.
65. *al-Akhbar* (Damascus) May 16, 1959 quoting *Akhbar al-Yawm* (Cairo); Haikal, 79; P. Seale, 321.
66. The title was mentioned in the telegram which Quwatli sent on February 5, 1958 to the National Assembly in Egypt saying that he considered it his duty to be the first citizen in the new state to propose the candidacy of Nasser for the presidency. See text of his telegram in Salaheddin Munajjed ed., *Suriyya wa Misr Bayn al-Wahdah wal Infisal,* (Syria and Egypt Between Unity and Separation), (Beirut, 1962), 19.
67. For Aflaq's declaration and the hopes of the Baath, see *L'Orient* (Beirut) February 25, 1958; Jargy, "Le Declin d'un Parti," *Orient,* no. 11 (1959, 3), 31-32.
68. Jargy, 29 ff.
69. See the prediction by Charles Issawi, "The United Arab Republic," *Current History,* February 1959, p. 69.
70. *al-Nasr,* October 4, 1961; *The Economist,* October 15, 1960, p. 259 said that the special police of Sarraj counted 12-15,000.
71. Haikal, 90 ff.
72. *al-Nasr,* October 11, 1961.
73. See declarations by Izzat al-Nousse, minister of education after secession, in Munajjed, 152 ff.
74. See declaration of Izzat Tarabulsi in *al-Hayat,* October 14, 1961, and in Munajjed, 185 ff.
75. See the declaration of the Grand Mufti, Abu'l Yusr Abdin, in Munajjed, 169; *al-Nasr,* October 2, 1961.
76. Complaints against the Baathist minister of agrarian reform led to the appointment of a committee of five persons after Amer's arrival in Damascus in October, 1959, to supervise the implementation of the reform. The committee was well-received except by the Baathists who resented its formation, and consequently the agrarian reform minister, Mustafa Hamdun, was the first to resign, and was followed by Hourani.
77. See Izzat Tarabulsi in Munajjed, 187 ff.

78. For details on these decrees and on the socialist system, Malcolm H. Kerr, "The Emergence of a Socialist Ideology in Egypt," *The Middle East Journal,* XVI (Spring, 1962), 128 ff; see infra ch. I of vol. III on Egypt, the section on socialism.
79. For details see Zahreddin's *Memoirs,* 17-21 where he mentions twelve causes for the officers' discontent and sixteen for that of the civilians.
80. Faris al-Khouri advised Nasser to stop his attacks against the other Arab countries and to encourage them to join the UAR, but he did the opposite. See *al-Hayat,* October 7, 1961. See President Quwatli's statement on his warnings to Nasser in *al-Nasr,* October 24, 1961.
81. On the story of Sarraj, see Haikal, 113 ff.; Zahreddin's *Memoirs,* 31 ff.
82. *Ibid.*, 25 ff for the military action during the coup.
83. *Ibid.*, 30; Reuter in *al-Hayat,* October 5, 1961 said 20 to 25 persons were killed and 100 or more were wounded.
84. The five dismissed by Nasser after communiqué no. 12 were: Brig. Genls. Abdul Ghani Dahman, Muwaffaq Assasa, Faisal Sirri al-Husseini, Lt. Cols. Abdul Karim Nahlawi and Haidar Kuzbari, according to Zahreddin's *Memoirs,* 65.
85. Declaration of the Revolutionary Command spokesman in the press conference, Brig. Gen. Dahman, on October 4, 1961; Munajjed, 136 ff; see Haikal, 127 on the alleged contacts between Lt. Col. Kuzbari and King Hussein, and between the latter and King Saud who provided the funds. When Saud knew about the success of the coup, he allegedly danced with the sword.
86. *Haqiqat al-Thawrah, op. cit.*, pp. 28-29.
87. Seven members of the cabinet had doctorates in law, medicine, or letters and the rest were engineers or lawyers. Only four of them had been cabinet ministers before.
88. *Haqiqat al-Thawrah,* 38; see the ministerial statement, pp. 36-41; also in Zahreddin's *Memoirs,* 84-87.
89. The first Syrian republic was founded in 1930 and continued, with an interruption (1939-43), until 1949. The second was established by the constitution of 1950 that followed the military coups of 1949. In December, 1951, the second Syrian republic was ended by the dictatorship of Shishakli, who introduced a presidential constitution in 1953. The second republic was resumed in February 1954, and lasted until 1958 and ended with unity.
90. Quoted in *The New York Times,* December 10, 1961.
91. See the manifesto in *Haqiqat al-Thawrah,* Vol. II, pp. 49-58; an analysis of the manifesto can be found in "Le liberalisme socialiste," by Doctor Albert Coudsi in *L'economie et les finances de la Syrie et des Pays Arabes,* October, 1961.
92. Nizar Arabi, in *al-Nasr,* October 16, 1961.
93. Text in *Haqiqat al-Thawrah,* 72. Among those who signed were Hourani, Asali, Bitar, Azme, and Azem.

94. Iran also recognized the new regime on the first day, but relations with Egypt were already broken.
95. See, in particular, the editorial of Rafiq al-Maaluf in *al-Zaman,* and quoted in *al-Nasr,* October 13, 1961. The editorial was entitled "The Government of Lebanon and the High Commissioner," (Abdul Hamid Ghaleb, the Ambassador of Egypt).
96. The text of his speech of October 5, in Munajjed, 294-305.
97. Jargy, "La Syrie province de la république arabe unie," *loc. cit.*, 18.
98. The two articles of Taha Hussein in *al-Gumhouriya,* October 7, and 14, 1961, quoted in Munajjed, 328 ff.
99. See the answers of Premier Kuzbari and cabinet ministers A. Barakat and I. Nousse in Munajjed, 139-143, 147-154.
100. See Marcel Colombe, "La république arabe syrienne à la lumière du coup d'état du 28 Mars," *Orient,* no. 21, (1962, 1) pp. 11 ff; Lenczowski, in *Current History,* April, 1962, p. 207; *al-Hayat,* March 29, 1962.
101. See Zahreddin's *Memoirs,* 159-161, 149.
102. *Ibid.*, 165, 185.
103. Text in *al-Nasr,* February 8 and 9, 1962; Eva Garzouzi, "Land Reform in Syria," *The Middle East Journal,* XVII, (Winter–Spring, 1963), 85-88.
104. Zahreddin's *Memoirs,* 186.
105. *Ibid.*, 164-176. Zahreddin admitted that two officers were sent to the meeting.
106. *al-Hayat,* March 22, 1962.
107. *al-Nasr,* February 19-21, 1962. As early as November 6, 1961, a Syrian official delegation went to Beirut to present a protest to Lebanese foreign affairs minister, Philip Taqla against the unfriendly attitude of the Lebanese government, and supported their protest by facts on the anti-Syrian activity of the Egyptian ambassador in Lebanon.
108. Haikal, 124; *al-Hayat,* April 3, 1962; Zahreddin's *Memoirs,* 144 ff.
109. See *al-Nasr,* April 3, August 28, 1962; Zahreddin, 164 ff.; Nasser claimed that he refused the Syrian officers' suggestion to restore unity through a coup. See *Proceedings of the Sessions on Unity Discussions,* 105.
110. *al-Hayat,* March 29, 1962; the trials were then dominated by political and partisan considerations and were made under a regime of martial law.
111. The communiqués and proclamations can be read in *al-Nasr,* March 29, 1962; some extracts are in *The New York Times,* March 29, 1962; see also Zahreddin, 196 ff; *al-Ahram,* March 29-31, 1962.
112. Akram Hourani who made this accusation in *al-Nasr,* June 14, 1962, says that he knew that the officers were planning a coup and he

warned them against Nasser's real intentions. Hourani also accused Nasser of wanting to conceal thereby his crime of allowing Israel a free hand in diverting the Jordan River waters; see also Zahreddin, 209, 232 on Nasser's double role and the revelations of Nahlawi himself.

113. See the report of the General Prosecutor in the trial of the officers in the Aleppo coup. *al-Nasr,* November 21, 1962.
114. *al-Hayat,* April 5, 1962, quoting the ABC Correspondent, said that 200 Nasserist officers were dismissed in the six months that followed the coup of September 28, 1961.
115. The director of police in Aleppo, Colonel Daghestani, testified in court in October, 1962, that officials of the U.S. Consulate in Aleppo participated in distributing Nasser's pictures. See *al-Nasr,* October 22, 1962. This was also mentioned in a report by the Public Prosecutor that appeared in *al-Nasr,* November 21, 1962.
116. General Zahreddin's *Memoirs* published in 1968, gave for the first time a possibly authoritative list of the resolutions but did not mention the question of Qudsi's return; see also *al-Bayan* (New York), April 7, 1962; *al-Hayat,* April 5 and 6, 1962.
117. The seven officers whose names were mentioned in *al-Hayat,* April 4, 1962, were Brig. Genls. Abdul Ghani Dahman, Hisham Abd Rabbu, Colonels Abdul Karim Nahlawi, Muhib Hindi, Fayez Rifai, Bassam Asali, and Adel Haj Ali.
118. Communiqués mentioned in the sentences against the Aleppo rebels, in *al-Nasr,* January 18, 1963; see also *al-Hayat,* and *The New York Times,* April 4, 1962.
119. The sentences and their preamble were published in *al-Nasr,* January 18, 1963. Louay Atassi was sent to Washington as military attaché directly after the collapse of the coup. He was brought back as a witness in early November 1962, and was arrested for his role in the coup.
120. The Prosecutor's report in *al-Nasr,* November 21, 1962.
121. *The New York Times,* April 4, 1962.
122. *al-Hayat,* April 6, 1962; *The New York Times,* April 8, 1962.
123. *The New York Times,* editorial of April 4, 1963.
124. Zahreddin's *Memoirs,* 240.
125. *al-Hayat,* April 12 and 13, 1962; Zahreddin, 245 said that more than half of the deputies resigned.
126. The decree gave the peasant immediate possession of the land, reduced his payment to half the amount, allowed the landlord to retain larger holdings in the northeastern provinces, and paid the landlord the price of his land over fifteen years instead of forty. *al-Nasr,* May 2, and 3, 1962.
127. The shares of the company were converted to state bonds payable in

fifteen years with 21/2 per cent interest. The Syrian Economic Organization was to supervise the company, and legislation was promised for giving shares to small stockholders and employees. *al-Nasr,* May 22, 1962.

128. *al-Nasr,* May 21, 1962. Already on April 26, a decree had appeared organizing the elections of workers' and employees' representatives to the board of directors of corporations. For the law on banking see *al-Nasr,* May 25, 1962.
129. *al-Hayat,* April 26, 1962.
130. *al-Nasr,* April 27, May 20, 1962. The still-born committee was called "committee on Arab affairs and unity."
131. *al-Hayat,* July 22, 1962; *al-Nasr,* August 16, 1962; see Zahreddin, 281-304 for details of the discovery of the conspiracy and the reports of the Syrian agents of the military intelligence.
132. See, for example, "Open Letter to the Ambassador of the United States in Damascus," by Rafiq Maqdisi, in *al-Nasr,* July 13, 1962.
133. *al-Nasr,* July 10, 1962.
134. See the declaration of Doctor Azmeh in *Time,* August 24, 1962, where he says, "Syrians will never again accept tyranny . . . by its very nature, Syria lives on commerce . . . we favor free enterprise and private business; we are against feudalism and exploitation."
135. For the Shtura Conference see *Documents of the Syrian Complaint Against Nasserist Intervention* (in Arabic), (Damascus: Ministry of Foreign Affairs, 1962).
136. *al-Nasr,* August 14, and 15, 1962.
137. See Zahreddin, 319-24 for the account of the meetings with Qudsi and the officers' conditions.
138. For a description of the meetings and the text of the amendments, *al-Hayat,* September 12, 13, 14, 1962; *al-Nasr,* September 9-14, 1962.
139. Quoted in *Time,* September 21, 1962. *Time* also referred to the restoration of constitutional rule and to the return of the army "to soldiering" as a result of the "quiet, legal coup." The restoration of constitutional life was mentioned in an editorial of *al-Nasr,* September 16, 1962.
140. In *al-Hayat,* March 14, 1963, the names of Dawalibi, Leon Zamariya and Rashad Jabri were cited as being the candidates whose appointment in the cabinet was vetoed by the army; see also Zahreddin, 324-325.
141. Ministerial statement in *al-Nasr,* September 14, 1962.
142. When the third conference of cooperation among afro-Asian peoples was held in Tanganyika on February 4, 1963, the two Baath leaders attended as representatives of the Syrian people. Their activities were supposedly financed by President Nasser.
143. Amin Nufuri and Akram Hourani in *al-Nasr,* January 6, 1963.
144. Zahreddin, 343-348.

145. *Ibid.*, 348-355. The Damascene press did not report the entire Nahlawi attempt. Details are given in Zahreddin, 355-370; *al- Hayat,* January 15-17, *N. Y. Times,* January 16, 17, 1963.
146. These Nasserist conditions for union had been proclaimed in March, 1962. Again in mid-January, 1963, Muhammad Hassanein Haikal wrote an article on them in *al-Ahram* as a reminder, and its contents were quoted in *al-Nasr,* January 20, 1963.
147. See the account of Zahreddin; 363 ff. and the reports in *al-Hayat* and *The N. Y. Times,* January 16, 17, 1963.

CHAPTER IV

The Baath Regime in Syria: Military Coups d'Etat and Popular Revolts 1963-1969

The Baath party succeeded as no other party has done in the recent history of Syria in imposing its exclusive rule over the country with the help of its military officers. The party was ultimately dominated by the officers who brought it to power. The military Baathists set out first to destroy the groups opposed to their party in three successive coups d'état, and then engaged in a power struggle among themselves that has produced so far four military coups. They imposed a socialist system that led to popular revolts and brought economic stagnation and weakness, while the chaos engendered by their factional struggles and arbitrary rule led to insecurity and defeat, and to the Israeli occupation of a part of Syrian territory.

I. The End of Semi-Constitutional Rule: The Coup d'Etat of March 8, 1963

The Azem cabinet continued in office for eight weeks after the riots of Deraa and the abortive Nahlawi coup. It was supported by substantial anti-Nasserist forces and was not ready to resign. The Syrian-Lebanese border through which "the winds of intrigue" and Nasserist agents passed to Syria was closed after the Deraa riots. On February 6, 1963 the secret Nasserist radio station established in the border village of Deir al-Ashayer in Lebanon for beaming propaganda against Syria was blown up by a Syrian force. In early February, Premier Azem made certain declarations that optimistically underestimated the power of his Nasserist adversaries and their Baathist allies. He referred to those insignificant few who "work for a fee," and who "sell their conscience to others." He predicted that the month of February which Nasser usually exploited for creating trouble–on the occasion of the anniversary of the defunct Syrian unity with Egypt–would pass peacefully.

The month of February did indeed pass without major incidents in Syria, but in Iraq a military coup d'état was successfully staged against the Kassem regime on February 8, 1963 by Baathist and pro-Nasserist officers. The presence of a new revolutionary government in Iraq that was friendly to Nasser lent support to the Syrian opposition and practically meant the doom of the Azem cabinet which managed to survive for another month. In early March 1963, a Syrian "central command of the unionist movement" appealed to its followers to "destroy the nests of treason, reaction, and vassalage, and of opportunism and separatism in Syria."[1]

In dealing with the plots and open attacks that sought to destroy it, the Syrian government was handicapped by political rivalries and disagreements between the radical Hourani socialists and the conservative Muslim Brethren within and outside the cabinet. Another basic cause of trouble was that the Hourani socialists had their eyes fixed already on the future elections and, in preparation for them, they wanted to eliminate their opponents from various sensitive posts in the administration. An acute cabinet crisis erupted before the end of January when the three socialist ministers resigned and were followed by the two ministers of the Muslim Brethren. The populist minister of education had already withdrawn from the cabinet. It was only on February 16 that the resignations of the six ministers were accepted, but the Azem cabinet decided to remain in power as a neutral cabinet rather than one of national union.

The Azem cabinet tried to conciliate the Aflaq wing of

the Baath and its leaders by giving them pensions for the few years, or even months, of service in the government, and by offering them cabinet posts during the ministerial crisis in early February. The Baathist leaders accepted the pensions but refused the posts. The Syrian government, furthermore, made a desperate but fruitless effort after the Iraqi coup of February 8, to reach an understanding with the new regime in Iraq in order to avert the formation of a hostile coalition of Egypt, Iraq, and the Syrian Baath. Moreover, the Syrian delegation that was sent to Baghdad to congratulate the new government never reached the Iraqi capital and was told to postpone the visit until conditions in Iraq become more settled.[2]

The Syrian traditional elite reacted, but too late, against the threatening danger and presented on February 16 a memoir to President Qudsi emphasizing the need for stability and national unity, and the necessity of defending the constitution by holding elections. The memoir was signed by political, economic and religious leaders and was handed to Qudsi by three leading personalities. The aim of the leaders was to form a Popular Organization movement to counteract the Nasserist-Baathist action and help restore the confidence of the people, and to prepare for the return of constitutional rule. The movement was supported by Premier Azem, but did not receive Qudsi's encouragement. The executive power was thus paralyzed by disagreement, not only between ministers and parties in the cabinet but also between the president and his prime minister.

The Azem cabinet had taken over the government in September 1962 in a peculiar, peaceful coup, and it managed to survive for about six eventful months. It was finally swept away by the coup d'état of March 8, 1963. It has been said that what happened on March 8 was "a coup by default produced by the utter exhaustion of all the forces that might have stood against it." [3] In reality, the forces that could have prevented the coup were not so much exhausted as corrupted by the plots, intrigues and incitements, from within and outside Syria, that created division and disloyalty in military ranks and weakened the morale of the cabinet. The coup d'état became inevitable and Damascus lived in the shadow of an expected army intervention because the officers of the Damascus region who could have defended the Azem regime and the capital were drawn to the conspiracy. The parties and factions that participated in preparing the coup were the Baathists, the Nasserists, the members of the Arab nationalists' movement, and the socialist unionists. The Baathists were the best organized and contributed most to the planning of the coup although their officers in the active service were few as a result of purges during the period of unity and immediately after the breakup of the United Arab Republic. The secretary general of the Baath party, Munif Razzaz, has told us, however, when he wrote later in 1967 that the coup of March 8, 1963 was a purely military coup and that the Baath party, i.e. the national civilian organization, neither planned nor executed it. He has also explained that the Baathist organization in the army, or the Baath military committee, acted independently and amounted to another Baath party, and this was the source of serious trouble later between the national leadership of the Baath and the Baathist officers.[4]

Among the four groups that prepared the coup of March 8, the Nasserists had the largest number of officers. They wanted the return of unity with Egypt, but had neither organization nor plan. The various issues, including those of unity and socialism, united these factions, military as well as civilian, against the Qudsi-Azem regime and in favor of a coup, but the same factions and cliques disagreed on the details and on the plans for what was to come after the coup. The lines often were not sharply drawn between their goals nor between the persons belonging to them. The affiliations of officers were often determined by personal rivalries and by loyalties to individual military leaders or to regional groups, and these affiliations and loyalties often changed.

The army included, moreover, a number of opportunists who were moved by ambition and the prospect of personal gain but who could be included in the general category of unionists. One of them was Colonel Ziad Hariri, commander of the southern front forces, whose name was mentioned in the rumors since early February as the officer most likely to stage the coup. He was chosen by the Nasserists and Baathists for his adventurous spirit, his self conceit, and his burning desire to exercise power. They tried to satisfy his ambition by placing him in the limelight and making him the equal of the Damascene director of internal security, Col. Muti al-Samman, the champion of the anti-Unionists who gave the government a false picture of the situation with his reassurances that coups d'état were no longer possible.[5] Hariri was chosen by the planners of the coup also because of his friendship with the director of military intelligence, Colonel Adnan Aqil, and his assistant, Colonel Marwan Kailani, and with several brigade commanders of the Damascus region who were all his colleagues at the Military Academy. The commander-in-chief, General Zahreddin, has related how the director of army intelligence, Colonel Aqil, deceived him when he was sent to inquire among the units along the front about the truth of the rumors relating to Hariri and then returned to say that the rumors were false and were intended only to disturb the government.[6] Hariri was not only plotting, but at times he and his colleagues also presented their demands and views openly to the cabinet on the question of unity and relations with Nasser. On the night of February 21 when Hariri was expected to march on Damascus, according to a rumor, he allegedly presented certain demands to the government.[7]

The Syrian government took precautions after the Iraqi coup of February 8, 1963 in anticipation of what might happen. Schools were kept closed even though the mid-year vacation had ended, in order to avoid students' demonstrations. Tanks and armored cars were sent to patrol the streets. The high command sent suspected officers to the front thinking that their duties near the Israeli border would detract them from attempting a rebellion. But the concentration of anti-government officers in one area made it easier to scheme and to plan a coup d'état.[8] The conspirators decided to use the units stationed at the front as a striking force precisely because the command in Damascus could not have imagined that these units would abandon their posts facing Israel one single hour, and also because, as it was said, their spirits were naturally mobilized for action in virtue of their position.[9] General Zahreddin naively found it difficult to believe that Colonel Hariri would stage a coup in view of the presence of several police and military posts along his way from the front to Damascus. He also was constantly reassured by the deceitful profession of loyalty expressed by his chief of military police and his brigade commanders in the Damascus region who came to his office during the day and to his home during the night, as he related, to tell him that conditions were normal and secure.[10]

The high command, supported by the officers' committee, found it expedient after mid February to send Colonel Hariri away from the country and to make other transfers that would include both rightists and leftists. On February 22 the list of transfers became known and it included the appointment of Hariri as military attaché in Baghdad, the return of Samman to the army, and the transfer of Brig. Gen. Rashed Qattini to the direction of military intelligence with Col. Aqil as his assistant. The group of Damascene rightist officers refused to accept Samman's transfer and similarly the Palace and the cabinet insisted on keeping him in his direction of internal security. The unionist officers who were preparing the coup refused in their turn Hariri's transfer. The only important one that materialized was that of the pro-Nasserist Brigadier Qattini who became director of military intelligence on March 1 and cooperated with the authors of the coup.[11]

The plotters from both the southern front and the Damascus region met in a half deserted village called Kafr Nafah between Damascus and the Syrian border to agree on the final arrangements. They decided to carry out their coup on Thursday, March 7, but the action was postponed to the following day because the air force commander of the Damascus area, Colonel Haytham Mahayni, and some armored units refused to cooperate. It was even reported that Hariri's forces had to return to the front after they had begun their March on Damascus.[12] In the first hours of Friday March 8, 1963 the insurgent forces moved from the front and this time reached Damascus, at some sixty miles, to the north, at 4 a.m. The chief of the Second Bureau (army intelligence) in Damascus evidently ordered the military posts on the way to allow the units to pass. They consisted of about 1800 troops or even less, with tanks, half tracks and anti-aircraft guns. Some of the units were assigned to block the entrances to the city, while others went to occupy the General Headquarters, the radio station, the directorate of police and other important government buildings. In the brief engagements that followed, three sentries were killed.[13] At 6:20 a.m. the operation was ended with the cooperation of certain elements of the Damascus command, and the coup was announced by the radio station. The air force opposed the operation but Mahayni ended the resistance in the afternoon because he realized he was alone in the opposition and he saw that the Dmeir air base near Damascus was surrounded and then it surrendered. In the camp of Qatana near the border there was some initial opposition to the coup but finally all rallied.

General Zahreddin has claimed that he did not cooperate with the authors of the coup, but was the victim of the deceit and treachery of his subordinates. According to him, any brigade of the Damascus region could have successfully broken the assault of Colonel Hariri if there had been no treason. One of the most powerful brigades was the one commanded by Colonel Nureddin Kenj—a Druze like Zahreddin—but Kenj was "bought" by Hariri. Zahreddin learned about the coup at 5 a.m. and wanted to reach Brigadier Qattini, director of military intelligence, but was unable to locate him. The commander of the military police, Colonel Saleh Agha, pretended that he informed the chief of staff when the coup first began, but General Namek Kemal, the chief of staff, did not communicate the news to the commander in chief. General Zahreddin's attitude towards the coup was evidently one of indifference. The coup makers, however, associated him with the "separatist" regime of President Qudsi and kept him in jail for over nine months.[14]

The coup d'état was immediately named the "revolution" of March 8 and it boasted in its radio statement that "the army put Syria back in its place in the procession of progressive countries under the banner of unity, freedom and socialism." Its leader, Colonel Hariri, and many of the officers who supported him were not partisans of the Baath, and he later emphasized the fact that the coup was not limited to one party or group. Yet, it was the Baath party that obtained most of the credit for making it.[15] According to one estimate, "Baathist officers from the south seemed to have got in ahead of Nasserists from the north by a short head."[16] The preponderance of Baath members and sympathizers in the National Council of Revolutionary Command and in the cabinet that was formed on the following day along with the repeated mention of the Baath slogan of "unity, freedom and socialism" tended to confirm this estimate. The Baath Party gave itself later the credit of having been in the forefront of the revolution of March 8.[17] The impact of the Iraqi revolt must have also helped reinforce the position of the Syrian Baath, as it had helped in providing the example and the encouragement for the coup itself.

The Syrian revolt of March 8 was the third upheaval in six months—after the coup of September 26, 1962 in Yemen and that of February 8, 1963 in Iraq—that succeeded in overthrowing regimes which Nasser was ruthlessly striving to destroy. Cairo was certainly aware of its role in preparing for the revolt in Syria. Orders were said to have been given to the Egyptian air force and navy, as soon as the news about the coup was known, to alert their forces in case the Syrian revolutionaries called for help.[18] Egypt and Iraq were the first to recognize the new regime as soon as a government was formed. At the same time, Egypt, in a warning to Jordan,

Saudi Arabia and Israel, announced that "any outside aggression on Syria is an aggression against the United Arab Republic."

The Syrian revolt was considered by Cairo ruling circles an Egyptian triumph and a "full vindication of President Nasser and his socialist policies." In the nationalized Egyptian press, entire pages of advertisements were published by the nationalized industrial and commercial corporations about the Syrian coup with a delirium of congratulations for the success of the revolt of the Syrian army and people. They included the standard slogans against what they called "the idols of secession and reaction.'"[19] Writers like Fikri Abaza, Habib Jamati, and Ihsan Abdul Quddus published articles on "the revolution that was absolutely bound to happen," and described how Syria had been rehabilitated and had "regained her genuine Arab face." They even called on the Jordanian army to do its duty–to revolt–because its turn had come.[20]

II. Baath Rule and the Problem of Arab Unity: The Federal Charter of April 1963

The government of Syria after the coup was in the hands of a national council of revolutionary command, and a cabinet. The Council signed the communiqués during the coup but, as in Iraq, it did not disclose the names and the number of its members. It is believed that it consisted of eleven members, but according to certain reporters it included about twenty to twenty-five members, half civilian and half military, with a Baathist majority. It was only on March 24 that Louay Atassi was officially mentioned as the president of the Council. He had been appointed commander-in-chief immediately after the coup and was promoted directly from Colonel to Lieutenant-General.[21] Similarly, Colonel Ziad Hariri who led the coup, was made chief-of-staff and promoted to Major General, while Rashed Qattini became his deputy and was also made Major General.

The national council of revolutionary command was a policy-planning body for internal and foreign affairs. The cabinet was its executive arm and was appointed by it. On the day that followed the coup, a cabinet of twenty members was formed with Salah Bitar, the Baath leader, as its prime minister. It included two officers, Lt. General Muhammad al-Soufi, a pro-Nasserist, as minister of defense and Colonel Amin Hafez, a Baathist who was recalled from his post of military attaché in Argentina, as interior minister. The cabinet had to be a compromise between four unionist parties or groups, but the Baath party was strongly represented in it by about eleven ministers. The other groups were first, the United Arab Front, whose members were referred to as the Nasserist *ghulats* (Ultra-Nasserists), because they wanted the immediate restoration of unity with Egypt and included the deputy prime minister, Nihad al-Qasim; second, the Arab Nationalists' Movement that favored unity with Egypt under certain conditions, and it included Hani Hindi who was awarded the ministry of planning; third, the Socialist Unionist Front with Abdul Halim Suwaidan, a professor of biology at the Syrian University as minister of agriculture. The last two groups stood between the Ultra-Nasserists and the Baathists.

The new cabinet was the first in the history of independent Syria to be dominated by an ideological party, which in this case was the Baath party. For the first time since the establishment of the Syrian Republic in 1930, the traditional parties from which the ruling elite came, were completely excluded from the government. The cabinet contained no declared enemies of Nasser or of unity with Egypt. Its members, Baathists as well as Nasserists, adopted the slogan of "unity, freedom, and socialism." The cabinet, however, soon proved to be a shaky coalition that lasted only two months. At no time in the history of modern Syria, have the government and the administration been so chaotic and unstable, the cabinets so short-lived, and the riots, conspiracies and attempted military coups so frequent as under the Baath-dominated regime. The causes are obvious. The Baath party was brought to power by a group of officers who were not all Baathists, and even the Baathists themselves were divided by rivalries and separate goals. The Baath party, moreover, came to power with the cooperation of other unitarian groups, because of its condemnation of "separatists and the disaster of separation" and its supposed readiness to restore unity with Egypt. It became evident, however, in the first three days after the coup, that although it deplored the divorce or "the separatist disaster," it did not move to announce the remarriage.[22] Nasser's popularity, which the Baath had exploited to fight the Azem regime, now became an object of Baathist concern and fear. In the course of negotiations for a federal union between Syria, Iraq and Egypt in March and April, it became evident that essential differences existed between the Baath on the one hand, and Nasser and his Syrian partisans on the other. Nasserist propaganda as a result provoked more riots and military coups to overthrow the Baath regime which in its turn resorted to more purges of officers who did not embrace its point of view.

One of the tragedies of the Baath party has been its ambition to rule and to maintain itself in power without being able to do so by due constitutional process. The first result was that it had always to resort to conspiracy and subversion and to seek the help of the military to reach its goals. Its rule therefore had to be tragically unstable owing to the instability of its alliances with the military. Another tragic result of its drive to reach the seat of authority has been its dependence on Nasser's stature and on projects of unity with Egypt that would earn for it Nasser's endorsement and support. But twice the Baath found out, to its great disappointment, that unity with Nasser's Egypt could only mean Baath weakness and subordination and even self-destruction. A third tragic result has been the glaring contrast, whenever the Baath attempted to govern, between the democracy and freedom which the party professes and the repressive rule it has practiced.

The Baath-dominated cabinet inaugurated its rule by

hunting down communists, anti-Nasserists, and other opponents of the new regime. The ex-Premier, Khalid al-Azem, sought political asylum in the Turkish Embassy in Damascus, while several former ministers went into hiding or left the country. The permits of seventeen newspapers were cancelled by a decree of the revolutionary council, and the publishers were denied the right to ask for an indemnity. Two months later, when relations with the Nasserists became strained, two daily newspapers that supported Nasser were closed on May 8 and their publishers were detained. The only newspaper left was *al-Baath,* the official publication of the party.

The unprecedented harsh treatment of the press was matched by measures that were similarly unprecedented in the history of Syria against politicians and army officers. Imitating the procedures followed by the Nasserist regime in Egypt, the new revolutionary government stripped morc than 140 leaders of their civil rights between the end of March and the beginning of May, and banned them from political activity for periods of five to ten years. At the same time, twenty-two persons who included the former president, three former prime ministers, and the officers who made the coup of September 28, 1961, were ordered to be tried as "enemies of the people," for disruption of the unity with Egypt, and for alleged usurpation and abuse of power, killing workers and peasants, and making contacts with foreign states. A national security tribunal was formed for the trial, and on October 5, 1963 the public prosecutor asked the death penalty for the former premier, Dr. Kuzbari, who was out of the country, and for thirteen retired officers, three of whom only were under arrest and included Col. Haidar Kuzbari. The death penalty was asked in the name of "the eternal Arab message . . . Arab history, and the Arab nation."[23]

The trial of the officers who had made the secessionist coup of September 1961, was comically illogical because it was conducted at a time when Nasser, as a result of his dispute with the Baath, was describing the Baath leaders themselves as separatists and their regime as fascist, immoral and inhuman. The Baath leaders, while trying others for secession, were attacking Nasser's dictatorship and misrule in Syria that led to that secession. In Lebanon, where the press was free, at least one publisher critically spoke of the Baath trials as "the Mahdawi trials in Syria." It was said, moreover, that the officer Salah Dalli, who presided over the trial of the separatists, had been seen dancing out of joy on the boat that brought back the Syrian officers from Egypt after the breakup of unity.[24] In Egypt itself, the trial of separatists and the renationalization of banks by the Baath government were judged hypocritical and insincere, and were viewed as only a cover for serious steps to liquidate the commanding officers who were opposed to the Baath. On the other hand, General Zahreddin has maintained that his own extended imprisonment and that of President Qudsi until December 1963 was the result of Cairo's continuous attacks against the ruling Baath regime for its alleged tolerant treatment of the separatists.

Baath rule in Syria, and similarly in Iraq, added to its guilt of persecuting persons for their opinions and attitudes that of indoctrination and partisanship in the armed forces, and brainwashing among the political prisoners.[25] The Baath party has attempted to do what no other Syrian political party or regime has done, namely, to impose one-party rule on the country. It has sought to do this not only by banning freedom of expression and association, and by indoctrination, but also by continuous purges of the administration and the armed forces and increasing the number of Baathist officers in the army and retaining their loyalty by promotions and other favors. Immediately after the coup of March 8, Baathist officers who had been dismissed under the preceding regimes were recalled and assigned to important posts. Similarly, because Baathist officers were not numerous, all reserve officers who belonged to the Baath were called to the service. Some reservists were related by family, clannish and sectarian ties to prominent Baath officers and most of them came from rural areas.[26] The Baath party has also tried to organize the student body and regiment it for its own benefit, and has encouraged the use of undemocratic methods in the direction of student assemblies. In both Syria and Iraq, the Baath youth were recruited to form a militia known as the national guard to support their party by military action when needed. The Baath ruling party in Syria and Iraq, moreover, attempted to evolve a theory of mutual armed support against rebellions and coups that could threaten their regimes.

The various devices employed by the Baath to ensure its exclusive rule of Syria have succeeded in keeping it in power, but its rule has been deplorably unstable and fragile. Instability has been illustrated first, by frequent changes of cabinets, and second, by the disorders and attempted coups, accompanied by much bloodshed, against the Baath regime. Four cabinets were formed in the first seven months that followed the coup of March 8, 1963. Three were formed by the Baath leader, Salah Bitar on March 9, May 13, and August 5, and the fourth was formed by General Amin Hafez on November 14. Popular and military disorders occurred in the first week of May in connection with the purging of forty-seven pro-Nasser officers, in the first week of July during the quarrel with General Hariri, and reached their climax in the bloody Nasserist coup of July 18, 1963, led by the retired Colonel Jassem Alwan. Changes of cabinet, as well as coups and disorders were accompanied and followed by changes in the revolutionary council and in the army command, and by the inevitable arrests, purges, investigations and trials.

The first Bitar cabinet resigned on May 11 as a result of a struggle that had been brewing for weeks between the Baath majority and the pro-Nasserists over the question of unity with Egypt. Soon after the coup of March 8, the two Ultra-Nasserist members of the cabinet–Nihad Qasim and Abdul Wahab Humad–addressed a memorandum to the prime minister asking for immediate restoration of unity with Egypt, "without loss of time and vain formalities." The cabinet did not permit the publication of the memorandum, but it was published in Cairo. The Baath party in reality needed some kind of unity or talk about unity because the coup of March 8 was proclaimed "a victory against separation and separatist logic." The party also needed unity in order to consolidate the new regimes, both in Syria and Iraq, with a guarantee of Nasser's support. On March 14, delegations from Syria and Iraq rushed to Cairo to open negotiations for a federal union, and were followed by another delegation on March 19 that included the Baath leaders Aflaq and Bitar. Egyptian leaders and Syrian Baathists confessed the mistakes made during the unity regime but no agreement was reached on the basic question of one-man, one-party rule versus collective leadership and the free functioning of political parties that involved the future of the Baath party.

The disagreement between Cairo and the Nasserists on the one hand, and the Baath on the other, soon became open and manifested itself in the wild demonstrations in favor of Nasser and against the Baath on April 1, 1963 when Houari Boumedienne, Algerian defense minister, visited Damascus. When the demonstrations failed, the Nasserists now openly asked to have an equal number of seats in the cabinet and in the Council. The Baath refused but the Nasserists were given equal representation in the Syrian delegation that was formed a few days later in order to participate with the Iraqi and Egyptian delegations in laying down the principles of the proposed federal union in Cairo. The seventeen-member delegation led by General Louay Atassi, president of the revolutionary council, thus went to Cairo to discuss the formation of a federal union before its members had settled their differences on the basic principles of rule in Syria. The Baath in other words, rushed to discuss unity with other countries before assuring unity within Syria itself and before putting order in its own house. Its strategy, however, was clear. It aimed at continuing the dialogue on Arab unity without surrendering power to Nasser. The prominent Baath leader, Munif Razzaz, commented later that it was the street demonstrations that impelled the government to send delegations to Cairo, and that the Baath military leaders did not participate in these delegations but they sent non-Baathists like Generals Atassi and Hariri while they stayed in Damascus to prepare the dismissal of Nasserist officers from the army.

The tri-partite conference for Arab union met in al-Qubba Palace in Cairo on April 6, 1963. After ten days of discussions, the delegations of Egypt, Syria, and Iraq agreed on the formation of a federal state that would retain the name of the United Arab Republic with Cairo as the capital. They signed, on April 17, a 5,000-word contradictory and unworkable charter for the proposed federation. The document was found by certain observers to be "a conglomerate of doctrines and republican procedures assembled from sources as divergent as Karl Marx and the founders of the Constitution of the United States." It was said that Nasser wanted to reject it but the Iraqi delegation begged him to sign it, and he did.[27] The federal state, according to the charter, was based on Arab socialism and western democracy, and Islam was proclaimed to be its religion. The federation was expected to be formed at the end of five months–September 17–when a new constitution and the name of the new president would be submitted to a popular referendum. This was to be followed by a transitional period of twenty months, during which the constitutional government would be established. The armed forces, economic planning, and conduct of foreign affairs were to be unified, and other details were to be worked out by special committees. The Baathists succeeded in winning the acceptance of a parliamentary, instead of a presidential form of government, and of a bi-cameral, instead of a unicameral legislature, but the president was given the right to name the cabinet ministers, not merely the prime minister. The provision for a five-month period during which the constitution was to be drafted, was a gain for the Baath who expected to use it in consolidating their position in both Syria and Iraq. The Baath obtained a vague right to co-exist with other socialist progressive parties, but the relationship of these parties with the single overall national political front remained unsettled. Nasser had thus to compromise in the question of immediate union and that of a single undisputed one-party system, but he won the acceptance of one federal political leadership and one president. More than a month later, editorialist Haikal wrote in *al-Ahram* that the charter "was neither a union, nor a scheme for union, but a project of action towards union."[28] The charter nevertheless enhanced Nasser's prestige and one of its results was that Jordan and Saudi Arabia made efforts for reconciliation with Nasser.[29]

III. The Aleppo Riots of May 1963 and the Anti-Nasserist Purge

The dreams of Arab unity contained in the charter of April 17 began to fade away three weeks after the return of the delegations to their capitals. Baathists and Nasserists distrusted each other, and unity could not be made by disunion. In early May, rumors of a pro-Nasser army coup were heard in Damascus. The ruling Baath, backed by the chief-of-staff, General Hariri, dismissed, pensioned, and transferred to the foreign service forty-seven Nasserist officers following reports that they were attempting to oust the dominant Baath from the government. Six Nasserist ministers, including the minister of defense, General Soufi, reacted immediately by resigning on May 3. The deputy chief-of-staff, General Qattini, and several members of the revolutionary council likewise withdrew. Pressure, in the form of riots and sit-in strikes was now brought against the Baathists to reinstate the officers and to give the pro-Nasser factions more voice in the government.

The Baath government held out against the riots that lasted for almost a week. It was backed by all those who hated Nasser and feared his domination, civilians as well as military. Many of them did not care particularly for Baathism, but considered it the lesser of two evils. The bloodiest of the riots was that of May 8 in Aleppo. It began in a poor section of the city called Kallasi, and was said to have been planned and financed by Nasserist retired officers.[30] The armed mob established road blocks, fired at policemen with machine guns and pistols, and was near taking over the city. The riot ended after a two-hour battle in which some fifty persons were killed. The military governor, General Hafez, who crushed it began since then to attract attention as the Baath strongman.

The ruling Baath party must have felt the need for ending the tension generated by the dispute with the Nasserists. It probably realized the dangers of its isolated position. This is why, on May 8, 1963, before the Aleppo riot had started, a Syrian four-man delegation under General Atassi reached Cairo to discuss the means of settling the dispute with the Nasserists. Nasser was then in Algeria, and the delegation was therefore received by Marshal Amer who is said to have stormed at the Syrian delegates saying, "Is Nasserism a crime in Syria now? If it is, how can we face the future together?" [31] The delegation returned to Damascus without achieving any positive results.

On May 11, 1963, three days after the Aleppo riot, the Bitar cabinet resigned following the withdrawal of two more cabinet ministers who belonged to the Socialist Unionist Front. It is significant that in Baghdad, the Baath prime minister, Ahmad Hasan Bakr, resigned on the same day, a few hours after Bitar's resignation as a result of a similar disagreement with Nasserists. The Syrian revolutionary council asked Sami Jundi, a forty-two year old dentist and minister of culture in Bitar's government to conciliate the Nasserists and form a middle-of-the-road cabinet but the attempt failed because the Baath party refused the conditions of the Nasserists for participation in the cabinet. The Baath desired a union with Nasser but without sharing power with the local Nasserists. In order to stand up to Nasser within the proposed union, the Baath wanted the exclusive control of both Syria and Iraq.

On Monday, May 13, Bitar was asked to form a new government. His second cabinet was ready a few hours after Ahmad Hassan Bakr had formed his own cabinet in Iraq. The

Nasserists were now excluded from both cabinets. The Baathist military governor, General Amin Hafez, who had sternly crushed the Nasserist riots became deputy prime minister as well as minister of interior. At the same time the independent chief of staff, General Ziad Hariri, became minister of defense.

In its press and radio attacks against the Baath government, Cairo made it clear that it wanted union with the Syrian people and not with a Baath-dominated Syria. In Cairo, Haikal writing in *al-Ahram* on June 14, 1963, declared that the Baath command was never sincere at any moment since March 8 in asking for union. The Baath socialists, on the other hand, accused the Egyptians of breaking up the proposed federation before its birth by refusing to cooperate with the new Syrian government. On May 19, the Syrian revolutionary council issued a statement warning politicians to keep the army out of their quarrels. The Baath rulers also accused their opponents of organizing conspiracies. On Wednesday, May 22, a plot was said to have been uncovered in Syria against the Baath regime. Three days later, on Saturday, May 25, the Iraqi revolutionary council announced that it thwarted a similar plot made by officers and nationalist groups supporting Nasser.

IV. The Baath Coup Against General Hariri

While the cold war between the Nasserists and their Baath opponents continued, the Baath government tried to complete the elimination of all organizations and officials who did not recognize the party's supremacy. The Baathist regime thought it could win over the Syrian people by defending the principle of equal authority with Egypt within the proposed union, but it soon became evident that it was doing this for its own benefit, and that it was becoming as authoritarian as the Egyptian regime whose domination it was trying to avert. Between April and July, 1963, several directors-general in the departments were replaced by Baathists. New agrarian laws were made to benefit the backward areas in the Jabal Druze and the Alawi region with the opportunistic aim of winning the support of officers from these regions.[32] The Baath regime then prepared a decisive purge of those officers who had supported it against the Nasserists but were, at the same time, opposed to the establishment of a Baathist state. Prominent among them was General Hariri.

In their systematic purging of officers, the Baathists were realistic and ruthless. Past experience had taught them that coups d'état were usually the work of dissident officers. Therefore they decided that only Baathist or pro-Baathist officers should be kept in the army. They began by purging first the separatist officers immediately after the coup of March 8. Then with the help of General Hariri they dismissed and retired the Nasserist officers in May. The third purge touched Hariri himself and his group of officers.

The showdown between General Hariri and the emerging Baath strongman, General Hafez, began in the last third of June and ended on July 8 with Hariri's deportation to Paris. The details of the struggle illustrate the increased perversion of the standards of military discipline under the Baath regime. On June 20, 1963, the Baathist leading officers, General Hafez and Colonel Muhammad Umran, commander of the 70th tank regiment, took advantage of Hariri's absence on an official mission in Algeria and dismissed twenty-seven of his supporters from the various commands. The Hariri officers were considered the most likely to conduct a coup against the Baath, but their dismissal or transfer to the foreign service was decided without consulting General Hariri, the chief of staff and minister of defense. It is even believed that Hariri himself found a decree appointing him military attaché when he arrived in Algeria, but he ignored the decree and returned to Damascus.[33] He refused to accept the transfers and dismissals and looked for allies among the remaining anti-Baath officers. The two camps–Harirists and Baathists–now faced each other in the army and maneuvered, but did not clash. Several cabinet and revolutionary council meetings were held to persuade Hariri to accept the decrees. He categorically refused and manifested clearly his opposition to Baathist policy. In early July, he is reported to have made the following demands: 1) Dismissal of General Atassi from the presidency of the revolutionary council, and General Hafez from his ministerial and military posts, 2) Return of the recently dismissed officers and putting an end to the cashiering of officers, civilian officials, and police, 3) Ending the political disqualification of at least sixty persons, 4) Holding elections within three months, 5) Implementing the original aims of the March 8 revolution.[34]

General Hariri made several trips to the front in southern Syria to contact his friends and enlist support. His two trips on July 2 and 3 were attended by rumors about his impending march on Damascus, but he returned alone every time. On July 4, the government began the first stage of the anti-Hariri coup. It surrounded Damascus with army units and placed strong detachments around General Army Headquarters and the radio station. On Saturday evening, July 6, the special guard that protected Hariri's house and consisted of his supporters was withdrawn and replaced by army commandos. Hariri since then was virtually under house arrest. On Sunday July 7, the revolutionary council decided to dismiss Hariri from his posts of minister of defense and chief of staff. A government delegation that included General Atassi and Premier Bitar went to his house to hand him the decree. Hariri accepted without resistance in order to safeguard, as he said, the unity of the army. On Monday morning, July 8, he was put aboard a regular Air France flight to Paris with his chief of army intelligence. In what was described as "a gesture typical of the spirit of Syria's coups and counter-coups," Premier Bitar and the minister of planning, Brig. Gen. Ghassan Haddad, were present at the airport to greet him. Less than two months later, on September 28, General Hariri was deprived of his military status and transferred to the ministry of foreign affairs where he was given ambassadorial rank.

The Baath thus proved to be stronger than the man who originally brought it to power. Hariri undoubtedly must have weighed his chances against the Baath and found them inadequate. His ambitious adventure of March 8 thus did not take him very far, and his dreams of power ended only four months after his fateful coup. It must be said that Hariri had originally succeeded in his coup of March 8 by taking a deceivingly unclear position at the head of a group of professional officers. He deluded the Nasserists by making them think that he was a Nasserist, and acted the same way with the Baathists. He even deluded the separatists and the conservatives and made them believe at one time that he was one of theirs.[35] In early May, he supported the Baath against the Nasserists because of the traditional officers' fear of external domination. He thought he would turn against the Baath later as he became critical of its attempt to dominate the country. His showdown with the Baath came too late, for the Baath had reinforced its position by installing its men in the strategic posts. It must be said also that none of the groups opposed to the Baath supported him. The separatists never forgave him for his coup of March 8, and the Nasserists had lost confidence in him.

The removal of Hariri gave more titles and power to the Baathist strongman Amin Hafez. In addition to his being deputy prime minister and minister of interior, he inherited Hariri's position of chief of staff and minister of defense, and was promoted to Major General. In the Bitar cabinet, three pro-Hariri ministers resigned, but Bitar remained in office until August 5. His government, in cooperation with the revolutionary council, made a last attempt to negotiate with Nasser and bring about a reconciliation that would preserve the proposed Arab union.

V. The Abortive Nasserist Coup of July 18, 1963

On July 18, 1963 a Syrian delegation under General

Louay Atassi left by plane to Egypt in order to hold talks with President Nasser. It was said that General Atassi was prepared to make concessions on the reinstatement of Nasserists in the army and in the cabinet, and on the formation of a political national front that would combine Nasserist groups and the Baath Party. But while the delegation was on its way to Cairo, the Nasserist forces in Damascus started a coup d'état to overthrow the Baath regime. The attempt was psychologically prepared by the continuous campaign of propaganda from Cairo against the Baath rulers which only strengthened the hostility of the hard core military Baathists against Nasser and even allowed them to accuse the Baathist unionists of pro-Nasserism.[36]

The abortive pro-Nasserist coup of Thursday, July 18, 1963 was the bloodiest among the thirteen coups that Syria witnessed until then since 1949. In the fighting between the rebels and the government forces, planes, tanks, and artillery were used. The battle raged for about four hours—10:15 a.m. to 2:00 p.m.—around the General Headquarters and the radio station, and in the Qabun military camp near Damascus. It ended in the defeat of the Nasserist forces. A first estimate put the number of victims at 170, but an official declaration later spoke of 19 killed and 45 wounded.[37] The four rebel planes that bombarded the General Headquarters with missiles were forced by a superior force of thirteen loyalist planes to leave the scene. Civilian elements, including Palestinians, cooperated with rebel military elements and units of the Signal Corps in the attack against the General Headquarters, but they were defeated by the tanks corps and a guard regiment. The rebel force that tried to march from the Qabun camp under the command of some dismissed officers, was defeated by the loyalists. For five days after the attempt, there was sporadic shooting in the city, and on July 24 the rebels attempted to capture Army Headquarters and the radio station buildings but were prevented.[38]

The leaders of the plot were almost all dismissed officers who had held important positions during the Syrian-Egyptian unity. They included ex-Colonel Jassem Alwan, who had instigated the Nasserist rebellion of April 1, 1962 in Aleppo, ex-General Muhammad Jarrah, former security chief under Sarraj, and ex-Colonel Akram Safadi, once an aide de camp of President Nasser in Syria. The prominent civilian accomplice was Yusif Muzahem, former minister of Wakfs under unity. The operations were led by Jassem Alwan, who was at the head of the military units, and Muhammad Jarrah, who directed the popular elements and had succeeded in transforming the Ghuta, outside Damascus, to a Nasserist stronghold. The operations on the government side were directed by General Amin Hafez in person. It can be noted that this was the second time—after May 8, 1963—that Nasserist violence broke out while a Syrian delegation was trying to negotiate and seek conciliation in Cairo.

The Baath regime and its strongman, General Hafez, reacted with what was called "un-Syrian harshness," against those involved in the atempted coup.[39] Previous abortive attempts to overthrow Syrian regimes were traditionally followed by the arrest and prolonged formal trial of those involved until they were released by another coup. Sometimes the losers in the attempt were even sent to lucrative diplomatic posts. General Hafez chose to act differently. Early on the morning of July 19, he spoke in person over the radio and declared, in the manner of al-Hajjaj of Umayyad fame, that "the heads of the plotters shall be crushed and the arm of conspiracy shall be amputated."[40] On the same day, twenty rebels, eight military and twelve civilians, were executed by a firing squad after summary trials by a military tribunal at the Mazze prison. Two days later, seven more, five military and two civilians, were executed. This was followed by an intensified purging of the army and the civil service, and the Baath filled the vacancies with its own men.

During the summary trials that followed the coup a rumor spread that certain members of the court martial were in favor of executing a few imprisoned separatists after a nominal trial in order to prove to Cairo that the Baath government was not prejudiced in favor of separatists and that it could execute both separatists and Nasserists. General Zahreddin who was then in the military hospital at Mazze—where distinguished political prisoners were given special treatment regardless of whether they were sick or not—has related that he was transferred on July 21 to the Mazze prison. Orders were also given to transfer President Qudsi, and the transfer could have meant trial and execution. Qudsi reportedly became hysterical and refused to be transferred except by the use of extreme force. He was finally allowed to stay, and three days later Zahreddin was returned to the hospital. The separatists, who also included cols. Kuzbari and Mahayni and Bridgadier Assassa, were reportedly saved because the assistant director of the military prison at Mazze refused an oral order from the court martial to proceed with the nominal trial and executions, and also because one of the members of the court, Captain Salim Hatum, was opposed to the operation.[41]

The main explanation for the ruthless trials and executions must have been the seriousness of the challenge made against Baath authority and the violence with which it was made. Nasserist success could have meant not only the end of Baath domination, but also the end of the Baath itself. The Nasserist rebels conducted a real military operation for the first time in the history of Syrian coups, and the Baathists consequently had to answer by dealing a severe blow. General Hafez was not frightened or taken by surprise when the Nasserists moved. Unlike the military commanders under the President Qudsi regime, he not only knew what was coming, but also prepared for it. This alertness and preparedness on the part of Hafez was a principal cause of Nasserist failure. Another cause was the refusal of officers and units to join the Nasserists because they feared the return to unconditional unity with Egypt. Thus they again supported the Baath without really being in favor of its rule.

Nasser's reaction against the Baathists and their use of

the firing squad was particularly violent. This was only natural. For the first time in his career, his supporters and agents in Syria were killed in battle or executed, and this was at the hands of the very leaders who at one time were considered his own supporters and agents. The previous coups of March 28 and April 1, 1962 were simply followed by trials that dragged for months and by sentences that were never executed. Nasser, therefore, continued to depend on army officers and their attempted coups for overthrowing the Qudsi regime as long as no danger was involved and the only sacrifice was a financial one. Under the Baath domination, the situation was different, for the Baathists were revolutionaries also and were acquainted with, and well-versed in Nasserist methods. When Cairo therefore accused the Baath government of drowning the nation in a sea of blood in suppressing the uprising of July 18, it had only itself to blame, for it had set the example by provoking and even boasting of the bloody outbreaks that its allies, including the Baathists, caused in Iraq, Lebanon, and elsewhere since 1955. The school of violence was indeed a creation of Nasser's Egypt, and Nasser himself, as it has been said, was the master of that school.[42]

The real leaders of the abortive coup of July 18 went into hiding after the failure of their attempt. Three of the most prominent among them, however, were seized during the ten days that followed the coup.[43] The court martial that was entrusted with their trial began its work on September 9. It accused them of provoking attack against the Command Headquarters and government establishments, inciting an armed rebellion, attempting to usurp authority, plotting to overthrow the government, and making contacts with a foreign government to start aggression against Syria. On October 17, 1963 the court martial condemned thirteen leaders of the coup to death, three to prison for life, and issued various sentences of one to twenty years in jail to twenty others.

Already before the coup of July 18, rumors had spread that Nasser was going to announce Egypt's withdrawal from the projected Arab federation in the speech he usually makes on July 22 on the anniversary of the Egyptian revolution. The Syrian delegation that had left for Cairo on the fateful morning of July 18 under General Atassi, had actually gone to plead with Nasser not to cancel the Charter of April 17. On its arrival in Cairo, the delegation knew about the Nasserist coup in Damascus, but it still wanted to meet Nasser and therefore continued its way to Alexandria, his summer capital. Nasser refused the pleas of the Syrian delegates and when the talks ended on July 19 he refused to issue a communiqué.

On July 22, 1963 Nasser made his expected speech and announced Egypt's withdrawal from the proposed tripartite Arab federation. He put the blame on the Baath for having destroyed the hopes of Arab unity and he referred to the Baath government of Syria as "the government of fascism, Mazze prison, firing squads, curfew, and terrorism." Nasser also claimed that most of those "ardent Syrians" who originally signed the charter of April 17 were now in jail, and that "we cannot possibly have any link, any alliance, or any unity of objective with a fascist state in Syria."[44] Certain Cairo newspapers such as *al-Akhbar* began at this time to promote a new slogan, "the unity of organization," as a guiding principle for Arab unity in replacement of the older slogan, "unity of objective." The new slogan meant that one ideology, particularly socialism, was not sufficient as a prerequisite for forming a federal union, and that a uniform political organization such as the Egyptian "Socialist Union" should exist prior to union.

It is significant that in the first few weeks after the abortive coup of July 18, the Baath government was cautious not to blame Nasser publicly for the attempt. Even after having executed twenty-seven Nasserist rebels, the Syrian government declared its intention to maintain the charter of April 17 and work for union. On July 24, it asked Nasser to reconsider his decision to pull out of the agreement of April 17. The purpose of this demand was to charge Nasser with the guilt of destroying the hopes of Arab unity, and to prove its own innocence.

Nasser and the Syrian Baath leaders since then concentrated most of their attacks and counter-attacks on two questions, first, the responsibility for the destruction of Arab unity, and second, the methods and aims of government in the two countries. In his statement of July 24, 1963, Bitar attacked the cult of personality and strongman rule. On August 16, the Cairo government was publicly accused for the first time for financing the Nasserist coup of July 18. It was General Amin Hafez himself who made the accusation and charged Nasser with squandering Egypt's money in financing conspiracies in other Arab countries instead of spending it for improving the living conditions of the Egyptian people.

Nasser at one time tried to win over Baathist Iraq with whom he maintained polite relations. He invited President Aref, who was known as a Nasser sympathizer, in late July to visit Egypt, but it seems that the Baath regime caused Aref to decline the invitation. Late in August, however, Aref was allowed to make the visit and was accompanied by an Iraqi delegation. His talks with Nasser did not produce positive results.[45] Nasser did not modify his attitude towards the Baath Party and its leaders. He believed that the Baath desired to rule and that they worked for the Baath state, not the Arab state. Observers, as a result, have wondered why the Baath continued to insist on a union that included Egypt instead of forming a union with Iraq. The explanation must be sought perhaps in the Baathist need for time in order to consolidate its position and do the necessary purges, and also in the Baathist belief in what they called "the interaction between the two revolutions," the Egyptian revolution and that of March 8, 1963 in Syria.[46]

On the eve of the anniversary of the Syrian secession on September 28, the Syrian Baath Party announced that, in as much as it considered Arab unity its raison d'etre, it could not stop its struggle for unity and wait for Nasser's wishes. Consequently, it decided to establish a union between Syria and Iraq in the form of a socialist, democratic, popular state. The union was to be achieved gradually by the conclusion of a military, economic, cultural and then political union. On October 8, 1963 the first step was taken with the signature of a pact of military union that created a supreme defense council of three members from each country, and a supreme commander of the unified army. The supreme command was given to Lt. Gen. Saleh Mahdi Ammash, Iraqi minister of defense, and Damascus was made the center of the unified command.[47] On the same day, a Syrian military force, that took the name of "The Yarmuk Brigade," entered Iraq to join in the war against the Kurds, but no Iraqi force entered Syria.

The Syro-Iraqi military union was not well received in Cairo. Nasser had until then avoided offending Iraq while he was attacking Syria, possibly in order not to have the two states against him, and also in the hope of winning over Iraq. But as Syria and Iraq were now being bound by military and other union agreements, Nasser decided to open his fire also against Iraq and overthrow its government in order to isolate Syria and bring about the end of its Baathist rule. One month after the Nasserist offensive began, events in Iraq evolved more rapidly than Cairo had expected. A week of quarrels between the Baathist leaders ended on November 18 with a bloody coup directed by President Aref against Baathist domination and its instrument, the Baathist national guard.[48] The resulting change in Iraqi leadership eventually increased the isolation of Syria and created more Arab hostility towards its ruling Baath regime. About one month after the coup of November 18, the Syrian brigade that had entered Iraq to help against the Kurdish rebels was withdrawn.

VI. Experiments and Quarrels Within the Baath State 1963-1965

A. The Origins of Baath Troubles

The Baath party ruled Syria without serious challenge after its victory over the Nasserists in the coup of July 18,

1963. Theoretically the source of authority was the regional command of the party that was chosen by the delegates of the Baath chapters, while the national or pan-Arab command that represented the Baath organization in the various Arab states had also a certain measure of influence and control over Baathist policy. The cabinet and the members of the revolutionary council, for example, were nominated by the regional command. This system of party rule, however, was illusory because power was effectively in the hands of the officers. Since the summer of 1963, Baath rule in Syria has been dominated by disagreements and quarrels between the civilian and military wings of the party, and between moderate and radical party members as well as between the national and regional Baath commands. The quarrels often took the aspect of a struggle for power between military strongmen supported by civilian allies who disagreed on the extent of cooperation with the various Arab countries and particularly with Nasser's Egypt, and with the Syrian political factions and personalities. They also disagreed on the implementation of socialist policy and on the appointment of Baath party members to the newly created organs of government and important positions.

At the root of the disagreements and the confusion under the Baath regime was the failure of the party to define its relation with the Baathist organization in the army or the Baath military committee that took part in the coup of March 8, 1963. Moreover, the party allowed the Baathist military organization to participate in the command and supervision of the civilian organization, while the Baath regional and national commands–consisting of civilian and military members–were not allowed to control or supervise the military organization. The Baath military as a result were independent under their own command or committee and formed practically a second Baath party of their own or, according to another view, acted as though the Baath party was their own property. This situation, according to the former secretary-general of the Baath national command, Munif Razzaz, explains the failures of the Baath party in both Syria and Iraq.[49]

The Baathist military organization was originally formed during the period of Syrian unity with Egypt when Baathist officers felt they were distrusted. Among the leaders of the organization were the three Alawi officers Muhammad Umran, Salah Jedid, and Hafez Asad, and they were joined later by the Sunni officer Amin Hafez after his return from Argentina where he was military attaché after the end of unity. They remained opposed to Nasser after the secession, but they were also against the secessionist regime because it abolished the socialist measures. In their reserved attitude towards unity with Nasser's Egypt, they were in agreement with those civilian Baathists who held their leaders, Bitar and Aflaq, responsible for having accepted unity without guarantees and called for a reorganization of the party. These civilians were influential in the regional (Syrian) command of the party which also included a number of military Baathists. On the other hand, the national leadership command of the party was more inclined to achieve unity and was less opposed to cooperation with Nasser. It also favored a milder and more gradual approach in implementing socialism. The military Baath organization thus remained closer to the "regionalists" and virtually dominated the regional (Syrian) command, but it had also some members in the national command.

In the attitudes of the Baath officers and regionalists and in their clashes with the national command of the Baath, it is possible to see the influence of religious, geographic, and social factors. The Muslim minority groups, the Druzes, Ismailis, and Alawis, and particularly the latter who had a superior numeric strength in the army after the purges of 1963, disliked the rapprochement with Nasser and feared that a union with Egypt could restore Sunni military leadership. In as much as they came from depressed rural and mountain areas and from the poor lower or lower-middle class, the Alawis were determined to implement socialism in order to weaken and impoverish the Sunni urban middle class. Their leading officers and members of the regional command were younger and more radical than those in the national command.

The situation was further complicated by the opportunistic behavior of some leading Baathists and by the admission of hundreds of new members who wanted to participate in the scramble for influential and profitable positions and to strengthen the following of certain Baath leaders. This is how, according to Razzaz, slogans replaced rational thinking, and party differences and divisions of personal and political nature were given an ideological coating, while the various manifestations of backwardness in society which the party originally sought to remove began to appear. Personal allegiance, feudal subservience, tribal and sectarian ties thus became the main ties in the party. The Baath officers formed a special class with a privileged position, and certain cities, regions, and departments in the army and the administration became the spheres of influence of some well known officers.[50]

One week after the Nasserist abortive coup of July 18, 1963, General Louay Atassi, who was not viewed as an official Baathist, resigned from his functions of president of the revolutionary council and commander in chief of the armed forces. The deputy premier in Iraq, Ali Saleh Saadi, commented by saying that General Atassi was "a good but confused man" and that he was hesitant and not fit to lead an Arab revolution.[51] Atassi was replaced by the Baathist leader, General Amin Hafez, who thus became the official head of state, and had in addition the two portfolios of defense and interior in the cabinet. A redistribution of cabinet positions became necessary especially after the withdrawal of the pro-Hariri ministers. On August 5, Salah Bitar formed his third cabinet of eighteen members, ten of whom were retained from the former government. General Hafez relinquished his cabinet posts but retained the titles he inherited from General Atassi. In the revolutionary council, disagreement developed between General Hafez who advocated the end of Baath isolation in Syria and reconciliation with other political groups and personalities, and Colonel Muhammad Umran, the commander of the 70th regiment of tanks, who held that the Baath alone should rule and should be friendly to Nasser. General Umran was consequently transferred on September 14 to a diplomatic post, but he refused. Both parties were said to have mobilized their units, but the affair ended peacefully and Umran remained.[52]

During his third term as prime minister, Bitar showed signs of dissatisfaction and offered to resign on more than one occasion. There seemed to be disagreement between Bitar and the other older veterans of the party on the one hand, and the younger generation of Baathists on the other, for the latter were impatient with Bitar's slowness in answering their wishes and particularly their demands for jobs. On September 26 and again on October 7, Bitar submitted his resignation but the revolutionary council refused to accept it. Bitar evidently felt he should relinquish his post because he was dropped from the national command council of the Baath Party in early October. Another possible reason was his disapproval of the role of General Hafez and of the military Baathist members around him because they outweighed the civilians in the party command. A pro-Nasserist conspiracy was discovered about this time and it caused Bitar to stay in office. The Nasserist plotters were said to have planned to seize the Homs radio and appeal to Nasser for air-borne assistance after proclaiming the resumption of unity with Egypt. Some two hundred officers, mostly retired, were reported arrested because of the plot.[53]

On October 5, 1963, the Baath Party held its sixth national congress in Damascus with delegates from the Baath in Syria, Iraq, Jordan, Lebanon, and even the Gulf States and North Africa. The congress lasted seventeen days and elected the party national command council where Aflaq was retained as secretary-general, but Premier Bitar was dropped. Early in November, Bitar again sought to resign. It is said that both General Hafez and Colonel Umran asked him to stay but he insisted on withdrawing from the premiership.[54] On November

12 his resignation became official. Two days later, a new Syrian cabinet—the fourth since the revolt of March 8—came into being under General Hafez who retained the presidency of the revolutionary council while Bitar became deputy president of that council. The cabinet had this time a record number of twenty-two members. Both the prime minister and his deputy, Colonel Umran, were taken from among the military, and so were the two ministers of defense and planning. The new chief of staff, Salah Jedid, was a member of the regional command council of the Baath and a member of the revolutionary council. He was promoted from Lieutenant-Colonel of the armored corps to Major-General. The new cabinet thus meant a larger concentration of power in the hands of the military and in General Hafez in particular. General Hafez had been only four days in office as prime minister when the coup of November 18 took place in Iraq. As he could no longer count on the unequivocal support of Iraq, he had to look for support from within Syria. He released President Qudsi from the Mazze prison-hospital, and allowed ex-premier Azem to emerge from his sanctuary at the Turkish Embassy. He is said to have favored reconciliation with Akram Hourani, leader of the other faction of the Baath that supported secession, but Hafez realized that certain officers in his own cabinet and council, like General Umran, opposed the reconciliation.

Among the aspects of disagreement and confusion in the Baath government was the fact that the Hafez cabinet that had been formed on November 14, had not succeeded in making its statement of policy by the end of 1963, forty-seven days after its formation. Another aspect was the series of orders and counter-orders to arrest Hourani in January 1964. On December 10, 1963, the cabinet, however, reached an agreement on ending the disqualification of the country's former political leaders by abolishing the decree that disqualified them from civil rights after the revolt of March 8. At the same time the revolutionary council issued an amnesty in favor of persons accused of various crimes against state security. Among those pardoned were the authors of the separatist coup of September 28, 1961 who had been under arrest such as Haidar Kuzbari and Muwaffaq Assassa. Disagreements within the Baath Party itself were marked by the purging out of Bitar, three times prime minister after the March 8 revolt, from the regional (Syrian) command of the Baath on February 5, 1964 during the meeting of the regional congress of the party. Bitar was also opposed by the Baath military committee and by the regionalists because of his efforts to negotiate with Egypt and because he tried to stand in the face of military intervention. Some members tried also to attack Aflaq and made allusions to his "petrified mentality" and "eternal trusteeship."

The Baath party had already proclaimed its exclusive rule over Syria and defined the foundations of its policy and the instruments of its power in the sixth national congress in October 1963, but the resolutions of that congress became the source of anti-Baathist trouble and of controversies within the party.[55] It was indeed in this congress that the Baath party became "the leader and director of the government general policy" and no other party was to be tolerated. The national guard was officially endorsed as the "bulwark for the protection of the revolution." The ideological education in the army was decided "in order to give a new revolutionary meaning to military discipline." Of particular importance was the decision to move from the stage of belief in socialism to that of action to implement socialism. The socialist transformation was to be on a "democratie basis" and with the participation of the masses. The Baath congress decided arbitrarily and in contradiction to well known facts that "the bourgeois middle class is no longer capable of playing any positive role in the economic field and its opposition has made it a new ally of imperialism." The congress mentioned the workers, peasants, educated revolutionaries–military and civilian–and the petty bourgeoisie as the forces that will make the socialist revolution in its first phase. It stressed the importance of democratic control by the workers of the means of production in order to avoid the stage of government capitalism through which most socialist experiments, including that of Egypt, have passed. The agricultural revolution was to continue and collective farms were to be run by peasants in the land covered by the agrarian reform. Moreover, the congress mentioned that the government departments would be run on revolutionary and democratic lines.

The socialist resolutions of the sixth national Baath party congress contained a large dose of Marxism and were made under the influence of Nasser's socialist charter of May 1962. They were intended to demonstrate that the Baathist state in Syria and Iraq was at least as radical and revolutionary as Nasser's Egypt. The controversy about the implementation of these resolutions in Iraq was partly responsible for the coup of 18 November 1963 that ended the Iraqi Baathist regime. In Syria the socialist measures of the Baath rulers were largely determined by their attempt to win friends and destroy enemies. Shortly after they assumed power in March 1963, they reassured the influential middle class that they would not alter the foundations of the Syrian economy. But as the delegations flocked to Cairo to talk on unity, the Baathists wanted to impress Nasser with their socialism, and they therefore restored the decree that had nationalized the banks during the period of unity after it had been canceled under the Qudsi regime. The Baathists were often moved by passion, hatred, and spite in dealing with landowners and businessmen. The officers who were mostly sons of peasants or belonged to the urban lower and lower-middle class certainly enjoyed seeing the wealthy bourgeois dispossessed and their power destroyed. In their attempt to emulate Nasser and to gain popularity they ignored the differences between Egypt and Syria, and they probably did not realize that Nasser's popularity was not based originally on his economic policy but on his successful international and inter-Arab maneuvers in the period between 1955 and 1958. The disorganized and erratic socialist policy of the Baath threatened economic ruin. The Damascus Chamber of Commerce painted a realistic picture of the crisis that was caused, among other things, by the inefficiency of the nationalized banking system in its memoir of late October 1963 to the government.

The conflict or cold war between Baathist Syria and Nasser's Egypt continued until May 1966 when the Soviet prime minister, Alexei Kosygin, during his visit to Cairo, used his influence to conclude a truce and, later in November, a military pact between the two feuding revolutionary socialist regimes. The Baathist rulers had been fortunate in obtaining the support of the majority of the Syrians when, at the beginning of their rule, the alternatives were either Baathist or Nasserist domination. The Syrians who had neither admiration nor respect for the Baath thought that Baathist rule would free them from the Nasserist personality cult and from the feeling of being under external domination. The Syrians undoubtedly expected that the Baath regime, like the preceding military regimes, would soon be overthrown by a new coup that could restore normal civilian rule. In that they were disappointed.

One of the early results of the Baathist quarrel with Nasser was the rapprochement between Jordan and Egypt in the fall of 1963 in the face of the common Baath foe. The talks that took place at King Hussein's initiative in the Hotel Crillon in Paris on September 26, 1963 with Nasser's unofficial spokesman, Muhammad Hassanein Haikal, ended for some time the hostility between Egypt and Jordan.[56] In Lebanon, those of the newspaper editors and other Nasserists who had been pro-Baathist when the Baath cooperated with Nasser, now turned against the Baath. Syrian government allegations that Nasserist elements opposed to the Baath regime were being trained in Lebanese border camps were denied by the Lebanese government. Incidents took place on the Syrian-Lebanese border and culminated on October 19, 1963 in the death of four Lebanese soldiers. The Baath party was finally banned in Lebanon in early December. It is significant that the minister of interior, Kemal Junblat, who issued the decree against the Baath, had been a supporter and admirer of the

Baath in the days of Baath cooperation with Junblat and the Nasserists.

While the Baathists condemned the autocratic and dictatorial nature of Nasser's regime, there was hardly an aspect of Nasserist authoritarian and totalitarian rule that they did not apply in Syria in spite of the collective leadership that only contributed to making their government more chaotic and disorganized. For more than one year after the coup of March 8, 1963 they mentioned nothing about drafting a new constitution or restoring the old one, and they have been unable until this writing to draft a permanent constitution or to conduct elections for a representative assembly. They abolished the freedom of expression and association, subjected Syria to one party rule, and replaced hundreds of dismissed officials in the administration by their own inexperienced partisans. They imposed on those who were appointed to responsible positions the obligation under oath to work for realizing the goals of "unity, freedom and socialism," included in their slogan. Labor unions were formed under their direction, and in these unions as well as in the armed forces and in the schools, classes and meetings were organized for indoctrination. Schools, moreover, were given names of certain Baathists such as Colonel Adnan Malki, and Yusra Thabit—a girl who was involved in the attempt to assassinate Kassem in Iraq. The date of the coup that brought the Baath to power—March 8—became an official holiday. The partisan policies of the Baath and the stifling of freedom, in addition to the implementation of socialism, led to popular revolts against which the Baath strongmen used particularly harsh repressive measures.

B. Baath Socialism and Popular Uprisings

The Syrians resented the restrictions on their personal and economic freedom and could not accept without some resistance the exclusive rule of one party that was made possible only through the military force of Baath strongmen. The Syrians were provoked every day by the constantly repeated Baath party slogans, the Baath indoctrination, the successive socialist measures and the resulting decline in the volume of business and increase of unemployment. The Syrian middle class consisting essentially of landowners, merchants and professional people, and all the traditional and ideological parties and groups, including the Muslim Brothers and the Nasserists, stood against the Baath monopoly of power.

Between January and April 1964 under the General Hafez cabinet regulations were issued concerning membership in the boards of directors of private corporations and in the chambers of commerce, industry and agriculture. Contracts for agricultural work were required between the landlord or the tenant and the worker and the area to be planted cotton was defined.[57] Various labor unions were formed by government decree and a labor union institute was established to prepare Baath-indoctrinated union leaders. In February 1964 labor disturbances occurred in Homs in central Syria and radio Baghdad claimed that twenty-five persons were killed. On February 23, five persons were sentenced by a military tribunal to penalties of ten to twenty years in jail for inciting the workers in Homs to strike.[58]

Nasserists remained moderately active against the Baath administration. On February 8, 1964 when the Alawi Baathists in Baniyas on the Syrian coast demonstrated to celebrate the first anniversary of the Baath coup against Kassem in Iraq, they were beaten up by Sunni Muslims. Five persons were reported killed and hundreds of Nasserists were arrested. The government sources mentioned fifty persons arrested as a result of a plot to stage acts of sabotage and threaten Syria's security. Attacks were made in March 1964, possibly by Nasserists, in Aleppo on police posts outside the city. Nine men including five retired non-commissioned officers and four civilians implicated in the attack were sentenced to death on April 30, but a week later they were reprieved.

The Syrian government claimed that the attackers were paid agents of Egypt.[59]

The uprising in the city of Hama in mid April 1964 was the most violent expression of general discontent with Baath rule. It began with student demonstrations on April 9 following the trial and sentencing of a high school student to one year in jail because he erased a Baathist party slogan that was written on the blackboard and was denounced by the Baathist teacher who wrote it. The anti-Baath student demonstrations in Hama were the first demonstrations to occur after one year of Baathist rule. They were immediately followed by rioting and clashes with army forces that came from neighboring Homs. General Hafez who was then prime minister and military governor went to Hama, ordered a curfew for twenty-four hours, and described the riots as a plot against public security. The curfew was lifted on April 16 after a meeting between him and the Hama leaders, and on April 17 he returned to Damascus for the celebrations of Evacuation Day. He vowed in his speech to crush the conspiracy and its heads and claimed that the feudalists were behind the riots because socialism frightened them.

Rioting resumed after the lifting of the curfew. General Hafez immediately left Damascus on April 17 and ordered the shelling of Hama with heavy guns as the fighting continued. Several quarters were damaged by the shelling and, according to anti-Baath reports, 300 persons were killed. Hafez gave specific orders to shell al-Sultan Mosque and its minaret and thereby raised a storm of protest in the Muslim world. The mosque was damaged and the minaret was partly destroyed. Anti-Baath writers reminded the Muslims that during twenty-five years of French colonial rule in Syria, the sanctity of houses of worship was never violated and that it was only under the uncivilized Mongol and Tatar invaders that mosques were destroyed. Hafez later explained on April 19 and in a press conference on April 25 that as soon as the curfew was lifted in Hama, the rebels poured into the streets to "commit slaughter and murder" against security forces and the national guard in isolated streets and alleys and mutilated their bodies. He said that the rebels killed a national guard and a security man, that they brought arms of all kinds and placed machine guns on the minarets. When the mosque was surrounded and they were ordered to surrender, they sent out youths between the ages of fourteen and seventeen to plead for them. Security forces then entered the mosque and they were ambushed and some soldiers were killed. This is why orders were given to shell the mosque and the city.[60]

Hafez admitted that on the government and army side five persons were killed and fifteen were wounded, and that among the civilians there were forty to sixty killed and wounded. On April 20 he ordered the distribution of half a million Syrian pounds ($120,000) to the poor of Hama to rebuild their homes and he allocated funds for repairing the damaged mosque. In good Baathist style, he blamed the imperialists outside, and their allies the feudalists inside the country for the uprising. The imperialists, he said, were helped by the Egyptian embassy in Beirut, and by President Aref in Iraq who paid "much money to the plotters." He spoke of the religious charlatans and of the Muslim Brothers who were bought by funds, while the Damascus radio compared President Aref to Nuri al-Said and accused him of conspiring to revive the Baghdad Pact.[61] In Baghdad, on the other hand, the press spoke of the "Syrian revolt" as the revolt of Arabism against those who deviated from its national mission, and not as a mere local revolt. It described the Baath government as a "gang" that ruled by "fire and iron." The Ulama sent telegrams to Hafez against the "shelling of God's houses and your killing of the Believers because of your difference of opinion with them."[62]

The riots of Hama were followed by the trial by court martial of nineteen persons who belonged to its prominent landowning families—the Barazis, Keilanis, Azems, Asheqs, Nassours and others. The Baath regime had issued a decree on April 14 expropriating some 2500 acres belonging to various landlords in Syria including those of Hama. The Baath government claimed that these "feudal criminals"—as the martial law order that brought them to trial called them—took advantage of the arrest of a student to "plot against state security, oppose socialist principles and cooperate with imperialism." On May 2, 1964 the court martial sitting in Homs sentenced twenty-one persons to death for taking part in the uprising, but on the following day the national revolutionary council in Damascus decided to commute the sentence in response to delegations of religious leaders and popular organizations. Other sentences condemned five participants to life in jail and several others to terms of seven to fifteen years.[63]

The shelling of Hama and its mosque, and the socialist measures taken by the Baath regime led to a protest movement in other cities. On April 18, Homs went on strike and was followed by Damascus where the shops closed on April 19 and 20, 1964. Ten merchants were arrested, their stores were confiscated and their contents were given away. On April 21 Damascus opened its stores to allow the people to shop for the four-day holidays of the Adha feast (feast of sacrifice). When the holidays ended the strike resumed on April 26 for four days, but on April 30 the bazaars opened because the government issued martial law order no. 83 that threatened to bring the strikers to trial in a military court and confiscate their property. The martial law order at the end of April stipulated that the strikers would be tried on charges of disturbing public security and shaking general confidence.[64] The harshness of the Baath regime in dealing with the strike was unprecedented in the modern history of Syria. The Syrian Bar Association presented a memoir of protest to the government against the unusual measures and on April 20, the "national democratic constitutional front" that combined the representatives of various parties appealed, in a published statement, to the people to unify their efforts to save the country from "the mad governing clique." On April 28, another group of Syrians who claimed to represent all parties forwarded a call from Amman in Jordan to the Arab kings and presidents to help in changing the regime in Syria because it was ruled by a group of officers who did not represent the people.[65]

In the course of the uprising in Hama and the strikes in other cities, the Baath regime issued several decrees for implementing socialism. These decrees increased the discontent that led to the merchants' strikes in late April 1964, but the government used them as an instrument for weakening the opposition by nationalizing the property of its members and ruining them socially and financially. The Baath regime first created a general organization on April 9, 1964 called "the directorate of the socialist industrial sector" that was attached to the ministry of industry. On April 16 the national revolutionary council issued the decree 55 that established the system of "self management" in industrial establishments. The self management *(al-Tasyir al-Dhati)* of an establishment was defined as its "collective ownership by the community whereby the workers replace the employer or owner in the ownership and administration of its affairs under state supervision." The decree 55 stipulated that the self managed establishment would be administered by a board of directors of seven members who represent the workers, the government, the labor union, and the Baath party for a two-year term. The government representative would be the chairman of the board and could refer any decision he disagrees with to the directorate of the socialist industrial sector. The decree also said that during the transitional period, the board would be appointed by the minister of labor and social affairs, which meant that the Baath government–and not the workers or producers–was to direct the establishment through a board of its own choosing.[66]

Several industrial establishments were nationalized immediately after the decree of April 16. Three spinning and weaving companies in Aleppo were nationalized on the same day. Three days later, two companies were nationalized in Damascus, and a decree of the ministry of labor and social affairs appointed their boards of directors that consisted of a director representing the government, one member representing the Baath party, another representing the spinning and weaving union, and four representing the workers.

Nationalization continued under the fourth Bitar cabinet that was appointed on May 13, 1964. Two more spinning and weaving companies in Aleppo were turned to the public sector on May 25. At the same time the Bitar cabinet found a compromise formula for socialism under the name of the "joint sector" in which the government entered as a partner with 25 per cent of the capital instead of complete nationalization. This is how fifteen companies were partially nationalized on May 25, 1964 and they included a variety of cement, glass, sugar refining, and spinning and weaving companies.[67]

The Bitar cabinet had to resign in early October under the pressure of the Baath military committee and General Hafez became prime minister for the second time. In the quarrels and struggle for power between the regional Baath command and the national command at the end of 1964, the regionalists and the military committee that dominated them claimed that the main difference between them and the national command was in their attitude towards socialism, and that while they were leftists, the national command was rightist. Former Baath secretary-general, Munif Razzaz, has claimed that it was in this atmosphere of quarrels and exchange of accusations between Baathist factions that the sweeping decrees of nationalization of early January 1965 were issued under the Hafez cabinet in order to prove the leftism of the regionalists and the rightism of the national command.[68]

The decrees of January 3 and 4, 1965 were issued at a time when a certain degree of economic stability had been reached in Syria towards the end of 1964. The people were aware of the struggle within the Baath, but they probably underestimated the influence of the younger radical officers and the party solidarity that prevented the older moderate leaders from openly denouncing at this time the party extremists. The decrees nationalized 107 industrial concerns on

January 3, and eight others on the following day. The owners and shareholders were to be compensated over a period of fifteen years by bonds bearing 3 per cent interest. The entire labor force in the 115 nationalized concerns was about 12,000 workers and the total capital was 243 million Syrian pounds (about $70 million at the time).

Although the nationalized companies represented a modest section of the national economy and the entire industrial sector contributed only 15 per cent of the national product, the nationalizations were met with consternation in economic circles and in a large section of the urban population. They violated the strong tradition of private initiative and free enterprise to which the Syrians were attached since the dawn of history. Moreover, they hurt thousands of shareholders in the companies who were not capitalists but persons of modest means including small employees, shopkeepers, government officials and jobless widows. Their number exceeded by far that of the factory workers whom the nationalizations wanted to protect. The socialist laws thus nationalized—which in practice meant confiscated—the holdings of 7,000 persons in the cement factory of Homs most of whom were people of low income under the pretext of protecting 200 workers whose financial condition and wages were often better than those of many shareholders.[69] The nationalizations, furthermore, were decided rashly and without a study of the basic data about the nationalized factories. Some of them were small family concerns where management and labor included no more than the owner and his sons. This is why the government quickly reacted to the ridicule caused by its hasty decrees and before the end of January 1965 it began issuing denationalization decrees that returned certain companies and "factories" to their owners.[70]

Among the false and misleading assumptions on which the nationalizations were based was the Baath claim that the national bourgeoisie was exploitive and incapable of contributing to economic development. The industrial and agricultural growth in Syria during the twenty years that preceded

Baath rule, and the establishment of scores of factories with national capital by the genuine efforts of persons who rose from modest origins contradict those assumptions. The economic growth, including the expansion of agriculture and the exportation of hundreds of millions of dollar's worth of industrial and agricultural products, would have continued if the socialist laws under the UAR in 1961 and later under Baath rule had not paralyzed it. Another reason given by the Baath government for the nationalizations was the flight of capital that reached an estimated $200 million and most of it was smuggled to Lebanon. The obvious reason for the flight of capital that began immediately after the Baath regime announced its intention to implement socialism in October 1963 was the fear of nationalization and confiscation. There was a time before the advent of the Baath and before the Nasserist socialist laws of 1961 when capital flowed into Syria mainly from Lebanon, to be invested, instead of Syrian capital leaving the country to find a safe refuge in Lebanon.

The nationlization decrees of early January 1965 were followed by the setting up of a military court of five members on January 8 for trying crimes of opposing the socialist system, countering the revolution, attacking nationalization, and smuggling funds. The crimes were punishable by death or life imprisonment. The Baath regime knew only too well that its socialist decrees would be defied and therefore prepared the instruments of repression. Troops and tanks were placed at the gates of factories. The merchants were told that the policy of the government was socialistic, but the rumor that foreign trade and privately owned buildings would be nationalized was denied. It became a standard policy of the Baath and other socialist regimes to reassure the people that there would be no more nationalizations after every stage in the socialist transformation—a clear proof that the people were opposed to socialism and that the government resorted to trickey in giving promises that there would be no further nationalizations without intending to keep the promises. One merchant had the courage to ask the interior minister about the difference between socialism and communism and the minister answered, "our socialism will not be communistic; it springs from our present condition" *(min waqi' ina)*.[71]

The Damascus business community went on strike on January 25 and 26, 1965 and the government reacted violently. Many merchants were arrested, eight were sentenced to death by the military court, sixty-nine striking shops were confiscated and sledge hammers were used to break their locks. The prime minister, General Hafez, made a speech on January 26 in the rally organized by the government to beat down the strike and said some violent and threatening words against those who struck. "We shall crush their heads," he said, "and we shall kill them . . . The sword will soon be in their neck . . . Exploiters have sucked the blood of the people . . . They have smuggled out 300 million Syrian pounds, but by God this money shall return or they will stay in prison until they die like dogs." The bazaars opened on January 27 on account of the harsh repression that included seizure of the striker's property and long prison terms. After mid-February the Baath government began to nationalize the foreign trade. On February 18, 1965, thirty-nine companies that imported drugs and six others engaged in importing commodities were nationalized. On March 4, nine oil distributor companies, six Syrian and three foreign, including Socony Mobil, Esso Standard, and Shell, were nationalized. Two months later, in early May, the government took over fifty-five ginning mills and the exportation of cotton, wheat and barley. In the fall of 1965, the Baath regime began to relax its socialist policy and in early September it returned fifteen business firms to their owners.

The Baath regime thought it could rally all the leftist and socialist parties and factions after the nationalization decrees of January 1965, but only the communists responded to its call for cooperation. Khalid Bakdash, secretary-general of the Syrian communist party, sent a telegram from Prague to General Hafez on January 19 expressing the support of his party for the socialist measures. The various pro-Nasserist socialist factions withheld their support and so did the Arab socialists of Akram Hourani.[72] The Baath friendship with the Soviet Union and the other communist countries became closer and was expressed in official declarations, exchanges of visits of various delegations, and technical aid agreements. In the statement of the eighth national congress of the Baath in April 1965, the party asserted that it was "a socialist movement and a liberation movement and this determines our attitude towards the socialist camp."[73] In the *Pravda* of July 21, 1965 the Baath party was praised for releasing all "progressives" from jail and for "creating the necessary conditions for Syria's progress towards socialism" through social reform and dominance of the public sector in industry.[74]

The Syrian uprisings, strikes, and protest movements against the Baath regime, particularly those of Hama in April 1964 and of Damascus in January 1965 were only partly the result of the socialist measures. Among those who closed their stores were many modest traders and small shopkeepers who form the majority of the bazaar population and were supposed to be the foundation of the socialist society, along with the laborers and peasants, according to Baath declarations. They nevertheless participated in the movement against the Baath because they also wanted freedom and could not tolerate the one party slogans and the dictatorship supported by the army, the police, and the Baath "Bashi-Buzuks" or national guard.

C. Struggle for Power Among Baathists and the Coup of December 1965

Internal quarrels and intrigues among Baath leaders and factions absorbed an important part of their time and activity. In the course of their struggles among themselves and against the opposition, the Baath elite tried to create organs of government that could guarantee the exclusive rule of the party. Membership and influence in these government institutions changed frequently according to the fluctuations of the struggle for power within the Baathist state.

On April 25, 1964 the Baath regime issued its first provisional constitution. The new document declared Syria or the "Syrian Region" a "democratic popular socialist republic," in which Islamic law was the main source of legislation and the religion of the chief of state had to be Islam, as in the former constitutions under the old regime.[75] The rights and freedoms of the citizens were guaranteed by law but they could be exercised only if they do not jeopardize "the popular objectives of the revolution and socialism." Socialism was emphasized in Article 18 where it was mentioned that the state "shall provide work for all and guarantee the same by building a nationalist, socialist economy . . .", and in Articles 23 to 29 where the collective ownership of the means of production was divided into state ownership, cooperative or producers' ownership, and private ownership, and the state was given the right to nationalize any establishment or project bearing on public interest.

The provisional constitution gave the national revolutionary council–which had been hitherto called national council of revolutionary command–legislative powers and the right to control the operation of the executive authorities. Its membership was to consist of the existing members and of representatives of the people's sectors whose number and manner of representation was to be defined by decree. The number was raised in mid-May 1964 to forty-five but it was not a representative council elected by the people. It was rather, as one scholar said, a secret parliament whose membership was not publicly known and was coopted mainly among the leaders of the Baath.[76] The national revolutionary council (NRC) was given the power to elect the presidency council, the new executive organ created by the constitution, and to grant confidence to the cabinet and withdraw it. The presidency council (sometimes called "the presidium") was to consist of a president, vice-president, and three members chosen by the

NRC from among its members. The constitution did not create a presidency of the republic, but it mentioned that the president of the presidency council would exercise the functions of chief of state. The presidium had the right to appoint and dismiss ministers, but both the cabinet and the presidium were responsible to the national revolutionary council.

The provisional constitution of Baathist Syria was issued one month after that of Nasserist Egypt. The Baath rulers often followed in the footsteps of the Egyptian regime in the adoption of certain measures. It was as if they had neither the courage nor the creativity needed to initiate policy and waited until Egypt gave them the green light. Already the implementation of socialism and the nationalizations were decided only after Egypt had taken the initiative. The Baathist principle of collective power remained, and the division of powers figured in the constitution but they were both theoretical as long as the strongman, General Hafez, who was elected chairman of the presidium—or head of state—was at the same time president of the national revolutionary council or legislative power and also prime minister. The constitution of April 1964 was met with indifference by the people of Syria who had been protesting against the shelling of Hama and preparing for more strikes. They, moreover, were aware that the organs created by the constitution were to be directed and staffed by the status seekers in the Baath military and civilian ranks and by the representatives of the unions of workers, peasants and intellectuals chosen under Baath party supervision. The membership of the national revolutionary council was later increased, on August 23, 1965, to ninety-five,[77] and it was since then known as the "national council." On February 14, 1966 it was again expanded by decree to 134 members in order to secure a majority vote of confidence for the Bitar cabinet formed on January 1, 1966. The critics in Damascus claimed that the deliberations of the NRC were confused, that its legislative work was mediocre, and that the most mediocre among its members were heard and obeyed.[78]

The provisional constitution was followed by the formation of a cabinet under a civilian prime minister. On May 13, 1964 Salah Bitar formed his fourth cabinet of ten Baath members and nine pro-Baath independents. it was said that the military gave the premiership to Bitar only when their policy led to the Hama riots.[79] The presidency council that was created by the constitution was also selected on May 13 with General Hafez as president and Bitar as vice-president. Both were Sunni Muslims. The three members were Nureddin Atassi, a Sunni, General Muhammad Umran, a Nusairi (or Alawi), and Mansur Atrash, a Druze. The presidium thus included two military and three civilian Baathists, but the president or head of state was a military and he was still president of the national revolutionary council. Friction developed between the military committee and Bitar's cabinet. The regional command under military influence made accusations against the national command and its secretary-general Michel Aflaq, who left the country in disgust and stayed in Bonn, where his brother was cultural attaché, for five months (June to November 1964). Aflaq later claimed that the "comrades of the military committee" wanted to remove the old leaders of the party and take their place.[80]

The Bitar cabinet remained in office for less than five months. It was forced to resign in early October 1964 when the national revolutionary council under the influence of the military committee withdrew its confidence. Bitar and his close colleague Mansur Atrash had also to leave the presidency council. The Baath extremists accused him of being soft on Iraq whose president, Abdul Salam Aref, persecuted the Baathists. Bitar is said also to have been friendly to Egypt. For a party whose basic creed was Arab unity it was paradoxical that a premier should be forced to leave office because he was friendly to two other Arab states with a progressive regime like that of the Baath.

During Bitar's premiership the Akram Hourani socialists published in August 1964 a declaration against the Baath regime accusing it of having imposed a terrorist atmosphere on the country, distorted socialism, and isolated Syria. Earlier in June, one of the founders and organizers of the Baath party, Jalad al-Sayyid, sent from his hometown in Deir al-Zor a very critical "open letter to the president of the Syrian presidency council" in which he mentioned in some forty pages the various deviations of the Baath and its abuses and mistakes and asked for a general amnesty for convicted or prosecuted politicians, withdrawal of the army from politics, formation of a neutral cabinet of all trends to conduct free elections for a chamber of deputies, dismissal of incompetent officials appointed after March 8, 1963, and the freezing of all laws passed by other than freely elected chambers of deputies.[81]

General Hafez formed his second cabinet on October 4, 1964 after Bitar's forced resignation. Among the twenty-two cabinet ministers, twelve were new and were described as non-entities. The cabinet included for the first time, after Egypt had set the example, a representative of the working class who was prominent in the labor unions. In the presidency council or presidium, the two ousted members, Bitar and Atrash, were replaced by Salah Jedid, the astute Alawi chief of staff, and Yusif Zuayyen, the young ally of the military. The officers in the presidium were now three and the civilians two with Nurreddin Atassi as vice-president. According to religious sects there were three Sunni Muslims and two Alawis (Umran and Jedid). General Hafez had acquired by the end of 1964 more titles and functions than any Syrian public servant ever did: he was the president of the presidium (head of state), the prime minister, the commander in chief of the army, the president of the national revolutionary council (head of the legislative power), secretary-general of the Baath regional command, and member of the national command. As it was said, these titles and powers represented a fusion in his person of the state, the army, and the ruling party.[82] The Hafez cabinet tried to conciliate public opinion by declaring a general amnesty for political prisoners on November 15, 1964. Hafez was unable, however, to follow a moderate policy with

Nasser or come to terms with him because of the hostility of the anti-Nasser group of younger officers who commanded the armored units. It was even said that they prepared to oust him when he wanted to include some moderate Nasserists in the cabinet.[83]

After the return of Aflaq from Bonn, the Baath national command met in December 1964 with the regional (Syrian) command that dominated the government to discuss their differences. General Umran who was either influenced by the popular revolution of October 1964 that ended military rule in the Sudan, or was moved by personal ambition, joined the Aflaq-Bitar group and disclosed the plans of the military to liquidate the old leaders and dominate the Baath party. He declared his opposition to the dictatorship of the military committee and of Hafez, but in so doing he was isolated as a moderate who, moreover, favored close relations with Egypt. The powerful military committee then decided to have him exiled from Syria and obtained the consent of the regional command. He had to resign from the regional and national party command and to take the first plane for a diplomatic assignment in Madrid. It was even said that he was beaten and harmed before his departure. The national command reacted by adopting several resolutions limiting the power of the military in the government and in the party and dissolved the regional command, but the threats of the military leaders, obliged it to withdraw the order of dissolution.[84]

Aflaq later explained that those regionalists who boasted of their radicalism were rightists during the secessionist period (1961-1963) and tried to press for some reforms under the Qudsi-Azem regime. Seven out of nine civilians in the regional command, moreover, joined the Baath party only after March 8, 1963, according to Aflaq, and they reached their position of leadership not because of their sacrifices, but because the military clique raised them to it to make of them a civilian facade for the military domination of the party.[85]

In the eighth national congress of the Baath party that met for ten days in April 1965 attempts were made to define the relations between the party and the government, and to restrict the authority of the military committee to military affairs and abolish its political and party role except for its right to represent the military sector in the national revolutionary council. The military committee accepted the restrictions because it was sure of its power in the regional command that virtually ruled Syria. Aflaq decided to withdraw at this time from his position as secretary-general of the national command because he felt that he was not wanted, and his resignation was described by *al-Jaridah* in Beirut as a "white coup" in which the Hafez group was victorious. Aflaq was given the honorific title of "founding leader of the party," and was succeeded by the Jordanian Baath leader, Munif al-Razzaz Aflaq was then fifty-five years old while Razzaz was forty-six.

The new Baath secretary-general continued the effort of the national command to reduce the military aspect of rule, isolate the army from politics, and define the relation of the party members with the government in order to dispel the general impression created by the behavior of party opportunists that "the party had become a mere gang interested only in dividing up positions, and that the acquisition of a membership card in the party was the best way to obtain a job".[86] He was supported in this last effort by General Hafez who, as prime minister, issued an order on June 17, 1965 forbidding party members to make direct or indirect contacts with cabinet ministers and department directors. On July 22, 1965 a long transitional program or plan of action for the future was broadcast by the Baath party national and regional commands. It provided for an enlarged national revolutionary council that would be called the "national council," and the provision was implemented on August 23, 1965 when a national council of 95 members was chosen. The program promised a new constitution to be approved by a plebiscite before the end of 1967. It prohibited interference by the party machinery in government or military affairs, and barred army interference in state affairs "except through the authorities concerned".[87] The program, moreover, proposed that no civilian or military could hold two posts at the same time.

General Hafez had until then supported the military committee and the regional command in order to dominate the Baath party in Syria and weaken the control of the national command and its older civilian leaders. He cooperated with Salah Jedid, the calculating and ambitious chief of staff, in the showdown with General Umran in December 1964 because Umran's alliance with the national command threatened his position as Syria's strongman. Hafez, however, tended to become the ally of the national command and to support its attempt to isolate the military from politics when General Jedid began to challenge his power with the help of the regional command. The struggle between the lieutenant-general (Hafez) and the major-general (Jedid) eventually produced two coups d'état, one in December 1965 against Jedid and the regional command, and the other, more decisive, in February 1966, against Hafez and the national command. The crisis ended only when one of the two rivals was defeated, because under military rule there can be only one strongman. Former Secretary-General Razzaz gave a picture of the situation when he said, "For two months we had no other work than hold successive meetings to reach a settlement of the dispute but in vain, for everytime we met the dispute became deeper and more serious on account of the accusations exchanged during the meeting."[88]

General Jedid has been compared by some to Stalin and by others to Robespierre. He was a shrewd calculator who knew how to create alliances and bring even his rival's supporters over to his side. He had definite Marxist ideas and was said to have been so hard, pure, and "incorruptible," that he broke with his own brother, Ghassan Jedid, an anti-communist leader of the Syrian Social National party.[89] Jedid claimed that he was only challenging the personal rule and dictatorship of Hafez. He was able to build up a following in the party and the army and to influence supporters by hurling accusations of separatism, Nasserism, and rightism against his rivals. Hafez accused him of exploiting the sectarian feeling of his fellow Alawi officers and of building a party within the party. He proposed that Jedid should not keep his two posts of chief of staff and member of the presidium and should abandon that of chief of staff. In return Hafez promised that he would also abandon his post of commander in chief of the armed forces and keep that of chairman of the presidium.

In early September 1965 General Hafez was no longer commander in chief of the armed forces. The post was attached to the minister of defense following the maneuvers of his opponents in the extraordinary regional congress of the Baath on August 8-14, 1965. In the national council (or Baath legislature) of 95 members which was chosen on August 23, Hafez was no longer the chairman. The council, however, under the chairmanship of Mansur Atrash re-elected him president of the presidium or head of state on September 2 and Nureddin Atassi vice-president, but General Jedid was excluded. General Hafez evidently used his influence to prevent the election of any military besides himself to the presidium. Hafez then proceeded to oust General Jedid from the post of chief of staff on September 4 and replaced him after some hesitation by Colonel Muhammad Shnaiwi, who was immediately promoted to major-general.

General Jedid, though excluded from the presidium and no longer chief of staff, was still powerful, for some of the members of the presidium, and several commanders of important army units were on his side. He also derived much authority from his influence in the new regional command that was elected by the regional congress in mid-August and in which six of the seven military members belonged to the old military committee. The regional command included both Hafez and Jedid and some of their respective partisans, and the discussions in its meetings were related mainly to the appointments to high public office. Each of the two sides worked frantically to have its candidates in key positions. Immediately after his return from the Arab summit conference at Casablanca Hafez, who had been in the premiership since October 1964, was replaced by a civilian prime minister allied to Jedid and chosen by the regional command. The new premier was thirty-five-year-old Yusif Zuayyen, a physician from the Jazirah region in northeastern Syria. His cabinet was formed on September 23, 1965 and included twenty-one ministers, eighteen of whom had been in the Hafez cabinet.

While Zuayyen was prime minister between September and December 1965, General Hafez was still at the head of the presidium and a member of both the national and the regional commands of the Baath, but his rival, General Jedid, succeeded in making the regional command the source of power, at the expense of the presidium, the cabinet, and the national command. The new cabinet won a vote of confidence in the national council on October 17, but twenty-two out of ninety-five members indicated their disapproval by not attending. They included Aflaq, Bitar and Hafez.[90]

Jedid continued to accuse Hafez of selling Syria out to Nasser and abandoning revolutionary policy and the Palestine cause after the third summit conference. He also began, through the regional command, to remove those provincial governors who were not loyal to the regionalists, and to transfer officers with the help of the minister of defense, Hamad Ubaid, and the director of officers' affairs, Ahmad Sweidani. Hafez indicated his disapproval of the measures that were being taken by the cabinet and the regional command by withdrawing from the public scene for rest at the mineral waters resort of Hamma in mid-October. When he returned to Damascus, it was said that his regime was again solidly in power and that his position with the officers had improved.[91]

The arrest of Akram Hourani and eighteen of his supporters on October 20, 1965 by a decision of the Jedid faction again vexed Hafez because he had hoped to broaden the civilian base of support for the Baath regime by cooperating with the Houranists. This was difficult, however, in view of Hourani's active criticism of the regime, his declaration against the government agreement with a British consortium to build a pipeline from the oil fields of Jazirah to Tartus on the coast,"[92] his popular reception in his native city, Hama, and the feeling that all the forces against the regime were centered around him. This is why Hourani was attacked so severely by the government press and radio as a man who lived on political charlatanism and for whom socialism was a weapon against his opponents. He was described by his former allies of the Baath as the person who was behind almost all the military coups d'état in Syria since 1949 for purely personal interests, and who used the officers for threatening Parliament in the period between 1954 and 1958.[93]

The measures taken by Jedid and the regional command were viewed as preparatory for a coup against Hafez for the domination of the party, the government, and the army. The action of Jedid and his supporters was determined and quick and this is why the reaction of Hafez and the national command against the regionalists had to be urgent. It was the Homs incident on December 19, 1965 that really revealed the seriousness of the situation and the intention of Jedid to carry out a coup. The incident showed that Jedid wanted to guarantee the cooperation of the armored brigade at Homs before attempting a coup. He therefore asked his supporters, the minister of defense, General Ubaid, and the chief of staff of the brigade, Lt. Col. Mustafa Tlass, to transfer three senior officers of the brigade who were not on his side. But when the order was given on December 19 the officers refused and were probably encouraged to do so by their commander and by General Hafez. It is claimed that a report reached Hafez about a certain order given to Lt. Col. Tlass to take over the brigade and kill its commander. Later a message from Tlass to Jedid was intercepted and it announced that the brigade was taken over. Its commander and another officer were arrested by Tlass and sent to Damascus.[94]

The Homs incident was the immediate cause of the coup of December 19, 1965 in which the national command mobilized the army, dissolved the regional Baath command, and announced that it was taking over all civil and military authority in the country. The national command also released the arrested officers of the armored brigade at Homs, and ordered the arrest of Colonel Ahmad al-Mir, commander of the 70th armored brigade near Damascus, and two other officers who supported Jedid and the defense minister, while Mustafa Tlass was recalled to the capital. The advocates of the national command have claimed that it had no other alternative but to cut short the developing coup that was about to be staged by Jedid, for otherwise the army forces and the factions would have fought against each other. The dissolution of the regional command was effective because Hafez and his supporters in the army were in favor. Jedid and the regionalists had therefore to prepare again for the coup that was cut short, or rather postponed, by the intervention of the national command.

The dissolution of the regional command was followed by the addition of five Syrian civilians, including Salah Bitar, to the national command to allow it to fulfill the functions of both commands. On December 21, the Zuayyen cabinet had to resign after it had been three months in office. It was replaced twelve days later by a record cabinet of twenty-six members under Salah Bitar. This was Bitar's fifth cabinet. Three members of the presidium–Atassi, Jassem, and Shiya–who were opponents of Hafez resigned and the national council elected three new members to take their place. One of them, a Druze called Shibli al-Aysami, replaced Atassi as vice-president. It is significant that the coup brought to light the identity of civilians and military who belonged to the two groups. The membership in the Hafez and Jedid groups, however, was not permanent. Those who became the strong supporters of Jedid such as General Hamad Ubaid and Colonel Tlass, were a few months earlier partisans of Hafez.

Under the Zuayyen cabinet, the Baath regime continued to outbid other Arab governments in the radical expression of its nationalism and thereby became increasingly isolated from its Middle Eastern neighbors and from the West. On November 9, 1965 the Shah of Iran recalled his ambassador from

Damascus because Khuzistan in Iran, or Arabistan, was mentioned in Zuayyen's ministerial statement as usurped Arab territory. On December 6, 1965 Morocco broke relations with Syria and declared that the Syrian diplomatic mission was not desirable. The guerillas of the *Saiqah* (Thunderbolt) units were encouraged by the Baath to start action from Lebanon against Israel in order to make Lebanon's position critical. Baath relations, on the other hand, were increasingly closer with the Communist camp and particularly with China. It was said at the time that Jedid's radical wing of the Baath favored China, while Hafez preferred to remain close to the Soviet Union as Egypt did. About 200 Chinese experts arrived in Damascus in mid-November 1965 to help in the planning department in the economic sector and in the military organizations, and Syria obtained credit facilities to buy Chinese equipment. Delegations of teachers and labor union members were invited to visit China under both Hafez and Zuayyen.

Between the Baath regime and the United States the relations seemed to be deteriorating. The Baathists' hostility to capitalism, imperialism and Zionism and their image of the United States as the worst representative of all three and as a supporter of Arab reaction and an enemy of revolution and socialism led to a long impassioned anti-American campaign. "It was," said one scholar, "as if disapproval of socialism by the United States were necessary to Syria's psychological well-being, or needed as a demonstration inside the Arab world of the greater Baathist ability to be independent of the West."[95] In February 1965, under the Hafez cabinet, the government arrested members of a spying ring who, it said, worked with the second secretary at the American embassy and included a naturalized American named Farhan Atassi. The U.S. Ambassador denied the charges, but Atassi was convicted and hanged on February 23, and so was his cousin, an officer in the army. Another spying case, on the other hand, brought discredit to the Baath regime because the spy, an Israeli named Eliahu Cohen, had introduced himself as a Syrian emigrant returning from Argentina and became the friend of higher officers and cabinet ministers including Hafez himself who allowed him to visit the Syrian front. Nothing was mentioned about his case except in the Beirut press. His trial was secret and he was hanged on May 18, 1965.[36]

The Baath regime under Zuayyen, moreover, dropped a barrier, which some called the "Damask curtain", between the Syrians and foreign diplomats. In mid-December 1965 it notified the embassies and consulates to address invitations to private or general parties to the director of protocol at the foreign ministry, and the Syrian officials were told not to receive diplomats except by appointment through the protocol department. The Baath had already under the Hafez cabinet banned "free masonry" and rotary clubs on August 9, 1965 and threatened the members with military trials on charges of belonging to international secret organizations. The fear of spying and of conspiracies led the Baath regime to be constantly hunting down potential plotters.

The Syrian economy had been stagnant since 1963. Zuayyen tried to reassure the people in October 1965 by promising to encourage and expand the private sector, and he denied that real estate would be nationalized. Public celebrations were organized in order to entertain the peasants and the workers and portray them as contented citizens. It seems, however, that the working people were less happy under the socialist system and they felt that their participation in production and management and in elections to the national revolutionary council was only in name. The government-owned factories were not making profit, and the retail business was hard hit. The Baath administration, by restricting itself to party and class considerations, denied itself the support, advice and participation of most of its competent and resourceful citizens by forcing them to leave, and it had to depend on mediocre, raw and inexperienced party members to transact its nationalized business.

VII. The Baath Extremists in Power: The Road to Disaster

A. The Fifteenth Coup D'Etat and the Fall of General Hafez February 1966

The fifth Bitar Cabinet of January 1, 1966 ruled Syria for fifty-three days. It was swept away along with the national command and the strongman, General Hafez, because they were unable to remove the powerful army commanders who supported General Jedid and his dissolved regional command. Bitar wanted to make their deportation a condition for forming his cabinet, but he was told that this was not reasonable since the old defense minister was still in office. Bitar's cabinet of twenty-six ministers consisted almost entirely of Baathists with five independents. General Umran was the defense minister and the only member of the old military committee who stood on the side of the national command. The only other military in the cabinet held the portfolio of presidential affairs.

The choice of Bitar as prime minister was well received among the people and so was the dissolution of the regional command. The people generally felt more secure and confident with Bitar. They were now able to talk freely and complain against the behavior of local party members in the towns. The new prime minister represented a national unionist trend. He was relatively more moderate and less fanatic than his opponents who called him a rightist. He criticized the regional character of socialism in Syria and what he called "police" and "extemporaneous" socialism. He complained, in an article published in *al-Ahram* before he became prime minister, that Marxist logic had influenced the spirit of certain Baathists and other Arab revolutionaries because they were able to read only the available Arabic translations of Marxist works. They eventually fell in the contradiction of wanting to be Arabs and Marxists at the same time and thereby resembled the crow who wanted to imitate the walk of the partridge and ended by not knowing how to walk.[97]

Bitar also expressed his dissatisfaction with military intervention in government shortly after he became prime minister. He then made the distinction between "the doctrinal army which is tied to a national revolutionary doctrine, and the political army which interferes in the country's administration." The army, according to Bitar, could interfere in politics only when it is out of loyalty to the revolution, but any interference should be stopped when it threatens the revolution itself.[98]

Other Baath leaders of the national command expressed views similar to those of Bitar. While they admitted the strong connection between Baath socialism and Marxism they complained, as Aflaq and Razzaz had done, that the socialism implemented by the military Baathist rulers consisted of issuing orders, appointing labor union members, and spreading intelligence agents in factories. The founding fathers of the national Baath command were particularly opposed to the "regional socialism" of the military as they were opposed to the international socialism of the Marxists.

The older leaders of the national command also believed in the doctrinal army that protects the revolution and receives its doctrinal spirit and orientation from the party organization. But they wanted to prevent the officers from combining their military status with leadership in the party or in the government. In his talk shortly before the fall of Hafez and of the national command, Aflaq asserted that there was no revolutionary party in the world whose leadership included military officers who were still in command of their units, but "with us," he said, "some of the military comrades were at one and the same time in the party command, in the cabinet, and in the army."[99]

The soundness of these arguments in the particular case of the Baath party has been doubted by Arab observers and writers. It was judged hardly possible for a military Baathist, who had been indoctrinated and "used" for achieving the political goals of a party with conflicting elements, to remain neutral in intra-party quarrels, or to refrain from seeking his share of power and prestige when civilian members were seeking theirs. Baathist officers, moreover, were aware of the fact that the party and its leaders had so little weight and following in the country, and their imposed policies, including socialism and one-party government, were so unpopular that their rule had to be constantly protected by the military against the people or against other military dissidents. In this light, the only picture that could represent the reality of the Syrian situation under the Baath was that of government by the military. Baath party rule had to be military rule, or else there would have been no ruling Baath party.

Bitar's fifth cabinet and the national command that supported it had to adopt various measures to strengthen their position in the party and in the armed forces and improve their image in the country. They had, according to Razzaz, to apply a gradualist program in implementing socialism, and promote an atmosphere of Arab unionism. In the army, they wanted to do away with military intervention in daily government affairs, restore discipline to the army after it had lost all sense of discipline, and especially remove the domineering officers who viewed their units as their private property.[100]

The action of the national command was weakened by division, suspicion and disputes among its members. General Amin Hafez disagreed constantly with General Hafez Asad who, with Ibrahim Makhous, represented the regionalists on the national command. The discussions lasted hours without reaching any decision and each of the two rival military leaders, Hafez and Asad, came to the meetings with an impressive number of private guardsmen—forty with Hafez and twenty with Asad—and this made the atmosphere heavy with threats. The maneuvers of General Umran, minister of defense, were particularly harmful to the cause of the national command and its leaders. According to Razzaz, secretary-general of the national command, Umran worked for his own self-interest, and was slow in making the necessary transfers, particularly those of Izzat Jedid, who commanded the armored units, and Selim Hatum who was at the head of the commandos in the suburbs of Damascus. When the transfers were finally ordered on February 21, 1966, they were not preceded by any preparatory movements among the smaller officers in the Damascus region that would have made the resistance of the transferred commanders, I. Jedid and Hatum, difficult. Moreover, when it was suggested in the national command to mobilize some reliable units in order to discourage resistance to the transfers, General Hafez disagreed because he feared that the mobilization could be used by Umran against him.

The former regional command under Salah Jedid's and Zuayyen's leadership naturally exploited the disagreements and mistakes of the national command. The regionalists, moreover, charged that the appointment of the Bitar cabinet was altogether illegal because the regional command normally nominated the cabinet, and they therefore demanded the election of a new regional command. The regionalists also led a campaign of accusations against the Bitar cabinet and claimed that it prepared to repeal the nationalization decrees and that it consisted of imperialist agents.

The two immediate causes of the regionalists' coup of February 23 against Hafez and the national command were the negotiations with Nasser and the transfer of officers. On February 17, Defense Minister Umran and five other officers left for Cairo to discuss the restoration of diplomatic relations with Egypt and the conclusion of a truce between Nasser and the Baath regime. In Syria the regionalists were not in favor of the rapprochement with Egypt. It was even said that Hafez Asad, commander of the air force, decisively turned to Jedid's side because of a pro-Nasser demonstration on February 21, and the balance of forces was consequently tipped in favor of Jedid. The two sides began to mobilize their supporters in the tense atmosphere of Sunday, February 20 when the elections planned for the regional command were postponed by Hafez because he felt that the candidates of the Jedid group would win.[101] The national command held its last meeting on the evening of February 20, 1966 and it lasted until the morning of February 21. The decision was taken after almost two months of hesitation to transfer Izzat Jedid, Selim Hatum, and Ahmad Swaidani who were the most effective supporters of General Salah Jedid, and two pro-Hafez officers in order to reduce the shock for the other side.[102] The transferred officers decided to resist in spite of the exhortations of Razzaz to save the party and the country from civil war.

The coup of Wednesday, February 23, 1966 was described by eye witnesses as "bloody and savage." The main fighting took place around the residence of General Hafez in the Abu-Rummane quarter. The desert forces, estimated at about 120 soldiers, were summoned during the night to guard it when rumors of the trouble reached Damascus. No other military forces offered any resistance to the movement except for some loyalists in two camps outside Damascus who were overcome and some opposition in Aleppo. The leaders of the coup were Major Selim Hatum whose commandos and paratroopers were stationed at Harasta, and Lt. Col. Izzat Jedid who commanded the armored units at Qabun, south of Damascus. The two officers at the head of some 600 men first occupied the General Headquarters and the broadcasting station in the early hours of Wednesday, February 23, and at about 4 a.m. the attack on the Hafez residence began. Machine guns and grenades were used at the beginning, but tanks were brought later because of the valiant resistance of the desert troops. Hafez himself participated in the battle with a machine gun until he received a bullet in his leg. The fighting lasted about four hours and was said to have been the bloodiest in the annals of Syrian coups. Rough guesses put the number of those who were killed between 300 and 1,000 but more sober estimates later mentioned fifty dead, and the official figure given by the government in early March was forty-one.[103]

The communiqués on the coup were broadcast in the name of the "provisional regional command of the Baath party." One of them mentioned the arrest of Hafez, Umran,

Aflaq, Razzaz, Bitar and other leaders of the national command. Two officers who played an important role in the coup were given their reward immediately on February 23 by the first decree of the provisional party command, even before the cabinet was formed. They were Major-General Hafez Asad who was appointed minister of defense and Colonel Ahmad Swaidani, former military intelligence chief, who was now promoted to major-general and to the post of chief of staff. General Asad, like the two Jedids, came from the Alawi rural areas near the Syrian coast, while Swaidani was a Sunnite from a village in Hauran. He was an extreme and austere Marxist, an admirer of Mao tse-Tung, and a believer in the doctrinal army.

The provisional regional command broadcast a long statement on February 23 to justify its action. The ousted leaders were accused of selfishness, weakness and right wing tendencies. The forces of reaction were said to have infiltrated the party and attempted to make the revolution deviate from its unavoidable path. These forces "were aided by the individualism of Amin Hafez, the weakness of Muhammad Umran, the rightism of Salah Bitar, and the egotism of Michel Aflaq." The new leaders claimed that these "deviationists" were asked to hold a regional congress or a national party congress to discuss their decisions and they refused. They also did not agree to the meeting of a special session of the national council. This is why it was finally "decided to wage the battle against them and crush them forever to make of them an example to those who try to undermine the party and destroy its revolution from within or from without."

The coup was later described by its authors as a "corrective movement" that sought to "rectify the deviation" within the Baath party. Behind the struggle was also the conflict between the moderate socialist Sunnite city dweller represented by Hafez, and the ultra-socialist rural Alawi or Druze or Ismaili villager represented by the two Jedids, Hatum, and Jundi. Moreover, a difference in Arab policy separated Hafez from Jedid. The coup of February 23 was viewed as a triumph of anti-Nasserism over the restrained pro-Nasserism of the Hafez regime. This is why, it was supposed, the French and the British favored the coup, according to the Arab saying, "not by love for Ali, but by hatred for Muawiya."

B. Baath Disagreements and the Attempted Coup of September 1966

The coup of February 23, 1966 did not end the disagreements among the Baath military leaders. Rivalries soon led to quarrels between the victorious Druze and Alawi officers, and later between the leading Alawi strongmen.

The new leaders suspended the provisional constitution of 1964 two days after their coup. On February 25 one of the civilian members of the command, Nureddin Atassi, was appointed head of state, and another, Yusif Zuayyen, became prime minister. Both were in their mid-thirties, as most of the other new leaders. The new forty-year-old strongman, Salah Jedid, who engineered the coup against Hafez, took no official position in the government but he acquired a leading role in the provisional party command that had the power to appoint and dismiss the head of state and the cabinet. On March 1, 1966 the 20-member cabinet of Zuayyen was formed. It included for the first time in Syrian history, a regular member of the Communist party, Samih Atiyah, and a strong Communist sympathizer, Ahmad Murad.

In its leadership, its program, and its declarations and policies, the new Syrian Baath regime was viewed as extremist and farther to the left than the ruling regime in Egypt and Iraq. The new cabinet proposed in its announced program of March 2 to improve the economy by "developing and deepening socialist experience." It also wanted a "majority of the armed forces to become an ideological instrument" while avoiding interference in daily political affairs. The new leaders made it their chief occupation to denounce reactionaries, capitalists, and imperialists in the press, over the radio, and in organized *mahrajans* (mass rallies) and military parades. On the third anniversary of the Baath takeover on March 8, 1966 Atassi claimed in his speech that the obstacles to "full socialism" in Syria were "the imperialist designs to obstruct the liberation movements," and the "obstinacy of capitalism and its insistance on retaining its illegal privileges."[104]

The provisional Baath command called for the meeting of a regional party congress in Damascus on March 10 in order to discuss the coup of February 23 and to elect a regular regional command. It elected a 16man command that consisted essentially of the military and civilian authors and supporters of the anti-Hafez coup of February 23, and included Nureddin Atassi, the head of state, as secretary-general, while the real strongman of the new regime, Major-General Salah Jedid, became assistant secretary-general.

Among the active participants in the coup of February 23, 1966, the two Druze officers Hamad Ubaid and Selim Hatum soon became disenchanted with the new regime and turned against it. Hamad Ubaid expected to become defense minister in the cabinet because he had held that post in the first Zuayyen cabinet in September 1965, and he, moreover, had helped quell the resistance in Aleppo at the beginning of the coup. He reportedly retired to a redoubt in Aleppo and decided to return to Damascus only if he was offered the defense ministry. Later in March he was discharged from the army and in May he was arrested and accused of plotting against the regime. Hatum, on the other hand, remained in the active service until early September 1966. He had led the attack on the residence of Hafez in the coup of February 23, but he was distrusted by the new regime that he helped bring to power. Suspicion between him and the new leaders developed into hostility and led eventually to an attempt to overthrow the regime.

The new Baath government conducted a series of purges and arrests in the army and party ranks. Razzaz has claimed that the rule of violence under the new regime had no equal in Syrian history and that it was similar only to that of Kassem in Iraq.[105] what the new regime did, however, was not basically different in its purges, arrests, and violence, from the actions of the preceding Baath regime under Hafez. Following the coup of February 23, about ninety officers were pensioned or transferred because of their diapproval of the movement. Generals Hafez and Umran, who were still in jail, were discharged from the army later in March.

The relations of the new Baath regime with the neighboring Arab states, even the revolutionary ones, were unfriendly and Syria consequently isolated itself, even more than under the Hafez regime, from the rest of the Arab world. The sympathies of the radical Baath were generally described as closer to the Communist camp than to the brother Arab governments. Nasser's attitude towards the new rulers, and towards the Baath in general, was one of "no confidence."

In his attacks against the Arab summit conferences of 1964 and 1965 in which royalist, bourgeois, and revolutionary regimes had tried to cooperate, Nureddin Atassi held that these conferences "evaded the responsibility for the liberation of Palestine." The Baath government encouraged and patronized the *Asifa* (Thunderstorm) commando organization that made five raids into Israel in June-July, 1966. Israel's planes retaliated on July 14 with an air attack against an anti-aircraft position eight miles inside Syria. Baathist Syria lost one MIG-21 fighter in the air battle and charged that this was a part of an imperialist conspiracy.

The alliance of the new Baath rulers with the local Communists, their dependence on the Soviet Union and close friendship with the Communist camp, and their uncomprising hostility to the West were among the outstanding features of the new radical Baath regime. The return of Khalid Bakdash, secretary-general of the Communist party to Damascus from Eastern Europe on April 14 after a long absence confirmed the alliance between the Baath and the local Communists, and at the same time was meant to prove the neutralism of the Syrian government in the Moscow-Peking dispute. On April 18, 1966 a delegation of twenty-eight persons including

Zuayyen and the foreign affairs and defense ministers left for Moscow on a six-day visit. Four days later the Soviet Union promised in an agreement for economic cooperation to advance 150 million dollars to Syria towards the construction of the Euphrates dam that was expected to irrigate one and a half million acres. The new agreement with the Soviet Union that came one week after the return of Bakdash gave rise to the rumor that his return to Syria was a condition for the Soviet aid, and Bakdash was referred to, at least in one article, as "the man who is worth a dam."[107]

The radical Baath government proudly announced in its newspaper, *al-Baath,* after the economic agreement with the Soviet Union, that Syria "has shattered the political blockade imposed by Western imperialism." The Soviet Union, at the same time, took a patronizing interest in the new Baath regime and considered itself its protector. It issued warnings to those powers who were suspected of plotting against Syria that it would not stay indifferent in the event of attempted action against the regime.

The Syrians generally disliked the isolationism and radicalism of the new regime. They resented the stifling of freedom, particularly in the economic domain, and the "deepening" of socialist experience. They watched with disgust the rule of the country by raw and inexperienced upstarts and the resulting instability and inefficiency. The leading businessmen–some four hundred in number–were prevented from leaving the country and were held for investigation. The small retailers were the victims of bureaucratic red tape and incompetence because most of the import-export business and the consumer business was directly controlled by the government. For the first time in recent Syrian history, people had to wait for hours at the bakeries to buy their bread. Political parties no longer existed to organize resistance against government policy, and most of the political leaders had left the country. Under these conditions popular dissatisfaction was voiced on the occasion of celebrations and receptions of various kinds and often took the aspect of Muslim opposition to the ruling Baath and to Communism. The return of the former Mufti of Syria, Sheikh Hasan Habannakeh, from the prilgrimage to Mecca at the end of April 1966 became the occasion for a colossal political demonstration in which the people shouted "No Communism, No Baathism, but Islamic unity." The government wanted, but evidently was unable to prevent the demonstration.[108]

It was in these conditions of division and dissatisfaction that civilian leaders of the deposed Baath national command, and some disgruntled military commanders tried to overthrow the radical Baath regime. On Tuesday September 6, 1966 the Zuayyen cabinet said that an attempt to oust the present regime had been foiled and the attempt was attributed to the "Aflaq-Bitar-Razzaz clique." The statement of the ruling Baath cabinet in Damascus mentioned that "armed workers, peasants, and national guardsmen were ordered to crush the counter-revolutionary adventures." The general federation of labor controlled by the ruling Baath party overreacted to the government orders and sent its bands of armed workers, in an action that was compared to that of the Chinese Red Guards, to purge the state administration of "all reactionary and conspiratorial elements hostile to the revolution and its socialist experience."

On September 7, the government-owned newspapers published a communiqué issued by the labor federation describing how a group of armed workers walked into the offices of a state-operated insurance company on the preceding day and ordered seven of its officials to resign. When they refused, the labor commando group marched them at gun point to the federation headquarters where the Ismaili president of the federation, Khalid al-Jundi, told them they should resign because they were "reactionaries." They finally submitted their resignations to the ministry of national economy that controlled their company.[109] Similar action was directed by the labor squads against other government officials and businessmen.

On September 8, 1966 another attempt was made against

the radical Baath regime, but it was evidently a part of the general plot in which Bitar and Aflaq were involved. The abortive coup of September 8 was led by Selim Hatum. The immediate cause of his attempt was the fear of losing power completely by dismissal or transfer from his command of the commando unit at Harasta. One of his partners in the attempted coup was another Druze officer, Talal Abu-Asli, who had just refused to be transferred from his command post at Deraa. On September 8, the two officers and their supporters left for Swaida in Jabal Druze to rally support. They broke into a Baath party meeting that was attended by Atassi and Jedid and arrested the two dignitaries and kept them most of the night of September 8-9 as hostages. The minister of defense, Hafez Asad, was alerted in Damascus and sent an ultimatum to the post commander at Swaida to have Atassi and Jedid released or else the Syrian forces would march on Jabal Druze. The two hostages were released and were able to return in the morning of Friday September 9 to Damascus.

In Damascus a curfew was suddenly ordered in the evening of September 8 at 9 p.m. It was probably a direct result of the arrest of Atassi and Jedid, and was also intended to round up the plotters who were preparing to go into action in the capital. Tanks were brought to town and the defense ministry and the radio station were cordoned by guards while the people were warned to be ready for the decisive battle for the victory of the revolution. In the suburb of Harasta, Hatum's command post exchanged fire with the government forces, but the rebels had to surrender when the post was surrounded by tanks. Some 200 military and civilian rebels and plotters were arrested and the commandos of the labor federation were said to have arrested another thirty people.[110]

With the surrender of the rebel forces at Harasta and the fear that the government troops could march against and damage the Jabal Druze region, Hatum and his supporters were forced to abandon the struggle and cross the border to Jordan where they were granted asylum. The Syrian government blamed "reactionary, imperialist and deviationist circles" for the attempt. Premier Zuayyen linked the effort to overthrow the Baath regime with the government demand for increased transit royalties from "the imperialist oil companies." The leader of the labor federation accused Jordan and Saudi Arabia of supporting the plot, and the editor of *al-Ahram* in Cairo later added the CIA to the picture. On the other hand, some have given a sectarian explanation to the Hatum attempt and viewed it as an aspect of the conflict between the Alawis who were in control of Syria, and the Druzes and Sunnis.

The trial of those who were involved in the abortive coup of September 8 and other plotters began on December 17, 1966 in a special military court. Other defendants were tried by the same court because they resisted the coup of February 23, and seven of these were sentenced to death on January 7, 1967 but only one was in custody. Hatum remained in Jordan until the beginning of the hostilities with Israel in early June 1967. He then returned to Syria, placed himself under the protection of Sultan al-Atrash, the Druze leader, and offered his services to the Syrian army. The Baath rulers summoned him to Damascus and then executed him after a summary trial on June 26, 1967. He was charged with a new crime, that of plotting to overthrow the Syrian regime with the help of the United States during the war with Israel. His execution increased the rift between the ruling regime and the Druzes.[111]

C. The Baath Regime and the Military Disaster of June 1967

The Baath military strongmen were able to maintain their rule after the failure of Hatum's attempt by the violent repression of dissenting movements and by purges and trials of potential opponents. They tried to persuade the Syrians and other Arabs, through angry and boastful speeches, marches, and mass meetings, that their regime was the Arab citadel in the struggle against imperialism and Zionism. The Syrians, however, remained unconvinced. The competitive radicalism and boastfulness of the Baath rulers had no basis of competence or strength. It ended by giving Israel an excuse to attack Syria and occupy a part of its territory. In the meantime, the military leaders continued to have their petty jealousies and quarrels, and they concentrated their efforts on the prevention of a possible hostile military coup rather than on the defense of their country.

In late 1966 and early 1967 the radical Baath rulers took an increasingly hostile attitude towards the non-socialist Arab countries, and their attacks against the monarchs of Jordan and Saudi Arabia became more violent. When the joint defense agreement with Egypt was signed on November 4, 1966, Premier Zuayyen declared that it was directed against the Arab "reactionaries" as well as Israel. In the new agreement, it was decided to coordinate the military and political affairs of the two states and to establish diplomatic relations. The Syrian Baath, nevertheless, remained suspicious of Nasser and the Syrian Nasserist exiles in Cairo were not allowed to return.[112]

The standard practice of the military Baath was to show more belligerence and stir up more external crises whenever it felt that its control of Syria was weakening or the internal conditions were becoming worse. The Baath rulers expected to draw various benefits such as enhanced prestige and badly needed foreign exchange out of their dispute with the Iraq Petroleum Company in late 1966. They sent an ultimatum to the IPC to answer their demands on November 22 for more transit and shipping royalties and for back payments of the increase since 1956. Their press spoke repeatedly of "imperialistic injustice embodied in the oil monopolies." On December 8 the Syrian government sequestrated the movable and immovable assets of the IPC and four days later it stopped the pumping of oil through the pipelines crossing Syria and the shipping of oil from the terminal at Baniyas. When a satisfactory agreement was reached with the IPC on March 2, 1967, the government organized a mass workers' rally to celebrate the Syrian victory.

The Baath regime continued its pressure against Jordan and sent its trained saboteurs there to incite trouble. It also encouraged Syrian-trained commandos to enter Israel from Jordan and then exploited the Israeli retaliation against the Jordanians—as in the raid against the village of Sammu' in November 1966—to attack the Jordanian government. Atassi actually made it clear in early December that the "liberation" of Jordan should be achieved before that of Palestine. The Soviet Union was given credit for preventing Israeli retaliation against Syria in November 1966. Soviet officials in Moscow were said to have told the Israeli ambassador at the time that their government "will not acquiesce to any Israeli move which could weaken the Damascus regime."[113]

As the relations of the Baath regime with the Soviet Union became closer, differences of opinion appeared among the leaders on the consequences of these relations, especially in what touches the ambitions of the local Communist party, and the attitude of Communist China. On January 22, 1967 Salah Jedid was invited by the Soviet Communist party to visit Moscow in order to study party affairs and the functioning of socialism in the Soviet Union. He left with a twenty-member delegation which the authorities in Moscow spoke of as representative of the Syrian people. On Jedid's return at the end of January, he was accused of aligning Syria with Moscow against Peking. Some of the Baath rulers, moreover, were apprehensive of the ambition of the local Communist party and of the Communist cabinet ministers. This is why 250 Communist teachers were dismissed in early April 1967.

The favorite Baathist theme that was often used to explain Israeli retaliatory attacks was that the imperialist forces, including The United States, were determined to destroy the Syrian regime and other progressive forces in the Arab world. This was the explanation given to the Israeli retaliatory air raid on Syria on April 7, 1967 in which six Syrian planes were reported shot down in a seven-hour air battle and Israeli planes flew over Damascus. In his note to the Security Council after the raid, the Syrian representative at The United Nations said that "Israel was encouraged by imperialist powers and the forces of reaction who see in the development of Syria factors threatening their strategic interests."[114] The Baath government tried to remove the effect of the humiliation by claiming victory over the Israelis and "shattering the myth of Israeli air superiority." This typical self-delusion and deceit on the part of the Baathist as well as other Arab revolutionary regimes was one of the serious causes of defeat in the war that broke out less than two months later.

A few days after the Israeli air raid, the Beirut press reported that the Syrian planes that fought against the Israelis had no live ammunition, and instead of real air-to-air missiles they had dummies. The Syrian pilots therefore were sent to fight in planes of the type used for training, and the conclusion drawn was that the Baath regime, in its permanent fear of a coup d'état, did not trust its own pilots and did not enable them to fight in regularly equipped aircraft.

The Baath regime persisted in emphasizing its radicalism and even its leadership of the Arab radical camp in an effort to ignore, or to make up for, its military and other reverses. The people remained unimpressed and showed their dissatisfaction with the regime on various occasions. When the Israeli planes appeared in the sky of Damascus on April 7, 1967 the people became happy at the thought that they were Syrian rebel planes participating in a coup against the ruling Baath.[115] Those of the Syrians who were able to leave the country, emigrated particularly to neighboring Lebanon, and by the spring of 1967 it was estimated that about 200,000 persons had left Syria since Baath rule began. The Syrian opposition found a valid cause for demonstrating against the Baath establishment when an official army publication, the People's Army magazine, published an article calling for atheism. The author of the article, Ibrahim Khlass, wrote that the only way to build Arab civilization and society is to create the new Arab socialist individual "who believes that God, religions, feudalism and capital, and all the values which dominated the previous society are only mummified dummies that should be kept in the historical museum.'"[116] The Ulama (religious scholars) reacted with an attack on "the atheistic Baath government" in their Friday sermons on May 5, and a demonstration followed. Two days later a strike began and clashes occurred in Hama and Damascus, particularly after the arrest of Sheikh Hasan Habannakeh, president of the Society of Ulama. On May 9 the confiscation of shops and the violent action of "armed workers" forced the shopkeepers to end the strike. Arrests continued until May 15 and touched a number of Ulama following the anti-Baath sermons of Friday May 12.

The Baath government claimed that it was not responsible for the "atheistic" article, and the writer was described as an agent of the CIA. The entire incident was portrayed as a Zionist-imperialist plot. At the height of the crisis between May 5 and 15, 1967 the Syrian government found it convenient to raise the spectre of an imminent Israeli aggression in order to end the internal disturbances, and the Soviet Union gave its approval. The Russians persuaded Egypt that Israel was concentrating forces on the Syrian border, and Egypt prepared to implement the mutual defense pact of November 1966 with Syria by mobilizing its forces.[117] The Baath government thus contributed to the development of the Middle East crisis that led to the Israeli attack on Sinai on June 5, 1967 and to Arab defeat. Its leaders were contented with making belligerent declarations and warnings. Their chief of staff claimed that Syria was fully prepared. At the United Nations, their representative charged the United States on May 15 with complicity in a CIA plot of the Suez type.[118]

When the war broke out on June 5, 1967 the Israelis destroyed fifty-two Syrian planes on the ground but they concentrated their operations first on the Egyptian and Jordanian fronts. It was only on Friday June 9 that they turned against the Syrian forces. In the meantime, the Baath rulers who had been urging military action against Israel before the outbreak of hostilities made no effort to open a front in order to relieve the pressure on the Jordanians or to gain some ground in Israel. They seemed to be more fearful of an internal military coup than of an Israeli attack. This is why, as it has been explained, they had only four brigades near the Israeli border on the Syrian Golan heights, while ten brigades were posted around Damascus. When Israel turned to occupy the fortified Golan region that overlooked its settlements in the Jordan valley on June 9, the Baath forces offered little resistance. It was said that the Syrian military used their artillery badly and that they withdrew quickly as soon as their lines were broken.[119] The Baath leaders had talked much about fighting but they were unable to fight. Under the Baath regime, the army lost its discipline and its morale as political and ideological considerations dominated military policy and influenced the promotion and transfer of officers. Scores of reserve officers who were mostly Baathist teachers were brought to the army to enhance the Baath position but their performance was poor in the short battle with Israel and the minister of defense was able to obtain their dismissal only in March 1969.[120]

The story of the Baath regime after the Arab-Israeli war has been one of unprecedented internal and external extremism that caused disagreements among Baath leaders and ended with the emergence of Hafez Asad, the defense minister, as Syria's strongman. Aspects of Baath extremism could be seen in its attitude towards the Arab disaster, its continued boastful belligerence without positive military action, its refusal to cooperate with the Arab states for reaching a political settlement or for the coordination of military measures against Israel, and its complete boycott of the West and increased dependence on the Communist camp. The Baath government under Premier Zuayyen and the strongman Salah Jedid boycotted the Arab summit conference that was held in Khartoum on August 29, 1967 to discuss the means for "erasing the consequences of aggression," and held a national Baath party congress in Damascus on the following day. The

Baath congress decided that a war of popular liberation was the only way to make the Israelis evacuate occupied Arab lands. On November 10, 1967 the Syrian government rejected King Hussein's declarations in New York and Washington about accepting Israel "as a fact of life," and on November 23 a Syrian government spokesman announced that Syria "categorically and firmly rejects" the Security Council resolution of November 22 which Egypt and Jordan have accepted as a basis for a peace settlement and for Israeli withdrawal. President Nasser criticized the Syrian Baath indirectly when he referred in his speech of November 23 to the countries "that talk about fighting but are unable to fight and indeed have no intention of fighting."

The declaration that ended the ninth Baath national congress–that represented the ruling Syrian Baath, not the ousted one–in early September 1967 explained in radical Baathist language the causes and goals of the "imperialist Zionist aggression" in June, outlined the factors and causes of "the setback," and presented suggestions for facing the challenge on the internal, inter-Arab, and international levels. The objectives of the aggression, said the declaration, was "to obstruct the march of the Arab revolution and overthrow the progressive regimes that represent the basis of this revolution in order to weaken the struggle and the hopes of the Arab masses to build up their united modern state."[121]

The declaration suggested general principles for facing the challenge on the basis of a long and continuous struggle. On the internal level, the congress suggested unity in the direction of the party and the revolution, the reinforcement of the regular and popular armies, continued build up of the economic foundation, and extreme firmness in dealing with the conspirators and enemies of the revolution. On the inter-Arab level, the declaration saw the need for a united Arab state with a socialist basis that would include the progressive Arab countries. It also proposed the unification of the military and economic potential in Syria, Egypt, Iraq and Algeria. It suggested that the Palestinian people should be in the vanguard of the armed struggle, that the colonialist countries that participated in the aggression should be boycotted, and the oil flow to the countries that supported the aggression should be stopped. On the international level, the declaration suggested the development of relations and cooperation with the socialist countries in all the domains because the need for resisting the colonialist plans requires a unified attitude of the progressive and socialist forces in the world.

The Baathist declaration thus emphasized in repetitive inflamed phrases the need for the struggle against the imperialist Western powers whom it made responsible for Israeli aggression. The Baath continued to blame imperialism and Arab "reactionary" regimes for Arab disunity and for the "setback" in June 1967, but at the same time it based the cooperation and unity between Arab states on ideological considerations and socialist brotherhood. The Baath regime stubbornly refused to realize that its monopoly of power, its Marxian notions of revolution, its imposed socialism, and the preoccupation of army officers with politics had divided the country, weakened the army, and failed to make the masses better fighters.

The radical Baath government immediately after the June war expressed its belligerence in a xenophobia that banned Western newsmen and even tourists. The Baathist minister of education pursued a policy of "foreign cultural evacuation," that meant the weakening of Western education patterns by sending no students to study in the West and taking control of some 900 private schools, mostly parochial and Western-oriented in October 1967 and imposing nationalized textbooks that included the Baathist socialist doctrine and interpretations of world events.

While the Baath government persisted in its verbal belligerence and xenophobic propaganda barrages, the Syrian ceasefire line with Israel remained singularly quiet in contrast to the artillery duels fought by Jordan and later by Egypt on the Jordan and Suez Canal fronts, and to the Israeli air strikes and commando raids that these two countries had to endure. The Palestinian commandos rarely operated from Syrian territory and consequently invited no Israeli retaliation until February 1969. Moreover, the Baathist rulers remained largely indifferent when heavy retaliation was visited by Israel upon Jordan, where most of the commando raids originated. The rulers in Damascus, however, continued to oppose a political settlement and they used violent language to express their opposition.

While the Baath government avoided active military involvement with Israel, it returned to its old favorite game of creating problems and sowing discord in the neighboring Arab countries that continued to live under a system of free economy and parliamentary democracy. In Lebanon its agents encouraged a young Lebanese from Tripoli named Muhammad Nabil Akkari, to assassinate the former president and active politician, Camille Chamoun, in order to create a dangerous crisis that might lead to civil strife. On May 31, 1969, Akkari was sentenced to death because the attempt was considered an act of aggression against state security.[122] Two months after the crime, the prime minister of Syria, Yusif Zuayyeh, made an attack on Lebanon because of the discovery of an anti-Baath plot organized by Syrian political refugees living on Lebanese territory. The Baath government in its desire to punish Lebanon for refusing to deny asylum to the political refugees imposed heavy tariffs on its transit trade through Syria and on Lebanese exports.

For most Lebanese nationalists, the greatest damage that the Syrian Baath regime was able to inflict on the unity and security of Lebanon after the Arab-Israeli war of 1967 was produced by the Syrian encouragement of Palestinian commando groups to operate on Lebanese territory, and the incitements of the Syrian radio in support of the commandos in order to aggravate the division and the tensions in Lebanon. The attempts of the Lebanese rulers to restrict commando action led to demonstrations and cabinet crises. The impression of most Arab observers was that the Syrian Baath was provoking the kind of internal tensions in Lebanon that led to the armed conflict of 1958, and that it was giving Israel a pretext to occupy southern Lebanon.

In Jordan, the Syrian Baath regime also used the commando group *al-Saiqa* that was affiliated with it to kidnap the Druze leader, Hasan al-Atrash, on October 8, 1968 and take him to Damascus. Under the name of *Kata'eb al-Nasr* (victory phalanges) this same group opened fire on a Jordanian patrol and incited the people to revolt against their government. On November 4, 1968 the Jordanian forces arrested these "phony" commandos, as King Hussein called them, because their target was Jordan's east bank, not the Israeli-occupied west bank.

The military disaster, under normal circumstances, should have swept away the Baath regime that was responsible for it In Syria the Baath military rulers, however, became even more entrenched as they maintained their control over the army and immediately took up their prewar belligerence—that was partly responsible for the Israeli attack—and their quarrels with the neighboring Arab countries. They also isolated themselves even more completely from the West by breaking relations with the United States, Britain and West Germany and raising the level of their attacks against them. Their dependence on the Soviet Union, on the other hand, became more complete because of their need for Soviet arms and for diplomatic economic, and moral support. Soviet arms and diplomatic support did not succeed in erasing the consequences of aggression, but certain development projects were started with Soviet help. On March 6, 1968 Premier Zuayyen inaugurated construction on the Euphrates dam project that was to be supervised by the Russians. The development of oil production was to be undertaken in cooperation with the Russians following the visit of a Soviet oil delegation on January 23, 1969 under the Soviet petroleum industry minister.

The Syrian Communist party naturally acclaimed the Soviet support, and its politbureau emphasized the need to consolidate the Syro-Russian friendship and protect it because this friendship alone "could eliminate the aftermath of the Israeli aggression and overcome all the difficulties."[123] Communist activity was tolerated by the Baath regime at a time when all political parties were prohibited. In early June 1969 the third congress of the Syrian Communist party was held in Damascus and its declaration sought to sow discord among the Arabs by suggesting that the Israeli aggression in 1967 was prepared by the imperialist powers and supported in many ways by the Arab reactionaries who wanted to deal a blow to the Arab liberation movement. The Syrian Baath gave the Soviet Union complete satisfaction in maintaining the intense propaganda barrage against the "imperialists" and in strengthening its friendship with the Soviet Bloc and other nations of the Communist camp. The Baath rulers, however, again disagreed on the extent of Soviet cooperation and the degree of participation and influence of the Syrian Communist party in government and society, and these differences were among the causes of the coup of March 1969.

VIII. Baath Quarrels and the "Frozen Coup" of March 1969

The Baath rulers who led Syria to the humiliating defeat of June 1967 soon resumed their internal quarrels while the rival socialist parties plotted to overthrow them. The Zuayyen cabinet was reshuffled on September 28, 1967 and among its ten new ministers were some independent unionists and some Arab socialists of the Hourani group. In the defense ministry, disagreements and quarrels occurred between Lt. Gen. Hafez Asad and his chief of staff Ahmad Swaidani, and on February 15, 1968 Swaidani was removed and was replaced by Major General Mustafa Tlass who became also first deputy defense minister while two other major generals became second deputy defense ministers.

The only parties that were left to challenge the Baath regime were the socialist parties because the former traditional parties were dealt heavy blows and their leaders were in exile. In May 1968 three radical parties attempted to join forces in order to remove the Baath government. They were: The Arab nationalists' movement, the Arab socialist party and the pro-Nasser socialist unionists. Some leaders of these parties were arrested, but Hourani was able to escape to Beirut. The Baath rulers became particularly alarmed when the Iraqi coup of July 1968 brought to power in Baghdad a different Baath regime that was more inclined to Aflaq's and Bitar's "national Baath." Before the end of July the government in Damascus mentioned a plot that was prepared by the Syrian political refugees in Lebanon, but no details were given. More serious was the plot of mid-August 1968 that was organized by Ahmad Swaidani, the former chief of staff, and other Baathist officers, but ended in failure. The Beirut *al-Nahar* reported that on August 15, 1968 nine MIG-17's and their pilots escaped to Iraq, and two days later three MIG-21's followed. The Syrian government feared the consequences of the departure of the former strongman, General Hafez, from Beirut to Iraq and posted tanks around the General Headquarters and the radio station.[124] The failure of the plot in August meant that Syria and Iraq would not cooperate under the same type of Baath rule or under one command, and this is what both the United States and Russia evidently wanted.[125]

In the fourth regional Baath congress in Damascus in September 1968 that was followed in October by the tenth national congress, new disagreements between the Baath leaders in Syria appeared. The clashes between General Asad and his supporters on one side, and Salah Jedid and Yusif Zuayyen and their supporters on the other led to the resignation of the Zuayyen cabinet in late October and the formation of a cabinet under the head of state, Nureddin Atassi. The causes of the dispute centered around the question of military cooperation with other Arab states and the problem of relations with the Soviet Union and with the local Communist party. General Asad as defense minister wanted Syria to cooperate with Iraq and Jordan and leave ideological considerations aside in the interest of the military effort. He also gave priority to the needs of the defense over those of development projects in industry and agriculture. It was common knowledge that the administration of new development projects such as the Euphrates dam and oil production was in the hands of Communist officials. Zuayyen wanted more emphasis on the projects and closer cooperation with the Soviet Union to the extent of granting it a naval base at Tartus and spending funds for deepening the harbor. He was also ready to grant the Communists the increased participation in the cabinet that they desired.[126]

Before the resignation of the Zuayyen cabinet it was rumored that General Asad ordered the transfer of Izzat Jedid from the command of the powerful 70th brigade, but Jedid refused and took refuge in the barracks of his brigade where he was joined by his cousin, Salah Jedid, and by Premier Zuayyen. Reports represented Asad so indignant at the attitudes and policies of Zuayyen and the two Jedids that he wanted them exiled but he was finally persuaded by mediators to be satisfied with Zuayyen's resignation.[127]

The cabinet of twenty-two members formed by the chief executive, Atassi, on October 29, 1968 retained General Asad in the defense ministry with three deputy defense ministers. The Communist party was represented by Wasel Faisal in the ministry of communications and by a "peace partisan" in the ministry of justice. The formation of a new cabinet evidently did not produce the changes in policy desired by General Asad. He probably saw the need for a coup in order to force a change in Baathist policy, but the coup came only after an Israeli air attack on the outskirts of Damascus had made his position untenable.

The Israeli air strike of February 24, 1969 was the first strike directed against Syria since the War in June 1967. The waves of Israeli fighter bombers attacked two commando bases at al-Hamah, six miles west of Damascus, and at Meissalun that was described as a training site for Fateh commandos further west on the road to Beirut. In a series of dog fights, Israel said it shot down two Syrian planes. The attack was particularly humiliating for General Asad, who was defense minister and air force commander, because the Syrian public questioned again, as it did on former occasions, the effectiveness of the Baath military organization and training, and the competence of its anti-aircraft units and its pilots. General Asad must have recalled how the Baath rulers withdrew his best brigades from the front in the war of June 1967 in order to protect their regime in Damascus. The showdown between him and Jedid approached when, as a result of his transfer of certain officers from the Latakia region, he was called by the Baath regional command to account for his action.

The military coup d'état directed by General Asad during the Adha Feast (Feast of Sacrifice) against the other ruling Baath leaders on March 1, 1968 was not announced over the radio in a series of communiques followed by martial music, as in other normal military coups, nor was it followed by a change in government and the arrest and trial of the ousted rulers. It took the aspect of a violent debate that was accompanied by a power play by General Asad and then ended in a new regional congress in which Asad's demands were largely satisfied. This is why it was called a "frozen coup." General Asad took advantage of the security measures that were taken during the Israeli air raid and kept his troops around the Damascus radio station and the General Headquarters, and replaced the police guards at the Central Bank with troops in order to guard the cash deposits. Most reports mentioned that the chief of state and prime minister, Nureddin Atassi, and the Baath party boss, Salah Jedid, were placed under house arrest.

By the evening of Saturday March 1, General Asad felt powerful enough to confront Atassi and Jedid with his demands. In the meeting of Baath leaders on that night of March 1 that lasted until the early hours of March 2, Asad accompanied by his chief of staff, General Tlass, reportedly presented the following demands: Closer cooperation with other Arab states without regard to ideologies, more serious preparation for war and the party's support for demanding MIG-21's from the Soviet Union, more friendly relations with Iraq and the establishment of an "eastern command," government resistance to Soviet interference in Syrian affairs, more support to Palestinian commandos, and the restoration of party unity.[128] In the course of the heated meeting the director of national security, Abdul Karim al-Jundi, was accused by Asad of having imposed a police state in Syria. In the early morning of Sunday, March 2, the thirty-nine year old Jundi committed suicide. His desperate action was the result of either the charges brought against him, or of his distress over the confrontation between thc two factions.[129] He was a member of the regional party command and an ally of Atassi and Jedid.

It is not known if General Asad really intended to carry out the coup until its natural end by forcing a change of government, or if he simply wanted to suspend the power of the ruling faction in a show of strength that would oblige it to accept his demands. The events tend to prove that Asad was not prepared to take over the government, or at least that he was not in a hurry to make the radical changes. The suicide of Abdul Karim al-Jundi also seems to have contributed to the freezing of the coup by providing a picture of the damaging effects of the conflict on the Baath party. On March 2, 1969 a truce was consequently reached between Asad and his opponents, and it was decided to resolve the dispute in a regional congress of the party. Asad must have felt sufficiently strong to allow this respite. General Asad received mediators from Egypt, Iraq and Algeria and they also must have helped in freezing the coup. Perhaps the strongest pressure on Asad was exerted by the Soviet ambassador who became fully involved in the crisis and strove to keep the regime within the limits of legality and under the control of the Baath party. It was even reported that the Soviet Union threatened to cut off all aid to

Syria in order to save the political lives of its men in the Baath leadership—Atassi and Jedid—and to retain its influence.[130]

The Baath regional congress met on March 20, 1969 for eleven days and was attended by 158 delegates. Its resolutions answered most of Asad's demands. It decided to draft a provisional constitution within a month because Syria had been without a constitution since the coup of February 1966, elect a popular assembly four months after the drafting of the provisional constitution, freeze the disagreements of Syria with other Arab countries, and accept military or financial aid from any Arab state to strengthen the Syrian and Arab front, and realize any possible step towards unity with the "progressive" Arab countries. The congress also decided to achieve the unity of the Baath party within and outside Syria and to recall all Baathist and other non-political officers who had been dismissed since 1966.[131] The statement of the congress spoke of freedom, and of opening channels of understanding with the people and punishing those who hurt it, but these declarations as well as those that mentioned elections and the constitution could not conceal the truth that the Baath party was working for itself and its own unity and was not prepared to abandon its monopoly of power or to grant any measure of political or economic freedom.

The congress ended its work by electing a new regional command. Most of the old members were re-elected—such as Atassi, Jedid, Zuayyen, Asad, and Makhous—and only three new ones replaced the ousted Ashawi, Nu'aisah and the deceased Jundi. During the meetings of the congress, it was felt that the Communist embassies tried to influence the voting on the resolutions. The political bureau of the Communist party issued a declaration, as the congress met, criticizing the military action at the beginning of the crisis, but the distribution of the declaration was not allowed. Certain Communists were arrested during the period that followed the coup and an anti-Communist wave was noticeable in the writing of slogans against the Communists on some buildings.[132] The Syrian public was generally behind Asad in his bid for cooperation with Iraq and Jordan, and his frozen coup achieved some successful results partly because of the popular support of his more moderate policies and views.

On May 1, 1969, one month after the resolutions of the regional congress, a provisional constitution of 81 articles was announced. It promised the election of a legislative "people's council," or popular assembly, by direct popular vote in four months. Under the Baath one-party rule, this assembly could not be expected to be freely elected and it would not therefore represent the country. In the meantime Asad continued to watch his rivals and on May 19 it was reported that Salah Jedid was placed under house arrest because he opposed the visit of a Syrian military delegation under the chief of staff, Mustafa Tlass, to Peking five days earlier.[133] The Syrian regime, however, demonstrated that it was maintaining close relations with the Soviet Union when it kept the Communist minister of communications, Wasel Faisal, in the new cabinet formed by Atassi on May 30, 1969 and when it officially recognized Communist East Germany on June 5, 1969 and prepared to establish diplomatic relations with it.

The era of Baath military rule since March 1963 has been perhaps the darkest period in modern Syrian history on account of the instability, insecurity, irresponsibility, and disregard for human rights that it brought with it, and the military, economic, and political chaos that it created. In the period of six years (1963-69), the Baath was responsible for six military coups d'état, two of which were staged against non-Baath regimes or personalities, and four were led by Baathist factions and strongmen against each other.[134] The Baath regime was also the target of one serious, but abortive, coup in July 1963 and several conspiracies and attempts made by Nasserists and other factions. Its policies provoked two revolts in Syria in mid 1964 and early 1965. Before it came to power in 1963, the Baath party contributed to the rise of most military regimes and supported their dictators until it became evident that it would not be allowed to rule the country under the shadow of the military ruler. The climax of its ineptitude was reached when it gave Israel the opportunity to attack Syria and other Arab lands and allowed Israeli forces to occupy Syrian territory.

Since they began ruling Syria, the Baath military leaders and their docile civilian allies have been responsible for four major developments that have reduced a prosperous and vibrant free country to apathetic drabness and humiliation. First, they destroyed parliamentary life, introduced political intolerance to a hitherto unknown degree, imposed the exclusive rule of their own party and tried to protect their monopoly of power by military and police force. They have ruled through provisional constitutions which they wrote, and were unable to conduct elections—free or even directed—to a truly representative assembly. Second, they have imposed Marxist socialism on Syria by decree and crushed the revolutionary attempts of the people to oppose it. Because of their poor organization and leadership, the original founders and other moderate elements were ousted and insulted, and a Marxist neo-Baath group took over and led the class struggle for the destruction of the productive middle class and for the close cooperation with the Soviet Union and the Communist camp. Third, the military Baath leaders distorted the national struggle by the use of Marxist slogans and colored Arab nationalism with violent radicalism, and they placed socialist above nationlist considerations. Fourth, they destroyed army discipline, paralyzed the military effort, and virtually ruined the army by frequent arbitrary transfers and purges or by undeserved fabulous promotions that were the result of the involvement of the army in politics and in ideological and factional disputes. They thereby diverted the military from their primary goal of defending the country. The result was the neglect and ineptitude demonstrated in the various clashes with Israel and particularly in the poor military performance in the war of June 1967.

CHAPTER IV
Notes

1. Extracts from the circular distributed by the "Central Command" and comments by *al-Nasr,* March 4, 1963.
2. *al-Hayat,* March 14, 1963; Zahreddin, *Memoirs,* 381.
3. See statements by J. H. Jansen, "A Farewell to Syrian Coups," *Middle East Forum,* (May, 1963), 13. Jansen hastily predicted that this may be the last coup on the basis that the union would be restored with Egypt, or as he expressed it, "while in 1958 Syria rushed headlong into union, this time she has collapsed backwards into it."
4. See Munif Razzaz, *al-Tajribah al-Murrah* (Beirut, 1967), 86-90.
5. See Zahreddin, 389-393.
6. *Ibid.*, 418.
7. *al-Hayat,* March 12, 1963. The publisher Kamil Mrowe mentioned that during his stay in Damascus on February 21, he heard that Hariri was marching on Damascus that same night, and that when he met President Qudsi a few hours later and told him about the rumor, Qudsi admitted that the rumors were current and he hoped to convince the military to avoid violence. Mrowe also mentioned that Hariri and his friends presented demands to the government that same night.
8. Compare this with the concentration of Young Turkish officers in Macedonia under Abdul Hamid and its impact on the revolution of 1908.
9. See for this interpretation, and especially the second part of it, the Egyptian reporter Fumil Labib in *al-Musawar,* March 15, 1963.
10. Zahreddin, 419.
11. On the transfers see *Ibid.*, 397 ff.
12. See account of the coup in Fumil Labib, *al-Musawar,* March 15, 1963, p. 15; Zahreddin, 428 ff.; *al-Hayat,* March 9-14; *The N.Y. Times,* March 11, 1963.
13. *The New York Times,* March 11, 1963; *al-Musawar,* March 15, 1963 said that five soldiers or armed guards who opposed the march were killed.
14. See for these details, Zahreddin, 430-442.
15. See for example Hariri's declaration to President Nasser in mid-March, in *The Proceedings of the Sessions for Unity Discussions,* 73-74, 80.
16. Jansen, *loc. cit.* , 13; similar view in *al-Hayat,* March 14, 1963 that the Baath had to speed the coup because Nasserist officers would have otherwise made it.
17. See the declaration of the Baath party in Syria on September 27, 1963, in *al-Hayat,* September 28, 1963.

18. *Time,*, March 29, 1963 on the orders to alert the bombers and fighters and to the Navy to steam northward and await orders.
19. *al-Musawar,*- March 15, 1963, for example, carried eleven pages out of a total of seventy-two for congratulatory advertisements.
20. Habib Jamati, "The Army of Jordan, Its Turn Has Come," *al-Musawar,* March 15, 1963, p. 47. *Rose al-Youssef,* March 18, 1963 published on its cover, the pictures of five Arab kings and prime ministers and an Arab holding a rifle directed towards the two remaining ones, Saud and Hussein, after having shot the three others who were Iman Ahmad, Kassem of Iraq, and Khalid al-Azem.
21. Atassi had been involved in the coup of April 1, 1962 in Aleppo and was sent as military attaché to Washington. He was recalled as witness in the trial of those accused of the murders and then he was sent to jail. He was released when the coup of March 8 took place.
22. *The New York Times,* March 11, 1963.
23. *al-Hayat,* October 6, 1963. The slogans used in the decree were clearly Baathist slogans.
24. See Zahreddin, 70; editorial by Selim Nassar in *al-Safa,* (Beirut), July 10, 1963. On Baath accusations against Nasser's regime in Syria, and Nasserist condemnation of the Baath, see *al-Hayat,* September 28 and 29, 1963, and also July 22, and 23, 1963.
25. Article in *Time,* November 22, 1963 on the soldiers spending two hours a day for being politically indoctrinated.
26. See Razzaz, 158; Zahreddin, 423.
27. Jay Walz in *The New York Times,* April 18, 1963; see also Khaldun Husry in M.E. Forum vol. 42 no. 3 (1966).
28. *al-Ahram,* May 24, 1963; for an analysis of this charter, see *The New York Times,* April 18, 1963, *The Daily Star,* April 18, 1963; Mohammad Mehdi, "The Cairo Declaration," *Middle East Forum,* (Summer 1963), pp. 31-40; for the text of the charter see *Middle East Forum,* (June and July, 1963), pp. 11-15, 11-15; *Arab Political Documents* 1963 (Beirut, 1963), 227-246; *Ibid.* 75-217 for the proceedings of unity discussions in Cairo.
29. King Hussein let 56 Nasserists and Baathists out of jail. In Saudi Arabia, Prince Faisal, as Prime Minister, allotted funds for compensating those who would free their slaves. *Time,* April 19, 1963.
30. *al-Hayat,* October 19, 1963 mentioned accusations brought against Abdallah Jassumi who came from Damascus and made a speech in the Kallassi section and urged the people to riot. The head of the rioting was Ahmad Adani.
31. *Time,* May 17, 1963.
32. *al-Hayat,* July 7, 1963, article "Syria Without the Hair of Muawiya," by An Old Arab Politician (pseud.).

33. See Bernard Vernier, *Armée et Politique au Moyen Orient* (Paris: Payot, 1966), 138.
34. *al-Hayat,* July 4 and 5, 1963.
35. *al-Hayat,* July 9, 1963.
36. Razzaz, 99-101.
37. The first estimate was given by *al-Hayat,* July 19, 1963; during the trial by court martial, the smaller figure was given. See al-Hayat, October 18, 1963; Vernier, *Armée et Politique au Moyen Orient,* 139 mentioned 300 victims.
38. See the description in *al-Hayat,* July 19, 1963: *The New York Times,* July 20, 1963.
39. *The New York Times,* editorial, July 22, 1963,
40. Quoted in *The New York Times,* July 20, 1963.
41. See the account in Zahreddin, 471-473.
42. *al-Safa,* July 25, 1963, editorial by Rushdi Maaluf who spoke of Nasser as "the sheikh of the *'tariqa'* of violence in the Arab World."
43. They were Muhammad Jarrah, Jassem Alwan, and Raef Maarri.
44. Quoted in *The New York Times,* July 29, 1963; see also *Time,* August 2, 1963.
45. On this visit, *al-Hayat,* August 25, 1963, article "From April 17 to Aref," The visit began on August 22, and it was followed by Aref's visit to Damascus.
46. See the Baath party declaration and that of the Revolutionary Council in *al-Hayat,* September 28 and 29, 1963.
47. On the Syrian-Iraqi military pact, see *Arab Political Documents* 1963, 421-25.
48. See Supra the chapter on Iraq.
49. See Razzaz, 92-94.
50. *Ibid.*, 62-64, 102-103; see also the text of Aflaq's description of the situation in his party on February 18, 1966 in a party meeting in Damascus, in *al-Hayat,* February 25, 1966.
51. Quoted in *Middle East Forum,* November 1963, Chronology, "The Arab Month."
52. *al-Hayat,* September 15, 1963.
53. *The New York Times,* October 7, 1963.
54. *al-Hayat,* November 8, 1963.
55. See text of the resolutions of the 6th national congress in *Arab Political Documents 1963,* pp. 438-444.
56. See *Time,* October 11, 1963; *The New York Times,* October 15, 1963. On September 29, the Damascus radio accused Nasser of seeking an alliance with Hussein against the Baath.
57. See the Syrian*Official Journal,* January 30, February 6 and 27, March 12, 1964.
58. *The New York Times,* February 24, 1964.

59. *Ibid; Mideast Mirror,* May 9, 1964.
60. See for the Hama uprising *Mideast Mirror,* April 18 and 25, 1964; *The N.Y. Times* and *al-Hayat,* April 16-20, 1964.
61. *al-Hayat,* April 26, 1964; *The N.Y. Times* April 21, *Mideast Mirror,* April 25, 1964.
62. *Mideast Mirror,* April 25, 1964.
63. See *The Official Journal,* April 30, 1964 for the text of martial law order no. 68 that brought the feudalists to trial; *Mideast Mirror,* May 9, 1964 for the sentences.
64. *The Official Journal,* May 7, 1964.
65. 'Mentioned by *al-Hayat,* April 29, 1964; see also *al-Hayat* April 22 and 25 for the other protests and appeals.
66. The text of decree 55 of April 16 in the *Official Journal,* April 30, 1964 p. 4181.
67. See the decree of May 25, 1964 in the *Official Journal,* June 11, 1964; *The N.Y. Times,* August 29, 1964.
68. See the explanation in Razzaz, 104-105, 116 ff.
69. See the section on "the new nationalizations in Syria," in Jubran Shamiyeh, *Ya Uqala' al-'Arab Ittahidu,* vol. II, (Beirut, 1965?), 245-258; *The N.Y. Times,* January 4 and 9, 1965.
70. Six establishments were returned to their owners and thirty others were expected to be returned; see *Afro-Mideast Economic Bulletin,* February 1, 1965.
71. *al-Hayat,* January 10, 1965; *The N.Y. Times,* January 9, 1965.
72. See *The N. Y. Times* January 21, February 18, 1965.
73. See statement in *Mideast Mirror,* May 8, 1965 and in *Orient* no. 34 (1965), 197-210.
74. Quoted in *Mizan* VIII, 8 (September, 1965), 11.
75. Text of the constitution of April 25, 1964 in the Syrian *Official Journal,* May 19, 1964 and an English translation in *Middle East Forum* (May, 1964), 10-12.
76. See Pierre Rondot, "Quelques remarques sur le Baath," *Orient* no. 31 (1964), 7-19.
77. The 95 members of the national revolutionary council in August 1965 included the six Syrian members of the Baath national leadership, all 16 members of the regional leadership, five members of the former NRC, five members of the party's military command, 14 representatives of the Baath-sponsored general federation of labor, 14 representing the federation of Syrian farmers, eight representatives of the "feminine sector," 13 independent personalities allied with the Baath, two delegates of the lawyers' Bar Association, one member of each of the associations of doctors, engineers, chemists, two university professors and seven representing the teachers' association. See *Arab News and Views,* September 15, 1965; *The N.Y. Times* August 24, 1965.

78. Rondot, "Quelques remarques . . .," p. 11.
79. Razzaz, 114.
80. See Aflaq's comments of February 18, 1966 in *al-Hayat,* February 25, 1966.
81. See Hourani's declaration in *al-Hayat,* September 17, 1964; Jalal al-Sayyid's open letter in a pamphlet entitled, *Articles and Memoirs published in the Lebanese Newspapers 1964* (in Arabic), (Beirut, 1964), 8-47.
82. See Bernard Vernier, *Armée et Politique au Moyen Orient* (Paris, Payot, 1966), 144.
83. See reports by D.A. Schmidt in *The N.Y. Times,* October 26 and December 20, 1964.
84. See the account in Razzaz, 115-119; *The N.Y. Times,* December 20, 1964.
85. See Aflaq in *al-Hayat,* February 25, 1966.
86. Razzaz, 130.
87. *Mideast Mirror,* July 24, 1965
88. Razzaz, 140.
89. *Ibid.*, 149; Vernier, *Armée et Politique,* 145.
90. For these developments, al-Hayat, October 19, 1965; *The N.Y. Times,* September 3, 1965; Razzaz 144 ff.; 152 ff.
91. See *The N.Y. Times* and *al-Hayat,* October 19, 1965.
92. The agreement with the British consortium (which was never implemented) was made on June 22, 1965. Hourani claimed that it sold the country to the British, and in several declarations accused the Baath government of cooperation with imperialism; *al-Baath* as well as *al-Thawrah* in Damascus attacked him in early October for spreading harmful rumors and undertaking sabotage.
93. See *al-Hayat,* October 21-24, 1965; *Mideast Mirror,* October 23, 1965. Hourani was interviewed in his house in Damascus in early July 1965 by a correspondent from Beirut and when he was pressed to comment on Baath rule in Syria after he had tried not to talk, he reportedly said, "You want me to say something on the rule in Syria, it is the rule of the Tatars!"; see *al-Sayyad,* July 8, 1965, p. 15.
94. See details of the incident of Homs and its results in Razzaz, 162 ff.; *N.Y. Times,* December 29, 1965.
95. Alan W. Horton, "A Note on Syria, the Sudan and the United Arab Republic," *American Universities Field Staff,* XII, 1 (June, 1965), 12.
96. See the account on the Atassi and the Cohen cases in *N.Y. Times* February 18-25, and May 19, 1965.
97. Article of Salaheddin Bitar on "Nationalism and Socialism," in *al-Ahram,* October 27, 1965; see French translation in *Orient* no. 36 (1965, 4), 163-167.
98. Bitar's statement on radio and television on January 4, 1966 in *Mideast Mirror,* January 8, 1966.

99. Aflaq's talk in *al-Hayat,* February 25, 1966.
100. See Razzaz, 183 ff.
101. *al-Hayat,* February 20 and 24 mentioned the postponement of the election meeting from February 20 to 25, whereas Razzaz, 196 mentioned a regional congress that the Jedid group wanted to hold on February 25 to decide the overthrow of the national command.
102. Razzaz, 194 said that the transfers were restricted to these officers, while *al-Hayat,* February 26, 1966 said the decree dismissed thirty officers and ordered them to leave the country.
103. See for these figures and for accounts of the coup,*al-Hayat* February 24-26; *The N.Y. Times,* February 24-27; *The Los Angeles Times* February 26; *Mideast Mirror,* February 26, March 5, 1966; Razzaz, 196-197.
104. See *Mideast Mirror* March 12, April 9, 1966.
105. Razzaz, 200-204.
106. *The N.Y. Times,* July 16, 1966.
107. See article by R.V. in *jeune Afrique* (Algiers), no. 281 (May 15, 1966), 11, and another article by Dr. Nicolas Sarkis, "The USSR has won the race to the Euphrates."
108. Report on the demonstration in *al-Jaridah* (Beirut), April 29, 1966.
109. See *al-Baath* and *al-Thowrah,* September 7, 1966; report by Thomas F. Brady in *The N.Y. Times,* September 8, 1966.
110. See details in *The N.Y. Times* and *Los Angeles Times,* September 9-11, 1966; *Near East Report,* September 20, 1966.
111. See the story of Hatum in the *N.Y. Times* June 26, 1967, August 19, 1968.
112. In the celebration that commemorated the unity of Syria and Egypt on February 25, 1967 at Hotel Semiramis in Cairo, I met some of my former Syrian students like Abdallah Jassumi and others who had held key positions under unity and then had to leave Syria after July 18, 1963. They told me that they were not allowed to go back home.
113. Patrick Seale in *The Observer,* November 20, 1966.
114. *The Daily Star* (Beirut), April 14, 1967.
115. I was then in Beirut and was told by eye witnesses from Damascus that even when the people realized that the planes were Israeli planes, they were not unhappy to see the Baath regime humiliated.
116. *People's Army Magazine* (Arabic), April 25, 2967 and *al-Hayat* May 5, 1967; cited also by Salaheddin Munajjed in *A'midat al-Nakbah* (The Pillars of the Disaster), 2nd edition (Beirut, February 1968), 62-63.
117. See the section on Egypt's motives in the war in June 1967, in Ch. 2 vol. 3
118. *The N.Y. Times* May 19, 24, 1967; *Daily Star,* April 22, 1967 for the declarations of Ahmad Swaidani, chief of staff and Nureddin Atassi,

head of state.

119. See John K. Cogley in *Christian Science Monitor,* November 16, 1967; Terence Smith in *N.Y. Times* June 26, 2967; Joseph Alsop column, September 17, 1967.
120. See account of the meetings of the Baath regional congress and Hafez Asad's statements and purges, in *al-Hayat,* March 23, 1969.
121. I am referring to the French text of the statement, *Declaration sur les travaux du qeme congrés national exceptionnel, September 1967,*" pp. 12-13.
122. See the detailed report of the tribunal (called judicial council) and the sentence in *al-Anwar,* June 1, 1969. The sentence was given exactly one year after the attempt.
123. *The N.Y. Times,* July 2, 1967.
124. See *Los Angeles Times* August 4, 1968; *al-Bayan* (New York), August 20, 1968.
125. See analysis of *al-Bayan,* August 20, September 3, 1968.
126. See *al-Anwar,* October 26, 29, 1968.
127. *al-Anwar,* October 26, 1968.
128. D.A. Schmidt in *N.Y. Times* March 3, 5, 1969; *al-Anwar,* March 2, 1969.
129. *Los Angeles Times, N.Y. Times,* March 3, 1969.
130. See *al-Hayat* column, April 6, 1969; United Press International dispatch, April 13, 1969.
131. For the resolutions of the congress,*al-Anwar,* April 1; *al-Hayat April 6, N.Y. Times,* April 1, 1969.
132. Reported by *al-Hayat,* March 23, 1969.
133. Reported by *al-Bairaq* (Beirut and quoted in *N.Y. Times,* May 20, 1969.
134. See the table of military coups at the end of the volume.

CHAPTER V

Revolutions and the Survival of Democracy in Lebanon

Like most of the other newly-independent Arab states of the Middle East, Lebanon has had its revolutions, rebellions, and abortive coups d' état. Three differences, however, have distinguished its revolutionary movements from those of its Arab neighbors. First, Lebanese upheavals were generally popular in nature, and military leadership played little direct role in them. Second, these movements were relatively few in number and consequently did not lead to chronic instability. This was partly due to the non-involvement of the military in politics. Third, revolutionary action did not bring with it any radical change in the political and social order. Liberal democratic constitutional rule of the western pattern survived in Lebanon and so did the system of free enterprise, while both were swept away by the military regimes in certain other areas.

The Lebanese movements, their background, aspects, and results can be best understood by a brief study of the nature of the Lebanese state and society.

I. State and Society in Lebanon

Within its present boundaries, Lebanon came into being on September 1, 1920 under the name of Greater Lebanon. Various parts of the newly-created state, the region of Mt. Lebanon in particular, had been ruled from about 1516 until

1841 by the local emirs (princes) of the Maanid and Shehab dynasties, and by a number of subordinate or rival feudal families, under Ottoman suzerainty. During this same period and even earlier in the Middle Ages, Mt. Lebanon became the home of several religious minorities, Christian as well as Muslim, but the most numerous among them were the Maronite Christians, and the Druzes who were related to a branch of the Shia Muslims. Centralized Ottoman rule after 1841 and the end of feudalism were accompanied by tensions and strife between the two leading religious communities that culminated in the massacres of 1860. Order was restored and tensions were weakened when Mt. Lebanon regained its autonomy in 1861 under the guarantee of the great powers. The autonomous sanjak (sub-province) was ruled until 1914 by an Ottoman Christian district-governor (muteserrif) appointed by the sultan, and by a council in which the religious communities were represented in proportion to their numeric strength.

The State of Greater Lebanon which was proclaimed by the French authorities in 1920 was three times the size of the Sanjak of Mt. Lebanon - or Smaller Lebanon as it is sometimes called - around which the new state was formed. The 6,930 square kilometers that were added to the original 3,200 sq. kms. of Mt. Lebanon included large portions of the coast from the north of Tripoli to the south of Tyre, the entire internal plain of the Beqa, and the foothills of the Anti-Lebanon. The newly-added areas, inhabited by a majority of Sunnite and Shiite Muslims, increased the Sunnite Muslim population of the new state by eight times, the Shiite Muslims by four times, and the Maronite Christians by only one-third of their original number in the sanjak.[1] Greater Lebanon thus did not have that clear Christian majority which the original sanjak had, and it became a land of religious minorities among whom the Maronites represented about thirty per cent of the population, followed in order of numeric strength by the Sunnite Muslims, the Shiite Muslims, the Greek Orthodox, the Druzes, the Greek Catholics, the Armenian Orthodox, and the smaller minorities of Armenian Catholics, Protestants, Syrian Orthodox and Catholics, Chaldeans, and Jews. The large concentrations of Muslims in Tripoli, Beirut and the northern Beqa were reluctant to participate in the new state which was intended to be primarily Christian in spirit and Western in outlook, and they were rather oriented to the Muslim community centered outside, and particularly to neighboring Syria with its overwhelming Muslim majority and Arab outlook.

The Syrian nationalists at the same time reacted bitterly to the creation of Greater Lebanon and considered it a manifestation of the old colonial policy of divide and rule, and a stratagem to prevent the unity of Syria or the greater Arab unity. They also resented the cession to Greater Lebanon of the four cazas or districts of the Beqa, Baalbek, Hasbaya, and Rashaya which had been a part of the vilayet (province) of Syria in Ottoman times. Although Lebanon had to be at least as large as it was in order to be viable, its creation within the boundaries assigned to it contained elements that could eventually lead to internal as well as external trouble.

In 1926 the French gave Greater Lebanon a republican constitution modelled after that of the Third French Republic, and the first Arab republic of modern times was thus born. In the new republic, membership in the Chamber of Deputies and appointments to the various government posts were based on the principle of the equitable representation of the various religious sects in proportion to their numeric strength.[2] The proportions were fixed by the French, and after independence, by the Lebanese authorities on the basis of the census taken in 1932 when the Christians were the majority. The number of deputies in the Lebanese Chamber from the period of independence in 1943 to the present time has been a multiple of eleven, six Christians to five non-Christians.

In November 1943, the first nationalist government of Lebanon clashed with the French over the question of complete sovereignty. In the heat of that struggle in which the Lebanese, supported by Britain, finally won, the Maronite president, Beshara al-Khouri and his sophisticated Muslim prime minister, Riad al-Solh, agreed on a guiding formula relative to the internal and external policy of Lebanon that would insure the coexistence of Muslims and Christians. The general meaning of the unwritten agreement, known as the National Pact, was that the Christians of Lebanon would no longer turn to France for protection, and the Muslims would renounce the thought of union with Syria. Lebanon's Christian majority would remain unchallenged, but Lebanon would be identified as a part of the Arab world and would allow itself to become "neither a base nor a gateway for imperialism." It was also agreed that the president of Lebanon would be a Christian, usually a Maronite, the prime minister a Sunnite Muslim, the Speaker of the Chamber a Shiite Muslim, and the deputy prime minister a Greek Orthodox.

The National Pact, in spite of its lack of precision, was honored and respected by the coexisting confessions, and it was strengthened by the charter of the League of Arab states that was signed in Cairo in March 1945, because the latter recognized the existing boundaries of the member states and stated that no Arab state could interfere in the internal affairs of another. The National Pact, however, did not erase the differences in orientation, education, and political outlook between the communities, nor did it reconcile the various conceptions held by the Lebanese on whether Lebanon should be viewed as a part of an Arab-Muslim whole, or as a part of a Greater Syria, or still as a distinct entity that stands midway between the Arab and the Western world.[3] Muslims continued to feel that the Christian majority was a myth and they expressed their resentment of their inferior position in writings and petitions.[4] The debates and the protests in the press and in the Chamber about the distribution of government posts between the confessions sometimes endangered the life of certain cabinets.[5] Arab states, in spite of the National Pact and the Arab League Charter, continued to view Lebanon with suspicion as an obstacle to Arab unity or to the unity of Greater Syria. Yet, as long as Lebanon did not have to take a stand in an acute ideological or political conflict, it continued to play the role of neutral mediator between the Arab countries, and between them and the West without incurring the displeasure of certain elements of its population. After 1955, Lebanon could not, or was not allowed to remain neutral. The Baghdad Pact and the controversy over the Western alliance, the Suez crisis and the rising prestige of Nasser, as well as the formation of the United Arab Republic had their deep influence on the attitude of the Muslim population of Lebanon toward the Lebanese identity and government, and ended by destroying the National Pact.

The political attitudes and behavior of the Lebanese, it must be said, were not always dictated by sectarian differences. The ideological parties in Lebanon such as the Syrian National Party that worked for Syrian unity, the Baath Party that advocated Pan-Arab unity, and the Communist Party included leaders and members from the various religious sects. Among those who were favorable to Nasser's policies, certain Christian leaders could be found. But one should not lose sight of the game of personal politics and clan rivalries that often caused persons and groups to shift allegiance and to espouse causes in which they did not particularly believe. A well known example of this was the alliance of the Maronite Frangie clan of Zghorta in northern Lebanon with the pro-Nasserist Muslims of Tripoli against their local Maronite rivals, the Duwayhis, in the mid and late 1950's. One should also recognize that the great majority of the Lebanese were not as politically minded as their fellow Arab neighbors, and that owing to the presence of a large and influential middle class and a higher standard of living, they were not inclined to take extreme positions on political and economic issues. They also placed high priority on economic prosperity and its prerequisites, stability and good relations with the outside world. Lebanon, moreover, had the highest percentage of literacy and university graduates in the Arab world, and its cultured elite was educated in western institutions either at home or abroad. They had consequently acquired an understanding and appreciation of the values of freedom and democracy in a country that considers itself the Middle Eastern gateway to the West. Totalitarian democracy, socialism, and military rule with their encroachment on liberty and private enterprise and their resulting instability could not appeal to them.

The composition, size and recruitment of the Lebanese army, moreover, largely differed from what they were in other Arab countries. In Lebanon, the army is recruited by voluntary service, not by conscription, and it has been largely influenced by western standards of discipline and professional ability. Its officers and men belong to the various religious communities, and their involvement in politics could lead to more factionalism and quarrels than has been the case in Arab armies. This involvement, on the other hand, could not possibly give rise to a military dictator or to a viable military regime, because the support of the various sects represented in the army would be hard to insure. The army officers themselves, moreover, with their limited cadres and military resources, have not apparently been conscious of the need to fulfill any particular role or mission. They have not developed any special sense of class superiority in a country that abounds with all kinds of technological and cultural elites, and they have entertained no ambitions for political action. One should perhaps recognize, moreover, that political leaders, local bosses, and heads of politico-religious groups have been too jealous of their leadership – with all the social prestige and material benefits it brought – to allow army officers to wrest it from them. The only parties that have showed any tendencies to ask for army intervention and support, were the ideological parties, but they evidently have not succeeded in infiltrating the armed forces of Lebanon to any large extent.

The Lebanese administration as well as Lebanon's system of parliamentary democracy have functioned in much the same way as in other Arab countries. Lebanese public life did not rise to the level of its large educated elite, and some of its aspects are virtually unique in the Middle East. The reason must be sought in its historical background and in the composition of its society. As a country of minorities in an area where religion is an important symbol of identification, it is dominated in its executive, legislative, and even judicial action by confessional considerations.[6] Minorities, large and small, guard jealously their right, guaranteed by the constitution, to representation in the Chamber and to appointment in the civil service. Their rights are championed, not only by their representatives in the cabinet and in the Chamber, but more realistically by the heads of their confessions and by the congresses which the members of each community hold to defend these rights. Ambitious persons whose small sects had no parliamentary representation have sometimes found themselves obliged to change their religious identity in order to gain a seat in the Chamber.[7] Similarly, as a region where feudalism flourished until the nineteenth century, Lebanon has remained the home of old influential families of emirs and sheikhs who have inherited the taste and social need for power and prestige which only a seat in the Chamber or in the cabinet or in some other high post could satisfy. In no other country in the Middle East the decorative titles of "emir" and "sheikh" are as jealously guarded as in Lebanon. In hardly any other country too, could the elections lead to as much violence or could be as costly.[8]

Although such political parties as the Constitutional Bloc, the National Bloc (both formed in 1932), the Progressive Socialist Party (1949), and the National Liberal Party (1959) have existed in Lebanon along with the ideological parties, they are mostly organized around individual leaders and their designations often cannot be taken seriously. Considerations of personal interests and clan rivalries have played a certain role in their formation and membership. The group that supports Kemal Junblat, leader of the Progressive Socialist Party, for example, supports him as the head of a Druze clan and not as the leader of a socialist party. Other parties and groupings have been formed on a politico-confessional basis such as the Maronite Kataeb (Phalanges), and the Muslim

Najjada (both formed in 1936), or on a regional-personal basis as the group of the South and that of the Beqa with a recognized local leader at their head. Certain groups and coalitions appear and then disappear at the beginning and at the end of every new Chamber. Until 1953, elections were made on the basis of the large multi-seat district where candidates of the various confessions in the district grouped themselves on the ticket which had the greatest chance of winning. The ticket or list was usually formed around a strong clan leader who could purchase votes, use threats and violence, and exert his clan influence to make his ticket succeed. This is what has been called feudality in Lebanese politics. The deputies of the various confessions in this large ticket system were elected, not by the votes of their own community, but by those of all the communities in the district. Their political behavior therefore had to win the approval of a large cross section of the population and also of the leader on whose ticket they presented themselves to the electorate. In 1953 the number of electoral districts or constituencies was increased from nine to thirty-three, and their size as well as the number of deputies they could return naturally decreased. The influence of a strong leader in returning a large number of deputies was thus reduced. Multi-seat districts, however, have continued to exist and their number has changed since 1953 with the change of the total number of deputies in Lebanon.

The president of the Lebanese Republic, elected as he has been by the Chamber of Deputies, had to be acceptable to the members of the Chamber, Muslims as well as Christians. In spite of his large powers that included the nomination and dismissal of the members of the cabinet as well as the dissolution of parliament, the president was bound by certain conventions in his appointments and in dealing with the Chamber. He naturally could influence the voting record of those deputies who aspired to become cabinet ministers, but neither he nor his cabinet could follow a policy that would be unacceptable to a strong religious group or to a strong clan without running into trouble. This is why the Lebanese government under the confessional and feudalist system has been described as government by compromise, characterized by indecision in legislation and cabinet action. This system has given place to, and tolerated nepotism, corruption, and the influence of feudal bosses and confessional leaders, and it has made administrative, political and social reforms impossible whenever they disagrèed with certain sectarian or clan interests. Above all, this system has prevented Lebanon from following an independent policy even when its executive and the majority of its legislative bodies thought that such policy was in the country's interest.

An important aspect of the freedom which Lebanon has enjoyed, in contrast with its neighbors, has been its free press. Yet, although certain newspaper publishers have distinguished themselves by their ability and integrity and by their constructive patriotism, others, less qualified, have disgraced the free press and damaged the interests of their country by allowing themselves to be the instruments of generous local and foreign interests, and resorting to blackmail in order to amass fortunes as rapidly as possible.[9] They consequently aggravated the difficulties that Lebanon had to face since its independence.

II. The Syrian National Party Revolt 1949

Among the four revolts and attempted coups d' état that Lebanon witnessed since the establishment of its nationalist administration in 1943 and the winning of complete sovereignty in 1946, one was the work of a doctrinal party in 1949, another in 1952 was a popular protest against corruption and monopoly of power, a third one in 1958 stemmed from internal political tensions and external intervention, and the fourth in 1961 was a joint attempt of military elements and a doctrinal party.

It is significant that the first armed revolt against government authority was made by a doctrinal non-sectarian party, the Syrian Social National Party, that advocated the unity of the Fertile Crescent countries, i.e. geographic Syria and Iraq. The party was founded in 1932 by Antun Saadeh, and for many years it was particularly opposed by the Lebanese Phalanges *(al-Kataeb al-Lubnaniyah)*, which was founded in 1936 and dedicated itself to preserve Lebanese independence and identity. The Phalangist Party was led by Pierre Gemayel and consisted almost entirely of Maronites. Between 1940 and 1947, Emir (later King) Abdallah of Jordan had made efforts to realize his dream of uniting Syria, Lebanon and Palestine with Transjordan in a Greater Syria. These efforts, however, remained fruitless. In Syria, the fall of President Quwatli, opponent of the Greater Syria project, at the end of March 1949, and the seizure of power by Colonel Zaim might have encouraged the Syrian Social National Party to attempt the implementation of their program with possible help from the military in Syria. Rivalries in Lebanon between the SSNP and the Phalangists produced incidents such as the burning of the SSNP printing press in Beirut by the Phalangists on June 9, 1949. The Lebanese government found in these incidents an occasion to liquidate the SSNP. An investigation at the party headquarters in Beirut led to the discovery of arms and the arrest of some members. The party leader, Saadeh, had managed in the meantime to escape to Damascus where he was given asylum by the Syrian government under Zaim.

In early July, 1949, Saadeh proclaimed the revolution against the government of Lebanon, and his party responded on July 3 and 4 by attacking gendarmerie and police posts in little towns in Mt. Lebanon like Aley and Mtein, and Mashghara in the Beqa.[10] The Lebanese army intervened and after minor engagements, the paramilitary units of the SSNP either escaped or were surrounded and two persons were killed. The revolt thus collapsed because its forces were not sufficiently equipped to fight against an organized army, and also because in this, as in other attempts, the people did not respond. The Syrian Social National cause was opposed, not only by the vested interests of the two governments of Lebanon and Syria, but also by the two doctrinal parties at the two opposite poles, the Lebanese Phalangists and the pan-Arab Baathists, while the people were largely indifferent.

Following the failure of this short revolt, the Lebanese government offered 25,000 Lebanese pounds ($8,300) to anyone who would deliver the SSNP leader, Antun Saadeh, to it alive or dead. Husni al-Zaim, who had become president of the Syrian Republic as a result of a referendum on June 25, was asked by the government of Lebanon to turn over Saadeh, but he refused. He and his prime minister, Muhsin al-Barazi, had encouraged Saadeh at the beginning and promised him financial and military aid, for Zaim had frequent quarrels with Lebanon since he came to power, and he was, moreover, supported by the SSNP. But in the night of July 6, for some uncertain reason, the unpredictable Zaim suddenly surrendered Saadeh to the Lebanese authorities. Certain rumors mentioned that he might have been tempted by the 25,000 pounds. Other rumors indicated that he came to the conclusion that the SSNP was not loyal to his regime.[11] It is perhaps more likely that Zaim submitted to the pressure of Egypt and France, both of whom were friends of Lebanon and opposed to the Greater Syria scheme advocated by the SSNP. Certain quarters have condemned Zaim's action as treachery and contrary to the rules of political asylum. Saadeh and some of his colleagues were summarily tried by a military tribunal that condemned him and eleven others to death on July 8, but six including himself were executed on the same day. It is said that the six victims were chosen on the basis of confessional balance! The SSNP was outlawed by the Lebanese government on July 18, but it continued to exist while its open activities shifted temporarily to Syria. The execution of Saadeh was followed by an attempt on the life of the Lebanese prime minister, Riad al-Solh, in March, 1950 and by Solh's assassination on July 16, 1951 while he was on his way to board a plane in Amman (Jordan) for Beirut. It was assumed that the assassins were members of the SSNP, but certain rumors, on the other hand, have accused the clique around President Beshara al-Khouri of Lebanon of this assassination.

III. The Popular Revolution of 1952

The revolution of September 1952 that forced the resignation of President Beshara al-Khouri in the middle of his second term has remained, in many ways, unique in the annals of Lebanese and Arab revolutionary movements. It was perhaps the only revolution that won almost the unanimous approval of the various religious sects and political parties and factions in the country. It was also singularly capable of producing a change of government by popular action and without any violencc and bloodshed. This is why it has been sometimes called "the rose water revolution." It was, furthermore, one of the rare revolutions in which neither military nor foreign interventions were involved.

President Beshara al-Khouri (1890-1964), much like his colleague, President Quwatli of Syria, was a respected national leader in the days of the French mandate. In September 1943, two years after the Free French had proclaimed the independence of Lebanon, a new chamber of deputies raised Khouri to the presidency of the republic for a six-year term. His government soon gained popularity following the abortive French attempt, in November 1943, to restrict Lebanese independence and intimidate the Lebanese rulers. When, at the end of 1946, the evacuation of French troops from Lebanon was completed and Lebanon became fully sovereign and independent, President Khouri, like his colleague Quwatli in Syria, was hailed as "The Hero of the Evacuation." This was the climax, and at the same time the beginning of the end, of his popularity. As the crucial stage of the struggle for independence ended, the critics felt free to comment on the President's conduct of the affairs of state.

President Khouri shrewdly used the prerogatives of his

office to maintain his personal control over the cabinet, the chamber of deputies, and the administration, and to grant favors to his family and friends. He appointed and dismissed cabinets, and often dealt personally with officials over the heads of his ministers. He rewarded his supporters in the chamber of deputies with various benefits and tried to intimidate his opponents.[12] The elections of May 1947, the first to take place after independence, were in the words of a prominent member of the opposition, "a black date in the history of Lebanon," because of open government interference.[13] President Khouri needed a two-thirds majority in the new chamber for voting a constitutional amendment that would allow him to succeed himself. The elections of 1947 returned the needed two-thirds majority. On May 22, 1948, the newly elected "puppet parliament" voted the constitutional amendment, and a week later it re-elected Khouri President one year before the end of his term. In Syria, President Quwatli had been re-elected in April 1948 by a similar procedure. The supporters of the constitutional amendment in each of the two cases found a justification of their action in the great national services of the two presidents, and in the fact that their respective countries were in a state of war with Israel over the Palestine problem.

In explaining the causes of the revolution against President Khouri, it has been mentioned that the Lebanese people usually begin to be tired of any president in the third year of his term. [44] Another explanation is based on the frustration of certain ambitious leaders who never forgave President Khouri for being re-elected, because they were preparing to present their candidacy for the presidency. The basic causes, however, were related to the people's attitude towards the president's rule. The Lebanese could not forgive the President's monopoly of power, the material advantages offered to his family, the sudden fortunes made by the presidential favorites, and the general indifference and corruption of the self-seeking rulers. After his re-election in 1948, President Khouri was accused of becoming more distant and ostentatious, and of encouraging a cult of his person. The critics began to compare the Lebanese state to a farm run for the benefit of the President's family. His brothers were appointed in high office or were elected to the Chamber. One of them, a fuel merchant named Selim, and aptly nicknamed "Sultan Selim," established what looked like a state within the state. He dispensed money and jobs to supporters, and provided the necessary means to chastise opponents. The President's son, Khalil, became the lawyer of the most powerful corporations, while the law courts were compared to political agencies. The members of "the royal family" – the President's wife, sisters-in-law, nephews and nieces – became middlemen and brokers for large transactions and openly concluded profitable deals and bargains.[15] The President's wife, on a trip to Europe, was allowed $100,000 in travel funds at official rate, which was about forty per cent less than the current rate, while many students in Europe and particularly in France were in urgent need of hard currency.

Lebanon at this same time was facing an economic crisis that reflected itself in unemployment and reduced prosperity caused by the closing of the Palestine border, and the decline of trade relations with Syria. The Lebanese attributed their worsening condition to the corruption of their rulers, and resented the ostentation of the President's favorites. The fall of President Quwatli of Syria at the end of March 1949, as a result of a military coup d' état, was a meaningful sign for the Lebanese. The Egyptian revolution of July 1952 against the corrupt rule of King Farouk had even more significant results, for it strengthened the Lebanese opposition and made it more popular, and it emphasized the need for changes in Lebanon.[16] President Khouri himself has recognized in his memoirs the dangerous impact of the Egyptian revolution on Lebanon and he quoted the popular proverb, "If a minaret falls down in Egypt, beware of its flying debris."[17]

The opposition against President Khouri's regime was led by only a few members of the chamber of deputies. The parliamentary majority after the elections of April 15, 1951 still consisted of presidential favorites and supporters who were not very representative of the people's wishes. The nine opposition deputies – out of seventy-seven deputies in the Chamber – included some strong-willed and popular leaders like Camille Chamoun, Kemal Junblat, Emile Bustani, Hamid Frangie. and Ghassan Twaini. Camille Chamoun was a brilliant Maronite lawyer and an architect of Lebanese independence in the 1943-46 period. In the presidential elections of 1943, he was a candidate and was supported by Britain, while the former president, Emile Edde, was supported by France. But it was the third candidate, Beshara al-Khouri, who was elected as a compromise. According to some accounts, Chamoun was promised at the time that he would become president after the end of Khouri's term.[18] Chamoun was appointed minister to Britain during the first years of independence, and then he returned to Lebanon in 1947 and became minister of the interior. He resigned his cabinet post in protest on the eve of President Khouri's re-election in May 1948. The other prominent opposition leader, Kemal Junblat, was a strange combination of a Druze feudal chieftain and an austere, reform- oriented socialist. He was well known for his fondness of contradicting others and for his negative criticism. In 1949 he organized the Progressive Socialist Party which was joined mainly by his Druze followers. The Sunnite Muslim leader, Riad al-Solh, who had accompanied President Khouri in the struggle for independence and then became his perennial prime minister since 1943, had to resign in February 1951 because of the coming elections. The President was afraid that Riad would join the opposition, and he therefore assured him that his absence from the premiership would not be long.[19] Riad al-Solh was assassinated in Jordan in July 1951, one year before the crisis against Khouri entered its decisive stage.

At the very beginning of the eventful year 1952, trouble began against the administration with a strike of lawyers, followed by the boycott of the electricity company. The cabinet of Abdallah al-Yafi resigned on February 9 in protest against the President's abuse of power. It was succeeded by a cabinet under Sami al-Solh who, according to President Khouri, was the choice of the opposition.[20] In the chamber of deputies the attacks on corruption and against the over-extended powers of the President became more frequent and more violent. Junblat's newspaper, *al-Anba'* (the News), was suspended because of its onslaught on Khouri's regime, and its editor was sentenced to fourteen months in jail. On June 13, some twenty-seven newspapers declared a strike in protest against the suspension of nine publications. In this tense atmosphere of mounting opposition, President Khouri called the Commander-in-Chief of the army, General Fuad Chehab, probably in order to sound him on the possibility of establishing military rule. In his memoirs, President Khouri has claimed that he expressed to General Chehab his readiness to leave the presidency and encouraged the general to become president in his place, but Chehab persuaded Khouri to stay.[21]

In June 1952, the various parties, factions, and independent politicians within and outside Parliament began to organize themselves in opposition fronts. The Socialist National Front, the first to be organized, included Junblat's Socialist Party, Raymond Edde's National Bloc, Ali Bezzi's National Call Party, and several independents like Camille Chamoun. Its program of radical reform that demanded the end of abuses and the purging of the administration, strongly appealed to the masses. In another opposition coalition, the Maronite "Phalanges" of Pierre Gemayel, and the predominantly Muslim "National Organization" and "National Congress" formed the Popular Front and asked for the dissolution of the Chamber.

Shortly after the Egyptian revolution of July 23, 1952 and the abdication of King Farouk, the leaders of the Socialist National Front decided to hold a mass rally at Deir al-Qamar, home town of Camille Chamoun and an old capital of Mt. Lebanon. The *mahrajan* (mass rally) was authorized by Prime Minister Solh and was held on August 17. It was attended by a crowd estimated at more than 30,000 persons. The speeches violently denounced the President's misrule, and warned that force could be used if no immediate reforms were introduced. The cabinet reacted by approving two days later the draft of a reform program that included the adoption of the smaller constituency for parliamentary elections, the establishment of an auditing department, and the re-organization of most of the departments of the administration. The opposition, however, had no faith in the ability of any government to implement reforms under Khouri's presidency, and concentrated on one single aim, the President's resignation.

The revolution against President Khouri was effectively started by the head of the government, Prime Minister Solh, in an extraordinary session of the Chamber on September 9, 1952 in which he was expected to ask for a vote of confidence in his cabinet. Instead of asking for confidence, Premier Solh made a speech pointed at the President and his favorites. He described the corruption, mismanagement, and peddling of influence even in judicial processes, and denounced the continuous interference of the President and the resulting inability to effect any reform. He ended his speech by announcing his intention to resign. He did not present his resignation to the President, and the latter reacted by issuing a decree dismissing him. The surprise speech, which was not published because of censorship, was evidently made without the knowledge or consent of the cabinet, and President Khouri has claimed that it was written by the opposition and that Premier Solh's action was motivated by his desire to guarantee his future.[22]

The Premier's attack and withdrawal were followed by a rapid succession of events that caught the President by surprise and ended in his downfall after nine days. The President tried to solve the ministerial crisis by first appointing an "emergency cabinet" on September 10 consisting of three heads of departments pending negotiations with the political parties.[23] Two days later, he requested Saeb Salam, a Sunnite leader in Beirut, to form a coalition cabinet, but while Salam attempted without enthusiasm to complete the formation of his cabinet, the decisive revolutionary action began. On Monday, September 15, 1952 a peaceful general strike was declared by the Popular Front. In a memorandum to the President, the Front explained that the strike was a protest against the postponement of reform and it asked for the formation of a neutral cabinet that would have power to dissolve the Chamber.[24] The strike involved the total closing of the cities in Lebanon where the shopkeepers and the people demonstrated their cooperation with the opposition. President Khouri has claimed that Colonel Shishakli of Syria contributed funds for carrying out the strike in order to weaken Lebanon.[25]

On the third day of the strike, September 17, petitions demanding the President's resignation began to reach President Khouri directly or through the Speaker of the Chamber. One of the petitions, signed by fifteen deputies, requested the Speaker, Ahmad al-Asaad, to ask the President to resign. On the evening of the same day, Premier Salam arrived at the presidential summer residence in Aley accompanied by General Chehab, Speaker Ahmad al-Asaad, and former premier Yafi, and handed the President a letter asking for his resignation. Salam at the same time presented his own resignation. As the fourth day approached, it was feared that clashes between the demonstrators and the police might take place, and it was therefore important for the President to know the attitude of the army. General Chehab discussed the issue with his staff and gave the President his decisive answer. The army, he said, would use force only to maintain order but would not shoot at the citizens if a massive outbreak occurred. President Khouri realized that Chehab's answer meant that he did not want to use force except to a certain extent. He also saw that the Sunnite notable, Hussein al-Uwayni, whom he approached for forming a cabinet, was unwilling to be premier under the circumstances. At 2 a.m., Thursday September 18, President Khouri retained General Chehab in his office, and went to pray. He then joined his wife and his brother Fuad and told them his decision to resign because he wanted to avoid bloodshed, preserve the force of the army, and respect the dignity of the Presidency and of the constitution. He went back to General Chehab and gave him a decree appointing him prime minister with two other ministers, Nazem Akkari and Basil Trad. He also gave General Chehab a copy of the constitution of Lebanon and told him, "Keep it and defend it!" He then presented his resignation to the Speaker of the Chamber.[26]

In spite of the irregularities of his political and administrative behavior, President Khouri, like the other men of his generation, was respectful of the constitutional system. He was happy that the constitution was preserved and that the military commander who accepted to become prime minister promised to defend it. The leaders of the opposition likewise preferred to end their revolution against Khouri in good constitutional manner. They neither suspended the constitution, nor did they dissolve the Chamber in order to establish their own personal rule. In contrast to most other revolutionary leaders, they did not force President Khouri to leave the country, nor did they bring him to trial in order to insult him and his regime and make propaganda for themselves.

General Chehab announced to the Lebanese that he would rule temporarily with the help of his two civilian ministers until the election of a new president. In the chamber of deputies, the majority that had supported Khouri was in favor of electing Chehab president, but he wisely refused to present his candidacy. When the Chamber met on September 23 to elect the new president, the majority consequently had no other choice but to follow the leadership of the former opposition and the mood of the time and elect Camille Chamoun who became president by 74 out of 77 votes.

The opposition coalitions and fronts began to disintegrate soon after they succeeded in overthrowing President Khouri. Differences appeared among them as to the advisability of introducing the radical reforms they once advocated, and Lebanon soon returned to its traditional pattern of politics. Following the resignation of General Chehab from the premiership on September 24, President Chamoun asked in succession three Sunnite political leaders, beginning with Yafi, to form a cabinet, and the three failed. The main reason seems to have been the intransigent position taken by Junblat, leader of the Progressive Socialist Party, who wanted half of the cabinet posts for his party before pledging support to any cabinet or becoming a cabinet member. Junblat also wanted the new cabinet to pledge that it would carry out his ten-point program which included the prosecution of the former president and of all profiteers and grafters under the old regime, the nationalization of foreign public utility concessions, the redistribution of large estates and the re-districting of seats for the Chamber on the basis of the small constituency. President Chamoun and many others were of the opinion that if the door of trials of profiteers were to be opened, it would never be possible to close it. The ministerial crisis was finally solved by the formation of a four-man cabinet from outside the Chamber on October 1, 1952, with Emir Khalid Chehab, former premier and diplomat, and three civil servants.[27] The cabinet asked for emergency powers for a period of six months in order to make certain reforms by decree. The old majority that had supported Khouri rallied slowly to Chamoun out of fear of being prosecuted, and the chamber of deputies was maintained until its dissolution on May 30, 1953. The new Chamber was elected in accordance with a new electoral law that divided Lebanon into smaller electoral districts, reduced the number of deputies to 44 instead of 77, and granted the right of vote to women with at least an elementary school education.

IV. The Rebellion of 1958 Against Chamoun

A. Background and Causes

The revolution of 1952 showed, among other things, that the Lebanese could agree on a common objective and line of action, in spite of sectarian and factional differences, when the ruling clique becomes flagrantly corrupt to the point of hurting the interests and dignities of the people and their leaders. The rebellion against President Chamoun that almost developed into a civil war in 1958 proved, on the other hand, that the Lebanese could disagree to the point of carrying arms against each other when political and sectarian passions are stirred by personal and ideological disputes and by external pressures.[28] The power struggle among Lebanese personalities and clans that reached its climax in the 1958 rebellion, was rendered more acute by the differences in the aspirations of the Christian and Muslim communities on both the internal and external levels. These differences manifested themselves openly when, as a result of the rising prestige of Nasser and his advocacy of neutralism and pan-Arabism, the majority of the Muslims of Lebanon gave him their enthusiastic support and allegiance, while the majority of the Christians reacted by expressing their fear for Lebanese independence and their opposition to pro-Nasserist activity. The leaders of the opposition against Chamoun, who included certain Christian personalities, rallied sometimes by mere opportunism to Nasserist policy, and sought, with Nasser's blessing and support, to weaken Chamoun's government and force its resignation by extra-legal means.

Chamoun was the president of a small country that traditionally tried to remain neutral in inter-Arab politics, and occasionally acted as mediator in conflicts between the Arab states. In spite of its western orientation, Lebanon usually ranged itself on the Arab side in conflicts between the Arab world and the West involving the legitimate rights and aspirations of the Arabs.[29] In the first three years of his presidency (1952-1955), President Chamoun succeeded in following the traditional Lebanese policy of neutrality. Lebanon did not join the controversial Baghdad Pact in 1955, but like most other Arab states, it refused to condemn Iraq for joining it. At the same time, Lebanon did not accept to participate in the military agreements signed between Egypt, Syria, and Saudi Arabia in October 1955, and refused to subscribe to a policy that would lead to the isolation of Iraq. Chamoun's relations with Iraq and Jordan remained friendly in spite of the violent Egyptian attacks against their Hashemite rulers. Lebanon, moreover, accepted to grant political asylum to the Syrians who were threatened by the purges and treason trials in Damascus.

In the last three years of his rule, President Chamoun found it increasingly difficult to pursue an independent neutral policy, and he was faced with two alternatives, either submit to Egyptian pressure and align his policy with that of Egypt and its ally, Syria – with all its involvements with the Sovietic bloc, its socialistic trends, and its violent hostility to the West and to the two Hashemite kingdoms – or follow an independent pro-Western policy. Chamoun ultimately chose the second alternative, because it was becoming clear that what Nasser wanted was the domination of the Arab East, if not its unification under his leadership, and the establishment in the satellite countries of regimes similar to his own. Relations remained officially normal for some time between the Egyptian and the Lebanese presidents, but the two distrusted and watched each other.

President Chamoun, it must be remembered, was a proud, strong-willed, and courageous man who had a high opinion of the freedom and independence of his country and of his duty to defend its interests and protect it from the dangers of communism and totalitarian rule. His task, however, was made difficult by the attitude of certain Muslim leaders who sought popularity among their constituents by paying homage to Nasser. It became a classical procedure for those who had any grudge against Chamoun to ingratiate themselves with Nasser by making a pilgrimage to Cairo or to Damascus where they were generously received, and their utterances against Chamoun and his policies were reproduced in provocative headlines. During the Suez crisis in November, 1956, Chamoun's government chose not to break diplomatic relations with Britain and France. Chamoun explained that this allowed him to maintain contact with the two powers and mediate in favor of Egypt, as he actually did, on Nasser's demand.[30] It has been explained, moreover, that Lebanon could not break relations with the western powers without isolating itself and damaging its economic interests and those of Lebanese residents in the British and French dependencies. During the summit conference of heads of Arab states which was convoked by Chamoun on October 30 and met on November 13 in Beirut to discuss the Suez crisis, the two Sunnite leaders, Prime Minister Abdallah al-Yafi, and the Minister of State Saeb Salam, presented their resignation as a protest against Chamoun's failure to break relations with Britain and France. The object of their well-timed resignation seems to have been to embarrass Chamoun, please Nasser, and gain public support as champions of Arab nationalism.[31] Their Arabism, and that of others who followed their course, was described by Chamoun as "a source for income, a springboard for obtaining a cheap popularity, and a stage for dwarfs and mountebanks."[32] The two leaders, it was reported, tried to have Chamoun refuse their resignation, by asking important persons to mediate,[33] but when Chamoun accepted the resignation on November 16, they left for Cairo to be acclaimed as heroes and martyrs.

The Egyptian press and radio campaign against Chamoun began immediately after the resignation of the Yafi cabinet. It was reinforced by a similar campaign from Syria where the leftist Baath minority had gained influence in June 1956 through its alliance with strong military men such as Colonel Sarraj, the director of military intelligence and a well-known admirer and agent of Nasser. In Beirut, bombs began to explode near public buildings, and the Egyptian military attaché furnished the dynamite and other explosives needed for sabotage, while the Egyptian Embassy became the meeting place for journalists, politicians, and terrorists opposed to Chamoun. The Egyptian ambassador was criticized by the loyalist and neutral press for having behaved as if he were the High Commissioner of Egypt in Lebanon. Agents of the Syrian military intelligence entered Lebanon to kidnap or murder Syrian political refugees, and in February 1957 they were able to shoot and kill the retired Colonel Ghassan Jedid in the streets of Beirut, because he had been implicated in the assassination of the Baathist officer, Colonel Malki, in 1955.

The Syro-Egyptian campaign increased in intensity when Chamoun made a tacit declaration of policy by giving the portfolio of foreign affairs in the newly formed cabinet to Charles Malek, outspoken defender of the free world and of Lebanese independence, who believed that freedom was the only justification of Lebanon's existence and that "whoever is about to suffocate must be able to breathe freely in Lebanon."[34] In the United Nations, where he had been Lebanon's chief delegate, Dr. Malek had been an ardent supporter of human rights and of the concept of human dignity against the principles of totalitarianism. At the same time, he had been an advocate of Arab legitimate rights and aspirations and had defended Egypt through the various phases of the Suez crisis. At the head of the new cabinet was the sixty-eight year old liberal statesman, Sami al-Solh, who courageously stood on Chamoun's side in spite of the calumnies and threats of his large Sunnite Muslim community.

In early 1957, Chamoun and his cabinet, supported by the majority in the Chamber, thought that the existence of Lebanon as a free and independent state was in need of support against the threat of aggression. The Eisenhower Doctrine, primarily designed to keep the Middle East open to the West by assisting its free nations to remain free in the face of communist subversion or aggression, was accepted by the government of Lebanon on March 16, 1957.[35] The agreement between the United States and Lebanon promised American economic and military aid and provided for American help against foreign intervention, international communism, and generally against the threat to Lebanese independence. The Doctrine imposed no obligations on Lebanon, and Chamoun believed it would have been a crime to deprive Lebanon of its advantages.[36] To the leaders of the opposition, however, it meant a violation of the National Pact of 1943, but it did not occur to them that the Pact had been already violated when they began to show more loyalty to Nasser than to their own rulers and when they allowed themselves and their followers to become instruments of external attack against their own country. The approval of the foreign policy of the Solh cabinet by the Lebanese chamber of deputies led to the resignation of seven deputies of the opposition on April 6, 1957, a few weeks before the end of the legislature, and two months before the election of a new chamber.[37] The Eisenhower Doctrine became a convenient weapon in the hands of the Lebanese opposition and its allies in Cairo and Damascus for condemning Chamoun and representing him as a traitor selling his country to imperialists. The acceptance of the Doctrine, which effectively produced no basic change in Lebanon's policy and brought Lebanon no direct relief against subversion and rebellion, would have been totally unnecessary if there had been no attempt to force Lebanon into the Nasserist camp.

The issue of Chamoun's re-election to the presidency, before the expiration of his term in September 1958, became the main pretext for the rebellion of 1958. It was raised shortly before the parliamentary elections which were to take place in June 1957, because of the direct relation between the presidential and the parliamentary elections. A two-thirds majority was needed in the coming chamber of deputies for voting the constitutional amendment that would allow the president's re-election. The opposition, mainly for reasons of personal influence and prestige, sought the defeat of Chamoun's supporters in the elections in order to destroy Chamoun's chances of running for a second term. In April 1957, the opposition organized the National Front, later known as the National Union Front. It included various Muslim organizations, as well as the parties favorable to Arab unity or opposed to the West, along with the followers of individual Christian leaders like Hamid Frangie, who expected to run for the presidency. In the same month, Chamoun's government published the electoral law that raised the number of deputies to 66, modified the boundaries of certain electoral districts, and maintained the small list system which was first introduced in 1953 in order to weaken political feudalism and strengthen popular representation. The gerrymandering that was attributed to Chamoun and designed to defeat his opponents, was largely prepared under the Yafi cabinet in 1956, and actually did not succeed in bringing about a complete defeat of Chamoun's opponents.

The opposition tried to influence public opinion and win the elections by holding mass rallies and demonstrations and stepping up its propaganda against the Chamoun regime with the help of Cairo and Damascus. It called for the appointment of a neutral cabinet to conduct the elections, and wanted the number of deputies to be raised to 88. On May 12, 1957 it held a *mahrajan* (mass rally) in Beirut where Nasser's portraits were displayed, accompanied by signs calling for union with the other Arab countries. A covenant consisting of several articles was read and sworn to by those present. It called for a return to the National Pact of 1943, declared its opposition to foreign pacts and bases, and warned the government against interference in the elections for returning a majority that would favor Chamoun's re-election.[38] On May 30, the opposition organized a violent demonstration in which seven persons were killed and sixty were wounded. The opposition leader, Saeb Salam, received an abrasion in his head as he was hit with the butt of a rifle after he had slapped a gendarmerie commander. He was arrested and released shortly after. The pro-Nasserist journalist, Abdallah Mashnuq, who had been dismissed from a highly remunerative post in the Iraq Petroleum Company, called for an insurrection. In the course of the elections in June 1957, the resourceful Cairo propaganda found a way to smear the reputation of the Lebanese foreign minister, Charles Malek, by publishing in the Egyptian and Syrian press photostats of forged documents which were said to contain correspondence between Malek and Abba Eban of Israel. The Lebanese foreign ministry denied the authenticity of the documents and sent its protests to Cairo for having published them. On Sunday, June 16, 1957, an ugly massacre took place in a church in the village of Mizyara in North

Lebanon in which members of the Frangie clan were the aggressors against their political rivals, the pro-Chamoun Duwayhis. The shooting match ended in the death of 23 persons on both sides.

The Lebanese elections of 9-30 June, 1957, in which the Syrian military intelligence under Sarraj is said to have squandered 65 million Syrian pounds,[39] ended in the victory of Chamoun's supporters and the defeat of four leading members of the opposition: the two Sunnite leaders in Beirut, Salam and Yafi, the Shiite leader of South Lebanon, Ahmad al-Asaad, and the Druze leader, Kemal Junblat. Chamoun's government was accused of interference in the elections on the basis of the argument that the four leaders could not have possibly failed to be elected under normal conditions. Other opposition leaders, however, like Rashid Karami in Tripoli, Sabri Hamadeh in the Beqa, and Hamid Frangie in North Lebanon did succeed. The contending parties engaged, as usual, in vote buying, and Chamoun's influence and resourcefulness must be given their due share in the victory. The government won, however, mainly because its supporters made it known clearly to the Lebanese public that the electoral battle was the battle of Lebanese independence, and that voting for the opposition candidates meant subservience to Egypt. The atmosphere of violence and tension caused by the intervention and exploits of the Egyptian embassy in Beirut and of the Syrian military intelligence certainly did not induce the average Lebanese citizen who cared for Lebanese independence to vote for the opposition.

The outcome of the elections of June 1957 frustrated the ambitions of many Lebanese leaders and wounded their dignity and thus contributed to the rebellion of 1958. For those who lost, and even for those members of the opposition who were elected, the prospect of Chamoun's re-election was intolerable because it would have meant their exclusion from the exercise of political power for several years to come. The Druze leader, Junblat, decided after his first defeat since he inherited the seat of his cousin, Hikmat Junblat, in 1943 that a revolution was inescapable, and so he began training his men, who were impatient to revolt, as he said.[40] During the rebellion, he told President Eisenhower's special envoy, Robert Murphy, that his defeat affected the prestige of his clan, and he complained that American money was used in the campaign against him.[41]

Between the end of the elections in the early summer of 1957 and the beginning of the rebellion in May 1958, sabotage in Beirut and clashes of armed bands in the country were continuous. Arms were smuggled mainly from Syria in preparation for an insurrection. The centers for collecting equipment and training partisans were in Mukhtara, fief of Junblat, in Deir al-Ashayer on the Syrian border, and in Hermel in the Beqa. The formation of the United Arab Republic in February 1958 had its special impact on various aspects of the situation in Lebanon. It strengthened the position of the opposition, intensified its conflicts with Chamoun, and accelerated the preparations for rebellion. At the same time, it fired the enthusiasm of the majority of the Muslims for Arab unity and demonstrated their shaky loyalty to the Lebanese entity. When Syria and Egypt celebrated their unity, Muslim schools in Lebanon closed and participated in the celebrations. Delegations of Lebanese Muslims carrying Egyptian and Syrian flags flocked to Damascus during Nasser's visit on February 24, 1958. On the following day, Saeb Salam, speaking for the National Union Front, told Nasser, "You are not responsible for this republic [UAR] alone, but you are responsible for all the Arab people everywhere. . . in particular for Lebanon, and the Lebanese people feel reassured by this responsibility."[42] In the heat of the celebrations for the UAR in the Lebanese city of Tyre, some youths tore the flag of Lebanon, trampled it and wiped their shoes with it. When three of them were sentenced to a jail term in late March, violent demonstrations took place against the government of Lebanon. The Christian population, on the other hand, resented the visits and the speeches and became apprehensive of their effect on Lebanese independence. The challenge posed by the UAR to the integrity of Lebanon was such that even the radical leftist journalist and opponent of Chamoun, Nasib Metni, had to draw the attention of "those going to Damascus" to their duty towards Lebanon and to the fact that the Christians were disturbed and should be given assurances.[43]

In fomenting trouble in Lebanon, Nasser must have been motivated by a revengeful design to punish Chamoun and force his resignation for refusing to submit to his influence and align Lebanon's policy with his own. He had already tried the same tactics with other Arab heads of state. After the formation of the UAR, he might have thought of scoring another success with the help of the Lebanese opposition by incorporating Lebanon in the United Arab States federation or, according to other views, by making Lebanon the third province of the United Arab Republic. Under these conditions, it is highly possible that Chamoun's supporters could have made plans to insure his re-election so that he might carry on the struggle for preserving the independence of Lebanon, which the loyalists thought was threatened by pan-Arabism as expressed in the formation of the UAR. The rumors about Chamoun's approval of the movement to amend the constitution in order to allow his re-election were evidently well founded.[44] It has even been said that he was encouraged by the United States and Britain, and by Iraq and Jordan to seek the renewal of his term, and that the United States set ten million dollars aside for the purpose on condition that they be sent to the Iraqi government and be spent as Arab money.[45] American interest in Chamoun's re-election, however, was weakened when his quarrel with the opposition became more serious in late 1957, and it was realized that "the pro-western orientation of Chamoun's government, while gratifying and helpful, had its dangers," as President Eisenhower expressed it later. On the other hand, as Nasser looked strong and popular after the unity with Syria, a rapprochement was outlined between Washington and Cairo before Nasser's trip to Moscow in May 1958.[46]

Chamoun, it has been said, never spoke publicly of the renewal of his presidency to anyone, and until the rebellion broke out, four months before the end of his term, neither he nor his government made proposals to amend the constitution.[47] When he was called upon to make an announcement about the issue of re-election after the rebellion had started, he refused to speak. He was probably too proud to make a denial of what he never proclaimed.[48] The opposition, however, continued to make of this issue their most potent pretext for the rebellion. On April 15, the Sunnite deputy of Sidon, Maaruf Saad, warned that those who support the re-election must give up the idea, or else an insurrection would be unavoidable. When, three weeks after the rebellion had broken out, Prime Minister Solh broadcast on May 27 a statement promising that the government would never make proposals for amending the constitution, the rebels remained indifferent and continued their rebellion. The re-election was thus proved to be only a pretext for the rebellion.

In a simple colloquial and current expression, Prime Minister Sami Solh described the basic motive for the rebellion as being the desire of the opposition to reach the "karassi"[49] (literally chairs) or occupy the positions of influence. To this he added the following motives: the greed for funds offered by the rulers of the UAR, the defeat of some leaders in the elections, and the refusal of the Lebanese government to follow Egyptian policy and to join the UAR. The struggle and rivalries for power between personalities were thus accompanied by the ideological-sectarian struggle between Arabism and Lebanism, and between Nasserist influence and Lebanon's freedom. Chamoun, at the center of the dispute, was accused of having tried to monopolize power and of having alienated the leaders, disturbed the sectarian balance, refused to compromise with Nasser, and sought western guarantees. Yet it is difficult to assert that Chamoun acted as he did merely for the purpose and pleasure of destroying his opponents and exercising personal power, or for serving the goals of western policy. Chamoun was known as a proud Lebanese Arab nationalist, and had worked for the Arab cause, but he and his supporters were committed to defending the independence of Lebanon against external interference and influence, and to keeping it free from socialism and dictatorship. Under the circumstances, a compromise with Nasser and with those Lebanese leaders who were on his side, became impracticable because the only compromise acceptable to Nasser was that Lebanon should follow a policy parallel to his own. The issue in Lebanon was not really Chamoun's re-election but the preservation of freedom threatened by Nasserist interference, which began actively in November 1956 and reached its climax in the decision that Chamoun should leave.

B. Characteristics and Developments of the Rebellion

In early May 1958, the Lebanese opposition leaders visited Damascus and it is supposed that they agreed with Abdul Hamid Sarraj, minister of interior in the Syrian province of the UAR, on a plan of action against Chamoun's regime. The common understanding was that a strike accompanied by rioting would force Chamoun's resignation in one week.[50] The strike had to be violent and bloody in order to be effective because it was not expected to be general as in 1952 owing to divided opinion and orientation. The strike indeed was accompanied by bloodshed, as expected, but it failed to overthrow Chamoun and turned into a large scale rebellion that lasted five months. Nasser realized that he made a miscalculation that was not to be the last, as his intervention in Yemen was to prove. The immediate pretext for the strike was the mysterious assassination on the night of 7-8 May, 1958 of the leftist journalist Nasib Metni, editor of *al-Teleghraf,* who regularly attacked the Chamoun regime in the same manner as the half-dozen Beirut newspapers subsidized by the UAR. The opposition immediately held the government responsible for Metni's assassination and ordered the indefinite closing of all shops and businesses until Chamoun resigns. Although the assassins were never found, certain persons believe that Metni was murdered by the UAR military intelligence in Syria with the knowledge of Sarraj in order to implicate Chamoun's government and provide an excuse for the rebellion.[51] Nasser joined the Lebanese opposition in blaming the government for the murder and told the Arab people on May 16, after his return from a visit to Moscow, that "The conscience of the people of Lebanon was shocked because it knew the assassins and the criminals."[52]

Violence and bomb throwing were used on the very first day of the strike against those who did not close their shops, and serious clashes started in Tripoli on May 10 between rebels and loyalists. On May 12, barricades were set up in the Beirut Muslim section, and the insurrection began. On the evening of May 11, the Belgian Consul-General in Damascus, M. de San, who had crossed the Lebanese border from Syria several times in the preceding week, was searched for the first time, and the trunk of his car was found to contain an arsenal of weapons destined to the rebels in Beirut, with a message from Syria instructing the opposition to continue terroristic acts.[53] In retaliation against the Lebanese customs officers, a band of two hundred armed persons attacked the Lebanese border post of Masna from Syria on the following night, seized the six Lebanese officers, killed and mutilated five of them and released the sixth who is said to have been a Muslim. They also burned six cistern trucks and destroyed the border post.

The rebellion acquired from the very beginning a number of hitherto unusual features. It took, in the first place, the aspect of a sectarian struggle between those who stood with Chamoun for the independence of Lebanon against external encroachment, and they were in majority Christians, and those who supported the opposition allied to Nasser, and they were in majority Muslims.[54] The leaders of the opposition, who were basically moved by their personal grievances against Chamoun, became the commanders of the rebellion in their respective regions. The Sunnite leader, Rashid Karami, commanded in Tripoli; Saeb Salam with his Sunnite colleagues held the large Muslim section of Beirut; and the two Shiite leaders, Sabri Hamadeh and his father-in-law Ahmad al-Asaad, both of whom had monopolized the presidency of the Chamber before Chamoun, commanded respectively in the Baalbek region and in southern Lebanon. The Druze leader, Kemal Junblat, controlled a great part of Mt. Lebanon, and with the help of his Druze colleague, Shebli al-Aryan in the region of Rashaya, commanded a vast area extending from the Syrian border to the mountains overlooking Beirut and Sidon.

The sectarian aspect of the struggle was mitigated, however, by the presence of the Frangie clan of Zghorta in North Lebanon on the side of the rebels, and by the hostility of the Maronite Patriarch, Paul Meouchi, to Chamoun and his endorsement of the opposition. The Patriarch's behaviour, described by a foreign observer as frenetic and unbecoming his Beatitude,[55] was motivated by a personal grudge against Chamoun, and possibly by instructions from the Vatican to avoid a sectarian war that would prejudice Catholic institutions in the Muslim Near East.[56] The Patriarch's attitude was not shared by his bishops and by the Maronite masses. Ideological parties such as the Baath Socialist Party in Lebanon and the communist party, including the Armenian leftist Hinchak faction, were naturally on the side of the rebels.

Chamoun, on the other hand, was supported more by regular parties than by urban bosses or feudal leaders. Effective support was given him by the Syrian Social National Party which normally advocated the unity of Greater Syria, but now chose to defend the independence of Lebanon after the party had been purged and outlawed in Syria. It also defended Lebanon because of its opposition to communism and to the threat of Nasserist domination. The SSNP members were well organized and trained, and played at times a more active role in fighting the rebels than the Lebanese army itself. The Phalangists under Pierre Gemayel, who stood for the defense of the Lebanese entity, as well as the Armenian anti-communist Tashnak faction, were on Chamoun's side. Two leaders in Mt. Lebanon, the Druze Emir Magid Arslan, and the Greek Catholic Naim Mughabghab fought against the rebels and challenged Junblat and his followers. The Druze leader, Arslan, concluded a truce early in the insurrection (May 18) with his rival, Junblat, as a result of the mediation of Druze religious leaders, while Mughabghab and his men held out until the end of the rebellion. Two years later he was treacherously assassinated by his former Druze opponents in Mt. Lebanon. The loyalists included a fraction of the Muslim population who supported the Prime Minister, Sami al-Solh, and the other Muslim ministers in the cabinet. Two of the Muslim cabinet ministers, Rashid Beydoun and Bashir Uthman, resigned under pressure in the latter part of May. Prime Minister Solh remained bravely in office until the very end of Chamoun's tenure, in spite of the attempts on his life, the burning and looting of his house in the Muslim quarter in Beirut on June 14, and the edict issued by the Muslim Ulama on June 6 accusing him of acting against the interests of the Muslims and calling on the people to disown him.[57]

Between the forces of the opposition and those of Chamoun stood the "Third Force" consisting of such prominent Christians as Henri Pharaon, George Naccache, Charles Helou and Raymond Edde, who vainly tried to find a solution that would end bloodshed. On May 27, Premier Solh, as a result of Raymond Edde's mediation, promised publicly that the government would never present a plan that would permit the re-election of Chamoun, but the opposition, acting in accordance with instructions from Nasser's agents in Syria, refused to end the violence. The struggle, it must be said, did not lose its confessional aspect in spite of the attitude of the Maronite Patriarch and the efforts of certain neutral Christians and Muslims to end the conflict. It was rendered even more serious by the participation of recruits from the Syrian province of the UAR on the rebels' side.

The struggle, in the second place, acquired an international aspect because of the active intervention of the UAR in the conflict and the subsequent presentation of a Lebanese complaint against that intervention to the United Nations Security Council. From the very beginning it became evident that the rebellion was encouraged, prepared, armed, and financed by the UAR whose flag replaced the Lebanese national flag in Tripoli and in the Basta Muslim quarter in Beirut. Recruits were sent from Syria to join the rebels in North Lebanon and in Beirut, and Syrian Druzes were recruited to reinforce Junblat in Mt. Lebanon. The borders of Lebanon, through the negligence of the Lebanese military command, were under rebel control, and the leaders of the rebellion moved freely to Damascus and Homs to recruit fighters and obtain funds, while their men sometimes crossed to Syria in order to receive payment for their services or to be hospitalized.[58] Military operations were directed by instructors from Syria, or by messages from Cairo, or even by the Voice of the Arabs in Cairo which adopted the singular technique of announcing that an attack against a certain objective had taken place and using the announcement as a signal for the attack in the following twenty-four hours. In the region of Tripoli, communists and Baath socialists operated under Syrian officers, sometimes independently of Rashid Karami's control, and disposed of powerful arms such as bazookas and anti-tank grenades, while Maaruf Saad in the Sidon region was equipped by sea from Gaza. Extortion, plunder, and acts of vandalism were committed by smaller rebel chiefs in the villages of North Lebanon, while the more important bosses like Saeb Salam and Adnan Hakim in Beirut allegedly enriched themselves with UAR funds to the point that their embezzlements were reported by Junblat and Sarraj to Nasser in Egypt.[59] At the height of the insurrection, the number of rebels was estimated at about 10,000 of whom 3,000 came from the Syrian province. The cost of the rebellion for the UAR, including the generous monthly payments to newspaper publishers, was about 200 million Syrian pounds (60 million dollars). The number of victims was about 3,000 killed of whom 1,000 were Syrians.

The Lebanese authorities were able since the first days of the rebellion to identify Syrian civilians and military men among those who were captured or killed. An official memoir of protest was sent to the UAR against the participation of Syrians, the role played by the UAR Embassy in Beirut, and the hostile press campaign in Cairo and Damascus, but the Lebanese government received no satisfactory answer. Nasser disclaimed any UAR responsibility for the bloodshed, and in his speech of May 16, 1958 declared, "You and I, brothers, do not accept and will not accept in any way the effusion of blood in Lebanon, because the blood of the people of Lebanon is precious and dear Arab blood."[60] On May 21, Lebanon complained to the Arab League Council, and on the following day it presented its complaint to the U.N. Security Council charging the UAR with various forms of intervention. In the meeting of the Arab League Council that began at Benghazi, Libya, on May 28, the UAR delegate denied any involvement in the rebellion. The Council passed a conciliatory resolution reasserting the principle of non-intervention in the affairs of other states, without censoring the UAR or mentioning its aggression against Lebanon.

The Lebanese government, dissatisfied with the outcome of the Arab League meeting, consequently brought its case before the Security Council on June 6. After a debate that lasted five days, the Security Council decided to set up a United Nations Observation Group in Lebanon (UNOGIL) in order to make sure that there was no smuggling of arms or infiltration of persons from Syria.[61] The UN Secretary, Dag Hammarskjold, was from the beginning of the rebellion against UN intervention in the Lebanese affair. During his visit to Lebanon and Egypt, June 19-24, he evidently became inclined to the opinion that the problem was a Lebanese internal problem and refused to consider the gravity of UAR intervention.[62] The Ecuadorian director of the UNOGIL, Galo Plaza, adopted the same attitude. In his report of July 3 to the

Security Council, he displayed a surprising inability or unwillingness to observe the situation objectively and thoroughly. He failed to recognize the role of the UAR in the rebellion, and minimized the extent of Syro-Egyptian infiltration and activities in Lebanon. At the same time his observers admitted that they did not inspect the borders, which were completely in the hands of the rebels, and that their inspection was never done at night. External support of the rebellion consequently continued in spite of the presence of the UN observers. The American marines who later landed in Lebanon have obtained sufficient proof of that external support when they tapped the telephone between the rebel headquarters in Beirut, and Damascus.[63]

The rebellion, in the third place, has remained unique in the annals of Middle Eastern revolts because of the peculiar attitude of the Lebanese army and its commander, General Fuad Chehab, who also commanded the gendarmerie and police since December 1956. The army was alerted by President Chamoun on the second day of the violent outbreaks, on May 9. It is believed that a good determined operation by the police or by the army against the centers of rebellion in the very first days would have ended the crisis. The Lebanese army was considered well-disciplined and trained and seemed to have the weapons and strength to end the insurrection, but its commander, General Chehab, refused to take decisive action which would have cost a few lives. Instead, he allowed the situation to deteriorate and end in the loss of some 3,000 lives and immense material damage in the course of the five-month rebellion.[64] General Chehab preferred to use the army as a screen against the rioters in the hope of containing the rebellion instead of attacking its centers. He allowed the rebels to enjoy the various government facilities including the use of the telephone system and electricity. His men brought water to the rebels and moved their wounded to the hospitals. His officers imposed censorship in favor of the army but gave the press of the opposition complete freedom to attack the government.

General Chehab did not succeed in containing the rebellion. He left the borders open and thus allowed the free infiltration of recruits from Syria. The "Operation Casbah", intended to isolate and control the "Basta" rebel stronghold in Beirut, was not complete. The rebels received arms from various sources including the Lebanese army itself. Terrorists left the "Casbah" freely to place bombs in the bazaars and tramways, threaten and assassinate opponents, and kidnap innocent pedestrians and execute them for confessional reasons. In the three-hour attack against the presidential palace in June, it is said that Chamoun himself had to help the palace guards and use a machine gun against his attackers. On June 14, the rebels destroyed, plundered, and burned the house of Premier Sami al-Solh which was left undefended by the army in spite of the President's warning about the impending attack.[65] In the rest of the country, the army remained on the defensive. At the end of June, the Druze forces of Junblat in Mt. Lebanon, supported by a Druze battalion from Syria, attempted in a double offensive to march down to the coast and occupy the airport, and also to occupy Aley on the Damascus road. They were stopped by the combined efforts of the army and the forces of the Syrian Social National Party. In North Lebanon, as well as in the Merjayoun region, the army commanders repulsed the attacks of the rebels but were not allowed to take the offensive against them. The Lebanese army command even protected the rebels, at times, by preventing such pro-government forces as those of the SSNP from attacking them in Beirut.

Certain observers were startled by the fact that the Lebanese president had no authority to order the commander of the army to take military action.[66] The mysterious and cautious behaviour of General Chehab has been the object of speculation and has been explained by a variety of motives. President Chamoun, without doubting General Chehab's competence, said that "He was afflicted with an irresolute character and a mental laziness that made him incapable of sustained effort."[67] The average Lebanese loyalist who expected the army to suppress the rebellion spoke contemptuously of Chehab as a weak and spineless commander. Some have explained Chehab's attitude by his consideration for the caliber of the opposition leaders who, moreover, were his personal friends. Another explanation was Chehab's determination "to preserve his own virginity as a neutral candidate for the presidency,"[68] because the elections were to take place within one to two months before the end of Chamoun's term on September 23. On the other hand, Chehab is said to have viewed the conflict as a squabble between politicians caused by the issue of Chamoun's re-election, and he therefore believed that the two sides should settle their difference without involving the army.[69] The decisive factor that is said to have influenced his inaction was his belief that any drastic action against the rebels would have caused his army – which was 40 per cent Muslim with a majority of Christian officers – to fall apart and break into religious factions, and that a sectarian massacre would have resulted. Chehab consequently was given the credit of saving Lebanon from such a massacre. In his speech before the chamber of deputies on the day of his election to the presidency of Lebanon, Chehab actually paid tribute to the army which, he said, "preserved the safety of the country and maintained the values of the state."[70]

General Chehab may have acted under the influence of the various preceding factors. He must have been, moreover, at the very beginning of the strike, under the impression that Chamoun would immediately resign, as President Khouri had done in 1952, without discerning the radical differences between the two men and between the two situations. The expectation of Chamoun's resignation must have led Chehab to consider all decisive action superfluous and conducive only to the alienation of the opposition that was already appealing to him to take over the government of the country.[71] Chehab was therefore guilty of making a faulty estimate of the situation and of the forces at work in the rebellion. He was especially guilty of placing himself and his army above the government, and above the state which he was supposed to serve. Chehab's dangerous passive attitude, moreover, forced Chamoun to ask the support of the United States after the Iraqi revolution of July 14 had strengthened the position of the rebels and raised the spectre of an ugly massacre in Lebanon.

Chehab's conduct under normal conditions can be viewed as betrayal and treason. In view of the confessional situation and the differences in the goals of the Lebanese population, opinions on Chehab's behavior, however, have differed, and will continue to differ, in accordance with each person's religious and party affiliation. One thing, however, is certain. The wisdom of General Chehab in keeping the country from civil war has been unduly exaggerated, for the rebellion did take the aspect of a civil war, and the army and the police were incapable of protecting the people's lives and property. Even after Chehab himself had been elected president at the end of July, kidnappings and terrorism continued to the very end of Chamoun's term on September 23. Four days before this date, Beirut was shocked by the disappearance of the columnist Fuad Haddad who wrote sharp critical, but humorous, comments about Nasser in the Phalangist newspaper, *al-'Amal.* The victim was kidnapped by the rebels, allegedly on Nasser's orders, and no traces of him were ever found.[72] Chehab's attitude, moreover, did not succeed in maintaining the needed discipline in the army. Certain soldiers and gendarmes deserted to the rebel side, and some officers actively spread direct Nasserist propaganda among their soldiers. On the other hand, many officers were disappointed with Chehab's inaction and questioned the wisdom of his policy, or even went to the extent of plotting to overthrow him. Discontent with Chehab and his policies was a primary factor in the abortive coup that took place later during his presidency on December 31, 1961.[73]

The direct intervention of the United States and its role in ending the conflict was a fourth feature of the rebellion. American intervention did not take place immediately after the beginning of the insurrection, and for two months the hopes of the Lebanese government based on the Eisenhower Doctrine were frustrated. When Chamoun's memoir inquired on May 13 about what the attitude of the United States would be if she were asked to intervene, Eisenhower evasively answered that another Arab state should support Lebanon's demand for American aid, and Chamoun was told that American forces would not come to secure a second term for him.[74] The State Department manifestly faced a difficult dilemma. It found it, on the one hand, dangerous to abandon Chamoun in the face of indirect external aggression because of the disheartening effect on pro-western governments. On the other hand, it wanted to avoid a clash with Nasser at a time when it had been trying to improve relations with him. John Foster Dulles felt, moreover, that the adverse reaction to the sending of American troops might lead to the blocking of the Suez Canal and the blowing up of the oil pipelines in Syria. The United States consequently did not give Lebanon its total support, and its ambassador in Beirut, Robert McClintock, refused to take position and expected a compromise solution to be worked out. The American government hoped, and so did UN Secretary Hammarskjold, that the situation could be frozen until July 23 when the elections for a new president could be held – two months before the end of Chamoun's term.[75] As the situation became more critical, the Lebanese cabinet authorized the President on June 16 to ask the help of the friendly powers, when necessary, to defend the country's sovereignty.

In the early morning of July 14, the news of the Iraqi revolution and the massacre of the royal family reached Beirut. The rebels in their quarters danced with joy and threatened the Lebanese President and his government with the same fate. In Damascus, rumors immediately spread, as this writer recalls, that Chamoun was surrendered by his palace guards to the opposition. Chamoun feared that the situation might easily get out of hand, and had a clear vision of the sinister results. He consequently decided to ask for

American intervention on the basis of legitimate self-defense in accordance with Article 41 of the UN Charter. The American ambassador was told that Lebanon expected support "not by words, but by acts," and that it desired an answer within twenty-four hours.[76] The answer came at 2 p.m. on the same day that the Sixth Fleet and the American marines were on their way. On July 15, the first 1700 marines landed on the beaches south of Beirut, and the number of American troops ultimately reached 14,000.

It was the revolution in Iraq, therefore, that brought American troops to Lebanon. Two days before the revolution, Nuri al-Said had asked the American ambassador, Waldemar Gallman, if the United States was doing anything to save the situation in Lebanon, and Gallman answered that he had nothing reassuring. Nuri then decided to dispatch troops to reinforce the Iraqi contingent on the Iraqi-Jordan border.[77] Instead of going to Jordan, the Iraqi troops entered Baghdad in the early hours of July 14 and overthrew the monarchy. The Iraqi revolution, as its leader Kassem admitted later, would not have taken place on July 14 if the marines had been in Lebanon before that day.[78]

The American response to Chamoun's request was primarily motivated by concern about American and western interests in the Arab countries, and by the fear that anti-western revolutions would spread in the entire area after the success of the Iraqi revolutionaries. As the marines landed in Lebanon, President Eisenhower proclaimed that the Lebanese republic was the victim of an indirect aggression and that American troops landed to "uphold the sovereignty and territorial integrity of Lebanon." His statement was a clear refutation of Hammarskjold's views and those of his UN observers. The American landing, according to Robert Murphy, Eisenhower's special envoy, was intended to prove that the United States could support her friends and carry out her pledges.[79] American troops did not participate in the conflict on Chamoun's side, but their mere presence certainly averted the violent overthrow of Chamoun, and the chaos and violence that would have followed. The American landing was an unpleasant surprise and a bitter disappointment for Nasser, for he could no longer expect to establish, with the help of the rebel leaders, a satellite regime, or any other regime in Lebanon on his own terms. He flew to Moscow hoping that, among other things, the Russians would move quickly in his favor, but they did not. On his return, he nevertheless emphasized the victory of the revolution in Iraq and assured those who came to hear him in Cairo and Damascus that "the banner of freedom will be soon raised over Amman, Beirut, and Algiers, as it is raised at this moment over Baghdad."[80]

The commander of the Lebanese army, General Chehab, was manifestly offended by the landing of the marines, while excited Lebanese officers considered it an insult to their army. They consequently prepared to take position near the Beirut airport on July 16 and to fire on the American troops during their march from the airport to the harbor. Chehab was prevailed upon to intervene, and an agreement was reached to save the face of the army.[81] Lebanese tanks and jeeps were placed in intervals between the moving American troops, while General Chehab rode in the procession with the American ambassador and Admiral Holloway, commander of the American forces landing in Lebanon, in order not to give the American intervention the aspect of an invasion.

The presence of American troops did not end the rebellion, but while some sporadic fighting continued, the recruits from Syria began to leave Lebanon and the rebels' hope of scoring a smashing victory over the loyalists faded away. Robert Murphy, at the same time, in cooperation with Admiral Holloway and Ambassador McClintock, sought a peaceful end to the conflict on the basis that there would be "neither victor nor vanquished," and pressed for holding the presidential elections at the end of July. The admiral of the Sixth Fleet, according to Chamoun, threatened to withdraw his forces if the elections were not held on that early date.[82] Chamoun declared to Robert Murphy about this time that he would not seek re-election. The only compromise candidate acceptable to the rebels and to Nasser was General Chehab, while the only other presidential candidate was Raymond Edde, leader of the National Bloc. The majority in the Chamber were reluctant to elect a man from among the military, because it was deemed a dangerous precedent that would give the army a taste of politics and power. Yet under the circumstances, it was considered that the cooperation of the officers was needed to restore peace to the country, and the officers were not prepared to cooperate except with their commander.[83] On July 31, General Chehab was elected President by a majority of forty-eight votes against eight for Edde. Ten deputies were absent. Prime Minister Solh opposed Chehab's election on the ground that it was not constitutional.[84]

The rebels continued their strike in spite of the election of their candidate, General Chehab, and pressed for the immediate withdrawal of Chamoun and his prime minister, but Chamoun carried out his determination to remain in office until the very last day of his term – September 23, 1958. Premier Solh likewise kept his post until three days before the end of Chamoun's regime, notwithstanding the renewed attempts of terrorist rebels to assassinate him. On September 20, he left Beirut for Istanbul and sent his resignation. His enemies found a way to gratify their hatred by treacherously murdering his nephew, Wahid al-Solh, on October 13, 1958 under Chehab's presidency.

The landing of the marines was the object of a heated debate in a special session of the UN General Assembly, 8-21 August. The debate was finally ended on August 20 when the ten Arab states represented in the UN presented a resolution to adhere to the principle of non-intervention in the affairs of other states, in accordance with Article 8 of the Arab League Charter. The American marines, on the other hand, left Lebanon completely on September 29, and the last American troops withdrew on October 25, 1958. The American landing is estimated to have cost 200 million dollars.[85]

C. Results and Countereffects of the Settlement

The Lebanese crisis ended by placing a general at the head of the state for the first time in the modern history of Lebanon. Unlike the two other generals who seized power in Iraq and Sudan during that same year, General Chehab was carried to the presidency, not by a real military coup d'état but, strangely enough, by a parliament whose majority was favorable to President Chamoun. It is generally believed that Chehab was elected because of his neutral attitude during the conflict and his lack of political ambition. One of his admirers even has mentioned that "he became President without wanting the presidency, and this was unprecedented in world history."[86] The truth, however, is that the election of Chehab was indirectly imposed by his officers who assumed the role of arbiters in the conflict, and by Robert Murphy who knew that Chehab would be the only candidate acceptable to the rebels – and American policy definitely sought to appease the rebels and behind them Nasser. In addition, the election was the result of a common desire to reach a compromise and end the crisis.

The new President was expected to observe the National Pact of 1943 as well as the slogan, "Neither victor nor vanquished," with which the rebellion ended, but he did not, largely because of his weak withdrawing attitude and his personal friendship with the rebel leaders and with Nasser who supported his election. Chehab inaugurated his rule by appointing the leader of the rebellion in Tripoli, Rashid Karami, as prime minister. The cabinet was formed of eight members who were either former rebel leaders, or sympathizers with the rebellion. The President's choice was totally unacceptable to the loyalists and to the Christians in general, because it implied that the rebels were victorious. The loyalists, moreover, feared that acts of vengeance, similar to the kidnapping and slaying of the Phalangist columnist Fuad Haddad that occurred on the eve of Chehab's inauguration, would multiply, and that the independence of Lebanon would be compromised. The Phalangists and other loyalists consequently declared a general strike against the Karami government. The closing of stores, the paralysis of business activity and of transportation and tourism were even more complete than under the former rebels because the Phalangists and their allies of the SSNP and other groups controlled most of the roads leading to Beirut and to the mountains. The counterrevolution, as this movement of the new opposition was called, lasted about three weeks. It isolated the capital from the rest of the world and ended only when Karami resigned on October 10. The new cabinet formed four days later was intended to reassure the Christian population. It consisted of two Maronite Christians and two Sunnite Muslims. It was thus drawn from the two largest Christian and Muslim sects, and was referred to by a New York Times editorial as "a balance of fear." The prime minister was still Karami and with him was the Sunnite leader Uwayni, but on the other side the cabinet included Pierre Gemayel, leader of the Phalangists, and Raymond Edde, National Bloc leader. The policy statement of the new cabinet promised to safeguard the sovereignty of Lebanon, but it emphasized that Lebanon would remain an independent Arab country.

The Chehab regime offended the susceptibilities of the former loyalists in many ways and catered to the wishes of the former rebels. The deserters from the army, for example, received indemnities equal to their salary during desertion, and many deserters from the police and the gendarmerie were returned to their posts. The former ambassador of the United Arab Republic, Abdul Hamid Ghaleb, who had been forced to leave Lebanon because of his support for the rebels against Chamoun, was returned immediately after Chehab's election. His influence reached such a point that his old nickname, "the High Commissioner," was revived in popular circles and in the critical press. In the elections of June 1960, rumors about UAR intervention and support for certain candidates were such that the caretaker cabinet of Ahmad Daouq had to issue a statement denying the charges.[87] In April 1961, the Lawyers' Syndicate in Beirut declared a strike against the Egyptian School of Law that opened in Beirut, but after a strike of nine months the school was maintained.

Under President Chehab, the government of Lebanon declared a policy of non-alignment in world affairs, and on December 10, 1958, it ended its commitment to the Eisenhower Doctrine and notified the American government of its decision. In spite of this theoretical non-alignment policy and the presence of a Lebanese delegation at the conference of non-aligned countries in Belgrade in September 1961, Lebanon remained basically, as it had always been, oriented towards the West. In Arab affairs, however, the Lebanese government seemed to have become a docile follower of Nasser particularly after Saeb Salam, the former rebel leader in Beirut, had been appointed prime minister in early August 1960. Certain Lebanese politicians and officers were said to have been during this period on the payroll of Sarraj, Nasser's chief supporter and minister of interior in Syria under the UAR.[88] Resentment against the Lebanese government policy expressed itself either by exploding bombs at the UAR consulate in Beirut, or by attempting to dynamite the house of Premier Salam, or still by attacking on the highway the caravans of Lebanese Nasserists who flocked to Damascus every time Nasser visited the capital of the Syrian province.[89] On February 26, 1961, Nasser hurled a strong attack from Damascus against his Lebanese opponents, the Phalangists and the Syrian Social National Party. On March 11, 1961, the independent Beirut newspaper, *al-Nahar,* was suspended for ten days for publishing a cartoon depicting Lebanon as a province of the UAR.

When Syria separated from the UAR after the coup of September 28, 1961, the government of Saeb Salam in Lebanon was the only Arab government to withhold recognition of the independent Syrian regime for fear of offending Nasser. Egyptian-subsidized newspapers in Lebanon led a violent attack against Syria and became the targets of bombs that were exploded in their office buildings by anti-Nasserist elements. The damages, it is said, were paid by the Egyptian Embassy. Lebanon remained even after Salam's resignation on October 23, 1961 the center of anti-Syrian subversion and the chief source of Nasserist infiltration into Syria. The notorious Sarraj, who fled to Egypt after Syria's secession, came twice to Beirut in the summer of 1962 to create disorder against Syria. The Lebanese cabinet ministers, Abdallah Mashnuq and Kemal Junblat, made of their newspapers instruments of anti-Syrian campaigns. In one editorial, Junblat spoke of the Syrians as "the descendants of Hulagu, the Mongol." In the Arab League conference of Shtura in August 1962, where Syria presented a complaint against Egyptian subversion, the Lebanese ambassador to Egypt, Joseph Abu-Khater, acted as though he were a member of the Egyptian delegation.

Lebanon, under Chehab's regime, became a party to the disputes of Nasser with other Arab states. Many Lebanese deputies could not see why Lebanon should isolate itself from Syria, Jordan, Iraq, Saudi Arabia, and Yemen and become hostile to them and act contrary to her own interests every time a quarrel erupted between Nasser and the rulers of these countries. Other Lebanese deputies were at a loss to comprehend why favors should be accorded to Egypt even after it had nationalized the property of Lebanese residents in November 1961 and restricted Egyptian tourism in Lebanon.[90] In Jordan, Prime Minister Wasfi Tell charged that Lebanon had become the center of activity on behalf of Nasser against other Arab states. In May 1962, the Saudi ambassador had to leave Lebanon in protest against Nasserist newspaper attacks against the person of King Saud. The Lebanese government had finally to pass a law at the end of May that provided for the suspension of newspapers for five days for libeling a foreign chief of state.[91]

Lebanon's pro-Nasserist policy after the rebellion, however, did not go to the extent of promoting unity or federation with Egypt even when its neighbors in Syria and Iraq did. The rulers of Lebanon made it clear that they would cooperate with the Arab states within the framework of the Arab League, but that Lebanon should remain independent and sovereign. The Muslim leaders of Lebanon also were reconciled to the idea that Lebanon was worth protecting provided they had their real share of power and that no other religious group dominated the country.

The end of the rebellion against Chamoun and the accession of General Chehab brought several rebel leaders who had been in eclipse under Chamoun to key posts. Sabri Hamadeh again became the perennial president of the Chamber, and Kemal Junblat became almost a permanent fixture in the various cabinets, while Karami, Salam, and Uwayni succeeded each other in the premiership. The rebellion, however, produced no change in the fundamental structures of Lebanon's parliamentary life. The confessional system was retained and Muslims made no more remonstrances against it. Their leaders were satisfied by the larger role played by the prime minister in view of Chehab's reluctance to govern, and by the apparent pro-Nasserist policy that pleased the Muslim masses. Political behaviour, as expressed in the elections, and in party and factional alignments and maneuvers, remained unchanged. The parliamentary elections of April 1964 were attended by fist fights, stoning of cars, and other incidents that prompted the Maronite Patriarch, Paul Meouchi, to declare that he was "grieved by reports about various irregularities made against freedom, dignity, and ethical and constitutional fundamentals."[92] The avidity of the politicans for posts and honors became even less inhibited under a weak and complacent president. The number of deputies was raised from 66 to 99, and for the first time in Lebanon, a cabinet was formed – under Salam in August 1960 – of eighteen members. In imitation of Egypt, ministries of municipal and rural affairs, information and guidance, and planning were created, but did not last long. Between the old Muslim allies in the rebellion, rivalries and quarrels soon resumed, and when the Sunnite leader, Yafi, was defeated in the elections of June 1960, he accused his former ally, Salam, of betrayal and double-dealing.

One month after the beginning of the rebellion in May 1958, the independent journalist, Ghassan Twaini, had predicted that it "promised nothing worth the shedding of a drop of blood."[93] When the rebellion ended, Kemal Junblat, one of its leaders, expressed his disenchantment with its results. According to him, "the revolution ended where it should not have ended," for he was against the re-establishment of political sectarianism, and even against the National Pact which he called, "a mutual exchange of lies," and he advocated a revolutionary reform of Lebanese institutions.[94]

The rebellion seems to have given the army an idea of its political importance and led to the intervention of the military in political and administrative affairs.[95] The officers, however, did not establish a military regime in Lebanon. Their leader, General Chehab, in spite of his little consideration for politicians – whom he called *fromagistes* (cheese eaters) – allowed them to rule and was the least interested among the Lebanese presidents in the exercise of power. He used various occasions to commend the officers of the army for being unselfish and "too noble to ask a price for fulfilling their duty," and for saving not only the country's sovereignty, but also "that institution so dear to the Lebanese, namely their democratic system." General Chehab declared that the army of Lebanon, as well as its people, were firmly attached to democracy which "they consider a foundation of life in Lebanon and the basis for Lebanon's radiance, prosperity, and dignity."[96] It is worth mentioning that under Chehab's presidency, the leaders of the preceding regime enjoyed full freedom and participation in the Lebanese democratic system. Former President Chamoun himself was elected to the chamber of deputies in June 1960 and became the leader of a new party group called the National Liberal Party.

In the elections of April 1964, Chamoun was defeated, and the general impression was that the elections were conducted on the basis of returning to the Chamber only those candidates who would be willing to amend the constitution and re-elect Chehab president. When the elections were over, President Chehab wisely overcame the temptation of running for a second term in spite of the motion made by the new Chamber for the amendment of the constitution in his favor. He evidently profited from the experience of his two predecessors and listened more to the warnings and advice of those who opposed his re-election than to the appeals of his supporters.

V. The Abortive Military Coup of December 1961

The attempted coup of December 31, 1961 was the first instance of direct military action in Lebanon against the established government. It differed, however, from the classical military coups of the neighboring Arab countries in that it was not the result of a widespread military conspiracy, or the expression of general military discontent with the civilian government. It involved the isolated action of four officers of lower rank and some forty soldiers. In a way, it can even be viewed as a protest by certain patriotic Lebanese officers against the army itself for its passive attitude during the rebellion of 1958, and against the intervention of the military in politics during Chehab's presidency. The two military leaders of the coup, Captains Fuad Awad and Shawqi Khairallah, also meant to express their opposition to the noticeable Egyptian influence in Lebanon under the Chehab regime, and to erase the humiliation and the sense of defeat which many Lebanese felt when, as a result of the rebellion, the former rebels left their barricades to become the rulers and acted as though they were the victors.[97]

The coup of December 31, 1961, furthermore, was attempted by Captain Awad only after the full participation of the Syrian Social National Party and its para-military forces had been assured. It was in fact viewed officially as a party coup, and as an act of aggression committed by armed civilians against the Lebanese army. The leaders of the SSNP, and the few officers involved in the coup shared the same views about the situation in Lebanon and agreed to overthrow Chehab's regime. The SSNP, it must be remembered, had defended the legal government of Lebanon against the rebellion and against the threat of Egyptian domination, but its goal continued to be the unity of geographic Syria under some sort of federation. Its emphasis on Syrian nationalism and unity ran against the prevailing currents of Lebanese nationalism on the one hand, and Arab nationalism on the other, and made it suspect in particular to the Maronite and Catholic Christians, as well as to the Sunnite Muslims of Lebanon. The party had no representative in the Chamber and very few supporters or sympathizers in the Lebanese army. The four officers who participated in the coup denied that they were members of the party but they subscribed to its moderate socialism. One of them, Captain Khairallah, had directed the SSNP magazine in 1945 before joining the army.

In the summer of 1961, Khairallah met Dr. Abdallah Saadeh, leader of the SSNP, and discussed with him the possibility of staging a coup. In the third meeting that took place after the Syrian army revolt of September 28, 1961 and the secession of Syria from the UAR, Captain Khairallah spoke to Dr. Saadeh of his colleague, Captain Awad, who commanded the garrison of Tyre and was evidently in a better position to start military action since he had an armored unit under his command. During the six meetings between Awad and the party leader, the idea of the coup took shape. Captain Awad presented a plan of action which he said was easy to execute, while Saadeh obtained at the end of October extraordinary powers from the supreme council of the party to carry out the plan and enlist the support of party members. The role of the armed members of the party in the ensuing operations was to occupy certain important government buildings, including the post office and the broadcasting station, and to arrest the key senior officers in their homes, while Captain Awad was to occupy the Defense Ministry and the 16th Army unit headquarters in the Seray (Government House). Captain Khairallah had been already detained for subversion by the army in the barracks of Fayyadie near Beirut since the end of November 1961.

The plotters chose the night of Saturday December 30, 1961 – the night before New Year's Eve – in order to strike. Many officers were on vacation either for the weekend, or because of the New Year's festivities. Captain Awad left his post in Tyre on the coast of southern Lebanon on December 30 at 11 p.m. at the head of a force of forty soldiers, who were told they were on a special mission, and eight armored cars and tanks. On the way, his men cut the Beirut-Tyre telephone lines, but already the chief of Army Intelligence, Colonel Antoine Saad, who had been attending a party, had received a report from Sidon about the movement and left for the Defense Ministry. The armored units of Captain Awad reached Beirut at 2 a.m., and went first to Colonel Saad's house. Finding that he had gone, they proceeded to the Fayyadie barracks to release Captain Khairallah from detention, and then returned to Beirut to storm and occupy the first floor of the Defense Ministry.

In the meantime, about 400 to 700 members of the SSNP had converged on Beirut armed with rifles and machine guns, and spent a part of the night in private homes in town. At 1 a.m., they left their homes in various directions. One group occupied the Post and Telegraph building and cut the telephone lines to the Ministry of Defense, but they did not cut a secret line between the Ministry and the Department of Internal Security, and evidently forgot to cut the connections with the suburbs which were served by the telephone numbers above 90,000. Another civilian group went to the Seray where the officers of the 16th Army unit had been ordered by two armored cars to leave. The civilians, however, did not occupy the broadcasting station because it had moved from the Seray and they had no knowledge of the change of address. Other armed party members succeeded in abducting several senior officers from their homes. Among them were General Yusif

Shmeit, chief of staff, and Colonel Abdul Qader Chehab, commander of the garrison in Beirut, who were released by a military patrol while they were being driven to Dik al-Mehdi, the headquarters of the party at some twenty miles to the northeast of Beirut. They were arrested again by Captain Awad when they were brought to the Defense Ministry. Seven other senior officers, including Major Tewfik Jalbut, director of public security, were also abducted.[98]

At the Defense Ministry, a floor-to-floor skirmish continued between Captain Awad's force on the first floor and the loyal officers on the second until 4 a.m., when reinforcements with army tanks arrived from the suburbs and surrounded the building. Captains Awad and Khairallah then left the Ministry of Defense in a car while most of their soldiers were arrested. Other government forces surrounded the post office where some 19 SSNP members surrendered. The operation thus ended in Beirut before 8 a.m. and quiet returned. By the evening of the same day – December 31 – all the abducted officers had been brought back, and the leader of the party, Dr. Saadeh, had been placed under arrest. The security forces who stopped him on the road to Tripoli found the equivalent of 50,000 dollars (150,000 Lebanese pounds) in his car. The two military leaders of the coup, Captains Khairallah and Awad, were arrested on January 11 and 20 respectively, and a reward of 5,000 Lebanese pounds was given, as promised, to each of their captors. The former party leader, Asad al-Ashqar, was apprehended on February 3, 1962. The headquarters of the party at Dik al-Mehdi held for two days after the movement had collapsed in Beirut. On January 2, 1962 it was attacked by fighter planes and tanks, and on the following day it was occupied by government forces.

Immediately after the attempted coup, the Syrian Social National Party in Lebanon was dissolved on January 1, 1962, and the camp where its para-military forces were trained was occupied and was found to contain some 90 large and small machine guns and 200 rifles. The Lebanese government displayed unusual activity in the arrest and questioning of

SSNP members and other suspects, including many Syrians, Jordanians, and Palestinians in addition to Lebanese citizens. Three weeks after the coup, the number of those who were arrested and questioned reached 4,000 out of whom 1700 were still detained. During the interrogation, five persons, including former President Chamoun, were asked not to leave the country. The government did not impose a curfew, nor did it declare a state of emergency during or after the coup, but it was nevertheless criticized for its violation of the constitution and the bill of rights in its indiscriminate arrests and intrusions into private homes after the quiet had been restored. The National Bloc Party manifested its indignation in the declaration it published on January 5, and called on the government to respect the constitution and human rights and return to the normal administration of justice.[99]

The attempted coup was not bloodless, as the SSNP leader had desired it to be. The government communique no. 4 on December 31 mentioned the death of five victims who fell near the Defense Ministry. The Ministry of Justice declared later on February 6, 1962 that 27 persons were killed during and shortly after the coup. They included six members of the Lebanese security forces, and nineteen persons who were not Lebanese.[100] The coup was condemned by the Lebanese Chamber in its meeting on January 2, as an act of aggression against state security. The Chamber, at the same time, greeted the unity of the Lebanese people, and praised the security forces and the army for fulfilling their duty. The coup seems to have strengthened the sense of unity within Lebanon and produced a reaction in support of the government inside and outside the country.[101]

The general impression was that the Syrian Social National Party, in spite of the training and courage of its members, was not prepared for the attempt, and its dependence on four isolated small officers for carrying the coup was frivolous. Its action damaged whatever popularity it had gained in the summer of 1958 when it defended the legal government of Chamoun against the rebels. Its opponents now were given the opportunity to destroy it. Even if the coup had succeeded, it is doubtful that the party could have been able to rally the army and the populace to its ultimate goals. Already before the coup had started, the SSNP and Captain Awad found it difficult to obtain the cooperation of a well-known Lebanese superior officer who would accept the military command and act as the head of the transitional government in case of success.[102] Certain rumors claimed that the party hoped to restore Chamoun to the presidency.

Speculation about the source and extent of external support for the coup was officially ended by the foreign minister, Philippe Taqla, who declared on February 15, 1962 that in accordance with the investigation conducted until then, no foreign country was associated with the plot.[103] Before this declaration the tendency, particularly in the pro-Egyptian press, was to accuse Britain or Jordan of supporting the movement. Both the British government and King Hussein of Jordan denied any relation with the coup. In spite of the official declaration and the denials, various circles in Lebanon continued to believe that the leader of the SSNP and his colleagues would not have attempted a coup without financial backing from outside and a guarantee of recognition of the new regime. The external source that was deemed most likely to give that guarantee would have been King Hussein of Jordan. The attempted coup significantly occurred shortly after the secession of Syria from the UAR, and it was probably hoped that this circumstance rendered the establishment of a Greater Syria Federation more feasible.

The failure of the attempt was followed by the trial of 309 defendants who, with the exception of 43 military and police participants, were all civilian members of the Syrian Social National Party. The trial began in June 1962 in a normal military tribunal, and ended on September 18, 1962 with 51 condemnations to death, of which 17 were commuted to life in prison, 16 acquittals, and varying sentences to the rest.[104] Eleven of those condemned to death were in custody and included Dr. Saadeh and Captains Awad and Khairallah.

The prosecutor and the tribunal did not view the crimes as political, and charged the principal defendants with the following: plotting against the state security, aggression against the state in order to change the constitution illegally and by violence, inciting armed rebellion against the authorities to prevent them from the exercise of their functions, usurping civil and military authority, forming armed units and participating in them and plotting for aggression against state property, abducting officers and restricting their freedom while they were in the exercise of their functions. Captain Awad, in addition to these, was charged with incitement to destroy telephone lines, abandoning his job in a province in a state of war (with Israel), usurping military command, and using violence with the military guards. The court refused the protests of the leaders of the coup who maintained that they wanted to bring about a change in government, not to destroy the integrity of Lebanon, and who affirmed their belief in both the statehood of Lebanon and Syrian nationalism.

In mid-December 1962, about 180 sentenced persons, including the eleven in custody who were condemned to death, were given a re-trial in the military Court of Cassation. The re-trial lasted eleven months, a record in the history of military trials. The court gave the sentence on November 15, 1963 after 97 hours of continuous secret deliberations during which the judges ate and slept in the court. Eight defendants, instead of eleven, were condemned to death. They included three military, and five civilian leaders.[105] The president of the tribunal, Emile Abu-Khair, gave a dissenting vote and considered the crime to be political. The condemnations to death were not immediately executed. They remained in the files of President Chehab until September 19, 1964 – three days before the end of his term – when he issued a decree replacing the death penalty by life at hard labor for all eight.

The trial and the re-trial of the participants in the coup of December 31, 1961 were marked by a spirit of tolerance and independence that contrasted sharply with what happened in the trial of the SSNP in Syria after the assassination of

Colonel Malki in 1955. In Syria, the party attempted no coup, and yet its members were dismissed from their jobs, its leaders were tried and insulted, and the trial itself became a political demonstration against western policies and against Iraq and the Baghdad Pact. In Lebanon, the trial was serious, dignified, and respectful of human rights. It illustrated the independence of the judiciary from external political pressures. The defendant Khairallah expressed the desire to be treated like the rebels of 1958 who fought against the government and yet were saved from detention and trial. He and his colleague, Captain Awad, spoke freely against the attitude of the military in the rebellion of 1958 and criticized the intervention of the army in politics under the Chehab regime.

The SSNP-military attempt, in spite of its failure, shook the Lebanese government and produced rumors about the possibility of replacing civilians by military cabinet ministers and establishing military rule in order to face the troubled conditions. Premier Karami, however, was quick to declare in February 1962 that the rumors were groundless. On the other hand, as a result of this attempt and of the 1958 rebellion, the cabinet minister and Phalangist leader, Pierre Gemayel, proposed on February 20, 1962 that Lebanon be declared a neutral state, like Switzerland and Austria, in order to avoid the dangers of external intervention and domination, but his proposal was rejected by the cabinet.[106] Lebanon continued to be ruled, as it had been, by a democratic parliamentary regime which, in Karami's words on February 24, 1962, the Lebanese insisted on preserving. Lebanese leaders similarly, before and after this coup, took pride in calling their country an oasis of democracy and freedom, in comparison with the neighboring Arab countries.[107]

VI. Democracy and the Arab Cold War in Lebanon

The survival of democracy in Lebanon can be explained, first, by the Lebanese confessional structure and the vested interests which all the communities have in the democratic system. Second, the economic development of Lebanon and the relatively higher standard of living of its people, in addition to the absence of agricultural feudalism, and the importance of trade and services in the national economy. Third, foreign intervention, mainly western, to safeguard the democratic regime.[108] Fourth, widespread education given until very recently either in foreign schools or in private western-oriented schools, and the presence of an influential educated leadership strongly attached to the values of democracy, human dignity, and freedom. Fifth, little or no interest of its officers in political ventures owing to their educational background, and to the hitherto overwhelming importance of political bosses who were not ready to share power, with all its prestige and advantages, with the military or to be displaced by them. Although the commander of the army, General Chehab, was invited to take power in two of Lebanon's crises – by President Khouri in 1952, and by the opposition in 1958 – the offers were declined either because they were not considered serious enough, or because the commander knew the kind of problems and the caliber of the opposition he would have had to struggle with if he had accepted.

Democracy in Lebanon has been accompanied, and perhaps reinforced, by a free economy and an emphasis on free private enterprise. Lebanon, however, has not remained unaffected by the socialist ideologies and systems in neighboring Syria and Egypt. In the period of close Lebanese-Egyptian friendship after the rebellion of 1958 and under Chehab's presidency, Nasserist social and economic theories influenced a number of Lebanese admirers. The Egyptian editorialist, Muhammad Hassanein Haikal, criticized more than once the socio-economic structure of Lebanon. At one time, he compared it to that of Egypt before the revolution of July 23, 1952, where a small minority enjoyed everything and exploited rule for its own benefit. At another time, in June 1965, he compared Lebanon to Hong Kong and described it as the refuge of frightened capital and people, and as an example of social contradictions in the heart of the Arab world.[109] The Cairo daily, *al-Ahram,* that carried Haikal's criticism was seized by the authorities in Beirut. The Baath Socialist Party has tried, during and after its honeymoon with Nasser, to gain followers in Lebanon through its Lebanese branch offices or by the action of Syrian infiltrators. Within Lebanon itself, the leader of the Socialist Progressive Party, Kemal Junblat, has advocated a massive change in the traditional economic policies of Lebanon, and has attempted in the summer of 1965 to gain support for his socialism by holding rallies in which communists found an opportunity to spread their propaganda under the cover of socialism. Junblat's activities and rallies in the late summer of 1965 in certain villages that were considered to be a good breeding ground for his views have been watched, and in certain cases prevented, by the government in which he was no longer a member. He continued nevertheless to advocate socialism for Lebanon in his weekly *al-Anba'* and in his lectures. He praised the Egyptian socialist system after a visit to Egypt in early 1967 and, in his lecture at the Lebanese Club, he viewed socialism as the only way to overcome the sectarian barriers, provincial partisanships, and local contradictions, and to transform the Lebanese community into a really united people with a unified political existence and a comprehensive general public opinion.[110]

The government of Lebanon has succeeded so far in fighting extremist leftists and preserving its free economic system. On December 6, 1963 the Baath Socialist Party in Lebanon was declared illegal and, ironically enough, the minister of interior who issued that declaration was Kemal Junblat, the former close friend of the Baath Party. The reason he gave for banning the party was not that it was socialist, but that "it advocated single party autocracy which is contrary to the principles of Lebanon's democracy." More than two years later, the security forces in Lebanon arrested on March 3, 1966 fifteen members of the Baath Party and then released them after a week, partly as a result of the protest of the Syrian Baath regime. By a special law of

January 17, 1962, the government of Lebanon was given the right to repeal, refuse, and restrict the right of political asylum, in order to take action against undesirable infiltrators, or against those who might trouble Lebanon's relations with other countries.

It must be said, however, that the threat of socialism and the concern of the Lebanese about their free economic system have led to a discussion about certain evil aspects of the free economy of Lebanon and the need to remove them. Columnists and political leaders, including former President Chehab, have discussed the unjust distribution of wealth in which 18 per cent of the population disposed of more than 60 per cent of the gross national product.[111] They have criticized the serious deficiences of the fiscal system, and the exploitation of political power for personal profit. Lebanon, in other words, has found that if capitalism and free enterprise, and even democracy, were to survive, they should be accompanied by social justice, economic and social reform, and a complete administrative re-organization. This attitude has been expressed in a brief statement of the Lebanese Phalangists – uncompromising defenders of independence, democracy, and free enterprise in Lebanon – on their twenty-ninth anniversary (November 28, 1965): "We reject imported socialism, but we will fight monopoly and exploitation." [112] This seems to be also the view of the Lebanese president, Charles Helou, in his declarations and articles.[113] On July 25, 1965 Rashid Karami was asked by President Helou to form a cabinet that would include in its program the purging and reform of the administration. None of the cabinet ministers were members of Parliament. In a series of decrees they were enabled by the judicial and administrative reform law to dismiss thirteen judges, fourteen members of the diplomatic corps, including eight ambassadors, forty-five civil servants, twelve public security officials, and fifty-eight policemen.[114] The purge succeeded largely because professional politicians were excluded from the cabinet. The *Economist* viewed it as "the disestablishment of an entire oligarchy, carried out without violence, and within the existing constitutional framework, but without the politicians."[115]

The great problem in Lebanon, in view of the Arab cold war that took a more violent turn after 1966, was to remain neutral and avoid participation in the disputes of the contending Arab states and protect Lebanese interests. But this it was not allowed to do because of the external intrigues and interventions of Egypt and Baathist Syria, and the presence of Lebanese socialists and certain Muslim groups who continued to consider Nasser as their leader and to find in his Arab leadership a source of strength for their religious identity even though they could be indifferent to his revolutionary socialism. The Lebanese patriots who defended the Lebanese system and urged the government to protect Lebanon against external and internal intrigues and to avoid intimidation by the Nasserist fifth columnists, became at times victims of terrorist acts committed by fanatic radicals or by organized groups. It was as if Lebanon, as a Lebanese columnist said, were "a screw driver in the eyes of the socialist military dictatorships and a challenge to their revolutionary regimes, and this is why they aimed at its destruction."[116] On May 16, 1966, Kamil Mrowe, publisher of *al-Hayat* in Beirut and a leading defender of the Lebanese system and a critic of Nasser and of the radical military regimes, was assassinated in his office. In his confession, which he later repudiated, the assassin, Adnan Sultani, said that the instigator of the murder, Ibrahim Qleilat, told him that the case was "very important for Nasserism as well as national causes," and that after committing the crime he could move to Egypt where he would be secure and would be given a house and a car.[117] In the course of the trial by the Lebanese State Security Court, the assassin said that Kamil Mrowe was an agent of imperialism and reaction and his articles were against national causes. On March 15, 1968 the court sentenced Sultani to death, acquitted Qleitat, and condemned the two accomplices, who were at large, to death in absentia.[118]

The attacks of Nasserist-subsidized newspapers and Lebanese terrorist agents, and even of foreign diplomats, against Arab rulers friendly to Lebanon and their embassies were an aspect of the cold war to which Lebanon was dragged. Saudi Arabia in particular was attacked and criticized on various occasions because of its dispute with Nasser's Egypt over Yemen and over King Faisal's call for Muslim solidarity. In January 1967 Abdul Rahman Beidani, ambassador of republican Yemen, made a speech in the Egyptian-financed Arab University in Beirut in which criticisms were voiced against the rulers of Saudi Arabia and Jordan. The Lebanese Government took no action against Beidani, but it was quickly reminded that it was abandoning its neutrality and following a double standard in dealing with ambassadors, because one year earlier it had declared the Iranian ambassador, Ali Fetouhi, persona non grata and asked him to leave the country for a statement he had made against Nasser.[119] When the newly elected Mufti of Lebanon, Sheikh Hasan Khalid, was invited to visit Egypt with a large Muslim Lebanese delegation, he made speeches and declarations that offended the Lebanese loyalists and irritated Saudi Arabia. During his visit to the Egyptian prime minister in Cairo, the Mufti declared that "as Muslims from Lebanon, we feel that we are with Egypt in all its policies, for we are really its sons and soldiers who carry its message." He then said, in a pointed statement against Saudi Arabia, "Egypt is responsible for the liberal Islamic trend. . . Egypt which was accused of having deviated from Islam is the very country that nourishes the spirit of Islam in the Islamic world."[120]

Lebanese personalities and the Lebanese loyalist press felt that their government, and particularly their president, were not doing what they should to keep Lebanon nonaligned in its Arab policy, and one publication, *al-Shara'*, even wrote an editorial on February 3, 1967 entitled "The ruler who is afraid should step down." On March 8, 1967 the Lebanese leader Pierre Gemayel published in *al-'Amal*, organ of his Kataeb Party, an open letter to the president of the republic in which he referred to the "Interventionist Embassy" (the Egyptian Embassy), that "has abandoned all diplomatic traditions, principles, and courtesies, and carried its manifold interventions to such an extent that it has become almost a state within the state." He then added, "Had the President stood in the face of intervention that led to Lebanon's deviation from its neutral course, we would not have reached this stage." Ten days later, the editorial of *al-'Amal* criticized with sarcasm the "Talleyrand of the Palais Bustros," (meaning George Hakim, the minister of foreign affairs of Lebanon) because he voted in the Arab League Council to censure and condemn Jordan for its restoration of diplomatic relations with Western Germany, and thus aligned Lebanon with the Nasserist socialist group instead of voting with the other Arab countries who refused to censure Jordan.

Two incidents inflamed the feelings of the loyalist Lebanese on March 18 and 19, 1967 and caused the intervention of the Maronite Patriarch, Paul Meouchi. The first was the noisy reception for the Mufti of Lebanon on his return from Egypt and the alleged tearing of the Lebanese flag during the reception in spite of the fact that the President of Lebanon sent his car to bring the Mufti from the Beirut airport. The second was the explosion that rocked the Saudi Embassy in Beirut on March 19, two days after the execution of a number of Egyptian-trained saboteurs in Saudi Arabia. The Maronite Patriarch, who traditionally speaks out in times of crisis in defense of the integrity of Lebanon, referred in his speech on Sunday March 19 at Anturah, in Mt. Lebanon, to the noises of explosion and the insult to the Lebanese flag. He then spoke of Lebanon as a country that believes in God, respects human freedom and dignity, and desires neither socialism nor communism. "Those who refuse to share with us this homeland and the faith in God," he said, "can take the way of the sea and it is wide open." He called on the rulers of other countries who insist on disturbing the security of Lebanon to leave Lebanon alone because it harbors no hostile feelings to them. The Muslim community was critical of certain statements in the Patriarch's speech but its leaders showed restraint and the Mufti himself made a speech two days later calling for national unity and cooperation.

The Afro-Asian Writers' Conference met in Beirut in this atmosphere of controversy on March 24, 1967 and was presided by Kemal Junblat. The Lebanese liberals and loyalists were critical of its meeting in their capital and soon found that it turned into a socialist-communist demonstration in which certain speakers felt free to attack the conservative countries. Some of them were refugees from those countries and lived in Cairo, such as the delegate who attacked the government of Saudi Arabia. The pro-Nasserists, on the other hand, thought that the conference was a demonstration for freedom and socialism and proved that Lebanon was a neutral country.[121] During the conference, the Lebanese liberal writer and former ambassador, Khalil Taqieddin, sent a telegram in the name of some writers in Lebanon urging the delegates to condemn the murder of Kamil Mrowe, to ask for the release of the Egyptian journalist Mustafa Amin from jail, and to condemn the presence of an occupying (Egyptian) army in Yemen, but the telegram was not given any consideration.

In the clouded atmosphere of this last week of March 1967, the three Maronite leaders of three Lebanese parties, Camille Chamoun, Pierre Gemayel, and Raymond Edde, visited President Helou to submit their suggestions for improving the situation in Lebanon. Although the brief communiqué at the end of the visit on March 28 did not mention the discussions and the president's replies, the leaders, it is believed, argued that Lebanon was deviating from its traditional non-alignment policy in Arab differences and was siding with Egypt in its dispute with Saudi Arabia, that the state failed to carry out its authority fully because of the interference of "non-official elements," and that the government hesitated in taking definite and firm stands in vitally important issues. It is also believed that the three leaders protested against the veto on the appointment of Chamoun's followers and of Raymond Edde in government posts. The president is said to have answered that internally he followed the correct rules of the parliamentary system, and in Arab affairs, Lebanon was bound by the decision of the majority of Arab countries.[122]

Between the interests of Lebanon, supported by Lebanese nationalists, and the decisions of the Arab League agencies and the desires of radical Arab nationalists, the Government of Lebanon sometimes hesitated to take a position. When the Arab League offices for the boycott of Israel held a conference in Kuwait in November 1966 and decided the boycott of the three American companies, RCA, Coca Cola, and Ford for their relations with Israel, it was rumored that the Lebanese Government was unwilling to implement the decision because of its effect on the Lebanese economy and the possible reaction of big American companies towards commercial relations with Lebanon.[123] Lebanon reached a final decision on the subject and announced its boycott of the three companies only on July 5, 1967 after the end of the war with Israel.

Another problem that produced more political reactions within and outside Lebanon was the question of the visit of the Sixth Fleet that usually took place in the past without arousing serious debates. The reaction against the proposed visit came first from Syria before the Lebanese Government could consider the request presented by the American Embassy. The Syrian Government was bitter against the free press of Lebanon because it had mentioned, in reports from the news agencies, the presence of dummies instead of real missiles in the Syrian planes during the Israeli air attack on Syria on April 7, 1967. On April 17 the Syrian president, Nureddin Atassi, followed two days later by his minister of foreign affairs, criticized Lebanon and the defamatory reports of its press on the Syrian armed forces and asked Lebanon to refuse the visit of the Sixth Fleet. The affair was complicated by a declaration that was made at this time by the Israeli prime minister, Levi Eshkol, on the Sixth Fleet and its role in the protection of Israel. The Government of Lebanon thus faced a critical situation and sent two memoirs to Damascus to explain its position. Strong Lebanese personalities, at the same time, warned their government against refusing the visit because that would mean submission to Syrian pressure. On the other hand, the anti-western Front of Nationalist and Progressive Parties, Organizations and Personalities in Lebanon issued a statement that condemned American policy and mentioned the Fleet's mission as one of aggression against small liberated nations, and called on the authorities to prevent the visit.[124] The three Lebanese parties, the *Kataeb* (Phalangists), the National Liberal Party, and the National Bloc came out in favor of the visit which was expected to be at the end of May. They argued that Lebanon had important commercial relations with the United States, in addition to 600,000 Lebanese emigrants whose interests should be protected. Lebanese nationalists became bitter against the Syrian Baath regime for its interventions, and observers noted that whenever Syria was on good terms with Egypt, Lebanon's relations with Syria deteriorated. In the meantime, the American ambassador, Dwight Porter, showed no desire to ask for the postponement or withdrawal of the request. The Lebanese Government at last had to take a decision when Egypt and other Arab countries began mobilizing their forces after the middle of May. The Lebanese foreign minister, George Hakim, then asked the American ambassador on May 18, 1967 to postpone the visit of the Sixth Fleet and added, "although in principle we do not object to it."

VII. The Arab-Israeli War and the Continued Arab Cold War in Lebanon

In the Arab-Israeli war of June 1967 Lebanon kept its small army in a state of emergency alert but it did not open a front with Israel.[125] In the course of the hostilities and after, disagreements appeared, as they often did, between the

Lebanese nationalists and the pro-Nasser Arab nationalists, while the Lebanese government stirred a moderate course between the desires of the two groups. When Egypt and five other Arab governments – mostly socialist military regimes – broke relations with the United States and Britain following Nasser's famous accusations on June 6, Lebanon did not go as far as they did but it withdrew its ambassador and asked Washington to withdraw hers. The three Christian leaders – Chamoun, Gemayel and Edde – were said to have used their influence in preventing the break of diplomatic relations.[126] On June 7-8 the American residents in Lebanon assembled for leaving the country and were evacuated in order within twenty-four hours. The pumping of oil from the pipeline terminals on the Lebanese coast was stopped. Anti-Western demonstrations occurred and violent incidents accompanied the big demonstration on June 10 that expressed loyalty to Nasser and asked him to return to power after his resignation. The government prevented the vehicles from carrying slogans, and when the situation deteriorated it proclaimed a curfew and placed troops and armored cars in the streets. When the war ended and the Mufti of Lebanon made the Muslims in Beirut swear in a mosque on June 16 that they would boycott Anglo-American products, the leader Gemayel reacted and criticized the boycott, and said that it was not confirmed that the Anglo-Americans helped Israel.[127] On August 8, 1967 the three leaders asked the President to restore full diplomatic relations with the United States. Relations were fully restored on September 6, 1967 – three months after their partial interruption – and the American residents returned. Nasserist active intervention in the affairs of Lebanon could no longer be sustained by generous spending and by Nasser's prestige, but Baathist Syria continued to be an irritated and irritating neighbor, while Junblat's socialist activities and opposition to the Lebanese system did not stop.

The attempt on the life of former President Camille Chamoun on May 31, 1968 was another aspect of the cold war tensions that continued to trouble Lebanon after the June war. The former Lebanese president was wounded in his jaw and his hands by a young man called Muhammad Nabil Akkari who was immediately arrested. Tension ran high after the attempt and the Army was alerted to prevent clashes which would have occurred if Chamoun had been killed. The investigation showed that the would-be assassin was encouraged and even taken to the scene of the crime by Syrian Baath agents. The Lebanese Judicial Council sentenced Akkari to death one year after the attempt.[128] Chamoun had been elected to Parliament in March 1968 and some had speculated that he might have entertained the idea of becoming the next president in 1970, but he evidently had no such intention.

The most serious problem that Lebanon had to face after the Arab-Israeli war of June 1967 was that of the activity of Arab guerillas on its southern borders and the fear of Israeli retaliation. The issue was a part of the more general question of Lebanon's role in the Arab military effort against Israel and became a standing source of tensions and crises in the Arab cold – and sometimes hot – war in Lebanon. The parliament that was elected in March-April 1968 and public opinion were divided on the policy to be followed. In mid-October 1968 President Charles Helou presented his resignation because the leftist, Arab nationalist, Muslim groups and the moderate conservative, Lebanese nationalist, Christian elements in Parliament could not agree on the formation of a new cabinet. He withdrew his resignation on October 20 when Parliament accepted a four-man cabinet of two Sunni Muslims and two Maronite Christians with Abdallah al-Yafi as prime minister. Three weeks later, the cabinet was shaken by university student demonstrations on November 7, 1968 in support of Arab commandos following the Jordanian government action against certain commando elements who had threatened public security three days earlier in Amman. Clashes occurred in Beirut and Tripoli when right wing students attempted to break the demonstrations and the tumult continued for five days before order was re-established.

The Israeli commando attack on December 28, 1968 on

the Beirut airport – which was an unwarranted act of retaliation for an Arab commando attack on an Israeli airliner in Athens – destroyed thirteen Lebanese airplanes on the ground and played into the hands of Lebanese and Arab militants. It led to a sharp increase in the number of Arab guerillas in the foothills of Mt. Hermon in south Lebanon near the Israeli border. They belonged mostly to the *Saiqah* (Thunderbolt) units sponsored by Syria. The UN Security Council condemned Israel on December 31, while in Beirut the university student militants and the Mufti of Lebanon, among others, asked for compulsory military service. The high military command responded to the public and official demand and presented before mid-January 1969 the draft of a conscription bill to be discussed by Parliament.[129] Opinion, however, remained divided between some Muslim leaders, leftists and students who wanted to pursue a strong military policy that does not depend on foreign protection, and Christian leaders including the Maronite Patriarch and other Lebanese patriots who did not want to turn Lebanon into a military state and believed that Lebanon enjoyed a special status and would obtain foreign protection in any showdown.

The Yafi cabinet resigned on January 8, 1969 and was succeeded on January 15 by a cabinet under Rashid Karami that had a record number of sixteen ministers all drawn from Parliament for the first time since 1964. The new cabinet faced one of the most serious crises since the 1958 rebellion when riots erupted on April 23, 1969 in protest against the attempt to restrict the activity of Arab guerillas. The clashes between Lebanese troops and the rioting Palestinian refugees around the refugee camps and other demonstrators in the cities on April 23 to 25 left sixteen dead and more than one hundred wounded in spite of the state of emergency and the curfew imposed by the government. Premier Karami resigned on April 25 declaring that he was unable to take a stand, without splitting the country, between those who urged him to give unqualified support to the guerillas and those who warned that Israel would use it as an excuse to occupy southern Lebanon. Karami remained for a record period of seven months after his resignation the head of a caretaker cabinet because of the inability to form a new cabinet before solving the problem of how to deal with the guerillas, and on account of the relation between this problem and that of internal unity and the fear of upsetting the delicate religious and political balance in Lebanon.

The clashes in April 1969 and the Lebanese crisis were complicated by the incitement of leftist revolutionary elements who exploited the emotional appeal of the Arab commando effort, and by the support given by the Syrian Baath in Damascus to the commando units affiliated with it in order to create chaos and destroy the democratic regime in Lebanon. In the clashes between guerillas and Lebanese troops that continued in the first week of May, Syria was accused of sending the guerillas to challenge and attack the Lebanese military patrols and police posts in southeastern Lebanon. It was even suspected that some of the *Saiqah* guerillas on Lebanese territory were camouflaged members of the Syrian armed forces.[130]

The Lebanese official position as expressed by the president of the republic continued to be one of support for guerilla action with a guarantee of Lebanese sovereignty and internal unity. In his television address on the occasion of Martyrs' Day on May 6, 1969, President Helou made it clear to commando groups and their admirers that Lebanon's support of the Palestinian people's struggle must remain "within the framework of our sovereignty and security." He rejected the guerilla policy of the "fait accompli" and the claim that they were free to operate from every Arab position around Israel as he rejected the Israeli contention that the Arab governments were responsible for the attacks of guerillas even if they took place outside Israel.[131] The Arab socialist revolutionaries, on the other hand, declared the Lebanese position to be "a naked counterrevolution" and a conspiracy against the Palestinian struggle, and claimed that Lebanon was afraid of the socialistic tendencies of the Palestine revolution.[132] The Baath government in Damascus seems to have disregarded the idea of Lebanese sovereignty in dealing with the guerillas, and its official daily, *al-Thawrah*, declared that "the solution of the question of Lebanon should be a pan-Arab responsibility."[133]

Negotiations between the Lebanese rulers and the guerilla leaders after May 9 and the mediation efforts of Nasser's special envoy in Lebanon produced no decisive solution. At one time on June 20, 1969 it was reported that the guerillas were withdrawing from Lebanon and Nasser was credited with having influenced the guerilla leadership and the Syrian Baath to arrange for the withdrawal, but this was denied one day later.[134] The problem remained in the hands of the supreme defense council of Lebanon and the Lebanese military command that continued to watch the activities of the guerillas until the clashes resumed on a larger scale in October 1969. In the meantime Israel carried out air attacks on Arab guerilla positions in south Lebanon on August 10 and 11, 1969 and for the first time Israeli infantry penetrated into Lebanese territory to attack a guerilla position on September 4 in retaliation for attacks on Israeli settlements. Lebanese Christian leaders showed at one time an inclination to call international forces to defend South Lebanon in view of the continued tension, while the U.S. chief delegate at the UN suggested the possibility of stationing UN truce observers along the Israel-Lebanon border.[135]

The bloody encounters of October 1969 between Lebanese armed forces and Palestinian guerillas and the reactions they produced within and outside Lebanon presented the Lebanese democratic regime with the most delicate and dangerous situation since the armed rebellion of 1958. The encounters were caused, as in April 1969, by the attempt of the guerillas to be more free in their operations and movements along the sixty-mile Lebanese border with Israel. The Lebanese military authorities noticed that the number of guerillas had increased to an estimated 5,000 fighters, and that they had moved their forces to villages beyond their restricted area on the western slopes of Mt. Hermon and were endangering the civilian communities. The guerillas were possibly looking for better winter quarters and supply routes between them and neighboring Syria and for more favorable positions for raids into Israel. When they were asked by the Lebanese army to move out of a village called Majdal Slim they refused, and in the engagement that followed on October 20, 1969 fourteen of the guerillas were killed and many more were wounded. The reaction in the revolutionary Arab countries under military rule was very violent against the Lebanese government. The radical Baath government in Syria closed the border with Lebanon on October 21 and took advantage of the Lebanese troubles with the guerillas to wage economic war against Lebanon and damage its transit and foreign trade. Demonstrations in Baghdad shouted "Death to the criminal rulers of Lebanon" and the Baath president of Syria threatened to take other measures against Lebanon "until it takes on a real Arab aspect, sweeps out its treasonable clique and takes its full role in the Arab battle for the liberation of occupied territory." The Voice of the Storm in Cairo that spoke for the Fateh commando group attacked the Lebanese rulers and accused them of paving the way for American protection and landing of troops. Other spokesmen of the Palestine Liberation Organization claimed that Lebanon acted in accord with the American government to liquidate the guerillas, and that the collusion was proved by the declaration of Joseph Sisco, assistant secretary of state for Near Eastern affairs, on October 10, 1969 that the United States "views any threat to the integrity of Lebanon from any source with the greatest concern." The radical government of South Yemen broke its relations with The United States.

For ten days the guerillas, reinforced and supplied from Syria, challenged the Lebanese security forces in various parts of Lebanon and in the camps of Palestinian refugees. At least one hundred persons were killed in the fighting and hundreds were wounded. Certain little towns in southeastern Lebanon were seized and the Lebanese frontier posts on the northern and eastern borders were raided by guerillas from Syria between October 23 and 25. The northern town of Tripoli partly fell in the hands of demonstrators and guerillas on October 24 in spite of the curfew that was ordered by the government in the cities of Lebanon on that same day. Most of the refugee camps were taken over by the refugees and the guerillas. In Beirut a group of Palestinian fighters hurled a stick of dynamite at the American embassy on October 28 and on the following day a serious quarrel erupted at the American university between students for and against guerilla activities in Lebanon. The most violent clashes occurred when the commandos besieged and tried to overrun the town of Rashaya, focal point on the all-weather road from Syria, but failed after a twelve-hour battle on October 30 in which dozens of them were killed. The Lebanese officers and their army stood up successfully to the commando challenge and their morale remained high throughout the crisis.

The Lebanese president protested angrily on October 24 to the president of Syria about the deployment of Syrian troops and tanks along the border of Lebanon. President Helou also told Yasir Arafat, the PLO leader, that he made accusations against Lebanon that were not founded on fact. The Soviet Union took advantage of the crisis to express its support for the commandos and to accuse the American embassy in Beirut of supporting Lebanon against them. It also warned the West not to interfere in the internal affairs of the Middle East. The United States government expressed its concern at the beginning of the crisis that the situation could run into a "major tragedy," and later asserted that what the Soviet Union said about the American role in the crisis was false. In Israel the deputy prime minister declared on October 24 that his country would not stand by if the government of Lebanon is overthrown and the Arab armies are stationed in Lebanon. President Nasser of Egypt sent his special envoy on October 26 to Damascus and Amman to strive for restraint and compromise. The curfew in Lebanon was relaxed except in Tripoli, and the guerilla leaders began to tell their partisans and supporters to restrain themselves.

The crisis ended with a ceasefire on November 2, and an agreement on November 3, 1969 between a Lebanese delegation in Cairo under the Army commander, General Emile Bustani, and the PLO and Fateh leader, Yasir Arafat. The seven-hour meeting that concluded the agreement was attended by the Egyptian ministers of war and of foreign affairs. The crisis thus lasted two weeks during which some speculation was heard on what would happen if the ruling regime in Lebanon were overthrown and whether the United States would land troops as in 1958. The Lebanese regime survived because its defense and security forces stood firmly and without hesitation on its side and did not allow the guerillas to score any major victory that would have allowed them to dictate their conditions. The Lebanese military forces were able to contain the limited popular unrest that never reached the proportion of a major popular uprising as it did in 1958. Public opinion, moreover, and even those who supported the guerillas, hated to see Lebanon fall apart. The Muslim leaders who had fought the government of Lebanon in 1958 were now trying to restrain the people instead of inciting them. For these leaders and for Nasser, who had been sobered by his bitter experiences, the basic goal was not to overthrow the government of Lebanon but to face the Israeli challenge. Among some of the guerillas, however, and in the circles of the radical Baath government in Syria and other socialist states, there was a desire to expand the social revolution and to see the breakup of the Lebanese regime, and there was even a measure of indifference towards a possible Israeli occupation of Lebanon.

The Cairo agreement of November 3, 1969 was not published but it is believed that it recognized the presence of the guerillas in Lebanese territory and their right to operate from the Arqoub region in the southeast of Lebanon across the border against Israel and to maintain a line of communication with Syria. The guerillas, however, had to "cooperate" with the Lebanese army and to observe certain rules that were designed to limit the danger of Israeli retaliation.[136] Shortly after the agreement, the guerilla forces evacuated the villages they had occupied during the crisis – such as Kafr Kouk and Yanta – and on November 13 Syria opened the border with Lebanon. On November 25, 1969 Rashid Karami formed a cabinet of sixteen ministers who represented all parliamentary groups except the National Bloc, and thus ended the ministerial crisis that began with his resignation on April 25, seven months earlier. Karami believed that the agreement of November 3 assured sovereignty and security for Lebanon and also provided for the support of the Palestine struggle. The new minister of interior, Kemal Junblat, known for his support of the guerillas, was able to curb their activities in the Lebanese towns and refugee camps. The guerillas, however, could not be expected to observe the limitations on their strikes across the border, and the agreement consequently did not insure the security of the 100,000 Lebanese villagers who lived along the Israeli border, nor could it prevent the renewal of the trouble between the guerillas and the Lebanese government.

Israel had warned immediately after the agreement of November 3 that Lebanon risked retaliation if the guerillas should attack. On December 3, one month after the Cairo agreement, the Israeli army staged an attack by artillery and infantry on two villages that were believed to be commando bases in southern Lebanon. Another Israeli attack by artillery and rockets on the village of al-Khiam on December 23, 1969 killed one person, wounded twelve others and destroyed forty houses. The Lebanese villagers complained that they were totally unprepared for the attacks because their villages lacked defenses and shelters and the border villagers were not trained for defense.[137] The Israeli retaliation for the guerilla kidnapping of a watchman from Metullah at the end of December took the form of several air attacks on the Arqoub area in S. E. Lebanon, and of an Israeli infantry attack on January 3, 1970 on the border town of Qala that resulted in the seizure of twenty-one Lebanese hostages – including ten soldiers and eleven civilians. The Lebanese were indignant either because of the inadequacy of military defenses on the border or because of guerilla activities that invited Israeli retaliation. Voices were heard criticizing the Cairo agreement of November 3 and calling for the withdrawal of the guerillas from southern Lebanon. The secret session of Parliament on January 6 resulted in the dismissal of General Bustani on the following day and the appointment of a younger general, Jean Nujaim, who was expected to be more tough with both the guerillas and the Israelis. An indicator of the trouble to come and of the continued cold war in Lebanon was the joint statement by Arab guerilla organizations from Amman on January 10, 1970 warning that a violation by the Lebanese authorities of the Cairo agreement of November 3, 1969 would mean the renewal of the Lebanon-guerilla crisis. The statement also accused the Lebanese authorities of restricting the movement of guerilla organizations.

The problem of the Arab guerilla activities in Lebanon and the various other problems that have resulted or could result from the Arab-Israeli war of 1967 have thus been added to the internal and external sources of tension in Lebanon. However, in spite of the tensions, irritations and sensitivities between Lebanese confessional and ideological groups, and despite the pressures of the Arab cold war from within and from outside Lebanon, the Lebanese have been able to retain their free economic system, their particular democratic regime, and their moderate course in Arab affairs. They will probably continue to do so in the foreseeable future unless an external force imposes a different system. Lebanon has profited in the meantime from the experience of its Arab neighbors and has watched carefully, and not without emotion, the destructive effects of military rule and revolutionary socialism. It has seen the refugees and the smuggled capital pour into Beirut from the neighboring totalitarian countries whose shortages, economic difficulties and loss of freedom have distressed and disturbed many a thoughtful Arab. The people of Lebanon have been aware of the fact that the country is too much involved culturally, economically, and ideologically with the West to be able to change drastically its outlook. They are proud of their relative prosperity and freedom and are careful to avoid entanglements that could threaten their existence. The presidents of Lebanon have learned from the rebellion in 1958 and other crises that they cannot pursue a fully Lebanese western-oriented policy because a large sector of the population is interested in a more active Arab policy. Lebanon has had therefore to live by compromise in the midst of tensions in order to survive, and it looks like the two major communities in Lebanon are agreed, in spite of the winds of the cold war that blow from within and from without, that Lebanon is worth keeping and that it should not be torn apart. In the choice between military dictatorship and socialism on the one hand, and freedom and democracy and private enterprise on the other, the majority of the Lebanese have chosen the latter. In fact, Lebanon would defeat the purpose of its existence if it were to lose its political, economic and cultural freedom.

1. General Bakr Sidqi (d. 1937), leader of the first military coup in Iraq and in the emerging Arab states (from "Time", August 23, 1937).

2. Rashid Ali al-Gailani 1892-1965 (From James Morris, "The Hashemite Kings", Faber and Faber, London, 1959).

3. General Nuri Pasha al-Said 1888-1958 (From James Morris, "The Hashemite Kings").

4. From the right: King Faisal II of Iraq (1935-1958), President Camille Chamoun of Lebanon, and a Lebanese dignitary (From H. B. Sharabi, "Governments and Politics in the Middle East in the 20th Century", Van Nostrand, Princeton, 1962).

5. From the left: Crown Prince and former regent Abdul Ilah of Iraq, President Hashem al-Atassi of Syria (1873-1960), King Faisal II of Iraq, Rushdi al-Kekhia and Nazem al-Qudsi leaders of the People's party in Syria (From Patrick Seale, "The Struggle for Syria", Oxford University Press, 1965).

6. Colonel (later Marshal and President) Abdul Salam Aref of Iraq 1921-1966 (From "Middle East Forum", Winter, 1965).

7. General Abdul Karim Kassem 1916-1963 (From James Morris, "The Hashemite Kings").

8. Air Force Commander Aref Abdul Razzaq (born 1914) leader of two abortive coups in Iraq (From "The New York Times", September 7, 1965).

9. General (later President) Ahmad Ḥasan al-Bakr (born 1914) of Iraq.

10. Colonel Husni al-Zaim (d. 1949), leader of the first coup d'état in Syria (From Patrick Seale, "The Struggle for Syria").

11. Akram al-Hourani (b. 1914) leader of the Arab socialist party in Syria (From Muhammad Hassanein Haikal, "Ma Lladhi Jara fi Suriyah", Cairo, 1962).

12. General (later President) Adib al-Shishakli (1909-1964) of Syria.

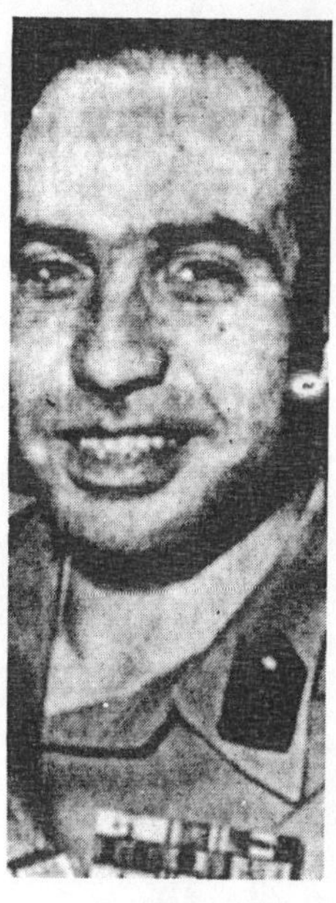

13. Colonel Abdul Hamid al-Sarraj, head of the Syrian Army Second Bureau or Military Intelligence (From M. H. Haikal, Ma Lladhi Jara fi Suriyah).

14. Akram al-Hourani and General Afif al-Bizri (born 1914) of Syria.

15. Michel Aflaq (born 1910) founder of the Arab Baath party (From "The New York Times", October 7, 1963).

16. Presidents Shukri al-Quwatli (1891-1967) and Gamal Abdul Nasser (born 1918) shaking hands after the proclamation of unity between Syria and Egypt, February 1958 (From "The Arab Observer", July 23, 1961).

17. Colonel (later General) Ziad al-Hariri leader of the coup of March 8, 1963 in Syria (Courtesy of George Atiyah, Library of Congress).

18. General Amin Hafez (born 1921) Syrian military strongman and head of state 1963-1966 (From "Time", March 4, 1966).

19. General Salah Jedid (born 1926) Syrian military strongman after the coup of February 1966 (From "Time", March 4, 1966).

20. General Hafez Asad (born 1930), Syrian minister of defense and military leader after February 1966 (From "Time", March 7, 1969).

21. President Beshara al-Khouri of Lebanon (1890-1964).

22. Antun Saadeh (1904-1949) leader of the Syrian Social National Party (courtesy of George Atiyah, Library of Congress).

23. Pierre Gemayel (born 1905) leader of the Lebanese Phalangist party.

24. Presidents Camille Chamoun (born 1900) and Fuad Chehab (born 1902) of Lebanon (From "The Middle East Journal", Late Autumn, 1963).

25. General (later President) Faud Chehab (From H. B. Sharabi, "Governments and Politics of the Middle East in the 20th Century").

26. King Abdallah ibn al-Hussein of Jordan 1882-1951 (From John Bagot Glubb, "Syria-Lebanon-Jordan", Walker and Co., New York, 1967).

27. King Hussein ibn Talal of Jordan (born 1935), (John Bagot Glubb, "Syria-Lebanon-Jordan").

28. General Ali Abu-Nawar of Jordan (b. 1923), (From James Morris, "The Hashemite Kings").

29. General John Bagot Glubb, Commander of the Arab Legion in Jordan 1939-1956 (From John Bagot Glubb, "Syria-Lebanon-Jordan").

CHAPTER V.
Notes

1. Fahim I. Qubain, *Crisis in Lebanon,* (Washington D.C.: The Middle East Institute, 1961), 16.
2. Article 95 of the constitution stipulated that "in order to guarantee justice and concord, the various confessions will be equitably represented in public offices and in the formation of the cabinet without causing prejudice to the interests of the state."
3. For these attitudes and differences: Francois Nour, "Particularisme Libanais et Nationalisme Arabe", in *Orient* no. 7 (1958, 3), 32; Moshe Zeltzer, *Aspects of Near East Society* (New York: Bookman Associates, 1962), 60ff.
4. In November, 1953, the pamphlet "Moslem Lebanon Today" by Dr. Mustafa Khalidi appeared; in March, 1953, Sheikh Shafiq Yamut issued a manifesto with thirteen demands relating to a census of the population, amendment of the constitution, status of the Lebanese emigrants etc.; see also, *Mudhakkarat Sami al-Solh* (Memoirs of Sami al-Solh), (Beirut, 1960), 452 concerning the petition of Muhammad Khalid, head of the National Organization, to Solh's fourth cabinet (September, 1954-July, 1955) including the same demands and speaking of the need for the removal of injustices between the sects.
5. A ministerial crisis almost occurred in December, 1959 after administrative appointments had been made, because certain sects felt that they did not receive their due share. Speaker Sabri Hamadeh complained that his community, the Shiites, received only one out of twenty-six appointments to the rank of director-general. Eighteen Shiite Ulama sent protests to the president of the republic against these appointments. A vote of confidence finally gave the cabinet twenty-six votes against nineteen with seven abstentions. See *al-Hayat,* December 17, 22, 1959.
6. Former President Camille Chamoun relates that when a summary military tribunal condemned twelve members of the Syrian Social National Party to death in July, 1949 and six of them were chosen for execution, the choice of the six victims was made on the basis of confessional balance! See Camille Chamoun, *Crise Au Moyen Orient* (Paris: Editions Gallimard, 1963), 239. For confessionalism and other aspects in Lebanese politics consult: Pierre Rondot, "Quelques Reflexions Sur Les Structures du Liban", *Orient* no. 6 (1958, 2), 24ff; C. G. Hess Jr. and H. L. Bodman Jr., "Confessionalism and Feudality in Lebanese Politics", *The Middle East Journal,* VIII, 1 (Winter, 1954), 10ff.; Arnold Hottinger, "Zuama and Parties in the Lebanese Crisis of 1958, "*The Middle East Journal,* XV, 2 (Spring, 1961), 127ff.;

J. C. Hurewitz, "Lebanese Democracy in Its International Setting," *The Middle East Journal,* XVII, 5 (1963), 488ff.

7. On December 22, 1959 *al-Hayat* of Beirut reported that the deputy Emile Bustani was criticized by an angry colleague for changing his religious sectarian identity to become deputy. Bustani frankly admitted that he wanted to serve his country, and as there was no seat then for Protestants, and finding that most of his family were Maronites, he changed his religious identity from Protestant to Maronite.
8. Certain deputies were known to have spent as much as six million Lebanese pounds (two million dollars) on their campaign; the general expenses in the election of a chamber of deputies could go to about twenty million dollars.
9. On June 10, 1962 *al-Nasr* of Damascus quoted a description of Lebanese newspapers by Muhammad Hassanein Haikal, editor of *al-Ahram* of Cairo, in the following prejudiced and exaggerated terms: "In Lebanon certain newspapers speak of freedom, and freedom for them is a trade; they sell it and Lebanon with it to the British Embassy in the morning, and at noon they sell it and Lebanon with it to the American Embassy, and at night they sell it and Lebanon with it to any reactionary with an oil well behind him and a purse of gold in his pocket." *al-Nasr* commented that Haikal forgot the newspapers that sell freedom and Lebanon and the Arab world with it to the High Commissioner (The Egyptian ambassador) in Beirut.
10. On this revolt, consult Beshara al-Khouri, *Haqaeq Lubnaniyah* (Lebanese Realities), vol. III (Beirut, 1961), 238; Chamoun, 238.
11. See Chamoun, 238-239; B. Khouri, 240 says that the Syrian Director of Security told his Lebanese colleague that he would deliver Saadeh on condition that he should be killed before reaching Beirut by the usual trick of pretending that he was running away and shooting him.
12. For a description of President Khouri's regime and the causes of the revolution, see Chamoun, 233ff; George Britt, "Lebanon's Popular Revolution", *Middle East Journal,* VII, 1 (Winter, 1953), 1-17; R. Mosseri, "The Struggle in Lebanon," *Middle Eastern Affairs* (November, 1952), 328-334.
13. Chamoun, 199.
14. Iskander Riyashi, *Ruasa' Lubnan Kama Ariftuhum* (Presidents of Lebanon as I Knew Them), (Beirut, 1961), 172ff.
15. Britt, 3; Riyashi, 156ff.; Chamoun, 233 says that President Khouri had the mentality of a dictator after his re-election.
16. Chamoun, 237, 242.
17. B. Khouri, III, 455.
18. Mentioned by Britt, 5.
19. Riyashi, 156 ff. says that President Khouri told Riad Solh that he would call him back after about one hundred days.

20. Khouri, III, 440.
21. *Ibid.,* 451; Britt, 11.
22. Khouri, III, 460 also claims that Premier Solh used to leave the cabinet meetings in Aley and go to Beirut to tell the opposition about what happened in the meetings.
23. The members of the three-man cabinet were Nazim Akkari, premier (Sunnite), Basil Trad (Greek Orthodox), and Moussa Mubarak (Maronite).
24. See the text of the memorandum in Muhammad Khalil, ed. *The Arab States and the Arab League, A Documentary Record,* vol. I (Beirut: Khayat's, 1962), 121.
25. Khouri, III, 471.
26. *Ibid.,* 476 ff.
27. The other three ministers were Moussa Mubarak, George Hakim, and Selim Haidar.
28. For the rebellion and its causes, see Qubain, *Crisis in Lebanon;* Chamoun, *Crise au Moyen Orient;* Sami Solh's *Memoirs;* Leila M. T. Meo, *Lebanon, Improbable Nation* (Bloomington: Indiana University Press, 1965); George Kirk, *Contemporary Arab Politics,* Ch. 7; George Lenczowski,, *The Middle East in World Affairs,* 337 ff.; Robert Murphy, *Diplomat Among Warriors* (New York: Doubleday, 1964), 396 ff; Marcel Colombe, "Panorama du Trimestre", *Orient* no. 6 (1958, 2), 7 ff; Dwight D. Eisenhower, *Waging Peace* (New York: Doubleday, 1965), 262 ff.; Desmond Stewart, *Turmoil in Beirut* (London: Allen and Wingate, 1958); Nadia and Nawaf Karami, *Waqi al-Thawrah al-Lubnaniyah* (The Reality of the Lebanese Revolution), (Beirut, 1959); Kemal Junblat, *Haqiqat al-Thawrah al-Lubnaniyah* (Truth about The Lebanese Revolt), (Beirut, 1959); Ghassan Twaini, *al-Ayyam al-Asibah* (Days of Crisis), (Beirut, n.d.); J.P. Alem, "Troubles Insurrectionnels au Liban," in *Orient,* no. 6 (1958, 2), 37-47.
29. Statement by foreign minister, Charles Malek, in the U.N. 12th General Assembly on October 8, 1957; *The New York Times,* October 9, 1957.
30. On the story of the Egyptian journalist, Mustafa Amin, who arrived in Beirut three days before the ceasefire with a message from Nasser asking Chamoun to mediate with the British and the French and ask for a ceasefire, see Leila Meo, 99-100; Chamoun, *Crise,* 300.
31. See the opinion of the late Lebanese deputy, Emile Bustani, quoted in Meo, 100.
32. Quoted in George Kirk, *Contemporary Arab Politics,* 126.
33. Solh, *Memoirs,* III, 377-378 says that Yafi and Salam sent Uwayni and asked King Saud to make Chamoun refuse their resignation.
34. Charles Malek, "The Near East: the Search for Truth," *Foreign*

Affairs, XXX (January, 1952), 239; see also Malek's declarations before the U. N. in *The New York Times,* October 9 and 26, 1957.

35. For the Eisenhower Doctrine, officially known as the Congressional Joint Resolution to Promote Peace and Stability in the Middle East, see the *Department of State Bulletin,* vol. 36 (1957) 481; for the Joint American-Lebanese Communique after the agreement with James P. Richards, see, *Department of State Bulletin,* vol. 36 (1957), 725-726.
36. Chamoun, 364; for a different opinion of the Eisenhower Doctrine, see Meo, 102-129.
37. The seven deputies who resigned and took the Damascus road to be hailed as martyrs were Abdallah al-Yafi, Ahmad al-Asaad, Kamel al-Asaad, Hamid Frangie, Rashid Karami, Sabri Hamadeh, and Abdallah al-Hajj.
38. For details of the covenant, see Solh, *Memoirs,* III, 410-11. The independent daily, *al-Nahar,* called the mahrajan a failure and spoke of its organizers as "candidates of Gamal Abdel Nasser," because of the display of his portraits.
39. Mentioned in article by Muttali (pseud.) in *al-Nasr,* November 27, 1962.
40. Mentioned in Solh, 424, 447.
41. Robert Murphy, 406. Mr. Murphy strangely concluded that a political error was made in ousting him; he evidently did not realize that it was an election! Mr. Murphy admitted that Junblat's political ideas were fuzzy. Chamoun has said that the main reason for Junblat's opposition was that the government refused to give him a permit to build a cement factory at Sibline near his property. Chamoun has spoken of Junblat's double personality, of his passivism and violence, of his pretended liberalism and his inability to tolerate ideas different from his own, and spoke of Junblat's mother who knew her son was not normal and asked Chamoun to treat him with patience. Saeb Salam himself, when harassed in October 1961 by Junblat's criticism, called him "The chronic Lebanese problem." See *al-Hayat,* October 24, 1961; Chamoun, 391.
42. Quoted in Qubain, 62.
43. Francois Nour, 37 ff. for Metni's statement; see also Meo, 159.
44. Eisenhower, 262 ff., believes that the rumor was well substantiated; J. P. Alem, 40; Lenczowski, *The Middle East in World Affairs,* 336; R. Murphy, 400.
45. Riyashi, 184 says that he heard this from the ambassador of Iraq in Beirut who complained that the Americans were late in paying the rest of the ten millions.
46. Colombe, "Panorama du Trimestre," 14; Eisenhower, 265 believed that the pro-western orientation of Chamoun's government, while

gratifying and helpful, had its dangers in that it increased the cleavage within Lebanon.

47. Solh, *Memoirs*, 523.
48. Meo, 175; Eisenhower, 262 ff., believes that Chamoun made a political error, and that he should have dispelled all rumors by a public announcement if he had not actively favored the constitutional amendment.
49. Solh, 454, 477.
50. Alem, 42; Chamoun, 399.
51. See *al-Sarraj wa Muamarat al-Nasiriyyah* (Sarraj and the Nasserist Conspiracies) by Muttali' (pseud.), 2nd ed. (Damascus, n.d.), 63-64, mentions that Abdu Hakim, of the Syrian military intelligence, accompanied by commandos, met with the Lebanese assassins in the home of Khairi al-Kaki, publisher of *al-Sharq*, and then proceeded to kill Metni. Abdu Hakim then went back to Damascus to tell Sarraj in presence of the director of security, Abdul Mejid Jamal al-Din; see also Nihad al-Ghadri, *al-Kitab al Aswad* (The Black Book), (Damascus, n.d.), 57-58.
52. Nasser's speech, published in *al-Ahram*, May 17, 1958.
53. Solh, 554 mentioned that the message instructed the opposition to continue firing all day, to dynamite Souk al-Tawile, Hamra and Sadat streets, the presidential palace, to explode hand grenades, and to kill Husni al-Barazi and Badawi al-Jabal, Syrian refugees in Beirut.
54. Riyashi, 192 arbitrarily estimates that 95 per cent of the Christians stood with Chamoun, and 95 per cent of the Muslims supported the opposition and Nasser.
55. Alem, 42 ff. Alem also believed that the Patriarch lost all sense of moderation and made declarations that served neither his prestige nor his authority. Already on April 19, 1958 the Patriarch had spoken against Chamoun and referred in a speech to "the destructive egotism of those in high places under the present regime."
56. I was told about the Vatican's message, at the time, by a Catholic member of the dissolved Syrian chamber of deputies who had heard it from a reliable Maronite source in Lebanon.
57. The refusal of some Muslim and Druze officials of the foreign ministry to join the Lebanese delegation to the Security Council to present the case of Lebanon made it difficult to follow the traditional sectarian basis in the formation of that delegation. The foreign ministry officials who were asked, and refused to be members of the U. N. delegation were Ibrahim Ahdab, Muhammad Sabra, and Muhammad Ali Hamadeh. See Solh, 519.

58. In Homs, a wing of Shahla Hospital was reserved for the wounded who were brought by the Shiite leader Sabri Hamadeh. See *al-Nasr,* September 14, 1962.
59. Alem, 46; Muttali (pseud.), 55; Ghadri, 60-61.
60. *al-Ahram,* May 17, 1958.
61. Charles Malek made a detailed speech on the proofs and aspects of UAR intervention; see Qubain, Appendix I, pp. 182 ff. Fadel Jamali of Iraq took advantage of the Lebanese complaint to urge the Security Council to protect the Arab countries against Nasserism and Communism.
62. It is related that when Hammarskjold visited the rebels in their Basta stronghold, the UAR flags that had been raised during the rebellion, were hastily replaced by Lebanese flags, and were then returned after his departure. See Solh, 571.
63. Robert Murphy, 402.
64. See on General Chehab's behavior, Eisenhower, 262 ff.; Qubain, 81, Chamoun, 399; Alem, 46.
65. Solh, 590 says that he wrote two letters to General Chehab asking if the army could protect the lives and property of the people. He also asked later to open an investigation on the source of negligence in defending the premier's house.
66. See, for example, Robert Murphy, 400.
67. Chamoun, 409.
68. G. Kirk, *Short History of the Middle East,* fifth ed. (New York: Praeger, 1959), 294; Qubain, 81.
69. Qubain, 81; Riyashi, 102; Meo, 176.
70. *al-Ahram,* September 24, 1958; Riyashi, 192, 209.
71. Sami Solh relates that he went at the beginning of the strike to the Ministry of Defense, and in presence of the chief of staff, Tewfik Salem, and of the deputy chief of staff, Abdul Qader Chehab, he asked for twenty-five men and two tanks to break the strike, but the answer of the military leaders was that a settlement would be soon reached, implying that the President would resign. Solh, 742.
72. It is believed that the victim was first tortured and then killed, dismembered, and his remains were disposed of so that no traces of him could be found.
73. See below, in section V of this chapter, the causes given by Captain Awad, who led the coup. See also Pierre Rondot, "Le Mouvement du 31 Décembre 1961 au Liban, a-t-il eté un coup d'état militaire?", *Orient,* no. 34 (1965, 2), 14 ff.
74. Eisenhower, 262 ff.
75. Colombe, "Panorama . . .", 18-22; Eisenhower, 262 ff; Kirk, *Contemporary Arab Politics,* 128 ff; Andrew Tully, *CIA The Inside Story*

(New York: William Morrow, 1962), 84 ff., said that Chamoun demanded U. S. aid at least on six occasions since the insurrection began.

76. Chamoun, 423.
77. See Waldemar J. Gallman, *Iraq Under General Nuri: My Recollections of Nuri al-Said* (Baltimore: Johns Hopkins Press, 1964), 146.
78. *Ibid.*, 210 quoting the answer of Kassem to a question about whether he would have struck on July 14 if the marines had been in Lebanon.
79. Murphy, 398 said that Nasser's respect for the United States was enhanced as a result of the landing; see also Eisenhower, 262 ff.
80. *al-Ahram,* July 20, 1958.
81. Chamoun, 426 said that he told General Chehab to end "the joke"; while Murphy, 401 said that it was Ambassador McClintock who induced Chehab to order his officers to hold their fire.
82. Chamoun, 428.
83. In spite of his dislike for Chehab, Chamoun claims that he personally intervened to convince the parliamentary majority to elect him. See *Ibid.,* 429.
84. According to Article 49 of the Lebanese Constitution, the candidate for the presidency is required to have the same qualifications as those of a deputy in the Chamber, and Article 24 of the electoral law prohibits officers and public security forces to present their candidacy except six months after their retirement. General Chehab became a candidate while he was in active service.
85. Murphy, 408.
86. Riyashi, 209.
87. *The Middle East Journal,* XIV, 4 (Autumn, 1960), 445 on Daouq's denial on June 28, 1960.
88. Rondot, "Le Mouvement du 31 Décembre," 16.
89. On September 10, 1960, a bomb exploded in the UAR Consulate in Beirut; on March 5, 1961, a convoy of Lebanese vehicles going to Damascus to congratulate Nasser on the third UAR anniversary was attacked at Kahale near Beirut; on March 7, 1961, a burning fuse leading to a pile of 105 sticks of dynamite to destroy Salam's house was extinguished by a Jordanian.
90. See, for example, the speech of Raymond Edde in the Lebanese Foreign Affairs Committee, reported in *al-Nasr,* February 7, 1963; other criticisms by Lebanese deputies appeared in *al-Nasr,* January 31, 1963.
91. *The New York Times,* June 1, 1962. Some Egyptian-subsidized newspapers were suspended or indicted for articles defaming President Qudsi of Syria in June 1962. See *The Middle East Journal,* XVI, 4 (Summer, 1962), 493.
92. *The Mideast Mirror,* April 11 and May 9, 1964.

93. Ghassan Twaini, *al-Ayyam al-Asibah,* quoted by Malcolm H. Kerr in "Lebanese Views on the 1958 Crisis," *The Middle East Journal,* XV, 2 (Spring, 1961), 217.
94. Kerr, "Lebanese Views", 213, quoting from Junblat's book, *Haqiqat al-Thawrah al-Lubnaniyah.*
95. Military intelligence, for example, is said to have supported certain candidates in the elections of 1960. This charge was made by Captain Fuad Awad, leader of the abortive coup of December 31, 1961, during his trial on June 16, 1962. The general idea in Lebanon is that there was widespread military interference in government during Chehab's presidency.
96. See the address of President Chehab to the graduates of the Military Academy in *al-Hayat,* September 15, 1962.
97. For some causes of this attempted coup, see Rondot, "Le Mouvement du 31 Décembre," 15-16.
98. The details of the coup and the government communiques appeared in *al-Hayat* January 3, 1962, and in the reports on the trial of the participants after June 1962. See also *The New York Times,* January 2, 1962.
99. The text of the declaration can be read in *al-Hayat,* January 6, 1962.
100. See *The Middle East Journal,* XVI, 2 (Spring, 1962), 200.
101. One of the manifestations of unity was the ending of the nine-month lawyers' strike against the Arab School of Law on January 18, 1962.
102. See Rondot, "Le Mouvement du 31 Décembre," 13 on the negotiations with Colonel Fuad Lahoud, and Colonel Ghattas Labaki, and the denial of the latter that he accepted the nomination.
103, *The Middle East Journal,* XVI, 2 (Spring, 1962), 200.
104. On the trial and sentences, see *al-Hayat,* September 19, 1962 and November 16, 1963; *The New York Times* September 19, 1962; *The Middle East Journal,* XVII, 1-2 (Winter-Spring, 1963), 121, and XVIII, 1 (Winter, 1964), 93.
105, The three military were Captains Fuad Awad, Shawqi Khairallah, and Ali Haj Hasan; the five civilians were Dr. Abdallah Saadeh, Muhammad Baalbaki, Bashir Ubaid, Jabra Atrash, and Muhsin Nuzha.
106. *al-Hayat* February 21, 25, 1965.
107. See Emile Bustani, "Lebanon on Oasis of Democracy," *Middle East Forum* (May, 1960), 9ff.; see also another declaration by Karami on June 19, 1962 on Lebanese freedom and democracy.
108. On these points, see Charles Issawi, "Economic Development and Liberalism in Lebanon," *The Middle East Journal,* XVIII, 3 (Summer, 1964), 279-292; Jacob C. Hurewitz, "Lebanese Democracy in its International Setting," *The Middle East Journal,* XVII, 5 (Late Autumn, 1963), 496-505.

109. The first criticism was quoted in *al-Nasr,* February 11, 1963; the second was reported in the Beirut press, and in *The Heritage* (New York), June 26, 1965.
110. See his article in praise of Egyptian socialism, and the text of his lecture in *al-Anba',* January 14, 1967; see also *al-Anba',* April 1, 1967.
111. See *al-Nahar,* October 30, 1965 for Chehab's declaration that the rising generations cannot be expected to be silent for long about this unfair and oppressive distribution of wealth.
112. *al-Nahar,* November 30, 1965.
113. See, for example, his "Lebanon's Development Policy," *Middle East Forum* (Late Autumn, 1965), 5-7.
114. These dismissals occurred between December 16, 1965 and March 9, 1966. The Karami cabinet resigned on March 30.
115. *The Economist,* April 1, 1966 quoted by *Mideast Mirror,* April 9, 1966.
116. From the words of Kamil Mrowe in *al-Hayat,* April 29, 1967.
117. See *Mideast Mirror,* July 2, 1966 for the indictment issued on June 25, 1966 by the Lebanon public prosecutor who called for the death sentence for the assassin, Qleilat, and the other two accomplices, the telephone operator of *al-Hayat,* and the driver of Qleilat's car.
118. See declarations of the assassin Sultani in *al-Hayat,* April 25, 1967, and the sentence in *The New York Times,* March 16, 1968.
119. This was on January 19, 1966 and the Government of Iran retaliated by expelling the Lebanese ambassador. Diplomatic relations were resumed between Iran and Lebanon at the end of October, 1966.
120. *al-Ahram,* March 7, 1967;see his other speeches in *al-Ahram* March 6-11, 1967.
121. See for the pro-Nasserist press *al-Anwar,* March 25, and *Kul Shay',* April 1, 1967 and for the Lebanese loyalist press *al-Zaman,* March 27, and *al-'Amal,* March 31, 1967.
122. See *The Daily Star* March 29, 1967, *Kul Shay',* April 1, 1967.
123. See *al-Ahram* February 13, 27, 1967; see also *al-Hayat,* January 7, 1967 for the proposal of the *Kataeb* deputies in Parliament to study the question of the boycott of Israel in the light of the interests of Lebanon which lives on trade and services.
124. On the reactions to the requested visit of the Sixth Fleet see *al-Zaman* 17, 24 April, *The Daily Star, al-Nahar, al-Anwar* 19-25 April, 1967.
125. *The Herald Tribune International,* June 22, 1967 published a report on how the Lebanese commander in chief of the army, Emile Bustani, refused the order of Premier Karami to open a front to help the hard pressed Syrians and threatened him with house arrest if he insisted.
126. *Ibid.*

127. See*Le Monde,* June 13 for a description of the demonstrations on June 10; and June 20, 1967 for the Mufti's boycott and Gemayel's response.
128. *al-Anwar,* June 1, 1969 for the detailed report of the tribunal and the sentence.
129. See details of the draft bill in the *Arab World Weekly* (Beirut, January 18, 1969.)
130. *Los Angeles Times,* May 8, 1969; Rowland Evans and Robert Novak, *Ibid.*, May 20, 1969.
131. *N.Y. Times,* May 7, 1969 for President Helou's declaration' February 20, 1969 for Israel's contention.
132. *Free Palestine,* (Washington, D.C.), July 1969, editorial.
133. *al-Thawrah,* September 7, quoted by D.A. Schmidt in the *N.Y. Times,* September 8, 1969.
134. *N.Y. Times,* June 21;*al-Anwar,* June 22, 1969.
135. *al-Hayat,* July 13, 1969; Ambassador Charles Yost's proposal on August 13 in the Security Council, in the *N.Y. Times,* August 15, 1969.
136. For the agreement of November 3, see D.A. Schmidt in *N.Y. Times,* 4 Nov. 1969.
137. *al-Nahar,* December 24, 28, 1969.

CHAPTER VI

JORDAN: THE GENIUS FOR SURVIVAL

The present Hashemite Kingdom of Jordan has been subjected since the early 1950's to internal and external pressures that succeeded in forcing the resignation of several cabinets. It has also known several attempts, mostly planned and subsidized by other Arab governments, against the very existence of the monarchy or even the state itself, but they all failed and the Jordanian monarchy has survived. The army emerged as a political power particularly after March 1956, but it has generally stood behind the monarchy and acted as a stabilizing force in spite of the successive plots of some of its dissident elements. The presence of Israel along its western borders and the Israeli occupation of the western Jordan bank in the war of June 1967, as well as the increasing militancy and independence of the Palestinian resistance groups established on its soil have aggravated the problems and challenges to Jordan's existence. A study of the particularities of the situation in Jordan and the attitudes of the neighboring countries would explain the causes and nature of these problems and challenges, and the relative success with which Jordan faced them.

I. Problems and Challenges in Jordan

The Jordanian state was first created as a separate political entity by Britain in April 1921 under the name of the Emirate of Transjordan. It was placed under the rule of the Hashemite leader, Emir Abdallah, who had acted as adviser and foreign minister under his father, Sherif Hussein, during the Arab revolt of 1916. The territory of Transjordan, with a population of some 300,000 inhabitants, had been before the First World War a sanjak (sub-province) of the Vilayet (province) of Syria. In the secret Sykes-Picot agreement in 1916, it had been included in the Zone B where Arab independence was to be recognized under British guidance. The post-war settlement placed this territory, as well as neighboring Palestine and Iraq, under the British mandate and thus enabled Britain to dominate a strategic area extending without interruption from the Mediterranean to the Persian Gulf. The new state was not to be covered by the provisions relative to the establishment of the Jewish national home in Palestine.

From the time of its creation in 1921 until after its complete independence in 1957, Transjordan was under the influence of special factors that often caused tensions to rise within and outside its borders. Transjordan was, in the first place, a part of geographic Syria that had been divided by the peace settlement after 1918 into four political entities: Syria and Lebanon under the French mandate, and Palestine and Transjordan under the British mandate. The ambitious and astute Emir Abdallah considered his rule over the poor and thinly populated principality as only a first step towards the rule of all Syria. He was patient and was prepared to wait for the appropriate occasion to achieve his dream. When it became known in 1941 that Syria would be granted independence by the Free French, Abdallah, who was now the only Hashemite survivor of the Arab revolt, began to press for the unification of Greater Syria. In several statements, speeches, and proclamations between 1941 and 1947, he announced that the Greater Syria scheme was a basic principle of Transjordan's policy. His efforts found sympathy in certain Syrian circles, but were opposed by the official rulers of the newly-independent Syrian republic, and by Lebanon, Egypt, and Saudi Arabia. In October 1947, he had to promise the Arab League states that he would not press his plan until after the solution of the Palestine problem. In the meantime, the prime minister of Iraq, Nuri al-Said, had been advocating a plan for a Fertile Crescent union that would include Greater Syria and Iraq as a first step towards a larger Arab unity. The plan, circulated in 1943 in a memorandum among Arab leaders, was opposed by the same states that had manifested their opposition to the Greater Syria scheme. [1]During the period of military and popular revolutions in Syria and Lebanon after 1949, the rulers of Jordan were often accused of supporting the change of regime in the two neighboring republics. In January 1962, Abdallah's grandson, King Hussein, denied that he had any role in the Syrian coup of September, and the Lebanese coup of December, 1961. In January 1963, he had to declare again that he had no ambitions in neighboring Syria.[2]

Jordan was thus unable to advance its plans for the unity of Greater Syria primarily because of the policies of what was known until the end of 1956 as the Cairo-Riyad-Damascus Axis. Saudi Arabia was apprehensive of any change in the status quo that would allow the Hashemites of Jordan or Iraq to grow stronger and acquire the means to avenge the Saudi annexation of Hejaz. In early 1957, Saudi Arabia became aware of the Egyptian revolutionary danger and of the Egyptian-Syrian threat to control Jordan, and it consequently became Jordan's ally. As for Egypt, its traditional policy was to keep the Fertile Crescent and geographic Syria divided and open for its own penetration. It therefore cultivated the independence of Lebanon, and supported President Quwatli and the Syrian ruling class whose vested interests demanded the preservation of the smaller Syrian state in order to resist either Abdallah's Greater Syria or Nuri's Fertile Crescent unity. Certain voices demanded the absorption of Jordan by Syria because of the tradition of close association between the two over the centuries, and even regarded Jordan as an artificial state that was carved out of Southern Syria to satisfy Britain's guilty conscience with regard to the promises she made to Sherif Hussein.

In the second place, the Emirate of Transjordan was

essentially a creation of Britain, and its Emir was appointed, subsidized and advised by the British. Militarily, the Arab Legion, which until 1939 was used as a gendarmerie force and was expanded into a fighting force in 1940, consisted of Transjordanian volunteers but was commanded since its establishment in 1921 by British officers – Captain F.G. Peake and later Major John Glubb after 1939. The British subsidy to the Arab Legion at the time of the British withdrawal in 1957 was about twelve million pounds sterling. Emir Abdallah recognized the agreement of February 28, 1928 and remained loyal to the British alliance when Transjordan became independent in accordance with the treaty of March 22, 1946 followed by that of March 15, 1948. The two countries were to cooperate in questions of defense, and Britain was allowed to maintain two military bases in Transjordan. On April 25, 1946, Abdallah assumed the title of King, and on March 1, 1947, the old Organic Law (Constitution) of 1928 was replaced by a monarchical constitution that provided for a bicameral legislature. Abdallah and the other rulers of Jordan, however, remained suspect in the eyes of certain Arab nationalists on account of the alliance with Britain. The Arab Legion was viewed in certain quarters as a symbol of imperialism as long as it continued to be subsidized by Britain and commanded by General Glubb, even though he was officially in the service of the Jordanian government. The participation of the Legion in the British action against the Iraqi revolution of 1941 certainly did not enhance its reputation, nor that of Abdallah among the Arabs.

In the third place, Jordan, of all the Arab states, was the most seriously affected by the impact of the Palestine war in 1948. The Arab Legion, which was generally recognized as the most disciplined and competent military force in the Arab world, fought valiantly against the Israelis and saved most of what the Arabs were able to save in Palestine. But the Legion and its commander, General Glubb, were made responsible for Arab defeat, and Glubb Pasha himself was accused of restraining his troops from military action and allowing certain towns, like Lydda and Ramle, to be occupied by the Israelis.[3] Towards the end of the Arab-Israeli war, which left more than 75 per cent of Palestine in the Jewish state, the Arab governments led by Egypt decided that the remaining part of Palestine should not be ruled by King Abdallah. On September 20, 1948, the Arab League announced the formation of an "Arab Government of All Palestine" with its center in Egyptian-occupied Gaza, and with a cabinet consisting almost entirely of supporters of Haj Amin al-Husseini, ex-Mufti of Jerusalem and declared enemy of King Abdallah. The new government existed only on paper, and was intended to be an instrument for the exercise of Egyptian control over Arab Palestine. King Abdallah and the Arabs of Palestine decided otherwise, for Jordanian troops alone occupied, and were in a position to defend Palestine after the withdrawal of the Iraqi troops from the Samaria sector. The remaining Arab part of Palestine had no common border with any Arab country except Transjordan, and the Palestinian Arabs, with no government and no army, had no other alternative but to unite with Abdallah's little kingdom. The resolution for unity was taken on December 1, 1948 in a conference of Arab Palestinian leaders in Jericho. On April 26, 1949 the new state was called the Hashemite Kingdom of Jordan. The unification was formally approved on April 24, 1950 by the new parliament of Jordan that gave equal representation to the Palestinians on the western bank of the River Jordan and to the Transjordanians of the eastern bank. King Abdallah incurred the wrath of Egypt, Saudi Arabia, and Syria in particular for his annexation of Arab Palestine, and his action was condemned by the Arab League Political Committee on May 15, 1950. Egypt even moved to expel Jordan from the Arab League, but the motion failed.

The annexation of the Palestinian territory that represented six per cent of the entire area of Jordan, added about half a million inhabitants to the population of the original Transjordan. At the same time, the Kingdom of Jordan opened its doors to another half million Palestinian refugees, mostly destitute, who originally lived in what became Israel. No Arab country bordering Palestine has received as many refugees as Jordan, and none has treated them as generously. The refugees, as well as the inhabitants of the western bank were soon integrated as Jordanian citizens and participated in the government of the country. The new Jordanians, however, had no deep feeling of allegiance to the Hashemite monarchy, and they remained critical of the Jordanian government and its action during and after the war with Israel.[4] Because of the serious injustice they had suffered at the hands of the western powers, who were considered responsible for the creation of Israel, they were bitter against the West and against Jordan because she followed a pro-western policy. They believed that their anti-Israeli objective and their desire for revenge required the elimination of British influence in Jordan. Some of them embraced communist and radical nationalist ideologies and advocated the use of violence to influence government decisions.

The rapid rise of Nasser of Egypt to a position of leadership and power in the Arab world – his violent verbal attacks against Israel, his defiance of the West, his arms deal with the Eastern Bloc, and his internal reforms and innovations – enabled him to interfere in the affairs of Jordan and other Arab states. The young Palestinian leaders, in their eagerness for revenge against Israel and in their impatience for the exercise of political power, cooperated with Nasser even at the expense of Jordan, their new country, and exploited the confused conditions that followed the Palestine war for their own advantage. The literate Palestinians influenced the life of Jordan in many ways. First, they tried to steer the country away from Hashemite Iraq and closer to Egypt, and succeeded for some time. Second, they weakened the royal prerogatives and strengthened the power of parliament and of the cabinet in the new Jordanian constitution of 1952. Third, they helped create an atmosphere of crisis and instability by their manipulation of the masses, their intrigues with anti-Hashemite forces, and their subversion of army officers. Fourth, the expansion of the Legion from some 9,000 soldiers in 1949 to about 25,000 in 1956 opened its ranks to new elements from among the Palestinians of the west bank and Jordanian city dwellers who eroded the cohesion of the Legion and brought politics into it. The new elements, however, were mostly in the technical and engineering services, while the infantry and armor divisions were largely of tribal and peasant composition and were loyal to the king.

The creation of Israel inflicted on Jordan far greater material damage than on any other Arab country. Jordan was the poorest among the major Arab countries and the smallest in population. Its commerce suffered because it had no more outlet to the sea except through the developing port of Aqaba. Its communications with the Mediterranean and with the West ran through Syria and Lebanon, and at times were cut off when relations with Syria became tense. Jordan received half the total number of Palestinian refugees and thereby aggravated its own political and economic problems. Skillful propaganda from outside Jordan urged both refugees and West-Bank Palestinians to demonstrate, and used them in various conspiracies against the rulers of Jordan. On its long border of 400 miles with Israel, the Jordanian state had to be militarily prepared against Israeli attacks which were frequent and particularly violent in the period 1948-1954. Jordan had to bear the burden of reprisals without help from the outside, and it had consequently to discourage Arab infiltration into Israel. Infiltrators from Jordan were sometimes paid by Egyptian agents, or by agents of the ex-Mufti to carry out sabotage in Israel. Some of these operations, it was reported, were financed by the Saudis in order to bring down reprisals from Israel and cause disturbances in Jordan.[5] Jordanian problems stemming from her attitude towards Israel or from the presence of a large Palestinian population in Jordan were almost endless. Between late 1965 and the Arab-Israeli war of 1967, disputes were continuous between King Hussein and the Palestine Liberation Organization, that had been created in 1964, about the question of separate recruiting of Palestinians resident in Jordan for a liberation army, and the imposition of a separate tax collection on them. King Hussein refused both measures on the grounds that they would split the unity of the country and divide the army.[6]

The atmosphere of crisis in which Jordan lived since the early 1950's, and the assassinations, conspiracies, riots, and abortive military coups that it witnessed were caused or planned in almost every case by external forces involving one or more neighboring Arab states. The pretexts were almost invariably connected with Jordan's relations with Britain and the West, or Jordan's attitude towards Israel. The general accusations, which became well known clichés for use in every case, were that Jordan was a servant of imperialism and its rulers were stooges of Britain and the United States and were soft on Israel and Zionism.

II. The Assassination of King Abdallah

The assassination of King Abdallah on July 20, 1951 was the first in a series of violent crises that shook the Jordanian monarchy without succeeding in destroying it. Violence in this case was not the outcome of a popular revolt or a successful military coup. It was instigated by a group of fanatics hostile to King Abdallah, and they possibly received encouragement or orders from the ex-Mufti, Haj Amin al-Husseini, who was then living in Cairo with other Palestinian personalities and never forgave the King of Jordan for his annexation of Arab Palestine and for having allegedly betrayed the Arab cause.

King Abdallah was sixty-nine years old at the time of his assassination. He had accompanied, and taken part in the national Arab movement before and after the First World War. He was known for his intelligence, courage, frankness, and tolerance. He was also a man of culture and of mature and broad political outlook. As a political realist, he recognized the weakness and shortcomings of the Arabs and the formidable forces they had to challenge. It is believed that he would have accepted the United Nations partition plan for Palestine in 1947 if he had been free to decide, but he went along with the other heads of Arab states and decided to send his forces across the Jordan into Palestine. When the war began, Egypt offered him the title of supreme commander of the Arab forces, but he soon realized that his supreme command was only nominal, for when he requested an order of battle of the Egyptian army, he received no reply.[7] He was not in favor of resuming the fighting after the end of the first truce on July 9, and so were the chiefs of staff of the Arab armies, as well as Nokrashy Pasha, prime minister of Egypt.[8] The fighting was resumed because of political pressure and ended in failure. The Arabs lost half of the area assigned to them in the Palestine U.N. partition, and Abdallah and his Arab Legion were made responsible for this disastrous result.

King Abdallah incurred the hostility of Egypt, Saudi Arabia, and Syria, and that of the ex-Mufti and his clique, and became a target for their attacks for several reasons. First, he annexed what remained of Palestine in spite of their protests and was permanently accused of harboring expansionist designs, with the encouragement of Britain, in other areas in Syria. Second, in the armistice agreement signed on April 3, 1949 with Israel, Abdallah had to accept, under Israeli military pressure, certain modifications of the border that gave Israel some agricultural land belonging to frontier villages. The armistice talks were conducted privately with the Israelis at his winter palace at Shunah, while his official delegation was at Rhodes. Third, it seems certain that Abdallah began negotiations for a peace treaty including a nonaggression pact for five years with Israel after having signed the armistice. The reason was the precarious position of Jordan in the face of a militarily stronger Israel along a border of four hundred miles with no prospect of Arab help, and his need for an outlet on the Mediterranean. The negotiations occurred between November 1949 and March 1950. According to General Glubb, who described King Abdallah as a practical man always ready to make a bargain, the King tried to explore the possibilities of peace with Israel and sent letters to certain Jews, whom he knew, through Colonel Abdallah al-Tell, military governor of Jerusalem. The King, however, could not make peace against the opposition of the Arab states unless he had valuable gains to show for it, and Israel evidently was not ready to make peace except on her own terms.[9] According to Walter Eytan, Director of the Israeli Foreign Office, the talks were intensive and a draft treaty was prepared and initialed, but the King, under the pressure of an extremism that scared his ministers, was unable to carry it through "despite the concessions Israel was ready to make."[10] When the news about the negotiations began to reach the Arab capitals in February 1950, a violent press campaign started against Abdallah, and the Cairo newspaper, *al-Misri,* called on the Arab League to "sever this decayed member [Jordan] from the body of the Arab world and to bury it and heap dung thereon", because it has betrayed Islam, Arab unity, and the Arab cause.[11] The reaction against the negotiations led to the resignation of the Abul Huda cabinet and the formation of another by him after an interlude during which Samir al-Rifai tried to form a cabinet. In the Arab League Council meeting, the Jordanian ambassador, Baha' al-Din Tuqan, denied on April 1, 1950 that his country had ever contemplated signing a final peace with Israel, and voted, along with the other delegates, the Lebanese draft resolution to expel from the League any member who signed a separate peace with Israel. King Abdallah's reputation naturally suffered as a result of this attempt. It was further damaged by the attacks of his old confident, Colonel Tell, who had resigned his post in Jerusalem and accepted a salary from Egypt in January 1950 to conduct propaganda against his king. Colonel Tell had evidently contemplated treachery when he was in the King's favor, for he took photostatic copies of the correspondence entrusted to him and later gave them to the Egyptian press. He also circulated accusations against the British officers in the Arab Legion and claimed that they prevented their units from fighting in order to help the Jews.

One Egyptian newspaper even went to the extent of accusing Abdallah and Glubb of selling the plans of the Arab armies to the Israelis.

King Abdallah, in spite of these accusations and attitudes, was supported by the Arab Legion and by a core of loyal subjects in Transjordan. On the west bank in Palestine, the common people liked his democratic and humane manner, for he liked to mix and talk freely with his subjects. In one of his visits to the front line villages, the people came out to meet him in large numbers, and their cheers were mixed with appeals for protection against Israel. General Glubb, who accompanied him, exclaimed, as he addressed the district governor of Nablus, "What an amazing reception, we are always told that the people of Palestine hate him." The governor is reported to have answered, "Don't believe it. The common people love him but they have no means of expressing their feelings except on occasions like this. It is the lawyers, politicians, and the newspapers who do this propaganda against him, and who are usually the only voices heard. But you can't blame them – they have to earn their living."[12]

King Abdallah loved to pray on Friday in the Aqsa Mosque, near the Dome of the Rock in Jerusalem. The conspirators evidently decided that this was the most convenient place to attack their victim. On Wednesday, July 18, 1951, the day before King Abdallah left for the Holy City, the American ambassador in Amman came to implore him not to go because he heard that there may be an attempt on his life. Abdallah did not heed the warning. "I will die when I am destined to die," he said.[13] To his prime minister, Samir Pasha al-Rifai, who begged him to be cautious during his visit, King Abdallah answered in the same terms, "I believe in God. My life is in His hands." King Abdallah, nevertheless, noticed that some of those whom he invited to go with him declined the invitation and gave unusually feeble excuses. He drove to Jerusalem on Thursday to spend the night, and on Friday morning July 20, he went to visit friends in Nablus. After his return to Jerusalem, he held an audience before starting to the mosque. Among those who came to see him was Dr. Moussa Abdallah al-Husseini, one of the conspirators, who bowed before the King and wished him a long life and happiness!

On his way to the mosque, King Abdallah was accompanied by the commander of the guard, Colonel Habis al-Majali, who tried to hold back the dense crowd while the King spoke to some men. As he stepped a few paces inside the main doors of the mosque with his young grandson, Prince Hussein, behind him, a man walked out from behind the door to his right and before anybody could do anything, he fired at very close range. The bullet hit the King in the head. He fell dead on the floor and his turban rolled away. The assassin fired wildly as he ran inside the mosque but he was shot dead by the King's escort.

King Abdallah's second son, Nayef, was proclaimed regent during the absence of his elder half-brother Talal, who was being treated in Switzerland for mental illness. The regent's first task was to try those implicated in the conspiracy. The chief conspirators were presumed to be Colonel Tell in Egypt, and Dr. Moussa Abdallah al-Husseini in Jerusalem. In all, ten persons went on trial, two of them in absentia. The accused included three members of the Husseini family, relatives of the ex-Mufti. The trial began on August 18 and ended ten days later with six death sentences, two in absentia including Colonel Tell. The sentences were confirmed by Prince Nayef on September 3, and the following day the four in custody were hanged. The anti-Hashemite forces within and outside the country tried to put pressure on Nayef to commute the sentences. On the other hand, the Hashemite loyalists believed that the execution was necessary to establish the king's power and to act as a deterrent. The British diplomatic representative, Sir Alec Kirkbride, believed that political crimes were popular because death sentences were regularly commuted. He therefore used his influence to encourage the regent to confirm the sentences.[14]

The death of King Abdallah gave rise to a struggle about the succession between those who preferred Talal because he was known to be anti-British and more likely to cooperate with Egypt, Saudi Arabia and Syria, and those, mainly in Transjordan, who wanted his half-brother Nayef. Iraq was mainly concerned about the preservation of the Jordanian state, while Syria under Shishakli, as well as Egypt and Saudi Arabia might have envisaged its dismemberment. Shortly before his death, King Abdallah is reported to have told the Iraqi statesman, Tewfik Swaidi, that Jordan should unite with Iraq because he had no suitable successors.[15] The Iraqi rulers became interested in union with Jordan only after Abdallah's death, but the Jordanian government under Tewfik Abul Huda, influenced probably by Saudi Arabia, showed no response. When it became known in early September that Talal and not Nayef was to be crowned as king, the commander of the Hashemite regiment of the Arab Legion, Colonel Habis al-Majali, prepared to surround the building where the government was to meet in order to force it to crown Nayef.[16] The government knew about Majali's plan and removed him from the command of the regiment. On September 5, 1951, Prince Talal was proclaimed King after a favorable report on his illness had been received. His son, Hussein, was proclaimed Crown Prince, and Prince Nayef's chances for succession were thus destroyed. Discipline in the army averted a coup that might have brought Nayef to the throne. King Talal was not able to continue his rule and had to return twice to Switzerland for treatment. On August 11, 1952, the bicameral legislature of Jordan dethroned him, proclaimed his seventeen year old son Hussein King, and appointed a regency council to rule the kingdom until May 2, 1953 when Hussein assumed his full powers.

III. The Anti-Baghdad Pact Riots: Three Cabinet Changes

The reign of King Hussein was seriously disturbed by problems of the Arab cold war and of Arab attitudes towards the West and the Soviet Union, as well as by the presence of Israel along the entire western border of Jordan. The security of Hussein's kingdom and of his throne was perhaps threatened, at this time and until May 1967, more by the Arab revolutionary governments in Egypt and Syria than by Israel. It is even ironic that at certain times the opposition of Israel to the elimination of Jordan, and the Israeli threat to invade the western bank in the event of Egyptian or Syrian intervention against Hussein's kingdom, contributed to reduce the pressure of the "sister" Arab states on Jordan and to preserve the Jordanian entity.[17]

King Hussein's rule was disturbed, moreover, by the activity of ideological anti-western and anti-royalist parties such as the Baath, and the National Socialist parties. Under the name of the "National Democratic Front", the communists and extreme leftists gained two seats in the elections of October 1954, and were responsible for the riots on election day. They came mainly from the western bank where they had been under Jewish leadership and favored partition before 1947, but had become pan-Arabists in the early 1950's and cooperated with the Baath Party in provoking violence and promoting pro-Egyptian and anti-western feeling.[18] They were challenged by the Muslim Brotherhood that became anti-Egyptian after 1954 and supported King Hussein. The leftist ideologists appealed to the refugees in Jordan and to most of those who resented western support for Israel or believed in the need to eliminate British influence. They were also aided by the growth in the techniques of mass communication, by the resources of the aggressive Egyptian propaganda, and by the willingness of King Hussein, at least in the first part of his rule, to grant more representative government and concentrate power in a cabinet responsible to parliament. King Hussein tried to observe the principle of parliamentary rule in accordance with the constitutional amendments of January 1952 and 1954, but in times of crisis he felt obliged to depend temporarily on emergency measures in order to maintain security and order and contain the action of subversive elements.

The first serious crisis in Hussein's reign was a result of the Jordanian attempt to join the Baghdad Pact in December 1955. Arab public opinion, influenced to a large extent by the violent Egyptian propaganda campaign against Iraq's participation in the Pact, became so hostile that no other Arab government was able to join. Membership in the Pact was represented as an alliance with those western powers who were responsible for the creation of Israel. Egyptian propaganda even told the Arabs that Israel would soon join the Pact.

King Hussein has admitted that it was a fatal mistake on the part of all countries involved in the Pact to rush into an agreement with Iraq only. He also agreed with Nasser that the hasty way in which the Pact had been conceived was unwise.[19] Yet Hussein was ready to explore any advantages he could obtain by joining the Pact. His small country needed arms, economic aid, and protection at a time when Israel directed most of its attacks against Jordan – Kibya in October 1953, and Nahalin in March 1954. The Arab neighbors, particularly Egypt and Iraq, on whom he was expected to depend, were quarreling. On the other hand, Iraq and Britain expected Jordan to join the Pact, the former because of Hashemite ties, and the latter on account of the heavy subsidy it paid to the Arab Legion and the traditional influence it enjoyed in the country. In the meantime, Nasser was gaining more prestige in the Arab world as a result of the neutralist policy he followed after the Bandung Conference of April 1955, and especially because of the Czech arms deal announced in September and applauded with enthusiasm in Syria and Jordan. At the same time, King Saud injected himself into Jordanian politics against the Baghdad Pact in solidarity with Egypt and in opposition to Iraq and Britain, and made generous payments to Jordanian politicians and journalists. His confidential adviser, Jamal al-Husseini, the ex-Mufti's cousin, supposedly organized the Saudi program against the Baghdad Pact in Jordan.

In spite of the pressures on Hussein to join the Pact, he did not rush into it. On November 2, 1955, President Bayar of Turkey visited Jordan in an attempt to add another Arab member to the Baghdad Pact.[20] The visit was immediately followed by Cairo radio attacks against Jordan. Early in December, Sir Gerald Templer, Chief of British Imperial General Staff, arrived in Jordan for military talks.[21] King Hussein discussed with him Jordan's need for arms and economic aid, and the modification of the Anglo-Jordanian treaty of 1948. The cabinet under Said al-Mufti was divided about the question of joining the Baghdad Pact. Hussein himself, who was evidently prepared to join, had claimed that he would not have taken a decision without informing Nasser of Egypt and seeking his views. He sent him a message explaining the Israeli danger, the Jordanian ties with Iraq, and the advantages he expected to obtain from Britain – the Arabization of the army, modification of the treaty, arms supplies, and protection against Israel. According to Hussein, Nasser sent back a message giving the idea his blessing, but then suddenly the Egyptian propaganda against Jordan became violent, and at the Egyptian Embassy there was money for anyone who wanted to work for the Egyptians.[22] Hussein was represented as selling out Jordan to the British. Four cabinet members from the western bank resigned, as a result of various inducements, from Mufti's cabinet on December 13, 1955 and then Premier Mufti himself had to resign.

King Hussein asked Hazza al-Majali, the young minister of the interior in the Mufti cabinet, to become prime minister. He was in favor of joining the Baghdad Pact because he found in it an occasion to abolish the treaty with Britain and to Arabize the Jordanian Arab Legion. He was also promised support by the four Muslim members of the Pact for implementing the United Nations resolutions on Palestine.[23] Those who accepted to join the cabinet from the western bank were mostly mayors of cities, and only one of them was a member of parliament. Several other deputies believed in the advantages of the Pact but were fearful of public opinion and therefore did not join the cabinet. Rioting broke out immediately after Majali became prime minister on December 15, and the Egyptian radio exhorted the people to "get rid of Hussein, the traitor." The riots, according to eye witnesses, were unusually violent and well organized. They were led by communists and Baathists and included attacks on the United States Consulate and the UNRWA headquarters in Jerusalem. The trouble began in Nablus on the west bank and spread to the major cities of Jordan. The Egyptian military attaché in Amman was reported by the police to have accosted individual policemen and told them not to disperse the crowds, and promised them pensions from Egypt if they lost their jobs.[21] Certain demonstrators were reported to have shouted, "Down with the monarchy, long live the republic."[25] According to the mayor of Nablus, Sulaiman Tuqan, King Hussein was heard saying on this occasion, "I am afraid the Palestinians will lose the rest of Palestine, and I regret that some big Palestinians get paid to oppose my policy." On December 19, three ministers of the Majali cabinet resigned, and as they were difficult to replace while the number of casualties was mounting, Premier Majali himself also resigned.[26] Responding to public pressure, King Hussein at the same time announced the dissolution of parliament. In Damascus, demonstrations were organized on two consecutive days in sympathy with Jordan, while the *Pravda* praised the Jordanians for their heroic stand against the Pact.

Majali's cabinet lasted only four days and was succeeded on December 20 by that of the elder statesman Ibrahim Hashem. After a relative quiet of more than two weeks, rioting broke out again in protest against the declaration by the Jordanian High Court on January 4, 1956 that the dissolution of parliament was found illegal. The disorders that began on January 7, 1956 were marked by looting, burning of government offices and private houses, and an attempt to storm the royal palace, in addition to the customary attacks on foreign consulates. In the course of the riots, certain Jordanians asked to be annexed to Syria, while some elements of the Arab Legion defected. The riots caused the resignation of Ibrahim Hashem's cabinet, and ended only when martial law was declared under the following cabinet formed by Samir al-Rifai. The intervention of the Arab Legion and a ten-day curfew soon ended the convulsions, and the new Premier reassured the people of Jordan that their country would never join the Baghdad Pact. A note of protest was sent to both Egypt and Saudi Arabia against the leading role they played in causing the riots, but the notes were of no avail.

Three cabinets thus fell in less than one month (December 13, 1955 to January 7, 1956) during the crisis of Jordan's unsuccessful attempt to join the Baghdad Pact. This was only one aspect of the impact of Nasserist intervention and incitement supported by Saudi money on the behavior of the masses in Jordan and other Arab countries. Jordan was forced later into still more serious crises by the same interventions and influences, but the interventionists were never able to score more than short term successes.

IV. The Abortive Coup of April 1957

King Hussein was induced by the experience of the Baghdad Pact riots and by various internal and external pressures to make concessions to radical Arab nationalists in Jordan, and to draw closer to the Egyptian-Syrian orbit. His first sensational act in this direction was the dismissal of General John Glubb (Glubb Pasha), who commanded the Arab Legion since 1939, along with fifteen British officers, on March 1, 1956. Hussein's action was a surprise to Britain as well as to the Arab world and it made him a popular national hero overnight. The dismissal was preceded by a violent Egyptian campaign against Glubb accusing him and Britain of all sorts of evil intentions. Behind the King's action were also the Jordanian officers led by Lt. Col. Ali Abu Nawar, the thirty-three-year-old aide of Hussein, who succeeded in influencing the King against Glubb and persuaded him that he could regain the popularity he lost in the Baghdad Pact riots by some act of defiance towards Britain. The King's jealousy was allegedly aroused by an article in the *Illustrated London News* that spoke of Glubb as the uncrowned king of Jordan.

King Hussein later explained in his autobiography that his decision to dismiss his fifty-nine-year-old commander-in-chief was on purely professional and national considerations. The King disagreed with Glubb's strategic plans for the defense of Jordan, and in particular with his alleged advocacy of withdrawal from the west bank in case of Israeli attack without fighting on the frontier. He believed, moreover, that Glubb was unable to stock the Jordanian ammunition depots, and that he followed the prevailing British policy of opposing the promotion of Jordanian officers to high military posts.[27] General Glubb, on the other hand, claimed that his stragetic plans were understood and approved by the King after clearing certain misconceptions. He attributed the King's action to the influence and intrigues of the young officers supported by Egypt. According to Glubb, the officers were later afraid that some units of the Arab Legion might march on the capital and dethrone the King after learning about the dismissal of their commander, and one or two units actually contemplated such an action.[28] As a result, Glubb was ordered to leave the country on the following morning (March 2) in order to discourage any attempts in his favor.

It was believed by some optimists at the time that the discharge of Glubb would take politics out of the army by removing the man who stood in the way of the officers' promotion to higher ranks and responsible military commands. What actually happened was the opposite, for the officers became more involved in political intrigues as they assumed more responsibility, and their intrigues were now directed against the King himself and the monarchy. The first Jordanian officer to replace General Glubb was General Radi Annab, but he was soon retired, and on May 25, 1956, Lt. Col.

Abu Nawar became the chief of staff after successful maneuvering. He had been a major only a few months before and was now promoted to major-general. Abu Nawar was known to Glubb as a Baathist and pro-Nasserist intriguer against the British and their subsidy to the Legion, and against the monarchy. This is why he sent him away as militaryattaché to Paris. In the French capital he occasionally accompanied young King Hussein in the course of his visits and was able to win his confidence and friendship. In the fall of 1955, King Hussein brought him back to Jordan and made him his aide in spite of Glubb's warnings.

As chief of staff of the Jordanian Arab Army (new name for the Arab Legion) from May 1956 until his escape from Jordan in April 1957, Abu Nawar and his clique worked hand in hand with the radical nationalists inside, and leftist Arab regimes outside Jordan and influenced King Hussein's policy of rapprochement with Egypt and Syria. In late May 1956, President Quwatli of Syria made a visit to Jordan that ended with a communique announcing closer cooperation between the two countries in the military and economic fields. During the troubled period that followed the nationalization of the Suez Canal, rallies were held in Jordan in support of Nasser, and on August 16, 1956 a nation-wide strike was organized in favor of Egypt and against the British and the French. The violent Israeli attacks on the Jordanian border between mid-September and early October were followed by a Jordanian agreement with Iraq that allowed the stationing of Iraqi troops and aircraft on the Jordanian border. Syria immediately reacted by announcing that her troops were ready to defend Jordan, and that she had moved heavy weapons into that country. On October 25, 1956, Jordan agreed with Syria and Egypt to place the armed forces of the three countries under one command – that of Marshal Amer of Egypt – in case of war with Israel. King Hussein, however, was careful to obtain the participation of Iraqi troops for the defense of Jordan as a guarantee against Syro-Egyptian pressure, and thus when the Israeli campaign against Egypt began, Iraq as well as Syria and Saudi Arabia sent troops to Jordan in early November for protection against Israel. At the same time, each army watched the other and tried to make sure that it did not take over Jordan.[29]

The decisive attempt to undermine the monarchy and operate a radical change in its orientation was the outcome of the elections for a new chamber of deputies on October 21, 1956. Although the radicals had no clear majority, one of their parties, that of the National Socialists, scored a greater success than any other party. Its deputies in the new chamber numbered eleven, while the communists – under the name of National Front – counted three deputies and the Baath Party counted two. The other members were drawn from the Muslim Brotherhood and the Arab Constitutional Party, or were independents, and some of these voted with the leftists. The leader of the National Socialists, Sulaiman al-Nabulsi, was defeated in the elections but owing to the success of his party, he became prime minister. The cabinet which he formed on October 29 was the first leftist popular front cabinet to be formed in any Arab country, and it included one communist minister.

The Nabulsi cabinet immediately began a campaign to end the Anglo-Jordanian treaty, establish diplomatic relations with Russia and Communist China, and form a federal union with Syria. The Suez crisis created an atmosphere of hostility to the West and a wave of admiration for Nasser and his neutralist-leftist policies that were exploited by the leftist cabinet. On November 15, Iraq was requested to withdraw her troops from Jordan, but no such request was made to Syria and Saudi Arabia. The Iraqi brigade left Jordan on December 10, 1956. Among its officers was Brigadier Kassem who established contacts with the radical Jordanian and Syrian officers and allegedly informed them about his plans to overthrow the Iraqi monarchy.[30]

The measures taken by the Nabulsi cabinet and the declarations of the prime minister himself clearly indicated the determination of the new government to modify the status of

Jordan as a sovereign entity and to follow the policies of the leftist regimes in Cairo and Damascus. On December 16, Nabulsi declared in his statement to Hanson Baldwin of *The New York Times* that Jordan could not live forever as Jordan, and that military, economic, and political connections had to be made with another Arab state.[31] In a political meeting in Amman five days later, Nabulsi stood up and for thirty minutes glorified President Nasser without mentioning a word about Jordan and its role.[32] The dismissal or forced retirement of officials by the new cabinet touched mainly those who were known to be loyal to the monarchy or of pro-western leanings. Soviet and Red Chinese movies soon appeared in the theaters, and the Tass Agency was allowed to set up a bureau in Jordan and distribute its bulletins freely, while a communist newspaper called *al-Jamahir* (the Masses) was given a license to publish in Amman. At the same time a campaign against the Iraqi government was organized, and on December 17 a two-hour strike was held in protest against the suppression of the opposition by Nuri's government and in honor of the "struggling people" of Iraq.

In preparation for the abrogation of the treaty with Britain, an agreement was concluded on December 19 between Egypt, Syria, and Saudi Arabia to share in the payment of the subsidy hitherto paid by Britain to the Arab Legion. It was decided that Egypt and Saudi Arabia would each pay 40 per cent of the total of 12.5 million pounds (about 35 million dollars), and Syria would pay 20 per cent. On January 19, 1957 the agreement was signed in Cairo by King Hussein and came to be known as the Pact of Arab Solidarity. As a result of the Anglo-Jordanian negotiations that began in early February, Britain accepted to terminate her 1948 treaty and withdraw British forces from their bases in Jordan. The payment of the British subsidy was to stop on the first day of March. The formal end of the treaty came on March 15 after an exchange of notes between the two governments, and the Nabulsi cabinet celebrated the occasion by declaring a three-day holiday. Jordan was thus completely emancipated from

British control, but at the same time it placed itself at the mercy of her more powerful neighbors. Hussein soon understood the dangers of his dependence on Cairo and Damascus from whom Premier Nabulsi seemed to draw encouragement and support to challenge the King and undermine the monarchy. President Chamoun of Lebanon has related that when Queen Zeine, Hussein's mother, came to Beirut about that time, he disclosed to her the Nasserist plan to weaken her son and isolate him before giving him the *coup de grace*.[33] King Saud, moreover, began to change his orientation in the first months of 1957. He was afraid that Egypt and Syria would control Jordan, and was disturbed by the leftist revolutionary trend of his allies in Cairo and Damascus. It is believed that during his visit to the United States in late January 1957, the Department of State opened his eyes to the danger of his close relations with radical allies and obtained from him two commitments, namely, to develop closer relations with Iraq, and to avoid working with Nasser for overthrowing Hussein.[34] Under these circumstances, the Solidarity Pact lasted a few months and King Saud was the only one to pay his share of the subsidy to Jordan.

The rising anti-western and pro-communist tide in Jordan alarmed the King and his loyal supporters, but it did not force them to acquiesce and drift with the tide as President Quwatli and his cabinets had been doing in Syria. King Hussein showed determination and courage when he challenged Nabulsi's policy and warned him against the dangers of communist infiltration in a letter that he made public on February 2, 1957. In his strongly worded message, King Hussein warned that unless the unwarranted principles, beliefs, and views that had infiltrated into the country were curtailed, "imperialism, which is about to die in the Arab East, will be replaced by a new kind of imperialism. If we are enslaved by this, we shall never be able to escape or overthrow it." Hussein also warned against the danger of "those who pretend to be Arab nationalists while they have nothing to do with Arabism."[35] Nabulsi paid no heed to the King's demands and warnings. President Nasser was upset by the King's attitude, and the foreign minister in Syria, Salah Bitar, criticized the King's views and even sent a message to the Jordanian government suggesting that Jordan become more friendly to the Russians and Chinese communists. Demonstrations and rallies were held in Jordan by the left wing parties on various occasions to attack the West and intimidate the King. The pro-western Syrian Social National Party was ordered by the cabinet to stop its activities, while anonymous threats were sent to newspapers for forcing them to ignore the King's stand on communism. At the end of March, the cabinet wanted to resign in protest against the King because he refused to dismiss "undesirable elements" from government service and tried to negotiate with foreign powers behind the cabinet's back. Nabulsi, however, received an order from Egypt not to resign. On April 2, the cabinet voted to establish diplomatic relations with the Soviet Union in spite of King Hussein's well known opposition. The decision came one day after Abu Nawar returned from Damascus with an offer of Soviet arms for Jordan.

The King was particularly disturbed by the disintegration of his once efficient and disciplined army into differing political factions. Key persons in the army and in the government had been brought under Syro-Egyptian and Soviet influence. Among them three in particular – General Ali Abu Nawar, chief of staff, Shafiq Rusheidat, minister of justice and education, and Abdallah Rimawi, minister of state for foreign affairs – were believed to have received money for themselves and for bribing others in Jordan. Their regular visits to Damascus did not escape the attention of secret service agents who reportedly told the chief of King Hussein's Diwan that "if the police open their bags at the Syrian-Jordanian frontier post of Ramtha, they will find money in any of their suitcases."[36] The chief of staff and the cabinet ministers each had his own agents among the higher officers of the security forces. In Beirut and Damascus, Jordanian officers were often seen in the night clubs spending large sums of money that they could not possibly have earned. As a sign of what was being planned, the cabinet minister Rimawi, according to a rumor which this writer heard about this time in Damascene circles, is said to have told his wife that she would soon become Jordan's First Lady.

The showdown between the King and his cabinet seemed inevitable in early April. The position of the two seemed irreconciliable: the cabinet supported by the left wing parties and Abu Nawar and his military clique followed a distinctly pro-Nasserist, pro-Soviet, and anti-western policy and wanted a federal union with Syria that was then under Egyptian and Baathist-Communist influence. It was ready to overthrow the monarchy if it did not conform to its plans. King Hussein, on the other hand, wanted Jordan to remain sovereign and free to decide its own policy without external pressure. He was determined to secure the country against direct or indirect communist influences. He was supported by conservative and moderate elements mainly on the right bank, and by loyal Bedouin regiments. He probably would have accepted American support under the Eisenhower Doctrine, but he was afraid of aggravating an already tense situation.

The outcome of the imminent showdown between the King and the Nabulsi cabinet depended much on the attitude of the army whose chief of general staff, Ali Abu Nawar, had increasingly become a central political figure. A plot was organized by him and some fourteen officers, each of whom was allegedly receiving secretly from Egypt a salary ten times as great as his regular pay.[37] The first attempt to carry out the plot occurred on April 8, 1957 when Abu Nawar ordered the First Armored Car Regiment to march from its headquarters at Zarqa to Amman. The regiment covered all the strategic roads and points around the capital and, according to certain reports, it surrounded the royal palace and the residence of the Queen Mother. When the King inquired from the prime minister and the defense minister about the purpose of this move, they professed ignorance. He then sent for Abu Nawar who explained that the action was merely a training exercise.

Hussein then suggested that the regiment be withdrawn and Abu Nawar agreed and left.[37] Those who believe that this was an attempted coup have mentioned that the commander of the regiment had the King's abdication in his pocket with instructions to have Hussein sign it. Their explanation for the failure of the attempt was that in the decisive confrontation of the King and Abu Nawar, the latter hesitated and lost his nerve. He probably was afraid that the rank and file of the regiment, who were unaware of the object of this operation, would have rallied to the throne if they had discovered the real motive.[39] Others believe that the move was a rehearsal of the coup that was set for overthrowing King Hussein in the following week.[40]

The fiasco of April 8 was followed by an attempted coup against the monarchy on April 13, but this attempt, known as the Zarqa incident, came only after the dismissal of the Nabulsi cabinet on April 10. King Hussein asked Nabulsi to resign only after a series of open challenges and intended acts of defiance on the part of the cabinet and the extremists.[41] At the same time, the King appointed Brigadier Muhammad Maaytah director general of public security in the place of Major General Bahjat Tabbarah. Nabulsi was in a meeting with the cabinet when the chief of the Royal Diwan, Bahjat Talhuni, delivered the King's message. The cabinet sent for Abu Nawar and two other officers to ask their advice. Abu Nawar evidently told Nabulsi to resign expecting that the ensuing ministerial crisis would give him the pretext to carry out his coup if the King did not call the same man back to form the cabinet. Nabulsi consequently went to the palace and submitted his resignation in spite of a cable allegedly sent by Nasser telling him, "Do not give in, remain in your position."

For three days King Hussein tried in vain to form a new government. He first asked the Palestinian leader, Dr. Hussein Khalidi, who soon abandoned the attempt because the National Socialists and other leftists backing Nabulsi issued a statement announcing their opposition to a government formed by Khalidi. The statement also spoke of their determination to achieve a federation with Egypt and Syria. The King then asked Abdul Rahim al-Nimr, leader of the National Socialists' moderate wing and minister of defense and interior in Nabulsi's cabinet, but he insisted on including extremists in his cabinet and his demands were emphasized by a demonstration led by the Baathists and Communists on April 12. On the following day Hussein next asked the veteran moderate politician and Circassian leader, Said al-Mufti, to form a government. Abu Nawar now stepped in and summoned Mufti to an army camp outside Amman and asked him to tell the King that unless a cabinet was formed by 9 o'clock that night by al-Nimr, he would not be able to prevent the army from taking "serious action."[42] Abu Nawar later repeated the same threat to the chief of the Royal Diwan in the palace and added, "you must consider this statement a final ultimatum."[43] The King then turned again to al-Nimr, who happened to be Nabulsi's uncle, but before his discussions with him were over, the attempted coup took place. The extremists, however, were so sure that the King would accept al-Nimr's terms that at 9 o'clock the Damascus radio announced the formation of a cabinet under al-Nimr and even gave the names of its ministers.[44]

In the turbulent atmosphere of severe tension that followed Nabulsi's resignation, the Jordanian extremist parties – communists, Baathists, and national socialists – and the Syro-Egyptian radio and press spread wild stories about western imperialist plots against Jordan. Parties distributed arms to their members, and students and refugees under radical influences were ready to demonstrate. Moderate elements were intimidated, but the Muslim Brotherhood, alarmed by the progress of communism, called on the people to support the King. In the army, the King was informed that a plot was being organized against him. He had communicated secretly with the loyal Bedouin units whose officers and soldiers were notably tough and straightforward, and had warned them of an imminent attempt against him. Abu Nawar feared these

Bedouin soldiers, but he thought that he could neutralize them by appointing his cousin, Lt. Col. Maan Abu Nawar, to command them.

The conspirators' plan in the coup of Saturday April 13 included two operations: first, to send the Armored Car Regiment, commanded by Nazir Rashid, a close friend of Abu Nawar, from the Zarqa camp at twenty miles northeast of Amman to surround the capital and capture the royal palace and the King if necessary; second, to remove the loyal Bedouin infantry regiments out of the way by sending them on a practice march to the Azrak oasis in the desert. It is said that new flags had been designed for the republic of Jordan that was to be proclaimed, and that two samples of them were found in Abu Nawar's office. He was so sure of success, it was claimed, that he did not try to conceal them.[45] The two operations that were expected to lead to the success of the coup failed.

The Bedouin regiments soon discovered the meaning of the strange orders they received about the desert exercise. The only explanation for sending them at night eighty miles into the desert without arms and in the month of Ramadan, when they had been fasting all day, was that a coup d'état was planned for that very night, and that the conspirators wanted to keep them away. The doubts and worries of the loyal infantry were communicated that same day to the King by Akif al-Fayez, son of the prominent sheikh of Banu Sakr, who was in touch with his tribesmen in the army. The King was also informed by one of the officers about the instructions given to the First Armored Regiment which was to march on Amman. By the time the King summoned General Abu Nawar in the evening for an explanation of the strange information he had heard, fighting had broken out in the Zarqa camp. The loyal Bedouin regiments had refused to parade for the desert exercise. They broke into ammunition depots and were now out of control. Some of them set out for Amman after they heard the rumor that the King had been assassinated, in order to find out the truth. The conspirators brought down the artillery units against the loyal infantry and told the artillery troops to attack them because they were starting a mutiny "against" the King. The fighting between the different units resulted in some thirty killed or wounded officers and soldiers.[46]

King Hussein heard about the fighting at Zarqa and immediately ordered Abu Nawar to accompany him to the camp at about 9 p.m. When they reached the Ruseifa Bridge over the Jabbok River, they met a column of troops heading towards Amman. On recognizing the King, the troops cheered with excitement when they saw that he was in perfect health, but when they recognized Abu Nawar they shouted, "Down with the traitor," and asked Hussein's permission to kill him. Abu Nawar implored the King's protection by touching his coat according to Bedouin custom. He pleaded with the King to send him back to Amman and the King agreed and told him to wait at the palace. Hussein continued to the camp where gunfire was still heard. He visited various units and addressed the troops at one time from the top of an armored car and received enthusiastic cheers. His visit to Zarqa resulted in a great triumph. Before he returned to Amman, he ordered the arrest of fourteen officers who led the conspiracy. In Amman, Abu Nawar again begged the King to save his life. The King did not want to make a martyr of him and allowed him to leave the country. He left for Damascus, and later for Cairo where he continued to plot against King Hussein. General Ali Hiyari was appointed to succeed Abu Nawar, but after a few days he escaped to Syria where other officers and political leaders involved in the conspiracy had been given asylum. The King finally placed General Habis al-Majali, one of his old and trusted friends, at the head of the armed forces. In Damascus, General Hiyari, who is believed to have been involved in the conspiracy, explained that he had to leave because he was unwilling to carry out a purge in the army. He also claimed that it was the palace that arranged the plot and began rumors about a coup in Zarqa in order to have a pretext for intervention and forming a new cabinet.[47]

In the days that followed the attempted coup, the King obtained pledges of loyalty from the various army units. He explained the nature of the conspiracy to the people of Jordan and answered the charges of the violent leftist propaganda from outside the country. He also had to deal with the threat posed by the Syrian troops who prepared to march southwards from their positions around Mafrak in northern Jordan. King Saud rallied to his support by placing the Saudi Brigade stationed in Jordan under his command, and the threat ended without serious incidents. The Syrian troops, estimated at 5,000 withdrew from Jordan on May 26 at Jordan's demand. They had come to support Jordan against a possible Israeli attack, but they were said to have engaged in various political activities and incitements against the Jordanian regime.

The ministerial crisis that began before the Zarqa incident ended with the formation of a cabinet by Dr. Hussein Khalidi on April 15. It was a coalition cabinet that included Nabulsi as foreign minister, but it was not destined to last long. The extremist leaders were concerned about the investigation relating to the attempted coup and feared the elimination of their supporters from the army. They consequently sought to secure their position and intimidate the King by holding a "national conference" of party representatives in Nablus on April 22 and presenting several resolutions and demands to the government. The demands included the expulsion of the American ambassador, Lester Mallory, and his military attaché, the rejection of the Eisenhower Doctrine and all imperialist schemes, federal union with Syria, the reinstatement of army officers who were in jail or in exile as a result of the crisis, and purging the government of all "imperialist agents." The demands, intended as a challenge to the monarchy, were reinforced by the announcement of a general strike and demonstrations for April 24. Premier Khalidi carried the demands to the palace where the King indicated his unwillingness to accept them. The decisive showdown with the extremists started on April 24 with the beginning of the strike. The loyal Bedouin infantry was stationed in various key points in the capital, while the demonstrators assembled near the prime minister's office and listened to speakers who defended the demands of the extremists. On one of the banners carried by the demonstrators, the following statement was inscribed, "Lift your criminal hands off the nationalist officers, release the arrested officers and return the exiled ones to their posts in the army." The government promised to give her answer to the demands on the following day, and the leaders accepted but threatened that they would raise rebellion in the country if their demands were not met. As a result of the crisis, Dr. Khalidi presented his resignation. At the same time, the United States government issued a statement saying that "the independence and integrity of Jordan are vital to American national interests," while the US Sixth Fleet began moving towards the eastern Mediterranean.

The King had to move fast before a bloody rebellion could start. He consulted the sheikhs of the leading tribes who promised their cooperation, and talked with his advisers. He then asked the loyal old politician Ibrahim Hashem to become prime minister, and Samir Rifai to be deputy prime minister and minister of foreign affairs. At 2:15 a.m., the cabinet announced a curfew in the main cities of Jordan while the loyal Bedouin troops prepared for action and began patrolling the streets. On the morning of April 25, martial law was imposed and parties were banned. The police force was placed under army command, and the defense minister, Sulaiman Tuqan, became military governor and began the arrest of communists and other extremist leaders. The demonstrators who violated the orders to stay indoors and prepared to assemble in an attempt to seize the city were met by soldiers with fixed bayonets and obliged to withdraw. It was said that the Bedouin soldiers had blackened their faces in order not to be recognized in case they were obliged to fire at the mob.[48]

The showdown ended with the King's triumph owing to the loyal support of the army. King Saud sent from Riyad a message of congratulations. Shortly after, the King flew to Riyad on April 28, and two weeks later King Saud paid a visit to Iraq. The reversal of alliances ending Saudi participation in the Damascus-Cairo-Riyad axis was now complete. Towards the end of April, Jordan's finances were bolstered by the announcement of a grant in aid of ten million dollars by the United States. On May 21, 1957 Saudi Arabia paid the balance of the first installment of the subsidy to Jordan under the Solidarity Pact, but Syria and Egypt never paid their share. Hussein's feeling about that pact and his agreement with Egypt and Syria was that "it was not worth the paper it was written on."[49] In Amman, the trade unions and employees' associations were banned on May 1, and Nabulsi was officially placed under house arrest. On May 7 the King refused to sign the document that established relations with the Soviet Union. The military tribunal that was set up in late April to try all cases relative to the attempted coup began the trials on July 27 with twenty-two defendants. It issued its sentences on September 25. Five persons including Rimawi, Abu Nawar, and Hiyari were sentenced in absentia to fifteen years imprisonment. Twelve officers (four in absentia) were condemned to ten years, and five were acquitted. The press, even in Syria, disclosed at the time certain profiteering scandals under the Nabulsi regime and one of them involved the Baathist minister Rimawi.[50]

V. The Anti-Hashemite Conspiracy of 1958 and Other Attempts

The abortive coup of April 13, 1957 was a blow to Nasser's prestige. His Jordanian allies were now either in jail or in exile. King Hussein was not forced to become a passive follower of Egypt's neutralist, or essentially anti-western policy. King Saud was now on Hussein's side, and Nasser became obssessed with the fear of being isolated. The United States, moreover, began pouring financial and military aid into Jordan which added to Nasser's resentment and desire to have a "second round" with the twenty-two-year-old King.

According to what he told Robert Murphy, Eisenhower's special envoy in the Lebanese crisis in 1958, Nasser did not believe in Jordan's continued existence as an independent state, nor did he believe that Hussein could really depend on the loyalty of his troops.[51] Plots to assassinate Hussein and destroy the Jordanian monarchy therefore multiplied and reached a climax in the summer of 1958. "So cunning and varied have been the plots against my person, and so constant," said King Hussein, "that sometimes I have felt like the central character in a detective novel." To this he added that these plots no longer deeply worried him – so long as he discovered them in time.[52]

King Hussein did indeed discover the plots in time, with the help of some faithful friends, loyal servants, and a reorganized intelligence service. On June 9, 1957, the Jordanian government ordered the expulsion of the Egyptian military attaché, Colonel Ahmad Fuad Hilal, on charges of bribing a Jordanian citizen to assassinate King Hussein. At the same time, Brigadier Muhammad Abdul Aziz, Egyptian Consul-General in Jerusalem, was expelled for organizing sabotage gangs and smuggling arms from the Gaza strip into Jordan, as the trial of nineteen persons revealed.[53] Jordan was then a participant in the joint command that included Egypt and Syria, but it had to withdraw troops from the Israeli border in order to guard her frontiers against the serious infiltration of hostile agents and the smuggling of arms from sister Arab states. The Jordanian government, moreover, claimed that it seized a letter from the Egyptian representative on the joint command in Amman, Colonel Yusri Kunsowa, to the Egyptian army headquarters in Cairo about plans under way to end the monarchy. Seventeen defendants in the trials that followed were said to have admitted that they had been sent from Syria to smuggle arms, blow up bridges and roads, and lead an attack against the palace.[54] In explaining the crisis between Egypt and Jordan, Abdul Munem Rifai, who was then Jordan's ambassador in Washington, declared on June

22, 1957 that it could be attributed to Egypt's over-confidence in its ability to coerce other Arab states with impunity.[55]

In November 1957, King Hussein became the target of a particularly vicious campaign of Egyptian and Syrian propaganda. For two weeks he was insulted and abused on radio and in the press, and was accused of the classical charge – often used by Arab leaders to berate each other – of holding secret negotiations with Israel for the liquidation of the Palestine question. The campaign called for the King's assassination and the overthrow of his government and aimed at eradicating western influence and bringing Jordan back to the Egyptian-Syrian camp. Hussein answered back by charging that the Egyptian rulers had sold themselves to Communism and have been exploiting Arab nationalism to divert Egyptian public opinion away from the deteriorating situation at home. At one time, the Jordanian radio spoke of Nasser as "a Don Quixote hopelessly striking with his wooden sword but hitting only himself."[56] In Jordan, the people did not rise to President Nasser's bidding. Large numbers of Jordanians were, on the contrary, shocked by the viciousness of the campaign and disillusioned by Nasser's "big lie" tactics, for the propaganda offensive abandoned mere distortion for outright invention, and the people realized that the Egyptian-fabricated reports of bloody clashes and riots in the cities of Jordan were not true.[57]

In explaining this campaign, it has been said that Nasser nurtured a desire for revenge against Jordan after the setback to Nasserism in the April abortive coup, and that he chose a time when the Soviet sputniks had lowered the prestige of the West upon which Hussein relied. In addition, it has been explained that a successful blow to Jordan would have also meant a blow to King Saud, friend of the United States and Jordan's new ally. The Egyptian campaign, however, was judged a failure because it was high handed, clumsy, and contained no basis of truth. The violent attacks against Hussein were finally called to a halt after a joint appeal of several Arab heads of state and personalities. President

Nasser, it has been claimed, also realized that the campaign was backfiring.

In the summer of 1958, Jordan faced one of its most serious challenges. Egypt and Syria had been merged on February 1 in one state to form the United Arab Republic. Jordan and Iraq reacted by forming the Arab Union on February 14. Jordan's union with Iraq, however, did not give it the security it was seeking, for conspiracies were organized against both countries and the Iraqi monarchy did fall during that fateful summer of 1958. Lebanon was then in the midst of a rebellion supported by the UAR, and Jordan was in imminent danger. In early July it is alleged that a Jordanian cadet, Ahmad Yusif al-Hiyari, of the Fourth Tank Regiment, was in charge of a plot to kill King Hussein and other officials by hurling grenades at a public function. In his confession, the cadet stated that a coup d'état instigated by the UAR would take place in Iraq in mid-July simultaneously with one in Jordan.[58] The Iraqi chief of staff who visited Amman after the confession did not take seriously the warning given by Hussein on the impending coup. In Jordan, twelve officers, followed by sixty army men, were sent to jail on and before July 12 and included a close friend of the King named Colonel Radi Abdallah. King Hussein asked for military support from Iraq, in accordance with the terms of the Arab Union, but the forces sent by Iraq, instead of proceeding to Jordan, entered Baghdad and overthrew the monarchy on July 14. Jordan felt insecure and her fate was uncertain after the success of the Iraqi revolution. King Hussein consequently obtained the approval of his cabinet and of parliament to ask military help from Britain and the United States for a limited period, and expected either of them to respond. The conspirators had planned their coup for July 14, but they received orders to postpone it until July 17. The Jordanian government was able to round up the conspirators on the night of July 16, and in the morning of July 17, two British battalions of paratroopers landed in Amman under the cover of some fifty American jet planes. The British landing was decided in the preceding night in an emergency meeting of the cabinet under Prime Minister Macmillan after a study of the intelligence reports on the plot and of Hussein's appeal. The British paratroops were ordered to Jordan from Cyprus and were flown over Israeli territory before the formalities of obtaining Israeli permission had been completed. British strategists believed that a successful revolution in Jordan would have caused the political situation in the Middle East to deteriorate and would have threatened the oil interests of the western countries.[59]

The presence of British troops in Jordan gave moral support to the harassed and threatened regime and allowed the British foreign minister, Selwyn Lloyd, to tell the House of Commons on July 22 that the foiling of a coup organized outside Jordan was achieved by the British intervention. In the Security Council, Jordan complained on July 17 over interference in her internal affairs by the United Arab Republic, and three days later Jordan broke diplomatic relations with the UAR. The British troops remained in Jordan until early November and, like the American forces in Lebanon, did not have to undertake any military action. In the meantime, twenty-seven men went on trial in Amman on August 3, on charges of having entered from Syria with arms and explosives to overthrow the government. Thirteen of them were sentenced to death on August 12, and the others received various sentences of five years to life imprisonment. The trial of a smaller group of five persons accused of terroristic acts began on August 13. The group included a girl named Nadia Salti. Her trial, which could have resulted in a death penalty, became the object of a campaign against Jordan in which the young terrorist girl became a national heroine overnight. Two of the five men were condemned to death, and Nadia Salti received seven and a half years in jail, but her sentence was commuted to one year.

King Hussein decided to take a short holiday in Europe after the crisis had abated. On November 10, 1958 he left Amman Airport in his old twin-engined plane after announcing his departure to his people. The plane, according to King

Hussein, contacted Damascus as it reached the Syrian frontier, reported its position, and got clearance to continue in direction of Cyprus. Shortly before arriving over Damascus, the plane was told by the Syrian authorities that it was not cleared to overfly and that it ought to land at Damascus. The order to land was repeated after a few minutes, and as King Hussein and his companion, Colonel Dalgleish, of the Jordanian Air Force, suspected a trap, they decided to return to Amman and turned their aircraft in that direction. As they were approaching the Jordanian border, they were attacked by two Mig 17's of the UAR Air Force. The King's De Havilland Dove twisted and turned several times to avoid the repeated attacks, and at one moment was about to crash into a hill. The two Migs finally flew away as the King's unarmed plane entered Jordanian air space. King Hussein has claimed that the two Migs were sent by the UAR authorities in Syria to kill him and thereby end the Hashemite kingdom of Jordan. He has argued that there was no question of mistaken identity, for his Dove was well known and it carried the Royal coat of arms and the Royal flag.[60] The UAR authorities, on the other hand, denied any knowledge of the identity of the plane and any intention of killing or capturing King Hussein, and accused him of having made this stunt in and out of the Syrian air space merely for the purpose of propaganda and for discrediting the UAR authorities in Syria.

In March 1959 while King Hussein prepared to make a five-week tour of the United States, he received strong evidence that his chief of staff, General Sadek al-Shara, and other officers planned to execute a coup against the throne with outside help while he was away.[61] When the time came for the King's departure, he decided to take the leader of the conspiracy with him as a part of his entourage, because he feared that the plot would be hatched during his absence. The King accepted no excuses for the General's attempt to decline the invitation. By the time King Hussein reached the United States, the conspirators in Jordan had been arrested, and General Shara became worried that they might implicate him.

King Hussein gave him no indication that he knew about his role in the plot and refused to allow him to break away from the group or even stay away from official engagements. On their return to Amman, the General was arrested, tried, and sentenced to death but the sentence was commuted to life imprisonment.

VI. Assassinations, Attacks, Reconcilations

The failure of the two conspiracies of April 1957 and July 1958, and of other plots planned by Hussein's internal and external opponents did not dissuade his enemies from trying again to destroy the Jordanian monarchy and its rulers. Having despaired of staging successful coups, they resorted to assassination and subversion. The cause was always the same – Hussein's refusal to accept blindly Nasser's policies. In March 1960, after seven months of relative calm during which diplomatic relations between Jordan and the UAR were restored in August 1959, the Egyptian press and radio resumed their attacks against King Hussein, "the stooge of Anglo-American imperialism," because he did not subscribe to the creation of a Palestine entity and continued to receive aid from the United States and Britain. The logic of the rulers in the UAR was that as long as Hussein received Anglo-American aid he would not fight Israel. Yet, Egypt itself had been receiving American aid, and in the years that followed the breakup of the UAR, it solicited and obtained more aid than all the Arab countries combined.

The hostile attitude of the UAR towards Jordan at this time can be illustrated by the text of the credentials accorded to a new UAR Consul in Jerusalem. The document, as described by Hazza al-Majali, Prime Minister of Jordan since May 1959, was addressed not to the King of Jordan, but "to whom it may concern," and the jurisdiction of the consulate was described in this same document of early March 1960 as "all the regions west of the River Jordan occupied by Jordanian forces."[62] The tone of Nasser's speech in Alexandria on June 24, 1960 was particularly insulting and included incitement to eliminate King Hussein. "There are still traitors in the Arab world," Nasser said, "who inherited kingdoms from their fathers and grandfathers, and the first duty of the Arabs is to get rid of these agents of imperialism." Hussein answered back two days later and described Nasser as a conceited tyrant and opportunist.

The men who were particularly marked for assassination in Jordan were King Hussein, his prime minister and friend, Hazza al-Majali, and his uncle Sharif Nasser. A plot to assassinate Majali and Sharif Nasser was discovered on April 1, 1960 when a restaurant waiter admitted that the exiled former minister Rimawi sent him from Syria to kill the prime minister and the King's uncle. The trial of those involved ended on May 14 and Rimawi was among those who were condemned in absentia to twenty years in prison. On Monday, August 29, 1960 the plotters succeeded in killing Premier Majali by putting time bombs in the drawer of his office desk in the government building. Twelve other persons were killed in the explosion that demolished half of the building. Among the victims were a ten year old child, a man of seventy, and an old woman who came to present a grievance. The plotters who planted the bombs on Sunday night knew very well that Majali would be in his office on Monday because it was the day of the week when he normally threw his doors open for people who wanted to see him. He had returned the day before from an Arab League foreign ministers' conference in Shtura (Lebanon) and was happy that an agreement was reached to remove the causes of strained relations between the Arab states and stop hostile broadcasts against each other. Forty minutes after the first explosion, another one occurred and caused damage and loss of life mainly among those who were trying to do rescue work in the building. King Hussein and some others believe that the plotters knew that he would rush to the building after hearing about his prime minister's death, and they therefore planted the other bomb intending to kill him. The King actually rushed from his farmhouse outside Amman, but as he reached the city he was stopped by General Habis al-Majali, cousin of the murdered premier, and was prevented from proceeding to the building on the grounds that it would be dangerous.

King Hussein accused the United Arab Republic of direct complicity in the crime. The two office messengers who supposedly planted the bombs were already on their way to Damascus when the explosion occurred, and this is why the Jordanian radio broadcast said that "Damascus was already harboring the murderers." In his speech of October 3, 1960 at the United Nations, King Hussein spoke bitterly against the UAR whose "incitements to overthrow our government and assassinate our leaders were daily broadcast on their government radio." He said that he "found considerable significance in the fact that our troubles with the UAR date from the time I denounced the growing menace of communism in the Arab world," and added, "I detect a significant parallel between tactics used against us and those used by communists the world over."[63]

The trial of those accused in the assassination opened in December 1960 before a special security tribunal. The prosecutor, Major Muhammad Rasoul Kailani, mentioned that five plots had been organized in Jordan in the past three years, and alleged that President Abdul Nasser of the UAR and his agents in Cairo and Damascus were responsible for "a chain of conspiracies against the entity of this country." Eleven of the sixteen defendants were accused of engineering the explosion. Seven of them were tried in absentia and included two men from the Syrian military intelligence, two office messengers from the government building in Amman, and Zakaria Taher, a Jordanian emigré in Damascus who hired a young news agent named Salah Safadi to arrange for the assassination. The news agent Safadi who was in custody, pleaded guilty and mentioned his meetings with Zakaria Taher and the two Syrian military intelligence officers in Damascus where it was agreed that he would take part in the conspiracy for blowing up the prime minister's office in return for a payment of 10,000 Jordanian dinars ($28,000) to be shared with other participants. The news agent Safadi admitted that he engaged the two office messengers and described how he received the bombs and the timing devices from Syrian agents, and how the bombs were planted. On December 29 eleven defendants, including the two Syrian officers, were sentenced to death and four of them who were in custody were hanged in Amman two days later.

Shortly after the assassination of the prime minister, the political intelligence in Jordan allegedly discovered evidence that the UAR Embassy in Amman recruited a man in King Hussein's residence to kill him. Two attempts on the King's life were made, according to King Hussein, but with no success. In the first instance, someone in the palace who had access to his bathroom, had emptied the bottle that contained his nose drops and filled it with a violent acid. It was discovered on time, but the culprit was not identified. In the second instance, an assistant cook in the palace kitchen who had a cousin in the military intelligence bureau in Damascus, was recruited for poisoning the King's food, but as the cook was no expert in poisons, he experimented on cats to find out what would be the fatal dose. In his confession, the cook allegedly admitted that the attempt on the King's life was not made because he could not judge the dose, for none of the cats had died quickly enough, and then he made the mistake of letting the cats wander off into the palace grounds to die, otherwise the plot might not have been discovered.[64]

The occasional plots against King Hussein and his men were discovered by the efficient intelligence service which was expanded and improved after 1956, and through the loyalty of individuals in the army and in other walks of life. The King has related that one plot was discovered when a father informed against his own son after the boy arrived from Syria on an assassination mission, and the plot was to shoot Premier Majali a few weeks before his office was blown up.

In October 1960, more than two years after the Iraqi revolution and the murder of the royal family in Baghdad, diplomatic relations were re-established between Jordan and Iraq. King Hussein was evidently satisfied by Kassem's reported declaration that he did not intend the murder of the royal family and that Aref was the one responsible for it. As Kassem's relations with the UAR were then at their worst, this rapprochement between Hussein and Kassem was not pleasing to Nasser who, moreover, was annoyed by the trial of the assassins of Premier Majali and by the involvement of two Syrian officers in it. During his tour of the cities of his Syrian province in mid-October 1960, Nasser attacked Hussein as "a hireling and an agent," and called on the Jordanians to rise against him. He reminded his listeners of King Abdallah's assassination and of how Abdul Ilah of Iraq "was trampled, torn to pieces, and thrown to the dogs," and added that the hireling King and the imperialist stooges would meet their expected fate.[65]

In 1961, Nasser observed a correct attitude towards Hussein. The UAR president was then having trouble in Syria and was frustrated by his inability to attract any Arab states to join the UAR or even the federation of the United Arab States. His relations with Kassem of Iraq were also worsening. King Hussein seized the opportunity to make a conciliatory move and was perhaps encouraged by the American government. He wrote his first letter to Nasser on February 23, 1961 – the eighth of the holy month of Ramadan – asking him to forget the past and work for Arab interests. Nasser answered with reserve on March 13 and mentioned that Arab divisions were not superficial but reflected contradictions in the Arab situation. The peaceful relations between Nasser and Hussein continued until the Syrian coup of September 28, 1961 and the breakup of the United Arab Republic. During this interval, King Hussein's second marriage took place – May 25, 1961. When Hussein announced his recognition of the Syrian separate regime immediately after the coup, Nasser angrily reacted by breaking relations with Jordan and declared that he never believed the good faith of Hussein's conciliatory letters. In his renewed attacks against the Jordanian king, Nasser claimed that Hussein secured Saudi money in order to finance the separatist Syrian coup against Egypt.

Although King Hussein denied in mid-January 1962 any role in the Syrian coup of September, 1961 and in the abortive Lebanese coup at the end of December, he did not conceal his feeling of satisfaction and relief particularly after the success of the Syrian secessionist coup. In his autobiography, he has written, "our Syrian neighbors are again a free people, having thrown away the Nasserite imperialism which threatened to destroy not only themselves but the rest of the Arab world."[66] Jordan was no longer the main target of Nasser's attacks after the breakup of Syro-Egyptian unity. Nasser's efforts were now primarily directed to discredit and overthrow the Syrian separatist regime. At the same time he engaged in a quarrel with Imam Ahmad of Yemen that led to the dissolution of the federation known as the United Arab States. Jordan itself attached little importance to Nasser's occasional diatribes as long as he was busy fighting other Arabs. Commenting humourously on the methods of Egyptian propaganda, Hussein explained that they sprang from "an under-estimation of the average intelligence of the Arab people."

The Jordanian government addressed itself to projects of economic development when it was not defending itself against internal and external subversion. The year 1961 saw the beginning of the five-year program for the development of the country's resources. The first phase of the East Ghor Canal was completed in August, the new oil refinery opened in March, the Arab Potash Company expanded its chemical plants, and a census of the population was taken. Already the Aqaba Harbor had been inaugurated, and work on a 220-mile asphalt road was begun – and was completed in 1962 – and the national income of Jordan had been showing a steady increase. Education had been expanding, Jordanian teachers were being loaned officially to Morocco and Algeria, and a Jordanian university was established in Amman.

In the relaxed atmosphere at the end of 1961 parliamentary elections took place and sixty deputies were elected on October 22. They were mostly right wingers and independents. King Hussein announced in his speech from the throne on December 2 that parties would be allowed to function – they were dissolved in 1957 – provided they served Jordan and did not act as agents or receive instructions from outside.

Towards the end of January 1962 King Hussein appointed a young and vigorous prime minister named Wasfi al-Tell with a team of new and young ministers. The King called his cabinet, which succeeded that of Bahjat al-Talhouni, "a new concept," and some American periodicals compared the new era it inaugurated to President Kennedy's "New Frontier." Internal conciliation and harmony was sought by inviting all the opponents and exiles, towards the end of February 1962, to return to Jordan for a new start. King Hussein, as a good sportsman, was not the type of person who could keep a grudge for long. He often jailed persons for subversion and for making attempts on his life, but shortly after he pardoned and released them. He also sought to secure Jordan against attack, and his interest in defending his country and maintaining the regional status quo coincided with that of King Saud and led to a mutual defense agreement signed at Taif in Saudi Arabia. In early 1963, Jordan felt it could consider establishing relations with the Soviet Union, and before the end of the year diplomatic representatives were exchanged by the two countries. Nasser, instead of applauding this move, tried to urge western bankers and incite the United States government against Jordan while the negotiations with the Soviet government were being conducted for establishing the new relationship. Hussein had to proclaim that in spite of the diplomatic relations with the USSR, no fundamental change in Jordanian policy would occur.

King Hussein had to weather another Nasserist storm before a more enduring truce could be reached with the Egyptian rulers. The successful coups d'état of February 8 and March 8, 1963 against Kassem in Iraq and Nazim al-Qudsi in

Syria respectively brought the pan-Arab Nasserists and Baathists in both countries to power. As Syria and Iraq opened negotiations with Egypt for a federal union between the three countries, Jordan was threatened by a serious crisis. The cabinet of Wasfi al-Tell resigned on April 15 because of "new developments" in the neighboring countries. King Hussein appointed the veteran sixty-two-year-old Samir Rifai to serve for the fifth time as prime minister. Rifai immediately began to speak of Jordan's attachment to Arab unity and ordered the end of attacks against Nasser. He suggested the availability of his country for participation in the planned federation and insinuated that the constitutional monarchic regime in Jordan should not be a hindrance to its membership in the union. Nasser received the Jordanian overtures coldly. On April 17 the charter for Arab federation between Egypt, Syria, and Iraq was signed in Cairo. The Jordanians had a feeling of isolation because they were not included in the federation, and in the meeting of the Jordanian Chamber of Deputies on April 22, thirty-one deputies voted no confidence in the Rifai cabinet. The King angrily reacted by dissolving the Chamber and appointing his uncle, Sharif Hussein ibn Nasser, to head a caretaker cabinet for the following elections.

The news of the Arab federation charter of April 17 created anti-government feeling and demonstrations in the cities of Jordan. Three persons in Jerusalem and twelve in Amman were reportedly killed. A counter-demonstration expressing loyalty to King Hussein took place in Amman on April 24 when about 10,000 Jordanians consisting of tribal chiefs, farmers, politicians, and workers marched to the courtyard of Basman Palace and cheered the King. Hussein prevented his supporters from shouting anti-Nasser slogans and declared that Jordan sought Arab unity. The anti-government demonstrators were dispersed by troops, gunfire, and the establishment of a curfew. The border with Syria and Iraq was closed. The American Embassy warned its citizens to keep off the streets and to build up emergency supplies for further disturbances. In the meantime, the Egyptian radio stations opened a particularly harsh campaign against Hussein, and the stations of Iraq and Syria followed. The hostile radio and press outside the country described the demonstrations in Jordan as though they were a spreading revolution or a guerilla war with pitched battles. The Baghdad radio and the Voice of the Arab Nation (a clandestine radio in Cairo) called for Hussein's assassination in a most cynical and crude fashion, and urged the Jordanian officers to revolt. The United States and Britain took military precautions towards the end of April fearing a potential coup by Jordanian officers.[67] Israel reportedly asked the American government at this time to warn Egypt that a move into Jordan would imperil peace, because Nasser in Jordan would be like the Soviet rockets in Cuba.[68] King Hussein was not frightened and at one time during the demonstrations, he drove through the streets in a white convertible car and was even cheered, and at other times he toured the Jordanian cities. The campaign subsided in early May and Hussein's regime survived while, on the other hand, trouble began between Egypt and the other members of the projected Arab federation.

Suspicions and exchanges of accusations in the press and radio between Egypt on the one hand, and Syria and Iraq on the other reached their climax in July 1963 in the abortive Nasserist coup against the Baath regime in Damascus. As the quarrels resumed between Nasser and Syria, the federation charter of April 17 became a dead letter, and Jordan was again able to live in peace. Diplomatic relations between Egypt and Jordan, which had been broken since September 1961, were resumed in mid-January 1964. Their resumption was prepared in a meeting in Paris between King Hussein and Muhammad Hassanein Haikal, editor of *al-Ahram* and Nasser's spokesman. Both Egypt and Jordan were hostile to the Baathist regime in Syria, and their common hositlity became the basis for a new truce.

Among the causes of tension between Egypt and Jordan was the Jordanian continued recognition and support of the royalist regime in Yemen after the republican coup of September 1962. This element of disagreement was gradually removed as Jordan stopped helping royalist Yemen in the fall of 1963 and finally recognized the republican regime on July 21, 1964. It is alleged that the King of Jordan had been threatened by the United States government with the ending of American assistance and protection if he did not cease helping the Yemeni royalists.[69] When the first Summit Conference of the heads of Arab states met in Cairo in January 1964, King Hussein was privately received in President Nasser's residence for one hour on January 12, the eve of the opening of the conference. The two chief executives are said to have settled then their personal and political differences. King Hussein later made a private four-day visit to Cairo in March 1964 and was received at the airport by a warm embrace from Nasser. This was followed by another private visit and series of talks in August. An ultimate expression of Hussein's chivalrous conduct with Nasser after enduring ten years of plots, threats, and abuse was his reported warning to Nasser in June 1965 against the conspiracies of the Muslim Brotherhood and other plotters who planned to overthrow the Nasserist regime in the following month.

As tension relaxed in 1964, Jordan was able to proceed with its economic and social projects and to demonstrate again its goodwill towards the detained or exiled Jordanians. In April 1964, fifty Baathist and communist detainees were released and included the Baathist leader Munif Razzaz. Later in September, Ali Abu Nawar was pardoned by the King and allowed to return to Jordan. In February, the Jordanian government decided to join the Arab Economic Unity Pact and the Arab financial organization for economic development. In October, work was inaugurated on a housing project near Aqaba for the benefit of some 25,000 persons. Jordan continued to lend teachers to the schools of Algeria and Morocco and to receive Algerian students in her schools.

The atmosphere of peaceful relations between Jordan and Egypt began to be disturbed in early 1966 when discussions on Islamic cooperation began between King Faisal of Saudi Arabia and the heads of some Middle Eastern states in a series of visits that included Jordan. Nasser viewed the reactivation of Islamic cooperation by King Faisal as an attempt on the part of the "reactionary" regimes to form an Islamic alliance and a conservative front against revolution and the revolutionary regimes. Nasser resumed his denunciations of Faisal and Hussein after a period of relative calm during which the Arab summit conferences were held in 1964-1965. The dangerous development for Jordan was the rapprochement between Egypt and the radical Baath regime in Syria after a period of conflict, and the signature of a mutual defense agreement, with the blessing of the Soviet Union, between the two revolutionary regimes on November 4, 1966. Jordan was bound to be in trouble as past experience proved every time Syria and Egypt came closer together. The head of the Palestine Liberation Organization, Ahmad Shuqairi, also took a more aggressive attitude towards King Hussein. The PLO was created in 1964 by the Arab summit conferences and, in the cold war between the Arab states, its chairman was on Nasser's side. Shuqairi complained on the "Voice of Palestine" radio in Cairo that Jordan was not doing what it should to help the PLO prepare for a war to liberate Palestine.[70] On June 29, 1966 he submitted a list of ten demands to the government of Jordan asking for the right to draft Palestinians living in Jordan for PLO service, the imposition of a tax collection on these Palestinians, and complete freedom of action and an independent status for PLO in Jordan. King Hussein could not accept the demands because the unity of Jordan would be in danger and the PLO would become a rival to the Jordanian government for the loyalty of the Palestinian residents. Shuqairi also claimed that King Hussein did not allow the Palestinian commandos to operate against Israel from Jordanian territory. The King of Jordan actually tried to avoid provoking an Israeli attack while his country was building up its forces, but Palestinian commandos did operate from Jordan, and Israel, after issuing some threats, made a heavy retaliatory attack on Jordan.

The Israeli punitive expedition of November 13, 1966 that destroyed most of the little town of Sammu' in the Hebron district was particularly serious on account of the heavy military action and the resulting losses in Jordanian lives and property, but especially because it produced a grave reaction among the Jordanians of the western bank against their own government. The radical regimes in Egypt and Syria, instead of helping Jordan or reacting in its favor, took advantage of the expedition to attack the Jordanian government and incite riots in the various cities. A state of siege was declared in most of Jordan, and the correspondent of the *Observer* believed that King Hussein faced on the week end of 25-27 November "the gravest political crisis since his near overthrow in 1957."[71] At the height of the crisis, Shuqairi sent an ultimatum from Cairo on November 22 to the ministers in the Jordan cabinet in Amman asking them to resign within twenty-four hours or face the consequences. They did not resign, and calm returned to Jordan after Hussein promised to arm the border villages, but the Syrian and Egyptian press and radio claimed that the revolt continued and that Hussein was about to lose his throne. In Cairo the *Gumhouriyah* said that the King of Jordan threatened to give the city of Nablus to Israel if the demonstrators did not surrender.[72]

The Israeli attack on Sammu' was followed by Jordanian complaints that neither the Unified Arab Command, created by the summit conferences, nor Syria and Egypt took action to help Jordan. In the Higher Defense Council of the Arab League in December 1966, Jordan asked for the removal of the United Nations emergency forces from Sinai as part of a general plan of Arab defense, in order to be able to concentrate Arab troops in Sinai and not only on the other Arab borders with Israel. Discussions in the Council were rendered useless because of antagonism between the two Arab camps. In the meantime, the Syrian radio claimed on November 29, 1966 that Saudi troops had entered Jordan accompanied by

American officers to help attack the Palestinians. It was an invention, but the Palestinian students in Algiers believed it and stormed their own embassy (Jordanian Embassy) and forced the charge d'affaires to send their telegram to Amman denouncing the arrival of "Saudi mercenaries in Jordan under the command of British and American officers."[73]

One of the stratagems of the cold war, frequently used by Egypt to embarass her Arab opponents, was to publicize and exploit the arrival of a military or political refugee from a rival Arab state and use him to denounce his country's government. In early February 1967, the headlines in the Cairo press carried the story of Captain Rashid al-Hamarsha, of the directorate of military operations in Jordan, who sought political asylum in Egypt because, as he said, his conscience "could not accept the missions he was asked to do for organizing sabotage in Syria or for killing Shuqairi." The Jordanian government explained that the fugitive must have been induced to leave by important cash payments, because he was known to be in financial trouble and suddenly began to act as a well-to-do officer. A few days later, an Egyptian plane was forced to land in Amman by what the Jordan government claimed to be an Egyptian Colonel, while Cairo said it was a man with a criminal record.[74]

Jordan broke its relations with republican Yemen on February 12, 1967 because its president, Sallal, was on Shuqairi's side in the dispute with King Hussein, and also because toxic gas and napalm bombs were used by the Yemeni republicans and by Egyptians. On February 26, the Jordanian ambassador was withdrawn from Cairo in protest against Nasser's insult to King Hussein, who was called, in a play on words of which Nasser was very fond, "the dissolute" man of Jordan *(aher al Urdun)* instead of the King of Jordan *(ahel al-Urdun)*. The insult was made in a broadcast speech on February 22 in which Nasser invented other nicknames for various rival Arab heads of state.

A serious break between Jordan and the revolutionary regimes occurred when its diplomatic relations with Bonn were restored at the end of February 1967. It thus joined the three other Arab states – Libya, Tunisia, and Morocco – that had refused to break relations with Western Germany after it had recognized Israel in May 1965. The West German action had come as a result of the crisis which erupted when Nasser invited Ulbricht, the president of East Germany, to visit Cairo earlier in 1965, and also because of German delivery of arms to Israel. King Hussein was immediately denounced on February 28, 1967 by Shuqairi for resuming relations with Western Germany, and Jordanian action was branded as "a new treason by the treacherous Hussein." The battle of liberation, said Shuqairi, "requires in the first place that Jordan be rescued from the puppet reactionary regime." In the forty-seventh session of the Arab League Council in Cairo in mid-March 1967, the Saudi and Jordanian delegates attacked Shuqairi and questioned his right of sitting with the other delegates. His right, however, was defended and maintained but the Jordanian delegate refused to sit and withdrew. A vote was taken to censure Jordan for resuming relations with Bonn and it obtained a majority. Jordan then explained in a memoir that the original breaking of relations with Western Germany was an artifical act imposed by Egypt as a part of a bargain with the Soviet Union for reaping material gain. The renewal of relations, said the Jordanian memoir, was useful for the higher Arab interests. The atmosphere was still tense between Jordan on the one hand, and Baathist Syria, Egypt, and Shuqairi's PLO on the other, when Nasser began moving troops to Sinai in May 1967.

VII. The Survival and Tragedy of Jordan

Jordan stands out as one of the few Arab countries in which the military failed to overthrow the constitutional western-oriented regime and establish a socialist revolutionary government. The Jordanian military leaders were divided over the questions of revolution and radical change, the orientation in regional and international politics, and generally over the future of their country. The supporters of the sovereign western-oriented monarchy have triumphed in spite of the recurring riots, assassinations, and attempted coups. Jordan, with a population of less than two million people and with limited resources, has thus given the Arab world the example of a brave leadership that refused to be intimidated by plots and threats, and succeeded in preserving its constitution and its freedoms. At one time, Jordan ended its military dependence on Britain by dismissing General Glubb and abrogating the Anglo-Jordanian treaty, but as it tried to compromise with her Arab neighbors and to depend on their aid, it was threatened with conspiracies and subversion. King Hussein's willingness to compromise could not be expected to go to the extent of accepting the destruction of the monarchy and of the Jordanian entity.

Compared to Iraq and Yemen, Jordan was more vulnerable to revolutionary ideas and more exposed to the loss of statehood. It was surrounded by revolutionary Arab states and by Israel, and its population consisted mostly of frustrated Palestinians who were inclined to believe in the possibilities of Arab unity and strength, and who were ready to listen to the charges against their own government. Jordan, moreover, was viewed as an artificial state owing to the circumstances of its creation by the British in 1921 and to its meager resources. The recurring plots and attempted coups by Jordanian civilians or by officers were partly an aspect of Jordan's vulnerability. The motives behind these attempts were a combination of frivolity and ambition, an expectation of liberating Palestine under a different regime, and a trend towards revolutionary socialism.

In spite of the many adverse factors, Jordan was able to survive and even prosper owing to the alertness and courage of its king, the character of its army and ruling elite, and the nature of the political alignments and developments that affected its contemporary history. King Hussein, in spite of the authoritarian regime that was needed to stem conspiracy and subversion, has been known to be basically democratic, liberal, and progressive in his outlook and temperament. He has been significantly close to his people and to those who served him, and could count on a large core of loyal supporters on the eastern bank, and even on the western bank, who wanted their country to remain free politically and economically. His grandfather, King Abdallah, had succeeded in the course of his long reign in establishing strong bonds of respect and friendship with his subjects on the eastern bank and with the Arab Legion, and in consolidating the Jordanian State. The army which included solid and tough units of loyal Bedouins and small townspeople shouldered the regime and frustrated the hopes of those of the officers who were known for their special conception of nationalism, or for their lust for power and wealth, and acted often on instructions from beyond the border. The Arab political alignments sometimes changed and evolved in Jordan's favor. A threat to Jordan existed whenever Egypt was on good terms with the Syrian and Iraqi regimes, but when Egyptian relations with these two, and especially with Syria, deteriorated, Jordan was relatively left in peace. Paradoxically, the survival of Jordan and its monarchy was due in part to the threatening attitude of Israel against any attempt to annex Jordan to another Arab state, and the inability of Egypt to defend Jordan against Israel and assure its future if Hussein were to be overthrown.

One should recognize, moreover, that the rulers and peoples of the Arab countries reacted differently to Nasser's appeal for revolution and change in the political and social order. In Syria and Iraq, and in Yemen to a smaller extent, the civilian and military opposition to the old regime was well organized and determined to operate a change and reacted favorably to Nasser's appeal. The old rulers of these countries were either unaware of the intrigues against them, or refused to believe in the imminent danger when it was brought to their attention, or were timid in taking measures to face it. In Jordan, the situation was different. King Hussein was usually well informed about the maneuvers and plots, and most of his supporters, civilian and military, were determined opponents of revolutionary action and were fanatically attached to their king and their country. They proved to have more courage to stand in the face of external intrigues and subversion than their moderate colleagues of the old ruling elite in Syria and Iraq, and they constituted a strong counter-balance to the designs of the revolutionary opposition. This is why the persistent attempts of Egyptian and Syrian agents in Jordan were so frequently frustrated, particularly in the Zarqa incident of April 1957. Nasser committed the mistake of refusing to admit that differences in political attitudes and social traditions did exist among the Arab countries and the Arab armies. The response to such a serious course of action as the imposition of revolutionary political and social change could not always be expected to be in his favor.

In Jordan, moreover, it should be noted that the end of the monarchy would have probably meant the end of the Jordanian state, whereas in Iraq and Yemen the state survived the fall of the monarchy. Depending on the kind of regional alignments at the time of a successful coup, Jordan could have been either dismembered and divided among its neighbors, or could have become a satellite of Egypt, or a part of Syria. The attitude and action of Israel in any change in the political or territorial status quo had to be given its due weight.

The belief that Jordan – or rather the original Transjordan – was an artificial, or a nonviable state was perhaps a factor in encouraging Syria and Egypt to deal with it in that highhanded manner. Yet Jordan was only artificial in the same sense as all the states that constituted a part of geographic Syria were – or for that matter all other states that have been created in the course of history by considerations of strategic, or religious, or ethnic expediency. The problem of the Jordanian entity could have been solved by the formation of a Greater Syrian federation. Since the early 1940's, King Abdallah proposed a union of Greater Syria, and Nuri al-Said of Iraq advanced the scheme for a federation between Greater Syria and Iraq. Any one of these two schemes, and especially the former, could have not only saved Palestine, but also avoided the various crises and tragedies that have continued to plague this area.

The tragedy of Jordan, whose problem was more serious than that of the other Arab countries that had to face the challenge of the revolutionary socialist Arab states, has been its inability to decide its own policy in case of Arab involvement with Israel. Jordanian Arab nationalism, the geographic position of Jordan along the Israeli eastern border, and the presence of a large Palestinian Arab population in it have obliged it to align its policy towards Israel with that of Egypt and Syria regardless of whether it took part in deciding that policy or not. Already in October 1966, when Israel and Syria were exchanging warlike delcarations because of the action of Arab commandos in Israel, and when the Cairo and Damascus press was accusing King Hussein of being in league with the Israelis, the King declared that Jordan would have to open a second front against Israel in case of an Israeli attack on Syria.[75] On May 21, 1967 a time bomb exploded in a car at the Jordanian frontier post killing fourteen Jordanians and injuring another twenty-eight persons. The car was reportedly sent by the intelligence officials of the radical Baath regime in Syria. Jordan broke relations with Syria, and Hussein condemned the Syrian action at a time when the Arabs were mobilizing their armies and preparing to face the possibility of war with Israel. Hussein's call on the Arabs to cooperate and forget their differences, and his expressed readiness to oppose Israel could not disarm the Syrian Baath efforts to stir a revolution against him even during the critical period of the Egyptian-Israeli crisis in May 1967.[76]

King Hussein could not remain indifferent to the critical crisis that followed Nasser's decision to close the Gulf of Aqaba to Israeli shipping on May 22. Jordan became automatically involved, more than any other Arab state, although it took no part in the crucial decisions that were approved, as it seems, by the Soviet Union and were primarily motivated by Nasserist and Russian interests. In the tense atmosphere of military preparations on the Arab and Israeli sides, Hussein made his dramatic flight to Cairo on May 30 to sign a mutual defense pact with Nasser. The pact provided for a joint defense council and joint chiefs of staff and an Egyptian supreme commander in time of war. Nasser commented after the agreement: "This is proof that the Arabs forget their differences at serious times.'"[7] Hussein met Shuqairi in Cairo and brought him back with him to Amman where they were met by joyful demonstrations. On June 2, Shuqairi spoke in the mosque in Jerusalem after the Friday prayers and exhorted the people to die for the homeland. He also declared that Jordan might fire the first shot for liberating Palestine. King Hussein was evidently annoyed by Shuqairi's talk and made it known that he gave orders to prevent anyone from taking advantage of the situation for personal political profit.

When Israel attacked Egypt in the direction of Sinai on the morning of June 5, King Hussein began military action on the western bank against Israel in accordance with the pact he had signed with Nasser. Hussein's forces fought gallantly for two days without air cover and with no substantial support from either Baathist Syria or Iraq. The participation of Jordan on Egypt's side was more active and prompt than that of any other Arab state, especially the revolutionary ones that had supported Egypt or were allied with it. King Hussein was the only Arab head of state who rushed in person to the battlefield and played in person his role of commander in chief. His army was defeated, his small air force was destroyed even before the fighting began, and on June 7, he accepted the proposed ceasefire. The Jordanian western bank, including the remaining Arab section of Jerusalem, was occupied by Israeli forces, and Jordan lost the important income from tourism and was deprived of 38 per cent of its productive capacity. More than 200,000 new refugees poured into the eastern bank and added to the problems and burdens of what remained of Jordan.

The war in June 1967 is an outstanding illustration of how Jordan could be led to destroy itself through no fault of its rulers. While other Arab leaders who participated in the war were discredited, Hussein emerged as a war hero and Nasser called him "a noble and courageous man." His status in the Arab world improved, but his internal problems have increased, and those related to his attempt to reach a settlement with Israel continued to be conditioned by the attitudes and decisions of other Arab states and by the Palestinian inhabitants of his reduced kingdom. Among the revolutionary socialist states, Egypt at least can no longer incite trouble against him. The attitude of the neighboring Baath rulers of Syria remained unfriendly. With another Baathist regime in Iraq since July 17, 1968 – although different from the radical Syrian Baath – troubles in Jordan might increase. Shuqairi left Jordan for Damascus when the first shot in the war was fired and was able to keep his position with The Palestine Liberation Organization until early 1968. When King Hussein made his peace offensive in Washington on 6-8 November 1967 and offered to accept Israel "as a fact of life," Shuqairi declared that Hussein was not empowered to speak for the Palestinian people. As much as Hussein and the rulers of Jordan might want to reach a settlement with Israel that would restore the western bank and normal life to the country, they would not be able to do so without the consensus of the other Arab states involved, or at least the consent of Egypt and of the Palestinian people in Jordan.

Within Jordan, Hussein's problem was aggravated by the failure of the United States to deliver the planes he needed, and by Soviet offers to supply arms to Jordan, because this strengthened the position of the elements opposed to the West on whom Jordan had traditionally depended. It was only in early June 1968 that the American government announced the resumption of arms deliveries to Jordan. King Hussein had visited Moscow in early October 1967 but made no formal agreements on war material, probably by fear of exposure to Soviet penetration.

Hussein's chief problem, however, has been connected with his attitude towards the guerilla organizations that became more active in Israel since its occupation of the western bank. They have operated mostly from the Jordanian eastern bank, and Jordan was warned by Israel about the consequences of their raids. On February 15, 1968 an eight-hour battle was fought between Israel and Jordan in which Israel used jet aircraft to bombard Jordanian positions. King Hussein warned his people that an end should be put "to giving Israel excuses to wage aggression," because the guerillas used Jordan as a jumping ground. The Jordanians were divided over Hussein's warning, and the Fateh guerilla organization[78] rejected it declaring that it "would not allow anyone or any regime to stop its operations against Israel." King Hussein was thus caught between Israeli warnings and the danger of massive retaliation on the one hand, and the feelings of the militant Palestinian refugees and other inhabitants of Jordan on the other.

On March 21, 1968 Israel invaded the Jordanian territory on the eastern bank for the first time. Its forces crossed the Jordan bridges and struck at four points east of the river, but the main target, where paratroopers were also dropped, was the guerilla camp, originally a refugee camp, at Karamah, about three miles east of the Jordan. The raid lasted thirteen hours, the casualties were relatively heavy on both sides, and the camp was almost completely destroyed. The other Arab neighbors of Israel did not react, and Hussein expressed his dissatisfaction saying, "Israel is aware that we are satisfied to talk of Arab unity without seriously working to build it up in union and strength."[79] The UN Security Council condemned the military action launched by Israel. Commenting on the Israeli threats to Jordan because of commando operations, King Hussein said, "We are in the ridiculous position of being blamed for not assuring Israel's safety." He added that he was unable to use his army against the Arab commandos, and he could not guarantee the security of Israeli soldiers while they occupied the heartland of his country.[80] While Hussein rejected the warning of Levi Eshkol, prime minister of Israel, who threatened to invade the land east of the Jordan again if the guerillas continued their operations, he (Hussein) was anxious to control guerilla activity and avoid being dragged to a war for which the Arabs were not ready. He was also afraid that the guerilla organizations might become a state within the state, and that the popularity of their raids against Israel might erode his control over his own kingdom.

Jordan and its king, Hussein, have so far survived the attacks of Arab socialist regimes and the attempts of dissident officers and groups, as well as the strain and stress and territorial losses caused by the war in June 1967 and its aftermath. The duels of artillery have been almost continuous across the Jordan with Israel, and on June 4, 1968 a severe Israeli attack on Jordanian artillery positions was made, and rockets and jet bombers were used. In mid-July a convention of the Palestine National Assembly representing guerilla organizations and other groups met in Cairo to coordinate their activities. In Jordan the Soviet Union has provided funds for an active pro-communist and anti-American organization called the National Charter Group. Although the campaigns of the Arab socialist neighbors of Jordan against King Hussein and his regime have stopped since the June war, other sources of danger have appeared in the increased number of restless refugees, the rising power of the guerilla organizations, and the remote possibility of Israeli occupation of the eastern bank in a new conflict and the obliteration of the Jordanian state.

In the face of the difficulties that Jordan has been encountering since June 1967, the Jordanian army has retained a remarkable cohesiveness and loyalty to King Hussein, whereas in the socialist Arab countries the army broke up into rival factions, and some cliques of officers have attempted, and others have succeeded in overthrowing the ruling regime. The Jordanian army without an adequate air force has had to challenge the frequent "search and destroy" air strikes by Israeli jets that attacked commando camps and artillery positions sometimes in the suburbs of cities as in the attacks of March 17 and 26, 1969 near Amman and al-Salt, respectively. The army was generally able, except in a few instances, to avoid serious confrontations with guerilla forces in Jordan, or with Palestinian refugees and Jordanians who supported them. King Hussein had also to take a favorable attitude towards commando activity although it invited serious Israeli retaliatory raids. On November 4, 1968 his forces, however, had to deal firmly with the members of the commando organization al-Saiqa (The Thunderbolt) that was affiliated with the Syrian Baath because they opened fire on a Jordanian patrol and incited with loudspeakers the people of Amman to revolt. The Jordanian army had to enforce a curfew in the capital and to arrest a number of "phony" commandos, as King Hussein called them, because their target was Jordan's east bank and not the Israeli-occupied west bank. They were denounced by the Fateh organization on the following day because of their attempt "to spread strife, sedition and lies".

An agreement was reached after the confrontation of November 4, 1968 between the government of Jordan and the commando organizations but it was not officially announced. The commandos were required to respect the Jordanian check points and submit to Jordanian security; they were expected to keep their uniformed men out of the town and allow Jordan's courts to deal with the crimes of commandos. Otherwise, the commandos were allowed to carry out their attacks against the Israelis without Jordanian government interference. The agreement in the view of certain observers gave the commando organizations a legal status in Jordan, and their influence increased later with the increase of their activity and popularity.[81] In early February 1969, the leader of the Fateh organization, Yasser Arafat, was elected in a meeting in Cairo chairman of a new executive committee of the Palestine Liberation Organization. In a discussion on the transfer of the PLO army of 3000 men from Egypt to join the commando forces, King Hussein indicated his disapproval, because the PLO forces would be transferred mainly to Jordan and their presence would upset the balance between commando and PLO forces on the one hand, and Jordanian regular troops on the other. Moreover, the Russian-trained PLO army in Egypt could bring with it Russian influence. The transfer of these forces was eventually postponed and when Arafat visited King Hussein in Amman on February 16, 1969 both of them went to visit commando camps where they were acclaimed, and it was said then that a new cordial relationship began between the commandos and the Jordanian government.

A serious confrontation almost occurred between the Fateh men and the Jordanian government forces on April 8, 1969 because of the Fateh rocket attack from the port of Aqaba in Jordan against neighboring Elath in Israel. A tacit agreement between Israel and Jordan had prohibited attacks from either side on the two cities. The commandos evidently waited until King Hussein left Jordan on a visit to Britain and the United States and launched their attack. A few hours later Israeli jets raided Aqaba in Jordan. The government was outraged by the Fateh attack and ordered the suspension of the traffic between Amman and Aqaba, while its forces began arresting commandos and an estimated forty-five of them were seized. The commandos answered by placing their units on a nation-wide alert. A secret high level conference was immediately called to avoid a confrontation and to prevent further rocket attacks, because Israeli retaliation could destroy Jordan's only seaport. An agreement was reached whereby the commandos promised not to attack Elath again, and the government promised to release those who were arrested.[82]

While King Hussein's government was obliged sometimes to restrict guerilla activities, as in the case of Elath, it was obliged to admit on various occasions that guerilla activity was legitimate and that "resistance to occupation," as Hussein said, "is safeguarded within this country." The Jordanian king continued his active search for a settlement with Israel and sometimes made bold peace proposals in international circles in spite of the declared opposition of the guerilla organizations to a political settlement. His government had to deny the rumors about his alleged meetings with Abba Eban, the Israeli foreign minister, in September 1968 and January 1969 and about his readiness to abandon a part of the west bank to

Israel.[83] On April 10, 1969 he spoke in Washington with the "personal authority" of President Nasser and presented a peace plan that included the end of all belligerency, respect for the sovereignty and independence of all states in the area, freedom of navigation in the Suez Canal and Gulf of Aqaba, just settlement for the refugees and the withdrawal of Israeli troops from occupied Arab territory. The guerilla organizations rejected the plan and took a hostile view of it but the king ignored the criticism because of his belief that the overwhelming majority of the people would agree to his proposals. Certain observers commented that Hussein's life, as a result, was in danger because no Arab leader spoke so boldly of a settlement, and that the threat to his life would be from Jordanian extremists or from Palestinian guerillas.@W

King Hussein, sometimes called "the durable pro-Western king", has outlasted all Arab chiefs of state who were in office at the time of his accession in 1953. He was able to survive in spite of all the conspiracies and attempts of the leftist Arab states and of his own dissident officers until the Arab-Israeli war of June 1967. Since then his authority has been seriously challenged and weakened, not by the former authors of plots and attempted coups but by the Palestinian guerilla organizations and their supporters within his own kingdom. In each of the confrontations following that of November 1968 he tried but was unable to impose on the guerillas the respect for law and order within the Jordanian state. He was accused everytime of pushing the country toward civil war and of cooperating with the American Central Intelligence Agency to liquidate the Palestinian resistance movement, although he usually did not interfere with the guerillas' freedom of operations against Israel. On February 12, 1970 a serious showdown was avoided when the king suspended a decree that his government had issued two days earlier to insure internal security but which the guerillas refused to obey. On April 15, 1970 the extremist guerilla elements turned a non-violent demonstration against the expected visit of Joseph Sisco, American assistant secretary of state for Near Eastern affairs, into a violent anti-American riot in which the U.S. Information Center and library were burned and the American embassy was attacked. The king's government felt insulted when the visit was canceled for the obvious reason that the ability of the security forces to protect the guest was doubtful. King Hussein subsequently demanded and obtained the recall of the American ambassador, Harrison Symmes, who was deemed responsible for the assessment of the conditions of security in Jordan, but this face-saving device did not conceal the essential facts about the lack of security and the weakness of government authority in Jordan.

In the most serious confrontation between King Hussein's forces and the guerillas that extended from June 6 to 12, 1970, about three hundred persons were killed and seven hundred were wounded in the fighting in Zarqa and Amman. An American diplomat was kidnapped on June 7 and was returned on the following day, King Hussein himself escaped an assassination attempt on Tuesday June 9 while he was on his way to the capital, the American military attache, Major Robert Perry, was murdered in his home on Wednesday June 10, and some of the guerillas participated in a rampage of looting, breaking into foreigners' homes, and stealing cars. About sixty foreign tourists and residents of the two largest hotels in Amman were held as hostages by the Marxist Popular Front for the Liberation of Palestine(PFLP) in order to impose on the king certain conditions including the dismissal of his uncle, Major General Sharif Nasir ibn Jamil, commander in chief of the army, and of his cousin Maj. Gen. Sharif Zayd ibn Shaker, commander of the third armored division, who were considered to be the guerillas' special foes particularly because of their shelling of the guerillas' headquarters within and around the refugee camps. The king accepted reluctantly to dismiss the two superior officers in order to enforce a ceasefire and to obtain the release of the hostages. He found it difficult at one time to enforce military obedience to his orders because of the dissatisfaction among the supporters of the dismissed officers. The departure of hundreds of Americans and other foreign residents from Amman on Friday June 12 meant that the future was uncertain after the continuous erosion of government authority and the difficulty of insuring security and order. The king's instructions to the new cabinet formed on June 28, 1970 indicated more surrender to the demands of the guerillas.

The showdown in June 1970 meant that it was too late for the king or for some of his loyal officers to attempt the breaking of the power of the Palestinian resistance organizations because their membership had increased to about 15,000 fighters and opinion in the Jordanian cabinet was divided. Moreover, it was not sure that other Arab countries, like neighboring Syria and Iraq, would have allowed the Jordanian army to suppress the guerilla organizations even if it had the power to do so. Civil war, in the case of a serious Jordanian attempt against the guerillas, would have probably been complicated by external intervention. The showdown also indicated the growing power of the PFLP and its leader, George Habash, who played an active role in the events of June and whose independent extremist action was based on the belief that an internal revolution against the Arab monarchies and "reactionary" regimes and the adoption of a Marxist program were as important as the struggle against Israel and should even precede the decisive action against Israel. The position of the PFLP was consequently different from that of the more numerous and prestigious Fateh guerilla organization led by Yasser Arafat who was at the same time the head of the Palestine Liberation Organization and the chairman of the central committee of guerilla organizations. The Fateh leader believed that the fight against Israel had priority over political ideologies, and he supposedly favored the survival of King Hussein's monarchy, at least for the present, because of the fear that the internal differences between the guerilla groups would widen and the task of ruling Jordan would prove impossible if the guerillas had to administer the country. Yet, the Fateh leader did not always succeed in moderating the extremism of the PFLP, and in the showdown of June he was even obliged to show a certain degree of solidarity with it.

The violent confrontation in June 1970, moreover, showed the concern of the Arab states about the fighting between the Jordanian army and the guerillas and considered it dangerous and damaging to the Arab struggle against Israel. President Nasser, who in the past was usually ready to throw the first stone at the rulers of Jordan, now told his National Assembly that the wrong actions of certain guerilla groups – meaning the PFLP – were intolerable and he called the fighting a "tragedy and a massacre." The Arab heads of state and delegates discussed earnestly the problem of King Hussein's relations with the guerillas in their meetings in Libya during the celebrations that followed the evacuation of Wheelus air base on June 11, 1970. They decided to dispatch a high level peace delegation that consisted of one member from each of Egypt, Libya, the Sudan, and Algeria to reconcile the Jordanian army and the guerillas. Israel, on the other hand, made it known more than once that it would not remain indifferent if Hussein should lose his throne and Jordan should fall into the hands of the Palestine resistance groups. Israel thus became, for different reasons, a factor in the preservation of the Jordanian monarchy under Hussein from the guerilla threat in the same way as it had been before the six day war when it stood for the preservation of the Jordanian monarchy against the threats of the socialist Arab states and their allies within Jordan.

King Hussein and his monarchy have thus survived the serious crisis of June 1970 through a combination of factors among which the protection of the United States and Britain was significantly absent. The King of Jordan, moreover, made it known on June 17 in spite of the precariousness of his position that he was not ready to abdicate because, as he said, "I am not the type of person who can quit. . .this nation is part of me and I am part of it and so is my family." His position will probably become more precarious, and the guerillas will grow more numerous and dangerous and will provoke more showdowns as long as the Arab conflict with Israel remains unsettled. The political settlement with Israel, however, will not be reached if the consent of the guerilla organizations is needed because they have declared their opposition to any solution that falls short of putting an end to the Zionist Jewish state and establishing a bi-national secular Palestinian state. King Hussein himself showed more hesitation in proposing, or commenting on peace plans but when the proposal of June 19, 1970 was presented by Secretary of State William Rogers and was accepted by Nasser on July 23, he gave his approval even though the guerillas disapproved. King Hussein will consequently need more than ever before the cohesiveness and loyalty of his army for the preservation of his monarchy during his arduous attempt to live with the guerillas and to face showdowns that could be even more serious than that of June 1970. Other factors in the survival of Hussein and his kingdom will continue to be the moderating influence of the Arab states on the guerillas, and the influence of Arafat and his Fateh and PLO organizations over the more extreme resistance groups. But the decisive factor that could remove the threat of the guerillas in Jordan as well as Lebanon and other Arab countries would be the ability of Israel and the Arabs with the help of the world powers to reach a settlement that would be not only acceptable to the Arab states but would enable these states to put pressure on the Palestinian resistance groups to modify their position and agree to the satisfactory agreement.

CHAPTER VI
Notes

1. *Memoirs of King Abdallah of Jordan* (London, 1950), 262, 266 ff.; *My Memoirs Completed* (Washington D.C., 1954), 33, 46; *al-Kitab al-Urduni al-Abiad: Suriyya al-Kubra* (The Jordanian White Book: Greater Syria) (Amman, 1947); Nuri al-Said, *Arab Independence and Unity* (Baghdad: Government Press, 1943); King Abdallah's proclamation to the Syrians, April 8, 1943 in *Mudhakkarat al-Malik Abdallah ibn al-Hussein* (Sao Paulo, 1953), 248-250; its circulation was prohibited by the British and French governments; see also Benjamin Shwadran, *Jordan: A State of Tension* (New York: Council for Middle Eastern Affairs, 1959), 223 ff.
2. *al-Nasr* (Damascus), January 13, 1963.
3. On the accusations against the Arab Legion, see John Bagot Glubb, *A Soldier With the Arabs* (New York: Harper, 1957), 243; for a view against the Legion, see Izzat Darwazah, *Hawl al-Harakah al-Arabiyyah al-Hadithah* (Around the Modern Arab Movement), vols. 4-5; 2nd ed. (Sidon, 1960), 185-188. Entire books were written on the role of Abdallah and the Hashemites in the loss of Palestine, mostly as a part of a blackmail campaign. See, Anis Sayegh, *al-Hashimiyun wa Qadiyat Falastin* (The Hashemites and the Palestine Question), (Beirut, 1966), who also quotes from books by Abdallah al-Tell.
4. On some aspects of the annexation and its results, and on the impatience of the West Bankers, see George L. Harris, *Jordan: Its People, Its Society, Its Culture* (New Haven, 1958), 71, 75, 88 ff; P.J. Vatikiotis, *Politics and the Military in Jordan* (New York: Praeger, 1967).
5. See Glubb, 306, 316, 381.
6. *Mideast Mirror,* January 8, 1966, p. 9; on March 1, 1966 the Government of Jordan and the PLO agreed to study the various issues in the dispute – conscription, training camps, frontier villages, propaganda, and levy of taxes – and Jordan seemed inclined to make concessions that would satisfy the PLO, but the disagreements resumed shortly after
7. Glubb, 85.
8. *Ibid.,* 150; see details in Anis Sayegh, 286 ff.
9. Glubb, 256, 341.
10. Walter Eytan *The First Ten Years,* 42-43, quoted in Shwadran, 152.
11. *al-Misri,* March 19, 1950, quoted in Shwadran, p. 292.
12. Glubb, 274.
13. For this and other details on the assassination, see King Hussein I, *Uneasy Lies the Head* (New York: Bernard Geis Associates, 1962), 7 ff; Glubb, 276 ff.

14. See Alec S. Kirkbride, *A Crackle of Thorns* (London, 1956), 167; Shwadran, 312, n. 9.
15. Nasir Nashashibi, *Madha Jara fil Sharq al-Awsat* (What happened in the Middle East), Beirut, 1961), 332 ff.
16. Shwadran, 313.
17. Robert Murphy, 415 has related that in 1958 Ben Gurion told him that if Nasser invaded Jordan by subversion or otherwise, Israel would feel obliged to seize the western bank.
18. See for the role played by the Communists, George L. Harris, 79 ff.
19. King Hussein I, 102, 105.
20. King Hussein, 108 says that during the talks he complained about the economic and military needs and difficulties and was encouraged by Bayar to write to Britain describing his demands and needs.
21. It is alleged that General Templer was disturbed about the security of Jordan because of the attempt of the Egyptian military attaché in cooperation with the superior officer, Ali Abu Nawar, to remove Glubb, and the danger of sending infiltrators to Israel with Egyptian encouragement and without Glubb's knowledge; see Shwadran, 326, n. 21 quoting *The Daily Mail.*
22. King Hussein, 108-111.
23. N. Nashashibi, 268,277.
24. Reported by Glubb, 398.
25. Nashashibi, 280.
26. Nashashibi, 277 ff. says that Majali had to resign when the number of persons killed reached fifty; King Hussein, p. 111 says that after the three ministers had resigned, he dissolved the cabinet.
27. King Hussein, 130-140.
28. Glubb, 365 ff., 421 ff.
29. For the clashes with Israel and the sending of Arab troops to Jordan, see Richard H. Sanger, *Where the Jordan Flows* (Washington D.C., The Middle East Institute, 1963), 376-377; Shwadran, 339 ff.
30. According to Colonel Afif Bizri, who commanded a Syrian unit in northern Transjordan, Kassem held meetings with him in a tent near the Mafraq airport; see *al-Nasr,* July 1, 1962.
31. For this declaration and the measures of the Nabulsi cabinet, see Richard Sanger, 378 ff.; Shwadran, 342 ff.
32. King Hussein, 154.
33. Camille Chamoun, *Crise au Moyen Orient,* 325-328; Chamoun believes that the three steps calculated to weaken King Hussein were: to convince him to admit Syrian units to Jordan, to dismiss Glubb, and to end the treaty with Britain.
34. Shwadran, 345
35. King Hussein, 159; Sanger, 379: see the text of the letter dated

January 31, 1957 in M. Khalil, *The Arab States and the Arab League,* II (Beirut: Khayat's, 1962), 916-919.

36. King Hussein, 157.
37. Glubb, 434.
38. King Hussein, 162; King Hussein did not mention that his palace and that of his mother were surrounded; for this see Glubb, 434.
39. Glubb, 434-435; Chamoun, 331.
40. See Sanger, 380-381.
41. The last of these acts was the decision of the cabinet to dismiss a number of senior officials known to be loyal to the throne. The list was sent to the king for approval and this was the last straw.
42. Sanger, 382. King Hussein's version p. 168, of Abu Nawar's words to Mufti mentioned neither al-Nimr nor the threat of army intervention; it said, "Unless a cabinet which will be satisfactory to the people and all parties is formed...by no later than 9 o'clock tonight, then I and my colleagues will not be responsible for anything that happens."
43. King Hussein, 169.
44. Sanger, 382 claims that al-Nimr proved even more uncompromising than before and the King therefore ended the talks, whereas King Hussein, 169 said that al-Nimr did not prove too difficult and admitted that he himself found his "friends" difficult, and then left for more disucssions. *The Middle East Journal* XI, 3 (1957), 297 mentions also the formation of a cabinet by al-Nimr and lists the ministers and then says that on April 14 it was dissolved by King Hussein before it could take office.
45. King Hussein, 183.
46. Sanger, 384; Glubb, 436 mentions two killed and twenty-five wounded; the *M.E.J.* XI, 3 (1957), 297 mentions three pro-Abu Nawar officers killed, ten wounded, and ten captured.
47. *M.E.J., Ibid.* 298.
48. For a summary of the developments, see Sanger, 386-387; *M.E.J., Ibid.,* 298 ff.
49. *The New York Times,* November 13, 1957.
50. The Damascene newspaper *Sawt al-Arab* May 18, 1957 mentioned a very profitable sugar deal obtained by Rimawi for a Baathist merchant in return for 21000 Jordanian dinars (about 60,000 dollars) paid to Rimawi.
51. See Murphy, *Diplomat Among Warriors,* 411-412.
52. King Hussein, 246, 212.
53. *Ibid., 212 ff.; M.E.J.,* XI, 3 (1957), 299.
54. King Hussein, 214.
55. *M.E.J.,* XI, 3 (1957), 299.
56. *The New York Times,* November 11, 1957; *M.E.J.,* XII, 1 (1958), 72.

57. See the articles by Sam Pope Brewer and Osgood Carruthers in *The New York Times,* November 17 and 24, 1957 respectively.
58. King Hussein, 194; Andrew Tully in *C.I.A.*, 82 claims that the C.I.A. uncovered the plot.
59. See the story in King Hussein, 206 ff; *M.E.J.*, XII, 4 (1958), 431.
60. King Hussein, ch. 15 "The Syrian MIG Attack," 218 ff.
61. The King's evidence came from an officer who, on the King's instructions, pretended to support the conspirator but kept the Jordanian government informed of every step; see King Hussein, 243.
62. *al-Hayat,* March 10, 1960.
63. *The New York Times,* October 4, 1960.
64. For these two attempts, King Hussein, 253 ff.
65. *The Christian Science Monitor,* October 15-18, 1960.
66. King Hussein, 305.
67. *The New York Times,* May 3, 1963; President Kennedy is said to have sent a personal message of support to Hussein, and the United States government was aroused by the harsh tenor of the campaign against Hussein and the U.S.
68. *The New York Times,* April 25, 1963.
69. C.L. Sulzberger in *The New York Times,* November 11, 1963.
70. *Mideast Mirror,* October 16, 1965.
71. Patrick Seale in *The Observer,* November 27, 1966.
72. Quoted in *L'Orient* (Beirut), November 28, 1966; see also the *Sunday Times,* November 27, 1966.
73. Syrian broadcast heard by this writer; see also *The Times,* November 28, *The New York Times,* November 29, 1966.
74. *al-Ahram,* February 2, 8, 1967; *The New York Times,* February 3, 1967.
75. *The New York Times,* October 12, 1966.
76. *Le Monde* (Paris), May 26, 1967 quoted the Lebanese press about a scheme of popular uprising against Hussein to be supported by the Jordanian officers and calls for revolution by the Damascus radio for mobilizing the refugees and Palestinians in Jordan, after which Shuqairi would proclaim a Palestinian republic in Gaza and claim the rest of Palestine including Jordan's western bank.
77. *The Herald Tribune,* May 31, 1967. For detailed information on the crisis, see the last sections of the second chapter on Egypt in vol.III.
78. The Fateh (Fath) organization is the most powerful among the guerilla organizations. Its name represents the three first letters in reverse of the *Harakat Tahrir Falastin* (the Palestine Liberation Movement).
79. *The San Francisco Examiner,* March 21, 1968.
80. *The New York Times,* March 25, 1968; Rowland Evans and Robert Novak column, March 27, 1968.

81. See the report of D.A. Schmidt in *N.Y. Times,* November 25, 1968.
82. *Los Angeles Times,* April 11, 1969.
83. *N.Y. Times,* March 25, 1969, Hedrick Smith said that King Hussein and Abba Eban held at least two meetings to arrange for a settlement and that Hussein was dissatisfied with Eban's terms.

APPENDIX

Chronology of Coups d'Etat and Revolutions

I. Iraq

1. October 29, 1963 Coup d'ètat of General Bakr Sidqi against the Yasin al-Hashimi cabinet; Hikmet Sulaiman became prime minister.

2. August 11, 1937 Coup against Bakr Sidqi by junta of seven officers assassination of Bakr Sidqi and fall of Hikmet Sulaiman six days later.

3. December 25, 1938 Resignation of Prime Minister Jamil Madfa'i after warning by plotting officers; Nuri al-Said became prime minister

4. 21 February 1940 Three officers against Nuri's participation in a new cabinet alert troops at Washash camp, while four other officers alert troops at Rashid camp near Baghdad; Nuri reappointed prime minister, three officers retired, the other four officers (Golden Square) dominate the government and appoint Rashid Ali Gailani prime minister at the end of March.

5. January 21, 1941 Pressure of the Golden Square colonels on Regent Abdul Ilah to retain Gailani as prime minister and threat to alert the army; Gailani retained but could not dissolve the hostile Chamber of Deputies because the Regent left Baghdad; Gailani had to resign January 30.

6. February 1, 1941 General Taha Hashimi appointed prime minister by the regent following threat by the four colonels.

7. April 1, 1941 General Hashimi had to resign following ultimatum of four colonels who wanted return of Gailani; regent left Iraq and was deposed and Gailani was appointed prime minister by new regent; war with Britain followed in May.

8. July 14, 1958 (The Iraqi revolution) Coup d'état led by Brig. Gen. Abdul-Karim Kassem and Col. Abdul-Salam Aref against the Hashemite monarchy; King Faisal II, Crown Prince Abdul Ilah and members of royal family massacred and Nuri al-Said killed following day; proclamation of a republic.

9. March 8, 1959 Abortive coup d'état of Col. Abdul Wahab Shawaf in Mosul against the Kassem regime.

10. February 8, 1963 (Revolution of 14 Ramadan): Coup by dissident officers including Aref against Kassem who was shot on following day.

11. July 3, 1963 Abortive attempt of Communists against the Baath regime after skirmish at Rashid camp.

12. November 13, 1963 Abortive attempt of the partisans of the radical Baathist, Ali Saleh al-Saadi, led by Mundhir al-Wandawi to overthrow the ruling Baath faction.

13. November 18, 1963 Coup by President Aref and moderate Baath officers against Baath national guard; end of the Baath regime.

14. September 16, 1965 Abortive coup by pro-Nasserist prime minister, Aref Abdul-Razzaq, against Aref regime in favor of unity with Egypt.

15. June 30, 1966 Second abortive coup by pro-Nasserist Abdul-Razzaq began in Mosul and ended in Baghdad.

16. July 17, 1968 Coup by moderate officers Ibrahim Daoud and Abdul-Razzaq Nayef in cooperation with Baath leader Ahmad Hasan al-Bakr against President Abdul-Rahman Aref.

17. July 30, 1968 President al-Bakr's coup against his former partners, Daoud and Nayef, and restoration of Baath rule.

II. Syria

1. March 30, 1949 Coup d'etat of Col. Husni al-Zaim against the government of President Shukri al-Quwatli.

2. August 14, 1949 Coup led by Col. Sami al-Hinnawi against Zaim who was shot along with his prime minister, Dr. Barazi.

3. December 19, 1949 Coup by Colonel Adib Shishakli against Hinnawi; constitutional parliamentary facade preserved.

4. November 29, 1951 Second coup by Colonel Shishakli against the constitutional regime of President Hashem al-Atassi.

5. February 25, 1954 Fall of Brig. Gen. (President) Shishakli; coup by dissident officers in northern Syria forced his resignation; restoration of constitutional parliamentary rule.

6. January 14, 1958 Syrian officers meet Nasser in Cairo and force the hand of the Quwatli government to accept unity with Egypt.

7. September 28, 1961 (Revolution of 28 September): Coup by Syrian officers against Nasserist regime; end of the unity with Egypt and restoration of normal parliamentary rule.

8. March 28, 1962 Coup by Col. Abdul-Karim Nahlawi against the parliamentary regime of President Qudsi; officers divided. Nahlawi and his group exiled, Parliament dissolved, Qudsi restored to presidency.

9. April 1, 1962 Abortive pro-Nasserist coup in Aleppo (coup within the previous coup).

10. January 13, 1963 Abortive coup of Nahlawi against Qudsi regime.

11. March 8, 1963 (Revolution of March 8): Coup by dissident Baathist, Nasserist and other officers led by Col. Ziad Hariri, and fall of semi-constitutional regime of Qudsi and his prime minister Khalid al-Azem.

12. July 4-8, 1963 Baath coup against General Hariri and his exile to Paris.

13. July 18, 1963 Abortive pro-Nasserist coup led by Jassem Alwan against Baath regime; General Amin Hafez emerged as Baath strongman.

14. December 19, 1965 Coup by Baath national command supported by Hafez and dissolution of regional (Syrian) command; resignation of Dr. Zuayyen's cabinet two days later.

15. February 23, 1966 Coup by dissolved Baath regional command led by Salah Jedid and Selim Hatoum against General Hafez and the national command; More leftist Baath elements dominant.

16. September 8, 1966 Abortive coup of Selim Hatoum against radical regime of Salah Jedid.

17. March 1, 1969 "Frozen Coup" of General Hafez Asad against General Jedid and his policies; General Asad emerged as the Baath strongman.

III. Lebanon

1. July 3-4 1949 Abortive revolt of Syrian Social National party led by Antun Saadeh against Beshara al-Khouri regime; execution of Saadeh and other SSNP leaders.

2. September 15-18, 1952 Popular Lebanese revolution and forced resignation of President Beshara al-Khouri.

3. May-October 1958 Rebellion of Lebanese dissidents against policies of President Camille Chamoun took aspect of civil war; ended in compromise after end of Chamoun's term and beginning of General Chehab's presidency.

4. 30-31 December, 1961 Abortive coup by Syrian Social National party junior officers and party members.

IV. Jordan

1. April 13, 1957 Abortive coup led by General Ali Abu-Nawar (Zarqa'incident) against King Hussein and the monarchy.

Other episodes in Jordan:

July 21, 1951 Assassination of King Abdallah.

December 15-19, 1955 Popular rioting against Baghdad Pact forced resignation of Hazza' Majali cabinet.

July 12, 1958 Conspiracy of dissident officers led by Col. Radi Abdallah discovered; coup was planned for July 14 and was postponed to July 17.

August 29, 1960 Prime Minister Majāli killed by time bomb in his office.

April 1963 Harsh Egyptian-Syrian campaign against King Hussein and demonstrations in Jordanian cities.

November 14-27, 1966 Riots and disorder instigated by Cairo and Damascus against Jordanian regime following Israeli attack on Sammu' on November 13.

November 4, 1968 Confrontation between Jordan armed forces and some Palestinian commando organizations ends in compromise.

February 10-11, 1970 Fighting between government forces and guerillas caused by decree restricting the freedom of guerillas; decree suspended in agreement of February 12.

June 6-12, 1970 Serious showdown between government forces and Palestinian guerillas; ca. 1000 killed and wounded; king's acceptance of guerilla conditions for a ceasefire and release of foreign hostages.

Documentary Records and Official Publicat...

Agwani, Mohammed Shafi, ed. *The Lebanese Crisis 1958, A Documentary Record.* London, 1965.

Arab Political Documents. Eds. W. Khalidi and Y. Ibish. Beirut. Annual since 1963.

Basic Documents of the Arab Unifications. New York, Arab Information Center, 1958.

"Congressional Joint Resolution to Promote Peace and Stability in the Middle East" (Eisenhower Doctrine), *Department of State Bulletin,* vol. 36 (1957).

"Constitution of the Hashemite Kingdom of Jordan", *ME Journal,* Winter 1952.

Dasatir al-Bilād al-Arabiyah (Constitutions of the Arab Countries). Cairo, League of Arab States, 1955.

Déclaration sur les Travaux du 9 me Congrès National Exceptionnel du Baath, Septembre 1967. Damascus, 1967.

Hanna, Sami A. and Gardner, George H. *Arab Socialism, A Documentary Survey.* Leiden, 1969.

Haqiqat al-Thawrah wa Ahdafuha (The Truth About the Revolution and its Goals). 2 vols. Dept. of Public Relations and Guidance of the Syrian Arab Army, Damascus 1961 (on the Syrian revolt of September 1961 and secession from UAR).

Hurewitz, J.C., ed. *Diplomacy in the Near and Middle East,* vol. II, Princeton, 1956.

"Iraqi Provisional Constitution of May 1964," *ME Forum,* June 1964.

al-Jaridah al-Rasmiyah (The Official Journal). Damascus: Syrian Republic (Weekly).

Khalil, Muhammad, ed. *The Arab States and the Arab League: A Documentary Record.* 2 vols. Beirut, 1962.

al-Kitab al-Urduni al-Abiad: Suriya al-Kubra (The Jordanian White Book: Greater Syria). Amman, 1947.

"Land Reform Legislation of Syria, Egypt and Iran," *ME Journal,* VII, Winter, 1953.

Laqueur, W. A. ed. *The Israeli-Arab Reader, A Documentary History of the Middle East Conflict.* New York, 1968.

Mahadir Jalsat Mubahathat al-Wahdah (Minutes of the Sessions on Unity Discussions) Cairo, 1963.

al-Marayati, Abid, ed. *Middle Eastern Constitutions and Electoral Laws.* New York, 1968.

Munajjed, Salaheddine, ed. *Suriyah Bayn al-Wahdah wa'l-Infisal* (Documents on the Unity and Secession of Syria). Beirut, 1962.

Nidal al-Baath (The Struggle of the Baath), 5 vols. Beirut 1963-65 (Includes Constitution of the Baath party and its many proclamations, manifestos, official policy statements in Syria and Iraq on Arab and local affairs).

Nusous wa Watha'eq al-Shakwa al-Suriyah (Texts and Documents of the Syrian Complaint: presented to the special session of the Arab League Council at Shtura on August 22-30, 1962 against Nasserist intervention in Syria). Damascus, Ministry of Foreign Affairs, 1962.

"Pact of Mutual Cooperation Between Iraq and Turkey" (Baghdad Pact), *ME Journal,* Spring, 1955.

al-Qawanin al-Ishtirakiyah (The Socialist Laws). Cairo, Information Dept. 1962.

Shamiyeh, Jubran ed. *Sijill al-Arā' wal-Waqa'i' al-Siyasiyah fil-Bilād al-Arabiyah* (Record of Political Opinion and Events in the Arab World. Beirut Monthly (Arabic text since 1966, now English issue since January 1969).

"Syrian Provisional Constitution of April 1964," *ME Forum,* May, 1964.

"Syrian Constitution of 1953 under Shishakli," *ME Journal,* Autumn, 1953.

A Select Chronology and Background Documents Relating to the Middle East. USGPO, Washington D. C. 1969 (covers the period April 1946 to April 1969).

Syrian Republic, Direct. Gen. Information. *First Statement, Second Statement.* Damascus, 1962 (On the achievements of the Shishakli regime).

Syrian Arab Republic, Planning Ministry. *Implementation Reports on the Five Years' Development Plan.* Damascus, 1963 and 1964.

United States Policy in the Near East Crisis (Documents and Policy Statements May-July 1967). Washington D. C. Dept. of State. 1967.

General Works

Atassi, Adnan. *Al-Dimuqratiyah al-Taqaddumiyah wal Ishtirakiyah al-Thawriyah* (Progressive Democracy and Revolutionary Socialism). Beirut, 1965.

Be'eri, Eliezer, *Army Officers in Arab Politics and Society.* Translation from Hebrew by Dov Ben-Abba. New York, 1970.

Berger, Monroe. "Les régimes militaires du Moyen Orient," *Orient* No. 4 (1960, 3).

Binder, Leonard. *The Ideological Revolution in the Middle East.* New York, 1964.

Bitar, Nadim. *al-Idiyologiyah al-Inqilabiyah* (Revolutionary Ideology). Beirut, 1964.

Dumont, Jean. ed. *Les Coups d'état.* Paris, 1963.

Finer, S. E. *The Man on Horseback: The Role of the Military in Politics.* New York, 1962.

Fisher, Sydney N. ed. *The Military in the Middle East, Problems in Society and Government.* Columbus (Ohio), 1967.

Goodspeed, Donald J. *The Conspirators: A Study of the Coup d'état.* New York, 1962.

Haliq̄, Umar. *Dawr al-Marxiyah fil Ishtirakiyah al-Arabiyah* (The Role of Marxism in Arab Socialism). Beirut, 1965; *al-Ishtirakiyun al-Arab wal Shuyu'iyah al-Duwaliyah.* (Arab Socialists and International Communism). Beirut, 1966.

Halpern, Manfred. *The Politics of Social Change in the Middle East and North Africa.* Princeton, 1963; "The Character and Scope of the Social Revolution in the Middle East," in William R. Polk ed., *The Developmental Revolution,* Washington D. C., 1963.

Hamon, Leo ed. *Le rôle extra-militaire de l'armée dans le Tiers Monde.* Paris, 1966.

Howard, Michael ed. *Soldiers and Governments.* Bloomington, Ind. 1961.

Hurewitz, J. C. *Middle East Politics: The Military Dimension.* New York, 1969.

Janowitz, Morris. *The Military in the Political Development of the New Nations.* Chicago, 1964.

Johnson, John J. ed. *The Role of the Military in Underdeveloped Countries.* Princeton, 1962.

Kerr, Malcolm. "Arab Radical Notions of Democracy," *St. Antony's Papers, ME Affairs* No. 3 Albert Hourani ed. Carbondale, Ill., 1963?; *The Arab Cold War 1958-1967.* 2nd ed. London, 1967.

Kirk, George E. *Contemporary Arab Politics.* New York, 1961.

Khadduri, Majid. "The Army Officer: His Role in Middle Eastern Politics," in *Social Forces in the Middle East,* ed. S. N. Fisher. Ithaca, 1955; *Political Trends in the Arab World: The Role of Ideas and Ideals in Politics.* Baltimore, 1970.

Lewis, Bernard. "The Middle East Reactions to Soviet Pressure," *ME Journal,* Spring 1956.

Lenczowski, George. "Radical Regimes in Egypt, Syria and Iraq: Some Comparative Observations on Ideologies and Practices," *Journal of Politics,* Gainesville, Fla., February, 1966.

Luttwak, Edward. *Coup d'Etat: A Practical Handbook – A Brilliant Guide to Taking Over a Nation.* Greenwich, Conn. 1969.

Munajjed, Salaheddin. *al-Tadlil al-Ishtiraki* (Socialist Deception). 2nd ed. Beirut, 1966; *Balshafat al-Islam* (The Bolshevization of Islam by Arab Marxists and Socialists) Beirut, 1966.

Nashashibi, Nasir. *Madha Jara fil Sharq al-Awsat* (What Happened in the Middle East). Beirut, 1961.

Rondot, Pierre. *The Changing Patterns of the Middle East.* New York, 1961.

Sebai, Mustafa. *Ishtirakiyat al-Islam* (Socialism in Islam). 2nd ed. Damascus, 1960.

Shaibani, Ahmad. *al-Akhlaqiyah al-Thawriyah wal Akhlaqiyah al-Arabiyah* (Revolutionary Ethics and Arab Ethics). Beirut, 1966.

Shamiyeh, Jubran. *Qadāyana al-Arabiyah* (Our Arab Problems). Beirut, 1965; *Ya 'Uqala' al-Arab Ittahidu* (O Thoughtful Arabs, Unite) 3 vols. Beirut, 1965?

Sharabi, Hisham B. *Nationalism and Revolution in the Arab World.* Princeton, 1966.

Tully, Andrew. *CIA: The Inside Story.* New York, 1962.

Vernier, Bernard. *Armée et politique au Moyen Orient.* Paris, 1966.

Chapter I

Abu-Jaber, Kemal S. *The Arab Ba ath Socialist Party.* Syracuse, 1966.

Aflaq, Michel. *Fi Sabil al-Baath* (For the Baath). 3rd. ed. Beirut, 1963; *Maarakat al-Masir al-Wahid* (The Battle of Common Destiny). 2nd ed. Beirut, 1959.

Anshen, Ruth Nanda ed. *Mid-East World Center,* New York, 1956 (Includes essays by G. Lenczowski on political institutions, Ernest Jackh on geographic and strategic importance of the Middle East, Ch. Issawi on economic and social conditions, and other useful essays).

Antonius, George. *The Arab Awakening.* New York, 1946.

Berger, Morroe. *The Arab World Today.* Garden City, N.Y., 1962.

Badeau, John. *An American Approach to the Arab World.* New York 1967.

Binder, Leonard. "Radical Reform Nationalism in Syria and Egypt," *The Muslim World,* vol. 49, April and July 1959.

Campbell, John C. *Defense of the Middle East.* New York, 1960.

Current History, February 1959 (Essays on nationalism in Jordan and Lebanon by Raphael Patai and Maurice Harari, respectively).

Faris, N.A. and Husayn, M. T. *The Crescent in Crisis.* Lawrence, Kansas, 1955.

Farzat, Muhammad Harb. *al-Hayat al-Hizbiyah fi Suriyah* (Political Parties in Syria). Damascus, 1955.

Fisher, Sydney N. ed. *Social Forces in the Middle East.* Ithaca, N.Y. 1955.

George, Lucien and Mokdessi, Toufic. *Les Partis Libanais en 1959.* Beirut, 1959 (French and Arabic texts in one volume).

Haim, Sylvia G. *Anthology on Arab Nationalism.* Berkeley, 1963.

Hamadi, Sania. *Temperament and Character of the Arabs.* New York, 1960.

Harris, Christina Phelps. *Nationalism and Revolution in Egypt; The Role of the Muslim Brotherhood.* The Hague, 1964.

Husaini, Ishaq Musa. *The Moslem Brethren.* Beirut, 1956.

Hourani, Albert. *Syria and Lebanon, A political essay.* London, 1947.

Hurewitz, J. C. ed. *Soviet-American Rivalry in the Middle East.* New York, 1969.

al-Husri, Sati', *Difa' 'an al-'Urubah* (Defense of Arabism). Beirut, 1956; *al-Iqlimiyah: Judhuruha wa Budhuruha* (Regionalism: Its Roots and its Seeds). Beirut, 1963.

Journal of International Affairs, vol. 13, no. 2, New York, 1959, (Includes essays by John Badeau on the revolt against democracy; Ch. Issawi on dilemmas in the Middle East; K. J. Newman on the new monarchies of the Middle East; and Richard Nolte on American policy in the Middle East); (vol. 19, no. 1, 1965 (Includes relevant essays on modernization by J. Badeau and H. Sharabi; population growth by J. C. Hurewitz; social structure and ideology in Iraq, Lebanon, Syria and UAR by Ch. Issawi; and the economics and politics of oil by S. H. Longrigg.)

Khadduri, Majid. "The Scheme of Fertile Crescent Unity: A Study in Inter-Arab Relations," in *The Near East and the Great Powers,* ed. Richard N. Frye. Cambridge, Mass. 1951.

Laqueur, Walter Z. *Communism and Nationalism in the Middle East,* New York, 1956; *The Middle East in Transition.* N. Y. 1958 (anthology of relevant background essays); *The Soviet Union and the Middle East.* N. Y. 1959.

Longrigg, S. H. *Oil in the Middle East.* 3rd. ed. London, 1965.

Macdonald, Robert W. *The League of Arab States,* Princeton, 1965.

Maksoud, Clovis. "Democracy and Military Regimes," *ME Forum,* April, 1960.

Marlowe, John. *Arab Nationalism and British Imperialism.* New York, 1961.

Marston, Elsa. "Fascist Tendencies in Pre-War Arab Politics," *ME Forum,* May, 1959.

Meyer, A. J. *Middle Eastern Capitalism.* Cambridge, Mass., 1959.

Niewenhuijze, C. A. O. *Social Stratification and the Middle East.* London, 1965.

Nutting, Anthony. *The Arabs.* New York, 1964.

Polk, William R. *The United States and the Arab World.* Rev. ed. Cambridge, Mass. 1969; *Perspective of the Arab World.* New York, 1956.

Qubain, Fahim I. ed. *Inside the Arab Mind.* Arlington Va., 1960 (Includes an annotated bibliographic survey on Arab issues).

Rivlin, B. and Szyliowicz, J. *The Contemporary Middle East: Tradition and Innovation.* New York, 1965 (Anthology of relevant selections and essays.)

Rondot, Pierre, "Parliamentary Regimes in the Middle East," *ME Affairs,* Aug.-Sept., 1953.

Saadeh, Autun. *Nushu' al-Umam* (The Rise of Nations). Damascus, 1951; *al-Muhadarat al-'Ashr* (The Ten Lectures), Damascus, n.d.

al-Said, Nuri. *Arab Independence and Unity.* Baghdad, 1943.

Sands, William ed. *Middle East Report: Nationalism, Neutralism, Communism, Struggle for Power.* Washington, D. C., 1959.

Sayegh, Fayez. *Arab Unity: Hope and Fulfillment.* New York, 1958; *The Dynamics of Neutralism in the Arab World.* San Francisco, 1964.

Sharabi, Hisham. "The Transformation of Ideology in the Arab World", *ME Journal* vol. 19, Autumn, 1965.

Siegman, Henry. "Arab Unity and Disunity," *ME Journal,* Winter 1962.

Safadi, Muta. *al-Thawri wal Thawri al-'Arabi* (The Revolutionary and the Arab Revolutionary). Beirut, 1961.

Stevens, Georgiana. "Arab Neutrality and Bandung," *ME Journal,* Spring 1957.

Tibawi, A. L. "Syria in War-Time Agreements and Disagreements," *ME Forum,* vol. 43 nos. 2-3, 1967.

Utley, Freda. *Will the Middle East Go West?* Chicago, 1957.

Von Grunebaum, G. E. *Modern Islam: The Search for Cultural Identity.* Los Angeles, 1963.

Warriner, Doreen. *Land Reform and Development in the Middle East.* 2nd ed. London, 1962.

Zartman, I. William. *Government and Politics in Northern Africa.* New York, 1963.

Zeltzer, Moshe. *Aspects of Near East Society.* New York, 1962.

Ziadeh, Nicola. *Syria and Lebanon.* London, 1957.

Zuwiyya-Yamak, Labib. *The Syrian Social Nationalist Party.* Cambridge, Mass., 1966.

Chapter II

Bagley, F. R. C. "Iraq's Revolution," *International Journal,* vol. 14, Autumn, 1959.

Bahri, Yunis. *al-Iraq al-Yawm* (Iraq Today). Beirut, 1938; *Sab'at Ashhur fi Sujun Baghdad* (Seven Months in the Prisons of Baghdad). Beirut, 1960; *Thawrat 14 Ramadan al-Mubarak* (The Revolution of 14 Ramadan). Beirut, 1963?

Bazzaz, Abdul-Rahman. *Safahat Min al-Ams al-Qarib* (Pages From the Recent Past). Beirut, 1960.

Lord Birdwood. *Nuri as-Said, A Study in Arab Leadership.* London, 1959.

Caractacus (Pseud.). *Revolution in Iraq.* London, 1959.

Caspar, Johann. "Baghdad's Year of Revolution," *Commentary.* September 1959.

Clin, George, "Situation de l'Irak," *Orient* no. 8, (1958, 4).

Delestre, Emile, "La republique Arabe unie face à l'Irak et au communnisme," *Orient* no. 9, (1959, 1).

De Gaury, Gerald. *Three Kings in Baghdad.* London, 1961.

Dann, Uriel. *Iraq under Qassem: A Political History 1958-1963.* New York, 1969.

al-Durrah, M. "The Mosul Revloution Seven Years Later," *Dirasat Arabiyah,* vol. 2 no. 6, April 1966.

Edmonds, C. J. "The Kurds and the Revolution in Iraq," *ME Journal,* vol. 13, Winter 1959.

Fawzi, Ahmad. *Thawrat 14 Ramadan* (The Revolution of 14 Ramadan). Cairo, 1963.

Gallman, Waldemar J. *Iraq Under General Nuri: My Recollections of Nuri al-Said 1954-1958.* Baltimore, 1964.

Ghaleb, Col. Sabih Ali. *Qissat Thawrat 14 Tammuz Wal Dubbat al-Ahrar* (The Story of the Revolution of 14 July and the Free Officers). Beirut, 1968.

Grassmuck, George. "The Electoral Process in Iraq 1952-1958," *ME Journal* vol. 14 no. 4, 1960.

Haddad, Uthman Kemal. *Harakat Rashid Ali al-Gailani* (The Gailani Revolt). Sidon, n.d.

Harbison, Frederick. "Two Centers of Arab Power", *Foreign Affairs,* vol. 37, July 1959 (On Egypt and Iraq and their rivalries).

Harris, George L. *Iraq, Its People, Its Society, Its Culture.* New Haven, 1958.

al-Hasani, Abdul-Razzaq. *Tarikh al-Wizarat al-Iraqiyah* (History of the Iraqi Cabinets). 10 vols. Sidon, 1953.

Heyworth-Dunne, J. "Partis politiques et gouvernements dans l'Irak d'aujourd'hui," *Orient,* 15, 1960, 3.

al-Hilali, Abdul-Razzaq. "Rural Development in Iraq," *al-Abhath,* vol. 17 no. 1, November 1964.

Hollingsworth, Clare. "The Baathist Revolution in Iraq," *The World Today,* vol. 19 no. 5, May 1963.

Husri, Khaldun. *The July 14 Revolution and the Truth About the Communists in Iraq* (Arabic). Beirut, 1963; "The Iraqi Revolution July 14, 1958," *ME Forum,* Winter 1965.

Husri, Sati. *Mudhakkirati fil-Iraq 1921-1941* (My Memoirs in Iraq). Beirut, 1968.

Jamali, Mohammed Fadel. "Iraq under General Nuri." *ME Forum*, Autumn 1964.

Jargy, Simon. "Une page d'histoire de la revolution Iraqienne: Le procès Abd al-Salam Aref," *Orient* no. 12, 1959, 4.

Kedourie, Elie. "Réflexions sur l'histoire du royaume d'Irak, 1921-1958," *Orient*, no. 11, 1959, 3.

Kennah, Khalil. *al-Iraq: Amsuhu wa Ghaduhu* (Iraq, Its Past and Future), Beirut, 1966.

Khadduri, Majid. "The Coup d'état of 1936," *ME Journal*, vol. 2, July 1948; *Independent Iraq 1932-1958*, 2nd ed. London, 1960; *Republican Iraq: A Study of Iraqi Politics Since the Revolution of 1958.* London, 1969.

Kubbah, Muhammad Mahdi. *Mudhakkirati fi Samim al-Ahdath 1918-1958* (My Memoirs in the Very Center of Events), Beirut, 1965.

Langley, Kathleen M. *The Industrialization of Iraq*, Cambridge, Mass., 1961; "Iraq: Some Aspects of the Economic Scene," *ME Journal*, vol. 18 no. 2, Spring, 1964.

Laqueur, W.Z. "As Iraq Goes Communist," *Commentary*, May, 1959.

Longrigg, Stephen H. *Iraq 1900-1950.* London, 1953; "Iraq under Kassim," *Current History*, April 1962.

Majzarat Qasr al-Rahab (The Massacre at the Rahab Palace); Dar al-Hayat, Beirut, 1960.

Mushtaq, Abdul Rahim. "Un aperçu sur les relations Iraqo-Egyptiennes," *Etudes Mediterranéennes*, Winter, 1959.

Morris, James. *The Hashemite Kings.* London, 1959.

Neumann, Robert G. "L'Iraq de Kassem," *Politique Etrangère*, 1960, 5.

Penrose, Ernest Francis. "Essai sur l'Irak." *Orient* no. 35 (1965, 3).

Polk, William R. "The Lesson of Iraq", *Atlantic Monthly*, December 1958.

Qubain, Fahim I. *The Reconstruction of Iraq 1950-57.* New York, 1958.

Ray, Alan. "Iraq After the Coup," *Commentary*, September, 1958; "The Great Arab Schism," *Commentary*, September, 1959.

Rihani, Amin. *Faisal al-Awwal.* Beirut, 1934.

Rossi, Pierre. "L'Irak devant la réforme agraire," *Orient* no. 7, (1958, 3).

Saab, Halim E. "Baghdad An II de la revolution," *Etudes Mediterraneennes,* Winter, 1959.

Schmidt, Dana Adams. *Journey Among Brave Men.* Boston, 1964 (On the Kurdish revolt).

Selim, Shaker Mustafa. *The Tribunal of Hasan the Cobbler and Other Events from the Record of Communism and Opportunism in Iraq* (in Arabic). Beirut n. d. (after 1963).

Shirri, Muhammad Baqir. *al-Iraq al-Tha'ir* (Iraq in Revolution). Beirut, 1963.

Shwadran, Benjamin. *The Power Struggle in Iraq.* New York, 1960.

Simmons, John L. "Agricultural Development in Iraq. Planning and Management Failures", *ME Journal,* vol. 19 no. 2, Spring 1965.

Troutbeck, John. "The Revolution in Iraq," *Current History,* February 1959.

Vernier, Bernard. *L'Irak d'aujourd'hui.* Paris, 1963.

Chapters III and IV

Abu-Mansur, Fadlallah, *A'asir* (Storms), n.p. Beirut?, n. d. 1959? (On the coups against Zaim and Hinnawi in Syria 1949).

Arabi, Nizar. *Madha Yajri fi Suriyah* (What is Happening in Syria). Damascus, 1962 (This is an answer to M. H. Haikal's book, *What Happened in Syria*).

Arslan, Emir Adel. *Dhikrayat al-Emir Adel Arslan 'an Husni al-Zaim* (Recollections of Emir Adel Arslan on Husni al-Zaim). Beirut, 1962.

Ben-Hanan, Eli. *Our Man in Damascus, The Story of Eli Cohen Israel's Greatest Spy.* New York, 1969.

Carleton, Alford. "The Syrian Coups d'Etat of 1949," *ME Journal* vol. 4 (January, 1950).

Colombe, Marcel, "La république arabe syrienne a la lumiere du coup d'état du 28 Mars," *Orient* no. 21 (1962, 1).

The Economic Development of Syria. IBRD Mission. Baltimore, 1955.

Farra, Adnan. *L'Industrialization en Syrie.* Geneva, 1950.

Garzouzi, Eva. "Land Reform in Syria." *ME Journal,* vol. 17 (Winter-Spring 1963).

Ghadri, Nihad. *al-Kitāb al-Aswad* (The Black Book). Damascus, n. d. 1962? (On Nasserist rule in Syria during the period of unity).

Haddad, George. *Fifty Years of Modern Syria and Lebanon*. Beirut, 1950.

Haikal, Muhammad Hassanein. *Ma Lladhi Jara fi Suriyah* (What Happened in Syria). Cairo, 1962.

Horton, Alan W. "Syrian Stability and the Baath," *American Universities Field Staff, S.W. Asia Series,* vol. 14 no. 1 (April 1965)

Issawi, Charles. "The United Arab Republic," *Current History,* February 1959.

Jansen, J. H. "A Farewell to Syrian Coups," *ME Forum,* May, 1963.

Jargy, Simon. "La Syrie province de la république arabe unie," *Orient* no. 8 1958, 4; "Le déclin d'un parti," *Orient*, no. 11 1959, 3 (deals with the decline of the Baath party under the UAR).

Khabbaz, Hanna and Haddad, George. *Faris al-Khouri, Hayatuhu wa Asruhu* (Faris al-Khouri, his life and Times), Beirut, 1952.

Khadduri, Majid. "Constitutional Development in Syria," *ME Journal,* Spring, 1950

Khalidi, Walid, "Political Trends in the Fertile Crescent," *The Middle East in Transition* ed. W. Z. Laqueur, New York, 1958.

Lenczowski, George. "Syria: A Crisis in Arab Unity," *Current History,* April 1962.

Mahdi, Mohammed. "The Cairo Declaration," *ME Forum,* Summer 1963 (On the charter for a federation of Egypt, Syria and Iraq April 1963).

Mahouk, Adnan. "Recent Agricultural Development and Bedouin Settlement in Syria," *ME Journal,* Spring, 1956.

Murad, Basim. *Abdul Nasser Bada' fi Dimashq wa Intaha fi Shtura* (Abdul-Nasser Began in Damascus and Ended in Shtura). Damascus, 1962.

Muttali (Pseud.). *al-Sarraj wa Mu'āmarāt al-Nasiriyah* (Sarraj and the Nasserist Conspiracies), 2nd ed. Damascus, n.d. 1962?

Porter, R. S. "The Growth of the Syrian Economy," *ME Forum,* November 1963.

Palmer, Monte. "The United Arab Republic: An Assessment of its Failure," *ME Journal,* Winter, 1966.

Razzaz, Munif. *al-Tajribah al-Murrah* (The Bitter Experiment). Beirut, 1967.

Rondot, Pierre. "Tendances particularistes et tendances unitaires en Syrie," *Orient* no. 5 (1958, 1); "Remarques sur le Baath," *Orient* no. 31 (1964).

Safadi, Muta. *Hizbal-Baath, Ma'sāt al-Mawled Ma-sāt al-Nihayah* (The Baath Party, The Tragedy of the Birth the Tragedy of the End), Beirut, 1964

Saqqal, Fathallah. *Min Dhikrayat al-Za'im Husni al-Za'im* (Recollections on Colonel Husni al-Za'im). Cairo, 1951.

al-Sayyid, Jalal. "Open Letter to the Chairman of the Syrian Presidential Council," in *Opinions and Studies on Economic and Social Problems: Articles and Memoirs Published in the Lebanese Newspapers.* Beirut, 1964 (Criticism of the Baathist regime in a 40-page letter to General Hafez by a disenchanted Baath leader).

Seale, Patrick. *The Struggle for Syria.* London, 1965.

Shamiyeh, Jubran. *Ya 'Uqalā' al-Arab Ittahidu, II Qadaya Suriyah* (O Thoughtful Arabs, Unite, vol. II Problems of Syria). Beirut, 1965?; *Mawqif al-Thawriyin Min Qadaya Falastin* (The Revolutionists and the Problems of Palestine), Beirut, 1965?

Takriti, Selim Taha, *Asrar al-Inqilāb al-Askari al-Akhir fi Suriyah* (Secrets of the last Military Coup in Syria). Baghdad, 1950.

Tibawi, A. L. *A Modern History of Syria.* London, 1969.

Torrey, Gordon H. *Syrian Politics and the Military 1945-1958.* Columbus, Ohio 1964; "The Ba'th: Ideology and Practice," *ME Journal* vol. 23 no. 4 (Autumn 1969).

Vernier, Bernard. "Le rôle politique de l'armée en Syrie," *Revue de Politique Etrangère,* vol. 29, nos. 5-6 (1964).

Winder, R. Bayly. "Syrian Deputies and Cabinet Ministers 1919-1959," *ME Journal* vols. 16 no. 4 and 17 no. 1 (Autumn 1962 and Winter 1963).

Zahreddin, Abdul Karim. *Mudhakkirati án Fitrat al-Infisāl* (My Memoirs on the Period of Separation), Beirut, 1968 (On the period that followed Syrian seccession from the UAR 1961-1963).

Chapter V

Alem, Jean-Pierre. "Troubles insurrectionnels au Liban," *Orient,* no. 6 (1958, 2).

Binder, Leonard, ed. *Politics in Lebanon.* New York, 1966.

Britt, George. "Lebanon's Popular Revolution." *ME Journal,* vol. 7 no. 1, (Winter, 1953).

Bustani, Emile. "Lebanon an Oasis of Democracy," *ME Forum,* May, 1960.

Chamoun, Camille, *Crise au Moyen Orient.* Paris, 1963.

Curtis, Gerald. "The United Nations Observation Group in Lebanon," *International Organization,* vol. 18 no. 4 (Autumn, 1964).

Eisenhower, Dwight D. *Waging Peace.* New York, 1965 (Includes chapter on the Lebanese crisis of 1958).

Hess, C. G. and Bodman, H. L. Jr. "Confessionalism and Feudality in Lebanese Politics," *ME Journal,* vol. 8, no. 1 (Winter, 1954).

Hottinger, Arnold. "Zuama and Parties in the Lebanese Crisis of 1958," *ME Journal,* vol. 15, no. 2 (Spring, 1961).

Hudson, Michael C. *The Precarious Republic: Political Modernization in Lebanon.* New York, 1968.

Hurewitz, J. C. "Lebanese Democracy in its International Setting," *ME Journal,* vol. 17, no. 5 (1963).

Issawi, Charles. "Economic Development and Liberalism in Lebanon," *ME Journal,* vol. 18, no. 3 (Summer, 1964).

Junblat, Kemal. *Haqiqat al-Thawrah al-Lubnaniyah* (Truth about the Lebanese Revolt). Beirut, 1959.

Karami, Nadia and Nawaf. *Waqi'al-Thawrạh al-Lubṅaniyah* (The Reality of the Lebanese Revolt). Beirut, 1959.

Kerr, Malcolm H. "Lebanese Views on the 1958 Crisis," *ME Journal,* vol. 15, no. 2 (Spring, 1961).

Khouri, Beshara. *Haqā'eq Lubnaniyah* (Lebanese Realities), 3 vols. Beirut, 1961. (Includes the memoirs of President Khouri and in vol. III the propular revolution against his regime).

Malek, Charles. "The Near East: The Search for Truth," *Foreign Affairs,* vol. 30 (January, 1952).

Meo, Leila M. T. *Lebanon, Improbable Nation.* Bloomington, Ind., 1965.

Mosseri, R. "The Struggle in Lebanon," *Middle Eastern Affairs,* November 1952.

Murphy, Robert. *Diplomat Among Warriors.* New York, 1964.

Nour, François. "Particularisme libanais et nationalisme arabe," *Orient,* no. 7 (1958, 3).

Persen, William. "Lebanese Economic Development Since 1950," *ME Journal,* Summer 1958.

Qubain, Fahim I. *Crisis in Lebanon.* Washington D.C., 1961.

Riyashi, Iskander. *Ru'a sā' Lubnān Kama 'Ariftuhum* (Presidents of Lebanon as I knew them). Beirut, 1961.

Rondot, Pierre. "Quelques réflexions sur les structures du Liban," *Orient* no. 6 (1958, 2); "Le mouvement du 31 Décembre 1961 au Liban a-t-il été uncoup d'état militaire?" *Orient* no. 34 (1965, 2); Quelques réflexions sur l'expérience politique du "Chéhabisme" au Liban," *Orient* no. 16 (1960, 4).

Salibi, Kamal S. *The Modern History of Lebanon.* London, 1966; "Lebanon Under Fuad Chehab 1958-1964," *Middle Eastern Studies,* vol. 2, no. 3 (April, 1966).

Solh, Sami. *Mudhakkirat Sami al-Solh* (Memoirs of Sami al-Solh), Beirut, 1960.

Stewart, Desmond. *Turmoil in Beirut.* London, 1958.

Suleiman, Michael W. *Political Parties in Lebanon.* Ithaca, N.Y., 1967.

Twaini, Ghassan. *al-Ayyam al-Asibah* (Days of Crisis), Beirut n.d. 1958?

Ziadeh, Nicola. "The Lebanese Elections 1960," *ME Journal,* Autumn, 1961.

Chapter VI

King Abdallah of Jordan. *Memoirs.* London, 1950; *My Memoirs Completed.* Washington D.C., 1954.

Abidi, Aqil Hyder Hasan. Jordan: *A Political Study 1948-57.* New York, 1965.

Dearden, Ann. *Jordan.* London, 1958.

Darwazah, Izzat. *Hawl al-Harakah al-Arabiyah al-Hadithah* (Around the Modern Arab Movement), vols. 4-5, 2nd ed. Sidon, 1960.

Glubb, John Bagot. *The Story of the Arab Legion.* London, 1948; *A Soldier with the Arabs,* New York, 1957.

Goichon, Amélie Marie. *Jordanie réelle.* Paris, 1967.

Harris, George L. *Jordan, Its People, Its Society, Its Culture.* New Haven, 1958.

King Hussein I. *Uneasy Lies the Head.* New York, 1962.

Kirkbride, Alec S. *A Crackle of Thorns.* London, 1956.

Patai, Raphael. *The Kingdom of Jordan.* Princeton, 1958.

Peake, Frederick G. *History and Tribes of Jordan.* Coral Gables, (Fla.), 1958.

Rouleau, Eric. "*Crisis in Jordan,*" World Today, vol. 23 no. 2 (February, 1967).

Sanger, Richard H. *Where the Jordan Flows.* Washington D.C., 1963.

Sayegh, Anis. *al-Hashimiyun wa Qadiyat Falastin* (The Hashemites and the Palestine Question). Beirut, 1966.

Shwadran, Benjamin. *Jordan, A State of Tension.* New York, 1959.

Sparrow, Gerald. *Modern Jordan.* London, 1961.

Vatikiotis, P.J. *Politics and the Military in Jordan: A Study of the Arab Legion 1921-57.* New York, 1967.

Wright, Esmond. "Abdallah's Jordan 1947-51," *ME Journal,* Autumn, 1951.

Other Publications

al-Nasr, al-Binā', al-Baath, al-Thawrah, al-Sarkhah (Damascus), al-Nahar, al-Anwar, al-Hayat, Daily Star, al-Safa, al-Zaman, al-Anbā', al-Jaridah, L'Orient, al-Sayyad, Mideast Mirror (Beirut), al-Ahram, Akhbar al-Yawm, al-Gumhouriyah, Rose al-Yusif, al-Misri, al-Musawwar, Egyptian Gazette (Cairo), Oriente Moderno (Rome), The Times, Daily Express, The Economist, The Observer, The Middle East and North Africa, Mizan Newsletter, The Daily Mail (London), Cahiers de l'Orient Contemporain, Le Figaro, Le Monde (Paris), Arab News and Views, al-Bayan, The Heritage, The New York Times, Time, Newsweek, Action (New York), The Los Angeles Times.

INDEX